WHICH KORAN?

EDITED BY

IBN WARRAQ

WHICH KORAN?

Variants, Manuscripts, and Linguistics

Prometheus Books
Essex, Connecticut

Prometheus Books

An imprint of The Globe Pequot Publishing Group, Inc.
64 South Main Street
Essex, CT 06426
www.globepequot.com

Cover design by Jacqueline Nasso Cooke

Library of Congress Cataloging-in-Publication Data

Which Koran : variants , manuscripts , linguistics / edited by Ibn Warraq.
p. cm.
Includes bibliographical references.
ISBN 978-1-59102-429-3 (hardcover)
ISBN 978–1–61592–977–1 (ebook)
1. Koran—History. 2. Koran—Language, style. 3. Koran—Criticism, interpretation, etc. 4. Islam—Controversial literature. I. Ibn Warraq.
BP131.W45 2008
297.1'224042—dc22 2006012124

To

Raphael and Benjamin

Incipit Vita Nova

Raphael

Un esprit courageux et une intelligence originale

De qui j'ai appris plus que de quiconque

Avec tout mon amour

Benjamin

Who, by his stoical example and encouragement, gave me the courage to persist, and banished despair as self-indulgence.

Avec tout mon amour.

Contents

PART 4. VARIANTS

APPENDIXES

Preface and Acknowledgments

My previous anthologies on the origins of the Koran and the beginnings of Islam were received enthusiastically by several distinguished scholars who found that my compilations fulfilled an important function, proving indispensable source books for researchers, teachers, students, and even making accessible to the educated public, in English translations, material buried in difficult to obtain nineteenth-century German journals.

The Quest for the Historical Muhammad,[1] an essay collection I edited, makes several appearances in the footnotes of Dr. Chase Robinson's *Islamic Historiography*.[2] *What the Koran Really Says*[3] was quoted at the opening talk of the International Conference at Notre Dame University on "Towards a New Reading of the *Qur'ān*" (Indiana, USA), which took place in April 2005 and was attended by some of the most distinguished Koranic scholars in the world. One speaker from the Middle East at the conference congratulated me on my efforts and confided that he had used my writings with his students. Two other teachers not present at the conference, Professor Peter von Sivers of the University of Utah and Professor Ervand Abramanian of City University of New York, also informed me a few years ago that they used *The Quest for the Historical Muhammad* with their students.

In his review in the *Times Literary Supplement* Dr. Chase Robinson, formerly of the University of Oxford, now provost and senior vice president at the Graduate Center of the City University of New York, offered this description of *What the Koran Really Says*: "Here, as in previous collections, his stated purpose is to historicize Islamic origins, and to do this by making accessible a range of (mostly European) nineteenth- and twentieth-century scholarship through re-publication, translation, and commentary (the present collection continues to the task taken up in *The Origins of the Koran: Classic Essays on Islam's Holy Book*: 1998,[4] with which it can usefully be considered a companion volume). For the professional Islamicist, it is enormously convenient to have all these articles assembled together in a single work. For anyone interested in the Koran, it will be a boon to understanding Islam, and it is for that reader, more than for the Islamicist, that Ibn Warraq intends the volume."[5]

Reviewing *The Quest for the Historical Muhamamd*, Professor Merlin Swartz of Boston University wrote something similar: "In this immensely valuable source, Ibn Warraq has collected seminal studies from several academic journals from the past 150 years. . . . Regardless of one's view, Ibn Warraq has performed a valuable service by bringing these important—and largely inaccessible—studies in a single volume, and by translating original German and French publications into English. . . . Highly recommended to all colleges and university libraries and to public libraries with collections in the history of religion."[6] In a personal letter, Günter Lüling wrote, and furthermore gave me permission to quote, the following, "I appreciate it very much what you have done with your anthologies for the progress of Islamic Studies."[7]

While it is always a pleasure to receive praise from whatever quarter it may come, surely the greater satisfaction must come when some scholar of Islam whom one expected to disapprove of one's skeptical forays into their chosen field of studies offers some murmur of approval. Hence my delight at reading that Angelika Neuwirth, professor at the Freie Universität, while disapproving of my "credulity" [*sic*][8] and my seeming endorsement of "*only attempts at deconstruction of the 'Qur'ānic narrative*,'" nonetheless found my collection *What the Koran Really Says* to be very meritorious.[9]

Even more memorable, for me, was the invitation I received to visit the great Semiticist and Islamologist Maxime Rodinson in his apartment, overflowing with books, in Rue Vaneau in Paris. Rodinson asked me to autograph my first work, one which he had been asked to review by the politically hypercorrect *Le Monde*. To the latter's chagrin, Rodinson wrote a very favorable review describing the book as "very learned," and expressing his desire for the book to be read widely. *Le Monde*, of course, refused to publish it, but it can be found now in the bimonthly journal *Panoramique*.[10]

Claude Gilliot, professor at the University of Aix-en-Provence, France, in an extended review of three of my books in *Arabica*[11] finds my approach "refreshing"[12] despite finding my "freethought" as applied to religion in general, and Islam in particular, a little negative. He applauds my efforts at rescuing from oblivion certain scholars. Gilliot concludes on an appreciative note, "One of the merits, and not the least, of this collection, *but also of Ibn Warraq's introduction* [my emphasis, I. W.] is to remind us, among other things, that we have yet to draw all the lessons [benefits] that we could from the theories and methodology of John Wansbrough and his school on the birth and rise of Islam."[13]

Jacques Berlinerblau, associate professor of comparative literature and languages at Hofstra University, wrote, "Ibn Warraq is to be lauded and admired for his critical heroism,"[14] and David N. Myers of Princeton University[15] wrote, "Armed with a healthy dose of disdain, Ibn Warraq has recently called attention to the reticence of Muslim scholars to undertake critical study of Muhammad and early Islamic sources."

The present work follows the pattern of the earlier ones. There are nineteen articles divided into four sections, some first translations from German and French; one (Schub) is an original article published here for the first time. I am particularly pleased to include Nöldeke's classic work on the language and style of the Koran. Nöldeke and Schulthess were especially difficult to edit since both scholars were astonishingly casual and cryptic in their references, on which I had to spend many hours. I have added my findings in square brackets in the footnotes—in fact, all content in square brackets in footnotes is my doing.

It is a particular pleasure to be able to include Pierre Larcher's contributions to linguistics and the Koran, since this is an abstruse subject avoided by all collections of the present kind. Larcher himself laments the lack of linguistic interest in the Koran, "For a linguist, even an Arabist or specialist of Arabic, the Koran is nothing other than a text written in Arabic; a text that he normally only consults to verify in context a quote found by way of another text. The indifference of the majority of Arabist linguists of today to the Koranic text, easy to verify statistically, is inexplicable by reasons at the same time internal and external to the discipline." Michael Schub has characteristically original observations on the difficult task of translation from the Arabic.

The work of Mingana and Jeffery on manuscripts and variants (parts 3 and 4) is well respected and continues to be of great importance, especially since the recent renewal of interest in these two domains thanks to the research and publications of, among others, Gerd-R. Puin. Jeffery's article on the Samarqand Koran will be of particular interest in the light of recent publications by Puin and Christoph Luxenberg.

Any anthology of this genre inevitably reflects personal choices of the editor. The selection of the present articles as well as the general introduction express my personal thoughts on these matters without my being limited to them. No scholar remains free of the consequences of his own choices and personal opinions. Nonetheless, my editorial decisions and closely argued comments are neither arbitrary nor perverse.

As on previous occasions, it would have been not only a duty but also a great pleasure to acknowledge all the kindness and generosity of all those scholars who helped me and saved me from sundry blunders. But once again not wishing to embroil them in any controversy I shall refrain from naming them. However, two such scholars, Marie-Thérèse Urvoy and Dominique Urvoy, upon reading my reticence to name any Islamologists, made it known to me that not only were they happy at having helped me but were equally content to be openly acknowledged if I so wished. So it is a great pleasure to thank Marie-Thérèse Urvoy for her advanced classes on the finer points of Arabic grammar, and her sense of humor and hospitality, and Dominique Urvoy, who spent long hours transliterating Arabic and lent me the difficult to obtain copy of Henri Lammens's *Fatima et les Filles de Muhammad* and his lecture notes on Islamic history. Having gained their permission, I am also able to thank Dr. Gerd-R. Puin and Dr. Elisabeth Puin for their patience in answering my endless questions and queries, for sending me innumerable copies of important articles by authors of whom I had never heard, and for their graciousness and kindness.

It remains for me to add that the opinions expressed, the very tone of the introduction, and any errors that persist are entirely my responsibility.

Ibn Warraq
June 2011

NOTES

1. Ibn Warraq, ed., *The Quest for the Historical Muhammad* (Amherst, NY: Prometheus Books, 2000).

2. Chase F. Robinson, *Islamic Historiography* (Cambridge: Cambridge University Press, 2003).

3. Ibn Warraq, ed., *What the Koran Really Says* (Amherst, NY: Prometheus Books, 2002).

4. Ibn Warraq, ed., *The Origins of the Koran* (Amherst, NY: Prometheus Books, 1998).

5. Chase Robinson, "From Hand to Hand," review of *What the Koran Really Says*, *Times Literary Supplement*, September 12, 2003, p. 28.

6. M. Swartz, review of *The Quest for the Historical Muhammad* in *Choice*, October 2000.

7. E-mail from Günter Lüling, November 24, 2005.

8. "Credulous," *Moi?* I am often accused of being too rationalistic and skeptical—Andrew Bostom once called me "The Amazing Randi" of Koranic studies. The Amazing Randi is a distinguished skeptic, long associated with magazines like the *Skeptical Inquirer* and the *Skeptic*. Randi is a debunker or rather tester of those who claim to possess special powers of a supernatural or paranormal nature, something he does with the help of rigorous experiments devised by himself.

9. Angelika Neuwirth, "Qur'ān and History—A Disputed Relationship: Some Reflections on Qur'anic History and History in the Qur'ān," *Journal of Quranic Studies* 5, no. 1 (2003): 1–18.

10. *Panoramique* (Paris), February 2000. An English translation can be found at http://www.secularislam.org/reviews/rodinson.htm.

11. C. Gilliot, "Review of *Why I Am Not a Muslim*, *The Origins of the Koran*, and *The Quest for the Historical Muhammad*," *Arabica* 47 (2000): 566–71.

12. Ibid., p. 568, end of second paragraph.

13. Ibid., p. 571.

14. Jacques Berlinerblau, *The Secular Bible: Why Nonbelievers Must Take Religion Seriously* (Cambridge: Cambridge University Press, 2005), p. 129.

15. David Myers, *Resisting History: Historicism and Its Discontents in German-Jewish Thought (Jews, Christians, and Muslims from the Ancient to the Modern World)* (Princeton, NJ: Princeton University Press, 2003).

Transliteration and Other Technical Matters

There is no universally accepted system of transliteration (transcription) of the Semitic scripts. The authors in this anthology use two different systems for the Arabic alphabet. As some editors in whose journals the articles first appeared insisted that we not change one single letter as a precondition for allowing us to reproduce them, I was unable to standardize all the articles and adopt just one system. However, the two systems are not that difficult to come to grips with. For Arabic they are:

(1) ʾ, b, t, th, j, ḥ, kh, d, dh, r, z, s, sh, ṣ, ḍ, ṭ, ẓ, ʿ, gh, f, q, k, l, m, n, h, w, y. *Short vowels*: a, u, i. *Long vowels*: ā, ū, ī

(2) ʾ, b, t, ṯ, ǧ, ḥ, ḫ, d, ḏ, r, z, s, š, ṣ, ḍ, ṭ, ẓ, ʿ, ġ, f, q, k, l, m, n, h, w, y. *Short vowels*: a, u, i. *Long vowels*: ā, ū, ī

The journal *Studia Islamica* uses and recommends system (1) on the whole I have used this system in my own introduction and translations.

The journal *Arabica*, on the other hand, uses system (2); thus, the articles from this journal included in this anthology follow suit. (Readers are also likely to encounter, though not often in this anthology, the following variations: *dj* for *j*, and *ḳ* for *q*, for example, in *EI2* [the second edition of *The Encyclopedia of Islam*].)

For the Hebrew and Syriac, I use the following:

ʾ, b, g, d, h, w, z, ḥ, ṭ, y, k, l, m, n, s, ʿ, p, ṣ, q, r, ś/š, t

All long vowels are overlined. The small raised ^{e} stands for a hurried or neutral vowel. Underlined letters (as in bēṯ) are pronounced as fricatives, thus ṯ = English "th" as in "thin"; p̱ = "ph" as in "phial."

Right up to the 1930s, Western scholars used the edition of the Koran by Gustav Flügel (sometimes spelled Fluegel), *Corani Textus Arabicus* (1834), whose numbering of verses differs from what has now become the "official" or Standard Egyptian edition, first published in 1924. Again, not only was it obviously much easier for me to leave the original Flügel numbering in the pre-1924 articles included in this anthology, but in some cases it was even essential not to interfere with the original numbering, since some pieces only referred to Flügel's edition. As one scholar reminded me, attempting to change the numbering would only have increased the possibility of further errors.

TRANSCRIPTION/TRANSLITERATION

Consonants

ا	alif		ض	ḍā d	ḍ
ب	bā᾽	b	ط	ṭā ᾽	ṭ
ت	tā᾽	t	ظ	ẓā᾽	ẓ
ث	thā᾽	th/ṯ	ع	ʿayn	ʿ
ج	jīm	j/ǧ/dj	غ	ghayn	gh/ġ
ح	ḥā᾽	ḥ	ف	fā᾽	f
خ	khā᾽	kh/ḫ/x	ق	qāf	q/ḳ
د	dāl	d	ك	kāf	k
ذ	dhāl	dh/ḏ	ل	lām	l
ر	rā᾽	r	م	mīm	m
ز	zay	z	ن	nūn	n
س	sīn	s	ه	hā᾽	h
ش	shīn	sh/š	و	wāw	w
ص	ṣād	ṣ	ى	yā᾽	y

(ء hamza ᾽)

Vowels

ا	ā/â	َ	fatḥa	a
و	ū	ُ	ḍamma	u
ى	ī	ِ	kasra	i

Dipthongs : aw, ay

آ	᾽alif-madda	᾽ā	لا	lām-᾽alif lā
ة	tā᾽marbūṭa	-at-	ّ	shadda (doubling consonant)

ى alif maqṣūra (pronounced like lengthening alif) ā

Part 1

Introduction

Introduction

Ibn Warraq

> It is an extraordinary thing that we still have no critical text of the Qur'ān for common use.
>
> Arthur Jeffery, 1937[1]

There is no such thing as *the* Koran. There is no, and there never has been, a *textus receptus ne varietur* of the holy book of the Muslims. We have two kinds of evidence for this claim. One comes from Muslims themselves. Many classical Muslim scholars–Koranic commentators, collectors of hadith, lexica, and *qirā'āt* books, for example, have acknowledged not only that many verses revealed to Muḥammad have been lost, and hence the Koran that we possess is incomplete, but also that the Koran assembled, whether by Abū Bakr, ʿUmar, ʿAlī, or ʿUthmān, is capable of being read in different ways—in other words, that variants exist. There are a number of hadiths that recount "the loss, withdrawal, or forgetting of this or that 'verse' said to have been revealed to the Prophet but not figuring"[2] in the Koran as it now exists. The other comes from extant Koranic manuscripts, inscriptions, and coins.

HADITH ON THE INCOMPLETENESS OF THE KORAN, VERSES MISSING, MUḤAMMAD'S FAULTY MEMORY

It is admitted by certain Muslim scholars that the Koran as we know it is incomplete:

Al-Suyūṭī, *Itqān fī 'ulūm al-Qur'ān*, two volumes in one, Cairo: Ḥalabī, 1935/1354, pt. 2, p. 25.

> ʿAbdullāh b. ʿUmar reportedly said, "Let none of you say, 'I have got the whole of the Koran.'" How does he know what all of it is? Much of the Koran has gone [Arabic: *ḏahaba*]. Let him say instead, "I have got what has survived."[3]

This sentiment is echoed by a hadith in al-Sijistānī, ʿAbd Allāh b. Sulaymān b. al-Ashʿath, Abū Bakr Ibn Abī Dāwūd's *Kitāb al-Maṣāḥif*:

> ʿUmar b. al-Khaṭṭāb enquired about a verse of the Book of God. On being informed that it had been in the possession of so-and-so who had been killed in the Yemāma wars, ʿUmar exclaimed the formula expressing loss, "We are God's and unto Him is our return." ʿUmar gave the command and the Qur'ān was collected. He was the first to collect the Qur'ān.[4]

Clearly, many verses were lost when those companions who had memorized parts of the divine revelation perished during the Yemāma wars.

Once again from al-Sijistānī, ʿAbd Allāh b. Sulaymān b. al-Ashʿath, Abū Bakr Ibn Abī Dāwūd's *Kitāb al-Maṣāḥif*:

> Zuhrī reports, "We have heard that many Qur'ān passages were revealed but that those who had memorised them fell in the Yemāma fighting. Those passages had not been written down and, following the deaths of those who knew them, were no longer known; nor had Abū Bakr, nor ʿUmar nor 'Uthmān as yet collected the texts of the Qur'ān.[5] Those lost passages were not to be found with anyone after the deaths of those who had memorised them. This, I understand, was one of the considerations which impelled them to pursue the Qur'ān during the reign of Abū Bakr, committing it to sheets for fear that there should perish in further theatres of war men who bore much of the Qur'ān which they would take to their grave with them on their fall, and which, with their passing, would not be found with any other."[6]

Here is Bukhārī on a certain verse that used to be recited as a part of the Koran but was somehow "canceled":

Bukhārī, *al-Ṣaḥīḥ,* vol. 5, book LXIV: *Al-Maghāzī*, chapter 29, hadith 4090, p. 254.

Narrated Anas bin Mālik: The tribes of Ri ʻl, Dhakwān, ʻUṣaiyya and Banī Liḥyān asked Allāh's Messenger to provide them with some men to support them against their enemy. He therefore provided them with seventy men from the Anṣār whom we used to call al-Qurrā' in their lifetime. They used to collect wood by daytime and offer *Ṣalāt* [prayer] at night. When they were at the well of Maʻūna, the infidels killed them by betraying them. When this news reached the Prophet, he said al-Qunūt for one month in the morning *Ṣalāt* [prayer], invoking evil upon some of the Arab tribes, upon Ri ʻl, Dhakwān, ʻUṣaiyya and Banī Liḥyān. We used to read a verse of the Qur'ān revealed in their connection, but later the verse was cancelled. It was: "convey to our people on our behalf the information that we have met our Lord, and He is pleased with us, and has made us pleased." Anas bin Mālik added: Allāh's Prophet said al-Qunūt for one month in the morning *Ṣalāt* [prayer], invoking evil upon some of the Arab tribes, upon Ri ʻl, Dhakwān, ʻUṣaiyya and Banī Liḥyān. Anas added: Those seventy Anṣārī men were killed at the well of *Maʻūna.*[7]

Both the Koran (LXXXVII, 6–7) and certain hadiths imply that Muḥammad himself was capable of forgetting some verses:

Bukhārī, *al-Ṣaḥīḥ,* vol. 6, book LXVI, *Kitāb Faḍā'il l-Qur'ān,* chapter 25, hadith 5037, p. 449.

Narrated ʻĀ'isha: The Prophet heard a man reciting the Qur'ān in the mosque, and he said, "May Allah bestow His Mercy upon him, as he has reminded me of such-and-such verses of such-and-such sura."

Narrated Hishām: [The same hadith, adding]: which I missed from such-and-such sura.

*

Bukhārī, *al-Ṣaḥīḥ,* vol. 6, book LXVI, *Kitāb Faḍā'il l-Qur'ān*, chapter 25, hadith 5038, p. 449. [See also Muslim, *Ṣaḥīḥ*, vol. 1, chapter 274, hadiths 1720 and 1721, p. 456.]

> Narrated ʿĀʾisha: Allah's Messenger heard a man reciting the Qurʾān at night, and said, "May Allah bestow His Mercy on him, as he has reminded me of such-and-such verses of such-and-such a Surah, which I was caused to forget."

*

Bukhārī, *al-Ṣaḥīḥ*, vol. 6, book LXVI, *Kitāb Faḍāʾil l-Qurʾān*, chapter 25, hadith 5039, p. 449.

> Narrated 'Abdullāh: The Prophet said, "Why does anyone of the people say, 'I have forgotten such-and-such verses [of the Qurʾān]?' He, in fact, is caused to forget."

*

Muslim, *Ṣaḥīḥ*. vol. 1, *Kitāb al-Ṣalāt*, chapter 274, hadith 1724, p. 457.

> 'Abdullah reported Allah's Messenger (may peace be upon him) as saying: What a wretched person is he amongst them who says: I have forgotten such-and-such a verse. [He should instead of using this expression say] I have been made to forgẹt it. Try to remember the Qurʾān for it is more apt to escape from men's minds than a hobbled camel.[8]

*

Abū Dāwūd, *Sunan*, book II: *Kitāb al-Ṣalāt*, chapter 347, number 1015, vol. I, pp. 260–61.

> Narrated ʿAbd Allah ibn Masʿūd: The Apostle of Allah (may peace be upon him) offered prayer. The version of the narrator ʾIbrāhīm goes: I do not know whether he increased or decreased [the *rak'ahs* of prayer]. When he gave the salutation, he was asked: Has something new happened in the prayer, Apostle of Allah? He said: What is it? They said: You prayed so many and so many [*rak'ahs*]. He then relented his foot and faced the Qiblah and made two prostrations. He then gave the salutation. When he turned

away [finished the prayer], he turned his face to us and said: Had anything new happened in prayer, I would have informed you. I am only a human being and I forget just as you do; so when I forget, remind me, and when any of you is in doubt about his prayer he should aim at what is correct, and complete his prayer in that respect, then give the salutation and afterwards make two prostrations.[9]

*

If the Prophet was capable of forgetting, then it is not at all surprising that his companions also avow to lapses of memory. Abū Mūsā, for instance, confesses [Muslim, *Ṣaḥīḥ. Kitāb al-Zakāt*, vol. 2, hadith 2286, pp. 602–603]:

Abū Ḥarb b. Abu al-Aswad reported on the authority of his father that Abū Mūsā al-Ash'arī sent for the reciters of Baṣra. They came to him and they were three hundred in number. They recited the Qur'ān and he said: You are among the best among the inhabitants of Baṣra, for you are the reciters among them. So continue to recite it. [But bear in mind] that your reciting for a long time may not harden your hearts as were hardened the hearts of those before you. We used to recite a surah which resembled in length and severity to Surah Barā'at. I have forgotten it with the exception of this which I remember out of it: "If there were two valleys full of riches, for the son of Adam, he would long for a third valley, and nothing would fill the stomach of the son of Adam but dust." And we used to recite a surah which resembled one of the surahs of Mushabbiḥāt,[10] and I have forgotten it, but remember [this much] out of it: "O people who believe, why do you say that which you do not practise" (LXI, 2) and "that is recorded in your necks as a witness [against you] and you would be asked about it on the Day of Resurrection" (XVII, 13).

*

Mālik in his *Muwaṭṭā'* also recounts how certain verses concerning prayers are missing from the Koran as we know it:

Mālik, *Muwaṭṭā'*, book I, *Kitāb al-Ṣalāt*, chapter 78, hadith 307, p. 64.

> Abū Yūnus, freedman of ʿĀʾishah, Mother of the Believers, reported: ʿĀʾishah ordered me to transcribe the Holy Qurʾān and asked me to let her know when I should arrive at the verse (II, 238) *ḥāfiẓū ʿalā –ṣ-ṣalawāti wa-ṣ-ṣalāti-l-wusṭā wa qūmū li-l-lāhi qānitīn* (Guard strictly your [habit of] prayers, especially the Middle Prayer;[11] and stand before God in a devout [frame of mind]).
>
> When I arrived at that verse, I informed her and she ordered: Write in this way:
>
> *ḥāfiẓū ʿalā –ṣ-ṣalawāti wa-ṣ-ṣalāti-l-wusṭā wa-ṣ-ṣalāti –l-ʿaṣri wa qūmū li-l-lāhi qānitīn* (Guard strictly your [habit of] prayers, especially the Middle Prayer and the *ʿaṣr* prayer and stand before God in a devout [frame of mind]).
>
> She added that she had heard it so from the Apostle of Allah (*mpbuh*).

Mālik has another hadith very similar to the above but this time with *Ḥafṣah* making the addition to the Koranic verse: Mālik, *Muwaṭṭāʾ*, book I: *Kitāb al-Ṣalāt*, chapter 78, hadith 308, pp. 64–65.[12]

Stoning Verses

The above is a clear acknowledgment that certain passages of verses revealed to the Prophet and memorized by his companions have been irrevocably lost. One such passage lost (left out deliberately) from the Koran but preserved in the hadith is the verse concerning stoning to death for adultery. The Sharia prescribes the penalty for adultery as death by stoning, which conflicts with the penalty mentioned in the Koran XXIV, 2, "The adulteress and the adulterer, flog each one of them one hundred strokes." Verse 15 of sura IV is also taken to apply to adultery; women found guilty of adultery were to be confined "in quarters until death release them or God appoint a way for them." The need to explain this contradiction between the Koran and actual practice led to the invention of a hadith sanctioning the latter. John Burton has argued that the story about the verse of stoning was put into circulation by the followers of Shāfiʿī "who did not accept that a sunna can abrogate a Quranic revelation and were forced to find a source with higher authority for the lawfulness of stoning for fornication."[13]

Muslim, *Ṣaḥīḥ*, *Kitāb al-Ḥudūd*, chapter 681, hadith 4194, p. 1100.

> ʿAbd Allāh b. al-ʿAbbās reported that ʿUmar b. al-Khaṭṭāb sat on the pulpit of Allah's Messenger and said: Verily Allah sent Muḥammad with truth and He sent down the Book upon him, and the verse of stoning was included in what was sent down to him. We recited it, retained it in our memory and understood it. Allah's Messenger awarded the punishment of stoning to death [to the married adulterer and adulteress] and, after him, we also awarded the punishment of stoning. I am afraid that, with the lapse of time, the people [may forget it] and may say: We do not find the punishment of stoning in the Book of Allah, and thus go astray by abandoning this duty prescribed by Allah. Stoning is a duty laid down in Allah's Book for married men and women who commit adultery when proof is established, or if there is pregnancy, or a confession.

*

Bukhārī, *al-Ṣaḥīḥ,* vol. 8, book LXXXVI: *Kitāb al-Ḥudūd*, chapter 31, hadith 6830, p. 431.

> Allah sent Muḥammad [saw] with the Truth and revealed the Holy Book to him, and among what Allah revealed, was the Verse of the Rajam [the stoning of married persons, male and female, who commit adultery] and we did recite this verse and understood and memorized it. Allah's Apostle [saw] did carry out the punishment of stoning and so did we after him. I am afraid that after a long time has passed, somebody will say, "By Allah, we do not find the Verse of the Rajam in Allah's Book," and thus they will go astray by leaving an obligation which Allah has revealed.

Ibn Isḥāq's biography of Muḥammad has ʿUmar saying, "Verily stoning in the book of God is a penalty laid on married men and women who commit adultery, if proof stands or pregnancy is clear or confession is made."[14]

The hadith collection of Mālik confirms that there was indeed a verse concerning stoning that is missing from the actual Koran.

Mālik, *Muwaṭṭāʾ*, book XXIX: *Kitāb al-Ḥudūd*, chapter 493, hadith 1519:

Mālik related to me from Nāfi' that 'Abd Allāh Ibn 'Umar said, "The Jews came to the Messenger of Allah, may Allah bless him and grant him peace, and mentioned to him that a man and woman from among them had committed adultery. The Messenger of Allah, may Allah bless him and grant him peace, asked them, 'What do you find in the Torah about stoning?' They said, 'We make their wrong action known and flog them.' 'Abd Allah ibn Salām said, 'You have lied! It has stoning for it, so bring the Torah.' They spread it out and one of them placed his hand over the ayat of stoning. Then he read what was before it and what was after it. 'Abd Allah ibn Salām told him to lift his hand. He lifted his hand and there was the ayat of stoning. They said, 'He has spoken the truth, Muḥammad. The ayat of stoning is in it.' So the Messenger of Allah, may Allah bless him and grant him peace, gave the order and they were stoned."

*

Mālik, *Muwaṭṭā'*, book XXIX: *Kitāb al-Ḥudūd*, chapter 493, hadith 1520.

Mālik related to me from Yaḥyā b. Sā'id from Sa'īd ibn al-Musayyab that a man from the Aslam tribe came to Abū Bakr as-Ṣiddīq and said to him, "I have committed adultery." Abū Bakr said to him, "Have you mentioned this to anyone else?" He said, "No." Abū Bakr said to him, "Then cover it up with the veil of Allah. Allah accepts tawba from his slaves." His self was still unsettled, so he went to 'Umar b. al-Khaṭṭāb. He told him the same as he had said to Abū Bakr, and 'Umar told him the same as Abū Bakr had said to him. His self was still not settled so he went to the Messenger of Allah, may Allah bless him and grant him peace, and said to him, "I have committed adultery," insistently. The Messenger of Allah, may Allah bless him and grant him peace, turned away from him three times. Each time the Messenger of Allah, may Allah bless him and grant him peace, turned away from him until it became too much. The Messenger of Allah, may Allah bless him and grant him peace, questioned his family, "Does he have an illness which affects his mind, or is he mad?" They said, "Messenger of Allah, by Allah, he is well." The Messenger of Allah, may Allah bless him and grant him peace, said, "Unmarried or married?" They said, "Married, Messenger of Allah." The Messenger of Allah, may Allah bless him and grant him peace, gave the order and he was stoned.

*

Mālik, *Muwaṭṭā'*, book XXIX: *Kitāb al-Ḥudūd*, chapter 493, hadith 1522.

Mālik related to me that Ibn Shihāb informed him that a man confessed that he had committed adultery in the time of the Messenger of Allah, may Allah bless him and grant him peace, and he testified against himself four times, so the Messenger of Allah, may Allah bless him and grant him peace, gave the order and he was stoned.

Ibn Shihāb said, "Because of this a man is to be taken for his own confession against himself."

*

Mālik, *Muwaṭṭā'*, book XXIX: *Kitāb al-Ḥudūd*, chapter 493, hadith 1523.

Mālik related to me from Yaqūb ibn Zayd ibn Talḥa from his father Zayd ibn Talḥa that ʿAbd Allah ibn Abī Mulayka informed him that a woman came to the Messenger of Allah, may Allah bless him and grant him peace, and informed him that she had committed adultery and was pregnant. The Messenger of Allah, may Allah bless him and grant him peace, said to her, "Go away until you give birth." When she had given birth, she came to him. The Messenger of Allah, may Allah bless him and grant him peace, said to her, "Go away until you have suckled and weaned the baby." When she had weaned the baby, she came to him. He said, "Go and entrust the baby to someone." She entrusted the baby to someone and then came to him. He gave the order and she was stoned.

*

Mālik, *Muwaṭṭā'*, book XXIX: *Kitāb al-Ḥudūd*, chapter 493, hadith 1524.

Mālik related to me from Ibn Shihāb from Ubayd Allah ibn ʿAbd Allah Ibn ʿUtba ibn Masʿūd that Abū Hurayra and Zayd ibn Khālid al-Juhanī informed him that two men brought a dispute to the Messenger of Allah, may Allah bless him and grant him peace. One of them said, "Messenger of Allah! Judge between us by the Book of Allah!" The other said, and he was the wiser of the two, "Yes, Messenger of Allah. Judge between us by the Book of Allah and give me permission to speak." He said, "Speak." He said, "My son was hired by this person and he committed fornication with his wife. He told me that my son deserved stoning, and I ransomed him for one hundred sheep and a slave girl. Then I asked the people of knowledge and they told me that my son deserved to be flogged with one hundred lashes and exiled for a year, and they informed me that the woman deserved to be stoned." The Messenger of Allah, may Allah bless him and grant him peace, said, "By him in whose Hand myself is, I will judge between you by the Book of Allah. As for your sheep and slave girl, they should be returned to you. Your son should have one hundred lashes and be exiled for a year." He ordered Unays al-Aslamī to go to the wife of the other man and to stone her if she confessed. She confessed and he stoned her.

*

ʿĀʾishah has an original explanation as to how the stoning verse came to be omitted:

> The stoning verse and another verse were revealed and recorded on a sheet (*ṣaḥīfa*) which was placed for safe-keeping under her bedding. When the Prophet fell ill and the household were preoccupied with nursing him, a domestic animal got in from the yard and gobbled up the sheet.[15]

Suckling Verse

Muslim, *Ṣaḥīḥ*, *Kitāb al-Nikāḥ*, chapter 565, hadith 3421.

> Narrated ʿĀʾishah: It had been revealed in the Qur'ān that ten clear sucklings make the marriage unlawful, then it was abrogated [and substituted] by five sucklings and Allah's Apostle (*pbuh*) died and it was before that time [found] in the Qur'ān [and recited by the Muslims].

Different Readings Allowed by Prophet: Seven Readings

Various hadiths recount how the Koran was revealed to the Prophet in seven different ways, in Arabic *Sab'atu aḥruf.* The word *aḥruf* is often translated as "seven sets of readings" or sometimes "dialects," though strictly speaking *aḥruf* is simply the plural of *ḥarf*, meaning "letter." By changing the inflections and accentuations of words, it is claimed, the Koranic text may be read in the seven dialects of the Quraysh, Ṭāʾī, Hawāzin, Yaman, Saqīf, Hudhayl, and Tamīm. More than forty interpretations have been offered for this enigmatic word.[16]

Bukhārī, *al-Ṣaḥīḥ*, vol. 6, book LXVI: *Kitāb Faḍāʾil l-Qurʾān*, chapter 5, hadith 4992, p. 428.

> Narrated ʿUmar b. al-Khaṭṭāb: I heard Hishām bin Ḥakīm bin Ḥizām reciting Surat-al-Furqān in a way different to that of mine. Allah's Messenger had taught it to me [in a different way]. So, I was about to quarrel with him [during the prayer] but I waited till he finished, then I tied his garment round his neck and seized him by it and brought him to Allah's Messenger and said, "I have heard him reciting Surat-al-Furqān in a way different to the way you taught it to me." The Prophet ordered me to release him and asked Hishām to recite it. When he recited it, Allah's Messenger said, "It was revealed in this way." He then asked me to recite it. When I recited it, he said, "It was revealed in this way. The Qurʾān has been revealed in seven different ways, so recite it in the way that is easier for you."

*

Bukhārī, *al-Ṣaḥīḥ*, vol. 6, book LXVI: *Kitāb Faḍāʾil l-Qurʾān*, chapter 5, hadith 4991, pp. 427–28.

> Narrated 'Abdullah bin *ʿAbbās*: Allah's Messenger said, "Gabriel recited the Qurʾān to me in one way. Then I requested him [to read it in another way], and continued asking him to recite it in other ways, and he recited it in several ways till he ultimately recited it in seven different ways."

If we do interpret these hadiths to mean merely differences of pronunciation, a question of different dialects—if truth be told, we have no idea what they really mean—we must distinguish them, however, from the variants recorded by Ibn Masʿūd, Ubai Ibn Ka'b, and others, which testify to real differences of substance and content, differences in the consonantal text, often lending different meanings to the Koranic text. The latter could not be dismissed as differences in pronunciation.

Ibn Mujāhid (died 935 CE), the influential imam of the readers in Baghdad, basing himself on the above hadith, banned the use of the codex of Ibn Masʿūd and other uncanonical readings, and recognized seven readers as authorities. He was supported by the government and the courts. Some scholars, such as Ibn Shannabūdh (died 939 CE), were literally flogged into submission, others were compelled, such as Ibn Miqsam (died 944 CE), to give up their own readings. To add to the confusion, each of the accepted seven readings was transmitted independently by two transmitters, giving us the following schema:

District	Reader	First Transmitter (Rawi)	Second Transmitter (Rawi)
Medina	Nāfi'(d. 785)	Warsh (812)	Qālūn (835)
Mecca	Ibn-Kathīr (737)	al-Bazzī (854)	Qunbul (903)
Damascus	Ibn- ʿĀmir (736)	Hishām (859)	Ibn-Dhakwān (856)
Basra	Abū ʿAmr (770)	ad-Dūrī (860)	as-Sūsī (874)
Kufa	ʿĀṣim (744)	Ḥafṣ (805)	Shu'ba (809)
Kufa	Ḥamza (772)	Khalaf (843)	Khallād (835)
Kufa	al-Kisāʾī (804)	ad-Dūrī (860)	Abū-l-Ḥārith (854)

However, not all Muslim scholars accepted the restriction to these seven readers; some spoke of ten readers (each with two transmitters), while others spoke of fourteen. We may tabulate these as follows:

The Three after the Seven

District	Reader	First Transmitter	Second Transmitter
Medina	Abū-Jaʿfar (d. 747)	ʿĪsā Ibn Wirdān (776)	Abū l-Rabīʿ ibn Jummāz (786)
Basra	Yaʿqūb al-Ḥaḍramī (820)	Ruways (852)[17]	Rawḥ Ibn ʿAbd-al-Muʾmin (848)
Kufa	Khalaf (843)	Isḥāq al-Warrāq (899)	Idrīs al-Ḥaddād (904)

The Four after the Ten

Mecca	Ibn Muḥayṣin (740)	al-Bazzī (854)	Ibn Shannabūdh (939)
Basra	al-Yazīdī (817)	al-Baghdādī (849)	Abū Jaʿfar al-Baghdādī (915)
Basra	al-Ḥasan al-Baṣrī (728)	al-Balkhī l-Baghdādī (806)	al-Dūrī (860)
Kufa	al-Aʿmash (765)	al-Baṣrī (981)	Shannabūdh l-Baghdādī (998)

Western scholars have yet to make a systematic study of the entire problem of these readings. Scholars sometimes omit to note that books composed on the Eight Readers, the Eleven Readers, or the Thirteen Readers include readers not mentioned in the above lists. Thus the *Raudat al-Huffaz* of al-Muʿaddil includes the readings of Ḥumayd b. Qays, Ibn as-Sumayfīʿ, and Ṭalḥa b. Muṣarrif. The *Kāmil* of al-Hudhalī is said to have contained readings of forty extra readers.[18] Other writers who have preserved old variants representing a different type of consonantal text from that of the ʻUthmānic text include al-ʻUkbarī (1219) of Baghdad, Ibn Khālawayh (980) of Aleppo, and Ibn Jinnī (1002).[19] *The Fihrist of al-Nadīm* lists a host of readers "with odd systems"[20] organized geographically. Thus the people of al-Madinah boasted five readers with their own readings; the people of Makkah had four readers with their own readings, the people of Basrah, five; the people of al-Kufah, five; the people of al-Sham, three; the people of al-Yaman, one; and so on. Not only were there disagreements among the seven primary readers as recorded by Abū Ṭāhir in his book *The Disagreement between Abū ʿAmr and al-Kisāʾī* but also between the primary readers and their own transmitters as recorded in the same author's *The Disagreement between the Adherents of ʿĀṣim and Ḥafṣ ibn Sulaymān.*[21] Ibn Miqsam (died 944 CE) and al-Naqqāsh (died 962 CE) both expressed their disagreement with the seven in books titled *The Seven with Their Defects.*[22] Al-Nadīm also lists more than thirty books[23] that discuss the ambiguous or obscure passages in the Koran; presumably these ambiguities can only be resolved by one or other of the countless readings proposed by the hundred or more readers.

In the fourth Islamic century we have the works of Ibn al-Anbārī, Ibn Ashta, and al-Sijistānī ʿAbd Allāh b. Sulaymān b. al-Ashʿath Abū Bakr Ibn Abī Dāwūd, all of whom wrote works on the old codices, though only that of al-Sijistānī ʿAbd Allāh b. Sulaymān b. al-Ashʿath, Abū Bakr Ibn Abī Dāwūd has survived in its entirety.[24]

Variants

The Arabic term *qirāʾa* can mean recitation (either of single parts of the Koran or the entire Koran), or a particular reading of a passage of the Koran, that is, a variant (plural = *qirāʾāt*) or even a particular reading of the entire Koran. In the latter case, we often speak of the *qirāʾa* of Ibn Masʿūd.[25]

As Jeffery has pointed out, we cannot easily dismiss these variants,

> for it's quite clear that the text which ʿUthmān canonized was only one out of many rival texts, and we needs must investigate what went before the canonical text. . . . [T]here is grave suspicion that ʿUthmān may have seriously edited the text that he canonized. It was therefore worth attempting an assembling of all the material that has survived from the rival texts. . . . Some of the variants seem linguistically impossible, and indeed are occasionally noted as such in the sources which quote them. Some give one the impression of being inventions of later philologers who fathered their

> inventions on these early authorities. The great majority, however, merit consideration as genuine survivals from the pre-ʻUthmānic stage of the text, though only after they have passed the most searching criticism of modern scholarship by scholars approaching them from different points of view, shall we be free to use them in the attempted reconstruction of the history of the text.[26]

Jeffery came across by chance the manuscript of al-Sijistānī, ʿAbd Allāh b. Sulaymān b. al-Ashʻath, Abū Bakr Ibn Abī Dāwūd's Kitāb al-Maṣāḥif, "which studied the state of the Qurʾān text prior to its canonization in the standard text of ʻUthmān."[27] Jeffery, drawing upon Abī Dāwūd's work, and other sources, established a list of fifteen primary codices and thirteen secondary ones. That there were indeed written codices that differed from the so-called ʻUthmānic text, or differed from manuscript to manuscript, is confirmed by al-Nadīm. The tenth-century scholar[28] al-Nadīm, in his celebrated work of reference, *The Fihrist*, gives a list of books devoted to discrepancies in the various Koranic manuscripts:

> Books Composed about Discrepancies of the [Koranic] Manuscripts.
>
> The Discrepancies between the *Manuscripts of the People of al-Madīnah, al-Kūfah, and al-Baṣrah*, according to al-Kisāʾī; book of Khalaf, *Discrepancies of the Manuscripts*; *Discrepancies of the People of al-Kūfah, al-Baṣrah, and Syria concerning the Manuscripts*, by al-Farrāʾ; *Discrepancies between the Manuscripts*, by Abū Dāʾūd al-Sijistānī; book of al-Madāʾinī about the discrepancies between the manuscripts and the compiling of the Qurʾān; *Discrepancies between the Manuscripts of Syria, al-Ḥijāz, and al-ʻIrāq*, by Ibn ʿāmir al-Yaḥṣubī Amir al-Yahsubi; book of Muḥammad ibn ʿAbd al-Raḥmān al-Iṣbahānī about discrepancy of the manuscripts.[29]

The written codex of Ibn Masʿūd (died 653 CE) was well regarded in Kufa whereas the codex of Ubai ibn Kaʻb (died 649 CE or 654 CE) was highly esteemed in most parts of Syria. However, we do not possess any of the early codices, and the variant readings of Ibn Masʿūd or Ubai ibn Kaʻb have only come down to us in the early scholarly literature.

Ibn Mas'ūd

I have seen a number of Quranic manuscripts, which the transcribers recorded as manuscripts of Ibn Mas'ūd. No two of the Quranic copies were in agreement.

—*The Fihrist of al-Nadīm*

Abdullah b. Mas'ūd was a companion of Muḥammad and claimed to have learned seventy suras directly from the mouth of the Prophet. According to tradition, Ibn Mas'ūd was the first to teach Koran reading. Later in Kūfah, he became famous as a traditionist and as an authority on the Koran. His codex was favored by the Shī'a.

There are several remarkable features about Ibn Mas'ūd's codex. First, it did not contain sura 1 (*the Fātiḥah)* and the last two suras, suras 113 and 114, known as the *Mu'awwidhatān* (since the principal word in them is *'a'ūdhu* [I take refuge]). Second, the order and even the name of the suras differed considerably from the 'Uthmān recension. The two lists that give the order of the suras do not agree either. The earlier list, that of al-Nadīm in *The Fihrist*,[30] leaves out suras 1, 15, 18, 20, 27, 42, 99, 113, and 114, while the list in the *Itqān* of as-Suyūṭī leaves out suras 1, 113, 114, 50, 57, and 69.[31]

Here we give some of the variants from Ibn Mas'ūd as collected by Arthur Jeffery from written sources, since we do not possess any manuscripts of Ibn Mas'ūd's version. The verses are quoted according to the Kufan verse numbering given in the 1342 Cairo edition of the Koran followed by the number of the verse in Flügel's edition; where Flügel's numbering agrees with the Kufan numbering, only one verse number is given. Jeffery prefaces his list of Ibn Mas'ūd's variants with these explanatory notes: "The variant readings which follow are necessarily arranged according to the order of the present official text [1342 Cairo edition]. Sometimes in the sources the variant is expressly said to come from the Codex of Ibn Mas'ūd. More often it is merely given as a reading (*ḥarf* or *qirā'a*) of Ibn Mas'ūd. Occasionally also readings are given as coming from the Companions of Ibn Mas'ūd, but as these obviously represent the tradition as to his text they are included here."[32]

SŪRA I

4/3: مَالِكِ — He agreed with TR against the alternative reading مَلِكِ which, however, some gave from him also.

6/5: إِهْدِنَا — أَرْشِدْنَا.

7/6: ٱلَّذِينَ — مَنْ. So read also by Zaid b. ᶜAlī and Ibn az-Zubair.

7: غَيْرِ — غَيْرَ. So read by ᶜAlī and Ibn az-Zubair.

SŪRA II

2/1: ذَٰلِكَ — تَنْزِيلُ, which involves ٱلْكِتَابِ.

7/6: غِشَٰوَةٌ — غَشْوَةً or some said غَشْيَةٌ. Given from Friends of Ibn Masᶜūd.

9/8: يُخَٰدِعُونَ — يَخْدَعُونَ. So read by Abū Ḥaiwa.

14/13: إِلَىٰ شَيَٰطِينِهِمْ — بِشَيَاطِينِهِمْ. So also Ubai.

17/16: فَلَمَّا أَضَاءَتْ — فَأَضَاءَتْ.

18/17: صُمٌّ بُكْمٌ عُمْيٌ — صُمًّا بُكْمًا عُمْيًا. So read by Ibn Abī Ṭalḥa and Ḥafṣa.

20/19: يَخْطَفُ — يَخْتَطِفُ. Thus read by ᶜAlī.

كُلَّمَا — كُلَّ مَا. Purely orthographic variant.

مَشَوْا فِيهِ — مَرُّوا فِيهِ وَمَضَوْا فِيهِ. See also Ubai's reading.

لَذَهَبَ — لَأَذْهَبَ, which makes the following بِ a zāᵓida.

23/21: نَزَّلْنَا عَلَىٰ عَبْدِنَا — أَنْزَلْنَا عَلَىٰ عِبَادِنَا.

24/22: أُعِدَّتْ — أُعْتِدَتْ or أُعِبِدَتْ.

25/23: مُطَهَّرَةٌ – مُطَهَّرَاتٌ. So read by Zaid b. ʿAlī.

26/24: مَا بَعُوضَةً – وَبَعُوضَةٌ, but others say he read بَعُوضَةٌ without و.
So read by Ruʾba b. al-ʿAjjāj and others.
يُضِلُّ بِهِ كَثِيرٌ وَيُهْدَى بِهِ كَثِيرٌ – يُضِلُّ بِهِ كَثِيرًا وَيَهْدِي بِهِ كَثِيرًا. So Zaid b. ʿAlī and Ubai.
مَا يُضِلُّ بِهِ إِلَّا ٱلْفَاسِقِينَ – مَا يَضِلُّ بِهِ إِلَّا ٱلْفَاسِقُونَ.

31/29: عَرَضَهُمْ – عَرَضَهُنَّ. See also Ubai's reading.

32/30: مَا عَلَّمْتَنَا – مَا أَعْلَمْتَنَا. See also Ubai.

36/34: فَأَزَلَّهُمَا – فَوَسْوَسَ لَهُمَا. So read also by al-Aʿmash.

40/38: بِعَهْدِي – بِعَهْدِيَ. So read by Ṭalḥa b. Muṣarrif.
اُذْكُرُوا – اِذَّكِرُوا.

42/39: تَكْتُمُوا – تَكْتُمُونَ.

46/43: يَظُنُّونَ – يَعْلَمُونَ.

48/45: لَا يُقْبَلُ – لَا يُؤْخَذُ.

49/46: يُذَبِّحُونَ – يُقَتِّلُونَ.

51/48: اتَّخَذْتُمْ – اتَّخَتُّمْ with Idghām.

60/57: تَعْثَوْا – تَعِيثُوا.

61/58: قِثَّائِهَا – قُثَّائِهَا. So Qatāda, Ibn Waththāb and others.
فُومِهَا – ثُومِهَا. As read by ʿAlqama and Ibn ʿAbbās.
مِصْرًا – مِصْرَ. So Ubai, al-Aʿmash and al-Ḥasan. It was also written thus in some of the ʿUthmānic Codices.

63/60: وَاذْكُرُوا – وَتَذَكَّرُوا or some said وَتَذَّكَّرُوا.

68/64: ادْعُ – سَلْ.

70/65: ٱلْبَقَرَ – ٱلْبَاقِرَ. So read by Ubai, ʿIkrima and Yaḥyā b. Yaʿmar.
تَشَٰبَهَ – تَشَّابَهُ or يَشَّابَهُ or مُتَشَابِهٌ which latter was the reading of al-Ḥasan and al-Aʿmash.

72/67: فَادَّارَأْتُمْ – فَتَدَارَأْتُمْ. Read thus by Abū Ḥaiwa.

74/69 : قَسَتْ — قَسَا. So read by Ubai and Zaid b. ʿAlī.

قَسْوَةً — قَسَاوَةً. So also Zaid b. ʿAlī.

83/77 : تَعْبُدُونَ — تَعْبُدُوا or يَعْبُدُوا or some said يَعْبُدُونَ.

حُسْنًا — حَسَنًا, supporting the reading of Ḥamza, al-Kisāʾī and Yaʿqūb.

تَوَلَّيْتُمْ — تَوَلَّوْا. (?). Al-Aʿmash تَوَلَّوْا عَنْهُ.

قَلِيلاً — قَلِيلٌ, a reading which some gave from Abū ʿAmr also.

85/79 : فَرِيقًا — طُوَيْفًا.

وَإِنْ يَأْتُوكُمْ أُسَارَى تُفَادُوهُمْ — وَإِنْ يُؤْخَذُوا تَفْدُوهُمْ. So read also by Al-Aʿmash.

مَنْ يَفْعَلُ — مَنْ فَعَلَ.

87/81 : أَفَكُلَّمَا — أَفَكُلَّ مَا. Purely orthographical variant.

89/83 : مُصَدِّقٌ — مُصَدِّقًا. So given in Ubai's Codex.

96/90 : بِمُزَحْزِحِهِ — بِمُنْزِحِهِ.

100/94 : نَبَذَهُ — نَقَضَهُ.

عَاهَدُوا — عُوهِدُوا. So read also by al-Ḥasan.

101/95 : مُصَدِّقٌ — مُصَدِّقًا. Thus also Ibn Abī ʿAbla.

102/96 : هُمْ بِضَارِّينَ — هُمَا بِضَارَّيْنِ.

104/98 : رَاعِنَا — رَاعُونَا or some said أَرْعُونَا.

105/99 : وَلَا ٱلْمُشْرِكِينَ — وَلَا ٱلْمُشْرِكُونَ. So read by Abū'l-ʿĀliya and al-Aʿmash also.

106/100: مَا نَنْسَخْ مِنْ آيَةٍ أَوْ نُنْسِهَا نَأْتِ بِخَيْرٍ مِنْهَا أَوْ مِثْلِهَا — مَا نُنْسِكَ مِنْ آيَةٍ أَوْ نَنْسَخْهَا نَجِيءْ بِمِثْلِهَا.

108/102: سُئِلَ — سَأَلَ, making Mūsā the one who asked.

111/105: هُودًا أَوْ نَصَارَى. Some say that he here read يَهُودِيًّا أَوْ نَصْرَانِيًّا as Ubai.

114/108: خَائِفِينَ — خُيَّفًا. (Ibn Khālawaih 155 wrongly gives it as حُنَفَاء).

119/113: وَلَا تُسْئَلُ – وَلَنْ تُسْأَلَ.

123/117: لَا تَجْزِى – لَا تُغْنِى.

124/118: ٱلظَّٰلِمِينَ – ٱلظَّالِمُونَ.

127/121: رَبَّنَا – يَقُولَانِ رَبَّنَا.

128/122: أَرِنَا مَنَاسِكَنَا وَتُبْ عَلَيْنَا – أَرِهِمْ مَنَاسِكَهُمْ وَتُبْ عَلَيْهِمْ.

132/126: وَوَصَّىٰ – He agrees with the Ḥafṣ text against the أَوْصَىٰ of the Syrian and Madīnan Codices.

يَا بَنِيَّ – أَنْ يَا بَنِيَّ. As read also by aḍ-Ḍaḥḥāk.

137/131: بِمِثْلِ مَا – بِمَا. As was read also by Ibn ᶜAbbās.

139/133: أَتُحَاجُّونَنَا – أَتُحَاجُّونَّا. So read by Ibn Muḥaiṣin and Abūʾs-Sammāl.

144/139: شَطْرَهُ – قِبَلَهُ (?) see Ubai's reading here.

148/143: وَلِكُلٍّ وِجْهَةٌ هُوَ مُوَلِّيهَا – وَلِكُلٍّ جَعَلْنَا قِبْلَةً يَرْضَوْنَهَا. Manṣūr from Ibn Masᶜūd.

149/144: فَوَلِّ – فَوَالِ.

150/145: حَيْثُ مَا – أَيْنَمَا.

158/153: أَنْ – أَنْ لَا. Similarly in Ubai's Codex.

يَطَّوَّفَ – يَطُوفَ. So Ubai, Ibn ᶜAbbās and Mujāhid.

تَطَوَّعَ خَيْرًا – يَتَطَوَّعْ بِخَيْرٍ

159/154: بَيَّنَّٰهُ – بَيَّنَهُ. Making Allah the subject. So read also by Ṭalḥa.

162/157: يُنْظَرُونَ – يُنْصَرُونَ.

177/172: لَيْسَ ٱلْبِرَّ – لَيْسَ ٱلْبِرُّ, as read by all save the Kūfans. Al-Aᶜmash, however, said that Ibn Masᶜūd read لَا تَحْسَبَنَّ ٱلْبِرَّ and Ibn Abī Dāwūd gives it as لَا تَحْسَبَنَّ أَنَّ ٱلْبِرَّ.

أَنْ – بِأَنْ. As read also by Ubai.

قِبَلَ – تِلْقَاءَ.

وَٱلْمُوفُونَ – وَٱلْمُوفِينَ.

بِعَهْدِهِمْ — بِعُهُودِهِمْ. So Ubai.

178/173: اَلْقِصَاصُ — اَلْقَصَصُ. So Abū'l-ʿĀlīya.

فَاتِّبَاعٌ — فَاتَّبَعَ taking it as a verb, so read by Muʿādh and Ibn Abī ʿAbla.

184/180: أَيَّامًا مَعْدُودَاتٍ — أَيَّامٌ مَعْدُودَاتٌ. So Ibn Dharr read.

أُخَرَ — أُخْرَى.

تَطَوَّعَ خَيْرًا — تَطَوَّعَ بِخَيْرٍ.

187/183: اَلرَّفَثُ — اَلرُّفُوثُ.

191/187: وَلَا تُقَاتِلُوهُمْ عِنْدَ ٱلْمَسْجِدِ ٱلْحَرَامِ حَتَّى يُقَاتِلُوكُمْ فِيهِ فَإِنْ قَاتَلُوكُمْ — لَا تَقْتُلُوهُمْ عِنْدَ ٱلْمَسْجِدِ ٱلْحَرَامِ حَتَّى يَقْتُلُوكُمْ فِيهِ فَإِنْ قَتَلُوكُمْ, which was the reading of Ḥamza and al-Kisāʾī.

196/192: أَتِمُّوا — أَقِيمُوا. So read by ʿAlī and ʿAlqama.

وَٱلْعُمْرَةَ لِلَّهِ — وَٱلْعُمْرَةُ إِلَى ٱلْبَيْتِ. Similarly ʿAlī read لِلْبَيْتِ which some gave from Ibn Masʿūd.

197/193: فَلَا رَفَثَ وَلَا فُسُوقَ وَلَا جِدَالَ — فَلَا رُفُوثٌ وَلَا فُسُوقٌ وَلَا جِدَالٌ.

وَخَيْرُ ٱلزَّادِ ٱلتَّقْوَى — فَإِنَّ خَيْرَ ٱلزَّادِ ٱلتَّقْوَى.

198/194: مِنْ رَبِّكُمْ — مِنْ رَبِّكُمْ فِي مَوَاسِمِ ٱلْحَجِّ. Abū ʿUbaid said he added وَمَنْ تَاجَرَ فلا اثمَ لمن اتقى الله and Ibn Abī Dāwūd says he read لا جناحَ عليكم ان تبتغوا فضلا من ربكم فى مواسم الحج فابتغوا حينئذ.

202/198: نَصِيبٌ مِمَّا كَسَبُوا — نَصِيبٌ مَا ٱكْتَسَبُوا. So read by al-Aʿmash also.

203/199: لِمَنِ ٱتَّقَى — لِمَنِ ٱتَّقَى ٱللَّهَ.

204/200: وَيُشْهِدُ ٱللَّهَ — وَيَسْتَشْهِدُ اللهَ, as the reading of Ubai.

The Koran according to Warsh, and Other Versions of the Koran Available in 2005

It is often a surprise for even educated Muslims to learn that there are printed Korans in the Islamic world that differ from one another. The extreme Muslim position as to the contents, form, and status of the Koran is best represented by Maududi [Mawdūdī, 1903–1979], the very influential Indo-Pakistani Islamist. He wrote, "The Qur'ān . . . exists exactly as it had been revealed to the Prophet; not a word—nay, not a dot of it—has been changed. It is available in its original text and the Word of God has now been preserved for all times to come."[33] He also wrote,

> The Qur'ān that we possess today corresponds exactly to the edition which was prepared on the orders of Abū Bakr and copies of which were officially sent, on the orders of 'Uthmān, to various cities and provinces. Several copies of this original edition of the Qur'ān still exist today. Anyone who entertains any doubt as to the authenticity of the Qur'ān can satisfy himself by obtaining a copy of the Qur'ān from any bookseller, say in West Africa, and then have a *ḥāfiẓ* [memorizer of the Qur'ān] recite it from memory, compare the two, and then compare these with the copies of the Qur'ān published through the centuries since the time of 'Uthmān. If he detects any discrepancy, even in a single letter or syllable, he should inform the whole world of his great discovery!
>
> Not even the most sceptical person has any reason to doubt that the Qur'ān as we know it today is identical with the Qur'ān which Muḥammad (peace be on him) set before the world; this is an unquestionable, objective, historical fact, and there is nothing in human history on which the evidence is so overwhelmingly strong and conclusive. To doubt the authenticity of the Qur'ān is like doubting the existence of the Roman Empire, the Mughals of India or Napoleon! To doubt historical facts like these is a sign of stark ignorance, not a mark of erudition and scholarship.[34]

The above claims are rather grand and also rather foolish. I have indeed gathered Korans from various parts of the Islamic world, and some of my results are presented below. It turns out to be surprisingly easy to refute Maududi's hyperboles.

Broadly speaking, the printed Korans now available fall into two transmission traditions: the Warsh transmission represents the Medinan tradition, and is found in West and Northwest Africa; the Ḥafṣ transmission stems from Kufa, and is found in the rest of the Islamic world. The so-called standard Egyptian edition of AH 1342/1924 CE is essentially the Ḥafṣ transmission, and is the most widely used Koran in the Islamic world. However, as Brockett has pointed out, "In the last decade . . . even in central Muslim countries like Saudi Arabia and Qatar, texts differing considerably in orthography from the 1342 Cairo text have been printed under official approval."[35]

For the basis of comparison between the Ḥafṣ and Warsh transmissions I have used the following Korans in Arabic acquired in the Islamic world in the last ten years:

The Noble Qur'ān. Arabic Text with English Translation by Dr. al-Hilali and Dr. Muhsin Khan. King Fahd Complex for the Printing of the Holy Qur'ān, Madinah, Kingdom of Saudi Arabia, AH 1419/1998 CE. [Saudi Koran]

The Noble Qur'ān. Arabic Text with English Translation by Dr. al-Hilali and Dr. Muhsin Khan. Published by Maktaba Darul Qurʾān Chitli Qabar, Delhi, India, 1993. [Saudi Koran II]

The Holy Qur'ān. Arabic Text, English Translation and Commentary by Maulana Muḥammad Ali. Ahmadiyyah Anjuman Isha'at Islam, Lahore, Inc., Columbus, Ohio, 1995. [Muḥammad Ali Koran]

The Holy Qur'ān. Text, Translation & Commentary by Abdullah Yusuf Ali. Lahore (Pakistan), Shaikh Muḥammad Ashraf, Kashmiri Bazar, 1938 CE. [Yusuf Ali Koran]

Uthmanic Qur'ān. Published Istanbul (Turkey). Arabic Text only. AH 1414/1993 CE. [Istanbul Koran]

The Noble Qur'ān. Published Tehran (Iran), Arabic Text only. Gulban Chap. 1978 CE. [Iranian Koran]

The Noble Qur'ān. Published Lahore (Pakistan). Arabic Text with Interlinear Urdu Translation. Taj Limited Company, 1956 CE. [Taj Koran].

The Noble Qur'ān as Transmitted by Warsh. Arabic Text only. Dar al-Qadriya, Damascus, Syria, Beirut, Lebanon; Dar Ibn Kathir, Damascus/ Beirut. AH 1419/1998 CE. [Warsh I]

The Noble Qur'ān as Transmitted by Warsh. Arabic Text only. Dar al-

Musahif Sharif. (No Date/No Place of Publication. Bought in Morocco in 1999). [Warsh II]

L'Interpretation du Coran. (Texte et Explication) D'Après Ibn Kathīr. Traduit par Fawzi Chaaban. Arabic Text with French Translation by Fawzi Chaaban. 6 Vols. Dar el Fiker, Beyrouth Liban (Lebanon), 1998. [Lebanese]

The Noble Qur'ān as Transmitted by Qālūn. Arabic Text only. Tunis (Tunisia), 1981. [Qālūn]

The Meaning of the Glorious Qur'ān. Text and Explanatory Translation. Marmaduke Pickthall. Distributed by the Muslim World League, UN Office, 300 East 44th Street, New York, NY 10017, 1977. [MWL]

Corani Textus Arabicus, ad fidem librorum manu scriptorum et impressorum et ad preacipuorum interpretum lectiones et auctoritatem recensuit indicesque triginta sectionum et suratarum. [Arabic Text only] Gustavus Fluegel. Editio Stereotypa C. Tauchnitzii. Lipsiae, 1883. [New Edition. Gregg Press Inc., New Jersey, 1965] [Flügel]

Readings according to Ḥafṣ and Warsh

Variants in Extant Printed Korans from the Islamic World. All the Arabic reproduced below was scanned directly from the Korans indicated.

[1] I,4: *Māliki* is written defectively with a dagger alif in the Saudi Koran I. According to Muḥammad Ali (see Koran number 3 in above list), there is a world of difference between *mālik* and *malik*, the former signifying master and the latter king; a master being more than a king. God is more than a king, and hence "master" is the correct translation. Many early Koranic manuscripts do not have the plene alif.

Saudi I مَـٰلِكِ يَوْمِ ٱلدِّينِ ﴿٤﴾ Istanbul مَالِكِ يَوْمِ الدِّينِ ﴿٤﴾

[2] I,6: *Aṣ-ṣirāta* is written defectively with a dagger alif in the Saudi Koran I. The verb *hada* is differently voweled, *ihdina* in the Istanbul Koran but *ahdina* in the Saudi Koran.

Saudi I اهْدِنَا الصِّرَاطَ الْمُسْتَقِيمَ ﴿٦﴾

Istanbul اِهْدِنَا الصِّرَاطَ الْمُسْتَقِيمَ ٧

[3] II,72: *faddāra'tum* is written defectively with a dagger alif in the Yusuf Ali Koran, while Warsh II has the scriptio plena, that is, the alifs in *faddāra'tum* are made explicit. There is also a discrepancy in the verse numbering, II,72 as opposed to II,71, respectively.

Yusuf Ali ٧٢- وَإِذْ قَتَلْتُمْ نَفْسًا فَادَّرَءْتُمْ فِيهَا

Warsh II نَفْسًا فَادَّارَأْتُمْ فِيهَا وَاللَّهُ

[4] II,125. The Ḥafṣ is in the Imperative [*'attakhidhū*], and means, "Take [as your place of worship the place where Abraham stood]. The Warsh is in the simple past [*'attakhadhū*], meaning "They have taken. . . ."

M. Ali وَاتَّخِذُوا Warsh I وَاتَّخَذُوا

[5] II,132: Yusuf Ali has *wa -waṣṣā* as opposed to *wa-'awṣā*, that is, Yusuf Ali Koran lacks an alif after the *wāw* at the beginning of the verse. Both Warsh and Yusuf Ali have *'Ibrāhīmu* written defectively. As Puin pointed out, it is clear that in a certain phase of the orthographic development of Arabic, it was no longer understood that *Yā'* in the Arabic script was nothing other than */a:/.* The original pronunciation of *Abrāhām* had to be altered, according to which *Yā'* now stood for /i:/ or /ay/.[36]

Yusuf Ali ١٣٢- وَوَصَّىٰ بِهَآ إِبْرَٰهِمُ Warsh I وَأَوْصَىٰ بِهَآ إِبْرَٰهِيمُ

[6] II,140: *ʾam taqūlūna* as opposed to *ʾam yaqūlūna,* giving the meaning "do you say. . . ?" or "do they say . . . ? respectively.

Yusuf Ali أَمْ تَقُولُونَ Warsh I أَمْ يَقُولُونَ

[7] II,259: *nunšizuhā,* as opposed to *nunširuhā.*

M. Ali نُنشِزُهَا Warsh I نُنشِرُهَا

[8] III,13. *yarawnahum* (they saw them) as opposed to *tarawnahum* (you saw them). This verse is said to be a reference to the miracle of the battle of Badr, when Muslims putatively defeated forces twice their own number. However, this interpretation is much easier if we read the verb as saying "you saw them" *tarawnahum*, as in the Warsh reading, and not *yarawnahum* (they saw them) as in the Ḥafṣ reading. Warsh gives us a miracle. Ḥafṣ gives us a confusion of pronouns. See discussion of this verse below, p. 57.

M. Ali يَرَوْنَهُم Warsh I تَرَوْنَهُم

[9] III,37. *yā maryamu* is written defectively with a dagger alif in the Yusuf Ali Koran; the alif is made explicit in the Istanbul Koran.

Yusuf Ali قَالَ يَٰمَرْيَمُ أَنَّىٰ Istanbul قَالَ يَا مَرْيَمُ أَنَّى

[10] III,80/81:

wa-ʾiḏ ʾakhaḏa l-lāhu mīṯāqa -n-nabiyyina lamā ʾataytukum

M. Ali Koran III, 80

wa-ʾiḏa ʾakhaḏa l-lāhu mīṯāqa –n-nabiyyina lamā ʾataynākum

Warsh I: III, 81.

wa-ʾiḏ / wa-ʾiḏa; ʾataytukum / ʾataynākum; *mīṯāqa* written defectively in Warsh I, and notice the difference in verse numbering.

M. Ali وَ اِذْ اَخَذَ اللّٰهُ مِيْثَاقَ Warsh وَإِذَ اَخَذَ اَللَّهُ مِيثَٰقَ

[11] III,133: *wa -sāri'ū* [M. Ali Koran III,132] as opposed to *sāri'ū* [Warsh I: III,133]

M. Ali وَسَارِعُوْٓا اِلٰى Warsh سَارِعُوٓاْ إِلَىٰ

[12] III,146 [M. Ali Koran] Ḥafṣ: Simple past tense giving the reading "fought" [*qātala*], while Warsh I is in the passive, meaning "were killed" [*qutila*]: an enormous difference in meaning. "And how many a prophet have there been a number of devoted men who fought (beside him)" or ". . . who were killed beside him," respectively.

M. Ali قٰتَلَ Warsh I قُتِّلَ

[13] III,158. *lā ʾila* as opposed to *laʾila;* the extra alif connected with *lām* in Yusuf Ali is not read. *lā* is normally the negative particle, and if read as such would give the reading "not to God"; it is read as "certainly to God."

Yusuf Ali لَاْ اِلَى اللّٰهِ Iranian لَإِلَى اَللَّهِ

[14] III,167. *lā ʾattaba'nākum* as opposed to *la-t-taba'nākum.* See note for III,158 above.

Yusuf Ali قِتَالًا لَّا اتَّبَعْنٰكُمْ Iranian قِتَالًا لَّاتَّبَعْنَٰكُمْ هُمْ

[15] V,53/V, 56. Yusuf Ali (V,56, note the difference of verse numbering) has *wa-yaqūlu,* Warsh I (V,53) lacks the *wāw* in front of *yaqūlu.*

Yusuf Ali وَيَقُولُ Warsh يَقُولُ

[16] V,54/V,57. Yusuf Ali has (V,57) *yartadda*, and Warsh I [V,54] *yartadid.*

Yusuf Ali مَنْ يَرْتَدَّ Warsh I مَنْ يَرْتَدِدْ

[17] VII,57. MWL Koran has *bushran* (Good News) and Warsh I *Nushran* (spread out/diffuse).

MWL بُشْرًا Warsh I نُشُرًا

[18] IX,47. *lā -ʾawḍaʿū* as opposed to *laʾawḍaʿū.* See note to III,158 above.

وَلَا أَوْضَعُوا خِلَالَكُمْ يَبْغُونَكُمُ الْفِتْنَةَ وَفِيكُمْ
M. Ali سَمَّاعُونَ لَهُمْ وَاللَّهُ عَلِيمٌ بِالظَّالِمِينَ ﴿٤٧﴾

وَلَأَوْضَعُوا
خِلَالَكُمْ يَبْغُونَكُمُ الْفِتْنَةَ وَفِيكُمْ سَمَّاعُونَ
Iranian لَهُمْ وَاللَّهُ عَلِيمٌ بِالظَّالِمِينَ

[19] IX,107. *wa-l-laḏīna* as opposed to *ʾilḏīna.*

M. Ali الَّذِينَ Warsh I وَالَّذِينَ

[20] XVIII,36. *minhā* as opposed to *minhumā.*

M. Ali مِّنْهَا   Warsh I مِّنْهُمَا

[21] XXI,4. Istanbul has *qāla*; M. Ali has *qāla* written defectively with dagger alif; Warsh I has *qul.* See pp. 69–72 for the full implications of these important variants.

Istanbul قَالَ   M. Ali قٰلَ   Warsh I قُلْ

[22] XXI,112. Istanbul has *qāla*; M. Ali has *qāla* written defectively with dagger alif; Warsh I has *qul.* See pp. 69–72 for the full implications of these important variants.

Istanbul قَالَ رَبِّ احْكُمْ   M. Ali قٰلَ رَبِّ احْكُمْ   Warsh قُل رَّبِّ اِحْكُمْ

[23] XXIII,8. *wa-l-laḏīna hum li-ʾamānātihim wa- ʿahidihim rāʿūna,* written defectively in Muḥammad Ali Koran. The scriptio plena of the Istanbul Koran in the writing of *li-ʾamānātihim* and *rāʿūna.* Note *liʾamānātihim* as opposed to *ʾalimānātihim* Warsh II.

M. Ali وَالَّذِيْنَ هُمْ لِاَمٰنٰتِهِمْ وَعَهْدِهِمْ رٰعُوْنَ

Istanbul وَالَّذِينَ هُمْ لِأَمَانَاتِهِمْ وَعَهْدِهِمْ رَاعُونَ

Warsh II وَالذِينَ هُمْ لِأَمَـٰنَـٰتِهِمْ

[24] XXIII,112. M. Ali has *qāla*, written defectively, translated by M. Ali as "He will say"; Warsh has *qāla*, written with scriptio plena.

M. Ali قٰلَ كَمۡ لَبِثۡتُمۡ Warsh قَالَ كَمْ لَبِثْتُمْ

[25] XXIII,114. M. Ali has *qāla*, written defectively, translated by M. Ali as "He will say"; Warsh has *qāla*, written with scriptio plena.

M. Ali قٰلَ اِنۡ لَّبِثۡتُمۡ Warsh I قَالَ إِن لَّبِثْتُمْ

[26] XXVI,217. *wa–tawakkal* (M. Ali) as opposed to *fa-tawakkal* (Warsh I).

M. Ali وَ تَوَكَّلۡ Warsh I فَتَوَكَّلْ

[27] XXVII,21. *lā-aḏbaḥannahu* (M. Ali), where *lā* is not to be read as the negative particle; *la-ʾaḏbaḥannahu* (Flügel). Ibn Khaldūn wrote: "No attention should be paid in this connection to the assumption of certain incompetent [scholars] that [the men around Muḥammad] knew well the art of writing and that the alleged discrepancies between their writing and the principles of orthography are not discrepancies, as has been alleged, but have a reason. For instance, they explain the addition of the alif in *la-ʾaḏbaḥannahu* 'I shall indeed slaughter him' as an indication that the slaughtering did *not take* place (*lā-aḏbaḥannahu*). The addition of the *yāʾ* in *bi-ayydin* 'with hands [power],' [LI,47, see below at 29. LI,47] they explain as an indication that the divine power is perfect. There are similar things based on nothing but purely arbitrary assumptions. The only reason that caused them to (assume such things) is their belief that [their explanations] would free the men around Muḥammad from the suspicion of deficiency, in the sense that they were not able to write well."[37]

M. Ali اَوۡ لَاَاذۡبَحَنَّهٗ Flügel أَوْ لَأَذْبَحَنَّهُ

[28] XXXVII,68. *lā ʾila* (M. Ali, with extra alif); *la-ʾila* (Iranian).

M. Ali لَاْاِلَى الْجَحِيْمِ Iranian لَإِلَى الْجَحِيمِ

[29] XL,26. *ʾaw ʾan* (M. Ali) as opposed to *wa-ʾan* (Warsh I).

M. Ali دِيْنَكُمْ اَوْ اَنْ يُّظْهِرَ Warsh I دِينَكُمْ وَأَنْ يُظْهِرَ

[30] XLII,30. *mā ʾaṣābakum . . . fa-bi-mā* (M. Ali, scriptio plena for the word *ʾaṣābakum*, using the alif, while Warsh I has the defective alif; Warsh has *bi-mā* as opposed to *fa-bi-mā* in M. Ali).

M. Ali وَمَآ اَصَابَكُمْ مِّنْ مُّصِيْبَةٍ فَبِمَا Warsh I وَمَآ أَصَٰبَكُم مِّن مُّصِيبَةٍ بِمَا

[31] XLIII,68. *yā ʿibādi* (M. Ali) as opposed to *yā ʿibādī* (Warsh I, note the long *–ī*).

M. Ali يٰعِبَادِ Warsh I يَٰعِبَادِے

[32] LI,47. *bi-ʾaydin* (M. Ali) as opposed to *bi-ʾayydin* (Warsh I, has an extra *yāʾ*). See Ibn Khaldūn's comments above at 27. XXVII,21.

M. Ali بِاَيْدٍ Warsh I بِأَيْيْدٍ

[33] LVII,24. *huwa -l-ghaniyyu* (M. Ali, has an extra word *huwa*) as opposed to *al-ghaniyyu* (Warsh I).

M. Ali اللّٰهَ هُوَ الْغَنِيُّ Warsh I أَللَّهَ الْغَنِيُّ

[34] LXXII,16. M. Ali has *wa-ʾan lawi staqāmu ʿalā ṭ-ṭarīqati la-ʾasqaynāhum māʾan ghadaqan.* Istanbul has the plene alif for both *staqāmu* and *ʾasqaynāhum.* Saudi 2 lacks the word *ʾan* before *lawi staqāmu*; the latter word is also written defectively, with a dagger alif.

M. Ali وَّأَنْ لَّوِ اسْتَقَامُوْا عَلَى الطَّرِيْقَةِ
لَأَسْقَيْنٰهُمْ مَّآءً غَدَقًا

Istanbul I وَأَنْ لَوِ اسْتَقَامُوا عَلَى الطَّرِيقَةِ لَأَسْقَيْنَاهُمْ مَاءً غَدَقًا

Saudi 2 وَأَلَّوِ اسْتَقَٰمُوا عَلَى الطَّرِيقَةِ لَأَسْقَيْنَٰهُم
مَّآءً غَدَقًا

Warsh I وَأَن لَّوِ اِسْتَقَٰمُواْ عَلَى الطَّرِيقَةِ لَأَسْقَيْنَٰهُم مَّآءً غَدَقًا

[35] LXXXV,22. (M. Ali) has *maḥfūẓin* as opposed to *maḥfūẓun* in Warsh I. The M. Ali Koran has *maḥfūẓin*, the genitive, giving the meaning "It is a glorious Koran on a preserved tablet." (This is a reference to the fundamental Muslim doctrine of the Preserved Tablet. But the Warsh transmission has the nominative ending *-un*, and we get "It is a glorious Koran preserved on a tablet." Did the doctrine arise out of the reading, or did the doctrine influence the choice of the reading?)

M. Ali فِيْ لَوْحٍ مَّحْفُوْظٍ Warsh I فِے لَوْحٍ مَّحْفُوظٌ

Do Variants Matter? What Is Their Significance?

The variants are not trifling, and are, in fact, of great significance. The problem is to work out what significance, and this proves to be no easy matter. For a flat-footed fundamentalist like Maududi, the admittance of any variant—whether in the extant printed Korans available in the Islamic world or in the manuscripts like the Samarqand Qurʾān or those recorded in the hadith, commentaries, and grammars—is, of course, devastating. Variants constitute an irrefutable, knock-down argument against his absurdly rigid position (already quoted above), a position not held by all Muslim scholars, however. I believe their significance lies in a wider context, in their profound implication for the sources of the rise of Islam, for the forging of Islamic identity, for the genesis of the Koran itself, for Islamic jurisprudence, for the so-called oral tradition, and for the history of the Arabic language and orthography. I shall leave these implications for later.

Even simply on their own terms, variants do result in significant differences in meaning that in turn have consequences for Islamic practice, ritual, and belief. Thus the variants in the printed Korans are not trivial. As an example of a variant reading on the level of vocalization though not of the underlying graphic shape (or, in Arabic, *rasm*), there are the last two verses of sura LXXXV, 21–22: (21) *bal huwa qur'ānun majīdun*; (22) *fī lawḥim maḥfūẓun* or *mahfuhẓin*. The last syllable is in doubt. The Ḥafṣ Koran has, as we saw above, *mahfuhẓin*, the genitive, giving the meaning "It is a glorious Koran on a preserved tablet." This is a reference to the fundamental Muslim doctrine of the Preserved Tablet. But the Warsh transmission has the nominative ending *-un*, and we get "It is a glorious Koran preserved on a tablet." Did the doctrine arise out of the reading, or did the doctrine influence the choice of the reading?

In sura III verse 13, there is much ambiguity as the exact reference of the pronoun is not clear:

> Bell: "You have already had a sign in two parties which met, one fighting in the way of Allah, another unbelieving, who saw them with their eyes twice as many as they were. . . ."
>
> Yusuf Ali: "There has already been for you a sign in the two armies that met [in combat]: One was fighting in the cause of God, the other Resisting God; these saw with their own eyes Twice their number."
>
> Arberry: "There has already been a sign for you in the two companies that encountered, one company fighting in the way of God and another unbelieving; they saw them twice the like of them, as the eye sees. . . ."

This verse is said to be a reference to the miracle of the battle of Badr, when Muslims putatively defeated forces twice their own number. However, this interpretation is much easier if we read the verb as saying "you saw them," *tarawnahum*, as in the Warsh reading, and not *yarawnahum* (they saw them); as in the Ḥafṣ reading. Warsh gives us a miracle, Ḥafṣ gives us a confusion of pronouns.

Ignaz Goldziher, one of the creators of modern Islamic studies, showed how hadith and Muslim tradition reflected "the social, political and religious ideals of transmitters themselves and of the societies or groups they served as spokesman. By Sunna was to be understood, not the inherited instruction of the Prophet, but the *ius consuetudinis* of a group or party, large or small. By hadith is meant the vehicle of that sunna, a report, verbal or written, conveying a description of the relevant practice, opinion or custom approved by the desseminators of the report."[38] Influenced by Goldziher's work, Joseph Schacht elaborated a thesis that "rather than spreading out from an original centre at Medina, Islamic Law originated in the provinces. Reference of the Sunna to the Prophet was the end rather than the beginning of a process. Its purpose was to verify some local legal viewpoint. In other words, the Sunna differed and was differently defined from region to region."[39]

Of course, the conclusions of scholars like Goldziher and Schacht are equally applicable to Koranic variants, many of which are known to us through hadith, rather than extant Koranic manuscripts. In other words, the variants reflect the ideology, as Burton shows, of groups that wish to argue for their own viewpoint, to establish a ruling, to settle conflict of sources. For example, the rite of *ṭawāf*, going round the two hills of Ṣafā and Marwa during *Hajj*, Pilgrimage, are considered obligatory by certain Muslim jurists despite a certain ambiguity in sura II, 158, which is interpreted by some to mean that the *ṭawāf* was optional. Others still also regarded the *ṭawāf* as optional, but this time the view "was explicitly derived from the variant reading of II,158 transmitted in the *muṣḥaf* of 'Abdullah Ibn Mas'ūd."[40]

Burton argues that when practice was at variance with the Koran, the partisans of the practice appealed to the Sunna of the Prophet, their opponents "improve the wording of the Qur'ān, inserting a word and appealing to the authority of a Companion of the Prophet, from whom not merely a variant reading, but a variant Qur'ān had apparently been transmitted. The alleged variant reading unmistakably proceeded from one of two rival and competing interpretations. To that extent the reading arose at a secondary stage."[41]

There is a similar exchange of argument and counterargument concerning the penalty for breach of oaths [sura V, 89], a three-day fast, ending as before with an appeal to a variant reading from Ibn Masʿūd. Al-Shāfiʿī argued that the Koran did not stipulate if the fast should be consecutive, hence Muslims were free to choose consecutive or separate days. Ḥanīfs argued that the fast should be consecutive, as a variant reading of Ibn Masʿūd indicates. The same variant reading was attributed to Ubayy.[42] Ubayy also had a very significant variant reading of sura IV, 24 concerning the Muslim Law on marriage; only with his interpolation does IV, 24 "sanction the doctrine of *mut'a*, or temporary marriage, rejection of which was elsewhere being propounded on the basis of information from a third Companion of the Prophet as a part of the Sunna. Evidently the Qurʾān, in the form of the Ubayy reading, is playing the role of a counter-sunna, rather, a counter-exegesis, the function of the Ubayy interpolation to gloss and bring out the full meaning of the root of *samta'tum, mt'*."[43]

As al-Suyūṭī put it, "The differences in the readings indicate the differences in the legal rulings."[44] Thus we have two opposing doctrines—the invalidation of the ritual purity [*wuḍūʾ*] and the contrary doctrine—depending on how we read a certain word in IV, 43 and V, 9 as *lāmastum* or *lamastum*; it is worth noting that all the printed Korans that I have listed above except the Flügel have the "defective" writing, with the long vowel after the letter *lām* indicated by a dagger *alif*; only the Flügel has the plene *alif*. Similarly, we have two opposing doctrines depending on how we read II, 222—*yaṭhurna* or *yaṭṭahirna*—concerning the permissibility of sexual intercourse with a menstruating woman at the expiry of her period but before she has cleansed herself.[45]

Finally, we have the example of V, 6, as al-Suyūṭī says, "The verse was revealed to sanction two distinct legal doctrines: *arjulakum*—enjoined the washing of the feet, *ajulikum*—permitted the wiping of the feet."[46] Herbert Berg summarizes the larger significance of these two interpretations,

> Al-Ṭabarī adduces 47 hadiths which seek to clarify the expression *wa-arjulakum ila al-ka'bayn* (and your feet to the ankles) of Qurʾān V,6. The first 27 hadiths read the passage as *arjulakum* (accusative); the other 20 hadiths read the passage as *arjulikum* (genitive). . . . Goldziher would see in these two sharply divided sets of hadiths the vestiges of a later debate within the Muslim community about the proper form of *wuḍūʾ* (ablution) that has

> been projected back to the earlier generations of Muslims. Schacht might trace this ablution debate in other texts to determine the relative chronology and the provenance of the hadiths. He might also, along with Juynboll, seek a common link to help date the debate. ʿIkrima is a candidate since he appears in five hadiths, though the *isnads* form more of a spider pattern. Wansbrough would abandon such use of the *isnad* except to note that their presence implies that the 47 hadiths reached their final form after AH 200 [9th century CE]. Moreover, the hadiths are primarily halakhic and masoretic: they contain pronouncements from the Prophet, his Companions and their Successors and have recourse to variant readings and grammatical explanations. Their presence implies a relatively late date as well.[47]

Burton, following al-Suyūṭī, argues that "the majority of variant readings came to be regarded as little more than exegeses that had gradually crept into the texts transmitted from the Companions."[48] While the latter observation may well explain some of the mechanism of how the companion texts came into being, I would go further and doubt the very existence of codices belonging to the companions; they have been conjured up by exegetical hadiths. In other words, the question of variants leads inexorably to the questions of the authenticity of hadiths relating them.

Koranic Manuscripts

In his translation of the Koran, the British convert to Islam Marmaduke Pickthall (1930) had the scholarly courtesy to tell us that the copy of the Koran (*muṣḥaf*) that he had used was a lithograph copy of that written by al-Hajj Muḥammad Shakarzadeh at the command of Sultan Mahmud of Turkey in AH 1246 (circa 1830 CE).[49] It does not tell us enough, however. We still do not know *which* Koran, which manuscript, the scribe al-Hajj had relied on. The situation is even worse with other translators of the Koran. George Sale (1734) in his note to the reader of his translation tells us, "As I have had no opportunity of consulting public libraries, the manuscripts of which I have made use throughout the whole work have been such as I had in my own study."[50] But he does not specify which manuscripts he had in his possession.

J. M. Rodwell (1861)[51] used Gustav Flügel's edition. Flügel published the Arabic text of the Koran in 1834, and a concordance in 1842. We no longer know on which Arabic manuscripts Flügel depended for his published text, but when Jeffery and Mendelsohn examined the orthography of the Samarqand Qur'ān Codex, a ninth-century CE work produced in Iraq, they found something astonishing:

> The most striking fact in this list [of verse endings] is the number of coincidences of verse endings in the Codex with those adopted by Flügel in his text. . . . Since we are entirely in the dark as to the source from which Flügel drew his verse divisions, these coincidences are significant. Flügel's verse endings agree with none of the known systems whose tradition has come down to us, nor with any that we have been able to trace in the Masoretic literature under the section Ru'ūs al-Ayy, and it has been generally assumed that he selected his verse endings on an arbitrary system of his own. The number of agreements between his system and that followed in this Codex, however, suggest that he may have been following the system of some MS in his possession which may have followed some divergent Oriental tradition. It must be admitted, however, that the table Shebunin [Russian scholar who studied the original manuscript in St. Petersburg in 1891] constructs of the divergences between the Samarqand Codex and the Flügel text in the matter of verse endings, is equally long and imposing, so that it is obvious that the question of Flügel's system of verse division awaits further elucidation.[52]

At any rate, Flügels's edition remained the standard one for reference for all of the nineteenth century.

While E. H. Palmer (1880)[53] and N. J. Dawood (1956)[54] do not indicate which Arabic text they were using, Yusuf Ali (1934) says he mainly used the "Egyptian edition published under the authority of the King of Egypt" for his *numbering* of the verses; there is no indication if he used the same edition for the translation itself.[55]

A. J. Arberry (1964), in the introduction[56] to his translation, makes the extraordinary claim worthy of an Islamic fundamentalist, "[T]he Koran as printed in the twentieth century is identical with the Koran as authorized by 'Uthmān more than 1300 years ago."[57] One wonders how Arberry knows that the present printed Koran (the Egyptian version of AH 1342?) is identical to the so-called ʻUthmānic one; did he look at and compare dated manuscripts that can be said to be genuinely ʻUthmānic? No wonder Arberry does not feel obliged to reveal which Arabic text he used, let alone which manuscript.

Régis Blachère, in his French version,[58] used the Arabic text of the Cairo edition of AH 1342/1923 CE.[59] However, the Cairo edition is not based on a comparison of manuscripts but a comparison of readings in written sources such as hadiths, Koranic commentaries, lexica, and so on, but ultimately derived from the reading of Ḥafṣ (805) and from ʿĀṣim (744), with a reliance on an Oral Tradition about the orthography of the Koran. Again, manuscripts do not seem to have played a significant role in arriving at a Koranic text. I shall come back to the 1342 Cairo text later.

Admittedly, some of the above translations were meant for a general public, but so was Gideon's Bible, and yet the latter gives the list of previous translations consulted and the original texts used; for Hebrew the celebrated R. Kittel edition of *Biblia Hebraica* was referred to, and for the Greek, the twenty-third edition of the Nestle Greek New Testament.[60] As for the *Biblia Hebraica* itself, in their forward to the new edition (1977), Wilhelm Rudolph and Karl Elliger wrote, "There is no need to defend the use of the Leningrad Codex B 19 A (L) as the basis of the Hebrew Bible, whatever one may think of its relationship to the Ben Asher text. . . . In any event, L is still 'the oldest dated manuscript of the complete Hebrew Bible' [dated 1009 or 1008 CE]."[61] If we consult the Greek New Testament edited by F. H. A. Scrivener (1903) we are informed on the title page that the text utilized is the one established by Stephanus in 1550 CE with variants from Bezae, Elzevir, Lachmann, Tischendorf, Tregelles, and Westcott-Hort.[62] Here we learn which texts were examined for translations, and if we go to the texts themselves, we are immediately apprised of the manuscript used.

The situation is different and, at present, far more difficult in the world of Islamic Studies. A Western scholar simply does not have a complete or comprehensive catalog of all the extant Koranic manuscripts around the world at his disposal. Many collections remain uncatalogued, such as the Damascus Korans of Istanbul.[63] There are also many private collections not inventoried, or inaccessible to scholars. There are scattered references to Koranic manuscripts in various articles in the two editions of the *Encyclo-*

pedia of Islam, such as those by Bernhard Moritz in the article *Arabia*, subsection *Arabic Writing* in the first edition, or Dominique Sourdel's *Khaṭṭ* in the second edition, but no comprehensive treatment of the subject. As Déroche remarks, "The bulk of the material, manuscripts without illumination or in more ordinary hands of later periods, have not even been examined or catalogued in spite of their importance for the study of a wide range of subjects, from popular piety to the diffusion of the book in the Islamic lands."[64] Déroche's own article in the *Encyclopedia of the Qur'ān* [EQ, henceforth] is perhaps the first of its kind, but Déroche also seems unaware of the significance of the variants, since he minimizes them. He writes, "[M]ost of the manuscripts currently known are very close to the canonical text," and yet adds immediately afterward the observation, "Some fragments of Ḥijāzī codices found in Ṣan'ā' are said to include some textual variants which were not recorded by later literature, and to offer an order of the suras differing from the arrangements of both the canonical text and the codices of Ibn Mas'ūd and Ubayy."[65] There is no further discussion of the Ṣan'ā' finds. It is clear Déroche is not interested in variants and what their wider meaning might be. Déroche's fellow contributor to the EQ, Fred Leemhuis, on the other hand, thinks there are variants and they are important, "Although the concept of the *'Uthmānic rasm* suggests a uniform and invariable text, such uniformity is not presented by most of the oldest extant codices. Considerable variation is found especially in connection with long *a* and words which in later classical Arabic orthography required a *hamza*. Even the word *Qur'ān* is found spelled as *qrn* (e.g. in Q 50,1 of the St. Petersburg fragment as reproduced in E. Rezwan, *Frühe Abschriften*, 120–21).[66] In addition to their value for study of the Qur'ān's textual history such evidential examples are important for the history of Arabic orthography."[67]

Even if they have access to the necessary catalogs, it is not certain that infidel researchers will be allowed to examine Koranic manuscripts with their skeptical, profane eyes. Then there is the additional problem of the dating of Koranic manuscripts; polemics and prejudice have penetrated this field as well. Presumably no revisionist who follows Wansbrough in his argument that the Koran was not put into its final form until the ninth century CE would accept an early date for any complete Koranic manuscript. There are indeed some leaves, folios, and Koranic inscriptions that have been dated to the eighth century CE or earlier but no complete Korans that can be dated with confidence to earlier than the ninth century CE.

But even if these difficulties are resolved, one has the impression that Western scholars, on the whole, are simply not interested in examining Koranic manuscripts for the sake of variants, to see what they might teach us about the history of that text, about the history of Arabic orthography, and about the history and nature of the Arabic language. Most scholars have uncritically accepted the Islamic version of the history of the text, and even believe, as Arberry does, that "the Koran as printed in the twentieth century is identical with the Koran as authorized by 'Uthmān more than 1300 years ago."

Werner Diem (born 1944) presumed to write the history of Arabic orthography *without, astonishingly enough, looking at a single manuscript*! He complacently announced, "Koranic manuscripts, however, have not been looked through, because they generally go back to a time after 'Uthmān, and because they do not preserve the old orthography as faithfully as the readers did."[68] How can he know that Koranic manuscripts did not preserve the old orthography without looking at the manuscripts? And how does one establish, without circularity, what the "old orthography" is in the first place? Brockett would answer, "by consulting the Oral Tradition." Brockett justifies taking the 1342 Cairo text as the basis for comparison with other printed texts that he wished to discuss and examine by pointing to "its clarity and faultless accuracy." How does he know it is accurate? Where is the original 'Uthmānic text to which it can be compared for its accuracy? The Egyptian scholars responsible for the 1342 Cairo relied on the Oral Tradition about the orthography of the Koran. Brockett then adds an unclear, even obscure note:

> Unlike the actual written Tradition of manuscript-copies, which had been exposed to an ongoing effect over fourteen centuries, and in various locations, this Oral Tradition about the graphic form [of the Koran] had begun to be preserved in writing since about the early third century AH. . . . Moreover, the record of this Oral Tradition about the orthography of the Qur'ān over the two and a quarter centuries is carefully documented in these written works, implying that the exposure to these centuries had no effect either. For the Egyptian scholars, therefore, the Tradition about the graphic form of the Qur'ān stretched right back to the times of the third caliph. The effect of time was, if possible, even less after the writing down of this Oral Tradition, so the written

sources used by the Egyptian scholars date from the fifth century AH and later does not diminish their justification in using them. Whatever free rein had existed would have been well before even the first writing down.[69]

One thing is clear: "No Manuscripts please, we are Koranic scholars!" A host of questions leap to mind. What is an "ongoing effect"? "The actual written Tradition of manuscript-copies"? There is also a naïve faith in Oral Tradition. All oral traditions are inherently unstable; you cannot rely upon Oral Tradition to scientifically reconstruct the events at the dawn of Islam. The chances are that the material transmitted will have undergone a considerable amount of change: people's memories—the most fragile of human faculties—may have failed them, and their prejudices, even fears of being accused of impiety, will have affected, distorted, or altered the contents of what was being transmitted. Finally, all the thousands of variants that we do have have also come putatively from Oral Tradition, later collected and written down—in other words, Oral Tradition can lead to alternative texts to that of the 1342 Cairo text. How do we choose from among them? In fact, as Gerd-R. Puin has argued, "the existence of variant readings indicates that neither the Oral Tradition nor the [textual] context were strong enough to rule out the emergence of alternative readings."[70]

The status that the 1342 Cairo text has acquired as the *textus receptus* has had unfortunate consequences. Here is how Arabist and linguist Pierre Larcher expresses his regrets:

> In theory, all Arabist linguists know (or should know) that the Koranic text, such as we know it today, is not *ne varietur*. The tradition of "seven canonical readings," laid down in the 10th century, is, as we have just suggested, all that remains of a variation, which was much more widespread and lasted much longer which wants to pass the thesis, ideologically more convenient than historically confirmed, off as true of an "ʿUthmānic recension." But, in practice, even this "residual" variation is not linguistically exploited. The exclusive citation of the Cairo edition (Ḥafṣ and ʿĀṣim, i.e., reading of ʿĀṣim transmitted by Ḥafṣ), recommended, when it is not imposed, by so many journals, has ended by conferring on the Koranic text an untouchability that historically it never had! A pity, even if the objective assigned by Rudi Paret[71] to the study of *qirāʾāt* ("to put to good use the known and

> still unknown variants with a view to studying the ancient Arabic dialects and, in general, with a view to preparing a historical grammar of Arabic") seems today excessively ambitious. Nonetheless, the simple collation of the Cairo edition with the Western version (N. Africa, W. Africa) of Warsh ʿan Nāfiʿ (reading of Nāfiʿ as transmitted by Warsh) is always fruitful from the linguistic point of view. To give one example: while in the Eastern Koran there are five occurrences of *salam,* with a short *a*, of which four occur in combination with the verb *ʾalqā* (IV,90 and 91; XVI,28 and 87), in the Western Koran, there are six: the latter reads in fact *salam* in IV,94 (where the word is equally combined with *ʾalqā*) while the former reads *salām* (with long *ā*), which suggests 1) that *salam* and *salām* are two variants of one and the same word and 2) that the collocation *ʾalqā al-sala(ā)m,* has everywhere the sense, not of "offering peace," as Masson would have it and with which her translation is sweetened, but really of "offering his submission," and 3) allows us to hypothesize on the way that the three concepts of "submission," "protection/preservation" and "peace" are connected to one another, and subsumed under the root *slm*. "Peace" is understood negatively as "preserving (the war)" and "protection" as a result of "submission."[72]

There is also a worrying tendency to interpret all manuscripts, inscriptions, and coins by the standard of the 1342 Cairo text. For instance, surely it is scientifically unsound to look at a Koranic manuscript and then judge a particular spelling or writing of a word as "incorrect," or a "scribal error," with the yardstick of the 1342 Cairo text, that is, to prejudge the issue. Perhaps the manuscript records a more ancient spelling or an entirely different word or text, and may have some significance that we cannot dismiss a priori as a mere scribal error in the way Jeffery and Mendelsohn do in their otherwise very valuable study of the Samarqand Qurʾān Codex.[73] For example, Jeffery and Mendelsohn note that at sura II, 119 the Samarqand Qurʾān has, intriguingly, some word ending in *sara*, but this is dismissed as a mistake since there is no such word in the 1342 Cairo text. Potentially significant orthographic variants are similarly brushed away, as at II, 171; II, 172; III, 78; III, 88; III, 167; III,174; XX, 47; and so on. And yet these two scholars note that the Samarqand Qurʾān, "Where it deviates it presents numerous points of interest, so that a detailed comparison is of a certain importance."[74]

François Déroche and Sergio Noseda have rendered all scholars an invaluable service with their facsimiles of the Korans from the British Library in London and the Bibliothèque Nationale in Paris.[75] None of these three Koranic manuscripts is pointed or voweled. Déroche and Noseda present the original manuscript facsimile on one side, and on the opposite side for comparison they reproduce the 1342 Cairo text with its full panoply of fatahs, shaddas, dots, and dagger alifs. Though for the scientific study of the manuscript the reproduction of the 1342 Cairo text is premature since it only prejudges the issue, Déroche and Noseda had no choice. For reference, research, and comparison purposes, they were surely correct in indicating the suras and verses of the Cairo Koran that enabled students and scholars to easily locate a passage in the original manuscript. Second, they were hoping for further permissions from various Egyptian and Yemeni authorities to reproduce facsimiles of ancient Korans in the latter's possession; thus they had to tread carefully, and had their London and Paris Koran facsimiles to show the respective religious authorities that they, Déroche and Noseda, were treating these ancient Korans with respect. Any indications of possible variants in these manuscripts would not have been appreciated by the *ulama*, the religious authorities. In fact, no scholar, with the noble exceptions of Adrian Brockett and Gerd-R. Puin, has ever considered how to represent an unpointed manuscript, short of drawing the basic shapes (*rasm*), so that proper scientific remarks can be directed to it. Here is how Brockett explains:

> Distinctions between Qur'ān readings can be fine and are sometimes a matter of subtle differences in the archaic orthography of the Qur'ān, so in order to write about them in English, it is necessary to have a precise system of transliteration. Since, moreover, the vocal form of the Qur'ān was not originally indicated in writing, it is useful to have a system which can highlight, where necessary, which elements are vocal and which are graphic. (The term "vocal form," with respect to the Qur'ān, is used throughout to signify the consonantal skeleton fully fleshed out with diacritical marks, vowels, and so on. The term "graphic form" refers to the bare consonantal skeleton).

Gerd-R. Puin, the German scholar most closely involved with the sixteen thousand sheets or parchments of Koranic fragments discovered in Ṣan'ā', Yemen, has uncovered even more variants in the *rasm* that are not found in the mammoth work of eight volumes, *Mu'jam al-qirā'āt al-qur'āniyyah*,[76] edited in Kuwait recently. This dictionary lists over ten thousand variants, of which about a thousand are variants of or deviations in the *rasm*. In just eighty-three sheets of Koranic fragments written in the Ḥijāzī or Mā'il style, tentatively dated on stylistic grounds to the early eighth century, Puin discovered at least five thousand deviations in the *rasm*, never recorded before, not even in the seven, ten, or fourteen readings tolerated by orthodoxy. The Ḥijāzī Korans show differences in the system of counting of verses from the two dozen or so schools of counting; even the sequence of suras is often at variance with not only the standard Egyptian edition but with the sequence of suras in the Korans of Ibn Mas'ūd and Ubayy. These deviations cannot be dismissed as mere scribal errors (*lapsus calami*) since the so-called errors are repeated with the same word several times in several fragments studied by Puin. Thus, as Puin emphasizes, it makes common philological sense to look for a rationale. The recurrent deviations from the standard Egyptian text must be taken seriously, and cannot be swept under the carpet and attributed to scribal inadequacy.[77]

One of Puin's conclusions is that though there was an Oral Tradition (otherwise the Koranic text could not have been read), there were deliberate changes in the Oral Tradition of the reading of the Koran. Thus this Oral Tradition was not very stable or elaborate—changes must have occurred as can be seen in the variant orthography to be found in the Ṣan'ā' manuscripts. Puin suggests that the long *a* sound could be rendered by the Arab letter *yā'*, and originally the name in the present Koran that is read as "*'Ibrāhīm*" must have been read "*Abrāhām*." In other words, at some stage the fact that the long *ā* was rendered with the *yā'* was forgotten—hence the so-called Oral Tradition was not strong or even nonexistent.[78]

It is clear that many hundreds of variants, though not all, were invented by Muslim grammarians, philologists, and exegetes of the third and fourth Muslim centuries to explain all sorts of obscurities of the Koran, whether of sense or reference, Koranic grammatical aberrations,[79] or even more seriously, for doctrinal reasons to defend some particular theological position.[80] A kind of ethics of variants had developed by the ninth century CE, according to which only variants that were not too far from Islamic orthodoxy or doctrines, or not too ungrammatical, were to be accepted and preserved. Hence, if there had been startling deviations or variants, they would have been suppressed. Thus the variants that do remain are not always very significant. But we need to make a distinction between the variants fabricated by the Muslim exegetes and the variants to be found in the *rasm* in manuscripts such as those examined by Puin. The sheer number of variants in the orthography in manuscripts dated as early as 715 CE seem to cast doubt on the traditional account of the compilation of the Koran. The Ṣan'ā' fragments seem to suggest that even in the eighth century CE, there was no definitive text of the Koran.

Andrew Rippin has drawn conclusions similar to Puin's. Referring to the Ṣan'ā' manuscripts, Rippin writes,

> The text contains variant readings of a minor nature that suggest to some scholars that the idea of an oral tradition running parallel to the written one cannot be given historical credence. What we may have evidence of is the interpretative nature of the detailed annotations that were added to the text later: that is, that the current text is the product of reflection upon a primitive written text and not upon the parallel transmission of an oral text as the Muslim tradition has suggested.[81]

Rippin goes on to discuss sura XXI, 4 and 112. Should the two verses begin with the imperative "Say!" (in Arabic: *qul*), thus indicating that God is the speaker, or should the word be read as "He said" (*qāla*)? What do the printed Korans say? Much depends on the answer to these deceptively trivial questions. Before quoting Rippin in full, here is a rapid survey of some of the translations and Arabic texts.

ARABIC TEXT:

1. Saudi: XXI,4: *qāla* with plene alif: translated as "He (Muḥammad, pbuh)[82] said . . ."

XXI,112: *qala* (to be read as *qāla*) with defective—dagger—alif translated as "He (Muḥammad, pbuh) said . . ."

2. Muḥammad Ali: XXI,4: *qala* (to be read as *qāla*) with defective—dagger—alif translated as "He said: . . ."

XXII,112 *qala* (to be read as *qāla*) with defective—dagger—alif translated as "He said: ..."

3. Yusuf Ali: XXI,4: *qala* (to be read as *qāla*) with defective—dagger—alif translated as "Say [*sic*, strictly speaking it should of course be translated, 'He said . . .']: . . ."

XXI,112: *qala* (to be read as *qāla*) with defective—dagger—alif translated as "Say [*sic*]: . . ."

4. Istanbul: XXI,4: *qāla* with plene alif
XXI,112: *qāla* with plene alif

5. Iranian: XXI,4: *qāla* with plene alif
XXI,112 *qāla* with plene alif

6. Taj: XXI,4: *qala* (to be read as *qāla*) with defective—dagger—alif translated as (in Urdu) "He said . . ."

XXI,112: *qala* (to be read as *qāla*) with defective—dagger—alif translated as (in Urdu) "The Prophet said . . ."

7. Warsh I: XXI,4: *qul* (Say)
XXI,112: *qul*

8. Warsh II: XXI,4: *qul*
XXI,112: *qul*

9. Lebanese: XXI,4: *qāla* with plene alif translated as "Say" [*sic*]

XXI,112: *qala* (to be read as *qāla*) with defective—dagger—alif translated as "Say" [*sic*]

10. Qalun: XXI,4: *qul*
XXI,112: *qul*

11. Flügel: XXI:4: *qāla* with plene alif
    XXI,112: *qāla* with plene alif

TRANSLATIONS:

George Sale
XXI,4: Say
XXI,112: Say

M. Pickthall
XXI,4: He saith
XXI,112: He saith

R. Blachère
XXI,4: *(Notre Apotre) a dit* = (Our Apostle)[83] said
XXI,112: *Dis* = Say

A. J. Arberry
XXI,4: He says
XXI,112: He said

M. Kasimirski
XXI,4: Dis = Say
XXI,112: Mon Seigneur dit = My Lord Says

D. Masson
XXI,4: Il a dit = He said
XXI,112: Dis = Say

N. J. Dawood
XXI,4: Say
XXI,112: Say

E. H. Palmer

XXI,4:	Say
XXI,112:	Say

R. Bell

XXI,4:	Say
XXI,112:	Say

M. Henning

XXI,4:	Sprich (German) = Say
XXI,112:	Sprich (German) = Say

Here is how Rippin analyzes the significance of this particular variant:

> The very last verse (112) of sura 21 starts "He said [*qāla*], 'My Lord, judge according to the truth. Our Lord is the All-Merciful.'" The reference to "My Lord" and "Our Lord" in the text indicates that the subject of "He said" cannot be God but is the reciter of the Qur'ān, in the first place understood to be Muḥammad. Such a passage, in fact, falls into a common form of Qur'ānic speech found in passages normally prefaced by the imperative "Say!" (*qul*). The significant point here is that in the text of the Qur'ān, the word here translated as "He said" is, in fact, more easily read as "Say!" due to the absence of the long "a" marker (something which commonly happens in the Qur'ān, to be sure, but the word *qāla* is spelled this way only twice—the other occasion being in Qur'ān 21,4 and that occurs in some of the traditions of the writing of the text). In the early Ṣan'ā' manuscripts, the absence of the long "a" in the word *qāla* is a marker of an entire set of early texts. But why should it be that this particular passage should be read in the way that it is? It really should read "Say!" to be parallel to the rest of the text. This opens the possibility that there was a time when the Qur'ān was understood not as the word of God (as with "Say!") but the word of Muḥammad as the speaking prophet. It would appear that in the process of editing the text, most passages were transformed from "He said" to "Say!" in both interpretation and writing with the exception of these two passages in sura 21 which were not changed. This could have occurred only because somebody was working on the basis of the written text in the absence of a parallel oral tradition.[84]

One cannot, I think, continue to maintain that variants are trivial and have no bearing on the meaning or that they are of no great significance. Several very important theses have emerged from the above discussions.

1. Variants have always been acknowledged: for example, Bukhārī, Abī Dāwūd, and al-Suyūṭī.

2. Manuscript variants show that the Koran, like any other text, has a history, a history different from the traditional Islamic account of the Koran's compilation.

3. Those variants that were invoked served many purposes:

(i) In August Fischer's opinion, Koranic textual variants "*for the most part* [Fischer's emphasis] consist of no more than attempts at emendation made by philologically trained Koran specialists on difficult passages in the 'Uthmānic redaction."[85]

(ii) Polemical, see A. Rippin, "Qur'ān 7:40, Until the Camel Passes through the Eye of the Needle," *Arabica* 27, no. 2 (1980): 107–13. "Variants such as those for surah 7,40 were created when polemically based pressures on the exegetes were the strongest and the attitudes towards the Qur'ānic text less confining," p. 113.

(iii) Doctrinal. The variants reflect the ideology, as Burton shows, of groups that wish to argue for their own viewpoint, to establish a legal ruling, to settle conflict of sources.

4. The existence of variants casts doubt on the existence of an Oral Tradition. Skepticism of an Oral Tradition has been expressed by Fritz Krenkow,[86] A. Rippin, C. Luxenberg, Gerd-R. Puin, and G. Lüling. The latter wrote, "It has long since been proven that there was in principle no Oral Tradition at all, either for Old Arabic Poetry or for the Koran, as now this book goes on to demonstrate by its reconstruction of the editorially reworked Christian hymnody in the Koran as well as of many (on the level of writing) reworked Old Arabic classical poems."[87]

5. This thesis leads to the conclusion that the redactor or redactors of the Koran was or were working on the basis of the written text in the absence of a parallel Oral Tradition.

6. The so-called Seven Readings of the Koran should not be taken too literally since seven has a symbolic value derived perhaps from ancient Babylonian times with their notion of the seven stars and planets. The Koran itself talks of the seven heavens (XVII, 44), seven gates to hell (XV, 44), seven oceans (XXXI, 27), and there is also the motif of seven in the story of Joseph.[88]

7. The story of the collection of the Koran under ʻUthmān is perhaps only a calque[89] on the story of the destruction of the heretical writings of Arius on the orders of Constantine as recounted in Socrates and Sozemenus. Socrates quotes this letter from Constantine to the bishops and the people,

> Since Arius has imitated wicked and impious persons, it is just that he should undergo the like ignominy. Wherefore as Porphyry, that enemy of piety, for having composed licentious treatises against religion, found a suitable recompense, and such as thenceforth branded him with infamy, overwhelming him with deserved reproach, his impious writings also having been destroyed; so now it seems fit both that Arius and such as hold his sentiments should be denominated Porphyrians, that they may take their appellation from those whose conduct they have imitated. And in addition to this, if any treatise composed by Arius should be discovered, let it be consigned to the flames, in order that not only his depraved doctrine may be suppressed but also that no memorial of him may be by any means left. This therefore I decree, that if anyone shall be detected in concealing a book compiled by Arius, and shall not instantly bring it forward and burn it, the penalty for this offense shall be death; for immediately after conviction the criminal shall suffer capital punishment. May God preserve you![90]

Sozomen tells us, "The emperor punished Arius with exile, and dispatched edicts to the bishops and people of every country, denouncing him and his adherents as ungodly, and commanding that their books should be destroyed."[91]

Under Theodosius II, the writings of Nestorius were also burned. Here is how Gibbon puts it, "After a residence at Antioch of four years, the hand of Theodosius subscribed an edict which ranked him [Nestorius] with Simon the magician, proscribed his opinions and followers, and condemned his writings to the flames, and banished his person first to Petra in Arabia, and at length to Oasis, one of the islands of the Libyan desert."[92]

None of the above theses lends credibility to the Traditional Islamic understanding of the Koran, its origins, its compilation, and its redaction.

Perhaps it is time to start taking variants and Koranic manuscripts seriously.

NOTES

1. A. Jeffery, *Materials for the History of the Text of the Qur'ān. The Old Codices* (Leiden: E. J. Brill, 1937), p. 4.

2. John Burton, *The Collection of the Qur'ān* (Cambridge: Cambridge University Press, 1977), p. 231.

3. Al-Suyūṭī, *Itqān fī 'ulūm al-Qur'ān*, 2 vols. in 1 (Cairo: Ḥalabī, 1935/1354), pt. 2, p. 25; quoted in Burton, *The Collection of the Qur'ān*, p. 117.

4. Al-Sijistānī, 'Abd Allāh b. Sulaymān b. al-Ash'ath, Abū Bakr Ibn Abī Dāwūd,' *Kitāb al-Maṣāḥif*, ed. A. Jeffery (Cairo, 1936/1355), p. 10; quoted in Burton, *The Collection of the Qur'ān*, p. 120.

5. John Burton's footnote: "The published text ought here to be amended: for *fa lammā jama'a Abū Bakr jama'a Abu Bakr*, I propose to read: *wa lammā yajma' Abū Bakr*, to follow: *lam yuktab*," in Burton, *The Collection of the Qur'ān*, p. 253.

6. Al-Sijistānī, 'Abd Allāh b. Sulaymān b. al-Ash'ath, Abū Bakr Ibn Abī Dāwūd', *Kitāb al-Maṣāḥif*, p. 23; quoted in Burton, *The Collection of the Qur'ān*, p. 127.

7. Bukhārī, *al-Ṣaḥīḥ,* trans. Dr. Muḥammad Muhsin Khan, 9 vols. (Riyadh, Saudi Arabia: Darussalam Publishers, 1997), vol. 5, book LXIV: *Al-Maghāzī*, chapter 29, hadith 4090, p. 254.

8. Muslim Ṣaḥīḥ, trans. 'Abdul Ḥamīd 'iddīqī, rev. ed. (New Delhi: Kitāb Bhavan, 2000).

9. Sunan, *Abū Dāwūd*, English translation with explanatory notes by Professor Ahmad Hasan, 3 vols. (New Delhi: Kitāb Bhavan, reprinted in 1997).

10. Mushabbiḥāt ("those which give praise"): those suras from the so-called Middle Medinan period, LVII, LIX, LXI, LXII, LXIV, so-named because they begin with the phrase *sabbaḥa* or *yusabbiḥu li' llāh.*

11. Middle Prayer sometimes translated as "the best or the most excellent prayer," e.g., by Muḥammad Ali.

12. Mālik, *Muwaṭṭā'*, trans. Professor Muḥammad Rahimuddin, 5th ed. (New Delhi: Kitāb Bhavan, 2003).

13. Article *Zinā* in *Encyclopedia of Islam*, 2nd ed.

14. Ibn Ishaq, *The Life of Muḥammad*, trans. A. Guillaume (Oxford: Oxford University Press, 1955), p. 684.

15. Burton, *The Collection of the Qur'ān*, p. 86, *Burhān al-Dīn al-Bājī, Jawāb, MS Dār al-Kutub, Taimūr majāmī' no. 207, f. 15.*

16. R. Blachère, *Introduction au Coran* (Paris: Maisonneuve & Larose, 1959), p. 124.

17. Muḥammad Ibn al-Mutawakkil.

18. A. Jeffery, *Materials for the History of the Text of the Qur'ān. The Old Codices* (Leiden: E. J. Brill, 1937), p. 2.

19. Ibid., pp. 2–3. Jeffery gives the full references to their works.

20. *The Fihrist of al-Nadīm*, trans. B. Dodge (New York: Columbia University Press, 1970), vol. 1, pp. 68ff.

21. Ibid., p. 73.

22. Ibid., p. 74.

23. Ibid., pp. 76–77.

24. Jeffery, *Materials for the History of the Text of the Qur'ān,* p. 10.

25. The entire section on variants has relied upon the terse article *Kira'a* by R. Paret in the second edition of *The Encyclopedia of Islam*.

26. Jeffery, *Materials for the History of the Text of the Qur'ān*, pp. ix–x.

27. Ibid., p. vii.

28. Al-Nadīm was probably born about 935 CE.

29. *The Fihrist of al-Nadīm*, vol. 1, p. 79.

30. Ibid., pp. 53–58.

31. Jeffery, *Materials for the History of the Text of the Qur'ān*, pp. 22–23.

32. Ibid., p. 24.

33. Abul Ala Mawdudi, *Towards Understanding Islam* (Gary, IN: International Islamic Federation of Student Organizations, 1970), p. 109.

34. Abul Ala Mawdudi, *Towards Understanding the Qur'ān*, vol. 1, trans. and ed. Zafar Ishaq Ansari (Leicester, UK: Islamic Foundation, 1988), p. 22.

See also Abul Ala Mawdudi, *Introduction, The Holy Qur'ān* (Leicester, UK: Islamic Foundation, 1975), p. xxxv. I have not personally verified this citation which is quoted in Brother Mark, *A Perfect Qur'ān*, 2000 [No place of publication or name of publisher given; place: probably UK], p. 13:

> The Qur'ān, which is now in use all over the world, is the exact copy of the Qur'ān which was compiled by the order of Hadrat Abū Bakr and copies of

which were officially sent by Hadrat 'Uthmān to different places. Even today many very old copies are found in the big libraries in different parts of the world and if anyone has any doubt as to whether the Qur'ān has remained absolutely safe and secure against every kind of change and alteration, he can compare any copy of the Qur'ān with any of these copies and reassure himself. Moreover, if one gets a copy of the Qur'ān from any bookseller, say, Algeria in Africa in the West and compares it with a copy obtained from a bookseller, say, of Java in the East, one will find both copies to be identical with each other and also with the copies of the Qur'ān made during the time of Hadrat 'Uthmān. If even then anyone has any doubt left in his mind, he is advised to take any copy of the Qur'ān from anywhere in the world and ask anyone, out of the millions who know the Qur'ān by heart, to recite it word for word from the beginning to the end. He will find that the recitation conforms word for word to the written text. This is a clear and irrefutable proof of the fact that the Qur'ān which is in use today is the same Qur'ān which was presented to the world by Muḥammad (Allah's peace be upon him). A sceptic might entertain a doubt about its revelation from Allah, but none can have any doubt whatsoever regarding its authenticity and immunity and purity from any and every kind of addition or omission or alteration, for there is nothing so authentic in the whole human history as this fact about the Qur'ān that it is the same Qur'ān that was presented by the Holy Prophet to the World.

35. A. Brockett, *Studies in Two Transmissions of the Qur'ān*, doctorate thesis, University of St. Andrews, Scotland, 1984, p. 13.

36. Gerd-R. Puin, "Neue Wege der Koranforschung: II. Über die Bedeutung der altesten Koranfragmente aus Sanaa (Jemen) fur die Orthographiegeschichte des Korans," *Universität des Saarlandes Magazin Forschung* 1 (1999): 37–40.

37. Ibn Khaldun, *The Muqaddimah* (Princeton, NJ: Princeton University Press, 2nd ed., 1967 [2nd printing, 1980]), vol. 2, pp. 382–83.

38. Burton, *The Collection of the Qur'ān*, p. 5.

39. Ibid., p. 6.

40. Ibid., p. 31.

41. Ibid., pp. 31–32.

42. Ibid., pp. 34–35.

43. Ibid., p. 36.

44. Jalāl al-Dīn 'Abd al-Raḥmān b. Abī Bakr al-Suyūṭī, *Itqān fī 'ulūm al-*

Qur'ān, 2 vols. in 1 (Cairo: Ḥalabī, 1935/1354), pt. 1, p. 82, quoted by Burton, *The Collection of the Qur'ān*, p. 36.

45. Burton, *The Collection of the Qur'ān*.

46. Al-Suyūṭī, *Itqān fī 'ulūm al-Qur'ān*, quoted by Burton, *The Collection of the Qur'ān*, p. 37.

47. Herbert Berg, *The Development of Exegesis in Early Islam* (Richmond, Surrey, UK: Curzon Press, 2000), p. 221.

48. Burton, *The Collection of the Qur'ān*, p. 39.

49. M. Pickthall, *The Meaning of the Glorious Koran* (London: George Allen and Unwin, 1930), p. viii.

50. George Sale, *The Koran* (London: Frederick Warne and Company [circa 1890] [1st ed., 1734]), p. ix.

51. J. M. Rodwell, *The Koran* (London: J. M. Dent & Sons Ltd., 1921 [1st ed., 1861]), preface, p. 16.

52. A. Jeffery and I. Mendelsohn, "The Orthography of the Samarkand Quran Codex," *Journal of the American Oriental Society* 62 (1942): 180–81.

53. E. H. Palmer, *The Koran* (Oxford: Oxford University Press, 1949 [1st ed., 1880]).

54. N. J. Dawood, *The Koran* (Harmondsworth, UK: Penguin, 1990 [1st ed., 1956]).

55. A. Yusuf Ali, *The Holy Koran* (Lahore, Pakistan: Shaikh Muḥammad Ashraf, 1938 [1st ed., 1934]), p. iv.

56. Arberry in his short introduction seems to have uncritically swallowed whole every single Islamic dogma on the Koran, from its being a revelation to its untranslatability. See A. J. Arberry, *The Koran Interpreted* (Oxford: Oxford University Press, 1964), introduction, pp. ix–xiii.

57. Ibid., p. ix.

58. Blachère, *Le Coran*, p. xii.

59. Cairo edition: Blachère and Jeffery give 1342/1923 as the date of publication; Jeffery and Mendelsohn (1942), however, give 1344/1925; R. S. Humphreys gives 1347/1928; G. Bowering and Brockett give 1924. Would postmodernists say all the dates are valid?!

[Blachère, *Le Coran*, p. xii; Jeffery, *Materials for the History of the Text of the Qur'ān*, 1937; Jeffery/Mendelsohn, "The Orthography of the Samarqand Quran Codex," p. 177, footnote 5; Brockett, *Studies in Two Transmisions of the Qur'ān*; R. S. Humphreys, *Islamic History* (Princeton, NJ: Princeton University Press, 1991), p. 21; G. Bowering, "Chronology and the Quran," in the *Encyclopaedia of the Qur'ān*, vol. 1 (Leiden: Brill, 2001), p. 334.]

60. The Holy Bible, placed by the Gideons (LaHabra, CA: Lockman Foundation, 1977), pp. xx–xxii.

61. K. Elliger and W. Rudolph, eds., *Biblia Hebraica Stuttgartensia*, new edition (Stuttgart: Bibelgesellschaft, 1967/77), p. xii.

62. F. H. A. Scrivener, ed., *Greek New Testament* (New York: H. Holt & Co., 1903).

63. *Encyclopedia of Islam*, 2nd ed., s.v. Khatt.

64. F. Déroche, "Manuscripts of the Qur'ān," in *Encyclopaedia of the Qur'ān*, vol. 3: J–O, ed. J. D. McAuliffe (Boston: Brill, Leiden, 2003), p. 255.

65. Ibid., p. 257, right-hand column.

66. E. A. Rezwan, "Frühe Abschriften des Korans," in *Von Bagdad bis Isfahan. Buchmalarei und Schriftkunst des Vorderen Orients (8.-18.Jh) aus dem Institut fur Orientalistik*, ed. J. A. Petrosjan et al. (St. Petersburg: Lugano, 1995), pp. 117–25.

67. F. Leemhuis, "Codices of the Qur'ān," in *Encyclopaedia of the Qur'ān*, vol. 1: A–D, ed. J. D. McAuliffe (Boston: Brill, Leiden, 2001), p. 350.

68. W. Diem, "Untersuchungen zur fruhen Geschichte der arabischen Orthographie. Teile I–IV," *Orientalia* 48–50, 52 (1979–81, 1983), Teil I, p. 211, translated and quoted by Gerd-R. Puin, *Variant Readings of the Koran*, in present volume, footnote 19.

69. Brockett, *Studies in Two Transmisions of the Qur'ān*, pp. 9–10.

70. Puin, *Variant Readings of the Koran*, in present volume.

71. V. "*Qirā'a*" in *Encyclopedia of Islam*.

72. P. Larcher, "Coran et Theorie Linguistique de l'enonciation," *Arabica* 47 (2000): 443–44.

73. Jeffery and Mendelsohn, "The Orthography of the Samarkand Quran Codex," pp. 175–94 passim.

74. Ibid., p. 182.

75. F. Déroche and S. Noja Noseda, eds., *Sources de la transmission du texte coranique. I. Les manuscrits du style higazi. vol. i. Lemanuscrit arabe 328 (a) de la Bibliothèque nationale de France*, Lesa 1998; vol. *ii Le manuscrit or.2165 (f. 1 a 61) de la British Library* (Lesa, 2001).

76. ʿAbd al-ʿ āl Sālim Makram (wa-) Aḥmad Mukhtār ʿUmar (Iʿdād), *Muʿjam al-qirā'āt al-Qur'āniyyah, maʿa maqadimmah fi l-qirā'āt wa-ashar al-qurrā'*, I–VIII (Al-Kuwayt: Dhāt as-Salāsil 1402–1405/1982–1985).

77. Puin, "Neue Wege der Koranforschung: II.Über die Bedeutung der ältesten Koranfragmente aus Sanaa (Jemen) für die Orthographiegeschichte des Korans," pp. 37–40.

78. Ibid., p. 40.

79. See A. Rippin, "Qur'ān 21: 95: A Ban Is Upon Any Town," *Journal of Semitic Studies* 24 (1979): 43–53:

> the variants still show traces of their original intention: to explain away grammatical and lexical difficulties. While obviously this is not true of all variant readings in the Qur'ān, many variants being too slight to alleviate any problem, in Sura 21:95 and in many others the exegetical nature of Qur'ānic variants is apparent. (p. 53)

80. See A. Rippin, "Qur'ān 7: 40, Until the Camel Passes through the Eye of the Needle," *Arabica* 27, no. 2 (1980): 107–13. "Variants such as those for Surah 7:40 were created when polemically based pressures on the exegetes were the strongest and the attitudes towards the Qur'ānic text less confining," p. 113.

81. A. Rippin, *Muslims: Their Religious Beliefs and Practices*, 2nd ed. (London: Routledge, 2001), p. 30.

82. Brackets in original.

83. Brackets in original.

84. Rippin, *Muslims: Their Religious Beliefs and Practices*, pp. 30–31.

85. A. Fischer in *Der Islam* 28 (1948): 5f. n. 4, quoted by R. Paret, *Ḳirā'a*, in *Encyclopedia of Islam*, 2nd ed.

86. F. Krenkow, "The Use of Writing for the Preservation of Ancient Arabic Poetry," in *A Volume of Oriental Studies, Presented to E. G. Browne on His 60th Birthday*, ed. T. W. Arnold and R. A. Nicholson (Cambridge: Cambridge University Press, 1922), pp. 261–68.

87. Günter Lüling, *A Challenge to Islam for Reformation* (Delhi: Motilal Banarsidass Publishers, 2003), pp. XLI–XLII.

88. A. Rippin, "Numbers and Enumeration," in *Encyclopedia of the Qur'ān*, vol. 3, p. 552.

89. I think it was Lawrence I. Conrad who first suggested such a thesis. At a conference at the University of Mainz, Germany, in 2002, a paper by Conrad was read out—he was unable to attend at the last moment because of a car accident—in which he puts forward this idea. I have not seen the paper in written form since that conference so I cannot say if he elaborates on this and explains what he meant. I do not know if he had the acts of Constantine and Theodosius in mind, they are my proposals.

90. Socrates, "Church History from A.D. 305–439," trans. A. C. Zenos, in *A Select Library of Nicene and Post-Nicene Fathers of the Christian Church*, ed. P. Schaff and H. Wace, vol. 2 (Michigan: W. E. Eerdmans, 1997), book I, chap. 8, p. 14.

91. Sozomen, "The Ecclesiastical History," trans. Chester D. Hartranft, in *A Select Library of Nicene and Post-Nicene Fathers of the Christian Church*, ed. P. Schaff and H. Wace, vol. 2 (Michigan: W. E. Eerdmans, 1997), book I, chap. 21, p. 255.

92. E. Gibbon, *The Decline and Fall of the Roman Empire* (New York: Modern Library, n.d.), vol. 2, chap. 47, p. 825. Gibbon's source was *The Imperial Letters in the Acts of the Synod of Ephesus* (Concil.tom.iii, pp. 1730–35).

Part 2

Language, Linguistics, and Translation

2.1

On the Language of the Koran[1]

Theodor Nöldeke

I. The Koran and Classical Arabic (ʿArabiyya)

In his work *Volkssprache und Schriftsprache im alten Arabien*[2] (The Vernacular and Literary Languages in Ancient Arabia) Karl Vollers sought to prove that the original text of the Koran was written in a popular dialect that prevailed in the *Ḥijāz*,[3] from which, inter alia, the inflections known by the name of *I'rāb* were absent, but that later on the form of Arabic literary language was worked into the text that now appears to us. That this view, which is presented with great certainty[4] and which can therefore easily impress the insufficiently prepared or discerning reader is untenable was proved in detail in particular by Rudolf Geyer.[5] I would like however here to underline a major point about which the excellent, all too prematurely deceased, scholar was in my view mistaken, since he was encumbered by a number of preconceived ideas.[6]

Vollers compares the "text" or "official" text of the Koran with the "variants" and finds in these many traces of the authentic vernacular spoken by the Prophet. He sees this text solely in Flügel's edition, without considering that Flügel merely reproduces the reading of the *Ḥafṣ* that is practically the most widespread in the Muslim world—unfortunately not completely accurately[7]—and without considering that alongside this one a whole series of other texts exists that are theoretically just as canonical, among which there is one, that by Nāfiʿ, which is the sole version still in use throughout the Maghreb. Most of the variants that are interpreted by Vollers as vestiges of an original *Ḥijāzic* vernacular are just as canonical as those he regards as belonging to an artificially arranged "official" text. This is also true of Abū ʿAmr's text in which the *idġām kabīr*,[8] the omission of short vowels in final position between two identical or similar consonants, is characteristic. This pronunciation that, according to *Sībawayhī*[9] often occurred, alongside which however the full preservation of the sounds was also usual, may have been used by Muḥammad both in the delivery and the recitation of the Koran. In any case, the different schools of thought have readily used all kinds of artifice in such matters. One can in no way infer the systematic omission of final-position short vowels from this. Even less should one follow Vollers in using pause and rhyme forms to support this thesis. This is also recognized by Geyer.

Unfortunately the work that gave the fullest overview of the different readings,[10] Ṭabarī's *kitāb al-qirāʾāt*, appears to be lost, but the sources that remain available to us provide rich material, much richer than that presented by Vollers, which was taken almost completely from Bayḍāwī's commentary. In these readings there is certainly much that was more or less foreign to the living language. The Oriental is inclined artificially to shape the solemn delivery of holy texts; the Jews and Syrians did the same. But the real language shows through everywhere. And this much can be said with certainty: had the Prophet and his contemporary believers spoken the Koran without the *Iʿrāb*, this tradition would not have disappeared without trace.[11]

In many instances with regard to Koranic variants it is a question of different conceptions of the meaning, in which case, as impartial observers, we often identify the correct one without difficulty. Many of the variants alter the meaning at most in very minor ways. Whether in II, 26 Muhammad said *ṯumma ʾilayhi turjaʿūn* or *tarjaʿūn* is fairly immaterial, even if verses II, 43, 151; XXI, 93; and XXIII, 62 with *rājiʿūn* make the active pronunciation more probable.[12]

But in particular, with regard to such variants that merely concern linguistic form, very often we have no idea which one reproduces the language of the Prophet himself. With the ancient poets we have to content ourselves entirely with the textbook vocalization, however probable it is that they themselves often deviated from this, with one saying it like this, another like that. When, for example, in the later tradition forms like *naḏkuru* predominate and are therefore quoted in our grammars alone or as the authentic or principle forms, this does not exclude the possibility that the poet from one tribe said *niḏkuru*, while that of another tribe said *nuḏkuru* (with equal vocalization). Here, we may trust the tradition that the forms in *a* are *Ḥijāzic*; therefore, Muḥammad would have said *naḏkur*.[13] Thus the authentic, entirely undotted consonant text of the Koran, which is a real skeleton, shows us that Muḥammad, as the tradition regarding the pronunciation of the *Ḥijāzers* has it, in many cases omitted, or softened, the Hamza. But whether he did the same with the initial sound, whether, for example, in XXIII, 1 he said *qaḏ ʾaflaḥa* or *qaḏa -flaḥa*, or in LXXII, 1 *qula ʾuḥiya* or *qulu -waḥiya* we cannot know, even if the omission of the Hamza, which Nāfiʿ, hands down and which therefore holds good for the Maghrebin Koran may be more likely.[14] The spelling of the *Muṣḥaf*[15] also gives us a fairly accurate idea of the instances in which the Quraysh used the so-called *Imāla*,[16] frequently differing from the usage of other Arabs.

But, of course, neither Muḥammad nor his "companions" demanded that Allah's words be pronounced exactly as he did, as long as one spoke authentic Arabic. Such a requirement would be more or less equivalent to expecting Goethe's poems to be read with a Frankfurt and Schiller's with a Swabian inflection, as the poets themselves recited them. In addition, I do not really believe that in ancient times, even after the establishment of the 'Uthmānic text, great offense was taken if, in reciting the Koran, someone used a phoneme that made no difference to the meaning, even if it did not entirely correspond to its primitive written form; for example, if they said *ʾafʿala*, where only *faʿala* was written. And that in II, 58 for *fūmihā* the pronunciation *ṯūmihā* occurred with the use of the original form[17] was also scarcely remarked, especially since the alternation between *ṯ* and *f* may in many cases have been more a question of individual than of dialect usage.[18] Among such inoffensive variants, I would like to include that in XLIX, 11 some people read the uninflected *ʿasa* either as *ʿasā* or as *ʿasayna*,[19] and other similar examples can be found. As we gather, particularly from Zamakhšarī's statements, many somewhat more divergent readings from pre-'Uthmanic times remained in people's memories, which may at least in part have derived just as much from Muḥammad as the ones adopted, or at least would not have been rejected by him, since they did not alter the meaning. Neither the Prophet nor his closest followers and successors had the slightest idea about philological meticulousness.

Nowhere among the variants do we find, however, a contrast between vernacular and literary modes of speech. And we find just as little of the contrast so strongly emphasized by Vollers between an original, *Ḥijāzic*, or Western style and an artificially imposed *Tamīmic* or Eastern style.

Moreover, I cannot concede to Geyer that Vollers had at least proved that in Mecca a language of the common man (the *ʿāmma*) existed, which differed greatly from the standard language of Muḥammad and those of his social rank. In a general way, one might suppose the existence of such a difference, but it is highly uncertain that this was the case, if one means more than perhaps that slaves brought in from Africa or other foreign countries did not express themselves entirely correctly or had their own linguistic idiosyncrasies. On the other hand, certain manifestations that are very clear through the spelling in the Koran indicate that in Mecca and also probably in Yathrib the evolution of the strict ʿArabiyya into the later vernacular had already begun. To this belong, apart from the already mentioned abandonment or transformation of the Hamza, the very widespread shortening of the final-position *ī*. This was, after all, only a continuation of a tendency that was apparent elsewhere in Arabic and the replacement that occurs twice, alongside numerous "correct" forms, of the nominative ending—*ūna* by *īna* in II, 172 and I, 160.[20] It is precisely through these forms, which caused the interpreters so much trouble, that we can see that the Koranic text has not been subjected to a process of linguistic polishing.

It remains the case, therefore, that the Koran was written in Classical Arabic (ʿArabīyya), a language that extended over a wide area[21] and which naturally exhibited many dialectical variations. These are also partly reflected in different readings of the Koran and have also persisted, either unchanged or transformed, in the dialects of today.[22]

II. Stylistic and Syntactic Peculiarities in the Language of the Koran

It is well known that for Muslims Allah's uncreated revelation, the Koran, constitutes the ideal of human expression,[23] and Europeans are also inclined to consider the book at least as the foremost example of Arabic literary style. But on closer examination, even this cannot be sustained. Of course, people will object: how can we who have painstakingly tried to immerse ourselves in the language of such an ancient people whose way of thinking is so far removed from our own contradict men who have imbibed their feeling for the Arabic tongue with their mother's milk and scholars of whatever origin living among the Arabs who completely devoted themselves to the study of the Arabic language and its monuments? We have, however, one particular advantage over them: freedom from religious prejudice or bias. And furthermore we have grown up in the school of scientific criticism. This allows us to recognize that the mode of expression of the Koran has great shortcomings, shortcomings that the ancient Arabic poems and tales (*ʾakhbār –l-ʿarab*) are free of. And this is entirely understandable. The poets and storytellers were using an established language that had been shaped by many predecessors; Muḥammad, on the other hand, arrived with a completely new literary genre and preached thoughts and ideas that were totally alien to his countrymen and thus he was unable to find an accomplished form of expression straightaway.

All beginnings are difficult.[24] The innovator allows himself much arbitrariness of expression, which may even have impressed the nonconverts but which was not in keeping with the spirit of the language. If he was already struggling in the description of his religious thoughts and even legends, it was even harder for him to express himself as a lawmaker and ruler. Muḥammad took from the soothsayers (*kāhin*), along with a number of other things, the use of short rhyming sentences. Already in the little care he takes with regard to rhyme and assonance,[25] he shows his lack of understanding of form; and this even more so in the fact that he retains this rhyme scheme even when his revelations turn naturally more and more into pure prose. On account of the rhyme, however imperfect it may be, the speech was subject to much constraint, while the individual verses of the same passage often varied greatly in length.[26] Muḥammad certainly reflected much on the content of his revelation before he presented it to the world, but little on its form.

It should, moreover, be noted that the Prophet had to battle with a very unwieldy medium. In spite of its incredibly rich vocabulary, Arabic was by its nature ill suited to the expression of long complete sequences of thought, especially with regard to matters spiritual. Certainly the serious work of people who came after turned Arabic into an appropriate tool for scientific description, but nevertheless certain weaknesses in the language have remained troublesome.[27]

On the whole, the sentences in the older suras flow easily and swiftly; here a few logical slips are not disconcerting. The narrative passages of the Meccan suras are tolerably smooth, especially when not much detail is given. But precisely in the description of "the most beautiful story" (sura XII) there is much to take issue with. Those with short verses are in general stylistically superior, for example, XXVI, XLIII, and LVI. In XXVI, certainly, we must take on board the fact that Abraham is speaking at length about the most recent law (verses 88–102), as well as the fact that all the prophets use the same formulations. The more Muḥammad speaks in prose, the poorer his style becomes. His lack of practice in sharp, logical thinking becomes increasingly apparent in his use of language. Here it can be clearly seen that no prose style yet existed for teachers and rulers.

One must furthermore bear in mind that the Prophet did not speak for educated Europeans and that the shortcomings in his mode of expression were not apparent to his contemporaries, who were not literary critics. The constant repetition of a few thoughts,[28] placed alongside one another in the book, also appears to much lesser advantage than was the case when originally uttered over a period of time. Indeed almost everything in it was new to the Arabs and, even if the hard-headed merchants from Mecca preferred the Persian heroic tales recited to them by Nadr to the prophet legends of his cousin Muḥammad, the latter's revelations nonetheless had a powerful impact. Not even his enemies noticed how unconvincing Muḥammad 's sentences were, how he indulged in circular arguments, let alone those won to his cause. It is precisely by virtue of his huge moral and material success that we recognize that, in spite of all of this, in all his activities he was also a ἐξουσίαν ἔχων καὶ οὐχ ὡς οἱ γραμματεῖς ["who has authority but not like the grammarians"].

Style and grammar can be separated in theory, but not in practice and certainly not in respect of this very singular work. At the outset, I wished only to deal with what was striking in terms of the grammar, but I soon saw that I had to refer to certain shortcomings in the style. This part then leads very gradually to the purely grammatical, in the discussion of which stylistic elements need also to be touched upon. In all of this, incidentally, I am by no means striving to be exhaustive, or even strictly systematic.

The fact that the Koran repeats its fundamental principles, readily using the same words, often makes it very boring for us. But Muḥammad had good reasons for this; it was precisely important for him to emphasize his teachings through such repetitions. And the Arabs, who were used to set formulations, were certainly not disconcerted by the fact that in different passages he used the same or essentially the same formulation, including in the mention of minor details, for example, in the introduction to a story:

XX, 8; LXXIX, 15:	*hal*[29] *ʾatāka ḥadīṯu Mūsā iḏ*;
LI, 24:	*hal ʾatāka ḥadīṯu ḍayfi ʾIbrāhīma-l-mukramīna iḏ*;
XXXVIII, 20:	*hal ʾatāka nabaʾu-l-khaṣmi iḏ*;
LXXXV, 17:	*hal ʾatāka ḥadīṯu l-junūdi*, to which also can be added the
LXXXVIII, 1:	*hal ʾatāka ḥadīṯu l-gāšiyati* indicating the *dies irae.*

On the other hand, one can criticize the fact that in the same passage he often uses the same words or expressions where this is not prompted by the meaning. When writing in haste, it can easily happen to the likes of us that we unnecessarily use the same word or phrase several times in quick succession, even if they are not ones that we use particularly often. Thus it is in many of the instances cited here, whereas in others the repetition is probably not undeliberate, but is rather clumsy. For example, the *qul* [say], which is certainly a favorite word in the Koran, with which God in a rather heavy-handed manner makes it easy for the Prophet to speak in his own name,[30] is to be found in sura VI[31] no less than forty-two times and *thumma* [yet, still, however, nevertheless] is found there twenty-one times. *ʾAm* [or] appears sixteen times in the passage LII, 30–43 in relation to very different matters and five times in LXVIII, 37–47. *Laʿallakum* [so that you . . .] is the closing sentence of verses 19, 49, 50, 53, 60, 68, 145, 175, 179, 181, 185, 217, 243, and 268 of sura II and in addition *laʿallahum* [so that they] in sura II, 182, 183, and 221 (in all seventeen times). *Ḥattā ʾidhā* [until, when] appears in XVIII, 70, 73, 76, 84, 92, and 95 (there twice). Forms of *istafazza* [to remove or expel] in XVII, 66, 78, and 105 (not found elsewhere in the Koran). *Tuqubbila* in V, 30, 40; *yutaqabbal* in V, 30; *yataqabbalu* also in V, 30 (the passive is only otherwise found in the Koran in IX, 53). Forms of *inqalaba* in III, 122, 138 (twice), 142, and 168. *Kafā bi-llāhi* with accusative of the Tamjiz of an adjective in IV, 7, 47 (twice), 72, 81, 131, 164, and 169 and *kafā bihi* (used differently) in IV, 53, 58. *Kidhdhāban* in LXXVIII, 28 and in another context verse 35 (not found elsewhere in the Koran).[32] *Lanansifannahū fū –l-yammi nasfan* in XX, 97 (the Golden Calf). *Yansifuhā rabbi nasfan* in XX, 106 (the mountains at the resurrection as in *nusifat*, LXXVII, 10). *Ḥijran maḥjūran* in XXV, 24 and used differently in verse 55. *Samiyyan* (homonym) is only found in XIX, 8 (John), 66 (God). *Sanurāwidu ʿanhu ʾabāhu* in XII, 61 after *rāwadatnū/rāwattuhū/rāwatunna ʿan nafsihū* (and small variations) in the sexual sense, XII, 12, 23, 26, 32, and 51 (twice); otherwise only *rāwadūhu ʿan ḍayfihī* in LIV, 37 (also sexual). *Wa ʾantum tanẓurūn* [while you saw/ while you looked on] in II, 52 is inappropriate or superfluous after verse 47 where it is appropriate. *Wama -l-lāhu bighāfilin ʿammā taʿmalūn* II, 2, 69, 79, 134, and 144 and with *yaʿmalūn* in verse 135 (otherwise only in III, 94 and with *rabbuka* instead of *Allāhu* in XI, 123; XXVII, 95). [Wa- or fa-] *lā khawfun ʿalayhim walā hum yaḥzanūn*, II, 36, 59, 106, 264, 275, and 277 (elsewhere five other times). *Li-l-Lāhi mā fū-s-samāwāti wamā fū-l-ʾarḍū*, IV, 125, 130 (twice), 131, 168, 169, 170, and 171 [with *lahū* instead of *lāhi*]. *Li-l-Lāhi mulku-s-samāwāti wa-l-ʾarḍī wama baynahumā*, V, 20, 21 and in very similar form in verses 44 and 120.

Some of the examples cited here are occasioned by the convenience of the rhyme. This is even more evident in other cases. *Sabūlan* is the rhyme word in XXV, 10, 29, 36, 44, 46, and 59 (where 36, 44, and 46 have *ʾaḍallu sabūlan*). In this sura other rhyme words are also repeated. Likewise in sura IV *sabūlan* is a rhyme word ten times or eleven times if the word is also used at the end of verse 38, and other rhyme words are also used several times. In sura XIX *Shayʾan* closes verses 10, 43, 61, and 68; in addition, there are other recurring rhyme words in sura XIX. In the short sura XLVII (forty verses), six verses rhyme with *ʾaʿmālahum* (verses 1 and 9: *ʾaḍalla ʾaʿmālahum*; verse 5: *yuḍilla ʾaʿmālahum*; verses 10 and 30: *fa ʾaḥbaṭa ʾaʿmālahum*; and verse 34: *sayuḥbiṭu ʾaʿmālahum*). To this can be added in IV, 52, 79 [in the latter slightly different]: *walā yuẓlamūna fatūlan / walā tuẓlamūna fatūlan*, respectively; *walā yuẓlamūna naqūran* in IV 123 and *lā yuʾtūna n-nāsa naqūran* in IV, 56 and so on.

That Muḥammad very often alters the word order because of the rhyme is his right; poets do likewise. The fact that for the sake of the rhyme he often employs different forms than he would do otherwise is also in order. But in so doing he makes it far too easy for himself. Occasionally this results in small inaccuracies. For example, *wa-ʾanā ma ʿakum mina-sh-shāhidūn* in III, 75, where it can only be a question of one witness. Likewise *ʾinnūmaʿakum mina-l- muntaẓirūna* in VII, 69 and X, 21, 102; *ʾinnū liʿamalikum mina-l-qālūna* in XXVI, 168; *latakūnanna mina-l-marjūmūna* in XXVI, 116; and *sawāʾun ʿalaynā ʾa-waʿaẓta ʾam lam takun mina l-wāʿẓūna* in XXVI, 136.[33] On account of the rhyme, there are often imperfects alongside perfects: *Kamā nasū liqāʾa yawmihim hādhā wamā kānū bi ʾāyātina yajḥadūna* in VII, 49; *fa-farūqan kadhdhabtum wa-farūqan taqtulūn* in II, 81; *farūqan kadhdhabū wa-farūqan yaqtulūn* in V, 74; *bi-mā ʿaṣaw wa kānū yaʿtadūn* in III, 108; and *wa-mā ẓalamūnā wa-lākin kānū ʾanfusahum yaẓlimūn* in II, 54 and VII, 160.

The Koran would also probably sometimes have the form *faʿalū* if the rhyme did not give rise to the composite *kānū yafʿalūn*.[34] The rhyme necessitates the massive use of duals in sura LV. One should also note *ʾinna l-muttaqūna fū jannātin wa-nahar* in LIV, 54, where the wholly inappropriate singular [*nahar*] that does not agree with *jannāt* is only there because the rhyme in this passage is *ar*, *ir*, *ur*.

The closing sentences of the verses often serve solely to fill out the rhyme, or at least to provide a certain rounding-off. Certainly, as has already been remarked, the Prophet is concerned to strongly emphasize many sentences through constant repetition; but how superfluous is, for example, the ending *wa-llāhu ʿazūzun ḥakūm* in II, 228, 241 in the middle of the laying down of laws and also the *wa-llāhu samū ʿun ʿalūm*, III, 30, in the story. Likewise a number of sentences with *laʿallakum* in sura II.[35] The phrases *ʾin kuntum taʿlamun* are only there to serve the rhyme in II, 180, 280; VI, 81; *ʾin kuntum fāʿilūn* in XII, 10; XXI, 68.[36] Similarly, *wa- kunnā fāʿilūn* in XXI, 79, 104 [with *ʾinna*]; *ʾin kuntum ṣādiqūn* is also superfluous following on from a conditional clause and exactly the same is true of *ʾin kunta mina ṣ-ṣādiqūn* in VII, 103. Likewise so, in the legal prescriptions: *wa -ʾinna llāha bi-mā taʿmalūna baṣūr* in II, 233, 238; *wa-llāhu bi-mā taʿmalūna khabir* in II, 234 and many similar instances. The closing sentence in *ʾafʾanta tahdū-l-ʿumya walaw kanū lā yubṣirūna*, X, 44, is frankly illogical, as though the inability of the blind to see were only hypothetical, and *wa-lā tusmiʿu-ṣ-*

ṣumma -d-duʿāʾa ʾidhā wallaw mudbirūna in XXVII, 82 and XXX, 51 is no better since the deaf do not hear even when they stand still.

The fact that the Koran has a tendency to switch rapidly from one subject to another will not have disconcerted the Arabs; they were accustomed to this with their poets. Certainly Muḥammad sometimes goes rather too far in this respect: he breaks off from one subject, takes up another, drops this one and goes back to the first, and so on. It is particularly odd that in XXXVII, 164 the angels suddenly speak without any introduction and then quickly withdraw. It is unclear in any case in sura LXXII that verse 15 marks the end of the djinns' speeches and that from then on Allah speaks directly again. In verse 16 *An* (*anna*) seems to come before the djinns words, whereas it belongs to the *qul* in verse 1. Perhaps Muḥammad did not really notice the transition himself.

The Koran is not very rigorous in the exact correspondence of the elements of a comparison. According to the wording, what is compared is sometimes equated with a secondary element of the image. Thus *mathalu-l-ladhūna yunfiqūna ʾamwālahum fū sabīli ạl- lāhi kamthali ḥabbatin ʾanbatat sabʿa sanābila fū kulli sunbulatin miʾatu ḥabbatin* in II, 263 while it is not the pious almsgivers but that which is piously given that resembles the seed that greatly multiplies. Exactly the same is true of the simile for those who do not give alms for the sake of God, II, 267. Furthermore, *mathalu mā yunfiqūna fū hādhihi ạl-hayāti-d-dunyā kamathali riḥin fūhā ṣirrun ʾaṣābat ḥartha qawmin ẓalamū ʾanfusahum faʾahlakathu*. III, 113, is not congruent either: the wind that brings about destruction is equated with its object, that is, the useless expenditure. *ʾInnamā mathalu -l- ḥayāti-d-dunyā kamā ʾin ʾanzalnāhu mina-s- samāʾi*, X, 25, where the fertilizing, but ultimately ineffective rain (instead of the field) serves as an image of worldly splendor; correspondingly XVIII, 43. In II, 16 et seqq. we first read *mathaluhum kamathali -l-ladhi -s-tawqada nāran*, etc. . . . [*They are like one who kindled a fire . . .*] but then it continues (verse 18): *ʾaw kaṣayyibin min as-samāʾi, etc. . . .* [*like a rainstorm from the sky . . .*], so that the unhappy unrepentant ones face the annihilating thunderstorm. In the question *mathalu-l-jannati -l- lati wuʿida -l-muttaqūna . . . kaman huwa khālidun fū n-nāri* in XLVII, 16 et seq. the meticulously described home of the blessed is compared to the damned rather than to their dwelling place, the fire of hell. Compare this with

ʾajaʿaltum siqāyata-l-ḥājji wa ʿimārata -l-masjidi-l-ḥarāmi kaman ʾāmana bi-llāhi wa-l-yawmi l-ʾākhiri wa- jāhada fū sabūli llāhi lā yastawūna ʿinda llāhi, IX, 19: here rather than the people that practice holy customs the customs themselves are compared to the true believers, but then both types of people are grouped together. Sentences like *mā khalaqakum walā baʿathakum ʾillā kanafsin wāḥidatin, your creation and your resurrection are those of a single soul* ["You were created but as one soul, and as one soul you shall be raised to life" (Dawood)], XXXI, 27, appear quite often in the Hebrew and Aramaic, but in Arabic this may be an isolated occurrence.[37]

In the language of the Koran, there are many other small inconsistencies. Thus of two linked or corresponding similar segments one is determined while the other isn't: *tilka ʾāyātu l- Qurʾāni wa kitābim-mubūnin*, XXVII, 1 ["THE Quran," as opposed to "book"]; *yahabu limay-yashāʾu ʾināthan wa -yahabu limay -yashāʾu-dh-dhukūra* ["THE boys," as opposed to "girls"], XLII, 48. One might assume here that the use of the article is supposed to emphasize male children as the only desirable ones. The close juxtaposition of a genitive subject and a genitive object is hardly striking in *la-huwa ʾahlu t-taqwā wa-ʾahlu l-maghfira, We owe Him Piety, and it is He who forgives*, LXXIV, 65. In *liyaʾkhudhū ḥidhrahum wa-ʾasliḥatahum*, IV, 103, the abstract noun *ḥidhr* is probably conceived in rather concrete terms so that it does not stand out too much next to the purely concrete noun.

The repetition of the same word with different meanings is not very pleasing in *ʾal-ladhūna qāla la-humu-n-nāsu ʾinna n-nāsa qad jamaʿū lakum*, III, 167: "for the people (friends) say: the people (enemies) are gathering against you." The repeated *min* in *fatarā -l-wadqa yakhruju min khilālihū wa -yunazzilu min -s-samāʾi, min jabālin fihā min baradin*, XXIV, 43, could hardly have corresponded to good Arabic style either, even though Arabic sentences often contain more than one *min* with different meanings alongside one another. Furthermore, *yā ʾayyuhā-l-ladhūna ʾāmanū ʾāmanū bi-l-lāhi wa rasūlihū wa-l-kitābi-* etc., *O you who believe, believe in Allah and His Messenger and the Book* . . . in IV, 135 appears clumsy in that those who are addressed as believers have yet to have recited to them the entire content of the belief they are supposed to have. The sentence *wa-mā kāna qawlahum illā an qālū* [literally: "*And their cry was only that they cried*: . . ."], III, 141, would not have struck the Arabs with their fondness for *figura etymologica* as strange. The *ka-dhālika* or *mitˀla qawlihim* in *ka-dhālika qāla lladhūna lā yaʿamūna mitˀla qawlihim* [literally: "So also those who have no knowledge, say much the same," i.e., "so also" on its own would be enough], II, 107, and *ka-dhālika qāla lladhūna qablahum mitˀla qawlihim*, II, 112, are superfluous; this tautology cannot be explained here as something like "exactly so."

Innū hadānū Rabbi ilā ṣirāṭin mustaqimin dūnan qayyiman [var. *qiyaman*] *millata Ibrāhūma ḥanūfan wa-mākāna min al-mushrikūn*, VI, 162, sounds very harsh where added to the construction of *hadā* with *ilā*, which follows with the accusative,[38] and then an accusative of state or condition (*ḥāl*),[39] and a circumstantial proposition of state: "while he (Abraham) was a real believer and not a polytheist."

Alladhū tassāˀ ˀalūna bihi wa-l-arḥāmi (literally: "concerning whom (God) you ask one another questions, and the ties of relationships"),[40] IV, 1, is at the least very inelegant.[41] *ˀIllā qalūlan mimmā taˀkulūna* in place of *ˀillā qalūlan taˀkulūnahu* (or *taˀkulūna*), XII, 47, is not pleasing and nor are the corresponding words in verse 48, in spite of the frequent switches from the partitive to the definite *min.*

Wa-lā yuʿammaru min muʿammarin walā yunqaṣu min ʿumurihi, XXXV, 12, is illogical, as if the man who lived a long time had his life cut short rather than he who lived for a short time. *Wa-lawlā ˀan thabbatnāka la-qad kidtta tarkanu ilayhim shayˀan qalūlan*, XVII, 76, a translation paraphrasing the general sense of these words would go something like this: "We made you steadfast and kept you from yielding anything to them, which you almost did." But this rendition conceals the imprecision of expression of the original.[42]

Exactly the same is true in *wa-lawlā faḍlu llāhi ʿalayka wa-raḥmatuhu la-hammat ṭāˀ ˀifatun minhum ˀan yuḍillūka*, IV, 113; the party really had the plan to lead him astray, only was unable to execute it. In *ˀinna lladhūna kafarū wa-mātū wa-hum kuffārun fa-lan yuqbala min aḥadihim milˀu l-arḍi dhahaban wa -law iftadā bihi*, III, 85, if only *law* were there, the last clause would be superfluous but not wrong, whereas the concessive *wa-law* certainly gives a false meaning.[43] In *khalaqakum min nafsin wāḥiddatin thumma jaʿala minha zawjaha*, XXXIX, 8, the sequence of tenses is reversed; Muḥammad could have avoided this if, in the place of the temporal or consecutive *thumma*, he had employed the simple *wa*. There is another *hysteron proteron*[44] in *man laʿanahu llāhu wa-ghaḍiba ʿalayhi wa-jaʿala min humu l-qiradata wa-l- khanāzūra wa-ʿabada ṭ-ṭāghūta*, V, 65, according to the meaning = *man ʿabada ṭ-ṭāghūta wa laʿanahu . . . -l- khanāzūra*. [The sense demands that the adoration of the *ṭāghūt* precede and not follow the metamorphosis into apes and swine.] Also in *wa-lawlā kalimatun sabaqat min rabbika lakāna li-zāman wa- ʾajalun musammā*, XX, 129, the last two words, which follow on from *kalimatun*, trail awkwardly behind.[45]

Fa -huwa jazāʾuhu, XII, 75, "he must atone for it with his own person," is a strange brachyology [extreme terseness leading to obscurity].[46]

Changes in grammatical number are very common in Arabic. For a sentence with *man* to be absorbed by one with *ulāʾika* or another plural, as, for example, in III, 76, 88; IV, 71; V, 49; III, 70, is certainly not contrary to the usage of the language. Neither are instances such as *wa-minhum man yastamiʿūna ilayka*, X, 43, completely without parallels outside of the Koran;[47] but note the inconsistency that immediately follows it: *wa-minhum man yanẓuru ilayka* (X, 44). The change is very abrupt in cases such as *man ʾaslama wajhahu li-llāhi wa-huwa muḥsinun fa-lahu ajruhu ʿinda rabbihi wa-lā khawfun ʿalayhim wa-lā hum yaḥzanūn*, II, 106, and even more so in *inna llāha lā yuḥibbu man kāna mukhtālan fakhūran alladhūna yabkhalūna*, and so on, IV, 40–41. In *man laʿanahu llāhu wa-ghaḍiba ʿalayhi wa-ja ʿala minhumu l-qiradata wa -l-khanāzūra*, V, 65, the plural in the partitive expression could hardly have been avoided. But the number changes very strikingly in *alladhūna yujādiluna fū ʾāyāti llāhi bi-ghayri sulṭānin ʾatāhum kabura maqtan*, XL, 37 (*Bayḍāwī* explains that difficulty in saying that there is there [in *alladhūna*] the pronominal value of *man*!:[48] *fīhī ḍamīru man*!!), and even more so in XXVII, 35–37: *ʾinnū mursilatun . . . irjiʿ* (the fact that Solomon uses the second person plural in verse 36 can, however, be justified since he may also have those that sent the envoy in mind). Furthermore, one should note *waqaḍā rabbuka allā taʿbudū illā iyyāha wa-bi-l- wālidayni iḥsānan immā yablughanna ʿindaka l-kūbara aḥaduhumā aw kilāhumā fa-lā taqul* and so on with the second person singular in XXIV, 24, 25, whereas in 26 the second person plural takes over again.The *kāf* of *rabbuka* is, admittedly, wholly acceptable since it refers to Muḥammad and not, like the other forms of the second person, people and believers in general. But the switch from singular to plural is strange in *alladhūna ttaqaw ʾidhā masshum ṭāʾifun min ash-shayṭāni tadhakkarū fa-idhā hum mubṣirūna wa-ikhwānuhum yamuddānahum fi l-ghayyi*, VII, 201 and the following verse, "When an attack[49] of Satan's strikes the god-fearing, they withdraw into themselves and then they are immediately insightful, but their (the Satans in the plural) brothers make them (the Satans) err ever more seriously."[50]

Saḥāban t'iqālan suqnāhu li-baladin mayyitin fa-'anzalnā bihi l-mā'a, LXXVII, 55, appears to me to be wholly without parallel. Genuine collective nouns like *saḥāb* (which through the addition of *tā' marbūṭa* become individual words) can be used as both masculine and feminine and, if need be, the plural of the adjective there is also permissible,[51] but this before the masculine singular is extremely disconcerting; in the end it is the singular *t'uqālan = t'āqūlan* that is meant. *Fa-mā minkum aḥadin 'anhu ḥājizina*, LXIX, 47, is also odd; such constructions occur quite often in Syriac, however.[52] It should furthermore be noted that Allah speaks of himself in the singular and the plural in rapid succession: *fa 'ammā –l-laḏīna kafarū fa'u'aḏḏibuhum 'aḏāban šadīdan fi-d-dunyā wa-l-'ākhirati wamā lahum min nāṣirīn wa 'ammā –l-laḏīna 'āmanū wa 'amilū –ṣ-ṣāliḥāti fanuwaf-fihim 'ujūrahum* . . . III, 49 and the following verse.[53]

The categories of grammatical person in the Koran also change, occasionally in an unusual and inelegant manner. Thus when Allah, speaking of himself, first uses the third and then the first person:

XXVII, 61: *'amman khalaqa s-samāwāti wa-l-'arḍa wa 'anzala lakum mina-s-samā'i mā'an fa'ambatnā bihī ḥadā'iqa*

XXXV, 25: *'alam tara 'anna-l-lāha 'anzala mina-s-samā'i mā'an fa'akhrajnā bihī ṯamarātin*

VI,99: *wahuwa –l-laḏī 'anzla mina-s-samā'i mā'an fa 'akhrajnā bihī nabātakulli šay'in*

In the similar *l-laḏī ja'ala lakumu-l-'arḍa mahdan wa salaka lakum fīhā subulan wa '-anzala mina –s-samā'i mā'an fa'akhrajnā bihī azwājam-min nabatīn šattā*, XX, 55, Muḥammad has in addition entirely forgotten that it is not Allah himself that is speaking, but Moses. Likewise in XXXI, 13 and the following verse. Allah speaks in the first person in the middle of words spoken by Loqman, and in XXIX, 19 God says *qul* within words spoken by Abraham. It is certainly possible that verses XXIX, 18–22 are not in the right place, but since in XI, 37 God also says *qul* in the middle of words spoken by Noah this is hardly likely.

In a few places the second and third persons change abruptly:

wamā ʾātaytum min zakātin turīdūna wajha-l-lāhi faʾūlāʾika humu-l-muḍʿifūna, XXX, 38; after a long address in the second person, *ʾūlāʾika humu-r-rāšidūna*, XLIX, 7.

huwa-l-laḏī yusayyirukum fi-l-barri wa-l-baḥri ḥattāʾiḏā kuntum fi-l-fulki wa jarayna bihim birīḥin ṭayyibatin wa farihū . . . , X, 23 (the people who are first addressed are the same as those who are then spoken about in the third person).

For examples of odd treatment of agreement with plurals and collective nouns in the Koran see *Zur Grammatik* (p. 81 et seq).[54]

The continuation of the participle by the verbum finitum in *ʾinna-l-muṣṣaddiqīna wa-l-muṣṣaddiqāti wa ʾaqraḍū-l-lāha qārḍan ḥasanan yuḍāʿafu lahum* . . . , LVII, 17, "the men and women and (those that) pay good obeisance to God will be doubly rewarded." *Wa-l-ʿadiyāti ḍabḥan fal muriyāti qadḥan fal mugīrāti ṣubḥan faʾaṯarna bihī naqʿan*, C, 1–4, "with those that run snorting and strike sparks and go out early into the field and stir up dust."

Wa bašširi-l-mukhbitīna l-laḏīna ʾiḏā ḏukira-l-lāhu wajilat qulūbuhum wa-ṣ-ṣābirīna ʿalā ināʾaṣābahum wa-l-muqīmī-ṣ-ṣalātiwa mimmā razaqnāhum yunfiqūna, XXII, 35 and the following verse.

It is not so shocking in *Ḥāl* in *ʾawalam yarawʾilā-ṭ-ṭayri fawqahum ṣāffātin wa yaqbiḍna* . . . , LXVII, 19.

Also *wala-kinna-l-birra man ʾāmana bi-l-lāhi* . . . *wa ʾātā-l-māla ʿalā ḥubbihī ḏawī –l-qurbā* . . . *wa ʾaqāma-ṣ-ṣalāta waʾāta-z-zakāta wa-l-mufūna biʿahdihim ʾiḏa ʿāhadū waṣ-ṣābirīna* . . . , II, 172, is less disconcerting; *al-birra man ʾāmana* "piety is he that believes," that is to say, "piety consists in what someone believes" is permissible and a participle can always be added to a sentence with *man* and a verbum finitum. What is infelicitous, if not exactly incorrect, is the alternation of participle and finite verb in VI, 95 and the following verse (where, incidentally, in verse 96 *waju'ila* is probably the correct reading).

Like the participle in these sentences, the infinitive is also continued here and there by a verbum finitum, that is, *kayfa yahdī llāhu qawman kafarū ba'da ʾ īmānihim wa šahidūʾ anna –r-rasūla ḥaqqun wa jāʾahuma l-bayy-inātu*, III, 80, "how is God to lead people rightly who have become infidels after they had accepted and recognized the belief that God's apostle is truth and after clear proof had come to them/reached them"[55] and *wamā ʾadrāka mā-l-'aqabatu fakku raqabatin ʾaw ʾiṭ'āmun fī yawmin ḏī masòabatin yatīman ḏā maqrabatin ʾaw miskīnan ḏā matrabatin ṯumma kāna mina-l-laḏīna ʾāmanū* XC, 12–17.

Whether there are other examples in ancient Arabic of the continuation of the participle by the verbum finitum (as is certainly not unknown in Hebrew),[56] I do not know. The examples given by Ewald in the Gramm. arab., 2, 547 are untenable.[57] In the place of Kosegartens's *Ṭabarī* 1, 14, 9, the Leiden edition 1, 1824, 17 correctly gives *illā murtaddun aw man qad kāda an yartadda* and in Kosegartens 2, 220, 7 is, of course, to be read as *abā* (with *alif maqṣūra) –l-ḥafḍi instead* of *abī l-ḥafḍi*; the Leiden edition 1, 1992, 14 gives even more clearly *abā* (with *alif* of prolongation) *l-ḥafḍi*.[58] For the corresponding infinitive connection, I have at least one other example:[59]

innī wa qatlī sulaykan ṯumma a'qiluhu kālṯawri yuḍrabu lammā 'āfati-l-baqaru [in *basīṭ* metre]

"Since I have killed the Sulaik and then paid the wergild for him, I am in the position of the bull when he is beaten because the cows did not wish to drink" *Ag.*[60] 18, 138, 6.[61]

The fact that poetically or rhetorically inspired speech is often content with incomplete sentences, or that a single noun, or even an adverb, can represent a whole sentence is perfectly acceptable. Ellipses are quite usual in lively conversation and cannot be dispensed with. Thus no one will take offence at incomplete sentences like *ṣummun bukmuns* II, 17,

matā'un qalilun, III, 196
matā'un fī-d-dunyā, X, 71
tā'atun IV, 83

balāġa, XLVI, 35, "enough!"
hāḏā, XXXVIII, 55, 57, "(it's) so"
'āl'āna, X, 52, 91, "yes, now!"
fakayfa ' iḏā, IV, 45, 65
XLVII, 29 "what if . . . ?"[62]
and so on.

Here belongs also the so-called nominative (and accusative) of praise and blame that the exegetes subject to all kinds of mischief but which in my view is to be recognized in IX, 113.[63] By means of *fa 'iḏā 'uḥṣinna fa'in 'atayna bifāḥišatin wa* . . . , IV 30, "when they respect marital fidelity (it is good); but if they behave unchastely . . ." a favorite abbreviation in parallel conditional clauses is represented, but not in a pure form since we read *'iḏā* here and not *'in*. And very often the Koran leaves out words and sentences that it would be difficult to omit in common usage. Thus in the place of *wa min aṣ-ṣādiqīn*, III, 41, *wa huwa min aṣ-ṣādiqīn* would have been expected. Likewise *mina-l-laḏīna hādū yuḥarrifūna –l-kalima 'an mawāḍi'ihī*, IV, 49, is odd where the word *qawmun* is to be understood before *yuḥarrifūna*: "among the Jews there are some who move the words from their places." This is even more striking in cases such as *warasulan*, IV, 61, where the verb "we have sent" (*arsalnā*) must be understood by analogy (ἀπὸ κοινοῦ) with *'awḥaynā 'ilā*, verse 160, in a not exactly obvious manner.[64] Similarly *arsalnāhu* must be understood in front of *rasūlan* in III, 43, but the very chaotic passage about Jesus, III, 40 and the following verses, must be regarded as a single unit, in spite of the interruption by verse 42. The word *muṣaddiqan* of verse 44 belongs to it too, although Jesus himself is now speaking. We lack the subject even more in *wa 'Adan wa Ṭamūda*, XXIX, 37, as well as in *wa Qārūna wa Fir'awna wa Hāmāna*, verse 38, since the corresponding accusatives in verses 13, 15, and 27 are governed by *walaqad arsalnā . . . ilā qawmihi* of verse 13. Thus *wa li Sulaymāna-r-rīḥa*, XXXIV, 11, has no verb and where commonly or usually *sakhkharnā* is understood by analogy with *walaqad ātaynā Dā'ūda minnā faḍlan* of verse 10;[65] in addition *wa ḥifẓan*, XXXVII, 7 and XLI, 11, in which a subject has to be taken from the preceding *zayyannā-s-samā'a-ddunyā bizīnati-l-kawākibi* (or *bimaṣābīḥa*). *Waṣiyyatan li 'azwājihim matā'an*, II, 241, is also in fact without an actor or subject. Just the same is the accusative, *'aynan* LXXVI, 6, 18; LXXXIII, 28;

that the word cannot be in apposition to one of the preceding accusatives is shown by LXXXIII, 28. Similarly *lā ta'budūna 'illā-l-lāha wa bi-l-wālidayni'iḥsānan*, II, 77, and the very similar passage in IV, 40. *'Atlu mā ḥarrama rabbukum 'alaykum 'allā tušrikū bihī šay'an wa bi-l-wālidayni 'iḥsānan*, VI, 152, sounds even harsher.[66] To these should be added *walākin raḥmatan* (variant *raḥmatun*), XXVIII, 46: "but (that happened) out of mercy."[67]

The words *lilfuqarā'i*, II, 274 (where in fact a new verse begins), are not governed by anything; they are to be completed with a demand like "give alms." *Wafī Mūsā* of LI, 38, and consequently *wafī 'Ādin* of verse 41, require some kind of complement, as according to the meaning they cannot follow on from *fīhā*, that is, "in the country," *wa taraknā fīhā ' āyatan –lil-la<u>d</u>īn ya'afūna-l-'a<u>d</u>āba-l-'alīma* of verse 37.

In II, 159 *wa ba<u>tt</u>a fīhā min kulli dābbatin* can only be linked grammatically with the rest of the verse if a *mā* is added between *wa* and *ba<u>tt</u>a*; in reality, Muḥammad has probably lost his thread. This may also be true of some of the cases mentioned above.

In Arabic, the pronominal object suffix is also occasionally used with expressions of time, in particular in relative clauses, for example, *hawājiru taktannīnahā wa 'asīruhā*, "At midday when you cover yourself up, I on the other hand am journeying."[68] The Koran dares to completely leave out the reflexive suffix having the meaning of a *ẓarf* [adverbial expression of place and time] from the relative clause, as the reflexive object suffix in a relative clause can always be omitted (*arrajulu –l-la<u>d</u>ī ḍarabtu* for *ḍarabtuhu*; *rajulun ḍarabtu* for *ḍarabtuhu*). It is thus we read *yawmal –lā tajzi nafsun 'an nafsin šay'an* in II, 45, 117, "a day on which no soul shall stand for another" (Dawood), *yawma-l-lā yajzī walidun 'an waladihī walā mawlūdun huwa jāzin 'an wālidihī šay'an* in XXXI, 32, and *hal 'atā 'alā-l-'insāni ḥīnun mina-d-dahri lam yakun šay'am ma<u>d</u>kūran* in LXXVI, 1. The omission of the reflexive form in this case is probably otherwise very rare in Arabic. I have found *wa'in kāna ḥawlan kullu yawmin 'azūruhā* even if every day I visit her is a year,"[69] *Amālī* 1, 130 penultimate line.[70] And in the Hadith *zamānum yakūnul-mawtu 'aḥabba ilā 'aḥadikum min a<u>d</u>-<u>d</u>ahabi*, "a time in which death will be preferable to one of you to gold," Ibn Sa'd[71] 4, 2, 61, 25 with variant line 26; the speech would in any case have been smoother with the addition of *fīhi*.[72]

However little Arabic objects to the constant repetition of *qāla*, this word (and *qālat* etc.) is also omitted when the context is clear. But *qālū* or (*Sulaymān*) *qāla* is missing inappropriately before *ʾūtīnā* in *falammā jāʾat qīlaʾahākaḏā ʿaršuki qālat kaʾannahū huwa wa ʾutīnā-l-ʿilma min qablihā wa kunnā muslimīna*, XXVII, 42.

We find a very particular kind of Koranic ellipse with some of the little words that introduce something new, whereby "something happened," "something will happen," or something similar needs to be added. These *ʾiḏ*, *waʾiḏ*, *wa yawma* and so on are to a certain extent left hanging in midair. The exegetes mainly supply *ʾuḏkur*, "speak of it." We can roughly translate it as "once" but in doing so we again cover up or disguise the ungainliness of the original expression. Most frequently it appears as *wa-ʾiḏ*, for example, in II, 28, 32; XVIII, 15, 48, 59, and so on. It nearly always introduces legends of legendary expeditions or campaigns; in III, 117, however, it refers to something that has occurred very shortly before. The *ʾiḏ* on its own without the *wa* is rare: XII, 4; XXVII, 7. *Wa yawma* in VI, 22, 128; X, 29, 46; XVI 86, 91; XVIII 45, 50; and XLI, 18 and *yawma* on its own without *wa* in V, 108; XVII, 54, 73 refers almost always to the resurrection and what is related to it. XVI, 91 refers certainly to the past, but the expressions are like those in verse 86, which deals with the law. The Prophet switches here from one thought to another while scarcely being aware of it himself. This construction is also to be inferred in XIX, 88 and *yawma naḥšuru-l-muttaqīna ʾilā –r-Raḥmāni wafdan* to be considered as the main clause like the others with *yawma naḥšuru*, although the words could there be linked to the preceding *ʾinnamā naʿuddu lahum ʿaddan*.[73]

A few times *ḥattā iḏā* (referred to by the commentators as *ḡāyatu maḥḏūfin* = limit of apocopation, the goal of a thing not expressed) is loosely tacked on, which can be roughly translated as "so finally" or "then finally" in XII, 110; XXIII, 101; and LXXII, 25.

Similarly, *wa li* is often found with the subjunctive: "and in order to," "and together with this is the intention that," II, 145, 181, 261; III, 134, 148; VI, 55; VIII, 11;[74] and so on. First of all, there is a case like *wa lakum fīhā manāfiʿu wa litablugū ʿalayhā ḥājatan fī ṣudurikum wa ʿalā –l-fulki tuḥmalūna*, XL, 80.

Likewise *ṯumma li* in *huwa-l-laḏī ʾalaqakum min turābin ṯumma min nutfatin tumma min ʿalaqatin tumma yuʾrijukum ṭiflan tumma litablugū ʾašuddakum tumma litakūnū šuyūʾan wa minkum may-yatawaffā min qablu wa litablugū ʾajalam –musamman*, XL, 69. It is very similar in XXII, 5. Also *walākinli*, "but that happens (happened) so that," V, 53; VIII, 43; and XLVII, 5.

Further references to something unexpressed are found in *kāma ʾakhrajaka rabbuka min baytika*, VIII, 5.

ʾAw ka-l-ladī marra ʿalā qaryatin in II, 261 follows on from *ʾalam taraʾilā-l-ladī* and so on (verse 260). If we had merely *aw-l- ladī marra* or *aw ilā-l-ladī marra* it would be a question of a simple list; but the Prophet had it in mind that here was a second example, so he puts *ka* (as) and leaves the whole thing hanging in midair.

In several places in the Koran an initial or final position clause, or even a main clause, is missing. Thus in IX, 108 and the following verses with *alladīna*: *wa-l-ladīna-t-takh adū masjidan ḍirāran wa kufran wa tafrīqam bayna-l- minīna wa ʾirṣāda-l-liman ḥāraba—l-lāha wa rasūlahū min qablu wa layḥlifunna ʾin ʾaradnā ʾilla-l-ḥusnā wa-l-lāhu yašhadu ʾinnahum lakādibūna lā taqum fīhi ʾabadan*. Here the clause belonging to *alladīna* basically breaks off from *min qablu*; the subsequent passage up to *lakādibūna* follows loosely on from it; the main clause is represented by *lā taqum fīhi ʾabadan*. One can add something before such as "with respect to the people, I say," *ʾinna –l-ladīna kafarū wa yaṣuddūna ʿan sabīli-l-lāhi wa-l-masjidi-l-ḥarāmi-l-ladī jaʿalnāhu li-n-nāsi sawāʾani-l- ʿākifu fīhi wa-l-bādi wa man-yurid fīhi bi ʾilḥādim-biẓulmin-nudiqhu min min ʿadābin ʾalīmin*, XXII, 25 and the following verse (in reality only one verse). Here *wa man-yurid* picks up the thread of the sentence beginning with *l-ladīna*. In *ʾinna –l-ladīna kafarū biddikri lammā jāʾahum wa ʾinnahū lakitābun ʿazīzun*, XLI, 41, the final three words represent the main clause.

With *man: ʾafaman huwa qāʾimun ʿalā kulli nafsim –bima kasabat wa jaʿalū* in XIII, 33 is completely discontinued. *Bayḍāwī* augments it with *kaman laysa kadālika*. Likewise *afaman kāna ʿalā bayyanatin min rabbihī wa yatlūhu šāhidun minhu wa min qablihī kitābu Mūsā ʾimāman wa raḥmatan ʾ ūlāʾika yuʾ minūna bihī* in XI, 20.

With *idā*: *wa-ʾidā qīla lahumu –t-taqū mā bayna ʾaydīkum wamā ʾalfakum laʿallakum turḥamūna* in XXXVI, 45 is completely detached from the rest.

With *lammā* following on from *falammāḏahbū bihī wa ʾajmaʿū ʾan –yajʿalūhu fī ġayābati-l-jubbi*, XII, 15, come sentences with *wa* that simply continue the narrative. If *lammā* were absent, everything would be as it should be. *Falammā ʾaslamā wa tallahū liljabīni wa nādaynāhu*, XXXVII, 103. Here *wa nādaynāhu* represents the postponed clause; here either *wa* or *lammā* in front should be missing.

The omission of the postponed clause with *law* is certainly sometimes effective[75] or at least admissible. *Law* occasionally takes on something of the meaning of *layta* or introduces an unassuming (or possibly ironically modest) question, in which cases no main clause is expected. And elsewhere such a main clause with *law* may be dispensable, for example, *nāru jahannama ʾašaddu ḥarran law kānū yafqahūna*, IX, 82: "Hell-fire is even hotter: (they would consider that) if they were sensible!" Likewise II, 96, 67 (which last admittedly contains a sentence with *law*), and so on. But this omission cannot be justified in every instance, for example, in *walaw innahum raḍū mā ʾatāhumu –llāhu warasūluhu wa qālū ḥasbunā –l-lāhu sayuʾtīnā –l-lāhu min faḍlihī wa rasūluhū ʾinnā ʾilā –l-lāhi rāġibūna ʾinnamā –ṣ-ṣadaqātu* and so on, IX, 59.

With the negatively hypothetical *lawlā* the postponed clause is missing in XXIV, 10 and 20. Here, however, the clause is taken up again by *walawlā faḍlu llāhi* in verse 14 and by the same words in verse 21, but between the two there is all kind of unrelated material. In XLVIII, 25 there is a real sentence missing: *walawlā rijālum muʾminūna wa nisāʾum muʾminātu-l-lam taʿlamuhum ʾan taṭaʾuhum fatuṣībakum minhum maʿarratum baġayri ʿilmi-l-liyudkhila-l-lāhu fī raḥmatihī man yašāʾu law tazayyalū laʿḏḏabna –l-laḏīna kafarū minhum ʿaḏāban ʾalīman*. The final phrase that goes from *liyukhila* to *man yašāʾu* lets itself strictly speaking join the preceding phrase; the result is a new conditional sentence. What follows is a muddle, probably the result of Muḥammad's confusion when the hoped-for, indeed promised, success failed to materialize.

The expression of negation diverges not infrequently from what we were expecting. We need, however, to distinguish between such cases that also occur now and again in ancient Arabic poetry and which therefore represent actual linguistic usage and infelicities of expression, which, of course, are occasionally found in the work of the poets. I refer here to *Zur Grammatik*

(p. 90 et seq).[76] To the Koranic passages XXXV, 20, 21; XL, 60; XLI, 34. To LVII, 29, cited on page 91, can be added *wa mā yuš'irukum 'annahā 'iḏā jā'at lā yu'minūna*, VI, 109, where the negative element of the question is once again expressed by *lā* since the meaning is "and how do you know that they, when it (the sign) comes, will believe?"

In the case of a certain number of verbs that to a certain extent carry a negative meaning, in Arabic (as is always the case in German) a dependent clause is for the most part expressed positively.[77] Thus *mana'a* is constructed with *'an* in II, 108; IX, 54; XVII, 61, 96; XVIII, 53; and XXXVIII, 75. But in contrast to *mā mana'ahum 'an tuqbala minhum nafaqātuhum* in IX, 54 we find, however, *mā mana'aka 'allā tasjuda* in VII, 11 and *mā mana'aka 'iḏ ra'aytahum ḍallū 'allā tattabi'anī* in XX, 94. Here too we must take account of the fact that the main clause is a question that signifies a negative/negation. But we also find in XXI, 95 *waḥarāmun 'alā qaryatin ahlaknāhā annahum lā yarji'ūn* where perhaps the variant *' innahum* would be preferable; what precedes it would then be an incomplete sentence of the kind referred to on page 88:[78] "it is denied to a place that we have annihilated: they will not return."

The Koran is particularly fond of using *'an* where we would expect *'allā*, even after clauses where the negative meaning is not so evident. This is probably the case to a certain extent with *waḥḏarhum an yaftinūka*, V, 54, "be on your guard with them, that they lead you astray";[79] *ma'kūfan 'allā yabluḡa maḥillahu*, XLVIII, 25, "held back from reaching his position," and other similar cases. Also in phrases expressing warding off such as *'a'ūḏu bi-llāhi*, II 63; *ma'āḏa-llāhi*, XII, 79; and in *subḥānahu* IV, 169 (cf also XI, 49; XLIV, 19) we find simply *'an*; in German the equivalent would be "bewahre Gott" ("God forbid") or simply "bewahre" followed by "dass" ("that").[80] But these constructions are used very extensively in the Koran, for example, *wa 'alqā fī l-arḍi rawāsiya 'an tamīda*, XVI, 15 and XXXI, 9 (and very similarly XXI, 32), "and set high places on the earth (for protection) lest it rocked."[81] In XLIX, 6, *fatabayyanū 'an tuṣībū qawman bijahālatin*, "keep a sharp lookout (guard against), so that you (do not) assail people out of ignorance," and other similar cases. This idiosyncratic or peculiar usage can also be found on its own elsewhere in ancient Arabic texts, for example, 'Omar b. AR 26, 17, 305, 16; *Amāli* 2, 265, 13. Other examples in Schwartz: 'Omar

b. AR, 4, 160, and Reckendorf: 577 et seq. One can perhaps simply reproach Muḥammad for being too fond of it.

The Koran also occasionally employs other particles in an idiosyncratic fashion. Thus it is fond of *wadda law*, which appears to be rare in other ancient Arabic writings. Ma'n b. Aus, 3, 37, admittedly writes *yawaddu law 'annī mu'dimun*, "he wishes that I were poor."[82] The verse in *Amāli* 1, 84, 13 with *wadda law* is certainly not old.[83] Among later writers *wadda* law is used by Farazdaq in *Naqāiḍ* 718, 7 = *Jarīr* 69, 1; *Jarīr* 1, 82 = *Naqāiḍ* 939, 14 and 'Omar b. AR 315, 4[84] and 299, 23 where we have *waddu law 'anna*.[85] The closing sentence of *Ḥarīrī*'s 39, *Maqāmāt*[86] [. . . *wuddu law kāna halaka 'l-janīnu wa ummuhu*] with the same construction can naturally not be taken as *ḥujja* [proof, evidence, or authoritative source] in the classical language. The usual word found there is *wadda 'an*.

Walaw seems in several places in the Koran to be substituted for *wa'in*: *walaw kariha -l-mušrikūn*, IX, 33; LXI, 9. *Walaw kariha-l-kāfirūn*, XL, 14 and LXI, 8. *Walaw kariha –l-mujrimūn* IX, 32 and X, 82. *'Awalaw kānū lā yamlikūna šay'an*, XXXIX, 44. In any case one might assume that the ostensibly established fact is here portrayed ironically as uncertain: "even if this is disagreeable to the idolaters" and so on. But it would be simply too awkward if Joseph's brothers themselves gave their father the idea that they were lying with the words: *wamā 'anta bimu'minin lanā wa law kunnā ṣādiqīn*, XII, 17, which one would have to translate as "but you wouldn't believe us even if we spoke the truth." They presumably mean to say: "although we are speaking the truth." Then we would also be able to understand *walaw* in the sentences cited above as elements of a genuine condition [and assimilate *walaw* to *wa in*]. Of course, it cannot be wholly excluded that in XII, 17 Muḥammad puts his own judgment of the speakers into their mouths. In this particular sura other oddities also appear. In that case *walaw* would have its usual meaning throughout.

The Koran is very fond of *lawlā* "if not?" "should not?" in the place of our "why not?"; elsewhere *hallā* is the usual expression for this meaning. I also know this use of *lawlā* from one of Jarir's verses [in the *ṭawīl* meter]:

ta'uddūna 'aqra –n-nībi 'afḍala majdikum. Banī ḍawṭarā lawlā-l kamīya-l-muqanna'ā

"You consider the butchering of the old camels to be among the most glorious of exploits, you riff-raff; why not the heavily-armoured warrior?" *Kāmil* 158, 1 = Ham. 540, 16 = Lis. 20, 360, 4 + Chiz 1, 129, 6.[87] I produce all of this evidence because Diwan's printed text 1, 158, 4 replaces the *lawlā* that *Jarīr* perhaps took from the Koran with the usual *hallā*. The former may have belonged particularly to the language of Mecca and possibly to that of Medina. One of Muḥammad's companions uses it in Ibn Sa 'd 4, 2, 37 = 38, 10. In its place Ibn Sa 'd, 2, 1, 87, 7, has *lawmā*, which is also used once in the Koran to stand for *lawlā* (XV, 7).

I am also tempted to assume that the negative *ʾin* that is very common in the Koran but otherwise rare was commonly used in Mecca and Medina. It is found in the mouth of a Meccan woman, *Ṭab*. 1, 1435, 9 (= Agh. 4, 42, 11, where in *Bukhārī*[88] (Krehl) 3, 62, 4 has been modified), and those of people from Medina and its immediate environs, Ibn *Hishām* 458, 8 (= *Ṭab* 1, 1335, 10);[89] 577, 3 (= *Ṭab*. 1, 1471, 8, where a codex has it thus).[90]

Not infrequently in the Koran we find a final *li* where we would expect a consecutive expression. Similarly, *waminkum man yaruddu ʾ ilā ʾarḏali -l-'umuri likaylā ya'lama min b'adi 'ilmin šayʾan*, XXII, 5, "and he (God) brings this one and that one of you back to the most miserable life so that after (earlier) knowledge he knows nothing anymore." One can certainly assume in these and similar instances that the Prophet is expressing the outcome here as God's intention. In fact he has scarcely distinguished between outcome and intention.

A similar ambiguity is apparent in *liya'lama ʾan qad ʾablagū risālāti rabbihim*, LXXII, 28, where "that" stands for "whether." Where Allah is concerned, admittedly, wanting-to-know and knowledge itself are hard to distinguish.

In the same way that the Koran often interrupts one subject by lengthy discussion of another, only to return to the first, it also contains many short parentheses. Occasionally these are to the point. Thus in LXXI, 9 the *ʾinnahu kāna gaffāran*, which does not upset the relationship between what comes after with what precedes it; the insertion of *bal ṭaba'a –l-lāhu 'alyhā bikufrihim falā yuʾminūna ʾillā qalīlan*, IV, 154, the second sentence of which contains the rhyme, seems to be redundant; similarly the justification in XXXVIII, 70. Even the energetic "there you have not to interfere," *laysa laka mina –l-ʾamri šayʾun*, III, 123, inserted in the middle of the description of the uncertainty regarding what God will do is apposite and in addition with reference to words that the believers disappointed in their hope of victory had expressed (verse 148). But parentheses like *wa-l-lāhu ʾaʿlamu bimā waḍāʿat wa laysa-ḏ-ḏakaru kalʾunṯā*, III, 31, or *qul ʾinna –l-hudā hudā –llāhi*, III, 66, are awkward. And this is true of many other cases. Many final sentences come into this category.

That many passages in the Koran are turned out to be ponderous or unclear is demonstrated by the various verses cited above. One should also consider VI, 99; XLVIII, 25 and, for example, X, 2, where the words *ʾan awḥaynā . . . ʿinda rabbihim* belong both to *ʾkāna li-n-nāsi ʿajaban* and *qāla-l-kāfirūn*, with the result that either the initial or the final words are missing. Or IX, 93, where, in order to maintain the fiction of a genuine sentence, *`qulta* is explained as being an expression of condition.

* * *

It is important that the healthy linguistic sense of the Arabs prevented them almost completely from imitating the oddities and weaknesses of the language of the Koran. Although they saw in it the most magnificent merits or attributes of the unmatchable word of God, it did not occur to them to incorporate them into human speech. Thus rhyme in prose was always formed in a pure fashion and never in the incomplete manner of the Prophet. The Koran constitutes a literature apart: it had no real antecedents and could have no successors.[91] However often Koranic verses and individual Koranic expressions were used for decorative effect by Arabic writers and however many affectations are found in the work of many of them, those linguistic peculiarities play no part.

III. Arbitrarily and Erroneously Used Foreign Words in the Koran

It is well known that Muḥammad, along with the teaching and stories of the Jews and Christians, also took over many non-Arabic words, in particular Hebrew and Aramaic ones, into his holy book. In this process, the meaning was occasionally changed because the overall perspective or outlook of the new religion required it; for example, the Christian *haymānūṯā*, faith [Syriac] (Greek πίστις, faith) is not quite the same as its Jewish prototype: ה י מ נ ותא [*hymnwt'—haymānūṯā*]. However here it is a question mostly of subtle shades. But in the case of some Koranic expressions, the change of meaning is greater. Muḥammad (really) deviated from their actual meaning regularly or at least occasionally. And then he completely misunderstood individual expressions of his foreign mentors or they were passed on to him in already misunderstood form.[92]

To that which is contained on our subject in A. Geiger's dissertation "Was hat Muḥammad aus dem Judentum aufgenommen?" (What Did Muḥammad Take from Juadaism?) and Siegmund Fraenkel's "De vocabulis in antiquis Arabum carminibus et in Corano peregrinis,"[93] I can add little; here and there, however, I formulate things a little differently from them. In any event, I hope that this survey is not entirely without value.

Geiger (p. 56) already recognized the Koranic *furqān*[94] as פורקן [Hebrew; *pwrqn –pūrqān*], this is "deliverance, release." The Christian Syriac *pūrqānā* –salvation (in Peshitta and Christian Palestinian) takes on in addition the higher meaning of "redemption" (it translates λύτρον,[95] λύτρωσις,[96] ἀπολύτρ ωσις,[97] σωτηρία[98]). However in the Meccan passages XXV,1; XXI, 49 *furqān* can hardly be anything other than "revelation, divine inspiration." This also fits the Medinan passages II, 181; III, 2. Muslims are therefore not wrong when they consider *furqān* to be a synonym for *al-qur'ān*. But in VIII, 42 the Day of Badr is *yawm al-furqān*. There "inspiration, revelation" hardly fits; here *furqān* probably means "decision." In *yaj'al lakum furqānan*, VIII, 29, the meaning perhaps reverts to that of "inspiration." Since *faraqa*, "to separate," was a very common root in Arabic, this use in *yawm al-furqān* may have suggested itself fairly easily to the Prophet. Also in the transformation of the meaning of פורקן [*pwrqn –pūrqān*] into "revelation," something like "divine decision" may have been in his mind. Note the combination with *bayyinātin* in II, 181 of which the meaning also goes back to "distinguish." Muḥammad was certainly not completely clear about these matters, but however one likes to interpret these individual passages, nowhere is it "redemption" or even "redemption from sins" as Geiger understands it in at least several passages.

Sakīna. Geiger (p. 54 et seq.) recognizes the Jewish ה ָנ י כ שׁ [Hebrew: *šeḵīnāh*] in this word. It is well known that this means first of all the "dwelling (of God)," then "(God's) presence," and is occasionally more or less hypostatized. The Christian Syrians also use their Syriac *šeḵīntā* with the usual meaning of "dwelling place" occasionally in the Jewish sense (cf. PSm. 4155, where to 2 Par. 7, 1–3 Syriac *'īqārā ḏa-šḵīnteh d-māryā* or Syriac *'īqār šḵīnteh d-māryā* for Hebrew *kbwd yhwh –kāḇūd Yahwa*[99] can also be added Syriac *dḵeh –(h)ū šaryā šḵīnteh d-māryā* [pure is presence of the Lord] Jac. Sar., Constantin [Frothingham][100] v. 807). The fact that Arabic did not know *Sakīna* at least not in a meaning that was possible in the Koran, emerges from the exegetes' uncertainty (cf. Lis. 17,76). Some, however, exhibit a certain acquaintance with the Jewish/Hebrew use of [skynh] ה נ י כ שׁ; into this are introduced some very bizarre notions. At least with a similar meaning to the Hebrew, somewhat mythical [skynh] ה ָנ י כ שׁ, *Sakīna* is used in II, 249. Here the Prophet says: in the *tābūt* that is coming to the Israelites (a reference to the story in which the Ark of the Covenant is sent back by the Philistines in 1 Samuel 6) there is: *sakīnatun min rabbikum wa baqiyyatum mimmā taraka Mūsā wa 'ālu Hārūna*. What Muḥammad means by the undetermined (!) expression is admittedly rather unclear, but it seems to be something that is sent down by God for the illumination of mankind and he appears to regard it as being a concrete object. On the other hand, in all other places he links *Sakīna* to the usual meaning of *sakana* and uses it to signify "tranquillity/reassurance (sent by God)." But since here *al-sakīna* or *sakīnata* ("his [i.e., God's] *sakīna* ") is always the object of '*anzala* with God as the subject, we are nonetheless led back to the Hebrew ירד ה שׁ כ י ָנ ה [Hebrew: *yrdh h škynh*] (cf. Levy 4,554).[101,102] Thus during the dangerous migration from Mekka to Yathrib, God sent down his *sakīna* on the Prophet, IX,40; similarly on him and the other believers in the uncomfortable situation in Ḥudaybiyya, XLVIII, 4, 18, 26, whereby the last verse indicates particularly clearly the meaning of inner peace/calm through the contrast with the "zealotry of the unbelievers," *ḥamiyyata-l-jāhiliyyati* [XLVIII, 26], and likewise at the Battle of Ḥunayn after the initial defeat [IX, 26].

A verse of Abū ' Uraif al-Kulaybī[103] cited by Lis. names *sakīna wa waqār* as high virtues of a man, and in a speech that must date from before Islam's first victories, *sakīna* stands in parallel to *waqār* Agh. 14, 3, 23.

Since the meanings that fit in the Koran do not work here and a dependence on the latter is therefore improbable, we can believe that this was genuine Arabic usage and suppose that Arabs took the word to mean "calm, steadfastness" or "inner dignity."

Zakāt renders the Hebrew זכות [*zkwt—zeḵūṯ*] (cf. Fraenkel, p. 22). It means "profit, credit," in particular "moral credit" or "virtue." Thus Muḥammad uses *zakāt* to mean something like "uprightness" or "justification," XVIII, 80; XIX, 14. But generally he uses it to mean "alms" or "tax for alms." Neither the Hebrew word nor the corresponding Syriac *zāḵūṯā* (whereby the זָכות [*zāḵūṯ*] would be vocalized זָכותָא [*zāḵūṯā*]) appears to have this meaning. The Syriac means first of all "innocence" Genesis 30:33 (= צדקה, *ṣdqh –ṣeḏāqā*), then "justification," and from there comes the usual Syrian meaning of "victory," from which all kinds of further usages follow on.[104] Muḥammad probably adopted the idiosyncratic and specialized meaning himself; however, it is nonetheless conceivable that Arabian Jews already called alms *zakāt*. Compare the corresponding use of צדקה—*ṣdqh –ṣeḏāqā* (Syriac *zeḏqeṯā*, Arabic: *ṣadaqah*), ἐλεημοσύ νη [Greek: pity, mercy: an alms] (traces of which, passed on through Latin, can be found in all Western European languages), מצוה [*mṣwh—miṣwā*] (accordingly ἐντολή, injunction, command).[105]

Rajīm is understood by Muḥammad with the Arabic meaning of "stoned" instead of "cursed"; see below on foreign words.

Burhān [Ethiopic: *berhān*], that is, "light" in the Koran like in the later Arabic "proof"; see below.

In the Koranic *milla* "religion" (a synonym for *dīn* derived from Persian) I am still inclined to see an erroneous or arbitrary usage of the Aramaic מִלה [*Millāh*], Syriac: *meltā* "word."[106] It is certainly possible that Muḥammad gave a genuine Arabic expression this meaning, if *milla* first of all really signifies "way" and then "order, custom." I must say, however, that what Lis. gives for it in 14,154 is not really persuasive or convincing. *Mumallun = maslūk ma'lūm* can in fact mean "that which through constant use has surfeit."[107] *Mumall* is "fatigued" (of the camel), Labid (Chalidi)[108] 6, 2 ; Wright, Opuscula ar. 117, 5.[109] And whether *al-malal* in this verse (which is also given in a somewhat different version in the margin of Lis) means *al-diyah* "the wergild" (as "order") is debatable. In addition, I would like further proof that *mall* "arranger" is really common (Hélot in Dozy).[110]

The Koranic *sūra* is presumably [Hebrew] שׁוּרָה [*šūrāh*] "row, correctness, order" (cf. Levy s.v. Muḥammad probably took it to mean "norm" or "order" and called the individual independent pieces of his revelation in this way). For the first time, at least for us, in XI, 16; then in X, 39; the remaining passages are of Medinan origin. The attempts of Arabs to explain the Koranic word from the meanings that *sūra* or even *suʿar* have elsewhere in the language (Lis. 6,52 et seq.) are unsuccessful. The expression has nothing to do with שׁוּר –*šūr* "wall," although *sūra* is supposed to be a row of stones in the wall: *ʿirqa min ʾaʿrāq –l-ḥāʾiṭi* (Lis 6, 52, 4 v. u). In *Jarīr* 1, 161, 3 V. u. = Ibn Sa ʿd 3, 1, 79, 18[111] *suwar* is really "walls," of which the singular is therefore simply *sūra* = *sūran*.[112]

About *maṯānin* in *kitāban mutašābihan maṯāniya*, XXXIX, 24, and *wa-laqad ʿātaynāka sabʿan mina –l-maṯānī wa-l-qurʾāna –l-ʿaẓīma*, XV, 87 (both passages being Meccan in origin), the commentators have nothing useful to say (Lis. 18, 428–30). Particular credit for having recognized in it the Jewish מַתְנִיתָא [*maṯnīṯā*] (= Hebrew מִשְׁנָה, *mišnāh*) goes to Geiger (p. 58 et seq.). Muḥammad, however, gave the word a further meaning than in Jewish usage; it meant for him something like "sayings" or simply small pieces (verses) of the revelation. The seven *Mathānī* are, as ancient exegetes already supposed, in all probability the seven verses of the Fatiha (including the Basmala); the first sura can very appropriately be called autonomous or independent alongside the rest of the Koran. On the other hand, the true Jewish meaning "rule of conduct, canon" would not be at all appropriate here and the same is true for XXXIX, 24.[113]

Al-jibt = (Ethiopic: *amlāka*) *gebt*, see below.

That *al-muhaymin* is the rendering of the Aramaic מהימן [*mhymn*], Syriac *mhymn*, is absolutely clear. The corresponding verb, even if it still constitutes an H-stem could only be *hāmana* if it were genuine Arabic.[114] But the exegetes still felt the close connection with *ʾāmana* In V, 52 *wa- ʾanzalnā ʾilayka –l-kitāba bil ḥaqqi muṣaddiqa –l-limā bayna yadayhi mina-l-kitābi wa muhayminan ʿalayhi* the word must mean roughly *muṣaddiq*, "confirming, verifying." This could at a stretch correspond to another Syrian use: Euseb., Theoph.[115] 3, 62 at the beginning (p. 116, 2 of the whole book) is Syriac *lšrrhwn hymnwhy (lašrārhōn haymnu(h)ī)* "confirmed their conviction," "showed that it was true."[116] But for sura LIX, 23, where Allah is called *al-*

maliku –l-quddūsu –s-salāmu –l—mu'minu-l-muhayminu, there is no meaning of ן מ י ה *hymn*, Syriac *hymn* that could be applied to God directly. Given the context, one can assume that Muḥammad uses the word to mean roughly the same as *mu'min*, which here can scarcely mean anything other than "giving certainty/safety." Nonetheless some say *muhayman* in both Koranic passages. This might be one "whom is trusted, who is considered reliable" (cf. Syriac *mehaymenā* a euphemistic designation for a eunuch).[117] Whether this is fitting for Allah according to the Prophet's way of thinking I find doubtful; the *al-mu'min* next to it also seems to me to make the passive voice/form untenable; the reading of *al-ma'man*, which is supposed to stand for *al-ma'man bihi*, cannot really be considered. And a passive voice or form in V, 52 is inconceivable. We need to bear in mind that *muhayman* was foreign to the Arabs and that they relied wholly on commentary for the ascertainment of its meaning. The other evidence produced by Lis. to support *haymana* is all independent from the Koranic verses or rather from its interpretation.[118]

In (variant *lilkutubi*) *yawma naṭwi—s-samā'a kaṭayyi –s-sijilli lil-kitābi*, sura XXI, 104, according to the context *al-sijill* can only be one person.[119] Fraenkel, Aram. Fremdwörter,[120] was probably not the first to recognize in the word *sigillum*, certificate, document of which the oriental form is σιγίλλιον, σιγίλλιν, Syriac *sygylywn –sīgīliyōn*. Muḥammad, however, misunderstood it and took it to mean the scribe. Rückert's translation "as the sealer folds the letter" retains the echo of *sigillum*, but I do not think that an Oriental would still think of the original meaning of *sigillum* that we have retained in our "seal." Incidentally, *sijill* in its correct meaning is wholly familiar to Muslim Arabs, for example, *'asjala bidalika sajllā*, "issued a certificate about it" (Jaq. 2, 819, 2),[121] and some commentators also attempt to force this meaning into the Koranic passage; but the *lil-kitābi* alongside it would then be incomprehensible. I do not believe, in any case, that it would be correct to see *al-sajill* as the big or great book, of which *al-kitāb* would only be a part, as *sijjīn* LXXXIII, 7 and the following verses explains verse 9 as *kitābum marqūmun* and Fraenkel in *Fremdwörter* p. 252 as another form of our word. Here, however, the special book of the evildoers *kitābu-l-fujjari* has its rightful place, whereas *lil-kitābi*, XXI,104, would be entirely meaningless in this reading. The replacement of *l* by *n* may be arbitrary, used on account of the rhyme: *sīnīna*, XCV, 2 (instead of *sīnā 'a* XXIII, 20), and

ʾil yāsīna, XXXVII, 130 (instead of *ʾIlyāsa*, XXXVII, 123; VI, 85). The absence of an article turns *sijjīn* into a proper noun. Here we have a fantastical world, different from (that) in the simple picture, XXI, 104.[122]

ʿIlliyyūna genitive *ʿilliyyīna*, LXXXIII, 18 and the following verse, Fraenkel (*De Vocabulis*, p. 23) sees the proper name of the great book of the pious *kitābu- l- abrāri* -as a misunderstood ליון [*ʿ lywn*] and there is really nothing definite that can be said to contradict this.

Al-māʿūna in *yamnaʿūna –l-māʿūna*,[123] CVII, 7, is interpreted variously (see Lis. 17, 297 et seq). It is supposed to be "charity, alms" or the like, or else "implements." The former meaning appears the most likely; in any event, we are not far from Muḥammad's own meaning with it. But it cannot be explained from the Arabic how the form indicates a word of foreign origin. Geiger (p. 58) sees *māʿūn* as the Hebrew מָעוֹן [*maʿōn*] and is certainly right to do so. But when he understands this word also to mean "refuge," which מָעוֹן [*maʿōn*] "dwelling"[124] can mean, we should not follow him. This meaning does not fit well in the passage and the article would surely be out of place. I would presume that Muḥammad had heard the word from a Jew and misunderstood it if the poet *Aʿshā* had not probably used *Al-māʿūn* similarly. For in his work as handed down by Abū ʿObaidas ("a big shipping canal is not") *bi-ʾajwada minhu bi-māʿūnihi* "more generous than he is with his *māʿūn*," which necessarily designates "charity" or "donation." This reading of *bi-māʿūnihi* has in any case more authority than the colorless *ʿindah* of Geyer (*Zwei Gedichte*, p. 144).[125] Since *Aʿshā* himself had been in Jerusalem, as he attests in the same *Qaṣīda* from which this words come, he himself, as Geyer also supposes, may have heard the word from a Jew and misunderstood it. The poet is fond of using foreign words generally and in this poem, according to Geyer's information, in particular. I should, in fact, not have discussed *māʿūn* here since it is highly probable that it was not Muḥammad but another who introduced it into the language. The attachment to *ʿāna, ʾaʿāna* "to help" was natural for the Arabs even if it is grammatically impossible. The verse with *yamujj ṣabīruhu l- māʿūna sabban*[126] (Lis. 17, 296) (twice) "his fixed clouds spews forth amply (actually 'as an outpouring') his benevolence" (from which it was erroneously supposed that *māʿūn* means simply "water" or "rain") is probably of Muslim origin and stems from the Koran. It is worthy of note, incidentally, that the in any case incorrect interpretation of our word as "implement," "tool" has, at least in the Maghreb, passed into actual usage (see Dozy sub voce).

Ṣallā "to pray" had presumably arrived from the Aramaic into Arabic long before Muḥammad (like *ṣallaya* into Ethiopian, see below). We find *ṣallā* in the work of the Christian *'Adī* b. Zayd Agh. 2, 25, 26; in *A'shā*, Jamhara 6, 12[127] and Geyer, Zwei Gedichte 203, 2, and in *Labīd* (Huber)[128] 13 v. 30. Even the special relationship of *ṣallā* [with alif *maqṣūra*] and *ṣallā* [*wāw and tāʾmarbūṭa*] with ritually organized prayer (as opposed to the free *du'āʾ*) may be very old; the trend toward this can be seen as early as Daniel 6:11. And even with God as the subject Muḥammad is not the first to use the verb. For already in the Talmud Ber. 7ᵃ above[129] we read of God that he prays מתפלל *mtpll –mitpallel* (explained by מ צ ל י *mṣly*), that his mercy may overcome his wrath with his people. The words *huwa –l-ladī yuṣallī 'alaykum wa malāʾikatuhū*, XXXIII, 42, where "he" designates God himself could be understood in the same manner, but *ʾinna-l-lāha wa malāʾikatahū yuṣallūna 'alā –n-nabiyyi yā ʾayyuhā-l-ladīna āmanū ṣallū 'alayhi*, XXXIII, 56, shows that this will not do. From this passage it emerges (much more) than in Muḥammad's text *ṣallā* with *'alā*, used of God and people can only mean "to give one's blessing." Thus the Prophet has used the expression very idiosyncratically, if he had heard at all that Jews used it of God.[130]

By way of appendix, let us consider the word *ḥanīf*, which appears many times in the Koran. There it designates the confessor of the old monotheistic religion of Abraham, in part in explicit contrast to Judaism and Christianity. Only in four places does it have no specific reference to Abraham: X, 105; XXII, 32 (in the plural); XXX, 29; and XCVIII, 4 (plural). It is well known that Muḥammad's immediate predecessors were called *ḥanīf* s. Certainly most of what is said about these should be treated with suspicion and the frequently quoted verse of Umayya b. aṣ-Ṣalt, who calls *al- ḥanīfah* the one true religion (Agh. 3, 187, 25 etc.) is as dubious as the majority of the verses ascribed to this poet. Nonetheless the expression as a designation of a person with a particular religious position is pre-Islamic. What the *ḥanīf* is who meets the carousing or inebriated (*yusāqawna*) Christians (Hudh. 18, 11), is not clear. But it may very well be a hermit or penitent, as Wellhausen in *Reste*[131] (p. 239), supposes and this meaning would also fit with Abū Dhuayb's verse (Lis. 6, 133), about which I admittedly would like further enlightenment. When the mortally wounded Christian Bisṭām cries out to his brother so that he does not likewise expose himself to certain death: *ʾ anā ḥanīfan ʾin rajaʿta*, "I am a *ḥanīf* if you come back," *Kāmil* = 131, 4 = Naqāiḍ 1, 314, 15, our word cannot mean anything other than "heathen." The cry is a compelling entreaty. And this *ḥanīf* follows on from the completely ordinary Syriac *hanpā* "heathen" (cf. the Mandaean הא נ י פ ותא [*h ʾ n y p w t ʾ - hānīpūṯā*] variant הא נאפ ותא [*h ʾ n ʾ p w t ʾ - hānāpūṯā*], the book of John 176:5; cf. Ethiopic: *ḥanāfi* see below). How from this original meaning the others arose is hard to say. But one must bear in mind that the naive Arab heathens had no idea about the real nature of other religions and could therefore easily misunderstand and misuse such expressions.

Notes

1. [Footnotes in square brackets by I. W. With help of G.-H. Bousquet's French translation of this article, "Remarques critiques sur le style et la syntaxe du Coran," Paris, 1953, I was able to correct Nöldeke's many errors concerning verse and even sura numbering. I have kept Nöldeke's Flügel verse numbering.]

2. K. Vollers, *Volkssprache und Schriftsprache im alten Arabien*, Strassburg, 1906.

3. *Ḥijāz* is, of course, always used here as the name of the larger province. As an actual name of a region, it does not include Mecca since its inhabitants considered and still consider that the town is part of Tihama.

4. One must therefore take care not to regard his striking claims about Arabic stress patterns as facts; he only used them to prove or support his new linguistic theories and thereby often goes round in circles.

5. R. Geyer, *Göttinger gelehrte Anzeigen*, 1909, pp.10ff. On this subject, cf. also Martin Hartmann's article in the *Orientalistische Literaturzeitung* 1909, nos. 1 and 2, p. 19, which, however, also contains some very debatable propositions.

6. I have gone through the book three times and subjected very many, although far from all, details to closer examination and found much that does not bear such scrutiny, including elements relating to quite different matters from those discussed by me in these pages.

7. A cursory investigation shows that the division and numbering of the verses is not always correct in Flügel's edition. [G. Flügel, *Corani textus arabicus* (Leipzig: Sumtibus Caroli Tauchnitii, 1834), new ed., 1906.] And one needs only to

cite a few other pieces of evidence from *Ḥafṣ*'s text to recognize that there several of the hypotheses Flügel provides are missing. But Vollers bases far-reaching conclusions on these hypotheses. He should at least have borne in mind that the division of verses varies according to different schools of thought, that originally it was not marked and even now is not marked in all editions. Geyer refutes in great detail Vollers's misconceptions regarding the ends of verses, or rather the end-rhymes.

8. [*idġām*: insertion, assimilation of two letters; *idġām kabīr fī –l-mutajānisayni*: assimilation of the last letter, even when not quiescent, with a homogenous letter beginning the next word; *idġām kabīr fī-l-maṯalayni*: assimilation of the last letter, even when not quiescent with the same letter beginning the next word.]

9. [Sībawayhi, *Al-Kitāb*, 2 vols., ed. Būlāq, 1318 AH [edited by H. Derenbourg, 2 vols. Paris: Imprimerie Nationale, 1881–1889], § 564.

10. It would be more accurate to speak of "modes of recitation" or "modes of delivery."

11. [But see Paul E.Kahle, "The Arabic Readers of the Koran," in *What the Koran Really Says*, edited by Ibn Warraq. Amherst, NY: Prometheus Books, 2002, pp. 201–10, where Kahle indeed recounts just such a tradition.]

12. In XLIV,15 *nabṭišu* is indisputably correct, as the *baṭaštum* that appears twice in XXVI, 130 and the *baṭšata*- [XLIV,15], *baṭša* [LXXXV,13] that occurs in many places in the Koran show. This is in contradiction with the notion that *nabṭiš* is Hijāzic and *nubṭiš* Tamimic, as Vollers (p. 108) maintains based on the Berlin manuscript of Muzhir (edition 2, 143, 3 v. u. is without vowel markers). [Referring to al-Suyūṭī, *Al-Muzhir fī ʿulūm al-luga*, 2 vols. Būlāq AH 1282/1865 CE; 2nd ed., Cairo 1325/1907: a philological encyclopaedia] Bayḍāwī [Beidhawii, *Commentarius in Coranum*, ed. H. O. Fleischer, 2 vols. (Lipsiae, 1846–1848)] understands this *nabṭiš* as having a somewhat different meaning, namely, a causative one. Ibn Manẓur, *Lisān al- ʿarab*, 20 vols. (Cairo, AH 1300–1308) records no *ʾabṭaša*. The fact that in ʿAmr's *Mu ʿallaqa* v. 130 only *nubṭiš* appears to be handed down is certainly of no significance. [ʿAmr b. Kulthūm, circa 6th century CE, belonged to the great Christian tribe of Taghlib of Syro-Mesopotamia. The latter was one of the five *Mu ʿallaqāt* translated and commented on by Nöldeke in 1899: T. Nöldeke. "Funf Mo' allaqat I–III," *SBWA* 140, 142, 144 (1899–1901).]

13. It is not the *i* of the prefixes, which is also almost exclusively attested by the related languages, that is striking but rather the *a* in the *Ḥijāzic naḏkuru* and the Hebrew, *yāqūm*, *yāsōḇ*. Added to this is the *u* in *yufʿilu*, *yufaʿʿilu, yufā ʿi lu*, etc., which is not in contradiction to/incompatible with the *a* in *yap̄ʿīl*, *nap̄ʿel* [Hebrew /Syriac] as Vollers supposes (p. 111); because *yufʿilu* derived from *yuʾafʿilu*, *yuhafʿil*,

as *yap̄ 'īl* [Hebrew] did from *yehap̄ 'īl* [Hebrew], which very possibly may originally have been *juhafʿil*. And so on. In his references to related languages, Vollers is also infelicitous in other instances. On the other hand, there are a few occasions where he does not take them into account when that would have been useful.

14. The omission of the *Hamza* is also not infrequent among the ancient poets, especially, it appears, those of Western Arabia (which, however, should not be understood in the narrow sense, as Vollers does). See Paul Schwarz, *Der Diwan des ʿUmar ibn Abi Rebiʿa* [ca. 644–712 CE] (Leipzig, 1909), 4, 106. Of course, his examples can easily be multiplied. This appears seldom among the old poets of the Rabiʿa's tribes, apart from forms such as *yarā*.

15. [*Muṣḥaf* (pl. *maṣāḥif*): a complete text of the Koran considered as a physical object; the written corpus of the Koran.]

16. [*Imāla*: "the sound of long *alif* inclines, in later times and in certain localities, from *ā* to *ē*, just as that of *fatḥa* does from *a* to *è* [as in pet]. This change is called *al-imāla*, 'the deflection' [or causing it to incline] of the sound of *a* and *ā* towards that of *i* and *ī*. The Magribī Arabs actually pronounce *ā* in many cases as *ī*. Hence *rikāb, lākin, bāb, līsan* are sounded *rikēb, lēkin, bīb, lisīn*. . . ." W. Wright, *A Grammar of the Arabic Language*, 3rd ed. (Cambridge: Cambridge University Press, 1967) (1st ed. 1859–1862), vol. 1, p. 10].

17. Ibn Manẓur, *Lisān al-ʿarab*. 20 vols. (Cairo, AH 1300–1308). 15,358,14; K. Vollers, *Volkssprache und Schriftsprache im alten Arabien* (Strassburg, 1906), p. 10.

18. This reading probably stayed in people's memories because it was used as proof that really garlic is meant here, which most exegetes fail to grasp.

19. According to Bayḍāwī XLVII, 24, inflection is *Ḥijāzic* and noninflection *Tamīmic* (the reverse, therefore of what Vollers 19 maintains). But in the Koran we have both—see II, 247 and XLVII, 24; the practice therefore also varied in the *Ḥijāz*.

20. The other cases mentioned by Vollers 163 fall within the usual rules. Uncertainty in the use of *ūna* and *īna* can also be seen in some verses, whether this stems from the poets themselves or from the Rāwīs—see Sībawayhi, *Al-Kitāb*, 2 vols., ed. Būlāq, AH 1318: 1, 210, 12 = 213, 8 and 213, 11. One is assisted here as with these Koranic passages by assuming the accusative form *ʿalā –l-madḥi wa -l-ḏammi*. I do not wish entirely to dispute this, but here this explanation is insufficient. (An accusative of this kind on its own was only inserted into the correct text through carelessness or grammatical affectation; cf. Hudh 92, 54 [= *The Hudsailian Poems*, ed. J. G. L. Kosegarten (numbers 1–138), vol. 1 (London 1854)] on the one hand with Sībawayhi. 1, 169, 3, and on the other with Sībawayhi. 1, 214, 4. The complete

text in the *Diwan* naturally has greater authority than an isolated quotation.) This explanation is also entirely refuted by the official documents written on papyrus from the year AH 91 published by C. H. Becker: there *īna* always stands for the nominative, just as *miʿatayn, miʿatayn* [with a silent alif] stands for miʿ*atān, miʿatān* [with a silent alif] *and* perhaps we would find even more such cases if we had the ancient poems in their original wording before us.

21. Significantly wider than Vollers supposes. Parts of the *Rabī ʿa* and *Ijād*, whose poets are regarded as *ḥujja* [proof citation], lived in the Mesopotamian desert. Sībawayhi quotes verses by ʿAmr b. Maʿdīkarib from the Murād who dwelt quite far south and by Ḥātim, just like the Ṭai, even though they were known to have certain dialectal particularities, were considered to belong to the people of the ʿArabīya. A comprehensive collection of all of the information regarding the ancient Arabic dialect forms would be very desirable. But one cannot accept it on trust without further ado. There is a difference, for example, between Aṣmaʿī saying, "I have heard a Bedouin from such and such a tribe say such and such" and an unconfirmed claim about phonetic and syntactical differences between *Ḥijāz* and Tamīm. Inaccurate observation, inadmissible generalization, and outright distortion of tradition may play a big part in this.

22. Incidentally, I stand by what I said in articles ("Das klassische Arabisch une die arabischen Dialekte"—Classical Arabic and the Arabic dialects in *Beiträge zur semitischen Sprachwissenschaft. Ignaz Goldziher Zeichen der Hochachtung und Freundschaft gewidmet*, Strassburg 1904.) in all of the essential points.

23. In the first centuries of Islam when many different spiritual and intellectual movements wrestled with one another, there was no shortage of free-thinkers who doubted or contested this dogma, see I. Goldzhier, *Muhammedanische Studien*, 2 vols. (Halle, 1889–1890), t.2, p.401 et seqq.

24. The book of the Qoheleth [Ecclesiastes], an attempt at coherent discourse, the like of which the Hebrews had hardly known or not at all, also displays much clumsiness of the novice, but its author was in the favorable position of having a large body of literature at his disposal and being able to draw on lyrical poetry.

25. The verse divisions should, of course, in many cases be corrected, both by reassembling wrongly separated verses and by separating wrongly assembled ones. The verse endings were not marked on the original text. In his *Volkssprache und Schriftsprache im alten Arabien*, Vollers commits many errors based on the fact that he takes the verse division in the European editions of the Koran as definitive, see above, note 5.

26. Regarding the unequal length of the individual verses, recent attempts to prove that the Koran's stanzas are evenly proportioned bundles of such verses have

little prospect of success. The Prophet's aforementioned lack of understanding of formal considerations suffices to counter such an assumption.

27. The language frequently simply juxtaposes clauses without making clear their exact conceptual relationship (*Ḥāl* with and without *wāw*; the *Ṣifa* clause). The important *fā'* sometimes connects and sometimes indicates a final clause. The expression of tense remains undetermined, and so on.

28. For later highly educated thinkers, the scanty intellectual content of the holy book and the plain childishness of ideas therein must have been a terrible bind, whether they believed they adhered to Islam or only maintained the appearance of doing so.

29. In this extract, I reproduce the Koranic spelling that was unfortunately "improved" in the European editions and which retained the final-position ى alif maqṣūra (pronounced like lengthening alif) ā also before object suffixes. In Mecca and Medina, people namely said *'atāka* and so on. Unfortunately, omission of the *alif* as a sign of the *ā*, where the authentic Koranic spelling does not give it, cannot for the time being be implemented.

30. This is particularly striking when God orders him to speak to God himself, III, 25 et seqq.

31. In sura VI, in the revised edition of my *Geschichte des Korans* (History of the Koran), I. Leipzig 1909, Schwally establishes proof for a whole series of repeatedly used expressions.

32. The original Semitic infinitive *fi''āl* has become very rare in Classical Arabic and been replaced by *taf'īl* (*taf'ilah, taf'āl*). But it is worthy of note that in the South *fi''ālun* and the corresponding *tifi''ālun* are still very much alive today. See Landberg's *Dialectes de l'Arabie méridionale* [I Ḥaḍramut, Leiden, 1907, II Daṯīnah eb.1905], II, 536 et seqq., 1396.

33. But without *man* the rhyme would still be good in *lakuntum mina l-khāsirīna*, II, 61 (in fact the end of the verse).

34. Without the need for a rhyme *wa mā tubdūna wa mā kuntum taktumūna* in II, 31. Is this *kuntum* used perhaps for the sake of a certain rhythmical feeling.

35. In II, 217 *la'allakum tatafakkarūna* does not, however, represent the end of a verse since 216–19 constitute in reality only a single verse.

36. XV, 17 has *' in kuntum fā'ilīna*, a positive meaning.

37. I was unaware of this in *Mandäische Grammatik* (Halle, 1875), p. 363, note 1.

38. *Dīnan* and *millatan* are not, as one might think, in the accusative.

39. [See Wright. *A Grammar of the Arabic Language*, II. 112 c.]

40. [The translations into English vary wildly, and most add further words in brackets to complete the sense:

M. Ali: "By whom you demand one of another (your rights) and (to) the ties of relationship."

R. Bell: "Concerning whom and the wombs ye bandy questions to and fro."

Dawood: "In whose name you plead with one another, and honour the mothers who bore you."

Rodwell: "In whose name ye ask mutual favours—and reverence the wombs that bore you."

Arberry: "By whom you demand one of another, and the wombs."

Palmer: "In whose name ye beg of one another, and the wombs."

Yusuf Ali: "Through whom ye demand your mutual (rights) and (reverence) the wombs (that bore you)."

Pickthall: "In whom ye claim (your rights) of one another, and toward the wombs (that bore you)].

41. Cf. *Zur Grammatik*, p. 74, where it is also stated. That *wal-ʾarḥām* is the only possible reading, however much the ancient philologists resist it.

42. A workable translation of the Koran has precisely to gloss over many such weaknesses.

43. Cf below p. 21 on *law* instead of *in*.

44. [In grammar and rhetoric, a figure of speech in which the word or phrase that should properly come last is put first.]

45. [Cf. Bell, *Commentary on the Qurʾān* (Manchester, 1991), vol. 1, p. 538, "*ʾajal musammā(n)* is in apposition to *kalimah*; the awkward separation and the fact that rhyme is given by *lizāmā(n)* makes it almost certain that this phrase has been added. Perhaps the two verses were originally one, and the rhyme-phrases were added later."]

46. *Qul li-llāhi* as an answer to the question *man rabb*, XXIII, 89, 91, I would prefer to regard as a clumsy spelling of *qulillāhu*, or rather (on account of the pause) *qulillāh*. *Li-llāhi* fits much too ill. *Mā ʾinna mafātihū latanūʾ u bi-l-ʿuṣbati ʾūlī-l-quwwati*, XXVIII, 76, literally "whose keys with a whole crowd of mighty people rose up heavily" for "which a crowd . . . could only lift heavily" would be regarded as a very clumsy turn of phrase if Aʿshā had not had the verse or expression, "a bottom lifts her with difficulty" instead of "she lifts the heavy bottom with difficulty, *tanūʾ a bihā būṣun* (Geyer, *Zwei Gedichte*, at the top of p. 162). We are therefore dealing with a fixed expression that perhaps was originally meant to be humorous.

47. Cf. T. Nöldeke, *Zur Grammatik des Klassischen Arabisch* (Wien, 1896) (Denkschriften der kais. Akad.der Wissenschaften zu Wien, philos.-hist.Classe, Bd. XLV.) p. 83.

48. [Cf. Bell, *Commentary*, vol. II, p. 204: "Barth would omit the first part of the verse here; the grammar is certainly out of order, as *kabura* ought to be plural (i.e., *kaburū*); but probably we have an anacoluthon, and the verb refers to the action of these people."]

49. *Ṭāʾ if* of an attack of madness, Amraalq. 4, 41 [See T. Nöldeke. *Funf Moʾallaqāt* übersetzt und erklärt Sitzungsber. der K. Akad.d.Wiss. in Wien, Phil.-hist.Kl.Bd. CXL,VII 1899, CXLII,V 1900, CXLIV, 1 1901. *Le Diwan d'Amro'lkais* par M. G. de Slane (Paris, 1837); *The Divans of the Six Ancient Arabic Poets*, ed. W. Ahlwardt (London, 1870)]; Ṭab. 1, 976, 18. [al-Ṭabarī, *Annales*, ed. De Goeje et al. 15 vols. (Leiden, 1879–1901).]

50. [Cf the diverse English translations of VII, 200–201:

Sale (1734): Verily they who fear God, when a temptation from Satan assaileth them remember the divine commands, and behold, they clearly see the danger of sin, and the wiles of the devil. But as for the brethren of the devils, they shall continue them in error; and afterwards they shall not preserve themselves therefrom.

Rodwell (1861, 1876): Verily, they who fear God, when some phantom from Satan toucheth them, remember Him, and lo! they see clearly. Their brethren (that is, those under Satanic influence) will only continue them in error, and cannot preserve themselves.

Palmer (1880): Verily, those who fear God, if a wraith from the devil touch, mention Him, and lo! they see. And their brethren he shall increase in error, then they shall not desist.

M. Ali (1917): Those who guard against evil, when a visitation from the devil afflicts them, they become mindful, then lo! they see. And their brethen (that is the brethren of the devils, or the devil's human associates) increase them in error, then they cease.

Abdullah Yusuf Ali (1934): Those who fear God, when a thought of evil from satan assaults them, bring God to remembrance, when lo! they see (aright)! But their brethren (the evil ones) plunge them deeper into error, and never relax (their efforts).

Pickthall (1930): Lo! those who ward off (evil), when a glamour from the devil troubleth them, they do but remember (Allah's guidance) and behold them seers! Then brethren plunge them further into error and cease not.

Bell (1937): Verily those who show piety, when a phantom from Satan touches them, recollect themselves (or remind themselves of Allah), and, lo, they see clearly.

But their (usually taken to refer to the Satans) brethren they lead further into perversity and then they do not stop short.

Arberry (1955): The godfearing, when a visitation of Satan troubles them, remember, and then see clearly; and their brothers they lead on into error, then they stop not short.

Dawood (1956): If those that guard themselves against evil are tempted by Satan, they have but to remember; and they shall see the light. As for their brothers, they shall be kept long in error, nor shall they ever desist.

Cf. French translations:

Blachère (1949–51): When those who are pious are touched by a legion of Satan, they reflect and behold they see clearly, while (the legion of Satan) maintains the brothers (of these Pure ones) in error where they afterwards do not cease (to get in deeper).

Montet (1929): Truly those who fear (Allah) when a phantom of Satan touches them, they remember (Allah) and behold they see. And he will push his brothers [(lit. he will increase them (the brothers of those who have gone over to Satan. The subject of the sentence is Allah)], further into error, and then they will not desist.

Cf. Bell's Comments from his commentary vol 1, p. 266:

> The suffix in *ʾikhwānuhum* is usually taken as referring to the satans, and this, though grammatically difficult, gives good sense. Otherwise, taking the suffix as referring to those who show piety, we have to suppose that their good conduct drives others further into perversity.]

51. Cf. *Zur Grammatik*, p. 84. The passage cited there, Hudh. 154 5 [J. Wellhausen, *Skizzen und Vorarbeiten I: Letzer Teil der Lieder der Hudhailiten* (Berlin, 1884), numbers 139–280], *gābun tašayyamahu kharīqun yubbasu*, "a dry reed into which a fire has entered," also constructs the collective noun in the masculine singular and the plural, but the big difference is that only the plural form follows.

52. T. Nöldeke, *Kurzgefasste Syrische Grammatik*, 2 vols. (Leipzig, 1898), § 319. Correspondingly in Persian *bāyūn mīrīn namānand kas* Shahn. (Vullers) 3, 1471, v. 486 [*Firdusii Liber Regum qui Inscribitur Schahname*, ed. J. A. Vullers: Bd. I. II (Lugduni Batavorum, 1877–79)] *wa an naqad kasy azan birun nah barad nandy*, Nasiri Chosrau, Sefername (Schefer) [Charles Schefer, ed. & tr., *Sefer nameh: relation du voyage de Nassiri Khosrau* (Paris, 1881)], 83, 13 (simple prose).

53. Thus most of the readers. The reading of our texts (*Hafs*) *fayuwaf fīhim* would be even less commendable. But cf. what follows.

54. Note in relation to this Muḥammad's prayer: *allāhumma rabba s-samawāti wa mā' aẓlalna, wa rabba l-' aradīna wa mā' aqlalna, wa rabba š-šayātīn wa mā 'aḍlalna* and so on. Ibn Hishām 756 ult.—757, 1, where on account of the rhyme the Satans are treated as a feminine plural. [Ibn Hishām, *Das Leben Muhammeds*, ed. F. Wustenfeld, 2 vols. (Göttingen 1858–1860).]

55. *Baiḍāwī.wa šahidū 'aṭf 'alā mā fī 'aymānihim min m'nā l-fi'l.*

56. E.g., Psalms 91:1; Isaiah 5, 8, 11, 23.

57. [G. H. A. Ewald, *Grammatica Critica Linguae Arabicae* vol. I/II (Lipsiae 1831/33).]

58. [*Ṭabarī*, Leiden edition = *Annales quos scripsit . . . at-Ṭabari.* cum aliis ed. M. J. de Goeje, series I–III, Lugd. Bat. 1879ff; *Ṭabari*, Kosegarten ed. = *Taberistanensis . . . Annales . . .* ed. J. G. L. Kosegarten, vols. I–III (Gryphisvaldiae 1831–53).]

59. 'Omar b. AR 137, 17 [*Dīwān* ʿUmar b.a.Rabīʿa (Cairo, 1311); see also Paul Schwarz, *Der Diwan des ʿUmar ibn Abi Rebi'a* [c. 644–712 CE] (Leipzig, 1909)], *jaryin* is to be read for *jarīy* in *ba'da jayrin ' ilaykum rasa-nī*: "after I had tightened up my reins to you."

60. [Al-Iṣbahānī, *Kitāb al-Agānī*, 20 vols. (Būlāq, 1285); vol. 21 ed. R. Brünnow (Leiden, 1888).]

61. This occurs often in Hebrew, e.g., Isaiah 5:24; 13:9; 17:5; 30:12.

62. See Reckendorf § 116 regarding such cases. [H. Reckendorf, *Die syntaktischen Verhältnisse des Arabischen.* 2 vols. (Leiden 1895–1898).]

63. See above, note 3.

64. One might think that at least some of these passages had been affected by damage to the text, in the scattered fragments that were used for editing the canonical copy at a very old period in this copy itself. But the large number of cases and in addition the recurrence of some of these in several passages guarantees/confirms the appearance itself and hardly leaves room for doubt in the individual instances.

65. On closer examination the reading of *ar-rīḥu* raises even greater difficulties.

66. In XVII, 24 *' iḥsānan* can be seen as the object of *qaḍā.*

67. This is similar to the loose connection with the meaning "but that doesn't concern," "but it is a different matter with," and other similar formulations. These are very popular in the Koran, but also elsewhere in ancient Arabic. See II, 73; IV, 29; XX, 108; XXIX, 114; LX, 4; XXXIV, 3 (*' illā fī*); IV, 33 (*' illā ' an*); XXXIV, 20 (*' illā lina'lama*); and other passages in the Koran.

68. See *Zur Grammatik*, p. 36, where further examples are given. In the Koran we find *falyaṣumhu*, II, 181. Also in 'Omar b. AR 150, 6. 195, 5. 292, 1.

69. I.e. "even if there is a year between visits"; cf the preceding verse. I have

replaced *kulla* of the edition with *kullun*. This verse is missing as far as I can see in the other places where longer or shorter extracts of this poem are quoted.

70. [*Amālī* . . . a.'Alī Isma'īl b. al-Qāsim al-Qālī, Kitāb al-Amālī, vols I/II, (Būlāq, 1324).]

71. [Ibn S'ad, *Ṭabaqāt* (Biographien Muhammeds, seiner Gefährten und der späteren Träger des Islams . . . ed. E. Sachau, et aliis, vols. I–VIII (Leiden, 1904–1915).]

72. [Arabic is unable to distinguish between "He struck him" (reflexive object suffix) and "He struck himself" (reflexive pronominal suffix).]

73. Otherwise *yawma yakūnu-n-nāsu kal-farāši* . . . in CI, 3. Although this is not a precise answer to the question *wa mā ʾadrāka mal-qāri'atu*, it follows on from it.

74. [Nöldeke also cites XV, 21 and XCII, 21, but he seems to have made a mistake in these references since there are no *wa li* in these verses.]

75. How moving is the verse: *fa law fī yawmi ma'rikatin ʾ uṣību wa lākin fī diyāri Banī Marīnā*, "And had they met their deaths in a battle—, but in the dwellings of Banu Marina!" *Ag*. 8, 64, 24. [Al-Iṣbahānī, *Kitāb al-Agānī*, 20 vols. (Büläq, 1285).]

76. On the subject of general usage cf. also Ibn Saʿd 5, 89, 11; Aḍdād 84, line 5 from below [Abū Bakr b. al-Anbārī (d. 327/939) *Kitābo-ʾl-Aḍdād*, ed. M. Th. Houtsma (Leiden, 1881).] [Aḍdād =words which have two meanings that are opposite to each other]. Verse 139/13 of Aḍdād quoted on p. 91 is not really objectionable, probably reading *falam yabqa bayna l-ḥayyi Saʿd ibn Mālikin wa-lā nahšalin ʾillā dimāʾa l-Asāwid* "and between the house of S. b. M. and the N. remained nothing but the blood of vipers."

77. Since these verbs (to fear, to impede, to forbid) without exception have a simple object that is positive, this mode of expression is more consistent than the manner of expressing a dependent clause negatively usual in Greek, Latin, and French and not unknown in modern Arabic dialects (cf. Landberg, *Dialectes de L'Arabie méridionale*, II Daṯīnah (Leiden, 1905)], p. 657 et seq.). "I fear going into decline" corresponds better to "I fear decline" than "not going (μή, *nē*, que—ne: *ʾ an lā*) into decline." But psychologically speaking, this construction is easy to explain, just as the negative in sentences that depend on a comparative (French que . . . ne) and after words like "before" (*'adlā, before* [Syriac]; modern Arabic *qabla lā* Landberg l. c. 467 etc.); both can occasionally occur in German too but should probably be regarded as gallicisms.

78. Thus Muḥammad says: *mā ' alaykum ʾ allā tamn'ū hu*, "Why do you insist on hindering him?" Ibn Hishām 580, line 3 from below. In a negative main clause *lam naʾ man ʾ an lā najida ʾ amnan*, Ṭab. 1, 1561, 15 (cited by Landberg l.c. p. 567); *faḥarāmun ' alayka ʾ an lā tanāla*, "so it is denied you to achieve your purpose,"

Omar b. AR 293, 12 (cited by Schwartz, 4, 158); and even *famā ʾ alūmu l-bīḍa ʾ allā taskharā*, "and I do not rebuke the pure (women) for their mockery," Abu Najm in Aḍdād 131, 1; but that is the daring undertaking of a Rajaz poet. Only *yalḥayna-nī ʾallā ʾ uḥibbahu.* Line 4 probably means "they revile me for not (any longer) loving him" and is therefore wholly regular. Incidentally, the Aḍdād or at least their sources display a rather crude grasp of these matters, with the exception of the perspicacious Farrāʾ. Cf Lis. 20, 353 et seqq.

79. Our (i.e., the German) "davor" carries with it the negative meaning; otherwise it would signify "be on your guard so that they (do not) lead you astray."

80. Cf., for example, *fa-taḥarrajī min qatli na ʾ an taʾ ṯamī*, "make our murder a matter of conscience that you do not sin" Omar b. AR 91, 8.

81. In a childlike conception of the earth, the mountains give the earth its necessary immobility, they act as ballast so to speak.

82. [Ma'n b. Aus., *Gedichte des Ma'n ibn Aus*, ed. P. Schwarz (Leipzig, 1903).]

83. [Al- Amālī, *Kitāb al-Amālī*, vols. I/II (Būlāq, 1324).]

84. [Dīwān Ǧarīr b.ʻAṭīya al-Ḫaṭafā, vols. I/II (Cairo, 1313); *The Naqāʾiḍ of Jarīr and al-Farazdaʾ*, ed. A. A. Bevan, vols. I/II (Leiden, 1905–1909).]

85. The editor was certainly right to dot/punctuate as *wudda law*: "it would be good if."

86. [*Kitāb Maqāmāt al-Ḥarīrī (mit Komm.)* (Beirüt, 1873); *Les Séances de Hariri*, ed. S. de Sacy, 2nd ed. Reinaud Derenbourg, vols. I/II (Paris 1847/53).]

87. [*Kāmil, The Kāmil of El-Mubarrad*, ed. W. Wright (Leipzig, 1864); Ham, *Hamasae Carmina*, ed. G. G. Freytag and P. I. Bonnae, 1828; Lis., *Lisān al-'Arab, Ibn Manẓūr*, 20 vols. (Būlāq, 1300–1308); Chiz, *Ḫizānat al-adab wa-lubb lubāb lisān al-'arab* by ʻUmar al-Bagdādī. 4 vols. (Būlāq, 1291).]

88. [*Bukhārī . . . Les Recueil des Traditions Mahomé tanes par el-Bokhāri,* vols. I–III, ed. L. Krehl, vol. IV, ed. T. W. Juynboll (Leiden, 1862–1908).]

89. [Ibn *Hishām Sīrat an-Nabī*, ed. F. Wustenfeld (Göttingen, 1858–1860).]

90. But the composite *mā ʾ in* is frequently used by poets as a simple particle of negation.

91. Later imitations of the Koran, which aspire like it to be of divine origin, like the Siite suras (*Geschichte des Qorans*, p. 221 et seqq.) and Bab's revelations cannot really be considered as being real continuations along this path/road.

92. Unfortunately we know nothing definite about the people in Mecca who informed him about Judaism and Christianity in sura X,105; XXV, 5 et seq. There were certainly no highly educated scholars among them. Incidentally, the Arabs

have misunderstood other individual foreign words and used them differently from how they were is in the language of origin. Thus *fakhkhār* should mean "potter" but in fact means "clay" (only the Christian Arab tradition has kept the word derived from *paḥārā –potter* in its original meaning; thus Matthew in the Roman edition of 1671 and the London edition of 1848). In the same way, *ḥānūṯā* = Syriac generally retains its old meaning of "booth, inn," but in two authors it is used to mean "innkeeper," Lis. 2,330, cf. Barth on *Kumayṭ* 4, 9. [Jakob Barth, *Sprachwissenschaftliche Untersuchungen zum Semitischen* (Leipzig, 1907–11). See also J. Barth, *Zur Kritik des Dīwāns der Hudeiliten* (Gedicht I–LV) ZA 26, 1912) pp. 277–86.] (The erroneous reading Syriac *ḥnwtyky- ḥanūṯayk(y)*, Jes. 1,22, does not even come into consideration in the face of the excellently proven Syriac *ḥnwyyky* (Syriac *ḥānwāyayk (y)*).

93. [A. Geiger, *Was hat Mohammed aus dem Judenthume aufgenommen*? (Bonn, 1883); S. Fraenkel. *De Vocabulis in antiquis Arabum carminibus et in Corano peregrinis* (Leiden, 1880).]

94. [For an alternative interpretation see C. Heger. Koran XXV, 1 in Warraq, *What the Koran Really Says*, pp. 387–90.]

95. [λύτρον (lutron): something to loosen with, i.e., a redemption price (fig. atonement) ransom.

96. [λύτρωσις (lutrosis): a ransoming (fig.): redeemed, redemption.]

97. [ἀπολύτρ ωσις (apolutrosis): (the act) ransom in full, i.e., (fig.) riddance, or spec. Christian salvation: deliverance, redemption.]

98. [σωτηρία (soteria): rescue or safety; deliver, health, salvation, save, saving.]

99. The Syrian translation of the chronicle (which does not belong to the old Syrian canon) is however merely a slightly reworked Jewish Targum.

100. [Jacob of *Sĕrūgh*. On the baptism of Constantine: A. L. Frothingham Jr., "L'Omelia di Giacomo di Sarûg sul battesimo di Costantino imperatore," *Atti della R. Accademia dei Lincei* ser. 3, Memorie della Classe di Scienze morali, storiche e filologiche vol. 8 (1883): 167–242—edited, with Italian translation and notes.]

101. Cod. M. establishes the usual meaning: Syriac *hwā šeāinteh* "it (the temple) is his dwelling." In the relevant passage of the Talmud, Sukk 5 a, although the coming-down of the *skynh* is denied, it is done so in explicit opposition to the belief in this idea.

102. [J. Levy, *Neuhebräisches und chaldäisches Wörterbuch über die Talmudim und Midraschim*, 4 vols. (Leipzig 1876–89).]

103. I do not know if this poet is Islamic or pre-Islamic.

104. Τροπαια, "martyrs' grave," Euseb., Hist eccl. 108, 9 et Seq. Syriac

meṯnaṣaḥ b-zāāūṯā, Greek: τροπαιου῍χος in the imperial title, Land 3,179, 20, and then even Syriac *zkwth –zāāūṯeh* "his (the Persian king's) rule." Statute della scuola di Nisibi 7, 3. 26, 3 v. u. 32, 14. In Payne Smith and also Brockelmann the different meanings of the word are not well set out.

105. In Arabic *zakā* [with *wāw*] or *zakā* [with alif *maqṣūra*] means "to thrive," Ham. [*Hamasae Carmina*, ed. G. G. Freytag and P. I. Bonn, 1828], 722, 4; Lis. 19, 77, 12; Dinawari 72 ult. [*Abū Ḥanīfa ad-Dīnawari, Kitāb al-Akhbār aṭ-Ṭiwāled.* V. Guirgass (Leiden, 1888).] Labid (Chalidi) [*Der Diwan des Lebīd*, ed. al-Chālidī (Wien, 1880)], 142,10 (the latter two passages usual prose) and "to be seemly" ibn Qot., Shi'r 236, 3 [Ibn Qotaiba, *Liber Poësis et Poëtarum*, ed. M. J. de Goeje (Leiden, 1904)]. The elative *ʾazkā* in sura II, 232; XVIII, 18; and XXIV, 28, 30 probably belongs to this meaning. On the other hand, I choose to regard the Koranic *zakā* "to be innocent" along with *zakiyyun* and *tazakkā* "to behave virtuously" and particularly *zakkā* "to make just, to explain as just, to justify" as borrowings from Jewish/Hebrew usage.

106. Certainly it is very possible to establish a close link between *ʾamalla* "to dictate," sura II, 282, and also the *ʾamlā* used more frequently with Syriac *malē*, *meltā* with this meaning, but this does not help to explain our *milla.*

107. Transferring the feeling or condition of a person onto a thing as in *layla nāʾm* etc. Perhaps *mumill* should be said in its fully active form.

108. [Al-Chālidī, *Der Diwan des Lebīd* (Wien, 1880).]

109. [W. Wright, ed. *Opuscula Arabica* (Leiden, 1859).]

110. [R. Dozy, *Supplément aux Dictionnaires Arabes*. 2 vols. (Leiden, 1881).]

111. Read here *suwar* instead of *sūr.*

112. That שׂוֹרָה, sūrā Isaiah 28:25, should be entirely excluded here had long been clear to me. Since we have known from the Panamu inscription that שׂורה *swrh –sorah*) is the name of a useful plant (presumably a variety of cereal) this has been certain; cf. Gesenius-Buhl (14th edition) sub voce. Incidentally, it is highly unlikely that this verse of Isaiah is intact.

113. Later Arabs better ascertained the meaning of the Jewish word; this is shown by the words put into 'Omar's mouth, Ibn Sa'd 5, 140, 5, as well as 'Obeidas' statement that the *maṯanāh kamaṯ nāh ʾahl –l-kitābi* was a work written by the Jewish teachings based on the teachings of Moses, see Lis 18, 429 below. By this the entire work of the Mishna is naturally understood.

114. Hardly *haʾamana.*

115. [Eusebius on the theophania, a Syriac version, ed. S. Lee (London, 1842), Vgl. H. Gressmann in Texte und Untersuch. zur Gesch. der altchr. Lit. hrsg. von

Gebhardt und Harnack N.F. VIII, 3. Leipzig, ders. Eusebius Theophania, die grieche. Bruchstücke und Übersetzung der syr (Überlieferung: Leipzig, 1904).]

116. In Wright's *Kalila wDimna*, 14, 22, Syriac *hymn* is causative of the usual meaning "to make the lie believable." [W. Wright, *The Book of Kalilah and Dimnah, translated from Arabic into Syriac* (Oxford: Clarendon Press, 1884).]

117. From this Syriac *mehamen* "castrated," Chabot, Synodes, 24, 1 (variant Syriac *mesares*) [*Synodicon orientale ou recueil des synodes nestoriens*, published, translated, and annotated by J. G. Chabot (Not. et extr. des mss. de la bibliothèque nationale 37) (Paris, 1902).]

118. In Jaq. 2, 51, 6 [*Yāqūt. Mu'jam al-Buldān*, ed. F.Wüstenfeld, 6 vols. (Leipzig, 1866–1870).] *Al-qass al- muhaymin* is to be read for *al-qassu al-muhaynimu* "the murmuring priest," cf. Agh. 16, 45, 8; Bekri 371, 7 [*Das geographische Wörterbuch des . . . el-Bekri*, ed. F. Wustenfeld, vols. I/II (Göttingen/Paris, 1876/77)]. The verses are incidentally Muslim in origin.

119. This was also felt by those who saw in Sigill the name of a scribe of the prophet or of an angel.

120. [S. Fraenkel, *Die Aramäischen Fremdwörter im Arabischen* (Leiden 1886).]

121. [Yāqūt, *Mu'jam al-Buldān*, ed. F. Wüstenfeld, 6 vols. (Leipzig, 1866–1870).]

122. Our word has nothing to do with *ḍarbun sijjīnun*, "mighty blow," or the like in Ibn Muqbil's verse, the Abū Zaid 209; Bucharī (Krehl) 3, 260, 9; Lis. 17, 65 (where there is a second verse that secures the form with the rhyme) and others cite it. Or else the poet, who survived 'Uthmān, would have to have first taken *sijjin* from the Koran and used it arbitarily.

123. Certainly a deliberate play on words.

124. It is well known that *ma'ānan*, "dwelling, residence" corresponds exactly to this word, Abū Zaid 254, 7; Agh. 18, 151, 7 (from *Manṣūr's* time); Harīrī beginning of second *Maqāma*, and in a verse quoted by Isḥāq b. Barūn, *Muwāzana*, 77 and seq.: *mu'ānu min 'aḥabbtinā ma'ānu. 'Awānan* "remaining" (in all senses) belongs to the root with this meaning. That *'una* "to help" is identical to this is very doubtful.

The Syriac *me'āwnā (me'ōnā)*, known to us from the glossaries BA (Hoffmann) no. 2185. 4834; BB 1124 et seq., is the Hebrew itself *mā'ōn*, just Syriac *merawmā* = מָרוֹם [Hebrew; *mārōm*]. In authentic Aramaic it must have read Syriac *merāmā, meānā.*

125. Geyer, who for some time has been preparing an edition of the *A'shā*, has most kindly given me information about this passage that I know from Lis. and whose identity with other citations (which read precisely *'indah*) I had not noticed.

126. Variant *majjan.*

127. [Kitāb, *Gamharat aš'ar al-'arab ta'līf a.Zaid . . . al-Qurašī* (Būlāq, 1308/11).]

128. [Die Gedichte des Lebīd, *uas dem Nachlasse des Dr. A. Huber*, ed. C. Brockelmann (Leiden, 1891).]

129. Since I could not remember where there was such a case in the old rabbinical literature, I turned to my friend Landauer who immediately named this passage for me and also indicated the existence of several other analogous passages.

130. *Ṣalawātun* "oratories," sura XXII, 41, and in the treaty with the Najrānian [Wellhausen, *Skizzen und Vorarbeiten* IV/3. Ibn Sa'd, *die Schreiben Muhammads und die Gesandtschaften an ihn* (arab.text) (Berlin, 1889)] 4, 26, 10) is indeed Aramaic: Syriac *ṣlwt' –ṣelūṯā*, Land 2, 333, 4 shortened from Syriac *byt ṣlwt' –beṯ ṣelūṯā*; likewise Peshitta and Christian Palestinian Syriac *byt ṣlwt' –beṯ ṣelūṯā* for π ρ οσ ευ χή [oratory, chapel, prayer, pray earnestly], Acts 15, 13, 16, which Greek expression presumably renders a simple popular א ת ו ל צ *ṣlwt' –ṣelūṯā* without ת י ב — *byt - beṯ*. My supposition that the Maltese *sella 'al*, "to greet someone," can be traced back to *ṣallā 'alā* (ZDMG. 58, 920) is one that I maintain (see Falzon s. V.; H. Stumme, *Maltesische Studien* 13, 33 [Leipzig, 1904]; Bertha Ilg and Hans Stumme, *Maltesische Volkslieder, im Urtext mit Deutscher Übersetzung* (Leipzig, 1909)] 347, 4). The *e* in spite of the original *ṣ* is also in *ṣandūq*, *ṣan'a.* The fact that in Maltese alongside this toned-down meaning the original "to pray" in the form of *salla* also appears does not constitute a counterargument. Falzon designates this an "arabismo"; it certainly made its way from the Islamic usage again.

131. These verses are Islamic. Hanīf means simply Muslim, like al-qas, the Christian priest. See below Jag 2, 515 = Agh. 16, 45 = Ibn Qot. shi'r 354 = Amāli 1, 78 (this is the best text.)

2.2

On Sura 91.9–10

Friedrich Schulthess[1]

verse 9. *qad 'aflaḥa man zakkāhā*
verse 10. *waqad khāba man dassāhā*

This brief exegetical study examines the question of the meaning of the two rhyming verbs in this context. The two other verbs will be given only secondary consideration.

The postulation of a stark contrast between verses 9 and 10 may be accepted as generally correct; it forms the basis for most translations without providing an accurate understanding of this contrast.

As far as the analysis of the Koranic *zakkā* is concerned, Snouck-Hurgronje's instructive and far-reaching essay may be cited.[2] It came by chance to my attention only after I had completed the present study, through the same scholar's critique of H. Grimme's *Mohammed* (1892)[3]. If, in spite of our extensive agreement, which suits me very well, I present these lines in their original version, I do so partly because Snouck-Hurgronje interprets our Koranic verses in the conventional manner, and partly to avoid the confusion of context constant consideration of his essay would have entailed for this study. Incidentally, he seems to be too little known here—if the critical works are anything to judge by!

The verses, which are introduced by an unusually long sequence of vows, have been translated in a fairly uniform manner. Almost all translators I have access to render *zakkāhā* and *dassāhā* as "to purify" (or "to keep pure," etc.) and "to spoil" ("to allow to perish," etc.), respectively.[4] Boysen

(1773) and Wahl (1828) translate *dassāhā* as "to allow to grow wild," Grimme (1892, I, p. 20) as "to allow to wither away," and Uhlmann (1881) as "to bury under sins."

Snouck-Hurgronje (1892, I, p. 372, n. 2) translates verse 9: "Wel hem, die haar (zijne ziel) vroom houdt of maakt." [Well to him who keeps or makes his soul pious.]

Grimme (1882, I, p. 15) is alone in rendering: "Blessed is he who purifies his soul through donations, lost he who (failing to do so) allows it to waste away."

The terms I have spaced out in type are double translations, for *zakkā* means either "to purify" or *zakāt* "to give alms" but not both, *dassāhā* either "to fail (to do)" or "to allow to wither away"; nonetheless, Grimme came close to the correct meaning, as shall be shown later.

Translations of the verbs *'aflaḥa* and *khāba* are even more extensively concurrent:

> Bibliander: "semper antecedit—gressus retrorsum efficitur";
> Boysen, Sale, Wahl, Kazimirski: "is blessed—is damned";
> Henning: "fares well—is bound for ignominy"; cf. Rodwell, Palmer.[5]

The Muslim interpretations in *Ṭabarī Tafsīr* XXX, 116 et seqq. and Lane I, 878 a. 1240 a. are partly correct, partly erroneous. It is completely wrong to consider Allah the subject of *zakkāhā: qad 'aflaḥa man zakkā 'illāhu nafsahū fa-kabbarahā bi-taṭhīrihā mina l-kufri wa-l-ma'āṣī wa-'aṣlaḥahā bi-l-ṣāli ḥāti mina l-'a'māli*, Ibn ʿAbbas and others after him, including Ṭabarī; *man zakkā llāhu nafsahū*, Ibn Zaid.[6] This would have the same implications for *dassāhā*: *man dassasa llāhu nafsahū fa-'akhmalahā*, and so on. Qatāda, Ibn ʿAbbās, Ibn Zaid. This interpretation, however, is not without foundation, since it is indeed the case that nowhere in the Koran is man really the subject of *zakkā*. It is worthy of note that al-Farrā' and az-Zajjāj (cf. Lane)[7] link *dassāhā* to the miser who keeps his dwelling and money secret, and Ibn al A'rābī, Ṯa'lab, Muḥkam, and Qāmūs[8] to the impure man or infidel who worms his way into the midst of the good, and that the dictionaries already give the meaning of *dassāhā* as "to fail to give alms" (T 'A[9], Lane 878 a.), as the opposite of *zakkā* "to pay the alms tax" (Lane 1240).

Since *dassāhā* is ambiguous, everything depends on the meaning of *zakkāhā*. The most frequent use of *zakkā* or √*zkw*[10] in the Koran is *zakāh* [*with tā'marbūṭa*], *zkwh* [*with tā'marbūṭa*]; in almost every case it has the meaning of "alms" or "poor tax," which, as has long been recognized, renders the Hebrew-Jewish זכות [zkwt (*zeḵūṯ*)], which probably already had this meaning in Hebrew. But in suras XVIII, 80; XIX, 14 it means "purity" or "uprightness," and combined with *zakiyyan* XVIII, 73: *nafsan zakiyyatam* "innocent blood."

Conversely, I would read *zakiyyan* XIX, 19 as "thriving";[11] combined with the elative *'azkā* "more fitting, better," II, 232; XXIV, 28, 30.

It is difficult to evaluate the etymological connections we have briefly to consider at this point. If דכא [Hebrew *dk'*], *dk'* [Syriac] is not to be dismissed, it corresponds to the Assyrian *zakū* "to be immune, free," and to the Hebrew זכה [*zkh*] and Arabic *ḏakā* "to thrive, to develop."[12] This is not contradicted by *ḏakā* meaning "to slaughter according to the rites"[13] in Muslim terminology and already in sura V, 4 (*'illā mā ḍakkaytum* . . . unless you are able to slaughter it . . .). The latter *ḏakkā*, however, is probably somehow of Jewish origin and the usual *ḏakā* the true equivalent, and—we cannot get round this—*zakā* only a variant form of it. Their meanings are indeed practically identical.[14] In this instance, [*Syriac*]*zk'* is a Hebrew-Jewish loanword. That its meaning "to be victorious" (cf. PSM.[15] and the instructive passage in Kalila and Dimna 29/18 = 45/14 in my edition,[16] where it means both "to be justified" and "to prevail")[17] is secondary is rightly emphasized by Nöldeke (1910).

Following on from this, *zakāh* "purity, uprightness," and *zakīy* "pure, innocent," would be just as much of Hebrew-Jewish origin as *zakāh* "alms" ("voluntary donation"), because *ḏakā*, of which *zakā* is a variant, did not develop this meaning, whereas *zakīyun* "thriving" and the above-mentioned elative may be explained by Arabic usage.

The same is true of the verb *zakā*: XXIV, 21, meaning "to be innocent" = *hkz* [Hebrew *zkh*] (from which *zk'*: Syriac).

It is of crucial importance for our understanding of verse XCI, 9 that in the Koran Allah is always the subject of the second stem *zakkā*, whether directly or indirectly (cf. p. 150, l. 9 above). Only Allah (LIII, 33) can "declare as just" (δικαιουν Greek = *hKz* Hebrew, Psalm 73:13), as he does at the Last Judgement II, 169 [*llāhu yawma –l-qiyāmati walā yuzakkihim . . .*]; III, 71. [*llāhu walā yanẓuru 'ilayhim yawma –l-qiyāmati walā yuzakkihim*]. When the Prophet and his precursors do so, it is explicitly in Allah's name and at his command (II, 123, 146; III, 158; LXII, 2; IX, 104). An ordinary man cannot and must not do so (LIII, 33; IV, 52), in the same way that his justified state derives only from Allah's grace (cf. above regarding the first stem).

If *zakkāhā*, in XCI, 9, meant "to justify," or even merely "to purify," with man as its subject, it would be contrary to general Koranic usage.

Man's task is to *yatazakkā* [to be purified]. The fifth stem is denominated by "alms" or "poor taxes." The proof for this assertion is provided by verses LXXXVII, 14; LXXX, 3; XXXV, 19, where *tazakkā* always appears alongside prayer or *ḏikr*,[18] or both. It is, therefore, not simply a question of belief but has a practical consequence everyone has to provide for his person XXXV, 19 (cf. XXXI, 32; II, 45, 117). The passage says the same as XXXV, 26, making *infāq* the third requirement, alongside prayer and *ḏikr*. Thus *tuzakkā* is "to practise charity, benevolence," which has nothing to do with "to justify" or "to purify," but refers only to *zakātun*, "alms." Since these passages are Meccan in origin, they cannot refer to the poor taxes standardized by law—as that would mean that XCII, 18 is tautologous next to *yu'tā mālahu*—but rather "voluntary charity."

Genetically *tazakkā* is in exactly the same relation to *zakātun* as *taṣaddaqa* (IX,76 etc.) is to *ṣadaqatun.*

Of the two other passages XX, 78; LXXIX, 18, the first confirms our understanding perfectly: the gardens of paradise are the eternal reward of he who *tazakkā* [who purifies himself]. This is simply a periphrasis of the preceding verse and demonstrates that *tazakkā* is not only a synonym for *'amalu-l-ṣāli ḥāti* "charity" but as closely linked to "to be a believer" (*mu'min*). Thus voluntary charity is the defining practical moment of faith in the Meccan period. Even later on, when the poor tax was in existence, Mohammed considered it in every way more important for the Bedouin than the profession of faith.—I do not wish to force verse LXXIX, 18, where Moses asks, or rather demands of, Pharaoh: *hal laka 'ilā 'an tazakkā*, but I believe that, in the light of what has just been said, this verb may be understood as "to become a believer," to the extent that Pharaoh is to be converted from paganism (*ṭagā*, verse 17).[19] In XX, 46, "to perform the *ḏikr*" is used instead, and XXIII, 49: *'anu'minu*. But even if *tazakkā* were to mean here "to purify oneself" or "to justify oneself" (for which there is no parallel in the Koran), this would not warrant reading *zakkāhā* XCI, 9 as "purifies, justifies (the soul)."

On the one hand, as we have seen, nowhere in the Koran is man the subject of *zakkā* and, on the other, this translation would not provide the necessary contrast with *dassāhā* however one chooses to understand it.[20]

It is more likely to be a stylistic blunder[21] occasioned not by the idea contained in the sura but solely by its form, in particular, by the rhyme[22] and the preceding *nafs*, which serves as an oath. The result of this restrictive influence is what appears to be *zakkā*, which, in its literal sense, would contradict the Koran (cf. above, p. 152 et seq.), but means, translated mechanically, "gives the soul as alms,"[23] in fact, "practises charity" or "gives alms." The verse has the same meaning as LXXXVII, 14: *qad 'aflaḥa man tazakkā* and would have been identical given the corresponding rhyme structure.

Since the analogy with *nafs* and the restriction imposed by the rhyme persisted, *dassāhā* was equally affected, whereas it means "he who puts the alms aside," that is, keeps for himself the part of his possessions destined for alms.

This explains the form and meaning of *dassāhā*. It is the rhyme form for *dassahā*[24] (cf. XVI, 61), not *dassasahā*, and neither is it the second stem of *dasā*.

Thus *nafs* had merely a mechanical influence. Hence there are no grounds for referring to *qaddama* and *'akhkhara* LXXV, 13 or IX, 112 (God bought from the believers their soul and their possessions in the form of alms).

Boysen and Grimme[25] seem to have had that *dasā* in mind, that is, *dassā*, "to allow to lie infertile, fallow" (cf. *dāsin* in the dictionaries). Consequently, *zakkāhā* would mean "to make thrive" (cf. above, p. 151 and n. 4). I have found no evidence for *dasā* that may be due to chance; in any case, the Koran gives no basis for this interpretation, and the parallel LXXXVII, 14 is too extreme.

Zakkā and *dassa* are used, not in the Koran but elsewhere, with reference to money, the former in the sense of "to examine for genuineness,"[26] the latter "to pass off as genuine, to smuggle in."[27] A use in this sense would result in our verses in the idea suggested above of a commercial transaction between God and man regarding the soul. However, the verbs are not opposites, and this interpretation, which may be attributed to one or the other Muslim (cf. p. 150/13 et seq.), seems rather far-fetched.

Finally, as far as *'aṣlaḥa* and *khāba* are concerned, finding fault with the commonly held view may be pedantic, since there can be no doubt about their meaning. It is not, however, out of the question that the Prophet had the more concrete meaning of these verbs in mind and that they belong to the Koran's commercial vocabulary, as collected by Ch. C. Torrey in 1892.[28] *Khāba* means, indeed, "to be unsuccessful, disappointed," literally also "to suffer a defeat" (cf. sura III, 122, the opposite of *naṣr* "victory"). In sport, the losing arrow is called *'akhyabu* (cf. *Proverbia* ed. Freytag II,[29] p. 678 bottom, and Huber, *Meisirspiel* p. 34). Similarly, *'aflaḥa*, like *'aṣlaḥa*, means originally "to triumph, to succeed." In any case, the Muslim theologians' exclusive use of these two verbs in reference to salvation is certainly very old.

I would translate the verses as follows:

A good deal (for the hereafter) is made by he who gives alms,
But losses are incurred by he who hides them.

Notes

1. [Footnotes in square brackets by I. W.]

2. Snouck-Hurgronje, "*Nieuwe bijdragen tot te kennis van den Islam*," in *Bijdragen tot te Taal-Land- en Volkenkunde van Nederlandsch-Indië*, Vierde Volgreeks 6, 1882, p. 356 et seqq., in particular p. 365 et seqq.

3. Snouck-Hurgronje's critique of H. Grimme in *Revue de l'Histoire des Religions* 15, 30 (1894): 163ff.

4. Thus Sale (1812), Kazimirski (according to Le Beaume, *Bibl. Orient.* IV, p. 217), Rodwell (1861), Palmer (1880), Rückert (1888), Henning (1901), Dieterici (*Handwörterbuch*, 1894) [Friedrich Dieterici, *Arabisch-deutsches Handworterbuch zum Ḳoran und Thier und Mensch vor dem Konig der Genien* (Walluf-Nendeln Sandig: 1894)].

5. [T. Bibliander, Basel, 1543; G. Sale, London, 1734; Fr, E. Boysen, Halle 1773, 1775; S. Fr. G. Wahl, Halle, 1828; L. Uhlmann, Bielefeld–Leipzig, 1881; M. Kazimirski, Paris, 1841; J. M. Rodwell, London, 1861; E. H. Palmer, Oxford, 1880; M. Henning, Leipzig, 1901.]

6. It is not entirely clear whether *zakkā* is taken to mean "to purify" or "to raise" [or expand, enlarge, etc.] (*kabbara*) in this context.

7. [E. W. Lane. *Arabic English Lexicon*, 8 vols. London, 1863–1893.]

8. [*Qāmūs The Qāmūs of al-Fairūzabādī*, 2 vols. Cairo, 1298.]

9. [*Tāj al-'Arūs. Arabic Lexicon of as-Sayyid Murtaḍa*, 10 vols. Cairo, 1307.]

10. Cf. apart from Snouck-Hurgronje also Nöldeke, *Neue Beiträge zur semitischen Sprachwissenschaft*, Strassburg 1910, p. 25.

11. Cf. the periphrasis in Umajja b. A. ṣ Ṣalt XXXVIII, 11, *gulāman sawiyya l-khalqi laysa bi-taw'ami.*

12. Used of man in a physical and spiritual sense, also of fire and war ("flare up, break through"), and of fragrances etc. References are unnecessary as generally available.

13. *Ḏakāh* Ag. XVI, 52. Cf. Wellhausen, *Skizzen und Vorarbeiten*, Heft IV, Berlin, 1889. III, 112. *Reste arabischen Heidentums*. 2 Aufl. Berlin. 1897. 114, no. 4.

14. Evidence for *zakā, zakā* [*with alif maqṣūra*] "to thrive" (also "to be capable, fitting") is given by Nöldeke (1910), no. 3. In addition, *zakā* "to develop, to sprout, to be productive, fertile" of the soil: Arnold, *Chrestom*. 26/14 [F. A. Arnold. *Chrestomathia arabica*. Halle, 1853] and several passages in the *Gloss. Bibl. Geogr.* IV, 254 [*Bibliotheca geographarum arabicorum*, pars quarta. Continens indices, glossarium et addenda et emendanda ad.part I–III, M. J. de Goeje. Lugduni Bat. 1879]. Similar in Ḥarīrī *Durra 3*, 5, according to al-Khafāgī (and likewise in A. J. Silvestre de Sacy, *Anthologie grammaticale arabe*. Paris, 1829, p. 63, cf. p. 123), whereas Thorbecke [H. A. Thorbecke, ed., *al- Ḥarīrī, Durrat al-gawwas* Leipzig, 1871] uses *zakkā* followed by the accusative *zākin* of Allah's glory: Umajja b. A. ṣ Ṣalt XXXII, 6; of rain, Wright *Opusc*. 31/5 [W. Wright, *Opuscula Arabica* (Leiden, 1859)]. Elative *'azkā* "most fertile, best land": *Iṣṭakhrī*, cf. *Gl. Geogr. zakkā* "to help thrive, to bless"; Umajja XXXVII, 6 (= Nasr. 226/17), *Durra* ibid.; stem IV "to further" (as opposed to *naqaṣa*, to diminish) *Huḏail*. 70/4 [*The Hudsailian Poems*, ed. J. G. L. Kosegarten (numbers 1–138), vol. I, London 1854].—In addition, *zakā* "to spend well," elative *'azkā* "magnificent" (especially of a smell, thus like *ḏakkā*): Socin *Diwan* Gloss. [H. Stumme (Hrsg.), A. Socin, *Diwan aus Centralarabien*, 3 Bde, Leipzig 1900–1901]—*zukwatun = najlun Naqā''iḍ* 157/7. *mazka'un* Khiz. IV, 115 [*The Naqā''iḍ of Jarīt and al-Farazdaq*, ed. A. A. Bevan, 2 vols, Leiden 1905–1909; *Ḫizānat al-adab wa-lubb lubāb lisān al-'arab, al-Bagdādī*. 4 vols., Būlāq, 1291] ("support": Nöldeke, 1910, p. 219) may possibly be connected to *zakā* in the sense of "asylum," "sanctuary" (Lane's translation following the dictionaries. [E. W. Lane, *Arabic English Lexicon*, 8 vols., London, 1863–1893]).

15. [R. Payne Smith, *Thesaurus Syriacus*, 2 vols., Oxford, 1879–1901.]

16. [Friedrich Schulthess, ed. and trans., *Kalila und Dimna* (Syriac), 2 vols., Berlin, 1911.]

17. There is a semasiological parallel to *zaku* "to be immune": *ḏkw* (*zkw*) "to thrive" in *bara'a* "to be immune," Syriac *brē* "free" (Mārā b. Sarapion: *Spicil. Syr.* 47 18), if not "to be cured" (or "immune") like the Christian-Palestinian *br'* "healthy": Assyrian *baru* "to be fertile" = Hebrew א ר ב *br'* (and *Hebrew* ה ר ב *brh*).

18. In the Koran *dikr* appears to be some form of practical expression of piety, apparently a memory of old prophets' tales and the like. (Cf. Goldziher, *Vorlesungen über den Islam*, Heidelberg, 1910. 153.—*Red.*)

19. As is the case in the entire Muslim tradition. Cf. Umajja XXXII, 14: *fa-'ad'uwa 'ilā l-lāhi fir'awna l-laḏī kāna ṭāġiyan.*

20. It certainly does not mean "to soil."

21. Cf. Nöldeke (1910), p. 15 et seqq. on this chapter.

22. *Matrabah* XC, 16 (like *maš'amah* and *maymanah* verses 18 and 19) is probably also due to the constraint imposed by the rhyme, for *ḏū matrabah* was hardly used, but rather *ḏū turābin* in the sense of *ibn ġabrā'i* Kāmil 710 top [*The Kāmil of al-Mubarrad*, ed. W. Wright (Leipzig, 1864–1892)] *Muraṣṣa'* Z. 2545 sq. (= *Kitāb al- Muraṣṣa'*, ed. C. F. Seybold [Weimar, 1896, *Semitistische Studien*, 10/11]). It is just as unlikely that *ḏū maqrabah* (verse 15) was used, but rather *ḏū l-qurbā*, as in XXX, 37. It would have been admissible in verse 15 in terms of the rhyme, but was untenable for reasons of rhythm.

23. This is reminiscent of the misunderstanding discovered by Wellhausen, *Skizzen und Vorarbeiten* VI, 189 (cf. J. Wellhausen. *Einleitung in die drei ersten Evangelien* [Berlin, 1905], p. 27). *But rather give alms of such things as you have; then indeed all things are clean to you:* Luke 11 41. In my view, translating *zakāhā* by "purifies it" would be doing little better than the Greek.

24. Well-known analogies in C. Brockelmann, *Grundriss der vergleichenden Grammatik der Semitischen Sprachen*, 2 vols. (Berlin, 1908–13), p. 633, no. 2.

25. Perhaps following Ibn 'Abbās and Ibn Zaid, cf. above, p. 150, no. 1.

26. *Gloss. Bibl. Geogr.* IV, 254; Dozy I, 597 a.b. [R. Dozy, *Supplément aux Dictionnaires arabes*, 2 vols. (Leiden, 1881). Many forms apparently belonging to *dassa* originated from *jassa* by dissimilation in the style of *jašīšah* > *dašīšah* (ZA XX, 190 et seq.). Thus *dasīs* "spy"; Jāḥiẓ *Bukhalā* XLV, 11 *dāsūs* and its modern dialect form *dīsūs* for *jāsūs* (Kämil 629, Mas'ūdī V, 242 paen.), *jūsūs* is also modern [Syriac *jsws'*] (actually "sensor"), in pure Arabic *ra'idu 'aynin*. Also *midass* "sonde/probe" instead of or alongside *mijass* etc. On *dazza, kazza* see Landberg

Etudes I, 126, N. [Carlo de Landberg, *Études sur les dialectes de l'Arabie méridionale*, 4 vols. (Leiden, 1901–1913).] Cf. also Ruzicka, BA VI, 4, p. 178.—Already in *Ḥam.* 219, v. 2: *dassū fārisan minhum* the Scholiast uses *dassa* as the denominative of *dāsūs* "to send out as a scout."

27. Gloss, *Balāḏurī*, Dozy I, 439 b.; cf. *madsūs* 440 b.

28. [C. C. Torrey. *The Commercial-Theological Terms in the Koran*, Leiden 1892]

29. [Q. W. Freytag, ed., *Arabum proverbia* II 1838–1843 Bonnae et Rhenum.]

2.3

The Koran and the Linguistic Theory of Utterance Act[1]

Pierre Larcher

1. Concerning "linguistic" usage(s) of the Koran

For a linguist, even[2] an Arabist or specialist of Arabic, the Koran is nothing other than a text written in Arabic; a text that he normally only consults to verify in context a quote found by way of another text. The indifference of the majority of Arabist linguists of today to the Koranic text, easy to verify statistically,[3] is explicable by reasons at the same time internal and external to the discipline. Internal: Arabic linguistics has today broken off from the conception, at one and the same time monist and autistic, of Arabic, inherited as is well known from Arabic linguistics tradition, and succinctly symbolized by the slogan "Arabic, language of the Koran." External: in so far as these Arabist linguists are Occidental, or, better still, Western Europeans, sprung from liberal and secular societies, the Koranic universe is culturally and, even more, intellectually, the exact opposite of theirs. . . . To this structural feature is added another, of contemporary relevance: there is no doubt that the phenomenon known under various names ("the return of Islam," "the rise of Islamism," etc.) acts like a powerful foil! While understandable, this indifference must not be pushed too far, at the risk of confusion, for which I can personally vouch: a specialist of modern Arabic coming across every day in the Arabic press the expression *ḥizb Allāh* referred it correctly to a Near Eastern Islamist movement, without being aware that it was a Koranic expression![4]

The second part of the "linguistic" definition of the Koran aims to remind one that the question remains unanswered, which is obviously not "taboo," of the composition of the Koranic corpus itself. If the theological ("revelation") or traditional ("'Uthmānic recension") replies satisfy the Muslim believer (who, it is true, does not have a possible binary choice),[5] they only have, for everyone else, beginning with the linguist, an anecdotal interest, on the whole. A "revelation," in the technical religious sense of the term, is not, by definition, an empirical fact: it is a belief—or a dogma. As to the "Uthmanic recension," we need, for it to pass from the status of a hypothesis to that of a fact, to have 'Uthmānic Korans. It is hardly necessary to note that the oldest ones that we know of are much later. In this context, a linguist is perfectly justified in formulating his own hypotheses, provided that they are linguistically grounded.

That is what our colleague Louis de Prémare has done recently, here, in a brief article with a thought-provoking title,[6] where he shows, on an essentially lexical basis, that an episode traditionally situated in a Yemeni context and before Islam would be better understood in a Mesopotamian context and after Islam. The logical consequences of such hypotheses, namely, that the Koran is not only a text but also that this text has a history, have been accepted for a long time across the Rhine,[7] across the Channel,[8] and even across the Atlantic;[9] all societies that do not call themselves secular have nonetheless preserved enough critical thought to make the necessary distinction between theological "truths" and historical facts. On the other hand, in France, one notes on these subjects an extreme cautiousness that, to my mind, can only be explained by the morbid fascination that closed societies exercise upon an intelligentsia, more shaped by Karl Marx than Karl Popper.[10]

In theory, all Arabist linguists know (or should know) that the Koranic text, such as we know it today, is not *ne varietur*. The tradition of "seven canonical readings," laid down in the tenth century, is, as we have just suggested, all that remains of a variation, which was much more widespread and lasted much longer that wants to pass the thesis, ideologically more convenient than historically confirmed, off as true of an "'Uthmānic recension." But, in practice, even this "residual" variation is not linguistically exploited. The exclusive citation of the Cairo edition (*Ḥafṣ 'an 'Āsim*, i.e., reading of *'Āsim* transmitted by *Ḥafṣ*), recommended, when it is not imposed, by so many journals, has ended by conferring on the Koranic text an untouchability that historically it never had! A pity, even if the objective assigned by Rudi Paret[11] to the study of *qirā'āt* ("to put to good use the known and still unknown variants with a view to studying the ancient Arabic dialects and, in general, with a view to preparing a historical grammar of Arabic") seems today excessively ambitious. Nonetheless, the simple collation of the Cairo edition with the Western version (N. Africa; W. Africa) of *Warš ʿan Nāfiʿ* (reading of *Nāfiʿ* as transmitted by *Warš*) is always fruitful from the linguistic point of view. To give one example: while in the Eastern Koran there are five occurrences of *salam*, with a short *a*, of which four occur in combination with the verb *'alqā* (IV, 90 and 91; XVI, 28 and 87), in the Western Koran, there are six: the latter reads in fact *salam* in IV, 94 (where the word is equally combined with *'alqā*) while the former reads *salām* (with long *ā*). This suggests (1) that *salam* and *salām* are two variants of one and the same word, (2) that the collocation *'alqā al-sala(ā)m*, has everywhere the sense, not of "mission," and (3) allows us to hypothesize on the way that the three concepts of "submission," "protection/preservation," and "peace" are connected to one another, and subsumed under the root √ *slm* as "preserving (the war)" and "protection" as a result of "submission."[12] Nevertheless, by way of the history of Arabic grammar, which in recent years has greatly interested Arabist linguists, one can suppose that the question of *qirā'āt* [readings] will soon be back in favor.

In short, the mention, in our linguistic definition of the Koran, of an "Arabic" not otherwise qualified aims to remind one that the question that historically has troubled Arabist linguists the most cannot be considered today as resolved. This question is obviously, what is Koranic Arabic? That is to say, what is its place and status in the historical picture of the Arabic language? Otherwise stated what are its relations with what the Arabists call the *poetical koine* on the one hand, and what they glimpse of the ancient Arabic dialects, and, among them, a hypothetical "dialect of the Quraysh" on the other? The well-known theological thesis that identifies Koranic Arabic with the "dialect of the Quraysh," itself identified with what was later to be called *al-luġa al-fuṣḥā*,[13] is in reality only the conclusion of a syllogism whose premiss is verse 4 of sura XIV.[14]

For the linguist, such a dialect is hypothetical, simply because it is not documented in an independent way.[15] A more credible hypothesis would appear to be that of the Arabists who see in Koranic Arabic a language, if not identical, at least very close, to the language of pre-Islamic poetry, which they call, because of its homogeneity, *a poetical koine.* An Arabist linguist, even devoted to the classical language, cannot not be, more or less, a sociolinguist. Consequently, he would readily accept the following two propositions: (1) the polysegmented character of traditional Arab society has as a linguistic correlative polydialectalism, and (2) inversely, the existence of contacts between these different segments results in the emergence from these vernaculars of an Arabic *lingua franca* (such phenomena can be observed today in the Arab world and elsewhere). But from there to admit, without more ado, the existence of commercials fairs, scenes of poetical contests in this language (notably that of Okâz, near Mecca, a localization that opportunely leads back to the *Ḥijāz*), is a step that he cannot take. There again, pre-Islamic poetry itself is not independently attested before Islam.[16] One is reduced to comparing the language of this poetry, such as we know it, with that of the epigraphic material preserved. Now, the latter is both very scant and superabundant. It is very scant in the case of the dated Arabic inscriptions (two, to be precise, that of *Namāra* and of *Ḥarrān*, others being datable only approximately). The inscription of *Namāra* (328 CE) bears witness to a classic feature: *lm yblgh*, universally recognized as the negative particle *lam*, followed by the imperfect. Superabundant, as regards to the 20000 Safaitique graffiti (1st to 4th centuries CE?), certain brief and repetitive, documentation of a north Arabian language, very close to the Arabic, but not identical with, if we take the article (*h*- or *hn*- and not *al*-) as a criterion, but which bears witness to many linguistic and cultural features of pre-Islamic poetry.[17] In this context, one cannot neglect a third hypothesis which, basically, was already that of Vollers,[18] that of the homogenization a posteriori of poetico-Koranic Arabic.[19]

The Arabist linguists are more interested in the language of the Koranic text than in the latter as *parole* [see glossary], to use Saussurien terminology, or, to use that of contemporary linguists, as *discourse*. No doubt we could find, yesterday as today, studies on "stylistics,"[20] "poetics,"[21] or "rhetoric."[22] Recently, Alan Jones, in his article already cited, reminds us how the Koranic discourse was, stylistically and argumentatively, a tributary of traditional discourses before Islam, such that one can get an idea of it through the scant extant material (Islam, like all "closed" systems, having made of the past a *tabula rasa*). Jones enumerates four of them: those of the *kāhin*, of the *khaṭīb*, of the *qāṣṣ*, and documentary.

Apart from these different "linguistic" usages of the Koran, there exists one, indirect, that I intimated in recalling above that the *qirā'āt* were used at the same time for the history of Arabic and that of the traditional Arabic grammar or, as one would say today, in directly imitating English, Arabic grammatical tradition. The majority of Arabist linguists today are at the same time historians of this grammatical tradition, and more generally, linguistic tradition.[23]

2. An "indirect" usage: the history of Arabic linguistic tradition

This traditional "Arabic linguistics" or Arabic linguistics tradition is obviously an object constructed by the historians, though it is not without precedent in the Arabo-Muslim space itself. One can cite the *Miftāḥ al-'ulūm* of Sakkākī († 626 /1229), which is a veritable encyclopedia of language sciences, combining grammar, rhetoric, logic and poetics.[24] One can equally cite the chapter of the *Muqaddima* (I. 1055–70) titled *fī 'ulūm al-lisān al-'arabī* ("Of the sciences of the Arabic language") also, according to Ibn Khaldūn, four in number: lexicography, grammar, syntax and style (*bayān*), and literature. The comparison of these two quadruplets shows that they have in common two disciplines, grammar and rhetoric, which constitute the hard core of the Arabic linguistic tradition, as well as a certain number of differences of which I shall only note two here. Sakkākī conceives (p. 2) these four disciplines as "a certain number of species of *'adab* forming a coherent whole" ("*'iddat 'anwā'* [*al- 'adab*] *muta'ākhiḏa*"). He thus gives to the whole the name *'adab* that Ibn Khaldūn gives to one of the parts of his construction. It is just that Sakkākī puts the accent on the relations uniting these different disciplines, bipartite rhetoric being understood as a "complement" (*tamām*) of the syntactical part of the grammar, the logic as a "complement" of *'ilm al-ma'ānī* and the poetics as a complement of *'ilmay al-ma'ānī wa-l-bayān*. Conversely, Ibn Khaldūn puts the accent on the relations uniting the properly linguistic disciplines with the disciplines not strictly speaking linguistic:

"knowledge of them all is necessary for religious scholars, since the source of all religious laws is the Qur'ān and the Sunnah, which are in Arabic. Their transmitters, the men around Muḥammad and the men of the second generation, were Arabs. Their difficulties are to be explained from the language they used. Thus, those who want to be religious scholars must know the sciences connected with the Arabic language."[25] (*wa - maʿrifatuhā ḍarūriyya ʿalā ʾahl al-sharī ʿa ʾidh maʾkhadh al-ʾaḥkām al- shar ʿiyya kullihā min al-kitāb wa- l-sunna wa-hiya bi-lughat al-ʿArab wa- naqalatuhā min al-Ṣaḥāba wa-l- Tābiʿīna ʿArab wa- sharḥ mushkilātihā min lughatihim fa-lā budda min maʿrifat al-ʿulūm al-mutaʿalliqa bi-hādhā l-lisān li-man ʾarāda ʿilm al-sharīʿa*).

Indeed, Ibn Khaldūn particularly underscores the link between Arabic linguistics and the discipline known as *ʾuṣūl al-fiqh*, which includes the Koran and the Sunna as two of its components. Ibn Khaldūn is interested in the role of Arabic linguistics in what has been termed juridical or normative hermeneutics.[26]

THE *ʾUṢŪL AL-FIQH*: PRAGMATICS AND JURIDICAL HERMENEUTICS

Opening the late encyclopedias, which are the *Kulliyyāt al-ʿulūm* of ʾAbū l-Baqāʾ al-Kaffawī († 1094 /1683)—a simple synthesis of a certain number of earlier works[27]—one finds this definition of *ḥukm*: "In the terminology of the scholars of *ʾuṣūl* it is the speech of God relating to acts of the subjugated, which imposes or gives a choice" (*fī ṣtilāḥ ʾaṣḥāb al-ʾuṣūl khiṭāb Allāh al-mutaʿalliq bi-ʾaf ʿāl al-mukallafīn bi-l-iqtiḍāʾwa-l-takhyīr*), Kaffawī adding: "It is also said that it is mental discourse and the signified of order and defense, of obligation and prohibition" (*yuqāllahu al-kalām al-nafsī wa-madlūl al-ʾamr wa-l-nahy wa-l-ʾījāb wa -l- taḥrīm*).[28]

We will come back to this double definition, but, at this point, what draws the linguist's attention is that these definitions closely mix strictly linguistic and nonstrictly linguistic vocabulary, beginning with, in the first case, the term, which for a speech act linguist is entirely appropriate, *khiṭāb*.

If one turns to the article *khiṭāb* in the same encyclopedia, one reads:

"*Kalām* said of the signifying expression by institution and its signified, remaining in the mind, the address is either the verbal discourse or the mental discourse directed towards the other, with the aim of making oneself understood." (*wa-l-kalām yuṭlaq ʿalā l-ʿibāra al-dālla bi-l-waḍʿ wa-ʿalā madlūli-hā al-qāʾim bi-l-nafs fa-l-khiṭāb ʾimmā al-kalām al-lafẓī ʾaw al-kalām al-nafsī al-muwajjah naḥwa l-ghayr li-l-ʾifhām*).

There again such a definition closely mixes the linguistic and the non-linguistic. The linguist is obviously interested in the exact definition of the address as discourse orientated toward the other. A priori, he is not interested in the distinction between the two discourses, which for him is a theological problem.[29] Nevertheless, the distinction between the two discourses is the solution contributed by Muslim theology to a dispute, that of *ṣifāt Allāh*, and a means of avoiding a contradiction: Allah being eternal, one cannot attribute to Him speech (*kalām*), meaning by the latter something verbal (which, by definition, occurs in time). Instead, one attributes to Him mental speech, which alone is eternal (*qadīm* (*fī l-ʾazal*)). But this distinction comes from far: from ancient philosophy, as Claude Chiesa[30] reminded us during a conference in Paris, in 1991, on "Linguistic Theories and Mental Operations" organized by the Societé d'Histoire et d'Epistémologie des Sciences du Langage (SHESL) (the History and Epistemology of the Language Sciences Society), which culminates in the Porphyrian theory of *tres orationes*, or the three states of discourse: written, oral, and mental. This is a theory that one meets again intact in the *ʾuṣūl al-fiqh*, where the *kitāba* (writing) and consequently the *kitāb* (Writing with a capital W) is understood as the signifier of a signified that is the *kalām lafẓī*, itself understood as the signifier of a signified that is the *kalām nafsī*.[31] This distinction is met again in medieval theology in the Latin West, and may I call attention to a colleague of SHESL, the Canadian Claude Panaccio, who is interested in this problem, using retrospectively, for heuristic reasons, the linguistic theories of the American Jerry Fodor on mental language.[32]

Objectively the *ḥukm sharʿī* is the juridical interpretation of a Koranic verse (or a saying of the Prophet) thus guaranteed, as moreover Ibn Khaldūn intimated when he said the legal norms were drawn from the *Kitab* and the Sunna. But when the *ʾuṣūliyyūn* assimilate the *ḥukm* to the *khiṭāb*, it is a question of, as the second definition of *ḥukm* indicates, *khiṭāb nafsī*, the signified of *khiṭāb lafẓī*, which is its signifier: the *ḥukm* thus comes before *khiṭāb lafẓī*. If thus the *ḥukm* is drawn from *Kitāb*, signifier of *kalām lafẓī*, of which it is the signified, itself signifying *khiṭāb nafsī*, which is the *ḥukm*, we then have a magnificent hermeneutic circle, the *ʾuṣūlī* pretending not to have done anything but recover the eternal "intention" of the legislator. In other words, Ibn Khaldūn recognizes that the *ḥukm sharʿī* is a juridical interpretation when he says that the *ḥukm sharʿī* is drawn from the *Kitab*, that is, going from *kitab* toward the *hukm*, but theologically we go from the *hukm* toward the *kitab*, the *khiṭāb lafẓī* expressing the *khiṭāb nafsī* (and the *khiṭāb nafsī* is the *ḥukm sharʿī*).

That is exactly what is happening when one sees an *ʾuṣūlī* like Asnawī (died 772/1371) write in the *Nihāya* referring to the *Maḥṣūl* of Fakhr al-Dīn al-Rāzī (died 606 / 1209):

> When we say "the *ḥukm* is eternal," that means, as [Fakhr al-Dīn al-Rāzī] declared in the *Maḥṣūl* that God the Most High has said in eternity, "I authorize [*ʾadhintu*] such and such man to have relations with such and such woman, if for example they are married" (*maʿnā qawlinā al-ḥukm qadīm kamāqāla fī l-Maḥṣūl ʾanna Allāha taʿālā qāla fī l-ʾazal ʾadhintu li-fulān ʾan yaṭaʾ fulāna mathalan ʾidhā jarā baynahumā nikāḥ*).[33]

The "hermeneutic" character of such a proposition follows directly from the fact that it is not a question of a *literal* utterance of the Koran. In placing in the field of a *qāla Allāh* (Allah said) something that is not literally said in the Koran, the *ʾuṣūlī* are going to the logical extreme of the two *kalām*: a *kalām nafsī* is still a *kalām*. There again, a linguist seems to have nothing to say. In fact, there is much to say. If this linguist is a "cognitivist," he could surely think of what Jerry Fodor calls "language of thought," but if he is an "utteringist," the doubling of *kalām*, such as practiced by the *ʾuṣūliyyūn*, will make him think of the doubling of the utterance, such as it appears in the works of the linguist Oswald Ducrot:[34]

> The central idea is that one ought to, in this description of utterance which constitutes the meaning of the utterance distinguish between the author of the words (speaker) and the agents of illocutionary acts (performer of illo-

cutionary acts) in a correlative way, namely, the person to whom the words are addressed (the "addressee ") and those who are the sufferers of acts (the "consignee").

The illocutionary act is a generalization of the category of "performative," inaugurated in the West by the English philosopher Austin.[35] I have shown, in my thesis,[36] summarized in a certain number of articles,[37] that the Arabic linguistic tradition had its exact analogue in the category of *ʾinshāʾ* (lit. "creation").

That for the *ʾuṣūlī* the juridical sense of the Koranic utterance is the equivalent of the act of its utterance is indicated by the form itself that he gives to the formula representing the latter, the form *ʾadhintu*, "I authorize." The latter is not in the "past tense" (*māḍī*) because it is followed by *ʾidhā*: the formula *p ʾidhā* "if" *q* (where *p* and *q* are propositions) must not be confused with *ʾidhā p, q*. In other words, we are not here in the system of the double sentence and more especially in a hypothetical system where a condition (*sharṭ*) serves to frame an assertion, the truth of *q* depending on that of *p*. We are on the contrary in what the jurists call a "performative" (*ʾinshāʾ*), "suspended" (*muʿallaq*) from a condition, for example, *allaqtu- ki ʾin dakhalti l-dāra* ("I repudiate you, if you enter the house.")[38] If there were any doubt that this is a performative, it would be allayed by another example that follows, again citing the *Maḥṣūl* of Fakhr al-Dīn al-Rāzī saying: "The fact that the act is lawful has no other meaning than that Allāh, the Most High says: 'I consider the perpetrator not at fault' and the divine norm, it is this statement and it is he who relates it to the human act" *(lā maʿnā li-kawn al-fiʿl ḥalāl ʾillā qawl Allāh taʿālā rafaʿtu l-ḥaraj ʿan fāʿilihi fa-ḥukm Allāh taʿālā huwa hādhā l-qawl wa-huwa mutaʿalliq bi-fiʿl al-ʿabd*). Let us remark that the form *faʿaltu* is the usual form only of the "operatives" (*ʾinshāʾ ʾīqāʿī*), type *biʿtu* "I sell." In adopting it to represent the *ḥukm sharʿī*, the *ʾuṣūliyyūn* are thus drawing a parallel between the creation of the contract and the creation of the norm, a parallel equally drawn by certain philosophers of law, having read Austin.[39]

In the same way as Allah is understood not as a speaker, but as an utterer, that is to say not the one responsible for the utterance, but one responsible for the illocutionary acts accomplished in the utterance, so the other protagonist of the process of utterance is not understood as a simple addressee or the addressed one (*mukhāṭab*) but more precisely as the consignee, in the Ducrot sense, that is to say, the one submitting to the illocutionary act. This consignee in fact has the Arabic name of *mukallaf*, which is the passive participle of the verb *kallafa*, whose verbal noun *taklīf* constitutes the first and principal category of *khiṭāb* or *ḥukm*.

It is not difficult to see that the classification of *khiṭāb* in the works of the *ʾuṣūliyyūn* is closely related to that of *kalām* in the works of the rhetoricians. Where the rhetoricians divide the *kalām* into *khabar* ("affirmation") and non-*khabar*, the *ʾuṣūliyyūn* divide the *khiṭāb* into *ṭalab* ("demand, request" synonymous with *ʾiqtiḍāʾ*)[40] and non-*ṭalab*.

The substitution of *khiṭāb* by *kalām* and the focusing on the *ṭalab* in place of *khabar* ("affirmation") obviously accentuates the pragmatic character of the classification. According as what is in its field "to do" (*fiʿl*) or "not to do, refrain" (*tark*) and as what is "categoric" (*jāzim*) or not (*ghayr jāzim*), the *ṭalab* is an "obligation" (*ījāb*) and a prohibition (*taḥrīm*), a "recommendation" (*nadb*), and a "reprimand" (*karāhiya*). In the same way that, in the works of the rhetoricians, the non-*khabar*, usually called *ʾinshāʾ*, is subdivided into *ṭalabī* jussive and *ghayr ṭalabī* (non jussive), in the works of the *ʾuṣūliyyūn*, the non-*ṭalab* is subdivided into *takhyīr* ("to give a choice") and *ʾikhbār* ("assertion"). In the first case, it is a "permission" (*ʾibāḥa*); in the second, it does not impose, but "states, sets down" (*waḍʿ*); it is no longer a prescription (limitation), but an "ascription."[41] These six legislative acts constitute the *ʾaḥkām al-shar ʿiyya*, five "prescriptives" and one "ascriptive" (*waḍʿī*). Although there were as many *ʾaḥkām al-shar ʿiyya*, "prescriptives," in the works of the *ʾuṣūliyyūn* as kinds of *ṭalab* in the works of the rhetoricians—five—one notes nevertheless only four among them that derive from *ṭalab*, the fifth derives from *takhyīr*. But the *takhyīr* is nothing other than giving the choice between acting and not acting, in other words, to say "do" and "not do": as a result of which the *takhyīr*, and consequently the *mubāḥ*, all being from another point of view simply the *ṭalab*, of which as noted was logically and meticulously organized, is no less related to the four other *ʾaḥkām*.

4. Toward a Polyphonic Analysis of Koranic Discourse

Once it is realized that (1) the mechanism of the juridical interpretation of the Koran was, from the linguistic point of view, a theory of utterance and more particularly of illocutionary acts (the juridical meaning of the sentence being the pragmatic value of its utterance) that there was from this point of view a close interaction between the *ʾuṣūl al-fiqh* and one of the two components of the *balāgha* called *ʿilm al-maʿānī*, and (2) that the theological distinction of the two *kalām* -s could be reinterpreted linguistically as a speaker/utterer distinction opening the way to a *polyphonic*[42] vision of the Koranic utterance, one would be tempted to continue to interrogate the Arabic linguistic tradition in this sense: then one would easily find elements belonging to what for today's linguist is a theory of verbal interactions on the one hand, and argumentation on the other.

In the first chapter of *ʿilm al-maʿānī*, devoted to *khabar,* one finds a distinction between *khabar ibtidāʾī, ṭalabī*, and *ʾinkārī*. The first is addressed to someone without an idea as to the contents of the proposition *p*; the second is addressed to someone having a questioning attitude as regards *p*; and finally the third is addressed to someone having an attitude of denial as regards *p*. In other words, the *khabar ṭalabī* and *ʾinkārī* derive their name, not from utterances having an affirmative form and imperative or renunciatory meaning, but from affirmations, according to the correct interpretation of Simon,[43] reacting to an attitude of interrogation (*ṭalabī*) or denial (*ʾinkārī*) of the interlocutor, a reaction that leaves a trace, optional or obligatory (*ʾinna, la-*), in the utterance. Thus, a rhetorician like Qazwīnī (died 739/1338), whom we quote here,[44] exemplifies all this with Koranic utterances (the *khabar ṭalabī* by Koran XXXVI, 14): *ʾinnā ʾilaykum mursalūna* (yes, we were sent to you) which replies to the first denial of the "inhabitants of the city," to whom had been sent two messengers, reinforced by a third, and the *khabar ʾinkārī* by Koran XXXVI, 16, *rabbunā yaʿlamu ʾinnā ʾilaykum la- mursalūna* ("Our Lord knows that we are surely sent to you"), which replies to the second denial, explicit, of the same inhabitants: *mā ʾantum ʾillā basharun mithlunā* ("you are only men like us etc."). The rhetoricians of the Arabic language themselves thus open the door to a polyphonic analysis of the Koran, unsurprisingly. The Koranic discourse being very frequently polemical, one "hears" the "voice" of the other, whether it concerns a historical opponent or a opponent constructed for a particular need.[45]

A pragmatist easily recognizes this polemical character, with a connective such as *bal*, which occurs 127 times in the Koran.[46] The names that the grammarians give to *bal* are quite appropriate to the description of the latter in coherent discourse (*p bal q*), where the same speaker-utterer "gives up" (*ʾiḍrāb*) determination for the other and "checks himself" (*tadāruk*), in other words corrects himself. They are far less appropriate when *bal* is used in a dialogue (*p- bal q*, which predominates in the Koran),[47] where *bal q* does not work by a simple correction, but a negation-correction (e.g., II, 135):

wa-qālū kūnū Hūdan ʾaw naṣārā tahtadū qul bal millata ʾIbrāhīma ḥanīfan wa-mā kāna mina l-mushrikīna: "They said: 'Be Jews or Christians, you will be on the right path.' Say: 'But no! . . . [Be] the community of Abraham, a true believer, he was not one of those associationists.'"

One becomes aware of this negation-correction in comparing the Koranic discourse, where the ellipsis of the negation is the rule, with classical and modern prose, where, most often, there is first negation, then correction (*p [= Neg. p'] bal q*), for example:

wālidat Ḥasan saʾalat-hu kayfa kāna ḥāluka yā waladī maʿ a hādhā l-ajamī fa-qāla lahā lam yakun ʿ ajamiyyan bal majūsiyyan yaʿbudu l-nārdūna l-malik al-jabbār: "'How did it go with this Persian, my son?' his mother asked Hassan. 'It was not a Persian, but a Zoroastrian, worshipper of Fire and not the All-Powerful Lord,' he replied to her."[48]

5. KORAN, LOGIC, AND ARGUMENTATION

The connective *bal* leads naturally to the other Arabic connective having a corrective function, *lākin (na)* (65 occurrences of each in the Koran). While *p bal q* corrects *p*, which it denies explicitly or implicitly, by means of *q*, *plākin (na) q* corrects preventitively (*istidrāk*), by means of *q*, the false conclusion *r*, which risks being drawn from *p*, according to the exact description of the grammarian Raḍī al-Dīn al-Astarābādhī (died after 688/1289).[49] Here we are not only in the heart of pragmatics, but further and more particularly in argumentation (see Larcher, 1996, pp. 494–96).

Claude Gilliot, in his review already quoted, reminded us that "we are still awaiting a serious study of the logic of the Koran." Insofar as logic is often understood in a restrictive sense (i.e., as the logic of the logicians), it would be better to speak of argumentation. The difference between the two orders will appear clearly with a connective such as *ʾin*, which often passes for logic, but which we shall show to be esssentially belonging to pragmatics and argumentation.

There are 692 occurrences of *ʾin* in the Koran, the great majority concerning *ʾin* as "a particle of condition," sign of the potential mood (the *Muʿjam al-ʾadawāt*, unfortunately, does not count the negative *ʾin* separately). If *ʾin* is on the whole conditional, the hypothetical systems in *ʾin* have on the whole, not the form *ʾin p, q*, but *ʾin p fa-q* (where between the protasis and apodosis appears a *fa-* termed "of the apodosis"). But, although this *fa-* appears as soon as there is a formal rupture of the system, this formal rupture is just as much semantic, as one can verify through IX, 80, *ʾin tastaghfir lahum sabʿīna marratin fa-lan yaghfira llāhu lahum*: "If you ask for forgiveness for them seventy times, God will not pardon them." If one interprets this system logically, that is, if one considers it as an assertion of a relation of implication between *p* and *q* (*p*? *q*), it amounts to saying that human prayers are not simply inefficacious, but they also achieve the opposite effect to what was intended! The presence of *fa-* tempts one to give an argumentative interpretation: *ʾin p* presents in fact here *p* as an argument in favor of the implicit conclusion *r* = "Allah will pardon them" (*lan* ʿ *lā ʾan* is structurally a modal negation). In other words, IX, 80 means in fact: "[Even] if you ask (were asking) forgiveness for them seventy times, Allah will not (would not) pardon them." We are here not in the logical order of the condition, but that of the argumentative concession. Another example of the system *ʾin p fa-q* operating a pragmatic connection and not a logical one is supplied by XII, 77: *ʾin yasriq fa-qad saraqa ʾakhun lahu min qablu* "If he steals, it is that a brother of his stole earlier." Such an example, as interesting as it is, is to the argumentative order, what contraposition is in the domain of Logic, in that there is, if not negation, at least permutation of the terms of the system. One sees in fact in this example that, not only is the truth of *q* independent of that of *p* (*q* is thus in no way the consequent of *p*), but even more that the assertion of *q* which serves in reality to justify the supposition of *p* (in other words, it is *q* which is the antecedent: the fact that a brother of his has stolen before justifies the hypothesis that he is himself a thief).

Conclusion

I have remarked in the introduction on the disinterest of the majority of Arabist linguists of today to the Koranic text. My conclusion could seem paradoxal. Between the two, in fact, I have put forward a certain number of arguments justifying why a linguist should interest himself in it and tried to show that, without ceasing to take an interest in it as a linguist, he could nonetheless make a useful contribution, even totally new, toward the restoration of an objective Islamology.

Notes

1. [Translated from the French by Ibn Warraq. Footnotes in square brackets by I.W.]

2. This *even* will only seem arguably strange to those who shut their eyes to certain Arabist complacency in linguistic matters and of which here is a recent example: at the end of the introduction to their translation of *l'Autobiographie d'un clerc chiite du Ǧabal ʿAmil* [*Autobiography of a Shiite scholar of Ǧabal ʿAmil*] (Damascus: Institut Français d'Etudes Arabes, 1998), the translators write: (p. 32): "all the references to the Koran are taken and freely adapted from the *attempts at translation* of Denise Masson et Jacques Berque" [my emphasis, Pierre Larcher]. In an Islamological context, the passage underlined by me is obviously an allusion to the dogma of *'Iǧāz al-Qur'ān*, one of whose avatars is its "untranslatability." Islamology, not having kept its distance, has been assimilated to Muslim apologetics—as the absence of quotation marks suggests. For a linguist, it goes without saying that there is translation (good, beautiful, faithful . . . or not) as soon as there is a transfer of one language into another.

3. Thus, out of the 293 and 329 items in the section Arabic Language of the *Index Islamicus* 1996 (published 1998) and 1997 (published 1999), respectively, one finds on each occasion just one dealing specifically with the Koran.

4. Koran V, 56, and LVIII, 22. In the second instance, it contrasts with a *ḥizb al-Šayṭān* (58: 19), where we can see that the "satanization" which has made the ayatollahs famous has Koranic foundations and, furthermore, how vain is the apology, of Muslim origin, but largely adopted by Islamologists and Islamic political scientists declaring that Islamic fundamentalism has nothing to do with the "true" Islam (just as "actual" socialism has nothing to do with "true" communism).

5. A Western Arabist obviously cannot ignore the fact that the Muslim world is, with what remains of "actual" socialism (and which is not nothing: Communist China, North Korea, Cuba . . .), the other great dogmatic universe existing on earth, where one cannot think this or that, but on the contrary must think this and not that. That limits de facto the relations that one can have with this world.

6. A.-L de Prémare, "Les éléphants de Qādisiyya," *Arabica* 45, no. 32: 61–69. To the hypothesis put forward, I willingly add one, regarding *siǧǧīl* which appears three times in the Koran (XI, 82; XV, 74; CV, 4), and three times in the context *ḥiǧāra min siǧǧīl*, stones of clay. Rather than a word of Persian or Sumerian origin, one can see there, with the hapax *siǧill* (XXI, 104) the doubling of a single Latin etymon *sigillum*, the "sigillified earth" being with *strata* (> *ṣirāṭ*), *castrum* (> *qaṣr*), *camisa* (>*qam īṣ*) . . . one of the signs of Romanness.

7. Besides the now classic *Geschichte des Qorans* (Leipzig, 1909, 1919, 1938) by T. Nöldeke et al, one could cite the recent *The Qur'ān as Text*, ed. Stefan Wild (Brill: Leiden, 1996) and notably, in this volume, the article by Gerd-R. Puin, "Observations on Early Qur'ān Manuscripts in Ṣan'ā'" [now also in Warraq, *What The Koran Really Says*].

8. Cf. the abrasive *Quranic Studies: Sources and Methods of Scriptural Interpretation* (Oxford, 1977) by John Wansbrough [new edition, with foreword, translations, and expanded notes by Andrew Rippin (Amherst, NY: Prometheus Books, 2004)] of which there is no French equivalent or even a French translation!

9. Cf. the recent article by Toby Lester "What Is the Koran?" in *Atlantic Monthly*, January 1999, pp. 43–56 [now also in Ibn Warraq, *What the Koran Really Says*].

10. A linguist can only be astonished to see so many Islamologists including the most distinguished, writing with capital letters and without quotation marks, Revelation, Recension of 'Uthmān, etc., while one should be doing the opposite, such terms only having in truth the status of a quotation.

11. V. "*Ḳirā'a*" in *EI*².

12. As the Koran suggests, IV, 91, counterbalancing IV, 90: *'in lam (. . .) yulqū 'ilaykumu l-salama (. . .) fa-khuḏūhum wa-qtulūhum* . . . "if they do not submit . . . , then seize them and kill them. . . ."

13. Cf. Ibn Khaldūn († 808 /1406), *Muqaddima,* I, p. 1072 (Beyrouth, 1967), "The speech of the Quraysh was the most pure and the most lucid of all the Arabic dialects because of their remoteness, on all sides, from the territory of the Non-Arabs . . ." (*li-hāḏā kānat lughat Qurayṣ 'afṣaḥ al-lughāt al-'arabiyya wa-'aṣraḥa-hā li-bu'dihim 'an bilād al-'ajam min jamī' jihātihim*).

14. Koran XIV, 4: *Mā 'arsalnā min rasūlin 'illā bi-lisāni qawmi-hi li-yubayyina lahum.* "We have sent you a messenger only in the language of his people so that he can make things clear."

15. This does not prevent (and this is another example of Arabist indulgence in linguistic matters) the cover of the new edition of the translation of the *Mou'allaqât* by J. J. Schmidt (L'esprit des péninsules, 1999) to carry this description: "this bouquet of flowers of the rhetoric of the desert" is "written in the same language as that of the Koran (the Arabic of the *Ḥijāz*)."

16. For completeness sake, the Ḥimyarite site of *Qāniya* in Yemen yielded a hymn dating from the first centuries of the Christian era, in a mixed language (Arabic / South Arabic) and presenting, apart from the differences, certain common characteristics with the *qaṣīda* (unity of meter and rhyme). Cf. Ch. Robin, "Les plus anciens monuments de la langue arabe" (the most ancient monuments of the Arabic language) in *L'Arabie antique de Karib'il à Mahomet. Nouvelles données sur l'histoire des Arabes grâce aux inscriptions REMMM* 61, no. 3 (1991): 3; Edisud, 1992, pp. 113–25, notably § 4. There is equally the inscription of 'En 'Avdat, Aramaeo-Arabic, which would not be later than 150 CE, and over which, since its discovery, a lot of ink has been spilled. James Bellamy, notably, wants to see there verses in the *ṭawīl* meter ("Arabic verses from the first /second century: the inscription of 'En 'Avdat," *JSS* 35 [1990]: 73–79). For the problems that this inscription poses see A. Ambros "Zur Inschrift von 'En 'Avdat –eine Mahnung zur Vorsicht," *ZAL* 27 (1994): 90–92.

17. M. C. A. Macdonald, "Safaitique," in *EI*[2].

18. Karl Vollers, *Volksprache und Schriftsprache im alten Arabien* (Strassburg, 1906; reprinted, Amsterdam, APA-Oriental Press, 1981).

19. For a recent overview of Koranic Arabic, cf. Alan Jones, "The Language of the Qur'ân," *Proceedings of the Colloquium on Arabic Lexicology and Lexicography (C.A.L.L.)*, ed. Kinga Devenyi, Tamas Ivanyi, and Avihai Shivtiel, part one, *The Arabist*, Budapest Studies in Arabic, 6–7, 1993, pp. 29–49.

20. Notably T. Nöldeke, "Zur Sprache des Korans" II. Stilistische und synktaktische Eigentümlichkeiten der Sprache des Korans in *Neue Beiträge zur Semitischen Sprachwissenschaft* (Strasburg: Trübner, 1910) (French translation under the title *Remarques critiques sur le style et la syntaxe du Coran*, translated with a postface

"Observations sociologiques sur le dogme de la précellence du Coran" by G. H. Bousquet (Paris: Maisonneuve, 1953). English translation now in present volume, chapter 2.1, pp. 73ff.).

21. For a recent example, cf. Michael Sells, "Sound and Meaning in *Sûrat al-Qâri'a*," *Arabica* 40, no. 3 (1993): 403–40.

22. For a recent example, cf. Michel Cuypers "Structures rhétoriques dans le Coran. Une analyse structurelle de la sourate 'Joseph' et de quelques sourates brèves," *MIDEO* 22 (1995): 107–95.

23. Under the influence of English we sometimes call in French "linguistique arabe" what in English we differentiate by Arabic Linguistics and Arab Linguistics. Cf. M. G. Carter, "Arab Linguistics and Arabic Linguistics," *Zeitschrift für Geschichte der arabisch -islamischen Wissenschaft* 4 (1987): 205–18.

24. *Miftāḥ al-ʿulūm* (Cairo, 1348H); (reprinted Beirut: Dar al-kutub al-'ilmiyya, n.d.).

25. [Ibn Khaldūn, *The Muqaddimah*, trans. Franz Rosenthal (Princeton, [abridged edn.] 1989), p. 433.]

26. Cf. Robert Brunschvig, "Herméneutique normative dans la judaïsme et dans l'islam," 1976, reprinted in *Etudes sur l'islam classique et l' Afrique du Nord* (London, 1986), pp. 233–52, and Claude Gilliot, "L'Herméneutique en islam," in *Encyclopédie des religions*, II, ed. Jean-Pierre Rosa (Paris: Bayard, 1997), pp. 2233–37.

27. Notably for the *ʾuṣūl al-fiqh*, the two of 'Âmidi († 631 /1233), *al-ʾIḥkām fī ʾuṣūl al-ʾaḥkām* (Cairo, 1487 / 1967), and *Muntahā al-sūl fī ʿilm al-ʾuṣūl* (Cairo, Muhammad 'Alī Ṣubayḥ, n.d.) and the two of Ibn al-Ḥājib (†646 / 1249), *Muntahā al-wuṣūl ʾilā ʿilmay al-jadal wa-l-ʾuṣūl* (Cairo, 1326H) and *Mukhtaṣar al- Muntahā al-ʾuṣūlī*, and the numerous commentaries of the latter, notably those of ʿAḍud al-din al-ʾIjī († 756 / 1355), Saʿd al-dīn al-Taftazānī († 791 /1389), and al-Sayyid al-Sharīf al-Jurjānī († 816 / 1413), collected together with the *matn* in *Shurūḥ al- Mukhtaṣar*, 2 vols. (Cairo, AH 1319).

28. ʿAdnān Darwīsh and Muḥammad al-Maṣrī, eds., *Kulliyyāt al-ʿulūm*, 5 vols. (Damascus, 1981).

29. This could also be the case of grammarians of the Arabic language, Muslims though they may be. Thus one reads in *Sharḥ qawāʿid al-ʾiʿrāb li-Ibn Hisham* of Muḥyī l-Dīn al-Kāfījī († 879 /1474–5) (Damascus, 1989), p. 65: "As to the fact of not applying 'speech' to the words of God, it is in order to safeguard morality and it is not legally permitted. One needs such an excuse, in fact, when one hears, through the speech of God, oral language" (*wa-ʾammā ʿadam ʾiṭlāq al-lafẓ ʿalā kalām Allāh taʿālā*

fa- li-riʿāyat al-ʾadab wa-li-ʿadam al-ʾidhn al-sharʿī fa-hādhā l-iʿtidhār ʾinnamā uḥtuyija ʾilayhi ʾidhā kāna al-murād min kalām Allāh huwa l-kalām al-lafẓi).

30. "Le problème du langage intérieur dans la philosophie antique de Platon à Porphyre," *Histoire Epistémologie Langage* 14, no. 2 (1992): 15–30.

31. *Shurūḥ al- Mukhtaṣar*, I, pp. 221sq. and II, pp. 48sq.

32. Cf. for example, "La philosophie du langage de Guillaume d'Occam," in *Geschichte der Sprachtheorie*, vol. 3, *Sprachtheorien in Spätantike und Mittelalter* (Tübingen, 1995), pp. 185–206. Panaccio distinguishes carefully between the Occam's theory and that of, further on, Boethius (who took up Porphyry) and that of St. Augustine (*verbum mentis*) and, of course, later still, that of Fodor. [J. Fodor, *The Language of Thought* (Harvard University Press, 1979); *Psychological Explanation* (New York, 1968)].

33. Bayḍāwī, *Nihāyat al-sūl fī sharḥ Minhāj al-wuṣūl ʾilā ʿilm al-ʾuṣūl* (Būlāq, AH 1316), I, p. 28.

34. Oswald Ducrot et al., *Les mots du discours* (Paris: Minuit, 1980), pp. 43–44.

35. John Langshaw Austin [1911–1960], *How to Do Things with Words* (Oxford: Oxford University Press, 1962) [French translation: *Quand dire, c'est faire* (Paris: Le Seuil, 1970)].

36. Pierre Larcher, *Information et performance en science arabo-islamique du langage*, PhD Thesis, University of Paris III, 1980, unpublished.

37. Notably in these pages, the series "Quand en arabe, on parlait de l'arabe . . . (I) Essai sur la méthodologie de l'histoire des métalangages arabes," "(II) "Essai sur la catégorie de *ʾinshā* (vs *Khabar*)," "(III) Grammaire, logique, rhétorique dans l'islam postclassique," *Arabica* 35, no. 2 (1988): 117–42; 38, no. 2 (1991): 246–73; 39, no. 3 (1992): 358–84. Cf. equally "Une pragmatique avant la pragmatique: 'médiévale,' 'arabe' et 'islamique,'" *Histoire Epistémologie Langage* 20, no. 1 (1998): 101–16 and "La relation entre la linguistique arabe et les autres sciences dans la société islamique," in *History of the Language Sciences*, *Handbücher zur Sprach- und Kommunikationswissenschaft* 18 (Berlin and New York: Walter de Gruyter, 2000), pp. 312–31.

38. Āmidī, *ʾIḥkām*, II, 131. We would get the same effect by putting *fa-* between the protasis and apodosis. On the other hand, without *fa-, ʾin dakhalti l-dāra ṭallaqtuki* would mean "if you enter the house, I shall repudiate you." That would no longer be a performative of "suspended" repudiation, but a simple threat of repudiation.

39. Christoph Grzegorzyk and Thomas Studnicki, "Les rapports entre la norme et la disposition légale," *Archives de philosophie du droit* 19 (1974): 243–56.

40. Cf. Āmidī, *'Iḥkām*, I, 91, who speaks of *khiṭāb al-'iqtiḍā' wa -l-ṭalab* and in *Muntahā*, p. 22 of *khiṭāb al-ṭalab*.

41. Cf. Āmidī who in *Muntahā*, p. 23, speaks of *khiṭāb al -waḍ' wa-l-'ikhbār*.

42. The reader interested by this concept and its history in modern Western linguistics should refer to my article "Le concept de polyphonie dans la théorie d' Oswald Ducrot," in *Les sujets et leurs discours*, edited by Robert Vion (Publications de l'Université de Provence, 1998), pp. 203–24.

43. Udo Gerald Simon, *Mittelalterliche arabische Sprachbetrachtung zwischen Grammatik und Rhetorik*: 'ilm al-ma'ānī *bei as-Sakkākī* (Heidelberg: Orientverlag, 1993).

44. 'A. al-Barqūqī, ed., *Talkhīṣ al-Miftāḥ* (Cairo, n.d.), pp. 41–42.

45. Cf., in these pages (*Arabica*, 46, no. 1 [1999]: 130–31) the review by Claude Gilliot of M.Radscheit 's work, *Die koranische Herausforderung. Die taḥaddī-Vers im Rahmen der Polemikenpassage des Korans* (Berlin, 1996).

46. According to the *Mu'jam al-'adawāt wa - l- ḍamā'ir fī l-Qur'ān al-karīm* (Beirut: Mu'assasat al-risāla, 1408/1986).

47. Thus the seven occurrences of *bal* in sura II are all of this type.

48. *'Alf layla wa -layla* (Beirut: Dār al-Hilāl), II, p. 268. That does not mean that we cannot find there the schema *p-bal q*. Thus in the same tale (p. 247), we have: *fa-qāla Ḥasan 'anā 'abduka wa-'abduhā fa-qāla al-'ajamī bal 'anā 'abdukumā* ("I am your servant and hers," said Hassan. "On the contrary, it is I who is yours," replied the Persian").

49. *Sharḥ al-Kāfiya* (Istanbul, AH 1310), II, p. 346. On this description, cf. "la particule *lākinna* vue par un grammairien arabe du XIIIe siècle ou comment une description de détail s'inscrit dans une théorie pragmatique" ["The particle *lākinna* as seen by an Arab grammarian of the XIII century or how a detailed description enters into a pragmatic theory"], *Historiographia Linguistica* 19, no. 1 (1992): 1–24, and "Du *mais* Français au lâkin(na) arabe et retour" ["From the French *mais* to the Arabic *lākin(na)* and back again. Fragment of a comparative history of linguistics."] *Revue Québécoise de linguistique* 20, no. 1 (1990): 171–93.

2.4

Linguistics and J. L. Austin

An Introductory Note and Glossary

Ibn Warraq

J. L. Austin (1911–1960), professor of moral philosophy at Oxford, began his investigations with the observation that not all sentences are used to make statements which are either true or false. "There are indeed utterances that do not describe or report or constate [*sic*] anything at all; moreover the uttering of these kinds of sentences is, or is a part of, the doing of an action."

Examples:

1. "I name this ship the *Queen Elizabeth*"—as uttered when smashing the bottle against the stern.
2. "I give and bequeath my watch to my brother"—as occurring in a will.
3. "I bet you sixpence it will rain tomorrow."

These utterances Austin called "performatives." They are the performance of some act and not the report of its performance. Here an action is performed by virtue of the sentence having been uttered, for example, *I apologize*, *I baptize you . . .* , *I promise you. . . .* None of the utterances cited is either true or false. These utterances are contrasted with constatives, which can be said to be true or false, and which are used to make statements. However, Austin found this distinction unsatisfactory, since constatives seemed to collapse into the performative. To remedy this situation, Austin introduced the theory of illocutionary forces. Whenever someone says anything, he or she performs a number of distinguishable acts, for example, the phonetic act of making certain noises and the phatic act of uttering words in conformity with grammar. Austin then distinguished three other kinds of acts that we may perform when we say something:

First, the LOCUTIONARY act of using an utterance with a more or less definite sense and reference, for example, saying "The door is open" as an English sentence with reference to a particular door; this is roughly equivalent to "meaning" in the traditional sense—the act of making a meaningful utterance.

Second, the ILLOCUTIONARY act, which is the act I may perform in performing the locutionary act; acts such as informing, ordering, warning, undertaking, promising, baptizing, and so on—that is, utterances that have a certain (conventional) force.

Third, the PERLOCUTIONARY act, which is the act I may succeed in performing by means of my illocutionary act; what we bring about or achieve by saying something, such as convincing, persuading, deterring, and even, say, surprising or misleading. In other words, this is an act that is performed when an utterance achieves a particular effect on the behavior, beliefs, feelings, and so on, of a listener; utterances which frighten, insult, ridicule, sympathize, or persuade.

Thus, in performing the locutionary act of saying that a door is open, I may be performing an illocutionary act of stating, or hinting, or exclaiming; by performing the illocutionary act of hinting I may succeed in performing the perlocutionary act of getting you to shut it.

Constatives, along with performatives, can be construed as members of one particular subclass of illocutionary forces.

GLOSSARY

Apodosis: a term that refers to the consequences or result expressed in the main clause of a conditional sentence; opposed to *protasis*. In the sentence *We shall get in if we queue*, *we shall get in* is the apodosis, *if we queue* is the protasis.

Discourse: a term used to refer to a continuous stretch of (especially spoken) language larger than a sentence; it is a set of utterances that constitutes any recognizable speech event (with no references to its linguistic structure).

Hermeneutics: the science of interpretation.

Linguistics: the scientific study of language; *diachronic linguistics* refers to the study of language change (also called historical linguistics), and *synchronic linguistics* to the study of the state of the language at any given point in time.

Parole: the concrete utterances produced by individual speakers in actual situations; distinguished from *langue*, which is the collective language system of a speech community.

Signifier/signified: According to F. Saussure (1857–1913), language is a system of signs, which communicates or expresses ideas. The sign is the union of a form that signifies, which Saussure calls the *signifiant* or signifier, and an idea or concept signified, the *signifié* or signified.

Utterance: a term used to refer to a length of speech about which there are no theoretical assumptions. (Cf., the notion of a sentence that receives its definition from a theory of grammar.)

2.5

A Note on the Root in Indo-European Studies and Semitics[1]

Pierre Larcher and Daniel Baggioni[2]

In Indo-European studies, the "root" is clearly a construction of the linguist. An Indo-Europeanist never speaks of an Indo-European root without preceding it with an asterisk.[3]

True, the same thing happens in Semitics. Semitic languages constitute a group of closely related languages. It is thus possible in using the techniques of comparative grammar (here particularly the correspondence of phonemes)[4] to (re-)construct the common roots of these languages that are supposed to belong to a common hypothetical Semitic ancestor.

But (for there is a but) the same word "root" is used in an entirely different manner: no longer in the context of comparative and historical grammar (the comparison serving primarily to go back in time) but in the context of a purely synchronic grammar of a particular Semitic language and, notably, Classical Arabic (which here will serve as a point of reference). The "root" is thus an element of the structure of the word. It is no longer a construction. It is at most an *abstraction*. It is an abstraction in two senses: first, in the sense given to it by American structuralism (to which French Semiticists and Arabicists usually pay insufficient attention). The same stem morpheme can in fact be realized by several *morphs*, which creates cases of opacity, to which we will come back. Second, it is the sense given to it by French structuralism (generally preferred by French Semiticists and Arabicists). A "root" not existing independently of the word that embodies it, its existence is brought out by analysis. Just as Cantineau (1950) who had read

Saussure (1916) had clearly seen, this analysis is of the *associative* kind, that is to say it is only possible for, on the one hand, a word to be associated to other words of the same "root," and, on the other hand, to other words of the same "form" or "scheme" (or "pattern") [French: *schème*].[5]

The aim of the present note is to show the harm that this dual use of "root" has done, as much in the pansemitic and diachronic way as in the monosemitic and synchronic.

2.

In 1939, from August 28 to September 2, right on the eve of the Second World War, the Fifth International Congress of Linguists was to take place in Belgium. On the agenda was the question of the "root." A questionnaire had been addressed to a certain number of linguists, generalists or specialists, being understood that generalists are often specialists without being aware of it, working in reality on a single group of languages, when not working on a single language. Thus we can pick out the names of Emile Benveniste, Jerzy Kurylowicz, Carl Brockelmann, and Marcel Cohen. Otherwise, the synthesis of the replies to the questionnaire was made in the form of a report. Although sixty years separate us from these texts, they have preserved all their relevance and we shall refer to them constantly here.

3.

Marcel Cohen's reply[6] begins with the phrase "in Hamito-Semitic languages, the root is apparent." As for Benveniste (1939, p. 5), comparing Indo-European and Semitic, he wrote: "The root constantly visible and identical with the word in Semitic is not evident and of indistinguishable structure in Indo-European, where the only perceptible reality is that of the stem." One remains staggered by these two affirmations, even more so by the latter (concerning at least the Semitic) than the former! In Semitic the root can only be said to be identical to the graphic word, and even then only where (i) the written form of the language is defective and (ii) the word does not comprise inscribed augment (such as gemination). But from the phonic point of view, the root never coincides with a word. Benveniste's remark—"in Indo-European, one speaks with words, and not with roots"—is equally true of Semitic! If the root never coincides with a word, the root is not always apparent either. Where does this belief in the obvious character of the root come from? It is from the fact that Arabic is usually taken as the model of Semitic languages. Now, in Arabic, dictionaries are classifed by alphabetical order of the roots. In order to find a word in a dictionary, one must first extract the root. Trained from the very beginning of their apprenticeship to extract the word roots, Arabicists end by seeing it even where it is not visible: all cases of opacity that however we encounter daily when reading the smallest text are forgotten! More serious: Arabicists take what is a metalinguistic operation as linguistic competence of the very speaker (this is the case each time the former speak of "feeling" or of "awareness" of the root of the latter). And even more seriously: the root serving as an entry to an item in the dictionaries, they believe it to be the basis of the lexical derivation in the language, hiding completely the fact that very many formations are not modeled on the root but on the form of another word. A simple example to sweep away this double myth of the perceptible and basic root will do. If we ask ourselves why *makān*, "place, location," has for a plural *'amākin*, we would reply that the latter is only indirectly the plural of *makān* via the other plural *'amkina*; and that this shows that *makān* is not treated, *in the language*, as a *maf'al* (place name) on the verbal root *kwn* (to be), which is the case for grammarians and lexicographers however, but directly like a *fa'ā l* form: the form *'af'ila* is a form of the plural associated with this form (e.g., *ṭa'ām*, *'aṭmi'a*, dish, dishes). What is true synchronically is also true diachronically. To *makān* corresponds the feminine *makāna*: that *makāna* can be analyzed as *makān* + *a* is attested by the fact that these two words have the same meaning, near enough the contrasts concrete/abstract—*makān* is a concrete place, *makāna* is an abstract position, a place, a location. In the same way, the superplural[7] *'amākin*, via *'amkina*, attests that *makān* is read synchronically like *fa'āl*, and not like *maf'al*, *makāna*, read, not like *maf'ala*, but like *fa'āla*, that is to say like a verbal noun of a stative verb, (*makāna*) is very certainly the origin of the verb *makuna* "to be *makīn* / influential, to have a position, authority over someone." In other words, in the same fashion that synchronically a form is the function of the other, diachronically a lexical family comes out of the other, via a pivotal form. In the two cases, the root did not play any part. . . .

4.

The second paragraph of M. Cohen's reply opens with the sentence "the root is generally verbal-nominal." First one fears the worst and that the French Semiticist is pulling a fast one in saying that the root is indistinguishably verbal or nominal. Such an idea exists and is a correlate to the concept of derivation-from-the-root. If one derives words, which are essentially divided between two large lexical categories of verb and noun, from a root, it could be tempting to attribute to the root a meaning, not lexical but infra-lexical, that is to say neutral concerning the category of words said to be derived from it. One is however reassured when one reads at the end of the same paragraph of M. Cohen: "A certain number of roots designating concrete objects are nominal-verbal, forming nouns,with derivatives formed from suffixes, and denominative verbs."

M. Cohen's formulation is however far from being satisfactory. A nominal-verbal root is in effect a root on which one constructs a noun, before forming, on the root of this noun, a verb (thus: Root > Noun > Verb).Which amounts to distinguishing in the derivational process two stages: the primary one where a word is directly taken from a root and the secondary one where a word is formed with the root of the other word. And, consequently, to dissociating, in the second case, the properly morphological aspect of the derivation (the word is constructed on a root) from the semantical aspect (the meaning of the root, in the derivation, is that of the noun-source).

M. Cohen introduces a second asymmetry. A verbal-nominal root is not, in fact, as one would expect, a root from which one extracts first a verb, on the root of which one would then form a noun (that is, Root > Verb > Noun),with, thus deverbal nouns, like, in the preceding case, denominative verbs: for M. Cohen, "It functions like a verb, with alternating vowels and affixes (prefixes, more rarely infixes, of voice; personal prefixes and personal suffixes; it functions as a noun with alternating vowels, suffixes of declension, formative prefixes and formative suffixes." Here the words, verbs and nouns, are all derived from the same roots, even if from the semantical point of view, a logical priority seems to be given to the verb over the noun.[8] One can represent M. Cohen's concept in this way:

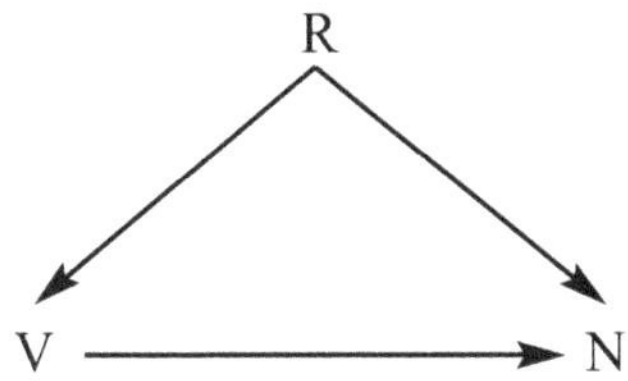

FIGURE 1

Sixty years later, one can say that this idea continues to dominate Semiticists and Arabicists, particularly French ones. Leaving aside nouns formed on another by suffixation, on the one hand, and denominative verbs (where the root is understood as the vestige of a noun in the verb), on the other, a lexical family is considered as the set of words, having such and such form derived from such and such root: if the root gives the fundamental sense, the form states precisely the meaning. M. Cohen does not use the word "form" when replying to a questionnaire on the root. It is nonetheless the consequence of the concept of root. As we have already remarked in section 1 above, Cantineau has shown how a word can be *analyzed* as a root and as a scheme (a term that seems more "scientific" than "form"), by association of this word with other words of the same root, on the one hand, and, of the same scheme, on the other. And D. Cohen (1964 [1970]), going in the same direction, but, in this sense, further than Cantineau, in that he goes explicitly from analysis to synthesis, presents the word as the product of crossing a root with a scheme (formula: word = root × scheme).We are here in the presence of a veritable theory of lexical derivation in CA, that is to say both the formation and the interpretation of words at the same time. It is thus legitimate to ask oneself if such a theory is descriptively adequate, not only from the morphological point of view, but even more so from the semantical. We have already indicated from the strictly morphological point of view it is at least partially inadequate: it does not give an account of the ensemble of the formations (far more numerous than the Arabicists realize), which model themselves, not on a root, but on the form of another word. If *makân* had been treated like the form *maf'al* on the root *kwn*, then it would have had the plural **makâwin*. The plural *'amkina* shows that *makân* is being treated like *fa'âl*, the association *makân / 'amkina* resulting in a new morpheme *mkn*, the vestige of one in the other. As to the super-plural *'amâkin*, it is a formation which models itself *directly* on the form *'amkina*, the prefix ['] being treated in the same manner as the stem morpheme *mkn*: a quadriliteral plural is a plural where what counts is the number of the consonants of the base, and absolutely not their nature. We should like to show now that this theory of lexical derivation is not only totally inadequate from a semantical point of view, but even more so that we cannot dissociate as easily as that the morphological and semantical aspects from the derivation.

5.

"The root," continues M. Cohen, "can be increased in its constitutive elements by gemination of a consonant, the repetition of one or two consonants—either with morphological value or with expressive value," adding: "The prefixes or infixes of derived verbal stems (with a voice meaning) could also be considered as augmentatives of the root—whence the easy equivalence of prefix and infix." What is interesting here is the use of double terminology. One inherited from traditional Arabic grammar, consists in distinguishing, in a word, next to stems, one or several augmentatives (*zāida*, pl. *zaw ā'id*). The other, inherited from the grammar of Indo-European languages, consists in distinguishing, in a word, a base (the stem), and affixes (prefixes, infixes, suffixes). The use of this double terminology à propos of "derived verbal stems" shows that the latter constitute the part of the morphology of Semitic languages in general and Classical Arabic in particular where one could hesitate between the two analyses, in root and scheme, on the one hand, and in the base and affixes, on the other. Besides, one can note that the famous Arabic grammars presenting simultaneously the "derived verbal forms" as derived from the root (including the form of the base numbered I) or as derived directly or indirectly from the ground-form (II, III, IV, VII, and VIII from I, but V, VI, and X from II, III, and IV). If one adds to that the fact that the quasi-totality of the grammatical schemes of Arabic could just as well be denominative as deverbal, it is clear that a root never has a meaning in itself, but always as a root of a verb or a noun, when it is not first one then the other, as in the case of *maktab* and *maktaba*. These two words have the same root, *ktb*, and the same grammatical form, that of noun of place. Thus they should have, if not the same meaning, at least for the only difference of meaning that resulting from the addition of the suffix *at(h)*, as is the case with *manzil* and *manzila*: both of them are nouns of place linked to the verb *nazal- / yanzil-* ("to get down, to settle") from which we get for the first word the classic meaning of "camp" or "encampment" and the modern "domicile," and for the second the more general and in a word more abstract meaning of "place, position." Not a single Arabicist however analyzes *maktaba* as *maktab + a*, simply because if *maktab* is a place where one writes, *maktaba* is a place where there are books. In other words, in *maktaba*, the root *ktb* represents the noun *kitāb-kutub* whereas in *maktab* it represents the verb *katab-yaktub*. Moreover, there is cause to ask how the same root goes from the meaning "to write" to the meaning "book." It does so via the pivotal form *kitāb*, which is a verbal noun and which according to its syntax could designate either the cause or the result ("writing"). But the meaning of "book" is only lexicalized when one associates with *kitāb* the plural *kutub*.[9] In passing from *kitāb* to *kutub*, one passes from a book to books, in other words from one form to another of the same noun: if the forms of noun exist concretely, the noun itself only exists in the abstract, in the association of the two forms. It is the association of the two that produces, here, the new meaning of an already existing root (the root, the verbal becoming on the way nominal), exactly like, in the latter case, the association of a plural to a loan word will produce a new root (e.g., the root *qms* / "shirt" when one passes from the singular *qamīṣ*, a shirt [< lat. *camisa*] to the plural *qumṣān*, shirts). To end let us add that the semantically deverbative formations that the Arabicists see derived more directly from the root than the semantically denominative formations are morphologically more related to the verb than the denominative formations are to the noun! Thus the deverbal noun of place conserves a formal correlation with the imperfect verb (e.g., *manzil / yanzil*), while the denominative noun of place has exclusively, at least in Classical Arabic, the form *maf'ala*. Likewise, the derived verbal forms, semantically deverbative could be morphologically present like the augmented forms of base (if one withdraws the augment, the form of base remains), while in derived verbal forms, semantically denominative, the noun is, in general, only represented by the root.[10]

6.

"The non-augmented Semitic root," continues M. Cohen, "is generally made up of three consonants (triliteral). But there exist roots increased by one consonant, constituting the quadriliterals." In the following paragraph, he indicates: "several facts, in Semitic itself, would tempt us to go back to a short type of root or at least suggesting the co-existence of a biliteral type with a triliteral type." There again, the question of whether the root in Semitic is fundamentally triliteral or not has no importance as soon as we place it in the framework of a particular Semitic language like Classical Arabic, and synchronically. What is important is to observe that we cannot derive from less than three stems, on the one hand, and from not more than four stems, on the other. But that does not at all prevent derivation from a biliteral base by adding a purely formal stem (it is clear in effect that it does not play a semantic role), nor to having a base with more than four consonants by reducing them to four.

The first case is represented by nouns belonging to the fundamental lexicon of Arabic and of Semitic. The third stem (in general *y ā'* or *wāw*), artificial, appears as soon as a plural is associated with the singular: for example, *yad*, a hand, *'aydiy-*, hands; *'akh*, a brother, *'ikhwa* or *'ikhwān*, brothers. The second case, quite the reverse, is represented by loan words. For example, the association with *barnāmaj*, a program, a word which has neither root nor form, of the plural *barāmij*, programs, producing a quadriliteral root *brmj* / program, that one comes across again in the verb *barmaja*, to program. If one adds that the quadriliteral forms are nothing other than variants of augmented triliteral roots (the augment of the triliteral becoming a stem in the quadriliteral), one is tempted to see in the famous "triliteral root" the result of the derivational process. It appears not like a point of departure, but a point of arrival, not like the base of derivation, but the vestige of the base in the derived, not like a fixed star in the lexical firmament from which words would descend, but the product, as much from the point of view of the signifier as the signified, of the movement of discourse.

7.

If the root, if not strictly at least functionally, plays the same role as the stem in Indo-European languages, why not substitute this term for that of root?

In reality, the notion of the stem is pertinent in Arabic. First because Arabic has derivation by affixation, which makes the stem appear. Thus on *ṭabī'a*, nature, one forms an adjective of relation *ṭabī 'yy*, natural revealing a stem *ṭabī '*, not coinciding, at least in the present state of the lexicon of Classical Arabic, with any word. The affixation could result in a deformation of the stem (e.g., *madīna*, city, gives *madaniyy*, civil). Second, because the notion of a stem is pertinent to the verbal system. An Arabic verb has at least two stems: that of the perfect (*fa'al-*) and that of the imperfect ((*ya)-f 'al*), which coincides with that of the imperative *(i)f 'al*. That this stem is either, alone, submitted to apophony (*fa'al* vs *fu'il-*, i.e., active vs. passive) or with augments (*yaf'al* vs. *yuf'al*, idem) makes no difference in the matter: the fact that in German one has *trinken*, *trank*, *getrunken* does not lead to the construction of a consonantal root TRNK, drink, but a stem—TRvNK. And, finally, something never noted before, the stem plays a role either in the creation of a new root or in the reinterpretation of an already existing root. If one wants to understand how one has *talyīb*, libyanization, one must start not from *Lībiy ā*, Libya, but from *lībiyy*, libyan, which reveals the stem *līb-* (*liyb*), at the base of three stems LYB.

Similarly, if one wants to understand why *tadwîl* signifies "internationalization" (and not "nationalization"), one must start not with the noun *dawla* (a state) or its plural *duwal* (states), not even the adjective of relation *duwaliyy* (relative to states, from which one gets "interstate, international "), but in fact from the ordinary realization of *duwaliyy* in *dawliyy*, which reveals a stem *dawl-* for the form, and *duwal* for the meaning![11] That is why we propose to substitute for root the term stem morpheme, to designate an element of the structure of the word in the context of the synchronic grammar of a Semitic language and to conserve the term root only to designate the archi-morpheme stem reconstructed in the context of a comparative grammar of Semitic languages. It is the latter, and only the latter, that should be compared to what one normally calls a root in Indo-European, as Petráček (1982) does admirably.[12]

Conclusion

We shall underline in conclusion the paradox of the root. From the point of view of the history of linguistics, the root is a concept born of the comparative and historical grammar of Indo-European languages. Its history, however, is more complicated. According to Rousseau (1984), this concept may have originated with Franz Bopp (1791–1867), the founder of comparative grammar (Bopp studied under Antoine–Isaac Silvestre de Sacy (1758–1838) for two years in Paris and thus was somewhat familiar with Semitic languages), and even though the Arabicists at the time did not use the concept of consonantal root but that of the verbal root coinciding with the third person masculine singular of the perfect, in other words not a root but a base. From Indo-European linguistics, it was imported into Semitic linguistics by the Semiticist Heinrich Ewald (1803–1875). There, this concept met again or thought it met again a concept of "root" already present in the traditional Arabic grammar and lexicography, under diverse names (besides by opposition to *ṣīgha*, form, those of *jawhar*, substance, or *mādda*, matter, than that of *'aṣl*, which designates most frequently a form considered basic in relation to another (cf. Troupeau [1984]). But if it is true that the root serves as an entry to items in dictionaries, it is not true on the other hand that it serves as an entry to derivation: grammarians and lexicographers derive in fact either from a *maṣdar*[13] (so-called moreover because understood as the "source" of the derivation [*ištiqāq*]), or from a *ism jāmid* (or a "fixed" noun, i.e., itself not derived from a *maṣdar*).[14] The *maṣdar* being a noun, but verbal, the "demasdarative" derivation hides in fact a deverbal derivation exactly like the derivation starting from *ism jāmid* hides a denominative derivation. It is the hybridization of two concepts (one of which is badly understood) that ended in the derivation—from-the-root ("deradicative"), but with a kind of inversion in respect to the comparative grammar of Indo-European languages. The term *root* is a vegetal metaphor. The root is that of a plant, coming out of the ground and branching out to the sky. If the movement is vertical, it is from the bottom to the top. But with Semiticists it is the opposite, if the movement is vertical, it is from top to bottom. It is not a historical interpretation but a "transcendental" one. A notion, born of a historical grammar, ends up, thus, being transposed into a descriptive grammar, quite the reverse: leads not to a historicization, but to an immobilization, the derivation from the root not allowing to take into account movement in the lexicon, as much morphological as semantical, as much synchronic as diachronic.

Notes

1. [Translated from the French by Ibn Warraq. Footnotes in square brackets by I.W.]

2. Our colleague Daniel Baggioni did not get the time to pass onto us the written version of his talk. This article is a result of both notes taken during the doctoral day, on the one hand, and numerous conversations that we have had together on this subject, on the other.

3. [Linguists use an initial asterisk to indicate sounds or combinations of sounds that do not occur in the language in question.]

4. [The minimal significant unit in the sound system of a language, or "a unit of sound which makes a difference in the meaning of words" (R. A. Hall, *Linguistics and Your Language*, New York, 1960, p. 37). This concept was introduced to determine the patterns of organization within the indefinitely large range of sounds heard in languages. See further David Crystal, *A Dictionary of Linguistics and Phonetics*, 4th ed. (Oxford: Basil Blackwell, 1997), pp. 287–88.]

5. Something that Massignon does not understand [Massignon, 1954, p. 10]. He had read without naming him, Cantineau, but not Saussure, and playing on the Greek and Latin etymology of the two words, finds the term itself of associative analysis "rather illogical."

6. Marcel Cohen 1939, 2:17.

7. W. Wright, *A Grammar of the Arabic Language*, Cambridge, 1967, p. 231: "The plural of the plural, or secondary plural."

8. This interpretation is confirmed by M. Cohen himself (1952, pp. 92–93,

taken practically word for word from M. Cohen, 1924, pp. 86–87): "there is no priority, in general, of the verb over the noun or the noun over the verb; one or the other can be derived independently of most roots; thus root such as the Ethiopic *ngr* provides as easily a stem noun, like *nagar*, word, thing, as a verb *nagara*, he said. . . ." This "general" case is nonetheless combined of two particular cases, that of "primitive" nouns and "denominative" verbs which are extracted from it (which takes us back to "nominal-verbal root") and that of "a great number of nouns not being directly attached to a root, but a verbal theme . . . , they are not only infinitives or nouns of action and nouns of agent, but even sometimes nouns of place and instrument." One can ask what then remains of the "general" case!

9. In reality, in the classical language, we already find the plural *kutub* associated with the noun *kitāb*, with the meaning of *letter(s)*. (Cf., for example, the extract from *Kitāb al-Kharāj* of Qudāma b. Jaf'ar [died after 320/932] quoted by R. Blachère and H. Darmaun, *Extraits des Principaux Géographes Arabes du Moyen Âge*, 2nd ed. [Paris: Klincksieck, 1957, p. 55]). On the other hand, we do not have in that case, unless we are mistaken, the noun *maktaba* with a meaning such as "* place where there are letters." That means that the same root can not only refer us back to the meaning of a verb or a noun but also to a particular designation of this noun.

10. There are however cases where it is the form itself of the nominal base that conditions that of the derived verb, as in the case of the verbs *f ā 'ala* linked to a noun *f ā 'il* (e.g., *sāḥil*, shore > *sāḥala*, reach the shore) or, more generally, having an *ā* in the first syllable (e.g., *bāl*, mind, attention > *bāl ā*, being careful).

11. [One should say, logically speaking, *duwaliyy*, but in reality one says *dawliyy*.]

12. This article commends itself also by the very large bibliography that it contains on the subject.

13. [Under Deverbal Nouns, W. Wright in his *A Grammar of the Arabic Language*, 3rd ed., Cambridge, 1967, p. 110, notes: "The nomina verbi are abstract substantives, which express the action, passion or state indicated by the corresponding verbs, without any reference to object, subject, or time. The nomen verbi is also called *al-maṣdar* (lit. the place whence anything goes forth, where it originates), because most Arab grammarians derive the compound idea of the finite verb from the simple idea of this substantive. We may compare with it the Greek Infinitive used with the article as a substantive."]

14. [W. Wright, ibid., pp. 106–107: "*ism jāmid* a noun that is stationary or incapable of growth, one that is not itself a nomen actionis or infinitive, nor derived from a nom. act., and which does not give birth to a nom. act. or verb, as: *rajulun*, a man;

baṭṭatun, a duck; opposed to *ism muštaqqun*, a noun that is derived from a nom. act. or verbal root, as: *kātibun*, a writer, *qatīlun*, slain.]

BIBLIOGRAPHY

Benveniste, Emile. 1939. "Sur la théorie de la racine en indo-européen." In *Réponses au questionnaire (suite), Première publication, Supplément*, Le problème de la racine, Vème congrès international des Linguistes, Bruxelles, August 28–September 2, 1939. Bruges: Imprimerie Sainte Catherine, p. 5.

Cantineau, Jean. 1950. "Racines et schèmes," Mélanges William Marçais. Paris: G. P. Maisonneuve et Cie, pp. 119–24.

Cohen, David. 1964 [1970]. "Remarques sur la dérivation nominale par affixes dans quelques langues sémitiques," *Semitica*. [Reprinted in *Études de linguistique sémitique et arabe*. The Hague-Paris: Mouton, 1970, pp. 31–48.]

———. 1968. "Les langues chamito-sémitiques." In *Le Langage*, with the assistance of d'André Martinet. Bibliothèque de la Pléiade. Paris: Gallimard, pp. 1288–1330.

———. 1996. "À propos de racines." In *Dictionnaire des racines sémitiques comprenant un fichier comparatif de Jean Cantineau*, edited by David Cohen, with the colloboration of François Bron and Antoine Lonnet, book 2, part 6: W-WLHP. Louvain: Peeters, pp. I–XV.

Cohen, Marcel. 1939. "Sur la racine dans les langues chamito-sémitiques." In *Réponses au questionnaire, Première publication*, "Le problème de la racine," V^{e} congrès international des Linguistes, Bruxelles, August 28–September 2, 1939. Bruges: Imprimerie Sainte Catherine, pp. 17–18.

———. 1924–1952. "Les langues chamito-sémitiques." In *Les langues du monde*, edited by A. Meillet and M. Cohen. Paris: Champion, 1924, pp. 81–151; 2nd ed. 1952, pp. 82–181.

Larcher, Pierre. 1995. "Où il est montré qu'en arabe classique la racine n'a pas de sens et qu'il n'y a pas de sens à dériver d'elle," *Arabica* 41, no. 3: 291–314.

Lecomte, Gérard. 1968. *Grammaire de l'arabe*, coll. *Que sais-je?* Paris: PUF.

Massignon, Louis. 1954. "Réflexions sur la structure primitive de l'analyse grammaticale en arabe," *Arabica* 1, no. 1: 3–10.

Petráček, Karel. 1982. "La racine en indoeuropéen et en chamitosémitique et leurs perspective comparatives." *Annali del Istituto Orientali di Napoli* 42, pp. 381–402.

Rousseau, Jean. 1984. "La racine arabe et son traitement par les grammairiens européens (1505–1831)." *Bulletin de la Societé de Linguistique de Paris* 89, no. 1: 285–321.

Saussure, Ferdinand de. 1916 [1972]. *Cours de linguistique générale*, published with Charles Bally and Albert Sechehaye, with the assistance of Albert Riedlinger. Critical edition prepared by Tullio de Mauro. Paris: Payot.

Troupeau, Gérard. 1984. "La notion de 'racine' chez les grammairiens arabes anciens." In *Matériaux pour une histoire des théories linguistiques*, edited by Sylvain Auroux, Michel Glatigny, André Joly, Anne Nicolas, and Irène Rosier. Lille: Presses Universitaires, pp. 239–45.

2.6

The Concept of Peace and Its Expressions in Arabic[1]

Pierre Larcher

1. *Salām/silmī*

It is not necessary to be an Arabist to know that in Arabic[1] "peace" is called *salām*, nor a Semitist to know that this is the exact equivalent of the Hebrew *shalom*. But an Arabist would note a primary asymmetry. In order to say "peaceful," one says *silmī*, an adjective derived not from the noun *salām* but from the related noun *silm*: thus "*ḥall silmī*" means "a peaceful solution."

2. *Salām/silm*

The question immediately arises: Is there a difference between *salām* and *silm*? And if so, what is it? A first answer to this question is supplied by the fact that Tolstoy's novel *War and Peace* is translated in Arabic by *al-ḥarb wa-s-silm*, not *al-ḥarb wa-l-salām*. Similarly, to designate a situation of "neither war nor peace," one says *lā ḥarb wa-lā silm*, rather than *lā ḥarb wa-lā salām*. These two examples seem to designate *silm* as the true antonym of *ḥarb*, "war."

3. *Silm/salm*

Several arguments point in this direction, first the fact that alongside *silm* there exists in the ancient language a variant, *salm*, twice occurring in the Koran, the first time in VIII, 61:

wa-ʾin janaḥū li-s-salmi fajnaḥ lahā

"If they [i.e., the unbelievers] incline to peace, incline thou also to it."

This verse is doubly interesting to the linguist. First, it shows that *salm* has the same form as *ḥarb*. One notes in the language a tendency to give a formal resemblance to words that are paired. Thus one has *bidāya*, "beginning," alongside *nihāya*, "end," in which the *y* of *bidāya*, linked to the verb *bada'a*, "to begin," can only be explained by the fact that the semantic relation of antinomy is translated into a formal relation of paronymy. And "time," *zamān* (with a long *ā*), is paired with *zaman* (with a short *a*), because it forms a couple with *makān* "space."[2] The same verse also shows that *salm* is here treated as a feminine noun (*la-hā*), just like *ḥarb*, of which it is the antonym in this context. Compare this with VIII, 57:

fa-'immā tathqafanna-hum fi-l-ḥarb fa-sharrid bi-him man khalfahum

"If thou comest on them in the war, deal with them so as to strike fear in those who are behind them."

The other occurrence is in XLVII, 35:

fa-lā tahinū wa-tad'ū 'ilā l-salmi wa-'antum al-'a'lawna

"So do not falter and cry out for peace when ye (will be) the uppermost."

The combination of *salm* with the verb *da'ā 'ilā*, "cry out for," suggests that we are here primarily in the realm of speech, which is confirmed by another variant of *silm/salām*: *salam* (with a short *a*).

4. *salam*

In addition to *silm*, *salm*, and *salām*, there also exists in the ancient language the variant *salam*, with five occurrences in the Koran, in IV, 90; IV, 91; XVI, 28; XVI, 87; and XXXIX, 29. Now in the first four of these five occurrences, the noun *salam* appears combined, as a direct object, with the verb *'alqā*, and in three of the four occurrences, a prepositional syntagm is added by *'ilā*. Therefore we are dealing here not with a simple combination, but with what in technical terms is called a veritable collocation, *'alqā ('ilayhi) al-salama*. Until the present time, the verb *'alqā* is preferentially combined with objects denoting a speech act. For example, it is used with *kalima* or *khiṭāb* in the sense of "making a speech." It implies among other things a certain elocutionary force. It is the same in the Koran, where the occurrence of *salam* in XVI, 87 is preceded in XVI, 86 by:

fa-'alqaw 'ilayhim al-qawla 'innakum la-kādhibūna

"They will fling to them the saying: Lo! Ye verily are liars." [Lit. "They will throw them the statement 'you are liars.'"]

All this suggests that *salam* is something that is shouted. But there is something else here. Denise Masson, author of the "authorized" translation of the Koran [into French], twice renders the term (in IV, 90 and IV, 91) as "offrir la paix" ["to offer peace"] and twice (in XVI, 28 and XVI, 87) as "faire/offrir sa soumission" ["to make/offer submission"].

The fact that the same word, in the same collocation, receives two such different translations raises a major question. But before answering it (or trying to), a prior issue arises: should *salam* be considered as another variant of *silm/salm* or else as a variant of *salām*? Perhaps of the latter, if we may judge from IV, 94:

wa-lā taqūlū li-man 'alqā 'ilaykumu s-salāma (salama) lasta mu'minan

"Say not unto one who offereth you peace: 'Thou are not a believer.'"

While the Koran of Cairo (cf. ʿAbd al-Bāqī's dictionary) reads *salām* with a long *ā*, the Maghreb Koran (Imām Warsh's recension)[3] has *salam* with a short *a*. This fact suggests not only that *salam* and *salām* are indeed two variants of one and the same word but also that there is a link between the two ideas of "peace" and "submission."

5. Noun/Verb Relations

In the ancient language, therefore, we have four nouns on a continuous axis: *salm* as variant of *silm*, and *salam* as the link in the chain between *salm* and *salām*. Etymologically, all these nouns are linked to a verb, the verb *salima-yaslamu*. In the ancient language, the relation between verb and noun is perfectly expressed, as revealed in poetic language, for example, verse 19 of the *Mu'allaqa* by Zuhayr (530–617?):

wa-qad qultumā 'in nudriki s-silma wāsi'an
bi-mālin wa-ma'rūfin mina l-qawli naslami

"If we hold, you have said, to a peace large
In goods, and customary remarks, we will be safe."

This is paraphrased by Zawzanī (d. 486 of the Hijra = 1093 CE), in his commentary on the *Mu'allaqāt* (p. 185), as:

'in 'adraknā al-ṣulḥ wāsi'an 'ay 'in ittafaqa lanā itmām al- ṣulḥ bayna l-qabīlatayni bi-badhl al-māl wa-'isdā' ma'rūf mina-l-khayr salimnā min tafānī al-'ashā'ir

"If we obtain a general arrangement, that is to say, if we reach a complete agreement between the two tribes by making unstinting use of material goods and fine words, we will be preserved from the mutual annihilation of clans."

In this paraphrase, two traits are telling: (1) the paraphrase of *silm* by *ṣulḥ* (cf. *infra* 8); and (2) the construction of the verb *salima* with *min*.

What Zawzanī puts into play with *min* is in fact a reference to the preceding verse (the noun *tafānī* responds to the verb *tafānaw* appearing in this verse):

tadāraktumā 'Absan wa-Dhubyānan ba'damā
tafānaw wa-daqqū baynahum 'iṭra Manshami

"You have again taken hold of 'Abs and Dhoubyān who
Were killing each other, grinding between them the drug of Manchem."

Some Arabists (e.g., Atallah, 1973), following after some Arab commentators ([Ibn] al-Naḥḥās, d. 338/950, I, p. 320), see in this verse an allusion to an old ritual oath of mutual extermination made by plunging the hand into perfume.

But beyond the contextual allusion, the fact that the verb *salima* cannot be understood apart from a construction with *min* permits the following hypotheses:

(1) *Al-silm* (or *al-salm*), in the sense of "peace," is the fact of being preserved from war.

(2) As for *salam/salām*, the Koranic collocation *'alqā ('ilayhi) al-salama/al-salāma* suggests that it means not to offer peace but to make proper submission, by crying something like "grace." In other words, *al-salam* or *al-salām* is the fact of being preserved from death, of being spared, of having one's life saved. This interpretation is confirmed by the first two occurrences of *salam*. In IV, 90, we have:

fa-'in i'tazalū -kum fa-lam yuqātilūkum wa-'alqaw 'ilaykumu s-salama fa-mā ja'ala llāhu lakum 'alayhim sabīlan

[So if they withdraw from you and fight you not and offer you peace, then Allah allows you no way against them.]

However, IV, 90 is balanced by IV, 91:

fa-'in lam ya'tazilū-kum wa-yulqū 'ilaykumu-s-salama wa-yakuffū 'aydiyahum fa-khudhūhum wa-qtulūhum ḥaythu thaqiftumūhum

"If they keep not aloof from you, nor offer you peace, nor hold their hands [lit. if they do not open the palms of their hands; in Masson's French translation: "if they do not lay down their arms"],[4] then take them and *kill them* wherever ye find them." [Larcher's emphasis]

[Denise Masson]:

> S' ils ne se retirent pas loin de vous;
> s' ils ne vous offrent pas le paix;
> s'ils ne déposent pas leurs armes;
> saisissez-les;
> *tuez-les* partout où vous les touverez. [P. Larcher's emphasis]

[Régis Blachère]: verses 90–91

Si (ces transfuges) se tiennent à l'écart de vous, s'ils ne vous combattent point et se rendent à vous à merci, Allah ne vous donne contre eux nulle justification (? Blachère's query) (pour les combattre) . . .

S'ils ne se tiennent pas à l'écart de vous, (s'ils ne) se rendent pas à vous à merci et (ne) déposent pas les armes, prenez-les et tuez-les où vous les acculiez!

[Régis Blachère's footnote:

ʾalqaw ʾilay-kumu s-salama "et se rendent à vous à merci." Il n'est pas possible de traduire l`expression par: "et vous offrent la paix," car il s'agit de gens qui, à l'avance, refusent le combat et qui sont donc prêts à se soumettre."]

[Arberry]:

"If they withdraw not from, and offer you peace, and restrain their hands, take them, slay them wherever you come on them . . ."

[Pickthall]:

"So, if they hold aloof from you and wage not war against you and offer you peace, Allah alloweth you no way against them."

While Masson's [and Pickthall's] translations are bowdlerized, that of Blachère (1980, p. 118) is more plausible: "and give themselves up to your mercy," to which this French Arabist adds a footnote: "it is not possible to translate the expression by 'and offer you peace,' because these are people who in advance refuse combat and who are thus ready to submit."

This interpretation is also confirmed by the two subsequent occurrences, which are placed in the context of the day of Resurrection, where it is a matter of being spared from Gehenna. First, XVI, 28:

fa-'alqaw s-salama mā kunnā na'malu min sū'in

"Then will they make full submission (saying): We used not to do any wrong." [actually, they cried grace]

Second, XVI, 87:

wa-'alqaw 'illā llāhi yawma'idhini s-salama wa-ḍalla 'anhum mā kānū yaftarūna

"And they proffer unto Allah submission on that day, and all that they used to invent hath failed them."

6. *salām/salāma*

That *salām*, currently employed today in the sense of "peace," may indeed be etymologically a verbal noun meaning "preservation" is attested to by a certain number of famous expressions.

In the first place, *al-salām* as one of the names of Allah should not be interpreted as signifying "peace" (cf. art *SALĀM* of *EI*²), but takes its noun, as written in the article SLM of Lisān al-'Arab (henceforth *LA*) by Ibn Manẓūr (d. 711/1311) "from the fact that he is preserved from defect, vice, and annihilation" (*li-salāmatihi min al-naqṣ wa-l-'īb wa-l-fanā'*).

Then there is *dār al-salām* as one of the names of Paradise, which should not be interpreted as the "house of peace," but takes its noun "from the fact that it is the house of preservation from evil" (*li-'annahā dār al-salām min al-' āfāt*) or "of preservation from death, decrepitude, and evil" (*dār al-salām min al-mawt wa-l-haram wa-l-'asqām*) (art. SLM of *LA*).

Finally, there is the famous salutation *(as)-salām 'alayka*, which should not be interpreted as a wish for peace, but as a wish for preservation: "and *salām* that is the active noun of the verb *sallamtu* has the meaning of a wish made in favor of an individual that he be preserved from afflictions acting on his religion or himself" (*wa-ma'nā al-salām alladhī maṣdar sallamtu 'annahu du'ā' li-l-'insān bi-'an yaslama min al-' āfāt fī dīnihi wa-nafsihi*) (*LA*, art. SLM). This paraphrase shows that the ancient Arab grammarians and lexicographers knew not only of the verbs that Benveniste (1958) called "delocutives" but also of what Cornulier (1975) calls "auto-delocutive reinterpetation"; the verb *sallama* (*'alayhi*) is indeed a delocutive of *salām 'alayka*, and the noun *salām*, in the sense of "salute/salutation," is the reinterpretation of *salām* in the sense of "preservation," through the "wish for preservation" amounting to the salutation that is *salām 'alayka*. One has the same movement in Latin with *salus*, which shifts from "health" to "salute/salutation," via the wish for health serving as a salutation in *Salus!* And in French, one moves from *the* mercy (= favor) to *a merci* (= thanks), via the recognition of favor, tantamount to granting thanks, in the medieval French *grant merci*.

In the two paraphrases of *salām* above, we have seen appear the noun *salāma*. On the morphologic level, this is nothing other than *salâm* + *a*, which is etymologically synonymous and relays it as the verbal noun *salima*, as *LA* sees very well (art. SLM): "*al-salām* is, at its root, *al-salāma,* one says *salima yaslamu salāman wa-salāmatan*."

Salāma is the fact of being preserved from all harm, hence the technical meanings of "health" (*'āfiya*) or, in the modern language, of integrity, for example, territorial integrity (*salāmat al-'araḍī*). In the meta-language of the grammarians, *salāma* refers as a verb to being *strong* (*sālim*), that is to say, preserved from this "infirmity" (*'illa*) that is the presence among its stems of a *w* or a *y*, and so on.

Therefore we must distrust the retrospective readings of which Arabists are victims more often than were the ancient Arab lexicographers, even if the latter are not spared from an "Islamicizing" tendency—visible, for example, in the paraphrase *salām*/salutation. *Salām 'alayka*, often presented as the

Islamic salutation par excellence, is only Islamic because it receives canonic sanction from the Koran. In truth, it can be found, well before Islam, in the Safaitic inscriptions documenting a north Arabic language very close to Arabic (cf. *EI*[2], art. Safaïtique), and still earlier, in other Semitic languages, starting with Hebrew (cf. Cassuto, 2001).

7. *silm/'islām*

Another example of this parasitism is supplied by sura II, 208 of the Koran, where we have the sole occurrence of *silm* (at least in the Cairo Koran, since the Maghreb Koran reads *salm*): *yā 'ayyuhā lladhīna ' āmanū dkhūlū fi-s-silmi kāffatan*. "O ye who believe! Come, all of you, into submission" [Pickthall]. Masson's French translation has *"ô vous qui croyez, entrez tous dans la paix,"* to which she adds a note: "*silm* is here put for *'islām*," a note that reflects the usual interpretation of Muslim commentators (cf. art SLM of *LA*, which [both for the *silm* reading as for *salm*] indicates that the meaning aimed for is really in fact *'islām*)—but there is nothing less certain than that they are interpreting it as "peace"!

'Islām is the noun of action of the verb IV *'aslama*, which signifies "to become Muslim," but as a metonymic reinterpretation of an implicitly reflexive verb: "to deliver oneself, to submit oneself [to Allah]" (*'aslama* = *'aslama 'amra-hu 'ilā llāhi*). This literal interpretation of *'aslama* is confirmed, moreover, by the existence, alongside IV, of a verb X *istaslama* that is etymologically derived from it by *-t-* and which is indeed an explicitly reflexive verb tending to mean "to deliver, to submit oneself," today employed in the sense of "to capitulate."

Which is where we again encounter the idea of submission, or better, of delivery/handing over. This is not the only location of this word family. In the same sense as IV, we have II *sallama*, currently employed in the ancient and modern languages in the sense of "delivering, remitting something (*-hā*) to someone (*'ilayhi*)" and to which corresponds the middle (voice) reflexive verb V *tasallama-hā* "to receive something." In legal language, one uses IV *'aslama* and II *sallama fīhā 'ilayhi* in the sense of *'aslafa*, described in this way by *LA*: "it is the fact of giving gold or silver for defined merchandise for a defined period of time" (*wa-huwa 'an tu'ṭī dhahaban wa-fiḍḍatan fī sil'a* *ma'lūma 'ilā 'amad ma'lūm*). Although in this sense these verbs function as denominatives of *salam* referring to a contract of anticipated payment for something material (cf. *EI*², art. SALAM), they can be interpreted as a specialization of the general meaning, as *LA* suggests: "In other words, one has *remitted* [my emphasis, P. L.] the price of the merchandise to its possessor" (*fa-ka'annaka qad 'aslamta al-thaman 'ilā ṣāḥib al-sil'a wa-sallamtuhu*).

We also have VIII *istalama* in the sense of "receiving." Since the verbs VIII are morphologically derivatives in *-t-* of the basic verb, of which they are semantically the reflexives, therefore one may reconstruct an I **salama*, itself conveying the sense of "to deliver." *Salima* would then be the middle voice of this **salama*, not by derivation but ablaut (apophony),[2] meaning "to be delivered," from whence "to be spared, preserved, have one's life saved." This interpretation is confirmed by the fifth and final occurrence in the Koran of *salam*, in XXXIX, 29, which consists of an adjectival use of the substantive, which was common in the ancient language:

wa-ḍaraba llāhu mathalan rajulan fīhi shurakā'u mutashākisūna wa-rajulan salaman li-rajulin wāḥidin

"Allah coineth a similitude: A man in relation to whom are several part-owners, quarrelling, and a man belonging wholly to one man. Are the two equal in similitude?"

Now, for this verse there also exists the reading *sāliman li-* (active participle of the verb *salima*). This vocalic middle voice existed in the archaic language (e.g., *ḥazana-hu* = "to sadden someone" vs. *ḥazina* = "to be saddened") and is encountered again in certain dialects (thus Egyptian contrasts *ta'abnī* = "he tired/fatigued me" with *te'eb* = "he is tired/fatigued"). Elsewhere, the attentive reading of the art. SLM of *LA* shows that *salam* really never has the sense of "peace" (and so the Masson translation is faulty), whereas *silm*, *salm*, and *salām*, while having the sense of "peace," may also all mean "submission." *LA* paraphrases them either by another term from the same family that is unambiguous (*istislām*), or by (para)synonyms such as *inqiyād* (the fact of letting oneself be led, docility), *idh'ān*, *istikhdhā'* (submission), which invites us to consider this latter meaning as primordial.

Our hypothesis may get support from a Semitic parallel: in the corresponding Hebrew family, Cassuto [2001] has noted here, too, the existence of a *shilem* (one occurrence in the Bible, meaning "retribution") and of a *shelem* (once in the singular and eighty-nine times in the plural in the Bible, with the sense of "sacrifice"), two meanings that easily carry the idea of "to deliver, remit something."

Other evidence, issuing from other Semitic languages, may come along to confirm or undermine our hypothesis, but, in any event, one must go beyond the idyllic and (frankly) irenic vision that Marcel Cohen (1947, p. 133) gave to the Semitic family *shlm* as "good health, salvation, peace." . . .

8. *silm/salām* vs *ṣulḥ*

In Zuhayr's commentary on the verse, the word *silm* is paraphrased by *ṣulḥ* because the verse, even while employing the word *silm*, indicates that there is a negotiation or more exactly a mediation of the two chiefs to result in a peace between the tribes of 'Abs and Dhubyân. The means are material compensation (*māl*) and diplomacy (*al-ma'rūf min al-qawl*).

There are only two occurrences of the word *ṣulḥ* in the Koran, in the same verse (IV, 128):

wa-'in imra'atun khāfat min ba'lihā nushūdhan 'aw 'i'rāḍan fa-lā junāḥa 'alayhimā 'an yuṣliḥā baynahumā ṣulḥan wa-l- ṣulḥu khayrun

"If a woman feareth ill-treatment from her husband, or desertion, it is no sin for them twain if they make terms of peace between themselves. Peace is better."

This is a matter of a negotiation between spouses. Thus it is the "household peace" (cf. Houdebine, 2001) that serves, Koranically, as a model for the peace negotiated between groups or states, as was later theorized by Muslim jurists (*EI*[2], art. *ṣulḥ*). One also comes across the collocation *'aṣlaḥa bayna-ṣulḥan* "to make an arrangement between . . . ," where the noun *ṣulḥ* is the internal object of the verb *'aṣlaḥa*. The Maghreb Koran reads *yaṣṣālaḥā* a homograph (in defective writing) of *yuṣliḥā*. This is the contracted form, by assimilation of the augment *t-* to the stem *ṣ*, of *yataṣālaḥūna*, "they arrange things between them" (which in this context is redundant). This demonstrates that the verbs IV *'aṣlaḥa*, III *ṣālaḥa*, VI *taṣālaḥa*, and VIII *iṣṭalaḥa* are heard as denominatives of *ṣulḥ* even if this noun might be attached to the verb *ṣaluḥa* or *ṣalaḥa*, "to be in good order," from which, for IV, "to put into good order, to arrange" (nowadays, "to reform").

CONCLUSION

The concept of peace, in classical Arabic, therefore appears to us to be broken up into two types of expression: on the one hand, a peace *by submission*, attenuating, by the metonymy between the process and its result, into preservation and, from there, ending up in the purely negative idea of peace as the absence of war; and on the other hand, a peace *by negotiation*.

The modern language is incomparably poorer. Only *salām* and *silmī* remain, with *silm* just the double of *salām* in ready-made expressions. The Islamically marked *ṣulḥ* has disappeared from the vocabulary for negotiated peace, even if some Islamist milieux no doubt dream of restoring it.[5] The collocations that are found in the press owe nothing to the Arab-Muslim tradition but everything to the copying of European languages, notably English, starting with *'amaliyyat al-salām* (peace process), but also *muḥādathāt/ mufāwaḍāt al-salām* = peace discussions / negotiations, and so on. . . .

NOTES

1. By Arabic we mean here both the classical and modern Arabic varieties of High Arabic, in historical continuity with one another. To be complete, one would have to include colloquial Arabic, understanding it, too, in continuity with classical and modern Arabic.

2. This last example is given by Joüon (1913, pp. 156–57). In *makān*, the *ā* is grammatical, due to the fact that it is a place name linked to the verb *kāna-yakūnu* (to be, to exist).

3. The Koranic text is not invariant. Of the tradition of the "seven canonic read-

ings," fixed in the tenth century, there remain essentially two "readings," respectively, in the East and West of the Muslim world (cf. *EI*[2], article QIRĀʾA). It is to these that I constantly refer here.

4. Since you have to open the palm of the hand to lay down arms (metonymic interpretation), it appears difficult not to see open palms as a gesture of submission.

5. On the other hand, there remain derivatives in the sense of *(re)concile*, for example, read recently in *al-Ahrām* (July 1, 2000), with respect to Sudan, *al-musālaḥa al-shāmila* "general reconciliation."

BIBLIOGRAPHY

ʿAbd al-Bāqī, Muḥammad Fu'ād (AH 1364). *Al-Mu'jam al-muhfaras li-'alfāẓ al-Qur'ān al-karīm*. Le Caire: Maṭba'at dār al-kutub al-miṣriyya.

Atallah, W. 1973. "Un rituel de serment chez les Arabes: *al-yamīn al-ghamūs*." *Arabica* 20, no. 1: 63–73.

Benveniste, Emile. 1958 [1966]. "Les verbes délocutifs." *Mélanges Spitzer* 5:63. [Reprinted in *Problèmes de linguistique génerale*, I, 277–85. Paris: Gallimard.]

Cassuto, Philippe. 2001. "Le concept de paix et ses expressions en hébreu." In *Redéfinir la paix à l'aube du XXIe siècle, actes du colloque de l' Université de la paix, Verdun 2, 3 et 4 Décembre 1999. Les Cahiers de la Paix* no. 8: 85–93. Nancy: Presses Universitaires.

Cohen, Marcel. 1947. *Essai comparatif sur le vocabulaire et la phonétique du chamito-sémitique*, Bibliothèque de l'Ecole des Hautes Etudes, Sciences historiques et philologiques, 291ème fascicule. Paris: Librairie ancienne Honoré Champion.

Cornulier, Benoît de. 1976. "La notion de dérivation délocutive." *Revue de linguistique romane* 40: 116–44.

EI[2] = *Encyclopédie de l'Islam*, nouvelle édition, 1960. Leyden: Brill.

Houdebine-Gravaud, Anne-Marie. 2001. "Des femmes et de la paix." In *Redéfinir la paix à l'aube du XXIe siècle, actes du colloque de l' Université de la paix, Verdun 2, 3 et 4 Décembre 1999, Les Cahiers de la Paix* no. 8: 119–35. Nancy: Presses Universitaires.

(Ibn) al-Naḥḥās = Abū Jaʿfar Aḥmad b. Muḥammad al- Naḥḥās. 1393/1973. *Sharḥ al-qaṣā'id al-tis' al-mashhūrāt*. Edited by Aḥmad Khaṭṭāb, 2 vols. Baghdad: Dār al-Ḥurriyya li-l-ṭibā'a & *Maṭba*'at al-hukûma.

Ibn Manẓūr, *LA* = Muḥammad b. Mukarram b. ʿAlī b. 'Aḥmad al-'Anṣārī al-'Ifrīqī al-Miṣrī Jamāl al-dīn 'Abū l-Faḍl Ibn Manẓūr. *Lisān al-'Arab al-muḥīṭ*. Edited by Yūsuf Khayyāṭ. 4 vols. Beirut: Dār Lisān al-'Arab. N.d.

Joüon, Paul. 1913. "Arabica. VIII. *zaman* et *zamān*," *Mélanges de l'Université Saint-Joseph* 6: 156–57.

Koran (Le). 1967. Traduction et notes, Denise Masson, I and II, coll. Folio. Paris: Gallimard.

Koran (Le). 1980. Traduction Régis Blachère. Paris: G. P. Maisonneuve et Larose.

Qur'ān (al-) 'alā riwāyat al-'imām Warsh. AH 1365. Tunis, Maṭba'at al-Manär wa-Maktabatuhä.

Zawzanī (al-). 1383/1963. *Sharḥ al-Mu'allaqāt al-sab'*. Edited by Muḥammad 'Alī Ḥamd Allāh. Damas: al-Maktaba al-'Umawiyya.

Zuhayr, *Mu'allaqa*, cf. Zawzanī.

2.7

Mauve Athena

The "Translation" of the Qur'ān into Modern Double-Standard Arabic

Michael Schub

> How the Koran is allowed to be interpreted—and how it isn't—has become everybody's business.[1]

> . . . history . . . will assign 9/11 a specificity of dating very much like that struck into our cultural calendar by the blows of Luther's hammer on the doors of Wittenberg.[2]

> Dr. Johnson wrote that men are very prone to believe what they do not understand.[3]

'Asal Ma'ānī Aṣl al-Aṣīl min Niḥal al-Waqf wal-Waṣl al-Nabīl

The main purpose of the present article is to compare the language of the Qur'ān[4] with the language of its "translation," or better said, its paraphrase (*cum* commentary)[5] into Modern Standard Arabic (MSA), (the modern avatar of Classical Arabic)—the *Muntakhab fī Tafsīr al-Qur'ān al-Karīm* (Mtkb, henceforth).[6] This work has the "seal of approval" of the al-Azhar[7] scholars.

Mtkb begins with a preface and an introduction, the first of which emphasizes repeatedly that the Qur'ān is a "Major Bounty"[8] for all mankind, the True Guidance toward all that is true of Islamic belief and practice; Mtkb is based on traditionally faithful commentaries, without burdening the reader with technical details of the religious sciences.[9] The introduction then relates that Mtkb's purpose is "the annihilation" of [religious] error[10] by obviating the reliance on translations of this "axis [*sic*!] of Islamic culture,"[11] "this unfathomable sea,"[12] into other languages, which are, *eo ipso*, "fraudulent and baseless."[13]

Despite the fact that the Qur'ān is often referred to as the archetype of Classical Arabic (CA) prose,[14] it, along with pre-Islamic poetry, should be considered "pre-Classical Arabic." We will see numerous examples of how Mtkb "corrects" the wording of the Qur'ān to make it conform to the rules of MSA.

In addition to affording us a great amount of invaluable linguistic material, Mtkb interprets Qur'ānic themes and doctrines, which give us unique insights into what modern "mainstream" Muslims believe.

[I] Mtkb's Themes

1.1. One recurring theme in Mtkb is that Muslims never fought [and, supposedly never will fight,] an aggressive *jihād*, but only engaged in defensive wars. Thus at Mtkb494 end [Q22, 39, note 1]: "only 'self-defense' is permissible" [*ad-difā' 'an*^{i} *n-nafs*]; and that "all of the wars of the Muslims were defensive, not aggressive, wars, and that they established and spread Islam [using only] clear proofs and pellucid demonstrations." Yet Muslims are obliged to fight constant *jihād* (Mtkb 120 mid; Q4, 66) and it is the duty of all Muslims to fight a constant *jihād* against the unbelievers [*qital al-mushrikin mustamirr*^{an} *wajib*: Mtkb 128 mid (Q4, 102)][15]

Mtkb391 (Q16, 41): "A fine, good life comes only with *jihād*" [*ḥayāt ṭayyiba ḥasana lā ta'tī illā bil-jihād*]. Muslims must oppose the Jews and Christians of *today* [*al-haliyyin* (*sic*): Mtkb 143 mid; Q5, 1].

1.2. A Muslim must never allow a non-Muslim to rule over them (Mtkb75 mid; Q3, 28/Mtkb 121 end; Q4, 75). He must emigrate to a Muslim land, because he should not live in humiliation and subjection (Mtkb127 mid; Q4, 97). Killing a Muslim, however, is "the most heinous crime in the world" [*akbar jarīma fī d-dunyā*: Mtkb126 mid; Q4, 93].[16]

1.3. [The purpose of the Hebrew Bible (Old Testament) dietary laws] is to punish[17] the Jews for their evil, and to wean their souls from their exuberance for lust (Mtkb199 mid; Q6, 196). Compare Ibn Kathīr quoting Abū Hurayra:[18] "Don't take on yourselves what the Jews have taken upon themselves: legally allow God's prohibitions using the basest of legal tricks" [*lā tartakibū mā rtakaba l-yahūd fa-tastaḥillu maḥārima l-Lāh bi-adnā l-ḥiyal*]. The Jews act only for themselves and in order to harm others, and they [now] control the international economy (Mtkb91 end; Q3, 191, note 1).

"God will judge the Jews on the Day of Resurrection, and each one of them will deserve what he gets" (Mtkb302 end; Q10, 94). "Those who have inherited the Torah are in confusion and far removed from the Truth" (Mtkb327 mid; Q11, 110).

1.4. Both Jews and Christians hide the "fact" that the coming of Muhammad is predicted in their respective Scriptures (Mtkb23 mid; Q2, 201/Mtkb18 mid; Q2, 76/Mtkb148 mid; Q5, 15/Mtkb174 end/Q6, 20). They must pay the *jizya* (head tax) "to contribute to building up the Islamic budget" [*li-yushimū fī binā' al-mīzānīya al-islāmiyya*: Mtkb263 mid; Q9, 25]. "This is not meant to humiliate or punish: that doesn't jibe with Islam's lofty goals" [Mtkb263 end; Q9, 29, note 1].

1.5. In sum, "[the Qur'ān] explicates everything that needs explaining in the realm of Religion." [*yubayyin kull mā yaḥtāju ilā tafṣīli-hi min umūr d-dīn*: Mtkb357 end; Q12, 111]. Thus one need not learn anything at all about other religions or philosophies. The revision of history is completed at M422 mid [Q29]: "In the most ancient House built on earth for the worship of God [i.e., the Ka'ba]" [*bi-aqdam bayt buniya li-'ibādat[i] l-Lāh fī l-arḍ*].

Egypt's present governmental system is far superior to France's because the former system is based on Quranic law (Mtkb96 end; Q3, 155, note 1).

[II] God, Women, and Punishments under Islam

2.1. Women are, and always were, weak (Mtkb133 mid; Q4, 127).

2.2. Good women are the ones who are obedient to God and to their husbands (Mtkb114 mid; Q4, 34).

2.3. Women should have no right of divorce, for this weakens the family (Mtkb53 end; Q2, 228, note 2).

2.4. "That they stay behind [from the *jihād*] like women [who are] weak" [*bi-an yaq'adu ma'a n-nisā' ḍ-ḍā'ifāt*] (Mtkb276 mid; Q9, 93).

2.5. "[God] favored them with the strongest children, the sons" [*fa-khaṣṣa-hum bi-aqwā l-awlād wa-hum^u l-banūn*] Mtkb415 mid; Q17, 40).

2.6. "Women must not let men see their chest, arms, or neck . . . or hair" (Mtkb522 mid; Q24, 31).

2.7. If one suspects his wife of adultery and cannot find four reliable eyewitnesses, he may testify himself four times [and have her stoned to death], unless she denies [the charge] . . . (Mtkb518 mid; Q24, 6).

2.8. "[The penalty for adultery] is one hundred lashes" (Q24, 2).

2.9. "[The *Sharīʿa* punishment for adultery is lapidation [stoning to death]" (Mtkb517 end). The contradiction is not explained. In actuality this ruling is from the Hebrew Bible.[19]

2.10. The *ḥadd* punishment for theft is the amputation of the right hand and the left foot, or vice versa. This is based on the expression *min khilāf* at Q5, 33 and Q7, 124. Asad[20] translates this expression, plausibly, as "as a result of their perverseness" (Mtkb224 end; Q7, 124) paraphrases: "a hand from one side and a leg from the other side are to be amputated" [*fa-uqṭiʿa l-yad^u min jānib^in war-rijl^u min jānib^in ākhar^a*]. Mtkb152 end (Q5, 33, note 2) states that the literal interpretation of this verse has had a deterrent effect, and thus "it is superior to any man-made legislation ever made."

2.11. (Mtkb523 mid; Q24, 32): "You may allow your slaves to marry." The Sharīʿa permits slavery.

2.12. God is incorporeal (Q20, 5): "Al-Raḥmān [God] sat on His Throne" [*ar-raḥmān ʿalā l-ʿarsh^i stawā*] is de-anthropomorphized. (Mtkb456 mid): "The Great of Mercy took possession of his property" [*ʿaẓīm^u r-raḥma ʿalā mulk^i-hi stawlā*].

[III] Suppression of the Isrāʾīliyyāt: "We have only one biblical midrash current in seventh-century Arabia, and that is the Koran itself."[21]

The Egyptian scholar Rashid Riḍā held that the *Isrāʾīliyyāt* or legends concerning biblical characters, from postbiblical Jewish collections or from the Bible itself, were "fabricated for the purpose of undermining Islam."[22] He "even attempted to refute some *Isrāʾīliyyāt* traditions with the help of original Biblical material."[23] *But the Isrā'īliyyāt are the warp and woof of Q.*[24]

3.1. At Q2, 63 God holds the *ṭūr*, that is, Mount Sinai over the Israelites' heads threatening to crush them if they do not accept the Torah. This legend is copied from the Babylonian Talmud, Tractate Shabbat 88a.[25]

3.2. At Q37, 100–13 Abraham is commanded to sacrifice "his son." A. Yusuf Ali 1149–50 tries, pathetically, to "prove" that this refers to Ismā'īl rather than Isaac, using the Bible account itself as a proof text. Mtkb449 end (Q19, 54) claims that Ismā'īl rather than Isḥāq, was the intended sacrifice of Abraham, although there is no indication of this is Q38, 101 itself: it has only "your son." Note that Bayḍāwī says that Isḥāq is the one to be sacrificed in his commentary on Q12, 7 (Beid. I 453, lines 3, 4).

3.3. Adam's wife is first introduced at Q2, 25 as "your wife."

[*zawju-ka*] Modern commentators are becoming more and more consistent in rejecting the traditional view that her name was "Eve" [*ḥawwā'*] because Q never states that explicitly. So at Mtkb10 end [Q2, 25] we have "and his spouse"; [*wa-zawjatu-hu*] and "and your wife"; [*wa-mra'atu-ka*] and verse 26 and verse 27 [Mtkb11 top], we again have *zawj*[26] referring to her. But about two hundred pages later, the editors drop the ball and call Adam's wife Eve [*ḥawwā'*] (at Mtkb204 mid/Q7, 1; also at Mtkb468 end/Q20, 117).

3.4. Sura 12, the Joseph story, does not mention the name of his full younger brother, Benjamin, but Mtkb does several times, for example, at Mtkb341 end [Q12, 59]: "He is Benjamin, Joseph's full brother" [*wa-huwa binyamīn shaqīq yūsuf*] Strangely, at Mtkb320 mid (Q11.71) we have: "[Sarah] would give birth to Isaac by Abraham . . . and from him also she would give birth to Jacob after Isaac [*sic*]."

3.5. The Seven Mathānī: "In Judaism, long before Sinai and the giving to Moses of the Law, there was Noah and the seven laws or *mishpaṭīm* that are presented, one by one, incident by incident, in the first eleven chapters of the book of Genesis. Known as the Seven Laws of Noah, they were the governing principles of Judaism before Sinai and, by their early coming, sketched in the first parameters of Jewish moral and religious thought. The Seven Laws of Noah are couched, as nine of the Ten Commandments are later, in terms of sins which must not be committed. In order of their Biblical occurrence, the first *mishpaṭ* or sin is blasphemy; the second is idolatry; the third, theft; the fourth, murder; the fifth, illicit sex; the sixth, false witness or duplicity in adjudication; and the last, the eating of flesh torn from a living beast."[27]

"The same religion He has established for you as that which He enjoined on Noah . . ." [Q42, 13]. Upon hearing of God's Covenant with Noah requiring all nations of the earth to abjure for all time the most horrific and abominable crimes known to mankind,[28] namely, living without a fixed system of laws, blasphemy, idolatry, incest and adultery, bloodshed, robbery, and eating a limb from a living animal,[29] Q's redactor [or Muhammad] came up with Q39, 23: "Allah has revealed the finest message, in the form of [*kitāb mutashābih*] a continually renewed Covenant [appropriate for and applicable to the warned people addressed]; [*mathānī*] repeating the prohibition on the most heinous crimes continually, [atrocities which] make the flesh of those who fear their Lord [*taqsha'irru min-hu*] crawl with horror. . . ."[30]

In his commentary[31] on Q, Qurṭubī states that the word *kitāb* (Scripture) at Q28, 43 refers to the Torah, and, more specifically, to six of the seven *mathānī* that are found in it; the seventh, he says, is found only in Q. He adds that Muḥammad was sent as a *mujaddid al-dīn*, that is, "a renewer of the Religion."[32]

At Q42, 13, Qurṭubī[33] notes that according to a crucial tradition Adam was the first *nabīy* [prophet], but Noah was the first *rasūl*, that is, a *nabīy* who brings a *risāla* [message] with him: "Allah had Noah bring the prohibition against marrying mothers, daughters, and sisters; and man's [moral] obligations and proper religious customs . . . ; and so on with the following *rasūls* culminating in Muhammad."

Traditional commentaries identify the seven mathānī as the seven verses of the *Fātiḥa*, the seven longest sūras of Q, the seven most prominent *Straflegenden* (the most prominent legends of previous peoples who failed to heed their Prophet, and subsequently perished; that is, the template of Muhammad's mission, etc.) At Q39, 23; Mtkb687 mid, the seven mathānī are identified as those Q verses that resemble each other in wording, repeating therein warnings and normative practices. At Q15, 87; Mtkb381 definitively identifies the seven mathānī with the seven verses of the *Fātiḥa*.[34]

3.6. M. Philonenko[35] has persuasively demonstrated that the expression at Q85, 4 "the men of the Pit" [*aṣḥāb al-ukhdūd*] is derived from a Hebrew expression in the Dead Sea Scrolls: *anshē hash-shaḥat.*

But what of the Arabic cognate of the Hebrew form *shaḥat* (= "Pit"), which appears at Q5, 62, 63: ". . . See, racing each other in sin and transgression, and eating of things forbidden (*wa-akli-him^u^ s-suḥt^a^*). . . . Why do the Rabbis and doctors of the Law forbid them from [their habit of] uttering sinful words and eating[36] things forbidden (*wa-akli-him^u^ s-suḥt*)?"

It is clearly a reflex of the Hebrew *shoḥad* at Isaiah 5:23: "They justify doing evil in exchange for bribes (*shoḥad*)."

The form now corresponding specifically to the evil of bribery, *rishwa*, does not appear in Q.[37]

3.7. Q6, 76–79 (Mtkb184–85) retells the *midrash*[38] that Abraham first worshipped the sun and then the moon, but when they set, he denied that they could be gods.

3.8. Mtkb remains clueless as to the import of "Messiah" in Judaism and Christianity: Mtkb78 mid [Q3, 45]: "his name is al-Masīḥ Jesus son of Mary" [*ism^u^-hu l-masīḥ 'īsā bn^u^ Maryam*]. Mtkb141 end [Q4, 171] notes that "the Messiah is an emissary just like all the other emissaries" [*fa-inna-mā l- masīḥ rasūl ka-sā'ir ar-rusul*]. Jesus was never crucified, much less resurrected, because (following the second-century docetic Basilidian Christian (!) heresy, a *Döppelganger* was executed in Jesus' place: "they [the Jews] absolutely never killed Jesus" [*mā qatalū 'īsā qaṭ'^an^*] (Mtkb139 end; Q4, 157).

Mtkb189 end [Q6, 100]: "Christians suppose that the Messiah is the son of God—this is ignorance" [*ẓa'ama n-naṣārā anna l-masīḥ^a^ bn^u^ l-Lah . . . wa-dhālika jahl*].

3.9. Q5, 60: "[God] transformed some of the unbelievers into apes and swine . . ." Mtkb157 end ameliorates: "*like* apes and swine." [*ka-l-qirada wal-khanāzīr*] God doesn't do magic tricks. Likewise at Q7, 166 [Mtkb233 end].

3.10. At Mtkb446 end on Q19, 28: "O sister of Aaron [Mary, mother of Jesus]," Mtkb notes that in "English scholarly circles" Q was said to be historically mistaken here for mistaking Miriam, the sister of Aaron (and Moses), with Mary, mother of Jesus: the Arabs give nicknames of this sort to people who resemble each other. Here the intent is that Mary is a sister to Aaron in "goodness and piety."

3.11. At Mtkb150 end [Q5, 31] Mtkb reports that Cain was at a loss as to what to do with Abel's dead body: "God sent a crow digging in the earth to bury a dead crow, in order to teach the killer how to dispose of his brother's body." This is a direct quotation of a *midrash* from *Pirkei De-Rabbi Eliezer*, chapter 21.[39] Curiously, at Mtkb564 mid [Q27, 18] we are enlightened to the fact that "ants comprise the only living species after man which buries their dead."

3.12. Mtkb's basic attitude is succinctly expressed at Mtkb184 mid [Q6, 71]: "It is Islam that is Right Guidance and Instruction—everything beside it is Error" [*innā l-islām huwa l-hudā war-rashād wa-mā 'adā-hu ḍalāl*].

3.13. At Q9, 30 we have the claim that "the Jews say that Ezra is the Son of God." Mtkb263 end repeats this oxymoron: had any Jews ever considered Ezra to be the Son of God, they would no longer have been called Jews," but "Ezranians," or something along these lines (à la "Christians").

[IV] SUPPRESSION OF ISLAMIC TRADITIONS

Mtkb almost never refers to the *asbāb an-nuzūl* (the "Occasions for the Revelation"), or the incident in the Prophet's career that prompted the revelation of a verse or verses, even though this is a major portion of the traditional commentaries. An exception occurs at Mtkb520 end [Q24, 22, note 1]: "This verse was revealed when Abū Bakr swore to withhold aid to his relative Mastaḥ ibn Uthātha because of his involvement in spreading the rumor about ʿĀʾisha['s infidelity to the Prophet]."

Likewise, Mtkb very rarely quotes from the *Ḥadīth* (Traditions), which also comprises a large portion of the classical commentaries. An exception occurs at Mtkb533 mid [Q24, note 1]: "[The Prophet said:] 'O Young Men! Those of you who are capable of *al-bā'a* (maintaining a household) should marry, and thus restrain your [roving] eyes and to fortify/restrain your *farj* (pudenda). He who is unable to should fast, so that he becomes *waja'* (gelded).'"

At Q49, 10: "If two parties fall into a quarrel, then make peace between them. . . ." All of commentators agree here; for example, the "standard" short commentary *Tafsīr al-Jalālayn* by the two Jalāls, Jalāl ad-Dīn as-Suyuti and Jalāl ad- Dīn al-Maḥallī, explains the incident that caused this revelation: "Riding a donkey, the Prophet passed by [a group of men led by] Ibn Ubayy. The donkey pissed, and then Ibn Ubayy held his nose. [One of the Prophet's companions,] Ibn Rawwāḥa, then said: 'By god! The piss of this man's camel smells better than your perfume.' The two groups began to brawl. . . ."[40]

Mtkb715 end does not mention this incident.

Q16, 103: "We know they say: 'a mortal taught him.' The man to whom speaks a foreign tongue, while this is eloquent Arabic speech." Mtkb403 end notes that this mortal is *shābb rūmī*, "a Byzantine young man," who probably spoke Syriac.[41]

[V] Mtkb's Structure

Mtkb begins with a preface, an introduction, and follows with the body of the work, each page of which is arranged into two or three horizontal sections: the text of Q on top, then the translation and brief commentary. The Q text is completely vocalized, that is, it has all the vowels indicated, but the following section is almost never vocalized at all. The following exceptions are an indication that the generally accepted unvocalized script is *incapable of expressing MSA expressions unequivocally.*

Very rare exceptions:

5.1. Mtkb43 end [Q2, 191]: *fa-inna l-islām lā yajubbu mā qabla-hu* = "for indeed Islam never cuts [itself] off from what came before it." Here *yajubbu* is fully vocalized with a *fatḥa*, two *ḍamma*s, and a *shadda*, to distinguish it from the much more common * yajibu, "must."[42]

5.2. Mtkb354 end [Q13, 9]: *ʿan ḥissi-na*, "from our senses": without vowels (the two *kasra*s and the *shadda* are written in, this could be easily misread as * *ʿan ḥusn^in^*, "out of goodness," etc.).

5.3. Mtkb78 end [Q3, 49]: *ʿalā yadayya*, "by my two hands" is written vowelless but with the *shadda*, lest one read * *ʿalā yadī*, "by my hand."

This is sometimes followed at the bottom of the page with a section of "scientific notes" (totally unvocalized), many of which are of the infantile apologetic genre of "modern archeology/geology/cosmology, and so on proves Q is true," "modern medicine proves that fasting is good for you," "Islam is the first religion to give women their rights," and so forth.[43] Thus at Q2, 13, after the law of inheritance states that the male's inheritance is twice that of the female's, Mtkb109, note 1: "The inheritance law which the noble Q sets forth is the most just inheritance law system ever known in world jurisprudence, and all European law scholars have acknowledged this fact [*sic*!]." Compare Ibn Bābūyā:[44] "Some among us claim that God created Eve from Adam's lowermost left rib. God forbid! He is far above that! . . . When God created Adam from clay, He ordered the angels to bow down to him. He caused a sleep to fall upon him, then He created Eve for him from the [*mawdi' al-nuqra a-latī bayna warakay-hi*] hole between his haunches, so that the woman would [always] be obedient to him . . ." [no airbrushing here].

Perhaps the first function of any translation is to render foreign terms into the target language. Q is so replete with foreignisms that "a fifth of the Koranic text is just incomprehensible."[45]

5.4. Thus at Q3, 77: [. . . *ulā'ika lā khalāq*[a] *la-hum fī l-ākhirat*[i] . . .] ". . . these have no portion in the world to come" (a direct quotation from the Mishna Sanhedrin 10, 1), Mtkb83 mid must translate the Hebrew term for "portion" [*kheleq]* to its Arabic equivalent: . . . *lā naṣīb*[a] *la-hum. . . .*[46]

5.5. At Q62, 1, Mtkb826 end insists on the traditional, but incorrect translation of *ummīyūna* as "illiterates," despite the fact that this word has long been recognized as a reflex of the Hebrew for "nations of the world; gentiles."[47] *Traduttore traditore.*[48]

5.6. At Q62, 5 we find the proverb that "those who accept the Torah but do not practice it are like a donkey carrying books, "*asfār*." This Hebrew term[49] is translated at Mtkb867 mid as *kutub*. (The Ethiopic [Ge'ez] term for book, *maṣḥaf*, also occurs in Q).

5.7. Q57, 13: *fa-ḍuriba bayna-hum bi-sūr*[in], "a wall was placed between them. Mtkb805 end paraphrases this "probably Syriac (Aramaic)"[50] word with *ḥājiz*, "partition."

5.8. At Q55, 20 the foreign[51] term *barzakh* is used for "barrier; wall." Mtkb792 mid paraphrases this also with *ḥājiz.*

5.9. At Q51, 40 the Hebrew word *yamm*, "sea," is correctly translated by Mtkb773 end as *baḥr.*

5.10. At Q52, 1 the Aramaic word for "mountain," *ṭūr*, is incorrectly rendered as *jabal ṭūr sinā'*, "the mountain [named] '*Ṭūr Sinā'* '[upon which God spoke directly to Moses]' . . ." (Mtkb231 mid [Q7, 155] uses *aṭ-ṭūr* in its commentary as if it were fully assimilated into modern vocabulary.)

5.11. At Q6, 14 the originally Ethiopic[52] usage of *fāṭir* as "creator" is paraphrased by Mtkb174 mid as *munshi*, "establisher." The same word appears at Q42, 11; Mtkb716 mid glosses it as *mubdi'*, "innovator." At Q39, 46 it is glossed as *khāliq*, "creator."

5.12. Q6, 95 and 96: the originally Syriac[53] expression *fāliq* is rendered *yashuqqu*, "splitting."

5.13. At Q6, 153, the originally Latin[54] and Syriac[55] words for "way," *ṣirāṭ . . . sabīl*, are glossed by Mtkb201 mid as *nahj . . . ṭarīq*.

5.14. Q39, 17 the originally Ethiopic or Aramaic[56] term *ṭaghūt*, "idolatry," is glossed at Mtkb686 mid as *al-aṣnāmm wash-shayāṭīn*, "idols and satans."

5.15. At Q39, 35 the transparently Hebrew/Aramaic *kaffara*, "to atone," is glossed by Mtkb688 mid as *li-yaghfira*, "so that [God] forgive."

5.16. Q7, 157 *'azzaru-hu*,[57] "He helped him" is translated by Mtkb231 end: *'azaru-hu wa-ayyadu-hu*, with the same meaning; Q23, 11: *firdaws*, from which we derive "Paradise," is glossed at Mtkb503 mid as *a'lā makān fī l-janna*, "the highest place in the Garden." ["'My paternal great-grandfather embraced Islam, ' as they say: Islam, that least huggable of faiths. As a result of that prickly embrace, . . . indeed every Muslim in the subcontinent . . . *lost his connection with history*."][58]

5.17. Some Quranic verses leave one up in the air, for example, Q11, 80: "[God said:] 'Had I power over you, or if I would repair to a strong pillar [*sic*]. '" Mtkb321 end completes the sentence: "then my situation with you would be different: I would have defended my guests from you, and prevented you from doing evil." Q20, 114: *rabbi zid-nī 'ilm^an^*, ". . . O my Lord, grant me knowledge." Mtkb468 mid clarifies: *bil-qur'ān wa-ma'ānī-hi*, "of Q and its meanings."

5.18. Other verses are unclear, for example, Q15, 4: "We have never destroyed a people, except that it had a *kitāb mubīn*." This phrase usually means "a clear Scripture." Here Mtkb372 end clarifies: *illā li-ajal qadara-hu ma'lūm 'inda-hu*, "except until the limit [God] had knowingly foreordained."

5.19. Still other verses have complicated syntax, for example, Q14, 47: *mukhlif^a^ wa'd^i^-hi rusul^a^-hu*, "break his pledge to his emissaries," is simplified at Mtkb371 mid: *mukhlif^u^ rusul^i^-hi mā wa'ada-hum bi-hi* with the same meaning. The obscure Q15, 65: *fa-asri bi-ahl*^{i}*-ka*, "take your family by night," is simplified at Mtkb379 mid: *fa-sir layl*^{an} *ma'a ahl*^{i}*-ka* with the same meaning.

5.20. Q17, 90: *adkhil-nī mudkhal*^{a} *ṣidq . . . wa-akhrij-nī mukhraj*^{a}, "Cause me to enter a true entering . . . and cause me to exit . . . an exiting." Here Mtkb421 end glosses the Form IV derived nouns of place (which equal their respective past participles) with the more common "absolute" accusatives, the verbal nouns: *idkhāl*^{an} and *ikhrāj*^{an}.

VI. Mtkb's Style

Early on in the commentary, Mtkb3 top [Q2, 1], Mtkb warns that blind faith in tradition is unwarranted because it leads to ignorance and group-think: *at-taqlīd al-a'mā bāṭil yu'addī ilā l-jahāla wal-'aṣabiyya*. Mtkb fails to follow its own advice:

6.1. Mtkb92 end blindly follows the Q text: *kayfa kāna 'āqibatu . . .*, "how was the punishment of . . . ," with an "incorrect" *kāna* for *kānat*. Later, Mtkb "corrects" this "error" (see below).

6.2. Q4, 47: *wa-kāna amr*^{u} *l-Lāhi maf'ūl*^{an}, "And God's order is always operative"; paraphrased at Mtkb117 mid: *wa-kāna qaḍā'*^{u} *l-Lāh nafīdh*^{an}, with the same meaning.

6.3. Q4, 39: *wa-kāna l-Lāh bi-him 'alīm*^{an}, "God is always knowledge-able"; is paraphrased at Mtkb115 end: *wal-Lāh 'alīm*^{un} . . . , with the same translation.

6.4. At Q4, 33: *innā l-Lāh kāna . . . shahīd*^{an}, "God is indeed witness," Mtkb113 end paraphrases: *innā l-Lāh kāna raqīb*^{an}, "God is indeed observer," keeping the otiose panchronic[59] form *kāna*.

6.5. Q17, 1: *asrā bi-'abd*^{i}*-hi*, "He took His servant by night." Mtkb309 end glosses: *sāra bi-'abd*^{i}*-hi muḥammad*^{an} *min juz' mina l-layl*, "He took His servant, Muhammad [accusative], by night." Fleischer[60] explains that this is a pre-Classical usage: *bi-na'lay-hi l-'utuq*^{a}, "with his sandals, the old ones."

VII. Apposition[61]

7.1. Mtkb507 mid [Q23, 47]: *wa-qawm*^{u}*-humā banū isrā'īl*, "and their [dual] people, the Children of Israel. "

7.2. Mtkb111 end repeats Q4, 57: *azwāj muṭahhara*, "purified wives," despite the fact that the rules of CA and MSA call for the feminine plural adjective here, *muṭahharāt* [unless "wives" are to be considered 'irrational beings'].

Mtkb is written in a very high-educated MSA style that adheres very closely to the syntax of CA; it only seldom employs "acceptable" simplifications[62] in Modern Written Arabic (MWA). Perfectly acceptable is the substitution of a simpler or less elevated Arabic word for the one in the Quranic text, for example, Q13, 14: *fā-hu,* "his mouth (accusative)";[63] Mtkb355 end: *fama-hu* ditto. See also Mtkb236 end [Q7, 176, note 1]:

min fam^{i}*-hi* instead of (the equally correct, but somewhat tricky): * *min fī-hi*, "from his mouth."[64]

Sometimes Mtkb disambiguates a Quranic phrase by adding a few words, for example, Q13, 22: *la-hum 'uqbā d-dār*, "theirs is the recompense of the Abode." But which Abode, Heaven or Hell? Mtkb357 end clarifies: . . . *bi-aḥsan*^{i} *d-dār*^{i} *wa-hiya l-janna*, "the best Abode, namely, Heaven."

VIII. Some Common Simplifications:

8.1. MSA uses the term *zawja* for "wife" rather than the Quranic *zawj*, for "spouse; wife," although Naguib Mahfuz is said to be an exception to this general rule.[65] See Mtkb77end [Q40]: *wa-'uqm zawj*^{i}*-hi* . . . , ". . . and his wife's barrenness . . ."[66]

8.2. In an *iḍāfa*, or annexation construction, the first member must be a monomial according to the rules of CA.[67] In MSA it is common for a binomial to occur here if it is considered as "one notion." Thus Q5, 18 [Mtkb148 top]: *abnā'*^{u} *L-lāh*^{i} *wa-aḥibbā'*^{u}*-hu*, "God's beloved children, rather than * *abnā'*^{u} *wa-aḥibbā'*^{u} *L-lāh*^{i}. Also, for example, *iḍlāl*^{u} *wa-fitnat*^{u} *l-mu'minīna* would be acceptable in MSA for "deceiving and inciting the believers." But the conservative Mtkb almost never uses this type of construction.

Exception #1: Mtkb163 end [Q5, 91]: *tanshīṭ wa-ta'wīq hādhihi l-marākiz*, "the excitation and obstruction of theses centers . . ."(!!);

Exception #2: Mtkb658 end [Q36, 67]: numuwwu *wa-naḍj*^{u} *wa-ḍumūr*^{u} *n-nasīj*^{i} *l-ḥashwi*, "growth, maturation, and atrophy of the intestinal tissue . . ." (!!)

Exception #3: Mtkb254 end [Q, 66]: *tanẓīm wa-ḍaf' junūd*^{i}*-hi*, "organizing and encouraging his troops."

It is remarkable that these exceptions occur mainly in the third part of a given page, that is, not in the commentary itself, but only in the additional notes, where a less frantic adhesion to the rules of CA could be expected. So at Mtkb81 end [Q3, 69] we have *idlāl*^{a} *al-mu'minīna wa-fitnat*^{a}*-hum* (with the same import).

8.3. Mtkb79 end [Q3, 53]: *aḥkām*^{u} *l-mudabbirīna wa-aqwā-hum*, "the most clever and powerful arranger."

8.4. Mtkb78 end [Q3, 49]: *bi-idhn*^{i} *L-lāh*^{i} *wa-irādat*^{i}*-hi* "with God's permission and will." This rule is maintained even when the binomial would comprise a single notion of "*itbā'* [imitative pleonasm][68] plus hendiadys:"[69] Mtkb842 [Q67, 14]: *mid*: . . . *bi-daqā'iq*^{i} *l-ashyā'*^{i} *wa-ḥaqā'iq*^{i}*-hā* . . . , ". . . with the detailed truth of matters. . . ."

8.5. Nor does it occur with merism(us):[71] Mtkb114 end [Q4, 34]: *ẓawāhir*^{i} *l- 'ibād*^{i} *wa-bawāṭin*^{i}*-him*, "the worshippers' exteriors and interiors"? Mtkb115 end [Q4, 39]: *bawāṭinu l-umūri wa-ẓawāhir*^{u}*-ha*, "the internals and externals of things."[71] Mtkb 356 mid [Q13, 15]: *li-amr*^{i} *L-lāh*^{i} *wa-nahy*^{i}*-hi*, "to God's positive and negative commandments."

8.6. Q6, 137: *qatl*^{a} *awlād*^{i}*-him shurakā'*^{u}*-hum*, "the slaughter of their children by their partners" is "corrected" at Mtkb196 end: *ẓa'amū shura'kā'*^{u} *lil-Lāh*^{i} *qatl*^{a} *awlād*^{i}*-him 'inda l-wilāda*, "those who ascribe partners to God supposed that the killing of their children at birth. . . ." But see Mtkb272 mid: *aḥibbā'*^{u} *wa-nuṣarā'*^{u} *ba'ḍ*^{in}, "lovers and victors for some" [Q9, 71]!!

8.7. Mtkb 286 mid [Q10, 10]: *tasbīḥ*^{u} *wa-tanzīh*^{u} *l-Lāh*^{i}, "praising and preserving God [from] . . ." (!!)

8.8. Mtkb 505 end [Q23, 20]: *afḍal*^{u} *wa-aḥsan*^{u} *anwā'*, "the most excellent and best types." (!!)

IX.

Almost never does Mtkb refer to grammatical questions per se. An exception is made at Q36, 36: "Glory to God Who created in pairs all things, *mim-mā tunbitu l-arḍ*[u] *wa-min anfus*[i]*-him wa-mim-mā lā ta'lamūna*, that the earth produces, as well as [He produces] you yourselves, and other things of which they have no knowledge." Of the three particles *min* here, Mtkb654 end identifies the second of the three (the other two are "partitive") as the "explicative *min*," that is, the one which has the "colon function" (or that can be glossed as "*viz.*"). Without this stipulation, one is liable to translate: ". . . that the earth and you produce, . . ."

X.

To a limited extent Mtkb "modernizes," or, perhaps better said, moves from Ferguson and Holes's Level 5 (Pristine Classical-Traditional Arabic) a bit lower toward Level 4 (Educated Modern Standard Arabic), for example, at M751 end [Q36, 1] by calling the "mysterious letters" which introduce some sūras as *al-ḥurūf al-muqaṭṭa'a* ("the interrupted letters") with the more frequent feminine singular adjective, rather than the traditional *al-ḥurūf al-muqaṭṭa'āt*.

XI. "Correcting" the Arabic Grammar of the Qur'ān

Classical Arabic (CA), a closed system by mid-tenth century CE,[72] as well as its contemporary avatar, Modern Standard Arabic (MSA), comprise "an art form for connoisseurs, where the spectator derives his pleasure from the appreciation of minor variations within the working out of a pre-established order."[73] "[The Arab grammarians] . . . had a strong sense that linguistic facts, for all their apparent disorder, were regulated by an underlying system which it was their task to make visible, in the form of explicit rules and principles."[74] "In giving prominence to Q, as divinely inspired text, as linguistic yardstick, and as motivation to record the pre-Islamic poetic tradition in written form, we acknowledge its central place in almost every aspect of the development of Arabic language and literature. In analyzing, albeit briefly, the beauty of the language and of Q, we may link the sacred book of Islam to recent literary-critical studies of religious texts."[75]

W. Fischer considers the language of Q and of pre-Islamic poetry to comprise "pre-classical Arabic."[76] Thus Mtkb must rephrase Quranic wording, which is "incorrect" according to the normative grammatical rules of CA ("CA represents the ancient poetic koine *frozen* [emphasis mine—MBS] at a particular moment of its existence . . .")[77] and MSA. (Like the Greeks, Hindus, and all other oriental peoples, the Arabs of old had no conception of language development over time).[78]

11.1. At Q20, 63: . . . *in hādhān*^{i} *la-sāḥirān*^{i} . . . ,[79] ". . . these two are verily sorcerers. . . ." Mtkb461 end must paraphrase[80] . . . *anna Mūsā wa-Harūn*^{a} *sāḥirān*^{i}. . . . The "error" in the Q text is a clear hypercorrection.

11.2. At Q2, 25: . . . *azwāj*^{un} *mṭtahharat*^{un}. . . . ". . . pure wives [in Paradise] . . ." Mtkb8 is constrained to paraphrase *zawjāt*^{un} *kamilāt*^{u} *l-ṭahārat*^{i} *laysa fi-hinna mā yu'ābu*, ". . . wives perfect in purity, in whom there is no blemish."

11.3. At Q2, 197: *ashhur*^{un} *ma'lūmāt*^{un}, "known months is corrected by Mtkb45 end to *ashhur*^{un} *ma'lūmat*^{un}. (See below for *ashhur*^{un} as a "plural of paucity.")

11.4. Likewise at Q2, 184: *ayyām*^{un} *ma'dūdāt*^{un}, "a few days" is "corrected" by Mtkb 41 mid to *ayyām*^{un} *ma'dūdat*^{un}.

Note: "[In CA] *all plurals which do not refer to rational beings* [are treated as feminine singular]." (Bateson, 12 mid; emphasis Bateson's.) This is called "deflected agreement," as opposed to "strict agreement." Brusted (53, n. 6) corrects: "It is reasonable to assume that these two types of agreement, deflected and plural, have coexisted for a long time." Yet the first statement is perfectly true for the dialects.[81]

11.5. Q58, 5: *ayāt bayyināt*, "clear signs;" M811 mid paraphrases with another noun-adjective phrase with a plural adjective: *dalā'il wāḍiḥāt.*

11.6. For "clear signs" Mtkb 699 mid [Q40, 34] has *ayāt wāḍiḥāt* /; at M702 mid [Q40, 69]: *ayāt wāḍiḥat*

11.7. At Q2, 275: *jā'a-hu maw'iẓat*^{un}, "an admonishment came to him," we have a masculine singular verb followed by a feminine singular noun.

Mtkb 66 mid: *fa-man jā'a-hu amr^u rabbi-hi*, "for to him to whom his Lord's command comes . . ."

11.8. Likewise at Q65, 9: *wa-kāna 'āqibat^u amr^i-ha khusr^an*, A285 mid: ". . . and the end of its affair was loss." Mtkb 835 end merely copies this "error."[82] But at Q6, 11 the same *kāna 'āqibatu* . . . is "corrected" by Mtkb 173 mid: *kāna l-halāk^u nihāyat^a l-mukadhdhibīna*, "perdition was the end of the disbelievers."

11.9. At Mtkb 218 end, Mtkb "corrects" Q7, 86: *kayfa kāna 'āqibat^u*, with *'āqibat^u* . . . *wa-kayfa kānat*. See also Q27, 14, where this formula is "corrected" at Mtkb 564 mid as: *kayfa kānat 'āqibat^u l-ladhīna da'abū* . . . , "how the punishment of those who behaved thusly was . . ." See also Q12, 30 [Mtkb335 top]: *wa-qāla niswa*, "women said."

11.10. Q11, 10: *dhahaba s-sayyi'āt^u 'annī*, "evil things have gone from me" is "corrected" at Mtkb 308 mid: *dhahaba mā kāna yasu'u-nī*, with the same meaning.

11.11. Mtkb 310 mid [Q11, 19]: Mtkb uses the word *sabīl*, "path, way, road," first as masculine, then as feminine: *sabil^u-hu l-mustaqīm wa-yaṭlubūna an takūna hādhihi s-sabīl muwāfaqat^an*, "His straight path (m.), and they want this path (f.) to be in agreement with . . ."

11.12. Q11, 114: *inna l-hasanāt^i yudhhibna a-sayyi'āt^i*, "the good deeds will vitiate the bad deeds." Mtkb327 end "corrects" this usage of the feminine plural verb: *wa-tamḥu āthār^a s-sayyiyāt^i l-latī* . . . , "they will erase the traces of the bad deeds which [feminine singular] "

11.13. Strangely at Q25, 36: *fa-dammarna-hum tadmīr^an*, "We utterly crushed them," Mtkb 536 mid paraphrases *fa-kāna 'āqibatu-hum* . . . , "their punishment was . . ."

11.14. At Mtkb555 mid [Q26, 148] we have the barbaric: *zurū' yāni'āt* . . . *wa-buyūt 'aliyāt*, "ripe seeds and high houses."

11.15. *Al-iltifat*: there is a switch in persons at Mtkb515 mid [Q23, 117]: *wa-inna-mā l-ladhī yufliḥu hum^u l-mu'minūn* -, "It is they the Believers [pl.] who are the one [sing.] who believes." [*sic*]

11.16. Q27, 9: *inna-hu anā L-lāh^u*, "Indeed, I am God" is "corrected" at Mtkb563 end to: *'innī anā L-lāh^u*. We note that Mtkb separates the printing of the first word in the Quranic text from the following two with a *tilde* (!!) under which is a comma (!!!)

11.17. At Q98, 5: *wa-dhālika dīn^u l-qayyimat^u*. A346: ". . . that is the religion of the True"; A. Yusuf Ali 1679: "And that is the Religion, Right and Straight."

This appears to be on the surface a masculine singular noun followed by a feminine singular adjective (most likely caused by *ḍarūra*, or *poesis causa* [poetic license, the necessity to preserve the rhyme, and thus, according to Nöldeke, the Prophet's "right]."[83] Mtkb 920 end is thus constrained to paraphrase: *wa-dhālika dīn^u l-millat^i l-qayyimat^i*, "that is the religion of the upright community." (Note that in the modern dialects of Syria and Kuwait, a feminine singular noun may be followed by a masculine singular adjective (!)[84] This may occur also in MWA through colloquial influence.[85] See Mtkb73 end [Q3, 19]: *al-dīn^u l-ḥaqq^u*, "the true religion"; and Mtkb87 end [Q3, 105]. Q12, 40 [Mtkb338 top]: *ad-dīn^u l-qayyim*, "The True Religion," which Mtkb paraphrases as *ad-dīn^u s-salīm^u l-qawīm*, "the Sound and Correct Religion."

11.18. Note that at Mtkb372 mid [Q15, 1] *jibāl rāsiyāt*, "high mountains," with a feminine plural adjective, and a few pages later, at Mtkb374 (Q15, 19) *jibāl thābita*, "firmly fixed mountains," with a feminine singular adjective.

11.19. At Q4, 1 we must read, according to Nöldeke, *wa-ttaqū L-lāh^a wal-ladhī tasa'alūna bi-hi wal-arḥāmi*[86] rather than with the generally accepted reading of . . . *wal-arḥāma*. Of all the translations I have checked, only Paret[87] provides this correct interpretation (as an alternative to the other one): ". . . or: 'Fear God, in Whose name—and in the name of the relatives by whom you demand of one another.'" Nöldeke (1963, 93 mid) compares the syntax of this verse to the oft-quoted line of the poet Ḥassān: *la'ana l-Lāh^u wa-zawja-hā ma'a-hā Hind^a l-Hunūd^i ṭawīlat^a l-biẓr^i*, "May God curse, together with her husband, Hindy-Hind with the long clitoris."

11.20. Compare: Q15, 20: *wa-ja'alnā la-kum fī-hā ma'āyish^a wa-man lastum la-hu bi-rāziqīna*, P191 end: "And We have given unto you livelihoods therein, and to those for whom ye provide not."

11.21. Q2, 217: . . . *wa-kufr^un fī-hi wal-masjid* . . . , ". . . and disbelief in it and in the mosque. . . ." Mtkb49 end "corrects" by paraphrasing . . . *man ṣadda 'an sabīl^i L-lāh^i wa-'an^i l-masjid* . . . , "whoever obstructs God's way and the mosque. . . ."[88] Or, for that matter, Q2, 133: . . . *na'budu ilāha-ka wa-ilāh^a abā'i-ka* . . . , ". . . we worship your God and your fathers'

God . . . : and Mtkb 33 mid [Q2, 148]: *qiblatu-ka waqiblatu ummati-ka*, ". . . your direction of prayer, and that of your nation . . ."

Q2, 127: *wa-idh rafa'a Ibrāhīm*[u] *qawā'id*[a] *min*[a] *l-bayt*[i] *wa-Ismā'īl*[u] . . . , "When Abraham raised the foundations of the House, and Isma'il [did too] . . ." It is clear that "and Ismā'īl" was tacked on later as a kind of "afterthought." Mtkb 28 end "corrects" with a "balanced nominal clause" (see below): *wa-idh rafa'a Ibrāhīm*[u] *huwa wa-bnū-h*[u] *Ismā'īl*[u] *qawā'id*[a] *l-bayt*[i] . . . , "And when Abraham, he and his son, Isma'il, raised the foundations of the House . . ."

Compare also: Q2, 210: *hal yanẓurūna illā an ya'tiya-humu L-lāh*[u] *fī ẓulal*[in] *min*[a] *l-ghanām*[i] *wal-malā'ikat*[u], "Do they not see that but God will come to them in the darkness of clouds, and [that] the angels [will come, too]" [Mtkb 48 mid].

XII. Negatives[89]

12.1. Q75, 31: *fa-lā ṣaddaqa wa-lā ṣallā*, "He neither believed nor prayed." Here the rules of CA require *mā* for the negation of the perfect tense, rather than *lā*. Mtkb 871 mid, deftly "corrects" to *ankara l-insān*[u] *l-ba'th*[a] *fa-lā ṣaddaqa bil-rasūli wal-qur'ān*[i] . . . , "They denied the resurrection and thus did not believe in the Emissary nor in Q. "

12.2. Q18, 56: *wa-mā nursilu*, "We never send" is "corrected" at Mtkb 435 mid: *lā yursilu*, "He never sends," with another negating particle. Fleischer (173 mid, §321) says that *mā* is used with the imperfect indicative to negate "the action or its possibility." Badawi (472 end, §4. 2. 2) claims that *mā* is used with the imperfect indicative only "to convey emotional intensity."

12.3. Q21, 111: *wa-in adrī* "and I do not know," is paraphrased at Mtkb 486 mid: *wa-mā adrī*, with the same meaning.

XIII. The Passive

13.1. In CA one may not mention the agent of a passive sentence. Hence the term for the passive voice in Arabic is *al-majhūl*, "the unknown."[90] but at (16, 1) Q2, 177, we have . . . *wa-man 'ufiya la-hu min akhī-hi shay'*^{un} . . . , A. Yusuf Ali (71 top): ". . . But if any remission is made by the brother . . ."

13.2. Q2, 136: . . . *wa-mā'ūti'a n-nabiyyūna min rabb*^{i}*-him* . . . ," . . . and what the prophets were given by their Lord . . ."

13.3. Q69, 5, 6: *fa-ammā Thamūd*^{u} *fa-uhlikū biṭ-ṭāghiya. wa-ammā 'Ād*^{u} *fa-uhlikū bi-rīḥ*^{in} *ṣarṣar*^{in} *'ātiya*? A297 top: "As for Thamood, they were destroyed by the Screamer; and as for Ad, they were destroyed by a wind clamorous, violent." Mtkb 848 end paraphrases with two similarly worded passive sentences mentioning the agents, despite Mtkb's arch-conservative grammatical stance.

13.4. Q13, 27: *unzila 'alay-hi āyat*^{un} *min rabbi-hi*, "a verse was revealed to him from his Lord," is paraphrased at Mtkb 358 end: *hal-lā unzila min l-Lāh mu'jiza*, "hasn't a miracle been revealed by God?"

13.5. At Q6, 34: *wa-la-qad kudhdhibat* . . . , "[Messengers from before you] were rejected," Mtkb 177 mid paraphrases by including the agent: *wa-la-qad qubila rusul*^{un} *min qabl*^{i}*-ka bit-takdhīb*^{i} *wal-idhā'*^{i} *min aqwām*^{i}*-him*, "Messengers from before you were received with denial and harassment *on the part of their peoples. . . .*"[91]

XIV. Balancing

Q permits only *balanced* nominative[92] phrases,[93] *unbalanced* accusative phrases, and *unbalanced* genitive phrases.[94]

14.1. Thus for the nominative, we may have Q2, 35: . . . *uskun anta wa-zawj*^{u}*-ka* . . . , ". . . dwell, you and your wife . . ." Not **uskun wa-zawju-ka* . . .

14.2. At Q3, 20 we actually have an anomalous unbalanced nominative phrase: *aslamtu wajhī wa-man ittaba'a-nī* . . . , "I surrendered myself and those who follow me [did also]. . . ." Mtkb73 end "corrects:" *akhlaṣtu 'ibādatī li-Llāh*^{i} *anā wa-man ittaba'a-nī*, "I dedicate my worship to God, I and those who follow me. . . ."[95] (!)

14.3. Mtkb 862 mid [Q73, 1]: *fa-qāma huwa wa-ṭā'ifat*^{un} . . . , "he and a group arose . . ."

14.4. Q58, 21: *la-aghlab-anna anā wa-rasūlī*, "I will overcome them, I and my emissary"; Mtkb 813 end paraphrases: *la-anṣur-anna anā wa-rasūli.*

14.5. Q53, 23: *sammaytumū-hā antum wa-abā'u-kum*, "You and your fathers named them . . ." Mtkb 782 mid copies verbatim.[96]

14.6. For the genitive: *Rara avis*: At Mtkb11 we read *'alay-kum antum wa-abā'^{i}-kum*, "upon your and your fathers." (!) This is a "balanced genitive phrase," a turn of phrase hardly ever found in any MSA discourse.

14.7. (Two other examples occur at Mtkb 568 end: [Q27, 47]: *tashā'um^{u}-na bi-ka anta wa-man ma'a-ka*, "our augury with you, you and those with you"; and [Q27, 49]: *'alay-hi huwa wa- ahl^{i}-hi*, "upon him, and upon his people.")

14.8. Most often we have expressions of the type at Mtkb562 mid [Q2, 71]: *'ibādat^{u}-hā wa-qawm^{i}-ha* . . . , "her, and her people's worship . . ." And *ibidem*: *wa-najāt^{u}-hu wa-qawm^{i}-hi*, "his and his people's salvation."

14.9. See also Mtkb21 end [Q2, 91]: . . . *'alay-hum hum* . . . , "upon *them* . . ."; at Mtkb 46 end [Q2, 202] we have the usual . . . *'alay-kum wa-'alā abā'^{i}-kum* . . . , ". . . upon you and your fathers . . ."

14.10. Perhaps most bizarre is Mtkb319 end [Q11, 69]: *bi-bashārat^{i}-hi huwa wa-zawjata-hu bi-mawlūd*, "in giving the glad tidings to [Abraham] and his wife of a child."

XV. Quibbles

15.1. *Form II v. Form IV:* Although Q itself uses both form II *nazzala* and Form IV *anzala* for "He revealed," M largely restricts himself to the latter, for example, Mtkb612 end [Q41, 10]. Both are used at Q3, 3 [Mtkb70 end], where Mtkb repeats Q. At Mtkb84 end [Q3, 84], where Q has *anzala* once, Mtkb has: *nazzala . . . anzala*. In the commentary of the following verse, Mtkb uses the form *anzala* no less than three times. In general, it prefers the usage of Form IV of this verb to Form II. At Q25, 32 *nuzzila* is paraphrased by Mtkb535 end by *anzalnā*. . . . At Q15, 9 we have for II: *nazzal-nā*, which Mtkb373 mid perhaps "hypercorrects"[97] to Form IV: *anzal-nā*. Leemhuis claims that Form II is preferable for the "frequentative" and Form IV for the "causative." "Why wasn't [Q] revealed all at once? We revealed it thus in installments . . ."[98]

15.2. The correct translation of Q43, 70: *tuḥbarūna*, is "are gathered together."[99] Mtkb 730 end glosses with the traditional "deliriously happy."

15.3. See Asad (220, note 92) [Q7, 124]: "The grammatical forms [II] *la-'uqaṭṭianna* and *la-uṣallibannakum* must be rendered as 'most certainly I shall cut off [your hands and feet] *in great numbers*' and 'crucify you *in great numbers* [emphasis Asad's].'"

15.4. Word order: Q12, 4: *ra'aytu-hum lī sajidīn*, "I saw them [that is, the stars, sun, and moon] bowing down to me," has its word order dictated by poetic license (see above). Mtkb 331 "corrects" this: *ra'aytu-hum jamī'* *an* *khāḍ'in lī sajidīn amāmī*, "I saw them humbling themselves to me, bowing down before me." Note the Mtkb does not "correct" the masculine plural forms for the feminine singular for irrational beings.

****

ABBREVIATIONS AND BIBLIOGRAPHY

A = Arberry, A. J. *The Koran Interpreted*. New York, 1955.

Allen, Roger. *The Arabic Literary Heritage*. Cambridge, 1998.

AYA = 'Ali, A. Yusuf. *The Meaning of the Holy Qur'ān*. Beltsville, MD, 1408/1989.

Badawi, E. *Modern Written Arabic: A Comprehensive Grammar*. London, 2004.

Baljon, J. M. S. *Modern Muslim Koran Interpretation* (1880–1960). Brill: Leiden, 1968.

Bateson, Mary C. *Arabic Language Handbook*. Georgetown, 2003.

Beck, Edmund. "'Arabiyya, Sunna und 'Amma in der Koranlesung des zweiten Jahrhunderts." *Orientalia* 15 (Rome, 1946): 180–224.

Bialik, Ch. N., and Y. Ch. Ravnitsky. *Sefer Ha-Aggadah*. [Hebrew.] Tel Aviv, 1987.

Blau, Joshua. *The Renaissance of Modern Hebrew and Modern Standard Arabic*. Berkeley, 1981.

Bloch, Ariel A. *Studies in Arabic Syntax and Semantics*. Wiesbaden, 1986.

Bohas, G., et al. *The Arabic Linguistic Tradition*. London and New York, 1990.

Brustad, Kristen E. *The Syntax of Spoken Arabic*. Washington, DC, 2000.

C = Cantarino, Vicente. *Syntax of Modern Arabic Prose*. 3 vols. Bloomington, 1975.

Carter, Michael. *Arab Linguistics*. Amsterdam, 1981.

Dickens, J., et al. *Thinking Arabic Translation* (= *TAT*). London, 2002.

Eickelman, Dale. "Islamic Liberalism Strikes Back." *MESA Bulletin* 27 (1993): 163–68. [Review of Shahrur]

Fischer, W. *A Grammar of Classical Arabic*. 3rd ed. New Haven, 2002.

Fleisch, Henri. *Traité de Philologie Arabe*. Beirut, 1961.

Geiger, Abraham. *Judaism and Islam*. Ktav: New York, 1970.

Glassé, Cyril. *The New Encyclopedia of Islam*. Walnut Creek, 2001.

Godbout, Patricia. "Entre la transparence et l'opacité . . ." *Meta* 47, no. 1 (2000): 29–36.

> She continues: "Cela nous rappelle en outre que ni l'activité traduisante ni le discourse qu'on tient sur celle-ci ne sont neuters ou anodins: ils participant a la redefinition des paradigms littéraires."

Hem. = Hemingway, Ernest. *Wa-la Tazal al-Shams Tashriq* (Arabic translation of *The Sun Also Rises*). Beirut, n.d.

Holes, Clive. *Modern Arabic*. London, 1995.

Ibn Babuya, Muhammad (died 381/991). *Man la Yahduru-hu al-Faqih* [*He Who Has no Jurist Present*]. 4 vols. Tehran, 390/1970. 5th printing [ed.] Al-Akhudi.

J = Al-Maktaba al-Sharqiyya. *Al-Kitab al-Muqaddas*. Beirut: Dar al-Mashriq, 1988. [Jesuit Bible Translation]

Jansen, J. J. G. *The Interpretation of the Koran in Modern Egypt*. Brill: Leiden, 1974.

Jeffrey, Arthur. *The Foreign Vocabulary of the Qur'ān*. Baroda, 1938.

Katsh, Abraham I. *Judaism in Islam*. New York, 1954.

L = Lane, Edward. *An Arabic-English Lexicon*. 2 vols. London, 1853. Reprint Cambridge, 1984.

Leemhuis, Frederik. *The D and H Stems in Koranic Arabic*. Brill: Leiden, 1977.

Lester, Tony. "What Is the Koran?" *Atlantic Monthly*, January 1999. http://www.theatlantic.com/issues/99jan/koran3.htm.

Lévy, Bernard-Henri. *Qui a tué Daniel Pearl?* Grasset: Paris, 2003.

Lloyd-Jones, Kenneth. *In Celebration of Language—A Symposium in Honor of Kenneth Lloyd-Jones*. Trinity College: Hartford, 2004.

Luxenburg, Christoph. *Die syro-aramäische Lesart des Koran*. Berlin, 2000.

Manji, Irshad. *The Trouble with Islam*. New York, 2003.

MSA = Modern Standard Arabic.

Mtkb = Lajnat al-Qur'ān wal-Sunna. *Al-Muntakhab fi Tafsir al-Qur'ān al-Karim*. Cairo, 1406/1985.

MWA = Modern Written Arabic.

Nafisi, Azar. *Reading Lolita in Tehran*. New York, 2004.

Nasr, Seyyed H. (aka "Sufi Sales"). *The Heart of Islam*. San Francisco, 2002.

Nöldeke, Th. *Neue Beiträge zur semitischen Sprachwissenschaft*. Strassburg, 1910.

———. *Zur Grammatik des classichen Arabisch*. Darmstadt, 1963.

P = Pickthall, M. M. *The Meaning of the Glorious Koran*. New York, n.d.

Paret, Rudi. *Der Koran. übersetzung*. Stuttgart, 1971, 1979.

———. *Der Koran. Kommentar und Konkordanz*. Stuttgart, 1971, 1980.

Rodinson, Maxime. *Mahomet*. Paris, 1968.

Rushdie, Salman. *The Ground Beneath her Feet*. New York, 1999.

Sabbagh, T. *La Métaphore dans le Coran*. Paris, 1943.

Said, Fast Edward (a.k.a. "Sammy Glick, al-Maqbur"). *Al-Ahram Weekly Online* 677, February 12–18, 2004.

Schub, Michael B. "Three Syntactic Discussions . . ." *Al-Andalus* 42, no. 2 (1977).

———. "Direct and Indirect Relative Clauses." *Al-'Arabiyya* 11, no. 1–2 (1978): 15–19.

———. "Panchronic Actions." *Journal of Semitic Studies* (= *JSS*) 27, no. 1. (1982a): 57–59.

———. "A Note on a Sextuple Plural . . ." *Al-'Arabiyya* 15 (1982b): 153–55.

———. "*Iqham* . . ." *ZAL* (= *Journal of Arabic Linguistics*) 13 (1984): 86–91.

———. "The Morphological Pattern *fi*^{c}*l*^{un} for Dichotomies." *ZAL* 16 (1987): 119–20.

———. "Ibn Ya`ish's Comment on a 'Balanced-Comitative' Sentence." *ZAL* 22 (1990): 79–80.

———. "The Buddha Comes to China." *ZAL* 29 (1995): 77–78.

———. "*Walad al-Balad* . . ." *ZAL* 38 (2000): 88–90.

———. "Impasse in Isnad-istan." Review of Herbert Berg, *The Development of Exegesis in Early Islam*. Richmond, Surrey: Curzon, 2000. In *JAL* (= *Journal of Arabic Literature*) 38, no. 3 (2002): 293–94.

———. "What Gets Lost in Translation." Review of H. Abdul-Raof, *Qur'ān Translation*. 2001. *Middle East Quarterly* 10, no. 4 (Fall 2003): 81–85.

Shattuck, Roger. *Candor & Perversion*. New York, 1999.

Speyer, Heinrich. *Die biblischen Erzählungen im Qoran*. Gräfenhainichen, 1931. Reprint: Hildesheim, 1988.

Suleiman, Yasir. *Arabic and Linguistics*. Richmond, Surrey: Curzon, 1999.

TAT = Dickens, see above.

Thackston, Wheeler. *An Introduction to Koranic and Classical Arabic*. Bethesda, MD, 1994.

Tickle, Phyllis. *Greed.* Oxford, 2004.
Ullmann, Manfred. *Sätze mit lau.* Munich, 1998.
V = United Bible Societies (Smith and Van Dyke). *Al-Kitab al-Muqaddas.* London, 1966.
W = Wright, W. *A Grammar of the Arabic Language.* Cambridge, 1967.
Warraq, Ibn *What the Koran Really Says.* Amherst, NY, 2002.
Zamakhshari, Mahmud ibn `Umar. *Al-Mufassal fii al-Nahw.* (Ed. J. P. Broch.) Christianiae, 1840.
Zammit, Martin. *A Comparative Lexical Study of Qur'ānic Arabic.* Leiden, 2002.

Notes

1. I. Manji, 183 mid.
2. Tickle, 45, 46.
3. Shattuck, 74 mid.
4. In 1993 a professor at Dartmouth—[Dale F. Eickelman, in *MESA* (*Mystical Elitist Spiritualist Assn.*) *Bulletin* 27 (1993): 163–67]—hailed the appearance of an Arabic book—[M. Shaḥrūr, *Al-Kitāb wa-l- Qur'ān: Qirā'a Mu`āṣira* [*The Book and the Qur'ān: A Contemporary Reading*]. Damascus, 1990]—which, he claimed, would revolutionize the way Muslims viewed the Qur'ān (hereinafter Q), and would pave the way toward mutual understanding and world peace (in the best tradition of the Miss America Pageant). The pedant asked whether one may regard, given the final eirenic effect of Shaḥrūr's work, "contemporary Islamic radicalism as a passing phenomenon." [Same 167 end. At 167 mid: "Is Shaḥrūr's book an intellectual equivalent in the Arab world to Allan Bloom's *The Closing of the American Mind*?" as if this last work had any appreciable lasting effect.]
5. "For the fact is that, far from being simply a matter of semantic substitution, all translation is at once an act of replicative writing, *and* an interpretative or hermeneutic act. The fundamental problem of translations lies less with how we choose to carry over original words into new words, but witth how we choose to convert original meanings into new meanings. If the translator's *inventio* pays homage to the target version it is translator's hermeneutic that honors the source text."—Kenneth Lloyd-Jones.
6. = *[The Most Authoritative] Culled Interpretations of the Noble Qur'ān.*
7. "The most important center of mainstream Islam in the modern world," Farid Zakaria, quoted in Manji, 176 top.

8. *Ni'ma kubrā*. Badawi 249, §2. 11. 3. Mktb511 end [Q23, 80], note 1: *dā'ira mulawwana kubrā*, "a major variegated circuit."

9. Jansen, 31, 32: "In ['Abduh's and Riḍā's] re-awakening the interest in Koran interpretation they also established a link between the Koran and the affairs of man's life in the world. This 'Abduh did by getting rid of the weight of erudition of the classical commentaries that were even too heavy a ballast even for many theologians. "

10. Mtkb, xi end.

11. Mtkb, xiii end.

12. Mtkb, xv top.

13. Mtkb, xvi top. Levy 351 mid: "Il hausse les épaules, manifestement dépassé par l'absurdité d'un Coran en français." [He shrugs his shoulders, obviously overcome by the absurdity of a Koran in French.]

14. "[The Qur'ān's] language became the basis of formal or classical Arabic, both literary and spoken. . . ." Glassé, 264 I, top.

15. A. Bostom, ed., *The Legacy of Jihad*, Amherst, NY: Prometheus Books, 2005.

16. But see note 36 below.

17. See also M306 mid [Q16, 118].

18. Ibn Kathīr, on Q7, 163; vol. VI, 260 top.

19. John Burton, in Hawting, 269–84.

20. Asad, 148 and 220.

21. F. E. Peters, "The Quest for the Historical Muhammad," *Der Islam* 68 (1991): 87–107. Reprinted in Ibn Warraq. *What the Koran Really Says* (Amherst, NY: Prometheus Books, 2002), 451 top.

22. Jansen, 27 top.

23. Jansen, 27, n. 35.

24. For the background of the Abraham saga see Q6, 74ff. and Geiger 95ff.; Speyer 120 ff., etc. Also Schub (1995), 78, n. 8

25. Katsh, 65.

26. Also at Mtkb372 mid [Q15, 1].

27. Tickle, 14–15.

28. Genesis 9:9ff.

29. Babylonian Talmud Sanhedrin, 56a.

30. For other views on the *mathānī*, here and at Q15, 87, see U. Rubin, "Exegesis and Ḥadīth: The Case of the Seven Mathānī," in G. Hawting and K. Shareef, *Approaches to the Qur'ān* (London, 1993), pp. 141–156. Some identified the "*Sabi'un*" at Q2, 62 as "the followers of Noah's religion." See Qurṭubī's Commentary, I, 300 mid (Beirut 1422/2002). See also Speyer, 96 end; and Rodinson 150–52.

31. Tome VII, vol. 13, 189 top.

32. Ibid., end.

33. Ibid., Tome VIII, vol. 16, 10, 11.

34. "After heated discussion, James issued the decree that Gentiles could become Christians without first becoming Jews, but they should observe the laws that the Torah assigns to Noah, the father of all humanity [the Noahide Laws] (Acts 15:28–29; see Genesis 9:3–7). Christianity would now inevitably become a largely Gentile movement"—Marshall D. Johnson, *The Evolution of Christianity* (New York, 2005).

35. *Atti del Terzo Congresso di Studi Arabi e Islamici*, Ravello, 1–6. September 1967. (Naples: Instituto Universaritario Orientale), 553–56. Translated into English and reprinted in Ibn Warraq, *What the Koran Really Says*, 238–87.

36. Note: One "eats" (*akl*) usury (*ar-riba'*) at Q2, 275 and Q3, 130.

37. Oddly, at Q2, 188; Mtkb42 end, note 1, the editors describe bribery as "mankind's gravest crime [*sic*]." At Mtkb217 end [Q7, 80] sodomy is awarded with the same epithet. See Asad's explanation of *suḥt* at Asad, 151, note 54.

38. *M'asei Avraham*. See Speyer, 124 mid ff.

39. Reported also in the *Yalqut Bereishit*. See Bialik, 19, col. 1 top.

40. Note that the Shī'ite commentator, al-Ṭabarsī, states that the donkey shat (*rātha*). Vol. IX–X, 132 end.

41. For which see Luxenberg, passim.

42. Which occurs (unvocalized) at, e.g., Mtkb334 end [Q12, 14]; Mtkb358 end [Q13, 62]; Mtkb372 mid [Q15, 1]; Mtkb384 end [Q16, 1]; Mtkb387 end [Q16, 22]; Mtkb402 mid [Q16, 97]; Mtkb405 mid [Q16, 113]; Mtkb484 mid [Q21, 92]; Mtkb509 end [Q23, 71]; etc.

43. *Pace* Nasr [the Sufi Sales of Middle Eastern Studies in the WEST, where he and his family live, despite his stated preference for the spirituality of the East] (xii mid): ". . . the so-called Age of Enlightenment . . . was in reality an age of the darkening of the soul and eclipse of the intellect . . ." [*sic*!]

44. III, 239 top, #1133.

45. G-R. Puin, in Lester, quoted in Ibn Warraq, *What the Koran Really Says*, pp. 107–28; and in Schub (2003), 82 II mid.

46. Katsh, 208; Jeffrey, 124.

47. Geiger, 20; Katsh, 75–76.

48. See Goodbout, 31 top: "Qui dit traduction dit trahison, n'est-ce pas?"

49. Jeffrey, 170–71; Geiger, 71 mid.

50. Jeffrey, 182 top; Nöldeke (1910), 26 mid.

51. Jeffrey, 77 top.

52. Nöldeke (1910), 49; Jeffrey, 221.

53. Jeffrey, 229.

54. Ibid., 196 top.

55. Ibid., 162 mid.

56. Ibid., 203.

57. Ibid., 213, 214.

58. Rushdie, 74 top. (MBSs emphasis); compare. S. Humphreys in Toby Lester, "What Is the Koran?" in *Atlantic Monthly*, January 1999. Reprinted in Ibn Warraq, *What the Koran Really Says*, 107–29: "If the Koran is a historical document, then the whole Islamic struggle of fourteen centuries is effectively meaningless. "

59. See Schub 1982.

60. Fleischer, 199 top, §383, note 3. Badawi, 123 ff., §2. 2ff. has nothing on this.

61. [*Apposition* is a figure of speech, in which two elements are placed side by side, with the second element serving to define or modify the first (ex: "My wife, a nurse by training . . ."). From Latin, appositio; *ad* ("near") and *positio* ("placement")

- My friend John
- John, my best friend in high school . . .
- John and Bob, both friends of mine . . .
- Your excuse, that your dog ate your homework, is pretty unbelievable. . . .
- His life, despite all its poverty of material possession, was rich in spirit. . . .
- You naughty boy, you.]

62. Bateson, 84 mid, ff.

63. Schub, 1979.

64. See also Mtkb487 end [Q22, 2]: /fī fam^{i}/ = "in the mouth of . . ."

65. Stetkevych, 91 mid.

66. But Mtkb858 end [Q72, 3]: *zawja*. Also at Mtkb334 end [Q12, 21]. Mtkb uses *zawj* for "wife" at Mtkb448 [Q19, 49]; Mtkb444 [Q19, 8 and 9]; at Mtkb483 end following Q21, 90; Mtkb469 mid [Q21, 120, 121, and 123]; Mtkb 448 end [Q21, 49].

67. See Schub, 1984; Stetkevych, 93 top.

68. [Pleonasm: tautology.]

69. [Hendiadys, from Greek *hen*, "one," *dia*, "through," *dis*, "two" (one by means of two): expressing a single idea by two nouns instead of a noun and its

qualifier—thus adding force. E.g., "The distinction and presence of the dignitary moved his audience" instead of "distinctive presence."] Schub (1984), 87.

70. [Merismus: the dividing of a whole into its parts.]

71. Also occurs at Mtkb184 end [Q6, 73].

72. Brustad, 63 mid.

73. Robert Warshow, "Movie Chronicle: The Westerner," cited in the *New York Times*, Friday, March 19, 2004, E1, IV top.

74. Bohas, 20; quoted by Suleiman, 35 end; Bloch, chap. 1.

75. Allen, 8 top.

76. Fischer, xv mid.

77. Bateson, 77 end.

78. Fleisch, 16 end: "Il a manqué aux grammairiens arabes, comme aux grecs, comme aux hindous, comme a toute la philologie occidentale jusqu'au commencement du XIX^{e}s., *la notion de changement historique* dans le langage . . ." [emphasis F's].

79. John Burton, "The Reading of Q20, 63," *ZAL* 19 (1998): 7–26.

80. Beck, 181 top.

81. Holes, 277ff.

82. Stetkevych, 92, 93.

83. Nöldeke (1910), 9 mid.

84. Brustad, 63 mid.

85. Badawi, 5 mid.

86. So Mtkb, 341 mid [Q12, 57]: *bi-hi wa-bi-rasūl^{i}-hi*, "with him and His Emissary"; Mtkb348 mid [Q12, 91]: *bi-ka wa-bi-akhī-ka* "with you and your brother"; Mtkb348 end [Q12, 93]: *bi-hi wa-bi-ahl^{i}-kum*, "with him and your family."

87. Paret (1979), 60 top: ". . . oder: Fürchtet Gott, in dessen Namen—und in dem der Blutvervandschaft—ihr einander zu bitten pflegt . . ."

88. Cited in Reckendorff

89. Gotthelf Bergsträsser, *Die Negationen im Kur'an.*

90. This is probably a much more recent term than *mā lam yusammā fā'il^{u}-hu*, "that whose agent is unnamed." Carter, 181 end. See Badawi, 383ff.

91. Mtkb728 mid [Q43, 47]: *qabalū-hu . . . bid-ḍaḥk*, "they would meet [a prophet] with scorn. "

92. Badawi is correct on the nominative (346 top), and stone-cold wrong on the accusative (372 top).

93. If one considers Q13, 23: *yadkhulūna-hā wa-man ṣalaḥa*, "they enter it, and those who did good works [too], "unbalanced," then Mtkb358 mid "corrects" it

to: *yakūnūna fī-hā hum wa-abā'ᵘ-hum*, "they will be in it, they and their Fathers [who did good works]." Compare Q11, 112: *staqim ka-mā umirta wa-man tāba ma'a-ka*, "stay as you were ordered to, and those who repented with you [too]" is paraphrased with a balanced Mtkb327 end: *fa-dāwim anta wa-man ma'a-ka*, "stay the course, you and those with you. "

94. See Bloch, chap. 1.

95. See Schub (1995), 77 n. 3.

96. See also Q5, 24: *idhhab anta wa-rabbb^{u}-ka*, "Go, you and your Lord"; Mtkb149 end copies; Q6, 91, Mtkb187 end copies; Mtkb160 mid [Q5, 75]. Q43, 70, Mtkb730 end paraphrases: *udkhulu antum ma'a azwaji-kum*, "enter, you *together with* your wives" for which see Schub 1995.

97. See Blau, *Pseudo-Corrections in the Semitic Languages.*

98. See also Mtkb507 edn [Q23, 50]: *anzalna-ha*, "We brought her down."

99. See Schub, 1995; Luxenberg, 229 top and note 251.

2.8

That Which Gets Lost in Translation[1]

Michael Schub

According to an "impregnable dogma" of early Islam, the Qur'ān has the quality of *i'jaz*, by which its rhetorical beauty in the Arabic language is "inimitable."[1] That is so because everything in the Qur'ān is an exact copy of the revelation preserved sempiternally on a "guarded tablet" in the highest heaven.

This outlook means that, for believers, the idea of translating the Qur'ān is absurd: "Arabic is not just the original language of the Qur'ān, it is the language of the Qur'ān."[2] English versions are therefore not titled *The Koran* but *The Koran Interpreted*, *The Meaning of the Glorious Koran*, and so on. This quality of being untranslatable, incidentally, makes the Qur'ān unlike the scripture of any other religion. About a decade before *Qur'ān Translation* was written, David Crystal effectively wrote a review of it in *The Cambridge Encyclopedia of Language*: "It would be self-evident that, as God chose Arabic as the vehicle of his revelation to his prophet, this must be the language used in heaven, and thus must be superior to all others."[3] Crystal then tellingly notes:

> A similar argument has been applied to several other languages, such as Sanskrit and classical Hebrew,[4] especially in relation to claims about which language is the oldest. For example, J. G. Becanus (1518–72) argued that German was superior to all other languages. It was the language Adam spoke in Eden, but it was not affected by the Babel event because the early Germans (the Cimbrians) did not assist in the construction of the tower.

> God later caused the Old Testament to be translated from the original German (no longer extant) into Hebrew.[5]

Abdul-Raof's contribution to knowledge is only a tad smaller than that of Becanus. (And, were Abdul-Raof capable of reading modern Cimbrian—as Becanus would be—his many trivial cavils would be obviated by perusing Rudi Paret's masterful two-part Qur'ān translation and commentary.)[6]

Of course, the Qur'ān cannot be fully translated. Robert Frost famously defined poetry as "that which gets lost in translation." Academic specialists agree that there is no such thing as a perfect translation of any work, poetry or prose. Abdul-Raof's study of Qur'ān translation is not a work of scholarship but rather one of pious apology: he claims, ad nauseum, that the Qur'ān presents a unique case of language not open to translation because it is God's own words (*ipsissima verba*) and the only true scripture for all humanity, forever.

G.-R. Puin of the University of Saarland, the scholar who worked on early Qur'ān manuscripts discovered in the wall of a mosque in Ṣan'ā', Yemen, has a much more plausible explanation for the inability to translate the Qur'ān, finding that "a fifth of the Koranic text is *just incomprehensible*."[7] A glance at the most popular and most reprinted of the Qur'ān commentaries, *Tafsīr al-Jalalayn*, clearly intimates this point. Concerning Qur'ān XI, 107, as-Suyuti (died, 1505 CE), possibly the greatest Arabist and Qur'ān commentator ever, writes words to the effect that: "I can't make heads or tails out of this blessed verse!"[8] And Abdul-Raof himself confirms this problem in the following delightful observation: "Al-Yazīdī . . . suggests the meaning 'black' instead of 'yellow.' "

Perhaps the most consequential effects of this opacity derive from Qur'ān XXXIII, 59, which advises the Prophet's wives to go veiled; and from Qur'ān XXIV, 31, which speaks of covering women's adornments from strangers outside the family. Women may be persecuted to the extent they were under the Taliban's recent regime in Afghanistan or enjoy equal rights with men in other venues, all depending on one's interpretation of these two verses. Half of the world's Muslim population is affected by this interpretation. In fact, "nowhere in the Muslim world are women treated as equals. . . . Part of the problem dates to Muḥammad. Even as he proclaimed new rights for women, he enshrined their inequality in immutable law, passed down as God's commandments and eventually recorded in scripture."[9]

Abdul-Raof's apologetics roll down like a mountain stream. To the famous admonition in Qur'ān, IV, 34, "if any of your wives prove disobedient, then beat her," our author adds on his own authority that this should be done "lightly." Likewise, "Your women are your fields: plow them however you want" (II, 223), whose plain text has always been understood by Muslim commentators to mean that a husband may have intercourse with his wife in any way he chooses, he reads as having intercourse in the "proper natural manner."

Abdul-Raof lives in a self-imposed cultural void in which he pretends that the Qur'ān has no historic precedents. While scholars may not know why consuming pig meat is forbidden in the Hebrew Torah, they do know the reason it is forbidden in the Qur'ān, at II, 173: because it is forbidden in the Torah. We also know why the direction of prayer, *al-qibla*, was changed from Jerusalem to Mecca in the Qur'ān, II, 142: as the historian Paul Johnson puts it, "Mohammad's development of a separate religion began when he realized the Jews of Medina were not prepared to accept his arbitrarily contrived version of Judaism."[10] Although Abdul-Raof does not mention it, all the Muslim commentators are in agreement that the original *qibla* was Jerusalem; indeed, Jerusalem's *laqab* (by-name) in Arabic is *ula al-qiblatayni*, "the first of the two *qibla*s."

The Qur'ān clearly relies on Jewish concepts, sometimes even the original Hebrew or Jewish Aramaic words,[11] for such basic Islamic concepts as monotheism, prophet, scripture, fast, prayer, alms, a specific direction of prayer, angels, the afterlife, hell, heaven, reward and punishment, the contents of all of the Ten Commandments, Bible narratives, and the sacredness of human life[12]—and translates them into Arabic (often putting a new spin on them). This dependence is hardly unique to the Qur'ān: "Any strong literary work creatively misreads and therefore misinterprets a precursor text or texts," writes the literary critic Harold Bloom.[13] Nor is Islam the only religion to take from its predecessors: "When individual DNA or the personal fingerprint of one author is present in another, we have the best available argument for dependence," writes John Dominic Crossan about Christianity.[14]

Abdul-Raof's apologetic stance shines through his entire text. Willfully ignoring the notoriously unsystematic nature of the Qur'ān, he claims that it represents structurally a unified coherent unit where each chapter enjoys a beginning, a middle, and an end and is correlated to the following chapter. At the interpersonal level, however, the tenor or Qurʾānic discourse is context-sensitive.

Translated into English, he is inadvertently echoing Thomas Carlyle, who observed of the Qurʾān that "it is as toilsome a reading as I ever undertook, a wearisome, confused jumble, crude, incondite."[15] The Arabic literary scholar R. A. Nicholson noted the almost unanimous opinion among European readers that the Qurʾān is "obscure, tiresome, uninteresting; a farrago of long-winded narratives and prosaic exhortations."[16] W. Montgomery Watt, a foremost biographer of the Prophet Muḥammad, remarked on its "disjointedness."[17] Issa Boullata notes that "some Western writers have criticized the Qurʾān" because of its perceived disjointedness[18] and adds that even Sayyid Qutb, one of the most influential Islamist thinkers, shared this opinion. Qutb, he writes,

> admits that there is no certainty about the authenticity of [the Qurʾān's] order, which he acknowledges is only approximate and not definitive; and he adds that even if there was certainty, the fact is that many *sura*s were not revealed as wholes but rather piecemeal at diverse occasions, of which there is no historical record agreed upon by scholars. Hence, the only option available to him, he says, is that of assumption and preponderation in this matter.[19]

Even as an apologist, Abdul-Raof fares poorly. How much superior is the argument of Cyril Glassé, a Muslim scholar on the salmagundi structure of the Qurʾān; he points out that the medieval mystic Jalal ad-Din ar-Rumi "suggested that it is this very nature, outwardly chaotic, that is a 'ruse' of the Koran to approximate the chaotic nature of the human soul, in order then to catch it, as a net catches a fish, and to bring it back to absorption in the divine from which the soul has wandered."[20]

In addition to suffering from terminal apologetics, Abdul-Raof's study has other problems. His prose can be completely unintelligible, as in this unintentional self-parody of lit-crit mumbo-jumbo:

> From a text linguistics point of view, the prepositional correlation among Qurʾānic chapters is seen as a positive textual feature of a cohesive text

where chapter-final and chapter-initial prepositional content is effectively employed as a form of textural cohesive link which feeds into the overall textuality and textness of Qur'ānic discourse.

Other howlers from *Qur'ān Translation* include:

The majority of the past tense in Qur'ānic discourse has a future meaning.

The source text, however, has not chosen other possible forms of noun such as (*/shajar|ashjar/*) which are generic plural nouns because the plural form does not signify the intended meaning.

These passages simply make no sense.

Abdul-Raof implies that the Qur'ān is a modern textbook of embryology, the last word in cosmology, the final authority on global warming, and supports the superstition of numerology. Here also is an implied approval of that most infantile of all modern genres, *at-tafsīr al-'ilmi* ("scientific interpretation"). This genre explains *jinn* as "electrons," and so forth.

Although Abdul-Raof's English is, to be kind, feckless, his Arabic is execrable. He uses *jam' al-kathra* to mean "paucity" in the plural, the direct opposite of what it means. Other mistakes include *wa-yahdi-kum* for *wa-yahdiya-kum*; *wa-l-nasala* for *wa-l-nasla*; *abwaba* for *abwabu*; *a-fa-Hukmi* for *a-fa-Hukma*; *bushshara* for *bushshira*; *sijjin* for *sijjīn*. There are wrongly placed *sukun*s (phonetic zeroes) once each on pages 63, 64, 71, 153, and 171; twice on page 86; and four times on page 38.

Why would Routledge-Curzon, a respected British academic publisher, publish such arrant nonsense? In part, because academic research on the Qur'ān lags centuries behind academic study of the Bible; there is, for example, no *textus receptus*, a generally accepted form of the text of the Qur'ān. In part, the reason has to do with universities shunning Orientalists, those scholars who know their subject matter and who realize with the French Orientalist Maxime Rodinson that "respect for the faith of sincere believers cannot be allowed either to block or deflect the investigation of the historian."[21]

The Qur'ān is not some musty manuscript but a vibrant document whose interpretation has direct consequences for the world at large. To permit authors like Hussein Abdul-Raof to publish with prestigious presses implies willingly blinding oneself to the realities. Sadly, Western academia is increasingly clueless about the realities of the Muslim world.

This is important for more than scholarly reasons: "Many former Soviet officers believe that the prime reason for the failure of their mission in Afghanistan was their profound ignorance about Islam. This is a lesson worth heeding."[22]

Notes

1. F. Buhl in H. A. R. Gibb and J. H. Kramers, *The Shorter Encyclopaedia of Islam* (Reading, UK: Ithaca Press, 1974), p. 276. Buhl goes on to note that the acknowledgment of that beauty "is not however easy to a reader with some stylistic training and a certain amount of taste. "

2. Michael Cook, *The Koran: A Very Short Introduction* (Oxford: Oxford University Press, 2000), p. 88.

3. David Crystal, ed., *The Cambridge Encyclopedia of Language* (Cambridge: Cambridge University Press, 1987), p. 7.

4. *Sofriim* (post-Talmudic rabbinic collection) I, 7: ". . . it is told that five elders wrote the Torah in Greek for King Ptolemy [the Septuagint; about 250 BCE] and that day was as hard for Israel as the day the golden calf was made, for the Torah could not be adequately translated. "

5. Crystal, *The Cambridge Encyclopedia*, p. 7.

6. Rudi Paret, *Der Koran*. I. *Uebersetzung* (Stuttgart, 1979); II. *Kommentar* (Stuttgart, 1980). German scholars must be especially *vorsichtig*: "the fog of language can be illuminated through footnotes that can be used in Qurʾān translation as demisting devices" (p. 139). See also the commonsense evaluation of English translations of the Qurʾān in Neal Robinson, *Discovering the Qurʾān: A Contemporary Approach to a Veiled Text* (London: SCM Press, 1996), p. 291.

7. Toby Lester, "What Is the Koran? *Atlantic Monthly*, January 1999, http://www.theatlantic.com/issues/99jan/koran3.htm, reprinted in Ibn Warraq, *What the Koran Really Says* (Amherst, NY: Prometheus Books, 2002), pp. 107–28; also "Scholars Are Quietly Offering New Theories of the Koran," *New York Times*, March 2, 2002.

8. Jalal ad-Din as-Suyuti and Jalal ad-Din al-Mahalli, *Tafsīr al-Jalalayn* (Beirut: Dar al-Maʿrifa, 1404/1984), p. 300.

9. Lisa Beyer in *Time*, cited in Jean Bethke Elshtain, *Just War against Terror: The Burden of American Power in a Violent World* (New York: Basic Books, 2003), p. 44.

10. Paul Johnson, *A History of the Jews* (New York: HarperCollins, 1987), p. 167.

11. So *zakat* and *sadaqat* are spelled with the original *waw* in the Qur'ānic manuscripts. Christian informants also contributed. See Arthur Jeffery, *The Foreign Vocabulary of the Qur'ān* (Baroda: Oriental Institute, 1935), pp. 153, 194.

12. Qur'ān V, 32–35: ". . . We ordained for the children of Israel that whoever killed a human being, except as a punishment for murder of other villainy in the land, shall be looked upon as though he had killed all mankind; and that whoever saved a human life shall be regarded as though he had saved all mankind." This is a direct quotation of *Mishna Sanhedrin* IV, 5. Since September 11, 2001, numerous imams and rabbis have quoted this verse on television.

13. Harold Bloom, *The Western Canon: The Books and School of the Ages* (New York: Harcourt, 1994), p. 8.

14. John Dominic Crossan, *The Birth of Christianity: Discovering What Happened in the Years Immediately after the Execution of Jesus* (San Francisco: Harper, 1999), p. 565.

15. Thomas Carlyle, *Sartor Resartus and on Heroes and Hero Worship* (London: Everyman, 1908), p. 299.

16. Reynold A. Nicholson, *A Literary History of the Arabs* (Cambridge: Cambridge University Press, 1969), p. 161.

17. W. Montgomery Watt and Richard Bell, *Introduction to the Qur'ān* (Edinburgh: Edinburgh University Press, 1970), p. 22.

18. Issa J. Boullata, "Sayyid Qutb's Literary Appreciation of the Qur'ān," in *Literary Structures of Religious Meaning in the Qur'ān*, ed. Issa J. Boullata (Richmond, Surrey: Curzon Press, 2002), p. 363.

19. Ibid., p. 359; on Sayyid Qutb, *Mashahid al-Qiyama fi al-Qur'ān* (Cairo: Dar al-Ma'arif, 1966, 1981), p. 11.

20. Cyril Glassé, *The New Encyclopaedia of Islam* (Walnut Creek, CA: AltaMira Press, 2001), s. v. "Koran," p. 267.

21. Maxime Rodinson, quoted in Ibn Warraq, *What the Koran Really Says*, p. 6.

22. Dmitri V. Trenin, review of *The Mission: Waging War and Keeping Peace with America's Military* by Dana Priest, *New York Times*, April 30, 2003.

Part 3

Manuscripts

3.1

Leaves from Three Ancient Qurâns

Possibly Pre-'Uthmānic with a List of Their Variants

Alphonse Mingana and Agnes Smith Lewis

PREFACE

The manuscript from which these leaves are taken was bought by me at Suez from a commercial antiquary on his travels in 1895. It is a palimpsest, the upper script being a series of closely written homilies in Arabic by early Christian Fathers, such as Theodosius, Chrysostom, and Mar Jacob. This was pronounced by Dr. Cowley, of Oxford, and Mr. Ellis, who was then at the British Museum, to be written in a style that is assigned to the very end of the ninth century, or to the beginning of the tenth one, and which was in vogue for a very short time.

Eighty-four leaves of the under script contain a text of the *Protevangelium Jacobi* and the *Transitus Mariae* in two columns of Estrangelo Syriac. I brought this up with a reagent, hydro-sulphide of ammonia, and published it in 1902 as no. XI *Studia Sinaitica*. It was not quite appropriate for that series; for I have no reason to think that it was ever at Sinai; but at that time I had no intention of returning to St. Catherine's Convent; and *Horae Semiticae* had not then been thought of.

Among the Syriac quires were six Arabic ones; while several miscellaneous leaves, in both languages, were scattered through the same volume, as is the manner of palimpsest manuscripts that were written when vellum was very scarce. The vellum of the *Protevangelium* and the *Transitus* did not suffice for the ninth-century scribe, for he pressed into his service one leaf of the Greek Septuagint, containing a text from Genesis 41, and several leaves that have been twice palimpsested with texts from the Syriac Old Testament; that is to say, there are three very good writings, crossing each other, on all these pages. I contented myself with deciphering only one of the under scripts, and thus obtained portions of Exodus and Isaiah, of which more may yet be heard. The under script of another leaf that I published in no. 11 was called by me a hymn. My friend Dr. Mingana considers it rather to be part of a commentary.

There are other curious things in it, the decipherment of which has baffled my own skill, and also that of some very capable Arabists. I am in the habit of exhibiting one leaf that has five different scripts on it, including the rough label of one of its commercial owners; three scripts, each of them covering the whole page; and some tiny lines, in a different hand, on the margin. Among this curious medley are what I took to be forty-four leaves of Kūfic Arabic, in six quires. As it lies crossways to the very clear ninth-century upper script, there are naturally four lines at least running along the margins on each page that are more easily read than the remainder. A little patient study revealed to me the fact that they were from the Qurân. I contented myself with verifying to which sūrah and which verse they belong; and with copying the lines at the top and bottom of each half-page. I found no less than forty-two words that I thought were wrongly spelt, such as اوليك for اولايك . What is generally called the Noun Agent of verbs in the first form, both in the singular and in the plural, is written without the usual Alif after the first radical letter, excepting where an ambiguity would otherwise ensue.

If the reader wishes to understand why I did not transcribe more of the text, he has only to glance at the tangle of cross-writings in my illustrations, and remember that while I am familiar with the Naskhi script of Arabic, and am not quite a stranger to Kūfic, this script is neither the one nor the other, but a kind of writing that, *me judice*, is very seldom seen. I was also prepossessed by the belief that all copies of the Qurân are in duty bound to be exactly alike. The same causes must have influenced all my Arabist friends, and all Oriental readers of no. XI *Studia Sinaitica*; for no suggestion has ever been made to me, during the eleven years that have elapsed since that book was published, that the subject might possibly repay further investigation.

It was on November 27, 1913, when Dr. Mingana spent two days in our house, that the idea occurred to me of showing him my book entitled *Apocrypha Syriaca*, that is, no. XI. As he turned its pages I was suddenly startled by the question, "What are you doing with *sics* in the Qurân?" "Because they are there," I replied, "and I can shew you where I got them." On comparing the manuscript with my printed lines, however, Dr. Mingana said that forty-one of the words to which I had put a *sic* are only archaic spellings; but that one in sūrah 7 can have a distinct difference of meaning; it is الله وكلمته , "God and His Word," instead of الله وكلماته, "God and His Words," as in the authorized text.

I was only too glad to find a learned Assyrian scholar, whose eyes are much younger and sharper than mine, and whose native language is Arabic, willing to undertake so difficult a task as the decipherment of my pages. The result has greatly surprised me. Few can read the list of variants given on pp. xxxvii–xli without perceiving that many of them fit better into their context, and are more likely to have been dictated by the Prophet and written by Zaid ibn Thâbit than those that have been doing duty for thirteen hundred years instead of them.

As Dr. Mingana's transcription has been made in our house, each variant, as he found it, was verified at once by me, and most of them also by my sister, Dr. Margaret Dunlop Gibson. Not till we were both satisfied did it go into this transcript.

We think that these leaves are pre-'Uthmānic for this reason. Muḥammad, when he believed that he was receiving supernatural revelations, employed Zaid ibn Thâbit to write them down for him, and this Zaid did, on potsherds, palm-leaves, strips of vellum, or whatever came handy. No doubt copies of the different sūrahs were afterward made by Zaid himself, when sufficient writing material had been obtained. It is not surprising if these contained some mistakes in spelling; especially as the rules of Arabic grammar were not then fixed. But after Muḥammad's death, Abu Bekr and 'Uthmān had all these writings properly copied out and arranged in the form with which we have become familiar. In this work, be it noted, they had the help of Zaid. 'Uthmān then ordered all the earlier copies to be destroyed; and the text of the Qurân, as it now stands, obtained a position of unique and unchallenged authority over the Muslim world. We therefore cannot imagine anyone attempting the useless task of writing out a text like ours, after the time of 'Uthmān.

Putting all the facts together, as they are known to ourselves, or as they have been handed down to us by a credible tradition, we think that these vellum leaves, now happily my property, were among those whose destruction was ordered by 'Uthmān and was incumbent on all true believers in Islâm. There are two ways of destroying manuscripts. The most effectual one is by burning; but in those early days vellum was scarce—especially in the desert—the papyrus reed had disappeared, having been utterly uprooted for the needs of literary folk; and paper was unknown, except in China. The owner of Qurâns that had been prematurely written was surely justified in thinking that if he got rid of their text, by means of pumice-stone or otherwise, the attenuated vellum might remain, and its price might help to equip himself for a *jehâd*. By sale therefore, or barter, this one passed into the hands of Christian monks; and then, toward the end of the ninth century, it was written clearly over with choice extracts from the Fathers of the Church; the pages being folded double, and some of them being clipped to a smaller size to make them fit in with those of the *Transitus Mariae*. I think it very probable that the writer of the second script did not suspect that any of the vellum he used had an earlier text on it. Dr. Rendel Harris, who was for several years lecturer in palaeography at the University of Cambridge, and who may be regarded as an expert in palimpsests, shares this opinion. There is no record, so far as I know, of the history of such documents; for in most cases their owners would never notice how long a period had elapsed between the effacement of the first writing and its reappearance.

The less the manuscript was exposed to the action of the air, the longer would be the time before this took place.

I have already given a description of the manuscript in no. XI *Studia Sinaitica*. The leaves of the Qurân are a very little smaller than those of the *Protevangelium*, that is, nearly 20 centimetres by 12. But those of Qurân A were certainly larger, and have been cut down to the size of their neighbors by the ninth-century scribe; Qurân A, called by me Qurân I, forms the two final quires of the volume, extending from folio 147 to folio 161; and being interrupted only by folios 155 and 162, which are taken from another manuscript whose script, being very small, is practically buried under the text of Mar Jacob, which forms the upper ninth-century writing. The thirty-one leaves in four quires, which I called Qurân II, have been found by Dr. Mingana to belong to two different manuscripts, and are therefore renamed B and C.

To those who have never handled a palimpsest it may be right to mention that I have followed the arrangement of the later script in numbering the pages of the whole book; thus two pages of the later Christian Arabic script correspond to one only of the earlier Qurân one; the original pages of the whole book having been folded double and turned sideways by the ninth-century scribe. Therefore the Qurân pages always bear two numbers, such as 18a and 15b.

I could have read no page of the Syriac *Protevangelium* nor of anything else completely, if I had not begun by cutting the cords that held the book together, and smoothing out the pages. These binding cords have made numerous holes in the inner margins. Qurân A, as I must now call it, is written on much stronger vellum than B and C are; some pages of the latter are beginning to split and crumble. This is not wonderful, since it was thin to begin with; and more than a thousand years ago it was rubbed hard with pumice-stone for the purpose of completely obliterating every word of the Qurân text that had been impressed on it.

After publishing no. XI in 1902, my first care was to place the manuscript in the hands of expert binders, Messrs Eyre and Spottiswoode, whose workshops are now attached to the British Museum. The vellum leaves have been by them set within strong paper ones, and the more ragged leaves have been mended with strips of very fine transparent white gauze. This gauze has been somewhat of an impediment to Dr. Mingana's work; yet without it some of the pages would not exist for him to decipher. Some of them have suffered so much from age and neglect that they have become undecipherable. In these cases we have indicated the missing text by a few rows of dots; but in places where only a word or two is undoubtedly there, although it is illegible, we have given the probable text from the standard Qurân; placing the borrowed words in square brackets, and adding a point of interrogation (?) where there is a doubt.

How did this manuscript come into my hands? And why should I have put it under the eyes of Dr. Mingana, who is, of all men I know, the most competent to decipher it? I leave others to explain this. Some may attribute it to what the Muslims call "Kismet," which is not exactly the same as what the Christians regard as Providence.

And now I must be allowed to congratulate heartily my Muslim fellow countrymen on the gift that, by the hands of Dr. Mingana, I now venture to offer them. The discovery of variants in our Jewish and Christian sacred books has been an untold blessing to our generation. If in Jerome's day the Roman pontiff had been sufficiently powerful or sufficiently ill-advised to order the destruction of every copy of the New Testament except the Vulgate, we should have been in a position analogous to that of the present-day Muslims. Try to imagine what we should have done without Codexes Sinaiticus, Vaticanus, Bezae, and so on, without the Old Latin, and without the Syriac Versions. We should have been doing penance for our sins, perhaps, without always truly repenting; and a powerful stimulus to the searching of the Scriptures would have been wanting. The existence of variants in Greek manuscripts and in the versions has been a means of waking us up; a thorough examination of the Bible text preceded and accompanied the Reformation of the sixteenth century, and accompanies also the present great activity of Christian missionaries. Uneducated people do not generally wish to think; they therefore welcome the idea of verbal and even of literal inspiration. Educated people, on the contrary, find no subject more engrossing than the study and elucidation of God's truth, whether by means of natural science, or human history, or of the text of His Word. The last of these subjects helps to keep highly trained minds imbued with religious thought. And when the best intellects in any nation cease to be religious, indifference and apathy creep downward among the multitude, and are closely followed by superstition. I therefore venture to indulge the hope that a search beneath the writing of ancient manuscripts in the libraries and museums of Europe may result in the discovery of more pre-'Uthmānic portions of the Qurân, and that ours may prove to be only the first drops of a shower; an occurrence which has happened already, in my own experience, to the Hebrew text of Ben-Sira, of which the first leaf was identified by Dr. S. Schechter.

The texts of the Qurân with which we have collated that of our fragments are those of the manuscripts numbered or. 1340 and or. 1401 in the British Museum; the Qurân of Tippoo Sahib in the Cambridge University Library, one of which belongs to Dr. Mingana; and the printed text of Gustav Flügel. Our thanks are due to my dear sister, Dr. Margaret D. Gibson, for help in revising proofs; and to the printers of the University Press, for their careful and accurate work.

Agnes Smith Lewis
Castle-Brae, Cambridge
May 1914

INTRODUCTION

I

About AD 611 an illustrious member of the Arabic tribe of Ḳuraish heard, in the cave of Ḥira, a voice giving him the solemn message: "Cry thou in the name of thy Lord who created, created man from clots of blood." Sūratul-'Alaḳ (XCVI, 1–2.)[1]

Whatever be the degree of credence that an impartial critic may bestow upon this tradition, held as an unshakable truth by more than two hundred and fifty million people, we must at least bear in mind that a tradition sanctioned during the long period of thirteen centuries should command a certain respect and trust.

The man who heard this secret voice was Muḥammad, and the result of the recital of the message that he received is Muḥammadanism, whose only foundation is the book entitled Al-Qur'ân, which originally means "recital" par excellence.

It is only during the last centuries that the Qurân has been studied scientifically, and the outcome of genuine research on this subject induces us to face the enthusiastic and often blind fascination that characterizes the Qurânic compositions of the Muḥammadan world. For this reason, we earnestly wish that the spirit of a higher criticism would soon be created among modern Muslim theologians, who, attracted by so many Christian theologians, commentators, and exegetes, will then give up the puerile servility in which they have lived and still live, and the low traditionalism of doctrine that tarnishes all the beauty of their writings.

Let us see what Muḥammad himself thinks of the inspired book by means of which he tried, if possible, to overthrow the Christian and the Jewish bulwarks, by sapping at their base, the foundations of all that the old Prophets and the Apostles handed down to their respective admirers:

> Say verily, were men and jinns assembled to produce the like of this Qurân they could not produce its like, though the one should help the other (Sūrat Bani Isrâ'il, XVII, 90).[2]

> If they say, "The Qurân is his own device" say, "Then bring ten Sūrahs like it of your own devising; call whom ye can to your aid besides Allah." (Sūrat Hūd, XI, 16).[3]

> If ye be in doubt as to that which we have sent down to our servant, then produce a Sūrah like it. (Sūratul-Baqarah, II, 21).[4]

"The Muḥammadan writers, in acknowledging the claims of the Qurân to be the direct utterance of the divinity, have made it impossible for any Moslem to criticise the work, and it became, on the contrary, the standard by which other literary compositions had to be judged. Grammarians, lexicographers, and rhetoricians started with the presumption that the Qurân could not be wrong, and that all works only approached excellence in proportion as they more or less successfully imitated its style."[5]

Before we examine the truth of these assertions, we would wish to direct the attention of every reader of the Qurân to the following points: (1) The sources of the Qurân. (2) If we strip from its text the historical events and the circumstances in which it was written, it becomes an inexplicable composition. (3) How were the verses of the Qurân preserved from 612 to 632? (4) Who is the compiler of the standard text that we have today, and is this compilation authentic?

The first point is very easily treated, and since the Prophet could probably neither read nor write,[6] the details that deal with the unity of God, and with the various forms of the Eastern conceptions of religious obligations, namely, prayer, alms, fasting, and so on must have been inspired chiefly by oral information drawn from Christians, and specially from the strong Jewish colony of Mecca and the neighboring districts. Besides the masterly book of Nöldeke, the reader will find trustworthy information on this subject in Geiger's *Was hat Mahomet aus dem Judenthum aufgenommen?* (1833) for the Jewish element in the Qurân, and in W. St. Clair Tisdall's *The original sources of the Qurân* (1905). Some good ideas may be found in Cl. Huart's *Une nouvelle source du Qorân* (1904). We have to draw attention to details.

Long before the time of the Prophet, the Ḳuraishites were mixed with the Christians, and about AD 485 a well-known Syrian writer, Narsai, the founder of the University of Nisibis, mentions the terrible raids that the forefathers of Muḥammad were wont to make in the district of Beith 'Arabayé, in Western Assyria: "The raid of the sons of Hagar was more cruel even than famine, and the blow that they gave was more sore than disease; the wound of the sons of Abram is like the venom of a serpent, and perhaps there is a remedy for the poison of reptiles, but not for theirs. . . . Let us always blame the foul inclination of the sons of Hagar, and specially the people (the tribe) of Ḳuraish who are like animals."[7]

The distance between Arabia and the desert of Syria will not astonish our reader if he thinks of the semi-nomadic life of every good Arab, when mounted on his swift mare. We read in *Synodicon Orientale*[8] that about AD 486 the famous Barṣauma of Nisibis was appointed with Ḳardagh Nakwergân, Roman *dux* and king of the Arabs, to settle the differences arising out of the rudimental delimitation of the Roman and Persian frontiers, in the East of Arabia. A letter from Barṣauma to Acacius, Catholicos of Seleucia, informs us that the Arabs called Ṭu'âites would not have permitted the inhabitants of the province of Beith 'Arabayé to live in peace through their continual raids. These Arabs, who are not to be confounded with Ṭayayés, Ṭay, and who molested so strangely the Western parts of the old Assyrian empire, were living in the sandy plains of the Southwestern land of the Sassanides, and by their proximity to the country of the Meccan prophet they must have shaken more than once the primitive religious authorities of central Arabia. In the districts adjoining the country where Mecca is situated, several small kingdoms were almost half Christian, and a document of supreme value[9] proves that Ḥîra was already a bishopric in AD 410.

In consideration of the meager scientific attainments of the Prophet, the question of the sources of the Qurân has been keenly debated by the old Christian communities. The outcome of some of their thoughts brought forth the curious *History of Rabban Beḥîra*. The second part of this legend, which tells of the interview of Muḥammad with this monk, and the epoch of whose composition may be the middle of the eighth century, is an irrefragable proof both of the ignorance of the Christian scholars of that time about the genuine sources of the Qurân, and of their conviction that it had a foreign origin. M. R. Gottheil, who printed this history in 1899,[10] remarks that its first part, containing the encounter of Beḥîra with Išo'iahb, and its third part, exhibiting some apocalyptic visions on Islâm, may date from the eleventh century, but its second part is much earlier. It would be interesting to know whether this second part has no historical value; but as this question is a digression from our subject, we content ourselves with a reference to it.

The internal criticism of the Qurân will easily show this elementary evidence of a foreign source; but what we can by no means explain are the wonderful anachronisms about the old Israelite history. The only possible way of accounting for these would be the distance that separated the moment of the inspiration of the verses from the moment when the Prophet received the oral communication. Who then will not be astonished to learn that in the Qurân, Miriam, the sister of Aaron, is confounded with the Virgin Mary? (Sūrat Ali-ʿImrân, III, 31 et seq.) and that Haman is given as minister of Pharaoh, instead of Ahasuerus? (Sūratul-Qaṣaṣ, XXVIII, 38. Sūratul-Mu'men, XL, 38 et passim.) The ignorance, too, of the author of the Qurân about everything outside of Arabia and some parts of Syria makes the fertility of Egypt, where rain is never missed, for the simple reason that it is very seldom seen, depend on rain instead of on the inundation of the Nile (Sūrat Yūsuf, XII, 49).[11] Moreover, the greatest honor that the Israelite tradition bestows upon Esdras is found in *Sanhedrin*, XXI, 22, where we read that "'Ezra would have been fully worthy to give the law, if Moses had not been before him";[12] but to state, as in Sūratut-Taubah, IX, 30, that the Jews believed that Esdras was the son of God, as the Christians thought of the Messiah, is a grave error hardly justifiable. All these historical mistakes receive another and not less topical support from the utter confusion that is made between Gideon and Saul in Sūratul-Baqarah, II, 250. Such mistakes are indelible stains on the pages of the sacred book that is the object of our study, and they are not wiped out by the following statement: "We (Allah) relate unto thee a most excellent history, by revealing unto thee this Qurân, whereas thou wast before one of the negligent" (Sūrat Yūsuf, XII, 3).[13] And again, "I (Muḥammad) had no knowledge of the exalted princes when they disputed about the creation of man; it is revealed unto me only as a proof that I am a public preacher" (Sūrat Ṣad, XXXVIII, 67–70).[14]

If we try to read the Qurân from beginning to end in the order in which it has been circulated from the latter half of the seventh century down to this day, we shall ascertain that it is the most incoherent of books, and the flagrant contradictions that we shall meet will astonish us. So in Sūratut-

Taubah, we read, "Make war upon the people unto whom the book has been delivered, who . . . forbid not what Allah and His Apostle have forbidden, and who profess not the profession of the truth, until they pay tribute out of hand in an humble condition."[15] And again in Sūratul-Baqarah, II, 189, it is said: "And fight against them till there be no more tumult, and the only worship be that of Allah."[16]

But in this same Sūratul-Baqarah, V, 257, it is said: "Let there by no compulsion in religion";[17] and in Sūratul-'Ankabūt, XXIX, 45: "And dispute ye not, except in kindliest sort with the people of the book."[18] (The Christians and the Jews, by allusion to the Torah and the Gospel, are called in the Qurân *the people of the book.*)

The Muḥammadan commentators noticed these contradictions, and found that the best way to remove them was that of the historical method, and availing themselves of the oldest lives of the Prophet by Zuhri, Mūsa Ibn 'Uqba, Abu Isḥâḳ, Madâ'ini, and the better-known books of Ibn Hishâm, Wâḳidi, and Ṭabari. They attempted to explain every verse by the circumstances in which it has been revealed, and they distributed the sūrahs of the Qurân into two distinct groups: those that were written in Mecca from AD 612 to 622, and those that were revealed in Medîna, from 622 to 632. The youthful and timid essay of Muḥammadan theologians has been in the last few years considerably expanded by many critics; special mention must be made here of Nöldeke's *Geschichte des Qorâns* (1860) and E. Sell's *The Historical Development of the Qorân* (1905).

By this synchronal method, the Qurân becomes a historical book, and the most trustworthy source of information about the Prophet. The touchstone of veracity for any given detail of the life of Muḥammad told by the historians of the period of decadence would be to find if this detail has any sufficient ground in the Islâmic book. But, at any rate, if by this criticism the chronological order is saved, the versatility of mind of the Prophet can by no means be excused, since, under the pressure of necessity, he cruelly contradicted sometimes what he had stated before. Can then the following verse inspired in Mecca excuse some flagrant contradictions of the Qurân? "And we have not sent an apostle or prophet before thee, among whose desires Satan injected not some wrong desire, but Allah shall bring to nought that which Satan has suggested" (Sūratul-Ḥajj, XXII, 51).[19]

We do not wish to discuss a youthful essay on the explanation of these difficulties, put forward by some pious commentators who say: "Allah commanded several things which were, for good reasons, afterwards revoked and abrogated." Those abrogated passages of the Qurân are distinguished by many of the rigid commentators, into three kinds, "the first, where the letter and the sense are both abrogated; the second, where the letter only is abrogated, but the sense remains; and the third, where the sense is abrogated, though the letter remains." The subtleties of the theological schools do not afford a profitable subject of study for a serious critic.

The most important question in the study of the Qurân is its unchallengeable authenticity. In this theme, the first step would be the following question: How could Muḥammad in all the wars by which his life was so unfortunately agitated, in all the displacements that he must have undergone, keep all the verses that had been previously revealed to him in his memory, after an interval of several years? A plausible and final answer will probably never be given to this question, and the only tenable hypothesis is that which discards the difficulty by the assumption of the prodigious memory of his followers, who are believed to have learned the strophes by heart, and that is a period lasting from 612 till 632. This hypothesis, which seems to be that of a *dernier ressort*, can be supported by the fact that the Prophet, who was more probably an unlettered man,[20] had never thought of writing a book, or of gathering together, in a complete code, the scattered verses that he had recited to his friends, in some circumstances of his life; so much so, that after his death, the emissaries of Abu Bekr, his successor in the Caliphate, could scarcely put together some separate bits of verses, despite the good memory, and the extreme care of Zaid ibn Thâbit, the real compiler of the Qurân of today.

This historical fact is suggested by the first refusal of Zaid to undertake the compilation of the Qurân, on the ground that the Prophet himself had never done so. "What right have I," said Zaid to Abu Bekr, "to gather in the form of a book what the Prophet has never intended to transmit to posterity by this channel? And since the Prophet never designed to give his message in this way, is it a lawful work that I am commanded to do?"

As to the prodigious memory of Eastern people who imperturbably and faithfully preserve verses of songs and poems, in their daily life, during a long space of time, we must say that this fact has been a little exaggerated;

and nearly always the rural ditties, used in our day among the Bedawin and the Kurdish population of the plains of Syria and Mesopotamia, are recited by different tribes in a different way, and the changes are often more or less sensible according to the remoteness of the tribes one from the other. So, for instance, how many significant various readings can we find in the well-known Arabic elegy called *'Itâbah*, in the divers Bedawin tribes of Albu-Ḥamad, Shammar, 'Aniza, Dleim? and so on, and, besides the various readings, how many new couplets of the Kurdish glee called *Mamo Zînê* are used in the deadly sept of Mîra, which are absolutely unknown in the tribes of Hâja, Zêwiki, Shakâki, and the like?

As to the faithfulness of a tradition among Eastern people, it has been, I think, accentuated too strongly, and the best comparison for this string of traditions would be, to anyone who has travelled in the arid deserts, a great caravan of big camels walking one after another, but all being guided by a small donkey. We cannot, indeed, understand why Eastern people should deviate in this matter from the natural law of a progressive evolution, and the tenacity with which some people cling to ancient religious creeds and habits of daily life has nothing to do with the change of words and the exaggeration of historical details; and for that matter, a serious man, who knows the domestic life of the nomads, will doubtless ascertain that the donkey, which conducts the imposing caravan of camels, is sometimes smaller in the East than in the West.

Besides the ordinary channel of the wonderful memory of the Arabs, many verses have been transmitted to Zaid by writing, a kind of writing that was in use at Mecca in the time of the Prophet; but since we cannot explain why some verses should have been written and others not, and especially since we are not told which are the verses transmitted to Zaid by writing, and which are those that he knew only from memory, this fact cannot come, till fuller light dawns, into the sphere of a scientific and positive study. To believe that several verses of the Qurân were written by friends of the Prophet during his lifetime is in accordance with some phrases of this sacred book, which mention clearly the name of *Kitâb* "what is written, scriptures," but to state that the fragmentary revelations were almost entirely written and "put promiscuously into a chest"[21] is in contradiction to the kind of life that Muḥammad led, and to early and authentic sources. In accepting such low and hardly disinterested traditions of Muslim authors, why should we not regard as true other and not less authoritative narratives which inform us that all the sūrahs were completed according to the directions of the angel Gabriel, who, on the other hand, brought only to Muḥammad, in parcels, a text written on a table of "vast bigness," styled the *Preserved Table* and existing from all eternity near Allah's throne? Muḥammadan pious annalists know, too, that a copy made from this eternal original has been sent to the lowest heaven, whence Gabriel was accustomed to show it once a year[22] to the Prophet, bound in silk and adorned with gold and precious stones of Paradise. The Prophet himself puts into the mouth of God the following sentences: "By the Luminous Book!—We (Allah) have made it an Arabic Qurân that ye may understand; and it is a transcript of the Archetypal Book kept by us" (Sūratuz-Zukhruf, XLIII, 1–3), and again: "We ourselves (Allah) have sent down to thee the Qurân as a missive from on high" (Sūratud-Dahr, LXXVI, 23), and again: "That this is the honourable Qurân, written on the *Preserved Table*; let no one touch it but the purified" (Sūratul-Wâḳi'ah, LVI, 77–78), and again: "Say, the Holy Spirit hath brought it down with truth, from thy Lord." (Sūratun-Naḥl XVI; V, 104), and so on, and so on.

We know the whole text of the Qurân has been drawn up twice by Zaid ibn Thâbit, who, it is said, was the amaneunsis of the Prophet. The first recension was made under the Caliphate of Abu Bekr, and at the instigation of 'Omar, his successor, between AH 11 and 15. "I fear," said this true believer, to the Caliph, "that slaughter may again wax hot amongst the reciters of the Qurân, on other fields of battle, and that much may be lost therefrom. Now therefore my advice is, that thou shouldst give speedy orders for the collection of the Qurân." Abu Bekr agreed, and addressing Zaid ibn Thâbit, he said, "Thou art a young man, and wise; against whom no one amongst us can cast an imputation. Wherefore now search out the Qurân, and bring it together." Yielding to the joint entreaties of Abu Bekr and 'Omar, Zaid sought out the fragments of the Qurân from every quarter and gathered them together, from date-leaves, bits of parchment, tablets of white stone, and from the hearts of men.[23]

The Qurân, so collected and drawn up by Zaid, was committed by 'Omar to the custody of his own daughter Ḥafṣa, the Prophet's widow. We are not told, by any contemporary outside writer, of what kind were these, tablets of white stone, or date-leaves, and the early sources do not suggest that the

Prophet had ever used such materials. It is quite possible, therefore, that the only source which Zaid had for the greater part of the text was "the hearts of men," and some scattered scraps of parchment. This hypothesis is supported by the absolute want of any chronological order in the Qurân; and this want suggests to us the idea that the book is not a result of one source of information, or of one Arab reciter, and that it has not been written in deep and laborious study, but that it is simply the outcome of many different recitals that Zaid heard day by day, and gradually wrote down in the measure and proportion that he received them. One day he received some verses "from the breast" of some inhabitants of Medîna dealing with the life of the Prophet in that city, and he wrote them quickly in his book; the next day, hearing some other recitals from some inhabitants of Mecca, he embodied them with the previous verses revealed in Medîna. For this reason, we can scarcely find a long sūrah of the Qurân that is not twice or thrice at least composite, that is, having verses dating from the time when the Prophet was still in native town, and some others referring to the time immediately following his flight to Yathrib. It is highly probably, too, that the bits of parchment used by Zaid contained sometimes a complete narrative of a biblical incident, and that the only work of the compiler was to put such well-digested material in one of the sūrahs of the book that he edited. In this category must be counted all the verses dealing with the history of Joseph, of the birth of the Christ, and many other stories.

Finally, if we understand correctly the following verse of Sūratul-Ḥijr (XV, 90–91): "As we sent down upon (punished) the dividers (of the Scripture?) who broke up the Qurân into parts,"[24] we are tempted to state that, even when the Prophet was alive, some changes were noticed in the recital of certain verses of his sacred book. There is nothing very surprising in this fact, since Muḥammad could not read nor write, and was at the mercy of friends for the writing of his revelations, or, more frequently, of some mercenary amaneunses.

The book, drawn up by this method, continued to be the authoritative and standard text till about AH 29–30 under the Caliphate of 'Uthmān. At this time the wonderful faithfulness of Arab memory was defective, and according to a general weakness of human nature, the *Believers* have been heard reciting the verses of the Qurân in a different way. This fact was due especially, it is said, to the hundreds of dialects used in Arabia. Zaid was again asked to put an end to these variations that had begun to scandalize the votaries of the Prophet. That indefatigable compiler, assisted by three men from the tribe of Ḳuraish,[25] started to do what he had already done more than fifteen years before. The previous copies made from the first one written under Abu Bekr were all destroyed by special order of the caliph: the Revelation sent down from heaven was one, and the book containing this Revelation must be one.

The critic remarks that the only guarantee of the authenticity of the Qurân is the testimony of Zaid; and for this reason, a scholar who doubts whether a given word has been really used by Muḥammad, or whether it has been only employed by Zaid on his own authority, or on the meager testimony of some Arab reciters, does not transgress the strict laws of high criticism. If the memory of the followers of the Prophet has been found defective from the year AH 15 to 30; when Islâm was proclaimed over all Arabia, why may it not have been defective from AD 612 to 632 when the Prophet was often obliged to defend his own life against terrible aggressors? And if the first recension of Zaid contained always the actual words of Muḥammad, why was this compiler not content with reestablishing it in its entirety, and why was the want of a new recension felt by 'Uthmān? How can it be that in the short space of fifteen years, such wonderful variants could have crept into the few copies preceding the reign of the third caliph that he found himself bound to destroy all those he could find? If 'Uthmān was certainly inspired only by religious purposes, why did his enemies call him "The tearer of the Books"? and why did they fasten on him the following stigma: "He found the Qurâns many and left one; he tore up the Book"?[26] We deem, therefore, as too categorical the following verdict of Von Hammer: "We hold the Qurân to be as surely Muḥammad's word, as the Muḥammadans hold it to be the word of God."

Though a convincing answer worthy of *twentieth*-century criticism cannot be given to the preceding questions, we believe that Zaid endeavored to reproduce, faithfully, so far as he could, the very words of Muḥammad. The imperfections of all kinds, and the want of historical order found in his book, are terrible witnesses against his intellectual proficiency; but, on the other hand, the fragmentary qualities of the last sūrahs, the good control of the first caliphs, and especially the suitable time of his compilation, when many believers were able to recite several verses by heart, testify to his faithfulness. We believe too, that if the historical attainments of the first Muslims and of Zaid himself had been less restricted, they would perhaps have modified in some way the historical and topographical errors that the Qurân contains.

Now, at what date has the Qurân been arranged in the order that it follows in our day? Professor D. S. Margoliouth remarks very justly that "the task of arranging the sacred texts in fixed groups might very well have appalled a Moslem; we could scarcely credit a contemporary of the Prophet with having the courage to attempt it. On the other hand, the notion that the Sūrahs existed as frames, which gradually became filled as revelations descended, has little to commend it, and involves the existence of an official copy, which we have seen to be excluded by the evidence."[27] We maintain, however, that this arrangement was made at the time of the first recension, and not at the second; the scandal that would have followed it at the time when the Qurân was known by many a Muḥammadan, and especially by believers in foreign countries, makes the contrary hypothesis very improbable.

> The recension of 'Uthmān has been handed down to us unaltered. So carefully, indeed, has it been preserved, that there are no variations of importance—we might almost say no variations at all—to be found in the innumerable copies scattered throughout the vast bounds of the Empire of Islâm; contending and embittered factions, taking their rise in the murder of 'Uthmān himself, within a quarter of a century after the death of Mahomet, have ever since rent the Moslem world; yet but *one Coran* has been current amongst them; and the consentaneous use by all of the same scripture, in every age, to the present day, is an irrefragable proof that we have now before us the very text prepared by command of the unfortunate Caliph. There is probably no other work in the world which has remained for twelve centuries with so pure a text. . . . It is one of the maxims of the Moslem world (supported perhaps by Surz XI, 2) that the Coran is incorruptible, and that it is preserved from error and variety of reading by the miraculous interposition of God himself. . . . According to the orthodox doctrine, every syllable of the Coran is of divine origin, eternal and uncreate as the Deity itself.[28]

From what we have said in the preceding pages, it is evident that if we find a manuscript of the Qurân presenting various readings of consonants and of complete words, and more especially if this manuscript offers some interpolations and omissions, it would not be too rash to suppose that it goes back to a pre-'Uthmānic period. The conclusion is clear and is corroborated by the constant history of the Muḥammadan world, from the seventh century down to our own day.

Viewing the linguistic wording of the text of the Qurân, we desire to examine a question that concerns us more than the others. Does the Qurân contain the flower of the Arabic language, and is the challenge given by the Prophet himself true? Besides the sentences quoted in the preceding pages, the Prophet repeats several times with a certain emphasis: "We gave a Qurân written in Arabic; it is in Arabic that this Qurân has been revealed, etc."[29] Philologists will not be much offended if we send our reader, for an answer to this question, to the excellent works of a man who deserves the gratitude of every Orientalist, Th. Nöldeke, and chiefly to his *Geschichte des Qorâns* already mentioned. We would wish only to draw attention to the following remarks: "The Arabic literature preceding the epoch of the Prophet is imperfectly known; but we may be allowed to state that it was not very flourishing, since the traces that it left for future generations are scanty in comparison with the formidable swarm of useful lucubrations of the post-Muḥammadan time. This being so, the Moslem authors are not to be blamed when they call that time the epoch of *Ignorance*[30] though they mean specially, by this qualification, an ignorance about Allah and his immediate attributes. The works of the best writers have been collected at the beginning of the ninth century by Aṣma'i and are Ṭarafa, Amrul-Ḳais, 'Antara, Zuhair, Nâbigha, 'Alḳama."[31] If we add to this number Ta'abbaṭa-Sharran[32] and Shanfarâ and some others found in the book of Louis Cheikho[33] but with some restriction about the authenticity of all their poems we may have the approximate number.

Now when we compare the style, the method of elocution, the purity of vocables, the happy adjustment of words, the choice of good rhymes in these pre-Islâmic writings with the Qurân, we are often tempted to give them an unchallengeable superiority; and it is only this kind of life, foreign to all learning, that can explain the great uneasiness that the author of the Qurân shows when he wishes to write in rhyme, and finds himself short of common lexicographical terms. So in Sūratul-Jinn the author had certainly an intention to write in rhymed prose (*saj'*), but his linguistic knowledge failing him, he repeats the word احدا six times at the end of twenty-eight short sentences. Besides the repetitions, being quite short of rhymes, even through this method, he changes the letter *Dâl* to a *bâ*, in verses 5, 8, 15, to a *qâf* in verses 6, 13, 16. This example, chosen among hundreds of others that are found frequently in the final sūrahs, is not weakened by some foreign and cacophonic terms of which the author of the Qurân is enamored, for example, سلسبيلا sūrah LXXVI, 18; فرقان from the Aramaic ܦܘܪܩܢܐ, sūrah VIII, 42; II, 181; III, 2 et passim; غسلين (!) sūrah LXIX, 36; سجين (!) LXXXIII, 7, 8; قمطريرا lxxvi, 70; الطاغوت Sūratun-Nisâ (IV, 78 et passim) inspired from the Aramaic ܛܥܘܬܐ; الحواريين Sūratul-Mâidah (V, 111–12, etc.) from the corresponding Ethiopic root, and so on, and so on.[34] We believe, moreover, that it is by the want of good literary attainments that we can explain the vulgar disfigurement of the names John (Yoḥannan), Jesus (Esho') into يحيى *Iaḥya* and عيسى *'Îsa*. Muḥammad seems to have taken the vulgar form of these names given in the popular language to children by some Christians of Jewish descent just as in English the name of Margaret becomes in colloquial fashion, Margie (*Scottice*, Maggie, Meg, Peggie), that of Elizabeth, Lizzie or Bessie, and Robert, Bob or Bertie.

Another and not less wonderful instance of spelling is used in Sūratut-Tîn, where the name of Mount Sinai (in Arabic سيناء as in Sūratul-Mū'minîn, xxiii, 20), is written سينين (!) to make it rhyme with the preceding verse and the following one, والتين والزيتون. وطور سينين وهذا البلد الامين. The disfigurement, too, of the name of Elijah (in Arabic الياس as in Sūratul-An'âm, VI, 85) into الياسين (!) to make it rhyme with the final words of the phrase, suggests on this point a systematic habit on the part of the Prophet: سلام على الياسين: انا كذلك نجزي المحسنين. (Sūratuṣ-Ṣâfât, xxxvii, 130).

This disfigurement of proper nouns is sometimes used in such an awkward manner that, if we wish to set aside an interminable tergiversation, we must attribute the origin of some unknown names, so strangely altered, to Muḥammad's own invention. So, who will easily be convinced that the Hūd of Sūratul-A'râf (VII, 63 et pas.) is the same man as the Eber of the Bible,[35] that the Ṣâleḥ of Sūrat Hūd (XI, 64, etc.) is the same man as Peleg of Genesis (XI, 16),[36] and that the Shu'aib of Sūratush-Shu'arâ (XXVI, 177, etc.) is the same name as Hobab[37] (Numb. X, 29)? No tradition, however corrupted it might have been, would have altered these biblical names in such a wonderfully different mould.

Other alterations of names may perhaps be sufficiently explained by a traditional Christian or Jewish channel; so in Sūratul-An'âm (VI, 74) Terah, Abraham's father, is called "Azar," and we know that in some Judaeo-Christian circles, Terah was called "Athar."[38] The Djâlūt, too, of Sūratul-Baqarah (II, 250) is unmistakably Goliath; likewise, the Ḳârūn of Sūratul-Qaṣaṣ (XXVIII, 76) seems to be the Korah of the Bible. At any rate, philology will be, for a long time, unable to explain convincingly how the name of Saul could become Ṭâlūt, as in Sūratul-Baqarah (II, 248, 250), nor how the name of Enoch could become Idrîs, as in Sūrat Mariam (XIX, 57, etc.), nor, finally, how the name of Obadiah (1 Kings 17:4) or of Ezechiel could become Dhul-Kifl, as in Sūratul-Anbiâ' (XXI, 85), in spite of a brilliant suggestion that Ezechiel is called by the Arabs Kefil (!).[39]

In any case, whatever view we may take of the claims of Muḥammad, no one can deny that he was a great man, ranking with men of the highest genius, as a skillful administrator after the Eastern fashion, and wielding every kind of spiritual weapon to attract and captivate his hearers and his countrymen. His legislation, though perhaps too theocratic for the democratic spirit of our day, was perfection at the time when he lived; *Exitus acta probat*. A man who put an end, in less than ten years, to two formidable kingdoms, the kingdom of the old Achemenides represented by the classic Sassanides, and that of the Roman Caesars of Eastern countries, by means of some camel-drivers of Arabia, must be, at any rate, taken into consideration.[40] A controller of conscience and soul to so many millions, and in the plain light of civilization, is indeed greater than Alexander and Bonaparte known only today in historical books. The proclamations of a semi-nomadic Arab of the obscure town of Mecca have been recited by the wide Islâmic world thirteen centuries ago, and are recited today; even the cross of the Messiah has been for many years nearly eclipsed by the Crescent, and the name of the *Praised One* of Arabia has been on many occasions on the point of overrunning the last refuge of Christianity. What history is unable to find, even in the twentieth century, is a name more terrible than that of *Muḥammad*.

II

For a scientific comprehension of the text of the Qurân, three kinds of study may be found useful: (1) The commentators of the Qurân; (2) the grammarians who applied to it the Arabic vowels and diacritical points; (3) the diverse forms of script formerly used in the Arabic language.

When the semi-nomadic Arabs started to conquer the world, they did not carry with them, on their camels, any productions of a progressive and latent literature, for they were not brought up in high schools of science and philology. The most picturesque figure among these first Arabs is that of the Caliph 'Omar entering the holy city of Jerusalem (637), mounted on his camel, a bag of dates and a skin of water by his side; this provision being judged sufficient for his simple wants. It is worth observing how exactly the Aramaeo-Syrian population of that period of conquests called these Arabs by derision: *Hagarians*, *Ishmaelites*, with the purpose of indicating precisely the semi-barbarous literary education that they had received.[41] But an end was soon made to this awkward situation; and the intelligent Arabs, attracted by the example of their neighbors, began to spread everywhere the language of the Qurân, and to devote themselves to the sciences that had long given to their new fellow-countrymen an unchallenged superiority. A well-known Syriac writer Bar Hebraeus tells us a significant fact, that the Umayyad Caliph Walîd ordered that the official acts of Damascus should henceforth be drawn up in Arabic, and no longer in Greek.[42] The sanguinary battles of Yarmûk (636) and Kadesia (637), in imposing a new rule over the remains of the once classic empires, gave them a new sacred language.

With regard to the commentaries on the Qurân, the only question in Arabic literature that concerns our subject, they are very important for the criticism of the text, since the commentators, when quoting and explaining a given verse in their books, quote it faithfully, and they often try to discuss it with all the resources of their science, literally and spiritually. The first commentator of the early epoch of Islâm was Ibn ʿAbbās, cousin of Muḥammad, who seems to have been the main source of the traditional exegesis of the Qurân. On theological grounds, a great number of his opinions have been considered heretical. He and his disciples deal with the sense and connection of a complete verse, and neglect the literal meaning of a separate word. His commentaries are therefore what Christian writers would call more spiritual than literal. No complete commentary either by the relatives of the Prohpet or by extraneous writers has come down to us from this period.

The greatest commentator of a later generation is the well-known Ṭabari (AD 839–923).[43] He is a mine for the knowledge of the wide Islâmic legislation, and has sometimes excellent views about the occasion of the revelation of several verses. He is first of all a historian, availing himself of the method of *Isnâd*, and by this channel he preserves several interesting traditions of the early age of Muḥammadanism.

Another good commentator is Az-Zamakhshari[44] (1075–1144). He is, according to the judgment of Nöldeke, too subtle a man, trying to apply his rhetorical and philosophical theories to the most practical of men: Muḥammad.

In our own days, the commentary most used by Moslem theologians is that of al-Baiḍhâwi (†1286) who employed the same method as that of Az-Zamakhshari in a more methodical manner.

The end of the thirteenth century, which marks the decadence and the close of the 'Abbâsside Caliphate, marks, too, the apogee of the Arabic investigations in the Qurân. The numerous commentators of a later date content themselves with quoting, abridging the old authors, and writing books more popular than original.

A good commentary needs good reading, and good reading, in the Semitic languages, involves an accurate knowledge of the right position of the vowels, with all the orthoepical signs of punctuation. We ought to say at once that according to the measure of scientific investigations of today, the Arabs, apart from seven or ten marks of intonation, never used the *rhetorical signs* employed sometimes so fantastically and so awkwardly by the Aramaeans. The Arabic language, possessing a kind of inflection like the Greek and the Latin, did not experience any great necessity for reaching even the fortieth part of the frightful number forty that the Aramaeans have invented for an intelligent reading of their Bible, and which are called by the curious and general name of *Puḥâmés*[45] "similarities, comparisons." A practical reason must have deterred the Arabs from adopting such a complicated system, and this reason is found in the script of their language, which distinguishes several consonants by means of one, two, or three dots placed either under or over a letter. The adoption of the *Puḥâmés* of the Aramaeans would have created an insurmountable mental difficulty in distinguishing a diacritical point from an orthoepical one dealing specially with a proper accent of voice in the reading of a sentence.

While the Aramaeans and the Hebrews admitted several vowels and invented a special sign for every vowel pronounced open or closed, short or long, the prudent Arabs adopted only three vowels, but these three vowels, represented by a stroke of the pen under or over the letter, respond quite sufficiently to all philological exigencies, since each one of them, when followed by a weak letter, is considered as long, for example, زَارُونِي "they have visited me," and it is considered short, when followed by a letter that is not quiescent, for example, قُتِلَ "he has been killed," and it is shortly closed when followed by a quiescent or reduplicated letter, for example, إِخْتَرْتُمْ "you have chosen." By this method, every vowel becomes quantitatively three, and so the system is more ingenious than that of the Hebrews, and of the Aramaeans, who by a long use and borrowing very often neglected the short vowel, so important in poetry and in euphonic sounds.

The history of the vowels is somewhat obscure. It is certain that their invention cannot go back to the period preceding the Umayyad Caliphate of Damascus. The period of conquest and of intestine war caused by the crucial question of the divine Caliphate, which covered the Muḥammadan world with blood, at the time of 'Uthmān and onward, was not very suitable for scientific research. The Umayyad Empire, though distinguished by some great productions of poetry and historical science, is unknown (except for some mere names such as that of Abul-Aswad Ad- Do'ali, or 'Abdur-Raḥmân ibn Ormiz, a Persian scholar, etc.) as a starting point for grammatical and morphological studies. The first period of conquest lasted from the death of the Prophet, AD 632 to 661, when Mu'âwiah entered Kūfa and became the sole representative of Muḥammad; the second period from 661 till January 25, AD 750, when the battle of Shaharzūr gave the scepter to the 'Abbâssides. Therefore, till the accession of Saffâḥ, no center of grammatical learning has left a trace to posterity. But at this time, the two other branches of the Semitic stock, the Israelites and the Aramaeans, had already passed the time of the careful elaboration of their Massorah, and their vowel-system had acquired a firm foundation, being, in fact, almost at the end of its final evolution.

From the middle of the sixth century, the Monophysite, Aḥud-Emmeh, Metropolitan of Tagrit, had opened a path for the Syriac grammar. Some years before him, the famous Joseph of Ahwâz had established, in the University of Nisibis, a solid foundation for the orthoepical studies and for the right pronunciation of the vowels. In the middle of the seventh century, a school founded by Abba Sabrowy, at Beth Shehak, near Nisibis, made the Nestorian system of vowels known even among the Monophysites, their enemies. Before AD 700 Jacob of Edessa, by his well-known sentence ܒܢܝܚܘ ܬܚܝܢ ܐܘܪܗܝ ܐܡܢ *Edessa, our mother, thou shalt live in quietness*, which represents all the vowels of the Aramaic language used today, marks the end of a systematic evolution of phonetic studies in the Syriac grammar. The school of Edessa, the University of Nisibis, and the monasteries of Tel'eda, Ḳennešrin, and Ḳarḳaphta, had then made complete, in the period lasting from 450 to 700 AD, the phonetic essays that the writers of a later period were content to abridge or to modify in some insignificant details.[46]

On the other hand, the strong Israelite colony that had remained behind from the old Babylonian captivity vied in a laudable zeal with the Aramaeans. By means of some prudently distributed bribes, they could always secure a satisfactory political condition under the Sassanide Sapor I and his successors. Their prestige was so widely felt that, in the fourth century, they contrived to be favored by the harem of the Queen Ephra Hormizd, to whom Christian writers of that time attribute the frightful ordeal that Sapor II, the enemy of the Roman legions, inflicted, in 341, on the Christians of the Persian Empire.[47] According to the Talmud, the Jews of Babylonia are from a purer race even than those of Palestine; we read, in fact, in the *Talm. Bab.* under the treatise *Ḳiddušin*, the following sentence:[48] "Tous les pays sont comme de la pâte relativement à la Palestine, mais ce pays l'est relativement à la Babylonie." By the works of Christian writers in Mesopotamia, we know how great was the influence that they exercised in that country and in the neighboring districts. Of the twenty-three homilies of Jacob Aphrahaṭ (fourth century) nine are devoted to the anti-Judaic controversy. Narsai (†502) has also some striking discourses against them.

The Torah was always the subject of a special study among the Jews of the Captivity either under the Arsacido-Parthians or under the Sassanido-Persians, but we know that from the third century and onward the study has been considerably extended. The great *Sidra* of Sora, founded in this epoch, acquired a worldwide renown, and could not be eclipsed by other celebrated schools established at Nehardea, Perozšabur, Maḥôzé (Seleucia), and Pumbaditha.[49] The Rabbinic Massorah flourished in these centers, if not more than in the highest schools of Galilee, at least in an equal degree with them, and the scientific investigations of Babylonian Jews contributed more to the final fixing and delimitation of the complicated Massoretic system as we have it today than the research of any other writers. In several manuscripts of the Old Testament, the work of these Israelite centers of learning is designated by the gloss מדנח *the East*, and we know that in the sacred books of the Jews, the "Babylonian punctuation" is in many cases better even than the "Tiberian punctuation."

When the 'Abbâsside dynasty appeared in the East, and new caliphs settled in Baghdâd, the grammatical studies of their neighbors were then at their apogee. The intestine dissentions about the caliphate having been at last cut short by the two-edged sword of Abu Muslim a new and deeper direction of studies was given to Arabic phonetics and morphology. Two celebrated centers of Arabic studies soon flourished in southern Mesopotamia: the school of Baṣrah and that of Kūfa. We do not wish our readers to understand that we positively deny that these two schools may have existed before the accession of the 'Abbâsside dynasty, but it is quite certain that to assign their foundation to the time immediately following Muḥammad's death, as some scholars state, and to believe that they exercised an influence as strong as that which they had, at a later time, under the eastern caliphate, would perhaps overstep the limits of safe criticism.

The first grammarian especially known for Arabic meter is Khalîl ibn Aḥmad (AD 718–791) of the school of Baṣrah. Besides having the glory of being considered the first Arabic grammarian, he is believed to have been the inventor, in the latter half of the eighth century, of the *hamza*, a semi-guttural consonant, in comparison with the weak Aliph. So far as I know, no complete grammatical treatise of his is extant today. Some grammatical sketches are attributed to him by authors of a late date, but their authenticity seems to be more than doubtful.[50] The earliest Arabic grammarian whose works have come down to us is Sibawaihi[51] (AD 753–793), a disciple of Khalîl.

The grammarians of the school of Kūfa seem to have paid more attention to the spoken dialect of the Bedawin, and for this reason their attempts could not influence, at the beginning, the right reading of the Qurân and could still less reach, in a later generation, a celebrity like that of the school of Baṣrah, in spite of the illustrious Kisâ'i, Ibn As-Sekkît, and Farrâ', who, according to a trustworthy tradition, pronounced to his friends the memorable sentence: "I shall die, and there is in my heart something yet unsettled about the particle حتّى." To some extent, their task was very difficult, and to Arabize all the Semitic and Aryan dialects, spoken in the old Chaldaean lands, such as the Mandaitic[52] and the Ḳatrian, was a harder task than many suppose.[53]

The foundation of the Arabic vowels is based on the vowels of the Aramaeans. The names given to these vowels is an irrefragable proof of the veracity of this assertion. So the *Phatḥ* (فتّح) corresponds in appellation and in sound to the Aramaic *Phtâḥa* (ܦܬܚܐ); the *Khaphedh* (خفض) is exactly the Aramaic *Ḥbâṣa* (ܚܒܨܐ). But though the Arabs imitated the Syrians in the verbal designation of their vowels, they recoiled, and very justly, from the absurd servility to Hellenism of their masters, who, after the time of Christological controversies and onward, could not shrink from the Greek method; and placing their morphology and syntax on fresh bases, they laid the first foundation of a high philology that excites our admiration in the present day. Viewing the intimate formation of words, they divided them into biliteral, triliteral, and quadriliteral with essential letters, in such a steady method that even the strongest philologists of the twentieth century are obliged to walk in their steps and to accept their impeccable terminology. Our thanks are due to the sagacity of scholars who in a short period of time perfected the delicate science of the deep constitution of their language.

The sagacity of the professors in the two schools of Baṣrah and of Kūfa was for a number of years challenged by a high seat of learning that the 'Abbâssides established in Baghdâd and that flourished greatly from the beginning of the ninth century and onward under the control of Christian physicians. This new school acquired a decided superiority over the others, because it taught several sciences derived from Greek and Syriac books translated into Arabic by the group of Nestorian doctors of the family of Bokhtîsho', Ḥunain, and Maswai.[54] Physicians have always had a preponderating authority at the courts of Eastern monarchs, and going back into past history, we shall find one man, Gabriel the Drustbed, eclipsing the prestige of all the formidable Dyophysite community, in the palace of the Sassanide Chosroes II Parwez.[55]

The first discoverer of the Arabic vowels is unknown to history. The opinions of Arab authors, on this point, are too worthless to be quoted; the critics of our day, too, have not clearly established their position on this subject. To find a way of unraveling this tangled question and to discern the truth among so many positively expressed opinions is by no means an easy task. If we may advance an opinion of our own, we think that a complete and systematic treatise on these vowels was not elaborated till the latter half of the eighth century, and we believe that such an attempt could have been successfully made only under the influence of the school of Baghdâd, at its very beginning. On the one hand, besides the insufficiency of the grounds for assuming an earlier date, we have not a manuscript that can be shown to be before that time adorned with vowels; on the other hand, the dependence of these vowels on those of the Aramaeans obliges us to find a center where the culture of the Aramaic language was flourishing, and this center is the school of Baghdâd, which was, as we have already stated, under the direction of Nestorian scholars, and where a treatise on Syriac grammar was written by the celebrated Ḥunain.

As to the forms of the Arabic script (we do not speak of the script used in the pre-Qurânic inscriptions), we can reduce them to three principal divisions: the Kūfi, the Naskhi, and the Kūfo-Naskhi. The Kūfi type is characterized by more square and more compact and united letters, and generally by thicker and bigger strokes of the pen. The Naskhi has smaller, thinner, and less compact strokes, and resembles more than other types the writing used, in our days, in printed books. The Kūfo-Naskhi is intermediate between these two scripts.[56] It is often very difficult to know, with certitude, the age of a manuscript only by its being written in one of these three types, since we find many documents written in each one of them and belonging to the same period. For instance, in *The Palaeographical Society*,[57] we meet with manuscripts written in these three scripts and dating from the eighth century; compare plates XIX, LIX, and V. Therefore, it is very often by the specific characters used in each of these three types, and especially by a more or less use of diacritical points, that we are guided when we ascribe a manuscript to a given epoch.[58]

For the diacritical points that distinguish the sound of many Arabic letters one from another, it is very puzzling to find a general and infallible criterion. Since many consonants, like the ض and the ص, which are distinguished today only by the dot on the letter, were generally distinguished in the early time by a somewhat different stroke of the pen, it may be supposed that the diacritical point has been invented at a late date; but can we assert the same for the case of the ت and the ث? The question thus becomes quite different, especially when these letters are followed or preceded, in the middle of the word, by a ي and a ن, which have almost the same form even in the most ancient manuscripts that we possess; for example, in how many different ways can the following word be read without diacritical points: اىسىا?

After this elemenatry dissertation, it becomes clear that a manuscript, and especially a manuscript of the Qurân, is sometimes to be considered more or less ancient according to the want or the existence of vowels, and according to the greater or less employment of diacritical points in its text, except perhaps in the case of letters that have exactly the same form, such as ت and ث.

III

Dr. Agnes Lewis, the discoverer of the Sinaitic Syriac version and of other valuable documents, has honored me with the task of deciphering an Arabic palimpsest that is in her own possession, and a good description of which has been given by herself, in the preface to this chapter. Palaeographically, we can reduce to three principal kinds of script the writing of this valuable palimpsest, the reading of which the following pages claim to give. Provisionally, these three different kinds of script will have the indications: Qurân A, Qurân B, and Qurân C.

Characteristics of the Writing in Qurân A

It is very similar to plate LIX of *The Palaeographical Society* quoted above, the kind of script that is assigned to the eighth century. The only differences are: (1) in that plate, l.10, the letter ث has three dots; in our manuscript this letter *Thâ* when punctuated has only two dots like a ت; (2) the red circle with red dots as in lines 1 and 9 of this plate, which marks larger divisions, never occurs in any of our copies of the Qurân; (3) the tail of the letter ق differs in a certain manner from that used in this plate; (4) the carelessness and somewhat archaic form of letters mark them as several years earlier than those used in that plate. The sūrahs exhibiting, in our manuscript, this kind of script are: Sūratun-Nūr (XXIV), Sūratul-Ḳaṣaṣ (XXVIII), Sūratul-'Ankabût (XXIX), Sūratul-Mu'men (XL), Sūratus-Sajdah (XLI), Sūratud-Dukkhân (XLIV), and Sūratul-Jâthiah (XLV).

Characteristics of the Writing in Qurân B

It has Kūfo-Naskhi letters as in Qurân A, with more diacritical points over the ت and the ن and very seldom any over the غ and the ذ, all the other letters being without them. Their characteristic note is that they are smaller, thinner, and more sloping to the left. The sūrahs exhibiting, in our manuscript, this kind of script are: Sūrat-Hūd (XI), Sūratur-Ra'd (XIII), Sūrat Ibrâhîm (XIV), Sūratul-Ḥijr (XV), Sūratun-Naḥl (XVI), and Sūratul-Asra (XVII).

Characteristics of the Writing in Qurân C

Its letters resemble those of Qurân B, but they are a little smaller, thinner, and taller. The peculiarities that seem to distinguish this type of script are: (1) the final ي, which, except in the case of في and some other words, is written in a perpendicular and zigzag form; (2) the final م, which is very often united to the words that immediately follow; this junction is used in some other words of this series, and in folios 151a and 150b of the series of Qurân A (II, 1, 2, and 4); (3) the complete absence of diacritical points. The sūrahs written in this kind of script are some parts of Sūratul-A'râf (VII) and some parts of Sūratut-Taubah (IX).

Besides these three general types of writing, of which we give a facsimile, we believe that there are some portions of the series Qurân B coming from a different manuscript. The considerations that suggest this idea are: (1) the kind of writing, which is not so thick as that used in other pages of this series; (2) the number of lines, which is not always identical; (3) the points that mark the separation of verses, which have a different form; (4) some words that are not spelled in the same manner. We believe also that even in the series of Qurân A some sūrahs do not belong to the same manuscript as other sūrahs do; the reasons why we think so are in most cases the same as those mentioned in the series of Qurân B. Thus it is very probable that folios 150a, 150b, and 151a, which contain some awkwardly united words, come from an outside source.

In addition to these special characteristics that we have enumerated, there are in our scraps of the Qurân some peculiarities common to them all that we wish our readers to observe:

(1) The Arabic hamza, possibly invented, as we have already stated, by Khalîl ibn Aḥmad, is not represented in them, even by the sign that doubles the vowel points generally used in the oldest manuscripts of the Qurân. Sometimes and in some places where the word may cause an equivocal meaning, instead of a hamza, we have simply a ي, for example, لين for لئن, since without this ي this particle would easily be confounded with that of the negative of the future tense لن; again in folio 161b we have ايمة because without this *yâ*, which takes the place of a hamza, we would read the word as امة "nation." When there is no fear of ambiguity, there is not even a trace of this strong consonant, for example, (folio 159a) يومذ for يومئذ; (fol. 55b) ولتسلن for ولتسألن; (ibid.) تستنسوا for تستأنسوا; (fol. 160a) يسوا for يئسوا; and so on.

(2) The ordinary marks of intonation and the old Massoretic signs are also quite absent. In the oldest manuscripts of the sacred book, the *Shadda* is expressed by a sign resembling a coarse Arab number, eight or seven; the *Waṣla* is expressed by a stroke of the pen upon the last letter of the first word, and the *Madda* is very often expressed by a horizontal line; but all these signs, so far as I know, are not found in our text.

(3) We were unable to find in these manuscripts even a shadow of a vowel. We know, too, that in the oldest manuscripts of the Qurân, the signs of vowels are very often represented by some dots, usually red, placed above or under the letter, and in the case of a *Ḍhamma*, between the first letter and that which immediately follows it; these marks are not found in series A and C, and are very seldom seen in series B.

(4) So far as I could ascertain, the red circles with the red dots that mark

a greater division in the sacred text are absolutely unknown to our scribes, as we stated above.

(5) Our manuscripts divide always the words, at the end of a line, in such an awkward fashion that we are tempted to believe that the ancient Syrian and Hebrew copyists had a certain superiority over the first Arab scribes in the art of arranging their sacred books; for example, folios 98 and 99, the words يسرف and ربك are divided into يسر and ف and ر and بك, and so on, and so on without any indication that they belong to each other.

(6) The long vowels (حروف المد) expressed by means of a و and a ي, as in the Aramaic language, are generally represented in our manuscripts, for example, غفور , رحيم , حليم , and so on. The case is different with the long vowel *â*, which is generally represented in the Aramaic Massorah by means of two perpendicular dots without an Alaph, for example, عبد for عباد, اولد for اولاد, سيت for سيئات, كلمت for كلمات, and so on. This fact establishes, once more, the dependence of the Arab vowels on those of the Aramaeans. The first grammarians noticing that the *Ḥibâṣa* (ܼ) and the *Ribâṣa* (ܿ) were expressed by means of letters, they expressed them, too, in their language by the same letters, but for the case of *Zeḳâpha*, since it was not represented generally by letters, they did not represent it at all; and they did not find a usual and obligatory sign for it, at the very beginning, and it was in a later period that the Aliph was invented to represent a long vowel, as the case was also not very rare in some old Syriac manuscripts.

This remark may be applied even to the rules dealing with the weak letters, called by the Arab grammarians قواعد الاعلال. These rules systematized in the schools of Baṣrah, Kūfa, and Baghdâd are not maintained by our manuscripts, since we have, for instance, هديه for هداه (fol. 101, l. 9) and افاصفيكم for افاصفاكم (fol. 99b, l. 8). But what distinguishes the orthography of some of our scraps of the Qurân from some other old Arabic manuscripts is the case of this long Aliph in the vocative particle يا, "O," which is joined to the following word by means of the complete rejection of the second letter, for example, ينوح instead of يانوح, "O Noah" (fol. 107a); يقوم instead of ياقوم, "O people" (fol. 106b, ll. 2, 5); يموسى instead of يا موسى, "O Moses" (fol. 59a, l. 3).

The diacritical points, as we have already said, in the series of Qurân C are utterly wanting. For the series of Quran B, since we suppose it to be a little more modern than the series of A, we think it unnecessary to enumerate all the letters that have one or two dots denoting their identity. We subjoin a list of all the words in series A that have a diacritical sign:

Folio 149a, l.1, a dot over the *nūn* of منا
Folio 149a, l.4, two dots over the *tâ* of نحست
Folio 150b, l.4, a dot over the *nūn* of تنزيل
Folio 150b, l.8, two dots over the *tâ* of موتها
Folio 159a, l.3, two dots over the *thâ* of للخبيثين
Folio 159a, l.6, two dots over the first and the second *tâ* of تستنسوا
Folio 159a, l.8, a dot over the *dhâl* of يوذن
Folio 156a, l.8, two dots over the *tâ* of يتبعون
Folio 158b, l.8, two dots over the *tâ* of ياتل
Folio 149b, l.7, a dot over the *nūn* of اذنا
Folio 152b, l.4, two dots over the *tâ* of اتيا and قلتا
Folio 152b, l.7, two dots over the *tâ* of تقدير
Folio 152b, l.10, a dot over the *nūn* of ربنا
Folio 160a, l.4, a dot over the *nūn* of ينشي
Folio 157b, l.5, two dots over the *tâ* of واتينه

Perhaps a list of fifteen diacritical points in fifteen folios, written in a Kūfo-Nashki script, may appear too long; I think that manuscripts of this type of writing offering fewer diacritical points are very rare in our days.

We know that in the oldest manuscripts of the Qurân the number of verses is not always identical; our manuscripts can hardly be an exception to this general rule. As to the points of separation placed at the end of one verse, and at the beginning of another, here are some specimens used in the diverse series of our portions of the Qurân, with indication of the page and of the line where they can be easily found.

sūrah VII, folio 59b, l.1
sūrah IX, folio 104a, l.8 
sūrah XLIV, folio 150b, l.1

sūrah XLI, folio 152b, l.4 //////
sūrah XVII, folio 102a, l.7 ///

As to the ornaments placed at the end of a sūrah, our manuscripts are very parsimonious. Sūrah XVII, which begins at the top of folio 101b, sūrah XIV, which similarly begins in folio 19b, and sūrah XVI, which begins in the middle of folio 15b, have absolutely no marks to distinguish them, except the space of one line. Sūrah XLV, which begins in the middle of folio 150b, has the following row of six circles: ° ° ° ° ° °, and sūrah XLI, which begins in folio 149b, has some strokes like these: 〰〰〰〰 .

The reader will easily find that we have followed, as faithfully as we could, the orthography used in our manuscripts. Besides the more scientific character of this method, it enables us to know the kind of spelling used in the early days of Arabic literature. Our transcription will show شاي for شئ , قرن for قرآن , ينللوا for ينالوا , اذنا for آذاننا, يوحا for يوحى , ان ما for امّا, عيلم (!) for علم , and so on. The lines of our transcription correspond exactly to those of the manuscript.

What seems to enhance the value of these scraps of vellum is that when we compare the text that they exhibit with the established *textus receptus* of the Qurân, as known today, we find some interesting various readings, and some omissions that, as stated above, will astonish more than one scholar. These various readings and omissions are more or less numerous according to the age of these scraps, that is, they are more accentuated in the series of Qurân A and C for the simple reason that these two series seem to be the more ancient. We will class the various readings roughly into two groups, those that offer a complete word different from that used in the *textus receptus* of the Qurân, and those that by means of one or two consonants give another meaning to the sentence used in this sacred book and constitute what we mean by the word *variant*.

FIRST GROUP OF VARIANTS

1. Qurân: Sūratul-Jâthiah, XLV, 18: شئا something
   Our MS. fol. 150a, l.6: هكما in (their) derision

2. Qurân: Sūratut-Taubah, IX, 43: وتعلم and you will know
Our MS. fol. 53b, l.9: ومنهم and who are

3. Qurân: Sūratul-A‘râf, VII, 153: ورحمة and mercy
Our MS. fol. 59b, l.6: وسلم and peace (or greeting)

4. Qurân: Sūratul-Jâthiah, XLV, 18: الله God
Our MS. fol. 150a, l.6: اللكم or اللك blow

Unless اللكم (or اللك) means *blow*, *fist*, or *boxing*, it is an obscure word. The sentence of the Qurân is as follows: انهم لن يغنوا عنك من الله شيأ. "They will not take the place of Allah in anything, for thee (Muḥammad)." Our text is: انهم لن يغنوا عنك من اللكم (or اللك) هكما. "In derision, they will not take the place of a blow, for thee." If this sense is rejected, the real meaning of this substantive would be problematic. The *Ḳâmūs* has simply: مجموعة واللكز والدفع الضرب باليد.

The abstract substantive هكْم, in its triliteral form instead of the form تفعّل, is not much used in the post-Qurânic compositions, but the adjective هكم is found in good writers.

SECOND GROUP OF VARIANTS

1. Qurân: Sūratur-Ra‘d, XIII, 26: الله God
Our MS. fol. 16b, l.9: والله and God

2. Qurân: Sūratun-Naḥl, XVI, 17: افلا do not you?
Our MS. fol. 15a, l.11: اولا (same meaning)

3. Qurân: Sūratun-Naḥl, XVI, 22: ايان when?[59]
Our MS. fol. 20a, l.4: اين where?

4. Qurân: Sūrat Ibrâhîm, XIV, 3: ضلا ل error
Our MS. fol. 19b, l.7: ضل (same meaning)

5. Qurân: Sūratul-Ḥijr, XV, 94:	واعرض	and oppose thou
Our MS. fol. 18a, l.10:	واعرضن	and do oppose thou (energ.)
6. Qurân: Sūratur-Ra'd, XIII, 33:	زين	was adorned
Our MS. fol. 16a, l.9:	فزين	verily, was adorned (energ.)
7. Qurân: Sūrat Hūd, XI, 24:	الاخسرون	the most in loss (superl.)
Our MS. fol. 107b, l.3:	لخسرون	verily, in loss (*Lâm* of energ.)
8. Qurân: Sūrat Hūd, XI, 25:	اخبتوا	they humbled (der. form)
Our MS. fol. 107b, l.4:	خبتوا	(same meaning, prim. form)
9. Qurân: Sūratun-Naḥl, XVI, 38:	فانظروا	and do look
Our MS. fol. 13, l.5:	وانظروا	and look (better in the context)
10. Qurân: Sūratut-Taubah, IX, 36:	فيهن	in them (fem. plur.)
Our MS. fol. 60a, l.4:	فيها	in them (fem. sing.)
11. Qurân: Sūratun-Naḥl, XVI, 36:	فاصابهم	and it happened to them (masc. sing.)
Our MS. fol. 20b, l.9:	فاصابتهم	and it happened to them (fem. sing.)
12. Qurân: Sūratut-Taubah, IX, 37:	لايهدي القوم	(God) will not guide the people . . .
Our MS. fol. 60a, l.8:	لايهدا لقوم	(God) will not be quiet towards the people . . .
13. Qurân: Sūratul-Asra, XVII, 52:	االّنا	are we?
Our MS. fol. 99a, l.7:	انّا	we are
14. Qurân: Sūratul-Asra, XVII, 24:	الاتعبدوا	that you might not serve
Our MS. fol. 97b, l.7:	فلاتعبدوا	do not serve then

15. Qurân: Sūrat Hūd, XI, 31:	اراكم	I find you (perhaps from رای)
Our MS. fol. 106b, l.7:	اريكم	I shall show you (perhaps from ارى)
16. Qurân: Sūrat Hūd, XI, 34:	جادلتنا	thou hast disputed with us
Our MS. fol. 107a, l.3:	جادلت	thou hast disputed
17. Qurân: Sūratul-Asra, XVII, 1:	باركنا حوله	we blessed round it
Our MS. fol. 101b, l.3:	بركنا حوله	we knelt down round it (cf. ܒܪܟ)[60]
18. Qurân: Sūratut-Taubah, IX, 23:	ومن	and he who
Our MS. fol. 104a, l. 9:	فمن	(same meaning)
19. Qurân: Sūratut-Taubah, IX, 24:	لايهدي القوم	(God) will not guide the people . . .
Our MS. fol. 109b, II, 3–4:	لايهدا لقوم	(God) will not be quiet towards the people . . .
20. Qurân: Sūratul-Mu'men, XL, 85:	فلمريك ينفعهم ايمانهم	their faith did not profit to them
Our MS. fol. 152a, l.11:	فلمريكن نفعهم ايمانهم	(same meaning in the case of the verb نَفَعَ, but with the infinitive نَفْع): their faith was of no utility to them
21. Qurân: Sūratus-Sajdah, XLI, 10:	فقال لها	he said to her
Our MS. fol. 152b, l.3:	فقيل لها	it has been said to her
22. Qurân: Sūratus-Sajdah, XLI, 5:	اننا	we
Our MS. fol. 149b, l.8:	انما	verily
23. Qurân: Sūratul-'Ankabūt XXIX, 24:	وقال	and he said
Our MS. fol. 160, l.12:	قال	he said

24. Qurân: Sūratun-Naḥl, XVI, 95: لجعلكم he would have made you
Our MS. fol. 55b, l.4: جعلكم (same meaning, but without energy)

25. Qurân: Sūratud-Dukkhân, XLIV, 44: اثيم iniquitous
Our MS. fol. 151a, l.5: اثم iniquity

26. Qurân: Sūratun-Naḥl, XVI, 24: يسرون they desire
Our MS. fol. 20a, l.7: تسرون you desire (the dots of the *Tâ* are clear)

27. Qurân: Sūratut-Taubah, IX, 54: وما and not
Our MS. fol. 53a, l.2: ما not

28. Qurân: Sūratun-Naḥl, XVI, 122: عملت (the soul) did
Our MS. fol. 56a, l.9: عملته (the soul) did it

29. Qurân: Sūratun-Naḥl, XVI, 30: بلى verily, yes
Our MS. fol. 13b, l.7: بل but

30. Qurân: Sūratun-Naḥl, XVI, 87–88: واذا and if, (and less frequently) when
Our MS. Fol. 55a, II, 4, 6: واذ and when, (and less frequently) if

There is, too, an omission in the standard text of the Qurân. In Sūratun-Naḥl, XVI, 95, we read ولكن يضل مَن يشآء, "but He misleads him whom He wishes (to mislead)," our manuscript folio 55b has the word الله "Allah" between يضل and مَن, so that the sentence runs thus: ولكن يضل الله مَن يشآء, "But Allah misleads him whom He wishes (to mislead)."

Let us now examine the interpolations that may be observed in the standard text of the Qurân, and compare them with our manuscript.

A.

In Sūratut-Taubah, IX, 38, we read يا ايها الذين آمنوا ما لكم اذا قيل لكم انفروا في سبيل الله اثاقلتم الى الارض, "O those who believed, what have you (had) when it was said[61] unto you 'Go forth for the religion of Allah,'[62] you inclined[63] heavily towards the earth." Our text (fol. 60a) has يا ايها الذين آمنوا اذا قيل لكم انفروا في سبيل الله اثاقلتم الى الارض, "O those who believed, when it has been said unto you 'Go forth for the religion of Allah,' you inclined heavily towards the earth." Here the words ما لكم are omitted; they do not suit the context.

B.

In Sūratut-Taubah, IX, 33, there is هو الذي ارسل رسوله, "it is He who sent His Apostle." Our manuscript (fol. 109a) had not the word هو, "He," originally, but this pronoun has been added in the margin by a different hand.

C.

In Sūratut-Taubah, IX, 36, we read وقاتلوا المشركين كافة كما يقاتلونكم كافة, "make war upon all the unbelievers, as they make war upon all of you." Our text (fol. 60a, ll. 4–5) has وقاتلوا المشركين كما يقاتلونكم كافة, "make war upon unbelievers as they make war upon all of you," in neglecting the first كافة.

It would be worthwhile to remark here that our manuscripts maintain the Aliph called الالف الفاصلة even when the verb is used in singular, for example, folio 161b, l.9, تتلوا, "that thou mightest recite" for تتلو; again on folio 17b, l.6, لتتلوا for لتتلو. On the other hand, we meed in folio 109a, l.5, with لياكلو, "verily they eat," instead of لياكلوا without a paragogic Aliph. This orthography, if a singular sense is intended in the former verbs, is highly ambiguous.

We leave the professional palaeographers to assign a definite and final date to these various scraps of parchment. The opinion that some portions of them may date from the very beginning of the eighth century is probable, and even alluring and tenable; critics generally own that hesitation and doubt make sometimes an integral part of palaeographical science, which often settles the date of a document only approximately, in centuries and not in precise years. Even if the *terminus ad quem* is fixed in some manuscripts by the date given in their colophon, yet the *terminus a quo* is still problematic, and it is always difficult to state with safety that a style used in the middle of the eighth or ninth century might not have been used likewise at the end of the seventh. *Servatis servandis*, some pages of our palimpsest may appropriate, at any rate, the aureole of a high antiquity and satisfy all the reasonable exigencies of historical researches. In a general sphere of scientific investigation, a man acquainted with historical and philological lucubrations on the sacred book of Islâm knows with certitude that a manuscript offering "in derision" instead of "something" deserves respect. Would it be possible to make some portions of our manuscript go back to a time preceding the epoch in which the Qurân has been officially edited in a fixed *textus receptus*? Or, if not, are they perhaps a transcription from some scraps of copies that had escaped the persecuting zeal of 'Uthmān? A categorical answer, affirmative or negative, would be, on our part, only premature.

In such a delicate matter, a serious caution was imperative; every variant found in the preceding pages has been verified with a magnifying glass, and sometimes by means of a fresh touch with the reagent, by the learned ladies Mrs. Lewis and Mrs. Gibson. The reading of an Arabic palimpsest—and the Arabic palimpsests are not very numerous—is far more difficult than that of a Greek or a Syriac one, since whereas in the old Greek letters and in the Estrangelo characters almost every letter is written separately, or if not, it is formed in a mold different from its neighbors, the Arabic language has many letters united with the preceding or with the following ones, and scarcely distinguishable by a different stroke of the pen. If then, in a contingent future, a scholar, guided by this first decipherment, notices that I have failed once or twice, I beg him to remember me in the following strophe:

لطافت بود کار صاحب دلان : لطافت بود پیشهٔ مقبلان

ALPHONSE MINGANA
Woodbrooke, Birmingham
May 1914

NOTES

1. اقرا باسم ربك الذى خلق: خلق الانسان من علق . See a striking narration in the annalist *Ibn Hishâm*, p. 152, l. 9 sqq., who represents the Prophet as responding to this voice: "What shall I cry?" We cannot help thinking of the following words found in the prophet Isaiah (40:6): קול אֹמר קרא: ואמר מה אקרא: "The voice of (one) saying, Cry, and he said What shall I cry?" The verb קרא, قرا , which is used in both texts in the same sense, will establish a curious and hardly accidental coincidence.

2. قل لئن اجتمعت الانس والجن على ان ياتوا بمثل هذا القران لا ياتون بمثله ولو كان بعضهم لبعضهم ظهيرا

3. ام يقولون افتراه قل فاتوا بعشر سور مثله مفتريات وادعوا من استطعتم من دون الله

4. وان كنتم في ريب مما نزلنا على عبدنا فاتوا بسورة من مثله

5. Palmer, *Sacred Books of the East*, vol. VI. pp. 55, 71, etc.

6. The question whether Muḥammad could read and write is discussed but not decided by Nöldeke, *Geschichte des Qorâns*, p. 7 sqq.

7. A. Mingana, *Narsai Homiliae et Carmina*, 1905, vol. I. pp. 115–16 and 117 n. 1 in changing ܡܪ̈ܥܝܐ into ܡܪ̈ܥܝܐ as the manuscript requires.

8. "Recueil des actes synodaux de l' Église de Perse," ed. Chabot, *Notice et extraits des manuscrits*, 37, pp. 532, 534, 536 et passim.

9. *Syn. Orient.* p. 275. Cf. on this question Duchesne, *Les Églises séparées*, pp. 337–52: "Les Missions Chrétiennes au Sud de l'empire romain, les Arabes."

10. *Zeitschr. für Assyriologie* XII, pp. 189–242.

11. عام فيه يغاث الناس وفيه يعصرون (that is in Egypt) ثم ياتي من بعد ذلك .

12. Cf. a passage of Josephus (Ant. XI, 5), which tells his high repute (δόξα) with the people.

13. نحن نقص عليك احسن القصص بما اوحينا اليك هذا القرآن وان كنت من قبله لمن الغافلين

14. ما كان لي من علم بالملا الاعلى اذ يختصمون. ان يوحى الي الا انما انا نذير مبين

15. قاتلوا الذين لا ... يحرمون ما حرم الله ورسوله ولا يدينون دين الحق من الذين اوتوا الكتاب حتى يعطوا الجزية عن يد وهم صاغرون

16. وقاتلوهم حتى لا تكون فتنة ويكون الدين لله

17. لا اكراه في الدين

18. ولا تجادلوا اهل الكتاب الا بالتي هي احسن

19. وما ارسلنا من قبلك من رسول ولا نبي الا اذا تمنى القى الشيطان في امنيته فينسخ الله ما يلقي الشيطان

20. Muḥammad often calls himself "the unlettered prophet" (النبي الامي). Cf. Nöldeke, ibid., p. 10.

21. G. Sale, *The Koran*, preliminary discourse, p. 46.

22. He showed it to him twice in his last year.

23. See *Fihrist*, ed. G. Flügel, p. 24. Other traditions:

افواه الرجال وجريد النخل
والجلود

24. كما انزلنا على المقتسمين. الذين جعلوا القرآن عضين

25. The annalists know them to be ʿAbdallah ibn Zobair, Sa'îd ibn Al-'Aṣ, and 'Abdur-Raḥmân ibn Al-Ḥâreth, followers of the Prophet (*Fihrist*, p. 25).

26. Ṭabari, I.2952, 10; 11, 516, 5; and Yāḳūt, *Dictionary of learned men*, VI.300, 499; see D. S. Margoliouth's *The Early Development of Mohammedanism*, 1914, p. 37.

27. Margoliouth, *Mohammedanism*, pp. 69–70.

28. Muir, *Life of Mahomet*, 1894, pp. xiv, xxi–xxii.

29. Expressions such as قرآنا عربيا or حكما عربيا and the like are sometimes used in the Qurân.

30. In Arabic الجاهلية. .

31. W. Ahlwardt, *The Divans of the Six Ancient Arabic Poets* (1870).

32. In Arabic تابط شرا..

33. *Les poètes Arabes chrétiens* (1890), cf. another Arbic book of the same writer, *Le Christianisme et la littérature Chrétienne en Arabic avant l'Islâm* (1912). Everybody knows the conscientious studies of Sir Charles Lyall, on this subject.

34. Cf. S. Fraenkel, *De vocalibus in antiquis Arabum carminibus et in Corano peregrinis*, 1880, p. 23 et passim.

35. Ita Geiger, *Oper. sup. laud.* pp. 113–19.

36. This name is perhaps an echo of *Shelah*.

37. Ita M. Rodwell, *The Koran*, p. 109.

38. Cf. Maracci, *Prodr*. IV. p. 90.

39. In Niebuhr's *Travels*, II. p. 265.

40. The Persian poet Saʿdi calls him *the earth conquering horseman with his chestnut Burâq*: سوار جهانگیر یکران براق .

41. Cf. A. Mingana, *Sources Syriaques*, vol. I, part II, p. 182 sqq.

42. *Chron. Syr.*, ed. Bruns, p. 120; and ed. Bedjan, p. 115.

43. Recently (1903) edited in Cairo, in thirty parts.

44. Edited in Calcutta (1859) by Nassau-Lees.

45. See A. Mingana, *Clef de la langue Araméenne*, 1905, pp. 33–34.

46. Cf. M. Merx, *Historia artis grammaticae apud Syros*, Leipzig, 1889; Duval, *Littérature Syriaque*, 3rd ed., p. 285 et seq.

47. Cf. Evod. Assemani, *Acta Martyr. Orient.* vol. I. pp. 19, 54; Nöldeke, *Geschichte der Perser und Araber zur Zeit der Sassaniden aus der Arabischen Chron. des Tabari*, p. 68, n. I.

48. Quoted in Neubauer's *Géographie du Talmud*, p. 320.

49. Cf. Graetz, *Histoire des Juifs* (translated by Bloch), 1888, vol. III, p. 165 et passim.

50. See Brockelmann's *Geschich. der Arabischen Litteratur*, I. p. 100; Weimar, 1898.

51. Edited by H. Derenbourg, Paris, 1881–1889.

52. About the relations of the Mandaeans with Christianity, see Brandt, *Die Mandäische Religion, ihre Entwickelung und Geschichtliche Bedeutung*, pp. 140–45 et passim.

53. For a general view on Arabic Literature, the reader will find good information in R. A. Nicholson's *A Literary History of the Arabs*, 1907; for some particular details, several articles written, in Arabic, in the review *Al Machriq*, Beirut, seem to be well documented and scientific.

54. See *Ibn Abi Uṣaibi'ah*, vol. I, p. 175 et passim; Bar Hebraeus, *Chron. Syr.* pp. 134 and 162.

55. See Labourt, *Le Christianisme dans l'empire Perse* (1904), p. 219 sqq.

56. See B. Moritz's *Arabic Palaeography* (with 188 plates), Cairo, 1906; and L. Cheikho, *Spécimens d'écriture Arabe pour la lecture des manuscrits anciens et modernes*, Beirut, 1911.

57. *Facsimiles of Ancient Manuscripts etc.* Oriental Series, part II, ed. W. Wright, London, 1877.

58. Cf. the valuable study of Professor Brockelmann, in the *Encyclopaedia of Islâm*, vol. I, p. 383 sqq.

59. Philologically a contraction of اي آن *at what time?*

60. This verb has been inserted here through our desire to know if there was, in early times, a sure philological criterion to distinguish the words from one another, which are distinguished today only by a long vowel; our text of the Qurân has many of these words.

61. Or, if it is said.
62. Literally, in the way of Allah.
63. Or, you incline.

إِنَّهُمْ كَانُوا إِذَا قِيلَ لَهُمْ

لَا إِلَٰهَ إِلَّا اللَّهُ يَسْتَكْبِرُونَ

وَيَقُولُونَ أَئِنَّا لَتَارِكُوا

3.2

An Important Old Turḳi Manuscript in the John Rylands Library

Alphonse Mingana

In the eastern parts of the country from which the actual Turks came, the inhabitants spoke the Uighur language of the Ḳudatḳu Bilik, or the so-called old Turḳi. This language has but slight affinity with the Osmanli Turkish used by the Turks in their official acts from the fifteenth century onward. The modern Turkish has a nearer ancestor in the language known as Chaghatāi, constituted in a literary form principally by the poet Mir 'Ali Shīr (AH 906). Even this last language a Turk of our days would hardly understand. The most common words are generally very different in their morphological form and in their lexicographic formation. For instance, the word used to express "God" is in modern Turkish either the Persian خدا or the Arabic الله, but I doubt whether many Turks of Constantinople or the neighboring districts are able to understand the word تنكري of the Chaghatāi.

At the time when the Turkish hordes settled in Asia Minor and pushed forward their success until the Byzantine hegemony was definitively overthrown in Stambūl and in the lands situated in the southwestern parts of the surrounding seas, a thick mist of ignorance enveloped their most enlightened circles. The constant intercourse with civilized nations occasioned, however, among them a progressive and salutary feeling toward scientific questions that gave their neighbors an unapproachable superiority. The first step in this direction was taken on the ground of their ancestral literature, and the poems of Mir 'Ali Shīr and of Bāber became the subject of the studies of many a Turkish patriot.

This language roused even greater interest among classic Persians, and few indeed are the books written in it that are not represented in the language of Saʿdi. Many useful lucubrations have been written by Persians to explain the philological difficulties of a language to which they were so curiously inclined. The catalogue of the British Museum and of other public libraries of Europe contain many Persian-Chaghatāi dictionaries and grammars (see Ch. Rieu's "Mus. Brit. Catalog." Add. 6646; 16, 759; 2892; 1021; 1712; 1912; 404, etc.).

The Turks themselves, attracted by their learned co-religionists, began, possibly toward the end of the fifteenth century, to devote themselves to the study of their mother-tongue, and some libraries fortunately show us the outcome of their researches. The manuscript (Mus. Brit. Add. 7886) is a small Turḳi dictionary compiled chiefly from the works of Mir ʿAli Shīr and explained in classic Turkish by an anonymous Turkish writer. The book is generally known under the title of "Abushḳa," which forms the first word explained in it. Its full title is اللغات النوائية والاستشهادات الجغتائية . A copy of it is found in Munich (no. 221), dated AH 960, and another one in Petrograd (no. 594) with the date of AH 967.

This language is on its broad lines fairly well understood by Orientalists. The Persians have smoothed the path of our access to it, and for this we are grateful to them. On this subject, the lexicographical works of the eminent Orientalists Vambéry, Zenker, and Pavet de Courteille, which explain hundreds of difficult words, are viewed with great esteem by their successors.

Of the old Uighur language of the semi-Mongols who inhabited the southwestern parts of Manchuria, little is known, owing to the scarcity of inscriptions and of historical and literary compositions referring with certainty to eastern Mongolia. It is, in a strict sense, this last country that gave birth to the famous Gengis Khan, who destroyed the Arab Empire of the East and stifled for a long time the attempts at domination of upstart descendants of some Kurdish and Turkish eponyms. As the origin of the peoples called Mongols, Tatars, Uighurians are very obscure, some useful purpose might be served by an attempt to throw a ray of light on the point that constitutes the aim of this article.

So far as our historical knowledge goes, we may assert that the Uighurians did not found an empire,[1] but having quickly followed the Mongols in their attempt to conquer the old world stretching from the northeastern parts of India as far as the valley of the Euphrates, they are justly incorporated in history with their Eastern conquerors, and counted as one of them. A Western branch of these Uighurians led by Ṭughrul and 'Uthmān occupied step by step the whole of Asia Minor, with all the Eastern provinces of the Roman Empire, and their successors were dreaming to add to their conquests the southern parts of Italy and the whole of Austria, when a complete defeat checked their audacious advance under the walls of Vienna (1683 CE). More than two hundred and fifty years earlier, some altercations about the right division of the occupied provinces had begun to have prejudicial results between the two clans, the old and the new, the Mongols and the Turks, and a fratricidal war (1402 CE) brought them to a premature exhaustion, the conclusion of which was the consolidation of the actual Empire of Persia. It would not be out of place here to remark that we believe the actual Ottomans never would have been able to settle so firmly round the littoral of the Black Sea, if the eastern Uighurians, or more accurately, the Tatars, had not inflicted a crushing defeat on the remnants of the ephemeral Empire of the Seljúḳs (1300). The acceptance of the rich inheritance that the Tatars had left was the only merit of the Osmanli Turks at their beginnings.

The inhabitants of eastern Uighuria and of Mongolia were some few years before Gengis Khān hardly more civilized than the antediluvian men: "They were dressed in the skins of dogs and wolves; they ate the flesh of mice and of other unclean animals, and they drank the milk of mares."[2] These primitive habits compared with the interesting legislation promulgated by the famous Gengis, the creator of the Tatarian Empire, will enhance the natural virtues of these "Asiatic Huns."[3]

"When you have to send a letter or a messenger to some rebels, do not threaten them with the greatness of your numbers or with your fighting force, but only say: 'If you submit, you will find goodness and peace; and if you rise, we will not be responsible for what will happen; the Eternal God only knows what will befall you.' In this way your confidence in the Lord will be made manifest, and you will win.

"You will honour and revere men who are pure, upright, learned and wise in all the nations, and you will despise the wicked and bad people amongst them.

"Do not use towards your kings and princes many titles of honour as other peoples do. The man sitting on the throne should be given only one name: *Khān*, and his brothers and relatives should be called by the name of their birth.

"When you are at peace with your enemies, give yourselves up to hunting, and teach also your children how to hunt beasts. In this way, you will be drilled in warfare, you will acquire endurance, and you will attack your enemies, without fear and pity, as wild beasts.

"If a man dies amongst you without a legitimate heir, all his possessions, and even his wife, should be given to the man who was attending to him. The king should not be given anything."

People brought up under such legislation could not fail to subjugate some decadent nations, worn out by intestine divisions and mutual strife. From the beginning of AH 617 to 619 many important places, such as Bukhāra, Samarḳand, and Khawarazm, were successively taken by storm, and some years later, the fall of Baghdâd (1258 CE) put an end to the Arabo-Persian domination in the south and threatened the Turkish possessions in the north.

These Mongols had no special literature, but they adopted the Uighur language to transmit their orders to the peoples that they had so easily subjugated.[4] By this method the Uighur acquired a wider field of extension than it could otherwise possess. Of the language itself, of the conquerors, not many literary compositions are known today, and it is by the language of the conquered nations that their own history is to be sketched in its most striking lines.

Between the old and imperfectly known language of the Ḳudatḳu Bilik poem, and the Chaghatāi, ancestral-tongue of the Osmanli-Turkish, there is an intermediary language that so far has not been very accurately studied in its general morphological features and in its distinct relations with the two dialects between which it keeps a *juste milieu.* It is well represented by the works of the famous writer Rabghūzi—of which a fourteenth-century good manuscript is found in the British Museum (Add. 7851) and it has been carefully described by the skilled hand of Dr. Rieu. The edition (1859) of Ilminsky from another manuscript belonging to the Imperial Library of Petrograd is not found in the public libraries of this country, and as Dr. Rieu says "is extremely rare, and no copy is accessible for purposes of comparison." About the value of Rabghūzi's work, Dr. Rieu writes (ibid. p. 271):—

> The early date of Rabghūzi's work gives it a great linguistic value. It forms an intermediate link between the old Turḳi, or so-called Uighur, and the Chaghatāi of Mir 'Ali Shīr and Bāber. Although written two centuries and a half after the former work, it preserves, with slight phonetic changes, much of its archaic vocabulary. It may be considered in that respect its lineal descendant, and a careful study of its language would throw light on many obscure points, which, in spite of the brilliant decipherment and interpreattion of Prof. Vambéry, still remain in the earliest document of the Turkish language.

Happily Rabghūzi is not the only man who can guide us safely in our investigations of the language of nations that played so important a rôle in the history of the world.

A manuscript in the John Rylands Library of Manchester contains the text of the Ḳurân with a literal translation into this Rabghūzi dialect, distant only a few steps from the Uighuric tongue. This manuscript numbered cod. 760–773 consists of fourteen volumes of 355 × 300 mm.

Nearly all the volumes are unfortunately truncated at the beginning and at the end, and all of them have many leaves missing in the middle, whilst the margins of many of the remaining leaves that were injured by worms have in consequence disappeared forever. But what is most to be regretted is the clumsiness of the last binder who arranged the volumes in the present order. Many leaves that properly belong to the beginning are placed at the end; and several leaves that contain verses of a sūrah and should have been bound, for instance, in volume 766, are bound through an incomprehensible blunder in volume 770, and so on. The following partial description of volume 772 will give a fair idea of the whole collection.

XXVIth juz' of the Ḳurân, from sūrah XLVI, 1, to sūrah LI, 30; with illuminated headings. Folio 1a, which is half torn away contains in the middle حم تنزيل الكتا[ب], at the top الاحقاف, and at the bottom وخمس اية. . . . Folio 26b, title of sūrah XLVIII. Folios 51b and 52a, a very large illuminated sūrah title. Folios 52b and 53a, beginning of sūrah XLIX called in the manuscript لا تقدموا; the two pages are completely illuminated. Folios 67b and 68a end with sūrahs XLIX and L, respectively, and in both cases with some curved sūrah titles. In folios 50b and 51a, a blank. Folio 74b, sūrah L, 60, omitted by the copyist but supplied by him on the margin.

Lacunæ. Folio 1a has only the second half of the title; one leaf, therefore, which contained the introductory words and سوره at the top, and ثلثون at the bottom, is lost. Folio 1b ends واجل (XLVI, 1); then follows a gap of about sixteen leaves, extending from verses 2–20 (عذاب). The next six leaves containing XLVI, 20–22 and 22–29 are wrongly bound as folios 84 and 79–83, respectively, of the volume 766. Folio 3b, the last two verses of the sūrah are altogether missing, with the heading of sūrah XLVII. At the top of the next page there is the following remark: "In the Kūfi, thirty-eight verses."

As the manuscript stands today, it would have occupied thirty volumes instead of fourteen if there were no lacunæ in it.

The manuscript seems to come from a country in which the Arabic was not the language of the people. The last owner of the manuscript has preserved his name in his seal found on folio 19a of volume 765: "'Abdul-Bâḳi son of 'Ali, the Arab." We suppose that according to the Oriental custom he would not have called himself "the Arab" if he were living in an Arab country.

One of the curious features of this manuscript is that the old Turḳi and the Persian translations do not correspond always with the Arabic text, in spite of the fact that one word is above the other, beginning with the Arabic and ending with the old Turḳi. If we mistake not, the Persian and the old Turḳi translations were made several years before the transcription of the Arabic sacred text, and the task of the scribe was in this case simply to transcribe from another manuscript a translation already in existence. Two reasons make this view highly probable:

1. There are Arabic sentences that do not give the same meaning as that of the translation. This fact would be very surprising, did we suppose that the divergence extends only to some very easy words, such as pronouns, and preformative letters of the Aorist. We know that in early times, and before the invention of the diacritical points in the Arabic language, there were in the Muḥammadan world different schools that read, for instance, the word مقتل as *Naḳtulu*, "we kill," or *Yaḳtulu*, "he kills," or *Taḳtulu*, "thou killest." When the context did not condemn one of these readings to death, they were generally admitted by the most rigid commentators; and the *Kutubul-Ḳira 'āt* have preserved scores of such words read in a different way. In the manu-

script with which we are dealing it happens sometimes that when the Arabic text gives "he kills" the translation exhibits "we kill." Let us take an example, which is even more amazing than a usual variant of a diacritical point. In volume 760, last line of folio 1, the Arabic words of sūrah III, 116 وان تصبهم are rendered in Persian واكر برسد شمارا and in old Turḳi واكر تكسا سيزكا. The Arabic text means "and if it befall them," and the Persian and the old Turḳi signify "and if it befall you." The old Turḳi and the Persian translations are therefore made from a copy of the Ḳurân that exhibited the reading of Flügel's edition, "and if it befall you."

2. In volume 771, folio 68a, the word "God" is omitted in the Arabic text in verse 18 of sūrah XLV, but it is rendered, in spite of the Arabic omission, into Persian and old Turḳi. This omission means also that the copyist was transcribing from two different manuscripts He has omitted the word in question in one of his transcriptions, but he has inserted it in the two other transcriptions. Here we find a curious coincidence to which we wish to draw attention.

In the book titled *Leaves from the ancient Qurâns*, which was printed some few months ago at the University Press of Cambridge, the word *Allah* which occurs in the above quoted verse of the Ḳurân has been read اللكم or اللك, "a blow." I was not quite satisfied with this reading, but the palimpsest that belongs to Dr. Agnes S. Lewis did not permit me to read the word otherwise. The letter ك is distinct and does not seem to suffer the existence of another word, or, at all events, I was not able to find a more suitable word. Everything considered, it appears that the scribe of our present manuscript found himself face to face with the same difficulty; having been unable to substitute another good vocable for the one that he could not decipher, he omitted it entirely. The hypothesis will become more plausible if we consider the extreme care the copyist has taken, throughout all the volumes, of the word *Allah* on which he has indeed profusely lavished all his skill; he writes it always in gilt letters, and sometimes he forms its letters in a curiously waving form, resembling a coarse zigzag. In any case such an omission in the text of the Ḳurân while both translations, the Old Turḳi and the Persian, are exact, is worthy of the attention of critics.

The note of the scribe referred to above informs us that the Arabic text has been transcribed from an old Kūfic manuscript, but the most elementary criterion is deficient as to the provenance of the old Turḳi version.

On the probable hypothesis that the translation was undertaken several years before the transcription of the Arabic text, the old Turḳi dialect becomes of an exceptional importance. The Arabic manuscript itself goes back to the time of Rabghūzi, or at latest, a few years after him, while the translation is very probably many decades earlier. Our manuscript is, therefore, from a linguistic point of view, more valuable than Rabghūzi's apocryphal stories.

A second reason that seems to establish a superiority of our manuscript over Rabghūzi's work is the facility with which it may be used for critical studies or scientific researches. Being simply a literal and interlinear translation of the Ḳurân, while the Old Turḳi word is placed immediately under the Persian and the Arabic words explained, it affords a most valuable field of investigation for the student who is by this method enabled to examine more thoroughly the old Chaghatāi dialect for purposes of comparison with the Uighur language.

Dr. Rieu (ibid., pp. 271–72) has gathered from Rabghūzi's book some stray words that he has compared with those of the Uighur of the Ḳudaḳu Bilik poem; we also will endeavor to compare some of these words with those used in our manuscript. The character of the Rabghūzian and even pre-Rabghūzian of the language of our manuscript and the importance that it deserves will then perhaps appear more striking. As is easily noticed from the following list, the dialect used in our manuscript corresponds, with a slight and explicable change of the letter ت into ذ, with the oldest form of the Uighur language. The Chaghatāi dialect, ancestor of the actual Turkish, has lost the majority of the under-mentioned words, and in the case of the few that it has preserved, it has softened to a simple vowel the strong consonants that characterize them. Let us take as our examples three words from the list: the word that means "after" has a ذ in the dialect of our manuscript and a ت in Uighur, but both consonants have been simply eliminated in Chaghatāi. Likewise the word meaning "foot" is in Chaghatāi اياق, and the word meaning "good" ايو, as in modern Turkish.

A. Rabghūzi dialect and that used in our manuscript		B. Uighur of the Ḳudaḳu Bilik
اذاق	foot (vol. 763, fol. 60a).	اتاق
بودون	people (vol. 763, fol. 17b).	بوتون
توريتمك	to create (vol. 763, fol. 58a).	توريتمك
ايذمق	to send (vol. 771, fol. 47a).	ايتمق
تيكم	everything (vol. 763, fol. 23b).	تيكم
كيذين	after (vol. 763, fol. 12b).	كيتين
اذكو	good (vol. 771, fol. 105a).	اتكو
يلاوج	prophet (vol. 763, fol. 33b).	چلاوج

There are even philological features that seem to establish a morphological ascendancy of the dialect of our manuscript over that used by Rabghūzi, for example, the particle of dative-accusative is in our manuscript always the letter ق followed by a paragogic *Alif*, for instance, موسى قا *to* Moses, ابراهيم قا *to Abraham* (vol. 771, fol. 8a); in Rabghūzi this archaic letter is softened sometimes into a غ as in Chaghatāi, for example, تنكريغا *to God.*

As a mere curiosity for students not accustomed to perusing an Old Turḳi manuscript we may mention the fact that the word "Arab" or "Arabic" is translated by the word *Târi*, for example, volume 771, folios 3b and 37a, the words قرانا عربيا, *an Arabic Ḳurân*, are translated into Persian ني تارى زبان and in Old Turḳi قران تارنجا .

We cannot conclude this study without comparing some grammatical topics of the text of our manuscript with the rules given by R. B. Shaw in his work titled *A Sketch of the Turki Language* (Lahore, 1875).

1. Against the rules of p. 52 dealing with the case of the "defective auxiliary" verb, compare the following example (sūrah, IX, 56): اندقارلر تنكرى توتا اولار سيزهز ارمان اولار سيزهز انجاى بارارلار بوذون لاركيم تورقارلر (vol. 764, fol. 40b).

2. Against the rules found on p. 8 about the pronouns in general, compare how the Arabic word اليه *to it* (IX. 57) is translated انكار (ibid., fol. 41a).

3. Against what is said (pp. 72–75) about post-positions and conjunctions, compare how the Arabic particle meaning *or* is translated twice by ازو (ibid.).

4. The possessive affix (p. 13), obsolete in the Old Turki, studied by Shaw, is generally maintained in our manuscript.

On the other hand, there are many lexicographical and grammatical similarities between the dialect exhibited in Shaw's Grammar and that used in our manuscript; but these similarities, so far as our short study of the text permits us to judge, do not seem to exceed in preponderating proportion those that unite all the Tatar dialects, the Chaghatâi and the Osmanli, for instance; and the main interest is precisely to ascertain the number of these similarities and dissimilarities and to know the epoch in which they have been gradually introduced by the general public whose linguistic knowledge was not so brilliant in ancient times as to fix all the disunited elements of words into a more common and stereotyped form of speech.

We could lay more stress on some grammatical peculiarities of this dialect, but we think that this short notice is sufficient to give an adequate idea of the manuscript and to stimulate the ardour of Ural-Altaic scholars, who by a careful study of its contents will perhaps be in a position to make substantial additions to the information published from time to time regarding the Turco-Tatar languages.

It should also be pointed out that in certain catalogs mention is made of a Kurân *cum Versione Turcicâ*;[5] but since it is not clearly stated what value we must attribute to this misleading term, we infer that it means simply Osmanli Turkish. At the time when such catalogs were prepared, few scholars were familiar with the Old Turki. These manuscripts, consisting of a single volume, cannot be compared with the thirty volumes of which our manuscript was composed. We cherish the hope that in the near future we shall learn more of the exact nature of these manuscripts.

Notes

1. Cf. N. Elias's "The Tarikh-I-Rashidi," 1895, pp. 72 sqq.
2. Barhebræus, "Chron. Syr.," ed., Bedjan, pp. 406–407.
3. Ibid., pp. 410–11.
4. Ibid., p. 410.
5. Cf. Cod. MDCXIII of *Lugd. Batav.* 1866, vol. IV, p. 2; Cod. XLIII of *Mus. Brit.* 1846, p. 38; Cod. 370, vol. I, p. 140 of *Berlin*.

3.3

Notes Upon Some of the Ḳurânic Manuscripts in the John Rylands Library

Alphonse Mingana

There are sixty manuscripts in the John Rylands Library that deal with the Ḳurân. Forty-six contain the sacred text, and fourteen treat of exegesis, orthography, and good reading. All Islamic compositions referring to Ḥadîth or oral traditions concerning the life and the saying of the Prohpet are excluded from the above heading.

I.

Among the first series of manuscripts we find some that commend themselves to the palæographer either on account of their very ancient date (eighth century) or the peculiarities of their script. More than one specimen of the writing that they exhibit is wanting in Dr. Moritz's valuable "Arabic Palæography" (1905), in the Palæographical Society's publications (1875–1883), and in other similar works.

There are also three volumes written from beginning to end in letters of gold, which by reason of the beauty of their execution will doubtless appeal to lovers of Eastern art. It would appear that the original collectors of these manuscripts displayed a special interest in this respect, with the result that many of the volumes easily take rank among the finest examples extant. One of these, which formerly belonged to Caussin of Perceval, was brought from the East in 1858. It was regarded as one of the most noteworthy exhibits in the Paris exhibition of 1867, and several of its pages have been reproduced in color in M. Prisse d'Avesnes's "Art Arabe." Furthermore, it has the distinction of being the largest Ḳurân known to exist, measuring as it does 860 × 540 mm.

There are two complete Ḳurâns written upon rolls of paper of the following dimensions: diameter of the cylinder when the paper is rolled up, 16 mm and 17 mm, respectively. Full length of the scrolls, 11 ft. 6½ in. and 12 ft. 3½ in., respectively, while the breadth is 60 mm and 77 mm.

The rolls consist of a series of ornamentations, sometimes continuous and sometimes interrupted, whose lines of demarcation are the sacred text. The sūrahs are introduced by the *Basmalah*, but there is no help to the eye to find them. Many such textual ornaments are shaped in red ink, but the text itself is in black. The words are so skillfully, but also so fantastically interwoven in the small blank spaces, that it is difficult to find out where a given verse is placed. The Ḳurân seems to have been written in this curious manner, in order that it may make a good amulet to be worn by a Muḥammadan prince. Some few other libraries contain *curiositatis causâ* one of these rolls,[1] but so far as we can judge from the descriptions given by the scholars who cataloged them, they differ somewhat from those now in Manchester.

There is one very curious manuscript of the Ḳurân that is deserving of special attention. It is that numbered Codex 52 in the Crawford collection, and Codex 133 in the Bland collection. It is written in an unusual form of slanting characters with very thick horizontal strokes. We doubt whether copies of the Ḳurân written in this character of script are numerous.

It is the most curiously written Ḳurân that we have ever met; it contains some wonderful anomalies of spelling attributable perhaps to the carelessness of the scribe; for instance, in Sūratul-Baḳarah, from verse 66 to verse 80, we find the following curiosities of spelling, which may easily touch the point of what we might call a *mistake*. كاد for كادوا; first منها of v. 69 omitted; final alif of قالوا omitted; فريقا for فريق; الصا الحات for الصالحات; واذ القربى for وذي القربى; the second member of ميثاقكم repeated twice.

The characteristic mark of this manuscript is that two nouns or a particle and a noun are frequently joined together, for example, النتمسنا for الن تمسنا; بلهم for بل هم. The letter ك, as is the case in many other manuscripts, is written like a ل, but a small ك is formed over it to distinguish it from the last letter. In the case of two *Hamzas*, at the beginning of a word, the first one is often written separately ءاله for االه.

The text exhibits sometimes archaic spelling to be put side by side with the oldest copies of the Ḳurân that we possess, and sometimes it offers readings that, by their undoubted internal value, and by their simultaneous homogeneity with the other kindred languages, would point to a very early period in Arabic literature. On the other hand, the manuscript dating only from the thirteenth to the sixteenth centuries may give rise by its carelessness to some perplexities on the ground of orthodoxy.

A large number of passages have been either erased or covered over with thin pieces of paper, throughout the volume, which numbers 882 pages, with eleven lines to the page, and measures 223 × 170 mm. As no later hand has touched it for the purpose of readjusting its lines to suit the standard text, since the space occupied by the lines that have been purposely erased is left blank, it would perhaps be useful to inquire as to the nature of the text eliminated in this strange manner.

Generally, when words have been obliterated, the space that they occupied is, as stated above, left blank, but a letter or two, at times a word or two, have been added by a later hand at the beginning and at the end of this space, to harmonize the text with the *textus receptus* of the Ḳurân. It is not, therefore, the first copyist who is responsible for all these changes. The following four instances will serve as specimens.

Folio 24b. There is one line blotted out that perhaps contained a text in addition to that of the Ḳurân, since the end of the line (في ذلك) and the beginning of the other line after the blank (ان ارادوا II, 227) correspond exactly to the standard text.

Folio 42a. A line has been blotted out; the last word of the blank space is (معكم III, 75) and the first word of the other line لتومنن; but after معكم the letter *waw* stands along and ought to be joined with the following word لتومنن, which is preceded by the blank line. This points to the probability of one line and a half having been purposely obliterated.

Folio 43b. Two lines and a half have been blotted out; the last word of the blank space is (مقام III, 91); the first word of the other line (ابراهيم) is found in the middle of the third line, leaving room for three or four more words.

Folio 109b. One line in the middle of the page has many obliterated words between خالصة and يوم (VII, 30), so that other words existed between the two; moreover, some letters appear from the erased words that cannot be safely supplied.

It may not be out of place here to remark that in the *al-Muḳniᶜ* of ad-Dâni (d. AH 444), there are some interesting variants of the Ḳurân about which, as is commonly admitted, al-Baiḍhâwi maintains silence. If the hope, expressed by a few scholars, for a critical edition of the sacred book of Islâm is someday to be realized, Dâni's composition will be found useful. A glance at one chapter of the manuscript under notice reveals three variant readings not mentioned by al-Baiḍhâwi:—

sūrah VII, 27; our manuscript, folio 96b, gives the reading وقال instead of قال.

sūrah X, 23; our manuscript, folio 97a, gives the reading ينشركم instead of يسيركم.

sūrah XLII, 29; our manuscript, folio 100a, gives the reading بما كسبت instead of فبما كسبت.

II.

Among the second series of manuscripts there are some very useful ones. If we mistake not, some of them are very rare and three unique, since they are not represented in the catalog of the rich Berlin collection compiled by W. Ahlwardt (1887–1899) and consisting of ten large volumes. Neither are they found in the catalog of the "Bibliothèque Nationale," compiled (1883– 1895) by Baron de Slane, nor in the two catalogs of the British Museum, by Cureton (1846) and by Dr. Rieu (1872 and 1894). They are also absent from the Library of Gotha, whose descriptive catalog is due to Dr. W. Pertsch (1878–1892), from Flügel's catalog of the Imperial Library of Vienna (1865–1867), and finally from the Khedivial Library of Cairo (AH 1310), and so on. In the following pages we shall offer a few remarks on each of these manuscripts, numbered, respectively, 347, 601, 337, and 729.

A.

Codex 347 has for its title حجة الاسلام, "Proof of Islâm." It is written in a clear Naskhi, and deals with the good writing and the pronunciation of the Ḳurân, arranged in sections under the sūrah headings. The author is called Muḥammad Bardul-Islâm, who explains the aim of his book in sentences which we translate thus:

> When I noticed that many people have neither the leisure nor the wish to peruse detailed books treating of the transcription of the Ḳurân, I compiled, in an abridged form, a small book, from such reliable compositions as the *Itḳân*, the *Shâṭibyyah*, the *Mudaḳḳik* and the *Djazaryyah*. I collected also interesting traditions which will appeal to the heart of the high and the common people, and which would be a source of meditation to men of understanding and thought. I entitled it: "Proof of Islâm," in the transcription of a text corresponding to that of the Imâm.[2]
>
> . . . It occurs in the Ḥadith that Gabriel—peace be with him—said: "Recite the Ḳurân in seven letters, each one being sufficient and efficient." Ibn Mas'ūd said that this Ḳurân came down in seven letters, each one having an apparent sense and one requiring development (Ḍhahrun wa Baṭnun). If you say: "What does he mean by seven letters?" I shall answer that many opinions have been expressed about that. . . . And Abu 'Ubaidah said: "The seven letters mean the seven dialects of the language of the Arabs." It does not imply that there are seven ways in which a letter may be found; this has not been heard of at all, but it does mean that these seven dialects are disseminated here and there in the Ḳurân. Some of them are in the dialect of Ḳuraish, some of them in the dialect of Hawâzen, some of them in the dialect of Hudhail, some of them in the dialect of Yaman, some of them in the dialect of Dūs, and some of them in the dialect of Tamîm. Some say that these seven letters are the seven readings that the seven Imâms have adopted; one of these is 'Âṣim b. Abin-Nujūd, and the name of his mother is Bahdalat, and he is called 'Âṣim son of Bahdalat; the second is Ḥamzah, son of Ḥabîb az-Zayyât; the third is 'Ali b. Ḥamzah al Kisâ'i; all these three

were from Kūfah. The fourth is ʿAbdallah b. Kathîr, the imâm of Maccah; the fifth is Nafiʿ b. ʿAbdur-Raḥmân b. Masʿūd, the imâm of Madînah; the sixth is ʿAmr. b. al-ʿAlâ', the imâm of Baṣrah, and his nickname is al-ʿAriân (= the naked) b. ʿAmmâr b. al-ʿAriân, and his surname is Abu ʿAmr; the seventh is ʿAbdallah b. ʿÂmer, the imâm of Damascus.

. . . Authors differ as to the number of the copies that ʿUthmān sent to various countries. It is a well-known tradition that they were five; b. Dâoūd, referring to Ḥamzah az-Zayyât, said that ʿUthmān sent four copies; b. Abi Dâoūd said also: "I heard abu Ḥâtim of Sijistan say: 'He wrote seven copies that he sent to Maddah, to Damascus, to Yaman, to Baḥrain, to Baṣrah, and to Kūfah; and he retained one in Madînah, and it is found at present in the *Enlightened Meadow*.'"

. . . Yazîd b. Abi Ḥabîb reports that the amanuensis of ʿAmr. b. al-ʿÂṣ wrote to (the caliph) ʿUmar—may Allah be pleased with him—*Bismillah*, without forming distinctly the (letter) *Sîn*, and ʿUmar—may Allah be pleased with him—struck him; he has been asked, with what did the Amîr of the faithful strike you? he said: He struck me with a *Sîn*.

B.

The title of Codex 601 is حاشية على البيضاوي, "Glosses on Al-Baiḍhâwi." The volume consists of glosses on part of *Anwâarut-Tanzîl* of al-Baiḍhâwi. Three rhymed lines are found at the end of the manuscript in the hand of a man weakened by age, with a note which we translate as follows:

"(The book) has been finished by the hand of its writer Aḥmad Shihâbud-Dîn b. Muḥammad al-Miṣri—may God forgive his sins."

The manuscript is, therefore, an autograph of the first author. There is an inscription in Turkish which shows that at the time when it was added (about AH 1075) the author was already dead: بو حاشيه شهابك اخريندده شهاب مرحومك خط لطيفلرى واردر.. In the pages that follow this note we are informed that a certain Sulaimân bought the book in 1192, for the sum of seven piastres and a half. In the catalog of the Khedivial Library (pp. 181–82) mention is made of this Shihâb as author of a commentary of al-Baiḍhâwi. He is there given the surname of al-Khaffaji, and he is said to have died in AH 1069. The author of our manuscript might be identified with him, but the books, judging from the quotation of the first words of the text, are different; they seem to represent two independent works by the same writer. An edition of the manuscript at Cairo was printed at Bulak (AH 1283) with al-Baiḍhâwi's text. From folio 7b and folio 8a we translate the following extract:

> About (al-Baiḍhâwi's) saying: "This is not accurate because (the Prophet) —prayer and peace be with him—stoned two Jews"—he (al-Baiḍhâwi) refers to what is in al-Bukhâri who quotes ʿAbdallah b. ʿUmar as saying: "The Jews came to God's Prophet and told him that a man and a woman from amongst them had committed adultery." God's Prophet said to them: "What do you find in the Torah about stoning?" They answered: "They must be stripped of their garments and be scourged." Then ʿAbdallah b. Salâm said: "You have lied; it is written that they should be stoned." They brought the Torah, and they opened it, and one of them put his hand on the verse containing the stoning. Then ʿAbdallah b. Salâm said to him: "Lift up your hand"; and he lifted up his hand, and, behold, the verse of the stoning was found in it. Then they said: "It is true, O Muḥammad, the verse of stoning is found in it." God's Prophet ordered, therefore, that they should be stoned.

C.

The title of Codex 337 is بحر العشق, "Sea of Love."[3] This title may be misleading, because the book is simply a commentary on Sūrat Yūsuf (XII). The author's name is not given. The manuscript was written in Lahore, by a certain Ḥaidar, surnamed Amir Muḍhaffar al-Khaibar, AH 1233. Some of the characteristics of the narration will be gathered from the following anecdotal tradition:

> And God the Most High revealed unto Joseph that he would send Gabriel with a message containing greetings and the information that God would reward him on account of Jacob his father. And Gabriel reached him before the she-camel, and offered him condolence as God the Most High had ordered him. And God the Most High had appointed an angel to protect the she-camel till she came to Joseph. And God the Most High caused her to speak. And she spoke in Hebrew and said: "Peace be with you, O Joseph,

> your father will greet you in the day of the Resurrection, and he is pleased with you." He was much afflicted with that, and he mourned during three days. The she-camel wept on Jacob. Then (Joseph) said: "My Lord, Thou hast given me power, and thou hast taught me the interpretation of ḥadîths; Creator of heavens and of earth, thou art my Protector in this world, and in the world to come, grant that I should die Moslem." He asked for death at that time, and God sent Gabriel to him and said to him: "God the Most High says that you will not die until from you, and from your child, and from your child's child, you may count six hundred (persons). At that time, your life will end." Then he called the inhabitants of Egypt into Islâm.

D.

The title of Codex 729 is كنز العباد في شرح الاوراد, "Treasury of Worshippers in a Commentary on the Awrâds."

Written in a rough Naskhi, about AD 1630, the margins are generally injured by worms, so also are many letters of the text itself. The last four leaves are supplied in a modern hand.

The Awrâds are the familiar citations from the Ḳurân occurring in some invocation of daily worship. A commentary was written upon them by the celebrated doctor ʿUmar b. Yaḥya as-Suhrawardi. The present work is a commentary by ʿAli b. Aḥmad al-Ghūri, in mingled Arabic and Persian, upon the commentary of Suhrawardi. A similar work is mentioned by Haji Khalîfa (*Haji Khalfae Lexicon Encyclopaedicum et Bibliographicum*, ed. Flügel, vol. V, pp. 254–55; two incomplete copies exist also in the Library of the India Office [cf. codd. 363, 364 in Loth's Cat.]).

From the contents of the present work it would appear to have a more appropriate place under the heading "Law," but the title, referring to divisions in the sacred text, justifies its inclusion under the heading "Ḳurânic literature." On the leaf preceding the first page of the text, there is a list of the sections of the book. From the following titles of a few chapters, it will be inferred that the author deals with points of casuistry and with Muḥammadan legislation in general:

A chapter on sneezing. A chapter on greetings. A chapter on forgiveness. A chapter on the traveller's prayer. A chapter on usury. A chapter on marriage.

Dhikr in the month of Sha'bân. Dhikr in the month of Ramaḍhân. A chapter on what spoils the fasting. A chapter on the prayer of Friday, and so on.

On folio 75b. we find the following passage:

> If some one sneezes, he must thank God and say: "Praise be to God, the Lord of the worlds; praise be to God in all events"; he is not to say other things. People who are present ought to say: "May God have pity on you"; then the sneezer will say: "May God forgive me and you, or, lead you in the right way and make good your condition." He must not say other things. In the *'Awârif*,[4] in the thirtieth chapter (the Prophet)—peace be with him—said: "He who sneezes or experiences a yawn and says: 'Praise be to God in all events,' God will take away from him seventy diseases, the easiest of which is elephantiasis." . . .
>
> It is written in the Ḥadîth that the sneezer deserves an utterance of prayer if he praises God when sneezing. If his companion has prayed for him, let him say: "May God lead you in the right way and make good your condition." In the Ḥadîth also it is written that he who sneezes three consecutive times, faith is solid in his heart. It is reported, too, in the Ḥadîth that if one sneezes more than three times, you can utter a prayer for him if you like, and if you like you may dispense with it. . . . It is reported that the Prophet—peace be with him—said: "Sneezing is from God and yawning is from Satan. If some one from amongst you yawns, let him put his hand on his mouth; and if he says: Ah, ah, Satan will laugh 'in his belly' (or) 'within him.'"

Folio 139a:

> 'Abdallah b. 'Umar is reported to have said that to swear by a thing other than God is an infidelity. He said also: "Nobody is allowed to swear except in case of necessity." It is written in the Shir'ah: "He who wishes to swear in truth, let him swear by God and be quiet. An oath taken by a thing other than God is a hidden infidelity. Let no one swear by his father, or by the life of somebody, or by the Ka'bah, or by his swerving from Islâm; because he who does that truly will not return to Islâm safely; and if he swears mendaciously, infidelity will cling to him." In the *Hidâyah* (title of a well-known work) it is written: "An oath taken in the name of God is right and lawful"; there also is the following saying of (the Prophet)—peace be with him—"He who swears falsely by God, God will get him into the fire."

From folio 146a:

Hospitality is one of the ways of acting in Islâm. If a man enters, as a guest, the house of his brother who is a believer, a thousand blessings and a thousand mercies enter with him. The first man who received guests is the Beloved One of God—peace be with him. He had built a house with four gates looking in the four directions of the earth. He used to go one mile or two miles in search of a guest. He did not eat (or, did not go away)[5] except with a guest. He did not show, in his hospitality, any preference to the rich, by excluding the poor. He used to know his guests with accuracy one day or two days before his invitation. He did not call from one family the father without the son and the brother, if they were grown up. . . . He never invited a man who, to his knowledge, would cause uneasiness to the other guests.

On folio 56a we read the following passage written about sūrah XXXIII, 9 sqq.:

The story runs thus: When the Prophet of God—may God pray on him and give him peace—returned from a certain conflict with one of the brave of Madînah, he made a covenant with Bani Ḳuraiḍhah and Naḍhîr[6] that they should not be for him nor against him; but they broke their engagement in the following manner: Ḥayya b. Akhṭab rode to Maccah with some of his companions and stirred up Abu Sufiân to fight against the Prophet. Then he went to Ghaṭafân and bani Kinânah and incited them also for the battle. In this way he formed seven armies which numbered, it is said, fifteen thousand men, who came and alighted near Madînah. Then (b. Akhṭab) cam to Bani Ḳuraiḍhah who had for chieftain Ka'b b. Asad. He went to him and said: "I have brought you all Ḳuraish, Kinânah, and Ghaṭafân; break, therefore, the covenant which exists between you and Muḥammad." He did not cease until (Ka'b) broke the covenant and tore up the paper.

The news reached the Prophet—peace be with him—who consulted his companions; they agreed to fight against them and to leave Madînah. Then Salmân rose up and said: "Did we not entrench ourselves, in the land of Persia, when horses frightened us? Do not you want us, O Prophet of God—peace be with you—to dig trenches round Madînah?" Then the Prophet of God—peace be with him—went out with the inhabitants of

Madînah, and the Prophet of God—peace be with him—took a pickaxe in his hands and said the formula: "In the name of God with whom we began; if we had another one besides him, we should have been unhappy." They dug trenches, and the *Companions* came and went to the back of them. They fought seven days. From the Infidels ʿAmr b. ʿAbduwaihi was killed; he was a warrior from amongst their chieftains. It is in that time that the Prophet of God—peace be with him—missed four of his prayers, on account of his occupation in the war. . . .

Notes

1. Cf. Codex 571, p. 135, of Baron de Slane's "Catalogue des Manuscrits Arabes de la Bibliothèque Nationale" (1883–1895).

2. The Imâm is the Caliph ʿUthmān under whose authority the Ḳurân was finally compiled.

3. From the citation of the first words of the text, this manuscript is not identical with that found in the Khedivial Library (ibid., p. 218, Codex 255).

4. Title of a work written by Suhrawardi.

5. The manuscript has يقطر, but this may be a mistake for يفطر.

6. Manuscript النضير but folio 56b بني النضر.

3.4

An Ancient Syriac Translation of the Ḳur'ān Exhibiting New Verses and Variants

Alphonse Mingana

FOREWORD

I.

Among the Syriac manuscripts brought recently from the East by the writer is one (numbered Mingana 89 and written about AD 1450) that contains controversial works against Jews, Nestorians, and Mohammedans by the West Syrian writer Barṣalībi, who died in AD 1171. The treatise against the Mohammedans is divided into three discourses (*maimré*), subdivided into thirty chapters, two-thirds of which would offer no compensation for the trouble taken by a diligent reader intent on perusing them thoroughly. The last discourse, comparising chapters 25–30, is entirely composed of quotations from the Ḳur'ān, translated into Syriac. These the author adduces for purposes either of refutation or of illustration, and he divides his page in this part into two columns, the first of which contains the Ḳur'ānic quotations, and the second his own refutations or illustrations.

As the verses in the tract are often quoted without any introductory or editorial words, it is sometimes difficult to make out when a quotation ends and another begins. The aim of Barṣalībi is making use of these quotations is threefold: to confirm a given Christian doctrine, to draw attention to some apparent contradictions of the Ḳur'ān, and to put before his readers the story of some biblical incidents as narrated in it.

Under the first head are all the Ḳur'ānic verses dealing with Jesus, His mother and His disciples, and with the Holy Spirit. The author often addresses in the second column the Christians or Mohammedans in some such phrases: "Examine what your (or: their, as the case may be) Prophet says about the Christ."

Under the second head fall all the passages in which the author puts side by side the apparently contradictory statements made by the Prophet. Here also the author addresses in the second column the Christians or the Mohammedans with some such words as: "Look how your (or, their) Prophet was inconsistent."

Under the third head occur all the passages dealing with the patriarchs Abraham, Noah, and others whose history is often narrated in a different way from that found in the Canonical Books of the Old and New Testaments. Here also the author interpellates the Christians or the Mohammedans with words similar to those used under the first two heads. If we add to these the didactic passages quoted for the benefit of Christian readers, in the matter of the creation of man and the universe, and of the life hereafter, we shall have a comprehensive synopsis of all the Ḳur'ānic citations, and a full abstract of the scope of Barṣalībi's work.

The Ḳur'ān in a Syriac garb greatly excited my curiosity and I began to peruse the above citations with some interest. I was not long in detecting the fact that they often represented a version that not only was not always in harmony with the *textus receptus* of the Ḳur'ān but also exhibited whole verses not found in it at all.

In 1914 when I edited some scraps of a palimpsest, the underwriting of which revealed scattered verses of the Ḳur'ān, I held to the traditional view, so ably maintained by Nöldeke in his classical *Geschichte des Qorāns*, that the sacred book of Islam was collected and standardized on the initiative of the third caliph by Zaid b. Thābit and other amaneunses.[1] In 1916, greatly under the influence of Professor Casanova's investigations I contributed a monograph to the *Journal of the Manchester Egyptian and Oriental Society*,[2] in which I suggested that the traditional view on the compilation of the Ḳur'ān was not always satisfactory, and set forth the hypothesis that the Ḳur'ān, as we have it today, was finally standardized at a much later date, under the Umayyad Caliph ʿAbd al-Malik b. Marwān. In the article *Qurān* in the late Dr. Hastings's *Encyclopædia of Religion and Ethics* (1918, pp. 547 sqq.), I endeavored to add more weight to this theory.

Before proceeding any further with the Ḳur'ān itself, it will be useful to discuss the all-important question of the origin, provenance, and antiquity of its Syriac translation. Unhappily Barṣalībi throws no light on the subject. He begins his section as follows:

> The third Discourse of the Treatise against the Muslims. Chapter 25, in which there are special parts of the Ḳur'ān in the upper column and a short refutation of them in the lower column, because a detailed refutation has been given in the previous chapters.

The colophon of the whole work is by the author himself and runs thus:

> Our Treatise against the Muslims has extended thus far. We have refuted their objection concerning the Trinity and the Incarnation of the Son, and by proofs taken from Nature and from Philosophical books we have demonstrated our truth. Then we have confuted them in many points from their own book. After that we have arranged in one systematic division parts of the Ḳur'ān, which has been translated from their language into Syriac, and we have succinctly refuted it in the column that is below, because in the previous chapters we have given a detailed refutation. The time has now come to put an end to our labour. Let any one who reads and understands, profits and makes others profit, pray for Mar Dionysius the stranger, who is Jacob Barṣalībi from Milīṭīni, Metropolitan of Amed.

Chapter 26 is entitled "From the Ḳur'ān," chapters 27–29 have no titles, and chapter 30 is headed "Further extracts from the Ḳur'ān."

It will be seen from the accompanying Syriac text of the colophon that the verb that we have rendered by "has been translated" with reference to the whole of the Ḳur'ān may equally well be rendered by "have been translated" with reference to "parts" only of the Ḳur'ān.[3] We are not, therefore, in a position to infer with certitude from the above headings and colophon whether Barṣalībi had before him all the Ḳur'ān translated into Syriac, or only parts of it; but from the comprehensive list of all the translated passages given below we are inclined to adhere to the first alternative. The contrary hypothesis would drive us into endless surmises involving the existence of *Testimony Books* consisting of extracts and selections from the Ḳur'ān for the benefit of Christian controversialists. Of the existence of such books there is no trace of any kind in the history of the Syrian Churches. What seems to lend color to our view is the fact that in the sentence following the one just reported (see the above colophon) the author clearly states that he has "succinctly refuted *it*," that is, the whole Ḳur'ān and not only "parts" of it spoken of in the previous sentence.

If, as seems probable, there was great necessity for early Christians to possess a thorough knowledge of the religion of their new masters and neighbors, is it not more natural to suppose that they had a complete version of the sacred book of Islam, rather than merely short portions of it that at best would prove a great hindrance in their religious discussions? We incline, therefore, to the belief that it is not intrinsically impossible to maintain the existence of a complete version of the Ḳur'ān in the hands of Christian doctors of the first centuries of the Hijrah. This hypothesis is rendered somewhat plausible by the fact that during the reign of some fanatical caliphs unclean Christians could hardly even touch a Ḳur'ān in the presence of Muslims for purposes of reference; and if all signs do not mislead us they would not be even allowed to possess officially Arabic Ḳur'ān, in their private houses. In how many ancient copies of the Ḳur'ān do we not find in large characters, on the first page, the verses 76–80 of sūrah LVI, which forbid even Muslims to touch it without having previously made their ablutions. (See Nīsābūri, *Gharāib*, XXVII, 113; ed. Cairo.)

The above remarks lead us naturally to the main point of our inquiry: when, where, and by whom was the Ḳur'ān translated into Syriac? We must dwell at the outset on the fact that we do not deem it probable to suppose that Barṣalībi had any share in this translation. Anyone who has read his Syriac works and noticed how careful he is to mention his name in sonorous phrases at the beginning or at the end of all of them would hesitate to believe that if he had anything to do with the translation of the Ḳur'ānic pericopes under consideration, he would not have used the phrase "has been translated," but he would have written something like "which we Dionysius the stranger . . . have by the Grace of God translated from Arabic into Syriac."

Furthermore, in the second column where he refutes or illustrates the Ḳur'ānic verses, he sometimes upholds the traditional Muslim interpretation against the meaning of the Syriac text that he had transcribed in the first column. If he was both the author and the translator he could not have commented in the way he did on verses that did not square with the meaning he adopts in the commentary. So, for instance, his refutation of verse 17 of surah LXIX, is in accordance with the Muslim traditional reading, which implies that the throne of God was borne by eight angels,[4] while the Syriac lying before him, and which he quotes, clearly refers the "eight" to days and says that "they shall bear the throne of thy Lord on the eighth day." In the same way the text used by the author in his refutations found in the second column of verses V, 50 and LXI, 14, seems to be different from that found in the first column.

There is in this connection a linguistic phenomenon to which we wish to draw attention. When in LII, 20 the translator wishes to illustrate the Arabic *Sururin* that he had rightly rendered by *Piryāwātha*, he adds to it the explanatory Persian word *awkaith takhthā* "that is to say *couches*." If the translator was Barṣalībi—born and brought up in Malaṭya—he would not have used at Amed a Persian word to explain a Syriac one. Does not this simple fact point to a time when Arabic had not yet supplanted Persian as a second language of the Christians of the Near East?

There is another linguistic feature worth mentioning. In the thirtieth chapter the author is evidently endeavoring to put side by side some apparently contradictory passages of the Ḳur'ān. This contradiction in terms, which he wishes to emphasize, is not always found in Arabic, but only in Syriac. If the author was working on an Arabic Ḳur'ān he would not have illustrated his point by wrong examples that did not prove his thesis. For instance, the Syriac verb ܛܥܐ means to *forget* (something), and the author finding it in his Syriac version used of the forgetfulness of God rightly quotes it in this sense in connection with Ḳur'ān XXXII, 14 or XLV, 33, where the Arabic has نسى ; but because he found this same Syriac verb in the Syriac version lying before him, he uses it in the form of ܛܥܝܐ ܠ, which means "something escaping one's notice; hidden from one "answering to the Arabic خفي على in connection with III, 4 and so on, where it does not fit in with his assertion. This simultaneous use of the same Syriac word in two different connections could not have arisen from an Arabic Ḳur'ān. The argument will hold good even if verses such as XLI, 53 and XXVII, 9 were alluded to by Barṣalībi. In XX, 54, the verb *yansa* is used of God as follows: "My Lord misleads not, nor forgets"; but the Ḳur'ān has "*my* Lord" while the Syriac has "*thy* Lord" with the addition of the word *nothing*, which is missing in the former; moreover, it is the existence of the *lamadh* before the verb that is the deciding factor. The only difficulty is that in all our other references from the Ḳur'ān the word "God" is used instead of "thy Lord." In such verses as VI, 132 and XI, 123, *ghāfil* is in evidence.

We will here allude to a palæographically archaic feature that seems to ascribe to the tenth Christian century at the latest the *terminus ad quem* of the Arabic manuscript of the Ḳur'ān from which our Syriac translation is derived, while the *terminus a quo* is lost in the mist of Ḳur'ānic antiquity: the first long quotation that the author gives from the Ḳur'ān embraces in a single whole, without any break in the text, all the first sūrah and verses 1–10 of sūrah II. Now the second sūrah is not introduced like the first by the ordinary formula: "In the name of Allah, the Compassionate, the Merciful," and although exhibiting the mysterious letters A.L.M. it is not preceded by its usual title and definition. We do not believe that any Arabic manuscript of the Ḳur'ān lacked all these features after the tenth century, and if Barṣalībi—who in his Syriac writings may always be taken as a faithful repertory of ancient records—was not playing havoc with all literary decency, it was hardly possible for him to have been the translator of the Ḳur'ānic periscopes under consideration (cf. Ṭabari, *Tafsīr*, I, 35, etc.). This refers only to the title and the description of the sūrah; for the absence of the introductory formula see below p. 310.

Finally, the fact that the Syriac version that the author quotes offers new verses not found in our Ḳur'āns, and various readings not mentioned by any Muslim commentator or reader, impedes us from ascribing it with any degree of probability to the time in which he lived, that is, the twelfth Christian century. It is well known that the sacred book of Islam was finally fixed and standardized about three hundred years before this date. See also pages 324–25.

In this respect we know how careful were the Muslim theologians and *Ḳurrā'* in their reading and transcribing of the Ḳur'ān at the period of the

'Abbasid dynasty, that is to say from the time when we have positive proofs of the existence of a standard text. Controversies among *Ḳurrā'* have since then been confined to one or two vowels, one or two consonants, but hardly ever to complete phrases, despite the verses that some Shī'ah writers have invented to bolster up the political aim of the 'Alids.

That all the early *Ḳurrā'*, however, were not always a model of accuracy in the performance of their work is borne out by the answer that Iyās b. Mu'āwiah gave to the Umayyad Caliph 'Umar b. 'Abd al-'Aziz (AD 717–720): "The *Ḳurrā'* are of two kinds: some of them do their work for the sake of the world to come, and these will not serve you; and some others do their work for the sake of this world, and on these you could not count."[5]

Islamic history has put on record cases of some doctors and *Ḳurrā'* who had different Ḳur'āns or knew verses of the Ḳur'ān not found in the official copies of the state. We will here mention Shanbūdh, whose case became famous in Baghdād because he read and taught the Ḳur'ān "with disgraceful readings and anomalies which were an addition to the *muṣḥaf*[6] of 'Uthmān," and who in AH 323 was seized by the sultan's emissaries and subjected to flogging.[7] Another instance is that of Ibn Ḳudaid (died AH 312), who had in his possession the Ḳur'ān of 'Uḳbah b. 'Āmir, which was different in composition (*'ala ghair ta'līf*) from that of 'Uthmān.[8] Others who ventured to register various readings had their books that contained them burned by order of the authorities.[9]

With Yākūt's account of the above unfortunate doctor should be coupled the important statement of the author of the *Fihrist* who informs us (pp. 31–32) that Ibn Shanbūdh died in the court prison in 328, and gives us some astounding variants, additions, and verbal differences found in the Ḳur'ān that he was using.

Our present knowledge of various readings in the Ḳur'ān is mostly derived from the commentators (chiefly Zamakhshari), from late books of *Ḳirā'āt* such as the *Muḳni'* of Dāni, and from stray quotations found in some early authors such as the *Mathālib*[10] of Ibn al-Kalbi and others, but these, as shown by the Ḳur'āns of 'Uḳbah b. 'Āmir and Ibn Shanbūdh, are not sufficient to enable us to form a clear opinion of the state of the sacred text in the time of its most critical period, which corresponds roughly with AD 660–710, and until some of those early works on the Ḳur'ān the existence—

even if not the actual wording—of which was known to the author of the *Fihrist* (pp. 28–30) are recovered, or something tangible turns up from an unexpected quarter, we will only be able to formulate more or less consistent hypotheses, which however good can hardly stand as established facts.

The above cases belong to the fourth Islamic century. Before this time we know also of the early existence of the (now lost or purposely destroyed) Ḳur'āns of Ubayy b. Ka'b, ʿAli b. a. Ṭālib, Ibn Masʿūd,[11] and of a few others, but is it likely that the Syriac translator would have chosen for the benefit of his co-religionists an unofficial and somewhat heretical text of which no Christian could make effective use in controversial discussions? What was there to tempt him in such an enterprise? Everything well considered we hold it, therefore, to be improbable that if a Syriac translation of the Ḳur'ān was in the hands of some Christian communities of the first centuries of the Hijrah, it was not made from a text that was in every respect official and acknowledged by the bulk of the Muslim testimony of the time.

Research in the domain of Syriac literature does not throw any important light on the point at issue. Most of the Syriac writers from the middle of the seventh century downward appear on the whole to be well acquainted with the religion of their new masters, although in the historical sphere a few of them fall into grave errors in their biographical essays on the genealogy of the first Arab caliphs and generals. From early times there have been, both in Syria and in Mesopotamia, discussions between Christians and Muslims, a commendable enumeration of which can be found in Steinschneider's *Polem. u. apol. lit.* (1877), with Goldziher's continuation of it in *Z.D.M.G.* (33), and in our Ṭabari's *Book of Religion and Empire* (1922),[12] but to our knowledge in none of them is there mention of a Syriac translation of the Ḳur'ān. The first mention of the refutation of a complete Ḳur'ān recorded in Syriac literature is that undertaken by the East Syrian writer Abū Nūḥ of Anbār, the secretary of the Muslim governor of Mosul, toward the end of the eighth Christian century, or about AD 790,[13] but since the work itself is lost we have no means for ascertaining the nature and the character of the sacred text that he used.

The above statement is subject, however, to an important qualification:

(*a*) From very early times Syriac writers, even those among them who knew no Arabic at all, referred to some statements made in the Ḳur'ān that it was very difficult for them to have discovered, unless they were either working direct upon a Syriac Ḳur'ān or upon firsthand Christian authorities versed in its knowledge. So, for instance, John of Phenek who was writing about AD 690 makes a clear mention of the fact that the Muslims had, from their leader Muḥammad, a special order in favor of the Christians and the monks.[14] This undoubtedly refers to Ḳur'ān V, 85. Now we cannot reasonably suppose that a monk living in the Bohtan district of Kurdistan, knowing no Arabic whatever, and writing purely for his fellow monks, could have expressed himself on a delicate subject in such a confident way, if he had no Ḳur'ānic knowledge of any kind derived either from a translated Ḳur'ān or from some of his co-religionists versed in its doctrine.

(*b*) Many Syriac writers quote complete Syriac sentences of the Ḳur'ān in their controversial works written, like the present one of Barṣalībi, for the exclusive benefit of their co-religionists. Now the Syriac phraseology used by them in such quotations is sometimes identical with that which we are publishing in this study, so that we must either advance the not very probable hypothesis that this coincidence in phraseology is always due to a fortuitous encounter in the intricate linguistic peculiarities of the Arabic Ḳur'ān, or else resort to the more likely surmise that the Syriac controversialists were drawing upon a Syriac translation known to them. So, for instance, Barhebraeus quotes in his *menārath Ḳudhshé*[15] Ḳur'ān IV, 169; V, 77; and CXII, 1–4 in words very akin to those that we are editing today. Since it is unlikely that this very famous West Syrian writer was referring to the present work of Barṣalībi, is it not reasonable to suppose that these two writers were working upon a Syriac translation of the Ḳur'ān that they knew was coming down to them from the times that followed the first onrush of Muslim invasions and conquests?

In this respect it is not very gratifying to notice the way our inquiry is proceeding on negative lines, but history being a science based on facts and positive records, in the absence of them we can only grope our way in all directions in search of any opening that is capable of shedding a ray of light on a previously unexplored theme. If we were allowed to express an opinion on the subject we should say, but only provisionally and with extreme reserve (until fuller light dawns), that in view of the character of the present document, and on condition that all the indications of the author are scrupulously correct, the most propitious time for the appearance of such a Syriac translation of the Ḳur'ān as that which it appears to represent would be the years of the reign of the Umayyad Caliph ʿAbd al-Malik b. Marwān, some time between AD 684 and 704, before the final effort of the caliphs to fix a text bearing the authoritative stamp of the first Orthodox believers. To this period would also more appropriately point the Syriac word translated into Persian, which we have already examined, and the general phraseology of the translation, which, although under Arabic influence (being a translation from Arabic), may nevertheless be considered good and moderately classical.

We will allude in this connection to the fact of the absence from sūrah II of the introductory formula, "in the name of God, the Compassionate, the Merciful." This formula is certainly very ancient and, if I mistake not, is found in all the old manuscripts of the Ḳur'ān that we possess—the oldest of which are by the way somewhat later than about the middle of the second century of the Hijrah, and correspond approximately with the first two decades that followed the 'Abbasid victory. Now unless we suppose, as we have already pointed out, that Barṣalībi was playing havoc with all literary decency, are we not allowed to argue from their absence that our Syriac translation was made from a Ḳur'ān in which the well-known formula was not, as at present, repeated before every sūrah (with the exception of the IXth), but was found once only at the beginning of sūrah I, that is, the *Fātiḥah*? If the answer be in the affirmative, would it not be improbable to suppose that this formula was missing from the second sūrah in any manuscript of the Ḳur'ān written after the first century of the Hijrah? And if so, could not our Syriac translation also be ascribed to the end of the first Islamic century, or to the time of Ḥajjāj?

We may here add that we do not believe that Barṣalībi purposely omitted to quote the above formula, or that he had anything in view in so doing, because he actually quotes it before the first sūrah and even gives us the three mysterious letters, beginning the second sūrah, as the only break in the text between the two sūrahs. See Nīsābūri's *Gharāib* (I, 76). That in the Ḳur'ān used by the author the first and second sūrahs were considered as one is established by the fact that he (see p. 326) calls the second sūrah as the first under the name of the *Cow*.

Of the same category of the apparently aimless omissions that might likewise tend to corroborate the point at issue is the refrain recurring after almost every verse of sūrah LV: "which of your Lord's bounties will ye deny," which is completely missing in Syriac. There are a few more textual phenomena of Ḳur'ānic phrases that are omitted in the translation. These the reader will easily notice for himself, and form his own judgment upon them without the aid of a Syriac scholar.

No one is more conscious than we are of the gravity of the above suggestion, as to the antiquity of the Syriac translation, and we hope that the care with which we have expressed ourselves will prove—as a Syriac saying has it—a healthy deterrent to any Arabic and Syriac scholar, whether Christian or Muslim, who might accuse us of lack of caution or of hasty conclusions. We are face to face with a Syriac text the character and the nature of which are not well defined. We have brought forward strong reasons for believing that it docs not emanate from Barṣalībi, but we are not able to ascertain with confidence the exact time of its appearance. The question, therefore, of authorship, and all the subsidiary points attaching to it, should be left open until further evidence is available. We shall always be thankful to any scientific worker who is able to explain more fully and more satisfactorily than we have done the difficulties inherent in the Syriac translation as compared with the traditional *textus receptus* of the Ḳur'ān and the various indications of the manuscripts. After this remark we will proceed to enumerate the historical data that we have so far found in Arabic literature concerning the work of the standardization of the Ḳur'ān that we firmly believe was undertaken by the Umayyad Caliph ʿAbd al-Malik b. Marwān and his powerful lieutenant Ḥajjāj.

Kindi, who was writing some forty years before Bukhāri, outlines the history of the Ḳur'ān briefly as follows:[16]

> Upon the Prophet's death, and at the instigation of the Jews, 'Ali refused to swear allegiance to Abu Bakr, but when he despaired of succeeding to the Caliphate, he presented himself before him, forty days (some say six months) after the Prophet's death. As he was swearing allegiance to him, he was asked, "O father of Ḥasan, what hath delayed thee so long?" He answered, "I was busy collecting the Book of God, for that the Prophet committed to my care." The men present about Abu Bakr represented that there were scraps and pieces of the Ḳur'ān with them as well as with 'Ali; and then it was

agreed to collect the whole from every quarter together. So they collected various parts from the memory of individuals (as *Surat al Barā'ah*, which they wrote out at the dictation of a certain Arab from the desert), and other portions from different people; besides that which was copied out from tablets of stone, and palm leaves, and shoulder bones, and such like. It was not at first collected in a volume, but remained in separate leaves. Then the people fell to variance in their reading; some read according to the version of 'Ali, which they follow to the present day; some read according to the collection of which we have made mention; one party read according to the text of Ibn Mas'ūd, and another according to that of Ubayy b. Ka'b.

When 'Uthmān came to power, and people everywhere differed in their reading, 'Ali sought grounds of accusation against him, compassing his death. One man would read a verse one way, and another man another way; and there was change and interpolation, some copies having more and some less. When this was represented to 'Uthmān, and the danger urged of division, strife, and apostacy, he thereupon caused to be collected together all the leaves and scraps that he could, together with the copy that was written out at the first. But they did not interfere with that which was in the hands of 'Ali, or of those who followed his reading. Ubayy was dead by this time; as for Ibn Mas'ūd, they demanded his exemplar, but he refused to give it up. Then they commanded Zaid b. Thābit, and with him 'Abdallah b. 'Abbās, to revise and correct the text, eliminating all that was corrupt; they were instructed, when they differed on any reading, word, or name, to follow the dialect of the Ḳuraish.

When the recension was completed, four exemplars were written out in large text; one was sent to Maccah, and another to Madīnah; the third was despatched to Syria, and is to this day at Malaṭya;[17] the fourth was deposited in Kūfah. People say that this last copy is still extant at Kūfah, but this is not the case, for it was lost in the insurrection of Mukhtār (AH 67). The copy at Maccah remained there till the city was stormed by Abū Sarāyah (AH 200); he did not carry it away, but it is supposed to have been burned in the conflagration. The Madīnah exemplar was lost in the reign of terror, that is, in the days of Yazīd b. Mu'āwiah (AH 60–64).

After what we have related above, 'Uthmān called in all the former leaves and copies, and destroyed them, threatening those who held any portion back and so only some scattered remains, concealed here and there, survived. Ibn Mas'ūd, however, retained his exemplar in his own hands, and it was inherited by his posterity, as it is this day; and likewise the collection of 'Ali has descended in his family.

Then followed the business of Ḥajjāj b. Yūsuf, who gathered together every single copy he could lay hold of, and caused to be omitted from the text a great many passages. Among these, they say, were verses revealed concerning the House of Umayyah with names of certain persons, and concerning the House of ʿAbbās also with names.[18] Six copies of the text thus revised were distributed to Egypt, Syria, Madīnah, Maccah, Kūfah, and Baṣrah. After that he called in and destroyed all the preceding copies, even as 'Uthmān had done before him. The enmity subsisting between 'Ali and Abu Bakr, ʿUmar and 'Uthmān is well known; now each of these entered in the text whatever favoured his own claims, and left out what was otherwise. How then can we distinguish between the genuine and the counterfeit? and what about the losses caused by Ḥajjāj? The kind of faith that this tyrant held in other matters is well known; how can we make an arbiter as to the Book of God a man who never ceased to play into the hands of the Umayyads whenever he found opportunity? All that I have said is drawn from your own authorities, and no single argument has been advanced but what is based on evidence accepted by yourselves; in proof thereof we have the Ḳur'ān itself, which is a confused heap, with neither system nor order.

Barhebræus[19] has preserved the interesting and important tradition: "ʿAbd al-Malik b. Marwān used to say, 'I fear death in the month of Ramaḍān—in it I was born, in it I was weaned, in it I have collected the Ḳur'ān (*Jama'tu*[20] *l' Ḳur'āna*), and in it I was elected Caliph.'" This is also reported by Jalāl ad-Dīn as-Suyūti,[21] as derived from Tha'ālibi.

Maḳrīzi,[22] Ibn Duḳmāḳ,[23] and Ibn Ḥajar al-'Asḳalāni[24] say about the Ḳur'ān of Asmā: "The reason why this Ḳur'ān was written is that Ḥajjāj b. Yūsuf Thaḳafi wrote Ḳur'āns and sent them to the head-provinces. One of them was sent to Egypt. ʿAbd al-'Azīz b. Marwān, who was then governor of Egypt in the name of his brother ʿAbd al-Malik, was irritated and said, 'How could he send a Ḳur'ān to a district of which I am the chief?'"

Ibn al-Athīr[25] relates that Ḥajjāj proscribed the Ḳur'ān according to the reading of Ibn Masʿūd; and Ibn Khallikān[26] reports that owing to some orthographical difficulties such various readings had crept into the Ḳur'ān in the time of Ḥajjāj that he was obliged to ask some people to put an end to them.

The Arabic manuscript of the John Rylands Library numbered 827[27] and dated (at the end of another work that precedes the one under consideration and that is written by the same hand) AH 732[28] AD 1331 contains an apparently unique work titled: *Laķāḥ al-Khawāṭir*: a collection of witty sayings, anecdotes, and traditions compiled by ʿAbdallah b. Yaḥya b. ʿAbdallah b. Muḥammad b. al-Muʿammir b. Jaʿfar who lived in the sixth Islamic century, because he has dedicated his work to the ʿAbbasid Caliph Mustaḍi (AD 1170–1180). On folio 99[a] of this manuscript occurs the following anecdote: "And Rabīʿ b. Khaitham[29] was of the number of the great *Tābiʿīn* and he had met with many of the *Ṣaḥābah* from whom he related traditions. The concubine of Rabīʿ b. Khaitham said that all the work of Rabīʿ was done in secret. If a man came to him while the exemplar of the Ķur'ān (*muṣḥaf*) was open he would cover it with his mantle and begin to recite it aloud and say: 'Until the reading of Ḥajjāj comes to us';[30] and if a noise was heard she (the concubine) was frightened."

We believe this to be a malicious allusion to the efforts made by Ḥajjāj for the standardization of the Ķur'ān, efforts of which Rabīʿ may or may not have approved.[31]

We will close all these quotations with a reference to an anecdote registered by Ṭabari,[32] in which Ḥajjāj is reported to have said in a speech that "Ibn Zubair had changed the Book of God"; whereupon Ibn ʿUmar, who was drowsing from the effect of the length of the speech, rose and challenged Ḥajjāj, saying: "Neither thou nor he are able to do that." The answer that Ḥājjāj gave was: "It has come to my knowledge that thou shalt do it." And the story ends with the sentence: "But when he approached him privately, he was silent."

This traditional anecdote, worded as it is in a somewhat veiled style, does not clearly show what was in the mind of Ṭabari when recording it, but it does prove without any doubt that the name of Ḥajjāj was associated, in the mind of his contemporaries, with changes of some kind in the Ķur'ān; this is all the more so because the anecdote is referred to in connection with Ķur'ān X, 65, which asserts that the words of God do not brook any change.

II.

The full list of the verses of the Ḳur'ān quoted in Syriac by Barṣalībi in the third discourse of his work is as follows: I, 1–7; II, 1–10, 28, 29–35, 44–45, 81, 109, 130–31, 132, 139, 172, 254; III, 2, 16, 18, 40–43, 45, 48–50, 52, 106, 109–10; IV, 50, 149, 154, 156–57, 162, 169; V, 16, 50–51, 69, 70, 72, 77, 85, 94, 109, 116; VI, 59, 76–78, 109; VII, 15–17, 171–72; IX, 34–35, 115; X, 94; XI, 9; XIII, 18; XV, 26–27, 39–43, 92–93; XVI, 104; XVII, 61, 87, 92–97; XIX, 29, 34–35, 61–63; XX, 114–18; XXI, 52–65, 66–72, 91–92; XXII, 8–9; XXIII, 14, 103; XXIV, 2, 24; XXVI, 83–85; XXVII, 24; XXIX, 13, 45; XXX, 7; XXXII, 14; XXXIII, 49–51; XXXIV, 3; XXXVI, 65; XXXVII, 14–15, 22–23, 97–113; XXXIX, 32, 67, 74; XL, 78; XLI, 8–11; XLII, 14; XLVI, 8; XLVII, 16–17; XLVIII, 10; LI, 47; LII, 19–21, 24; LIII, 7–17; LV, 39, 46–56; LVI, 20–22; LVII, 4, 21–22, 24; LIX, 7; LXIX, 17; LXI, 14; LXVI, 12; LXXI, 14, 27–29; LXXII, 3, 26–28; LXXVI, 1, 16–20; LXXVII, 35; lXXXVI, 5, 16–20; XC, 1–4; XCVI, 1–3; XCVIII, 1–7; XCIX, 7–8; CXII, 1–4.

Interspersed among the Ḳur'ānic passages referred to in the above list are certain verses that the author, according to his own indications, quotes as from the Ḳur'ān, that he genuinely believes to be Ḳur'ānic, and that he treats in every respect as he treats the authentic verses of the Ḳur'ān, but that, on verification, prove not to be found in the Ḳur'ān of our days. Among them are some the origin of which cannot be traced to any other source but that of the Ḳur'ān. They appear to be Ḳur'ānic in the spirit and in the letter, and are not, and (with the possible exception of no. 1) even could not be, found in the tradition, to the taste of which they appear to be somewhat foreign; at all events we have not been able to account for them through the channel of the *Ḥadīth*. They are the following, with the exclusion of the verse (in p. 230) that cannot be reconstructed except by a reference to two distinct sūrahs, XI, 2 and XIII 43:

1°

"If all men gathered together from the East as far as the West to change one letter from the words of God, they will not be able to do it."

2°

"The Holy Spirit brought down from the Lord grace and light."[33]

3°

"No one understands the meaning of the Garden[34] except God."

4°

"He[35] is sitting on a throne."

The last verse needs some explanation. The word used for "throne" is *Kursya*, which answers to the Arabic *Kursi*, and the nearest verse containing this word is II, 256, which is, however, very remote in meaning, not having even a reference to "sitting." There are in the Syriac translation two other verses, XI, 9 and LVII, 4, which mention God's throne, but the Arabic word used in the Ḳur'ān for sitting is *istawa*, rendered into Syriac by *ittarraṣ*. The Arabic and the Syriac words are far from being the same thing as "sitting." Further, in the two passages mentioned above, the Arabic word for "throne" is *'Arsh*, rendered into Syriac by *'Arsa*, which most generally means "bed, bier, and litter" and hardly ever "throne."

That the Ḳur'ān translated into Syriac had another verse in which the Arabic sentence used had *Kursi* and not *'Arsh* seems probable from the fact that Barṣalībi quotes two distinct Ḳur'ānic passages (see p. 328) in which it was stated that God's throne was upon water, in one of which he uses the word *Kursya* and in the other *'Arsa*, and he introduces the second by saying: "and in another place he (Muḥammad) wrote." As a matter of fact, there is no other passage of the Ḳur'ān in which the throne of God is set up upon water.[36] The great imam Abu Ḥanīfah says in his *Waṣīyah* (fol. 12^b of Arabic manuscript 614 of the John Rylands Library) that this act of God making for and standing on the throne is to be believed as an article of faith, and he introduces it by the formula *nuḳirru*, "we profess."

There is another group of verses that it is useful here to examine. We are all aware of the fact that as the Gospels do not contain all the sayings of

Christ, so the Ḳur'ān does not contain all the sayings of Muḥammad. Indeed Muslim tradition testifies to this in asserting that even the revealed passages are not consigned in their totality in the Ḳur'ān. Nöldeke[37] has long ago collected many such uncanonical passages that were scattered here and there in the tradition. In our present state of knowledge we are not in a position to affirm or to deny their existence in some early copies of the Ḳur'ān of the end of the first century of the Hijrah, but there seems to be a certain possibility in asserting that some ancient genuine sayings of the Prophet, now found only in the early tradition, might, in the heroic times of conquest, have constituted an integral part of some old Ḳur'āns.

Among the verses quoted by Barṣalībi as Ḳur'ānic there are some that, like those mentioned above, are not found in our traditional and official Ḳur'ān, but which are attested in the tradition to have been actually uttered by the Prophet. They are treated by the author as genuine and authentic, and said by him to have been excerpted, like the rest of the verses, from the Ḳur'ān that he was using. Since they are so treated by him, and since they are found in the first column of his work, we will retain and consider them as such till fuller light dawns.

They are the following:

1° "And Adam was fashioned and was lying on the earth forty years without soul, and the angels passed by him and saw him."

This is in our days only a traditional saying and is reported by ancient and reliable authorities.[38]

Another verse of this category is the one relating to the creation of the pen before every other created thing; and it is as follows:

2° "He first created the pen of the writer, and He said to the pen, 'Walk and write'; and the pen answered, 'What shall I write?' and He said, 'Write concerning what happens till the end.'"

This is also reported by Ṭabari and others as a saying of the Prophet.[39] A special section is devoted to it in the *Waṣīyah* of the great imam Abu Ḥanīfah (fol. 20ª in the Arabic manuscript 614 of the John Rylands Library) where it is treated as an article of faith and introduced by the formula *nuḳirru*, "we profess." (Cf. Muttaḳi's *Kanz*, II, 449 [edit. Cairo].)

Of the same kind is the following verse dealing with the creation of seven heavens and seven earths:

3° "And seven heavens and seven earths were created like coverings one upon another."

A saying of the Prophet to this effect is also found in Ṭabari[40] and others.

There is another verse that is likewise treated by the author as Ḳur'ānic, but which has a pronounced traditional savor, and is undoubtedly traditional:

4° "My nation among Gentiles is like a white spot in a black ox."

The work titled *Taysīr al-Wuṣūl ila jāmi' al-Uṣūl* of Wajīh ad-Dīn as-Shaibāni (edit. Cawnpore, II, 163 in the chapter of *Faḍā'il*) contains the following saying of the Prophet: "You are among men like a black hair in a white ox, or like a white hair in a black ox." This is doubtless taken from Bukhāri (edit. Krehl, II, 338).

At the end of all these uncanonical passages we will permit ourselves the observation that we do not believe that we have yet sufficient evidence to pronounce any verdict in favor of the view deduced from our Syriac authorities to the effect that the above traditional verses formed, at an unknown period preceding the time of Ḥajjāj, an integral part of some early copies of the Ḳur'ān. We are in complete ignorance both of the true state of the Ḳur'ān at that period and of the exact provenance of the Syriac translation. In the present state of our knowledge, as we have already ventured to remark, we must follow the indications of the manuscripts and look to the future for final results, in keeping constantly in our mind the important fact that we are dealing on the one hand with a sacred text, which, at least from the middle of the eighth Christian century downward, can with great justice lay claim to an uncontestable traditional authenticity, and on the other hand, with a Metropolitan of high integrity and unquestionable erudition and scholarship, who could not possibly have, or have been, deceived in a way that was as futile as it was stupid.

We will now discuss very briefly *some* of the variants in the genuine text of the Ḳur'ān. For the sake of conciseness we will divide them into two categories: (*a*) those that arise from Arabic words, mostly Ḳur'ānic, the nature of which may to a certain extent be safely conjectured; (*b*) those that arise from an Arabic text, the nature of which we are not able to ascertain with any degree of probability. Both categories are sometimes found in one single sentence. We will illustrate each group of such variants with examples:

First Category.

In XCVI, 3–4, the Ḳur'ānic sentence "Read, and thy Lord the most generous, who *taught* by the pen" is rendered by "Read by thy Lord the noble who *is versed* in the knowledge of the pen that writes." The second member of the sentence is reminiscent of عَلِمَ for عَلَّمَ. The phrase "that writes" may be an explanatory addition on the part of the translator who wanted to stress the fact that the Syriac word *Ḳanya* that he uses is here to be understood in the sense of "pen" and not of that of any other various meanings that the Syriac vocable possesses. According to Zamakhshari (II, 1621), Ibn Zubair's copy actually read: "Who taught *writing* by the pen."

In II, 131, the Ḳur'ānic verse "And if they turn back, then they are *in a schism*" is in Syriac "And if they turn back and do not accept, they are *damned*." This seems to denote a reading شقاء for شقاق. Compare Ṭabari, *Tafsīr*, I, 444.

In XLI, 9, the sentence of the Ḳur'ān that reads: "And he placed on the earth *firm mountains* above it, and blessed it, and apportioned therein its food in four days *alike* for those who ask" is translated thus: "And He made *administrators* on the earth, and He blessed it, and apportioned its food in four days, as an *answer* to those who asked (or: ask)." The first variant seems to represent the word روساء for رواسي, and the second the word سؤال for سواء.

In II, 30, the verse of the Ḳur'ān that means "No knowledge is ours, but what Thou *hast taught* us, Thou art the knowing, the wise," is found in Syriac as: "No knowledge is ours except *the knowledge* that Thou art the knowing and the wise." The word علّمتنا seems here to have stood as علْمنا.

In XCVIII, 1–2, the Ḳur'ān says: "Those of the people of the Book and the idolaters who disbelieved did not *fall off* until there came to them the demonstration, an apostle from God reading *purified* sheets (or: rolls), in which are solid Books," while the Syriac translation is: "Those who disbelieved among the readers of the Books and the idolaters who say two, will not *come back* until a proof of apostleship from God comes to them, that we (or: he) should read the Sacred Books in which are written *demonstrating* texts." In the last part of the verse the word مطهّرة seems to have been understood as مُظْهِرة. As to the beginning of the verse the word *munfakkīn* appears to have been understood with a meaning somewhat different from that given to it by commentators (see Zamakhshari, II, 1624, etc.). The clause "who say two" is nowhere found in the Ḳur'ān, and doubtless refers to Manichœans and Magians.

In II, 1 and 4, the sentences of the Ḳur'ān that mean "A *guidance* to the pious" and "These are on *guidance* from their Lord" are rendered into Syriac by "A *guide* to the truthful" and "These are on the *guide* from their Lord." This implies reading هادى for هدى. The translation refers the two phrases to the Ḳur'ān that is the actual guide.

In XXXVII, 101, the Ḳur'ān is "O my boy, I have seen in a dream that I should sacrifice thee, *look then* what thou seest right," but the Syriac translation means "O my boy, I saw in my dream that I should sacrifice thee, and *I vowed* what I saw." Here فانظر has evidently been فأنْذُر.

In III, 43, the Ḳur'ānic sentence that means "And I will tell you what you eat and what you *store up* in your houses" is found in Syriac as "And I will tell you what you eat and what you *talk about* in your houses." Probably تذكرون for تذخرون.

In XXVI, 84, the Ḳur'ān says: "And give me a tongue of truth *among the last ones*," but the Syriac translation is: "And give me a true tongue *in the end* (or: hereafter)." Probably الآخرة for الآخرين.

Second Category.

In II, 131, the phrase of the Ḳur'ān "but God will suffice thee against them" is found in Syriac as "*But without pain and torment.* God will deliver thee from them." This seems to emanate from a totally different source.

In xcix., 8, the Ḳur'ān says: "And he who does the weight of an atom of good shall see it, and he who does the weight of an atom of evil *shall see it*," The Syriac reads for the last "shall see it" as follows: "*God shall see it*," which seems to denote a different text. Something of the restrictrive meaning of the Syriac may be found in Ṭabari (*Tafsīr*, XXX, 173–75), who quotes authorities to the effect that only the unbeliever will see in the day of Resurrection the weight of an atom of evil.

In LXIX, 17, the Ḳur'ānic "Above them on that day *shall eight* bear the throne of thy Lord" is in Syriac written as "They shall bear the throne of thy Lord above them *on the eighth day*." See about this p. 305.

In II, 34, the Ḳur'ān says: "And you have an abode and a provision *for a time*," while the Syriac has: "And you have (on the earth) a dwelling *till the end of time*." Such a meaning has much in its favor. Zamakhshari (I, 70), distinctly states that the Ḳur'ānic *ila ḥīn* means "till the day of Resurrection," in other words, "till the end of time." The same thing is also asserted by Ṭabari (*Tafsīr*, I, 192).

In XV, 39–41, the sentence of the Ḳur'ān that reads "I will make it seem seemly for them on earth, and I will seduce them all together, *save* such of Thy servants amongst them as are sincere . . . ," is found in Syriac as: "I will lead them in the bad way, and I will seduce them all *even* Thy chosen servants . . . and He said, 'The right way is that Thou shouldst have no power over my servants.'"

In LXXI, 28, the sentence of the Ḳur'ān that is generally understood to mean "And they will only bear for children such as are voluptuous and unbelievers" reads in Syriac "And of the voluptuous and licentious only unbelievers are born."

In LXI, 14, the Ḳur'ān says: "O ye who have believed, be ye the helpers of God," while the Syriac is "O ye who have believed, be ye the Nazarenes of God, the *disciples of God*." The last sentence is not found in the Ḳur'ān and, if not an interpolation, seems to emanate from a source different from our Ḳur'ān of today. The translation in this verse of the word *anṣār* by *naṣrāyé* which generally means "Nazarenes," is curious. In other passages (III, 45, etc.) the word is translated by *m'addrāné*, "helpers."

To these two categories of variants we may add a third one, and that is the possible overemphasizing by the Syrian translator of the meaning of the Ḳur'ānic passages referring to Christians. In this connection, however, we are completely in the dark, and anything new we may advance should be taken as purely conjectural. We have indeed no reason to question the fairness of the translator, who, as everyone may remark for himself, is endeavoring to give as accurate and faithful a rendering of the sacred text as could possibly be given by any ancient *Ḳāri*. What seems to establish his impartiality is his confidence that he is writing a work that is in every respect genuine, and his ignorance of the fact that what he is doing is in reality in conflict with the traditional interpretation of the *Ḳurrā'*. Indeed, in none of the following verses is the author drawing any hostile conclusion in the second column from Ḳur'ānic premises enunciated in the first column.

Following this preliminary remark we may include under this head the fact that in verses where Moses and Jesus are mentioned simultaneously in a Ḳur'ānic verse, the latter invariably precedes the former. As the contrary is the case in the Ḳur'ān one may well ask the question: Why has this anomaly occurred in the Syriac translation? Is it possible to suppose that some early Ḳur'āns were worded in a way that violated the chronological order of events? Is it not more likely to assume that this is due to the zeal of the Syrian translator for stressing the fact that Jesus is far greater than Moses? But does this obvious chronological anomaly really help any Christian cause? On the contrary, does it not weaken it in all directions? One could hardly imagine a more stupid way of furthering a Christian cause, and I do not know any Syrian writer so dull-witted as to resort to such ridiculous methods. The point, therefore, remains in the category of unsolved mysteries.

In the same category of mysteries is to be included the fact that the name of Jesus appears always in the translation as *'Īsa*, as it figures in the Arabic of the Ḳur'ān, and not *Īshō'*, as it is invariably written in Syriac; and this in spite of the fact that the names of all the Patriarchs and Prophets of the Old Testament are given in the usual Syriac, and not in the Ḳur'ānic, form; so we have *Mūshé* and not *Mūsa* (except in II, 130 and XXX, 7) for Moses, *'Amram* and not *'Imrān* for his father, *Abrāham* and not *Ibrāhīm*, and so on.

Another point that requires some explanation is the translation of XVI, 104 by: "The descent of the Holy Spirit is from thy Lord in truth to confirm the believers in Him." The Ḳur'ānic text of our days does not present any difficulty and reads: "The Holy Spirit brought it (the Ḳur'ān) from thy Lord. . . ." I consulted the commentators (Ṭabari, Zamakhshari, and Baiḍāwi), but found no variants for the beginning of the verse. Either, therefore, the Ḳur'ān lying before the translator read تنزيل for نزّله, or the translator himself deliberately read the word in this way, in order to refer the verse to the Holy Spirit instead of the Ḳur'ān. But could he really further his cause in the eyes of Muslims with such mistranslations, or rather blunders?

A much more important verse for theological controversies is IV, 169. In the first half of it the Ḳur'ān has: "Believe then in God and in his *apostles*," but the Syriac translation reads: "Believe then in God and in His *Messiah*." Both readings are in conformity with the letter and the spirit of the Ḳur'ān, but the Syriac "Messiah" is more in harmony with the particular verse that deals with Christians and their Christ, to the exclusion of any other prophet or apostle. Is it possible that an ancient Ḳur'ān exhibited ومسيحه for ورسله? Is it not also possible to suppose that the important variant is due to a slip on the part of the translator in whose mind the Christian formula "God and His Messiah" may have been constantly vibrating?

Another important passage is that dealing with the *Ḳiblah*, II, 139. The Ḳur'ān reads: "Turn thy face towards the place of worship of holiness." All the commentators[41] understand the last words to mean the mosque of the Ka'bah, and Ṭabari[42] quotes ancient traditions to the effect that the precise direction toward which prayer is to be instituted is that of the door of the Ka'bah, which, according to Burckhardt,[43] looks to the east. The Syriac translation of this passage actually reads: "Turn thy face towards the east of holiness." But we should perhaps be expecting too much from the ingenuity of the Syrian translator were we to assume that he knew the direction of the door of the Kabah and all the intricate Muslim questions affecting it.

The problem may be approached from another angle. Is it possible to suppose that a confusion has been made between the words المسجد and المشرق? This should not look utterly impossible with old and undotted Kūfi characters. Is it also possible to contend that the Christian translator wished to insinuate to his readers the fact that the Muslims also did turn, or had to turn, toward the east in their prayers, as the Eastern Christians did in that time?[44] If only we were justified in translating the Syriac word *Madhnḥa*, "east," by *Ḳiblah*, more than half of the problem would be solved. It is probably along this line that the right solution of the problem is to be sought. In the preceding discourse the author has a whole chapter on *madhnḥa* in the sense of "direction of prayer," or something equivalent to *Ḳiblah*.

Before closing this short study it would be useful to remark that unfortunately the Syriac translation has not elucidated the meaning of some difficult words found in the Ḳur'ān. So the words used for the problematic *Houris* of paradise are simply transliterated as ܚܘܪ̈ܥܝܢ (with *siāmé*), and the words

Salsabīl and *Zanjabīl* are quoted as *Salibasīl* and *Zanjibal*, respectively. So is the case with *ḥanīf* (name of the traditional religion of Abraham in the Ḳur'ān), which is once translated by *Kashshīra*, "diligent," and once omitted in the translation of the first column but registered verbally in the refutation of the second column. The word *Ṣamad* occurs as *Ṣmīdha* and *Kāfūr* as *Kafru*.

We should also note the fact that the mysterious letters found at the beginning of sūrah II appear also in the translation. As far as the names of sūrahs are concerned only four are mentioned: II, IV, V, XXIX, and this mention, in the case of two of them, may even be due to the copyist who seemed to know something about Islam.

There are some passages in which there is clear proof of a double translation,—a phenomenon found more or less frequently in almost all translations. See for instance I, 5; II, 2, 3, 5, and so on.

An explanatory word resembling the case of a double translation is also found in III, 109, and LII, 20. See also in this connection II, 2, 7 and XCVI, 3–4. We have no means of ascertaining whether such words should be fathered on Barṣalībi or on the translation of the Ḳur'ān that he was using. See what has been said above concerning LII, 20.

In the following pages we will give a literal translation of the first column of all the third discourse of Barṣalībi, with the introductory and editorial words, as found in the Syriac text that accompanies it. In this way the reader who is not familiar with Syriac will have before him every detail likely to enable him to form an independent judgment. Of the text of the second column, however, we give no translation because it is of little importance for the study of the Ḳur'ān, having been solely written for controversial purposes between Christians and Muslims; but for the benefit of Syriac scholars we have deemed it advisable to give a facsimile of the Syriac text of all the third discourse of Barṣalībi containing both the first and the second columns.

Toward the middle of his discourse, the author, in order to illustrate the queerness of some Muslim beliefs concerning biblical events, has registered the fabulous story of an individual called 'Auṣ b. 'Anaḳ who was the only human being, apart from those sheltered in Noah's ark, who was not drowned in the Flood. The copyist, evidently to save space, or perhaps also by inadvertence, has written the first half of the story in the first column and the other half in the second column of the previous page(!) He noticed his error in time and corrected it.

This 'Auṣ b. 'Anaḳ is evidently 'Auj b. 'Anaḳ or A'naḳ spoken of by Ṭabari and others.[45] Barṣalībi's Christian authority seems to have been well acquainted with Islamic history, since he records about 'Ạus the following saying: "No one remained from mankind except Noah and those who were with him in the ark, and 'Auṣ, son of 'Anaḳ, as the People of the Book say." This is an exact translation of a tradition reported by Ṭabari in the pages referred to above.

We say deliberately "Barṣalībi's Christian authority" because his own knowledge of Muslim religious and historical books seems to have been extremely meager. Here is what he writes on this subject in the preliminary note of his third discourse (see facsimile): "And 'Uthmān wrote this book (i.e., the Ḳur'ān), and it has been called the 'Uthmānic book. And the Muslims say that they have two other books apart from their Ḳur'ān: the book called *Maghāzi* in which are the deeds and the battles of Muḥammad. At the end of the other book which they call *Mukhtāra* they show the image of Muḥammad whom also they call Aḥmad." Of the innumerable Muslim works of *ḥadīth* and history, preceding the twelfth century, the author had apparently heard only of the *Maghāzi* and the *Mukhtāra*(*!*), and even these he had not seen and read; he was aware of their existence only by hearsay: "the Muslims say that they have . . ."

A man of this caliber would hardly be able to translate the Ḳur'ān, or to use the early works of tradition in a controversial work between Christians and Muslims.

A reader has added on the margins some words or phrases of the Ḳur'ān in Garshūni, often in a perpendicular direction.

There are in the Syriac text some errors of the copyist to which we wish here to draw attention in the order in which they occur in the manuscript. We refer only to the text of the first column, and even there omit the slight grammatical mistakes, most of which are found more or less frequently in almost every Syriac manuscript.

ܠܥܒܕܬܐ	read	ܠܥܒܕ̈ܬܐ (possibly)
ܘܪܫܬܐ	,,	ܕܪܫܬܐ
ܩܪܝܡ	,,	ܬܪܝܡ
ܚܒܪܘ	,,	ܚܒܪ
ܕܐܒܗ̈ܬܗܘܢ	,,	ܘܐܒܗ̈ܬܗܘܢ
ܠܒܠܝ̈ܡܬܐ (twice)	,,	ܠܒܠܩ̈ܬܐ
ܕܝܕܥ	,,	ܕܝܕܥܬܐ
ܫܠܡܬܐ	,,	ܫܠܡܗ (possibly)
ܐ̄ܚܪ̈ܢܐ	,,	ܐ̄ܚܪ̈ܢܬܐ
ܬܫܒܚܘܢ	,,	ܬܫܒܩܘܢ (possibly)
ܘܠܡܡܠܠܘ	,,	ܘܠܡܫܒܠܘ
ܕܡܬܚܘܝܢ	,,	ܕܡܬܚܪܝܢ

ܢܬܠܒܟ̈ܘܢ	read	ܢܬܠܒ̈ܟܘܢ
ܬܝܡܢܬܐ	,,	ܕܝܡܢܬܐ
ܕܡܡܠܠ	,,	ܕܡܝܠܠ
ܕܪܘܚܬܐ	,,	ܕܪܘܚܬܐ
ܡܢ ܝܡܝܢܝܢ	,,	ܡܢ ܝܡܝܢܝܢ
ܠܝ	,,	ܠܟ
ܕܡܒܒ	,,	ܕܫܒܒ
ܕܐܡܪ	,,	ܕܐܡܪܬ
ܫܠܬܐ	,,	ܕܫܠܬܐ (?)
ܚܫܡܘ	,,	ܚܫܦ
ܘܠܐ	,,	ܐܠܐ

III.

Translation

[*The italics denote the author's editorial words.*]

The third discourse of the Treatise against the Muslims. Chapter 25 in which there are special parts of the Ḳur'ān in the upper column, and a short refutation of them in the lower column, because a detailed refutation (of them) has been given in the previous chapters.

"In the name of God the merciful and the compassionate. Thanks to God, the lord of the worlds, the merciful and the compassionate, the King of the day of judgment. Thee we serve and thee we ask for help. Show us, and guide us in, the path of those on whom Thou hast lavished graces, and not of those Thou art wroth with, nor those who go astray" (I, 1–7).

"Alaph, Lām, Mīm. That book in which there is no doubt, a guide to the truthful. Those who believe in the thing that is hidden and unseen, and set up prayer, and from the victuals or rations that we gave, spend and feed; and who believe in what came down to, and was bestowed on, thee, and in what was revealed to those before thee, and believe in the hereafter. Those are on the guide[46] from their Lord (and) these are who are the prosperous. But those who disbelieved, it is one and the same for them if ye warn them; and if ye advise them they will not believe. God has set a seal upon their heart and upon their hearing, and on their sight is dimness, and for them are grievous torments. And there are people who say 'we believe in God and in the day of judgment or trial,' but they are not believers. They deceive God and the believers, but they do not deceive except themselves, and they do not preceive and feel. In their heart is sickness, and God will make them still more sick. And they have grievous torments in what they lied. And when we said to them, 'Do not evil in the earth' they say 'It is we who do right things'" (II, 1–10).

And then: "Those who disbelieved among the readers of the Books and the idolaters who say two,[47] will not come back until a proof of apostleship from God comes to them, that we[48] should read the sacred books in which are written texts which demonstrate. And the readers of the Books were not divided except after knowledge came to them. And they were not ordered to worship except God, in pure conscience, and to set up prayer and to give alms; and this is the true religion. But those of the readers of the Books who disbelieved and the idolaters are in hell forever, and they are the most wretched of all the creatures. And those who believed and did good things, they are the best of all creatures, and their reward from their Lord is the paradise of Eden" (XCVIII, 1–7).

The "Surat al-Baḳarah," that is, "cow" is the first book of theirs in which it is written thus: "Say 'We believed in God and in what came down to us and in what came down to Abraham, and Ishmael, and Isaac, and Jacob, and the Tribes, and what was brought to Jesus[49] and Moses and what was brought unto the prophets from their Lord. And we will not distinguish between them, and we are "mashlmāné"[50] to Him.' And if they believe as you have believed in Him, they are guided, and if they turn back and do not accept, they are lost; but without pain and torment; God will deliver thee from them, for He is hearer and wise" (II, 130–31).—"For each one of *the prophets* we have made a law and a different pathway, and had God pleased He would have made all of *them* one nation" (V, 52–53).

And when he wished to speak of the creation he said: "He first created the pen of the writer and he said to the pen, 'Walk and write,' and the pen answered, 'What shall I write,' and He said, 'Write concerning what happens till the end.'"[51]—"Read by the name of thy Lord who created man from a moist clay. Read by thy Lord, the noble, who is versed in the knowledge of the pen that writes"[52] (XCVI, 1–3).—"And seven heavens and seven earths were created like coverings one upon another."[53]—*And* "the earth was made in two days" (XLI, 8).—"And His throne was upon the water" (XI, 9).

And in another place[54] *he wrote*: "He made the heavens and the earth in six days, and His throne was upon the water" (XI, 9).—"Say, 'Do you disbelieve in Him who made the earth in two days, and do you make partners to Him the Lord of the worlds!' And He made administrators on the earth, and He blessed it and apportioned its food in four days, as an answer to those who ask. Then He stretched in heaven which was but smoke; and He said to heaven and to earth 'Submit either willingly or forcibly'; and they answered Him 'We come having submitted.' And He decreed and ordered seven heavens in two days, and revealed in every heaven what was necessary to it" (XLI, 8–11).—"It will not be what you will, but what God wills" (LXXVI, 30, and LXXXI, 29, etc.).

"And he who does the weight of an atom of good shall see it, and he who does the same of evil God shall see it" (XCIX, 7–8).—*And in another place he said: God* "it is who created the heavens and the earth and all therein in six days, and then He stretched on the throne" (LVII, 4).—"And they shall bear the throne of thy Lord above them on the eighth day" (LXIX, 17).

Chapter 26

From the Ḳur'ān

"The Lord said to the angels, 'I am about to establish a vicegerent in the earth,' and the angels answered, 'Wilt thou establish therein one who will do evil therein, and shed blood therein, and we have glorified Thee, Confessed Thee, and hallowed Thee'" (II, 28).—*And again he said*: "'I know what ye know not.' And He taught Adam all the names; then He showed the names to the angels and asked them, 'Declare to me these names if ye are truthful.' And the angels said, 'Glory be to Thee, no knowledge is ours except the knowledge that Thou art the knowing and the wise. And God said to Adam, 'Declare to them these names.' And God said to the angels, 'Did I not say to you that I know the secrets of the heavens and of the earth, and I know what you wish to say, and what is still in you before it is said?' And when we said to the angels, 'Adore Adam,' all adored him save only Satan, who refused and was too proud and became one of the unbelievers. And we said to Adam, 'Enter thou and thy wife into Paradise, and eat what you want and wish to eat; but do not draw near this tree or ye will be of the transgressors.' And Satan deceived them and drove them out, and we said to them, 'Go down together, one of you the enemy of the other, and in the earth there will be a dwelling for you till the end of the time'" (II, 29–35).

"When we warned Adam from the beginning concerning the commandment, he forgot; and we did not find the warning in him. And when we said to the angels, 'Adore Adam,' they adored, save Satan, who became recalcitrant. And we said to Adam, 'Lo, he is a foe to thee and to thy wife. Take care that he should not drive you out of Paradise or thou wilt be wretched. And thou hast not to be hungry there, nor naked, nor thirsty; and thou wilt be in happiness (and immune) from heat and pain.' But Satan deceived him and beguiled him and said to him, 'I shall tell thee about the tree that it will be immortal, and a kingdom that shall not wane or perish'" (XX, 114–18).

And: "When thy Lord said to the angels, 'I am about to create a man out of clay; and when I have fashioned him, and breathed into him of my spirit, then fall ye down and adore him.' And all adored him, save Satan, and he became of the unbelievers" (XXXVIII, 71–74).—"That future abode, we have made it for those who do not seek haughtiness nor do evil in this world" (XXVIII, 83).—"'O Satan, what prevented thee from adoring whom I have fashioned with my hands? Hast thou been too big with pride, or hast thou been amongst the exalted?' Satan said, 'I am better, because Thou hast created me from fire, and him Thou hast fashioned from clay'" (XXXVIII, 75–77).—"And when we created man from hard clay and from putrid mud" (XV, 26).

"And the spirits that dwell in the air,[55] which we have created before from sharp wind" (XV, 27).—"And Adam was fashioned, and was lying on the earth forty years without soul, and the angels passed by him and saw him."[56]—"A long time passed over the man, and there was nothing worth remembering about him" (LXXVI, 1).—*And Satan said*: "O Lord, because Thou hast deceived me I will direct them in the wrong way, and I will deceive them all, even Thy chosen servants; and He said, 'This is the right way that thou shouldst have no authority over my servants, save over those who follow thee or such as go astray; and hell is the trysting-place of all of them'" (XV, 39–43. Cf. XXXVIII, 71–85).

"He said, 'For Thou hast deceived me, I will lie in wait for them in the straight path; then I will approach them from before their hands and from behind them, from their right and from their left, and Thou shalt not find many of them uttering thankfulness.' He said, 'Go forth therefrom, despised and expelled for those who follow thee; I will fill hell with you together'" (VII, 15–17).—"And Satan made their deeds and their work pleasing to them" (XXVII, 24; XXIX, 37).—"And when we sent Noah to his people, he remained and was among them nine hundred and fifty years; and the deluge overtook them while they were unjust" (XXIX, 13).

Chapter 27

"And Noah said, 'My Lord, leave not upon the earth one of the unbelievers; if Thou shouldst leave them, they will lead astray Thy servants, and of the voluptuous and licentious only unbelievers are born. My Lord, pardon me and my father and my mother, and whomsoever enters my house believing, and (pardon) the believers men and women, and do not increase to the unjust except destruction'" (LXXI, 27–29).

"And Noah cried to his son who had gone aside, 'O my boy, come with us into the ark, and be not of the unbelievers,' and he said, 'I will climb a mountain and I will be saved from the water'; and Noah said, 'There is no one that can be saved from His command except the one on whom He may have mercy';[57] and the waters came between them" (XI, 44–45).—*(And he said of Noah's wife that she was of the unbelievers like the wife of Lot,*[58] *and that she was drowned in water because she did not go into the ark,*[59] *and also that one of Noah's sons did not go into the ark and was drowned.*[60] *And he further wrote:* "And if thou art in doubt of that which we *God* have sent down unto thee, ask those that were before you" (X, 94).—*He said*: "The Book has come down to thee in the justice and truth of that which was before it, and from the Torah and the Gospel; and the Torah and the Gospel were sent as guides to men" (III, 2).

"What your Apostle orders you do (it), and what I order you not to do, desist from" (LIX, 7).—"And when thy Lord took from the children of Adam, out of their loins, a grain for their children, and God made them bear witness against themselves and said, 'Am I not your God'? And they said, 'Yea, we bear witness,' lest you should say, 'Our fathers made partners to God, and we were but (their) children after them: wilt Thou then destroy us for what the vaindoers did'" (VII, 171–72).—"And when we took from the prophets their compact and their covenant, from thee and from Noah, and Abraham, and Jesus,[61] and Moses son of 'Amram, and took from them a rigid and truthful compact" (XXXIII, 7).

Chapter 28

"And when we showed Abraham all the heavenly Kingdoms and those of the earth that he should not be of those who doubt. But when the night fell on him and he saw a star he said, 'This is my Lord'; and after it had set he said, 'I love not those that go and come.' And when he saw the moon rising and shining he said, 'This is my Lord,' but when he saw it setting he said, 'If God does not become my guide I shall be of the people who err.' And when he saw again the sun rising from its place he said, 'This is my Lord, this is the greatest'; and after it had set he said, 'O people, I am clear of the partner that you are associating with God; I have turned my face to Him who commanded and created the heavens and the earth, and I am diligent to Him, and I am not of those who associate others with God'" (VI, 76–78).

"And when we bestowed on Abraham revelation before, we knew him. And he said to his father and to the people of his father, 'What is this image which you continually worship?' And they said, 'We found our fathers worshipping it.' He said to them, 'Both you and your fathers have been in an error that is obvious.' They said to him, 'Hast thou brought the truth to us, or art thou but of those who jest?' He said to them, 'Nay, but your Lord is Lord of the heavens and the earth and their maker; and I am one of the witnesses; and by God I will plot against[62] your idols that you took back from me. And he brake them all except the largest of the images, that they may not go back to it (or: him) and search (for it?). And the idolaters said, 'Who has done this with our gods? because he is of the evildoers.' They said, 'We heard a youth whom they remembered, Abraham by name.' They said, 'Bring him before the eyes of every man that they may haply bear witness.' They said to Abraham, 'Was it thou who did this to our gods, O Abraham? And Abraham answered them, 'It was the largest of them that did this to them, but ask them if they can answer.' The idolaters thought then in their mind and said, 'You are the wrongdoers of yourselves.' And then they bent their heads to the earth. And they said to Abraham, 'Thou knowest; are these able to speak?' And Abraham answered and said to them, 'Will ye serve, beside God, what cannot profit you nor harm you? fie upon you and what ye serve beside God, while you do not see it.' And the idolaters got angry and said, 'Burn him and you will find your gods, if ye are going to do so.' And God said to the fire, 'Be thou cold in safety over Abraham, and wish him good.' And we contended for him, and we delivered Abraham and Lot to the land which we blessed for the worlds, and we bestowed upon Abraham, Isaac and Jacob, his grandson, and all of them we made righteous from the body" (XXI, 52–72).

"But after the time of the promise that his father made to him, and after it was made manifest to him that he was an enemy to God, he freed himself from him" (IX, 115).—"My Lord, grant me wisdom, and mix me with the righteous, and give me an honest tongue in the hereafter (or: in the end), and make me of the heirs of the Paradise of pleasures, and pardon my father who was of those who err" (XXVI, 83–85).—"I am going to my Lord, and He will guide me. O my Lord, grant me sons from the righteous; and we gave him glad tidings of a submissive boy. And when Abraham reached the spot, while walking he said to his son, 'O my boy, I have seen in my dream that I should sacrifice thee, and I vowed what I saw.' Then his son answered him, 'O my father, do what thou hast been bidden, and thou wilt find me, if God wills, one of the patient.'

"And when he made his son lie on his cheek upon his side we called, 'O Abraham, thou hast verified and fulfilled thy dream, and we are the rewarders of those who do good things; but if this deed were to be done, a great wrong would be done.' And we ransomed his son with a mighty sacrifice, and we left his son for him to the future generations. And peace be upon Abraham, for we have rewarded him with a reward that is due to the righteous; and he is one of our believing servants. And we gave him glad tidings of Isaac, a prophet from the righteous; and we blessed him and Isaac, and of their seeds is one who is righteous and one who is an obvious wronger of himself" (XXXVII, 97–113).

In Surat al-Baḳarah God said: "We gave Moses the book and we followed him up with the prophets, and we gave Jesus,[63] son of Mary, the truth, and we fortified him with the Holy Spirit. And when the prophets came to you, you were proud in your souls without pity, and some of them you killed and some of them you charged with lying" (II, 81).—*The followers of Muḥammad said*: "We believed in God, and in what He revealed to us and in what He revealed to Abraham, to Ishmael, to Isaac, to Jacob, and to the Tribes, and in what was brought to Jesus[64] and to Moses, and in what was brought unto the prophets. We have not distinguished between any one of them, and we are faithful to them" (II, 130).—"It is the baptism of God, and whose baptism is better than God's, and we worship Him" (II, 132).

Chapter 29

In the same "Cow" God said: "These apostles whom we sent, some of them are higher than the others; of them is one to whom God spake; but Jesus,[65] son of Mary, we gave him the knowledge of truth, and fortified him by the Holy Spirit" (II, 254).—*In the "Table"*: "And we announced to Abraham Jesus,[66] son of Mary, and we sent him after the prophets in order that he might confirm that which was given before him in the Torah; and we brought him the Gospel wherein there is the tradition of light, in order to confirm what was given before him in the Torah; and to guide and admonish the faithful" (V, 50).—*God said:* "O readers of the Books! Ye rest on nought until ye confirm the Torah and the Gospel, and all things given in them by their Lord" (V, 72).

And God said to Muḥammad: "We sent many prophets before thee, the names of some of whom we have told thee, and of some of whom we have not told thee; and no prophet that I sent was ever able to work miracles except by my order; and when my order came, he decided with truth" (XL, 78).—*And Muḥammad said*: "I believed in every Book which has been given by God, and I am bidden to put straightness[67] between you; our God is your God. We have no argument with you, because to Him we will eventually go" (XLII, 14).—*Muḥammad said*: "I said nothing from the apostles, and I do not know what will be done with me or with you, and I am but a warner and a preacher" (XLVI, 8).—*And God said*: "O ye who have believed, be ye the Nazarenes of God, the disciples of God" (LXI, 14).—"And a party of the children of Israel believed, and a party did not believe; and we aided those who believed against their enemies, and when the morning came, they ruled over them" (LXI, 14).

And the angel said to Mary: "God gives thee the glad tidings of a Word from Him whose name is the Messiah Jesus,[68] son of Mary, living in this world and in the world to come; and he is of those who are near (to God). And he shall speak to people even when in the cradle, and in the assembly he is of the righteous. And Mary said, 'How can I have a son, when man has not touched me?' And he said to her, 'Thus God creates what He pleaseth; and when He decrees a thing He says: Be and it is; and He will teach him the Book, and the wisdom, and the Torah, and the Gospel; and he shall be an apostle to the children of Israel, and he shall say to them, "I have brought to you a command from your Lord that I will create from clay something in the form of a bird, and I blow thereon, and it shall become a bird by God's command; and I will heal those affected with elephantiasis and the lepers; and I will bring the dead to life, by God's command; and I will tell you what you eat, and what you talk about in your houses. In these there is knowledge and miracle if ye be believers"'" (III, 40–43).

And God said to Jesus:[69] "I will make thee die and take thee up to me, and I will clear thee of those who disbelieved, and will make those who believed in thee and followed thee above those who disbelieved in thee, in the day of Resurrection. Then you will come to me, and I will decide between you concerning all that about which you disagreed. And as for those who disbelieved in thee, I will punish them with grievous and bitter punishment in this world and the next, and they shall have none to help them. But as for those who believed and did good things, He will pay them their reward, and God loves not the unjust" (III, 48–50).

And in Sūrah of Women "Nisā'" the Jews say: "We have killed the Messiah, Jesus,[70] son of Mary, the apostle of God; but they did not kill him and they did not crucify him, but in appearance it appeared to them in this way. And those who differed in his story are in doubt. But God took him up with Him, and God is mighty and wise. For there shall not be one of the holders of the Books but shall believe in him before he dies; and in the day of Resurrection he shall be a witness against them" (IV, 156–57).—"The Messiah, son of Mary, the apostle of God, the Word and Spirit from Him, and He sent it to Mary; believe then in God and in His Messiah" (IV, 169).—*Jesus*[71] *said*: "Peace be upon me the day I was born, and the day I die, and the day I shall be raised up alive." *And God said*: "The word of Jesus[72] is the word of truth concerning which[73] they dispute" (XIX, 34–35).

"Those who repent and believe and act aright, these I shall admit into the Garden, and I shall not wrong them in anything; and they shall not hear there the voice of fear and fright, but that of joy and of peace; and they have therein their provision, morning and evening (XIX, 61–63).—*And God said that Mary*: "guarded her virginity, and we breathed into her[74] our spirit, and we made her and her son a sign unto the worlds. This is your religion and it is one religion, I am your Lord, and serve me" (XXI, 91–92).—*And God said*: "Mary, daughter of 'Amram, who guarded her virginity, and we breathed into her[75] our spirit, and she believed in God and in His Book, and became of the saints" (LXVI, 12).—*And God said to Muḥammad*: "The descent of the Holy Spirit is from thy Lord in truth, to confirm the believers in Him" (XVI, 104).—*And God said to Muḥammad*: "If they ask thee concerning the Spirit say to them, 'He is from my Lord, and I have been given but little from[76] His knowledge" (XVII, 87).

Chapter 30

Further excerpts from the Ḳur'ān, from various places.

About whom who studies their book without knowledge he said thus: "Amongst men there is one who wrangles concerning God without knowledge or straightforwardness or an illuminating book; and he turned from that to stray away from the path of God;[77] for him there is disgrace in this world, and in that day of Resurrection we will make him taste the torment of burning" (XXII, 8–9).—*And he said*: "Come to our word and yours which is (laid down) plainly, that we will serve God alone" (III, 57).—"They disbelieve who say, 'God is Trinity'" (cf. V, 77).[79]—*And Muḥammad said*: "My nation among Gentiles is like a white spot in a black ox."[79]—*If they ask thee concerning signs,* "say to them, 'Signs are with God'" (VI, 109).—"Naught hindered us from sending signs, save that those of old said they were lies" (XVII, 61).

"And the unbelievers say 'Unless a sign come down upon him from his Lord.' Thou art nothing but a warner, and every nation has its guide" (XIII, 8).—"The *Ṣmīdha* is one; He begets not and He is not begotten, and there is no one similar or like unto Him" (CX, 1–4).—"O prophet, we have made lawful (for thee) thy wives whose dowry thou hast given, and every thing that thy right hand possesses from what God has lavished on thee, and the daughters of thy paternal uncle and the daughters of thy paternal aunts, and the daughters of thy maternal uncle and the daughters of thy maternal aunts who fled[80] with thee, and any believing woman if she gives herself up exclusively to the Prophet, if the Prophet desires to approach her; she is given to thee in a special manner to the exclusion of all the believers. We know what we ordained for them concerning their wives and what their right hand possesses, that there should be no blame on thee; and God permits and forgives. Put off whomsoever thou wilt of them and take with thyself whomsoever thou wilt, and if thou desirest to take one of those thou hast divorced, thou wilt be without blame if thou takest her" (XXXIII, 49–51).

"Those who disbelieve in God and His apostles desire to make a distinction between God and His apostles and say, that they believe in part and disbelieve in part, and desire to take a midway course between this and that" (IV, 149).—"Had they maintained the Torah and the Gospel, what has come down to them from their Lord, they would have eaten from above their heads and from below their feet. Among them is a righteous nation, and the majority of them profess badly" (V, 70).—"Had the holders of the Books believed it would have been better for them. There are believers among them, but the majority of them are wicked" (III, 106).—"You pervert the words from their places" (IV, 48; V, 16).—*Jesus said:* "Who will be my helper with God? And the apostles said, 'We are the helpers with God'" (LXI, 14; III, 45).—"O ye who have been given the Books, believe in what we have brought down, for it confirms that which you have with you" (IV, 50).

"And if thou art in doubt of that which we have brought down to thee, ask those who read the Books before thee; because the truth has come to thee from thy Lord, be not of those who are in doubt" (X, 94).—"And those to whom the Books were given did not contradict one another until after knowledge came to them, through their mutual bickering" (III, 16).—"On that day neither man nor demon[81] shall be asked about his crime" (LV, 39).—"Truly we will question them, one and all, about what they were doing before" (XV, 92–93).—"We have forgotten you as you have forgotten this day" (XXXII, 14; XLV, 33).—"There is nothing hidden from thy Lord" (III, 4, etc.).[82]—"This is the day in which you may not speak" (LXXXVII, 35).—"In the day of Resurrection you will dispute with one another before your Lord" (XXXIX, 32).—"On that day we will seal their mouths" (XXXVI, 65).—*And he said further*: "Their tongues shall bear witness against them" (XXIV, 24).—"There is no relationship between *men* on that day nor shall they ask one another anything" (XXIII, 103).—"The day when he shall flee from his brother and his mother and his father" (LXXX, 34–35).—"And they began to question each other" (XXXVII, 27).

"Any of your women who committed adultery, if they raise against them four witnesses about it,—the women such as these are to be kept in houses until death takes them or God shall make for them a dissolution" (IV, 19).—"The adulterer and the adulteress, scourge each of them with a hundred stripes" (XXIV, 2).—"And while he was in the high storey he drew near and hovered, as of the[83] angle of a bow, or nigher still, and he inspired his servant what he inspired him, and will ye dispute with him on what he saw? And he saw him on another descent towards the Garden, near the tree, and the sight swerved not nor wandered" (LIII, 7–17).—"And when he came to it he was called from the right side of the valley, in the blessed watery plain, out of the tree, 'O Moses, I am the God of the worlds'" (XXVIII, 30).

And Jesus said to the Jews: "I will create for you from clay something in the form of a bird, and I blow thereon, and it shall become a bird by God's command" (III, 43).—"Naught precluded men from believing when guidance came to them save their saying 'Has God sent a man as His apostle?' say, 'Were there angels on the earth walking in quiet, we had sent them an angel as an apostle'" (XVII, 96–97).—"The good luck of our Lord was raised, because He possesses neither consort nor son" (LXXII, 3).—*And*: "He knows the hidden things, and no one knows the hidden things of His knowledge, save such apostle as is chosen by Him. He sends a guard before him and after him, that he may know that they have delivered the apostleship of their Lord" (LXXII, 26–28).—"Do ye not see how God has created the seven heavens in stories, and has set therein the moon for light" (LXXI, 14).

When God swears, He says thus: "I swear by the Lord of the easts and the wests that I am able" (LXX, 40).—"Bring the unjust and all who follow them and all what they used to serve, and direct them to the way of hell" (XXXVII, 22–23).—"I did not say; if I had said, Thou wouldst have known it, because there is nothing hidden from Thee" (V, 116).—"Then we made *the man* a new creation; blessed be God the best of creators" (XXIII, 14).—"And we have wedded them to wives 'ḥur'ain'" (XLIV, 54).—"And we sent to them abundantly fruits and meat such as they like" (LII, 22).—"And round them shall go their sons who resemble beautiful pearls" (LII, 24).

And: "Garden, whose breadth is as the breadth of the heavens and of the earth" (LVII, 21).—"No one understands it but God."[84]—"Righteousness is not that ye turn your faces towards the east or the west, but righteousness is this: that one believes in God and in the last day" (II, 172).—"Turn thy face towards the east[85] of sacredness; wherever ye be, turn your faces towards it" (II, 139).—"God's are the easts and the wests; and towards whatever directions you turn your faces, there is the face of God, because God is broad and knowing" (II, 109).—"If all men gathered together from the East as far as the

West to change one letter from the words of God, they will not be able (to do it)."[86]

"Is it thou who didst say to men, 'Know me and my mother as two gods, and serve us instead of God" (V, 116).—*From the Sūrah of the "Spider"*: "Do not dispute with the holders of the Books except with the nicest of words" (XXIX, 45).—"Do good works because God loves those who do good works" (V, 94).—"And they say, 'We will not believe in thee until He make a fountain gush forth for thee from the earth; or there be made for thee a garden of palms and grapes, and thou make rivers flow round it; or thou make heaven to fall as thou saidst; or thou bring us God or receiving angels; or there be made for thee a house of gold; or thou climb up into the heaven. And we will not believe in thee until thou bring down to us a book from heaven that we may read.' Say to them, 'Praise be to my Lord! am I anything but a man messenger?[87] What precluded men from believing when guidance came to them . . .'" (XVII, 92–96).—"Say *to them, God* is a sufficient witness between me and you that I am His messenger to you" (cf. XI, 2; XIII, 43; XLVI, 7, 8).—"And when they see a sign they doubt and say, 'This is obvious sorcery'" (XXXVII, 14).[88]

"Mary, daughter of 'Amram, who guarded her private parts, and we breathed therein of our spirit, and she verified the words of her Lord and his Book and was of the devout" (LXVI, 12).—"O sister of Aaron, thy father was not a bad man, nor thy mother a blasphemer" (XIX, 29).—"The heavens *are* rolled up in His right hand" (XXXIX, 67).—*And* "the hands *of God* are outspread" (V, 69).—*And* "the hands of God are above their hands" (XLVIII, 10).—"And heaven—we have built it with hands" (LI, 47).—*And* "the good luck of the Lord is high" (LXXII, 3).—*And* "He is sitting on a throne."[89]—And "He ascended to heaven while it was but smoke" (XLI, 10).

"I do not swear by this land, and thou dwellest in this land; and the Father and the one who is begotten of Him. We have created man in anger"[90] (XC, 1–4).—"The Holy Spirit brought down from the Lord grace and light."[91]—*And* "God said, 'O Jesus,[92] son of Mary, remember my grace towards thee and towards thy mother, when I fortified thee with the Holy Spirit'" (V, 109).—"Are unbelievers who say 'God is the third of three" (V, 77).—"Of the holders of the Books there is a nation, *that is to say a community*, who stand all the night and recite the miracles of God; and they adore, and believe in, God, and in the last day, and bid good things and forbid bad things, and do charitable things with ease; and they are righteous" (III, 109–10).

"The Jews said, 'God's hands are fettered'; the hands of Jews are fettered, and they are cursed for what they said" (V, 69).—"*The Jews'* disbelief in God's signs, and their killing of the prophets undeservedly, and their saying, that *their* hearts are uncircumcised,—nay, (God) has stamped their unbelief on their *hearts*" (IV, 154).—"And thou wilt find the nearest in love to those who have believed to be those who say, 'We are Christians'; and among them there are priests and monks, and they will not be proud" (V, 85).—"There is nothing that is moist nor aught that is dry which is not known in this Book" (VI, 59).—"Even the weight of a grain of mustard does not escape from thy Lord, in heavens and in earth; and there is nothing, small or great, that is not known in this Book" (XXXIV, 3).—"And if thou art in doubt of that which we have brought down unto thee, ask those who read the Books before thee" (X, 94).

A garden whose breadth is as the breadth of the heavens and the earth" (LVII, 21; III, 127).—"In it are rivers of water without corruption, and rivers of milk the taste whereof has not changed, and rivers of wine delicious and pleasing to those who drink it, and rivers of honey clarified, and there they have of all fruits" (XLVII, 16–17).—"Eat and drink with pleasure for that which you have done; and reclining on couches, *that is to say 'takhthā*,'[93] which are put in rows; and we have wedded them to wives 'ḥur'ain'" (LII, 19–20).—"And we have abundantly sent them fruits and meat such as they like" (LII, 22).—"And round them shall go their boys who resemble beautiful pearls" (LII, 24).

"And for him who fears the standing up before his Lord are gardens twain in which there are two flowing springs in which there are two pairs of every fruit" (LV, 46–52).—"In them are women beautiful in sight, whom no corporeal nor spiritual being has approached" (LV, 56).—*And there in the Garden*: "fruits such as they choose, and meat of fowl as they desire and women 'ḥur'ain' who resemble beautiful pearls" (LVI, 20–22).—"The righteous shall drink *in the Garden* of a cup the mixture of which is Kafru[94] (LXXVI, 5).—"And flagons of silver made with symmetry; and they shall be given to drink in the *Garden* a cup the mixture of which is Zangibla;[95] and there is in it a spring called Salibasīla;[96] and there shall go round them boys continually; and when thou seest them thou wilt think them scattered pearls" (LXXVI, 16–20).—"Praise be to the One who hath made good His promise to us, and hath given us the earth as inheritance; for we dwell in the Garden wherever we please" (XXXIX, 74).

Our Dissertation against the Arabs, that is, Muslims, has extended as far as here. We have refuted their objection concerning the Trinity and the Incarnation of the Son, and by proofs taken from nature and from philosophical books we have demonstrated our truth; then we have confuted them in many points from their own book; after that we have arranged in one systematic division parts of the Ḳur'ān, which has been translated from their language into Syriac, and we have shortly refuted it in the column that is below it; because in the previous chapters we have given a detailed refutation. The time has now come to put an end to our labor. Let anyone who reads and understands, profits and makes others profit, pray for Mar Dionysius the stranger, who is Jacob Barṣalībi of Milīṭīni, Metropolitan of Amed.

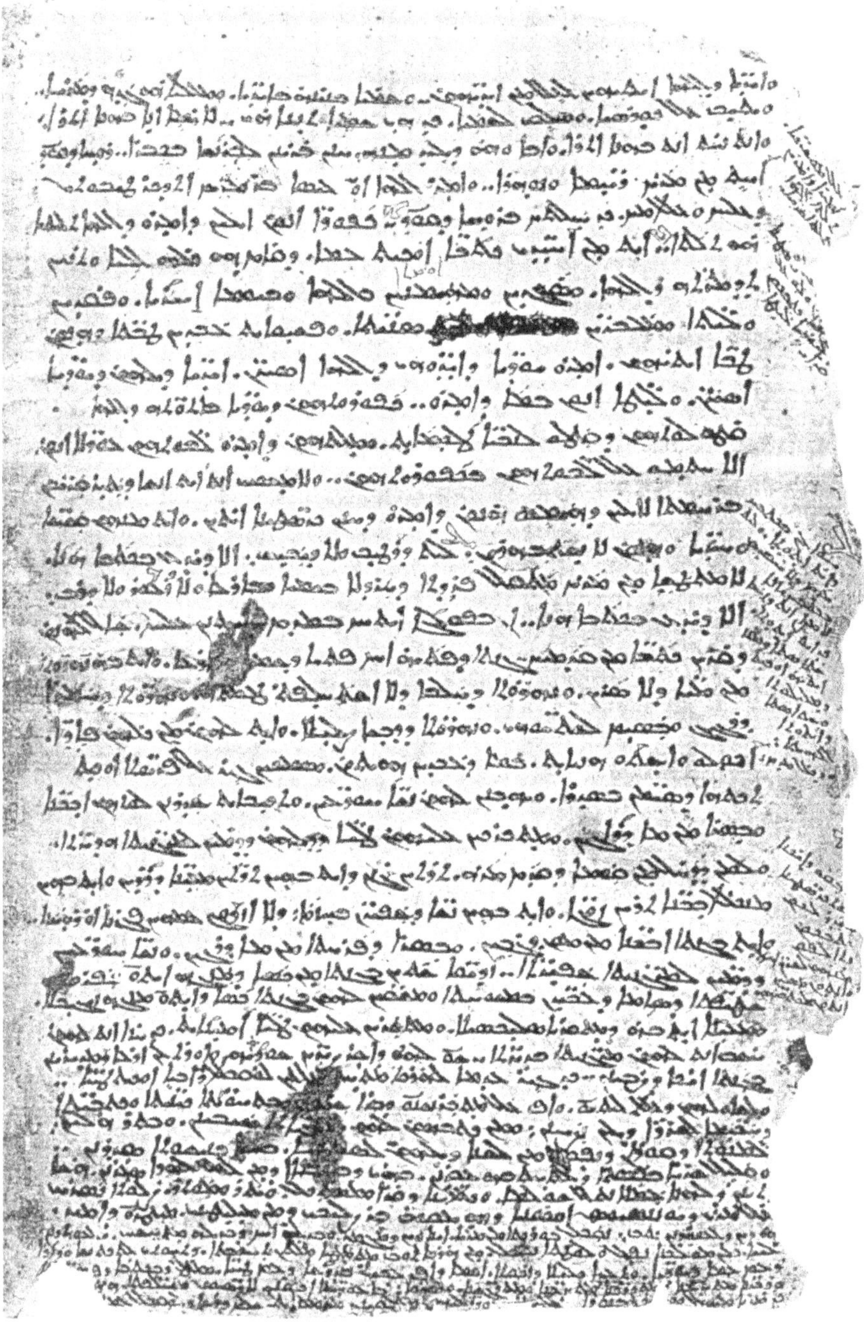

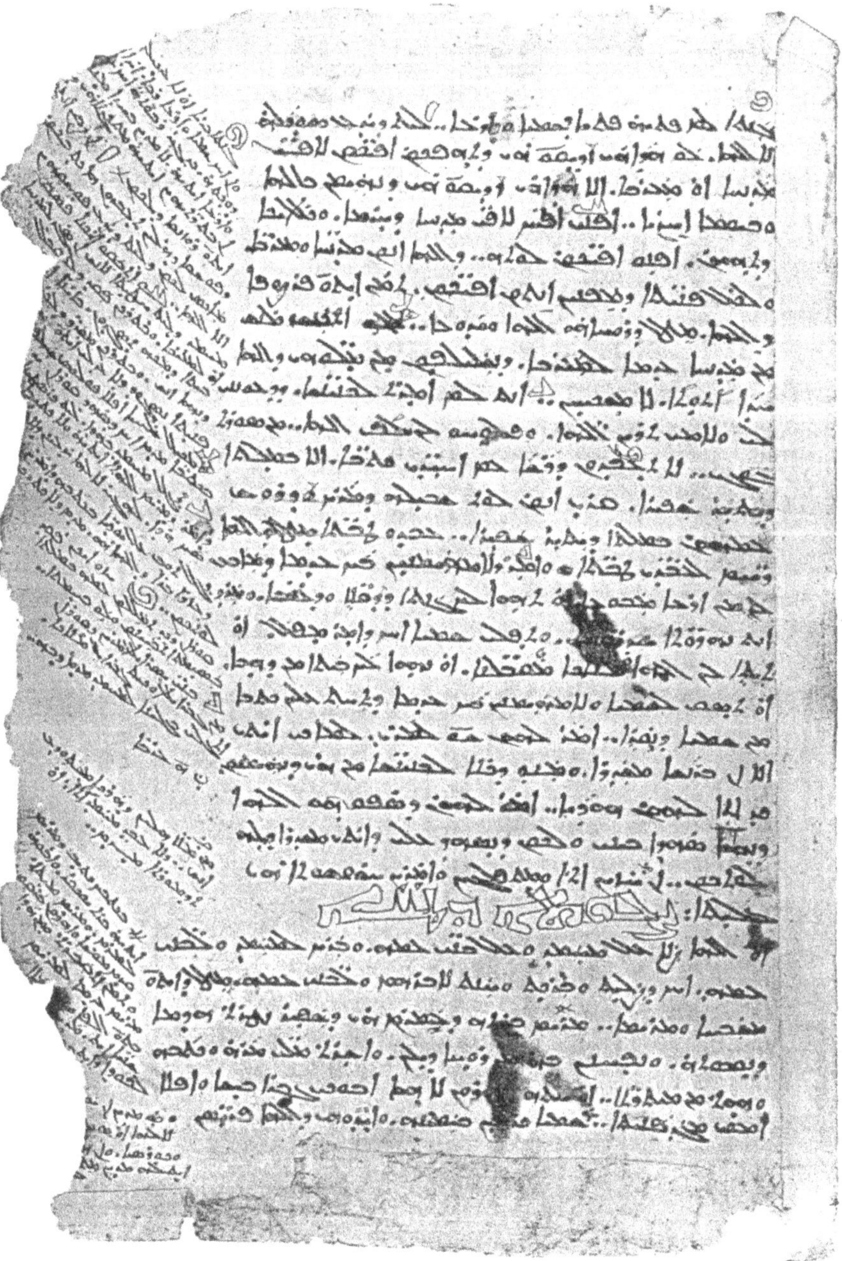

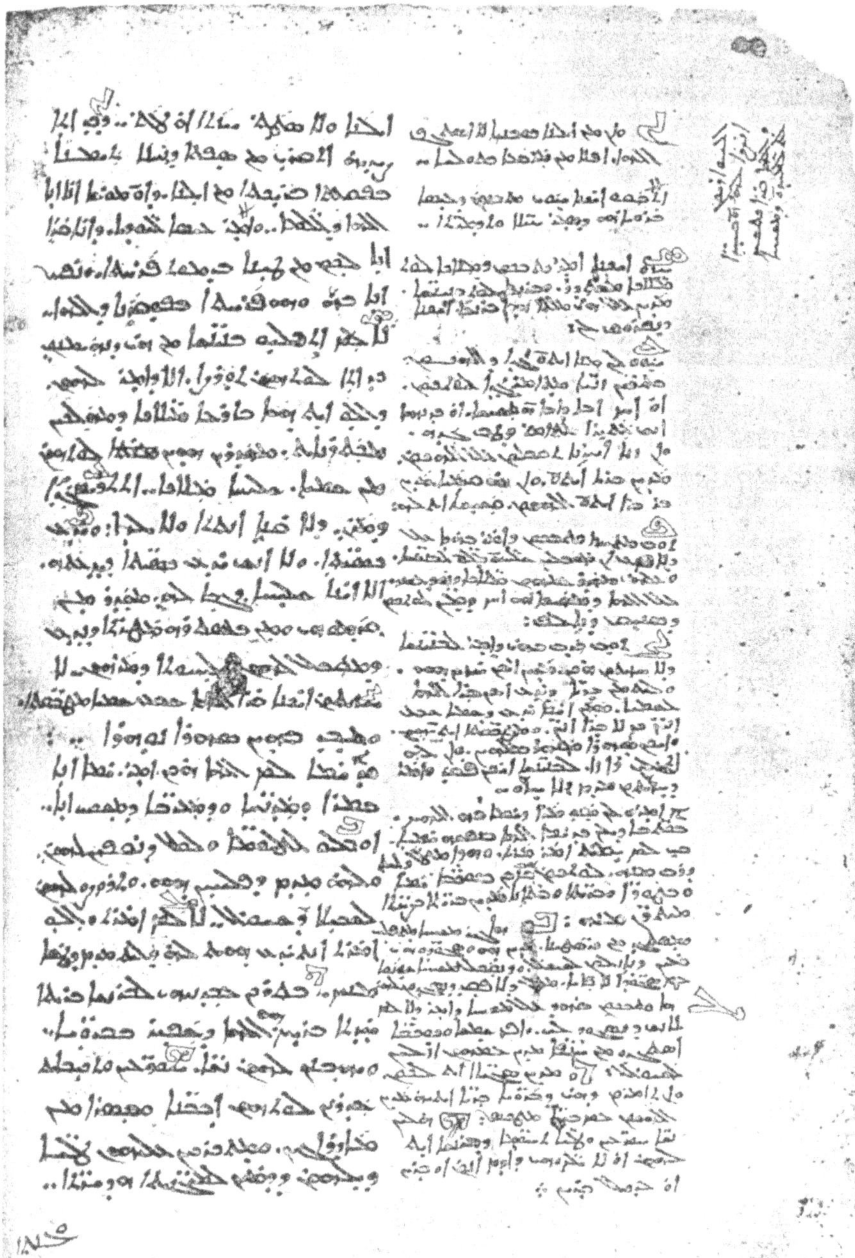

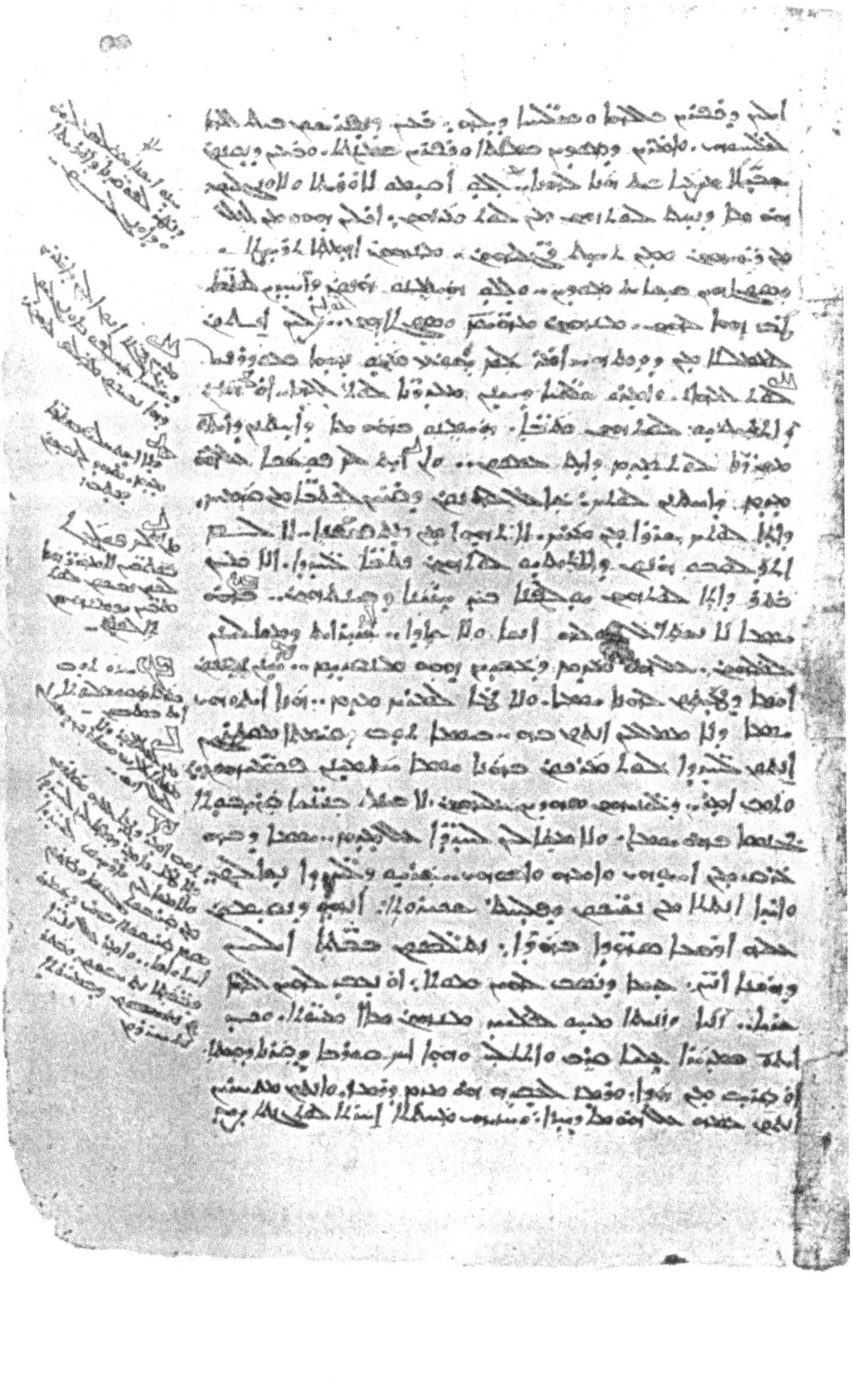

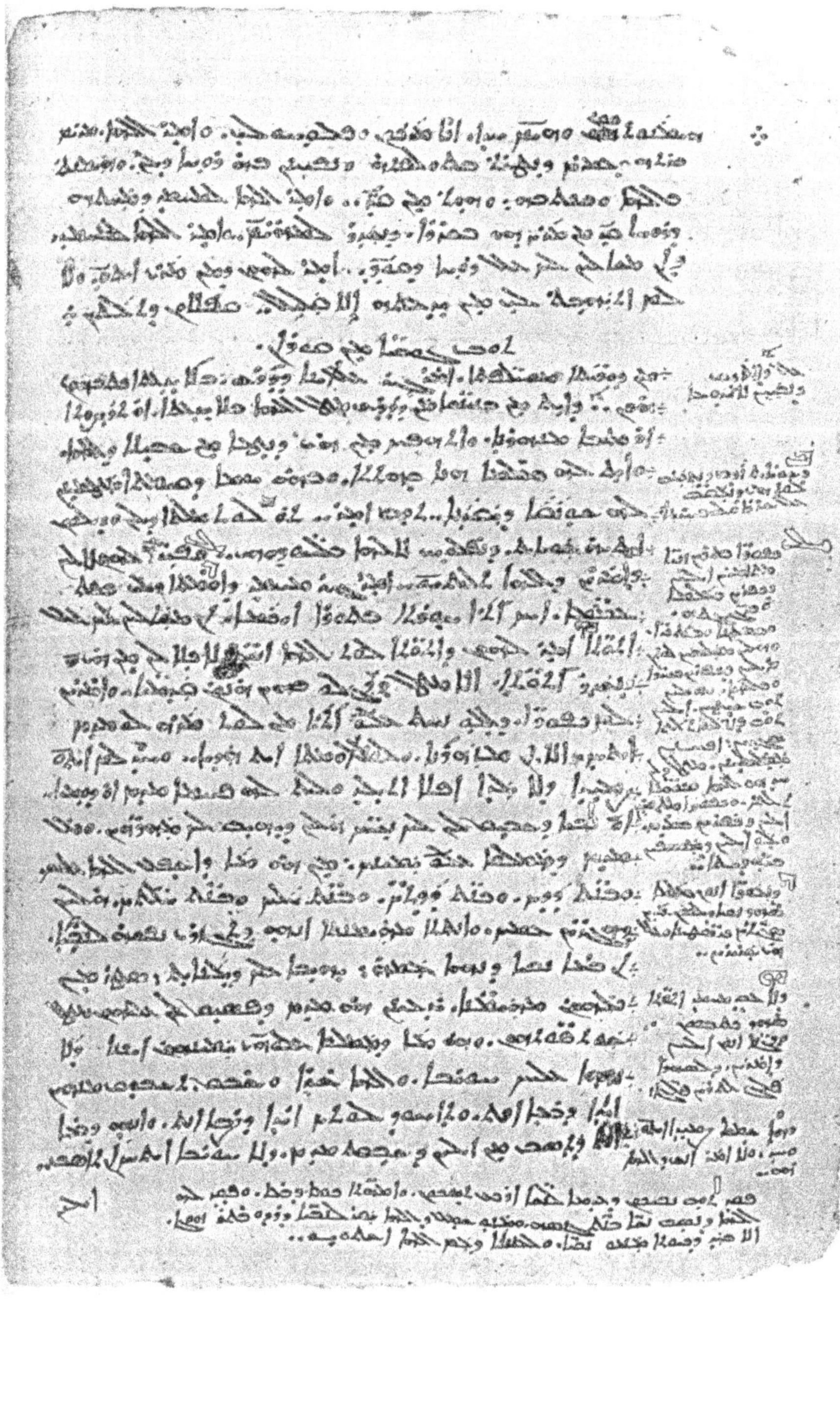

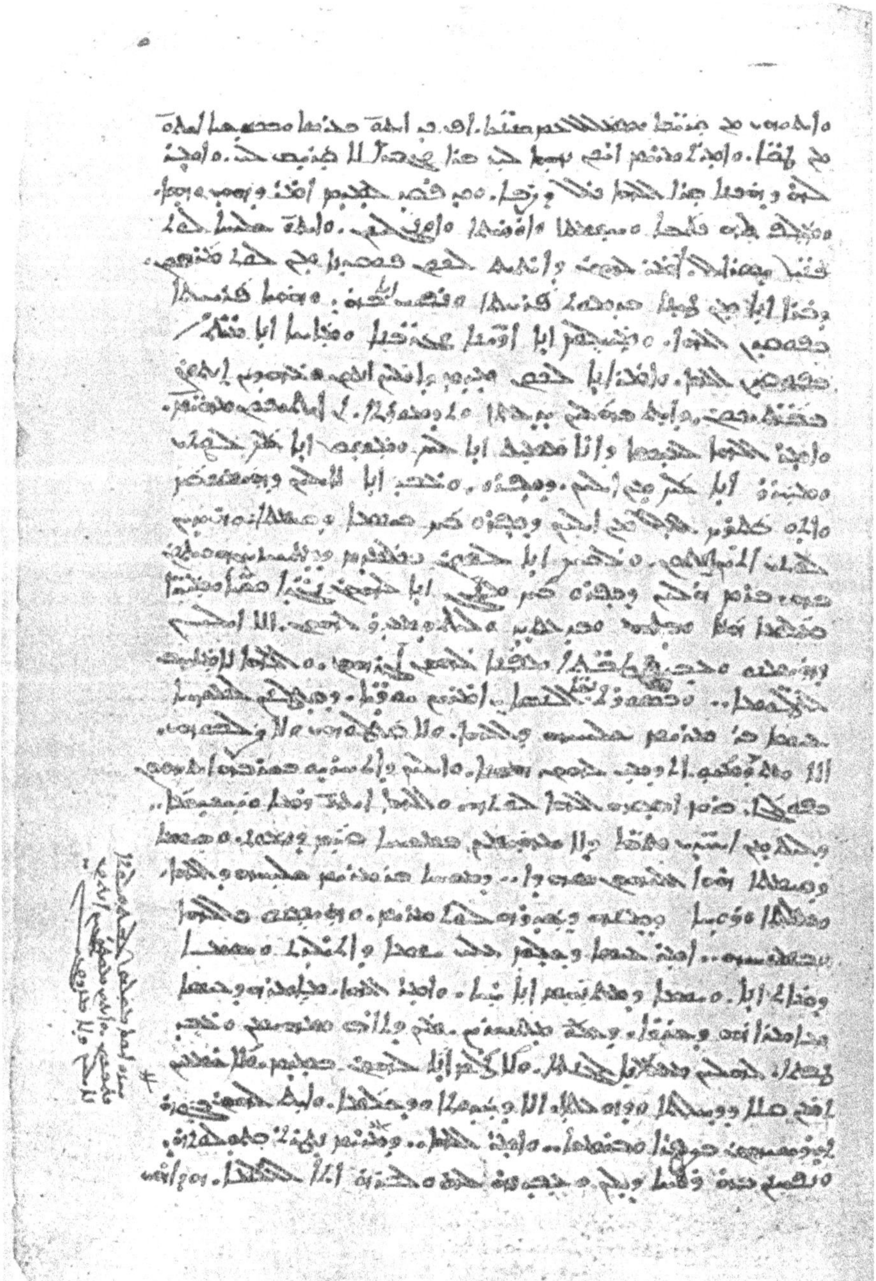

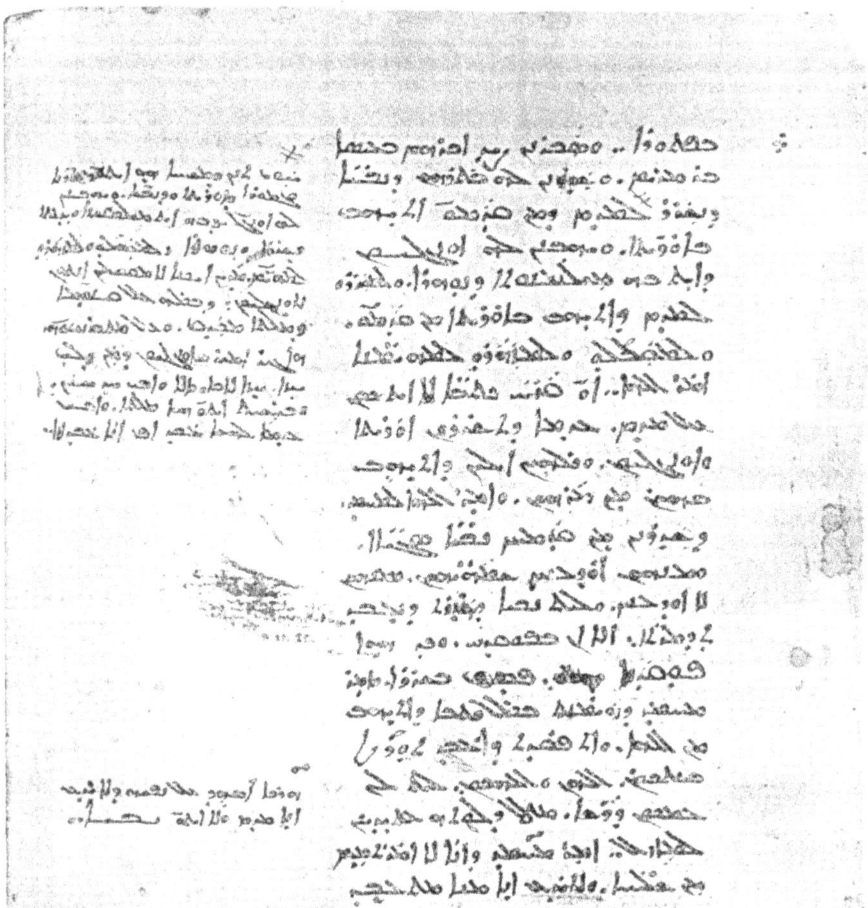

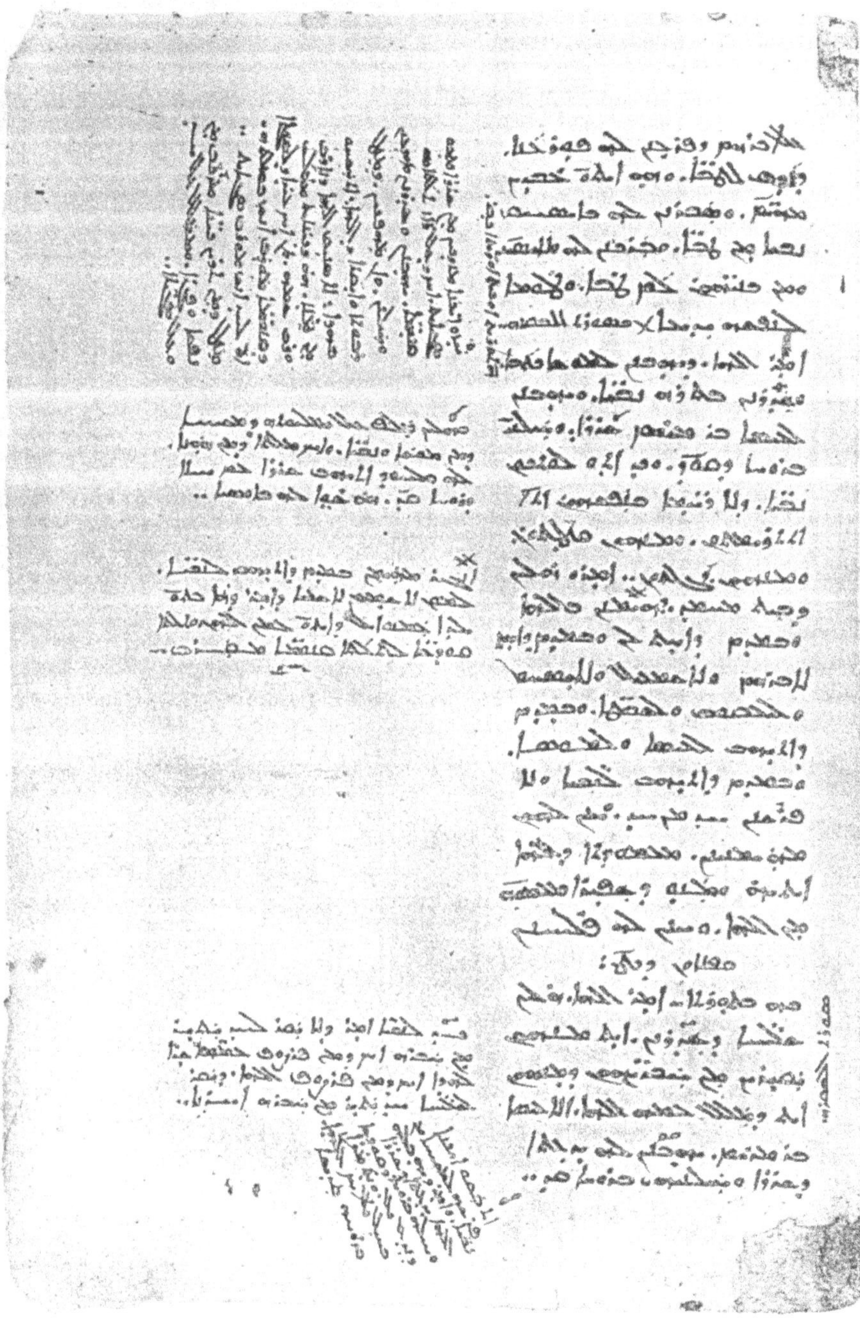

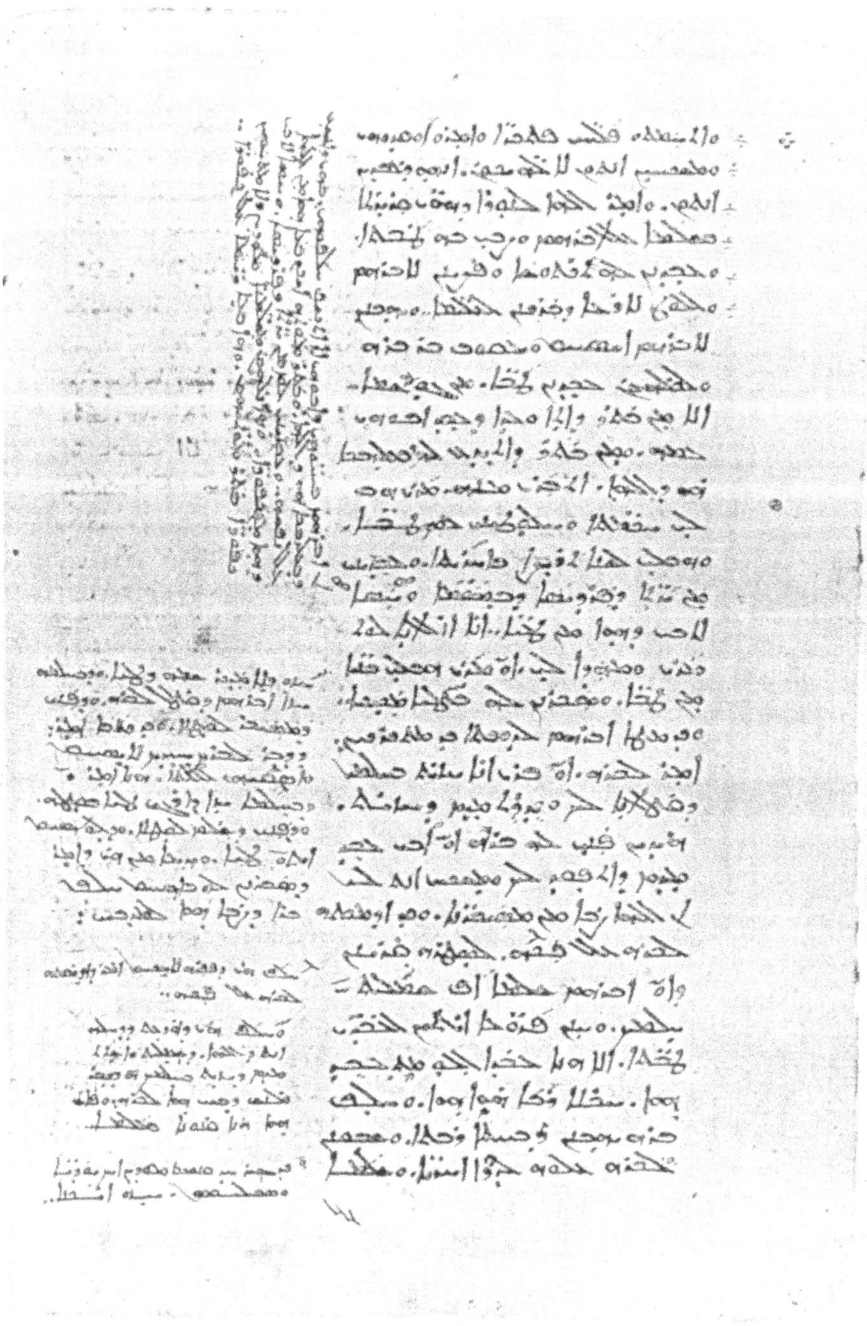

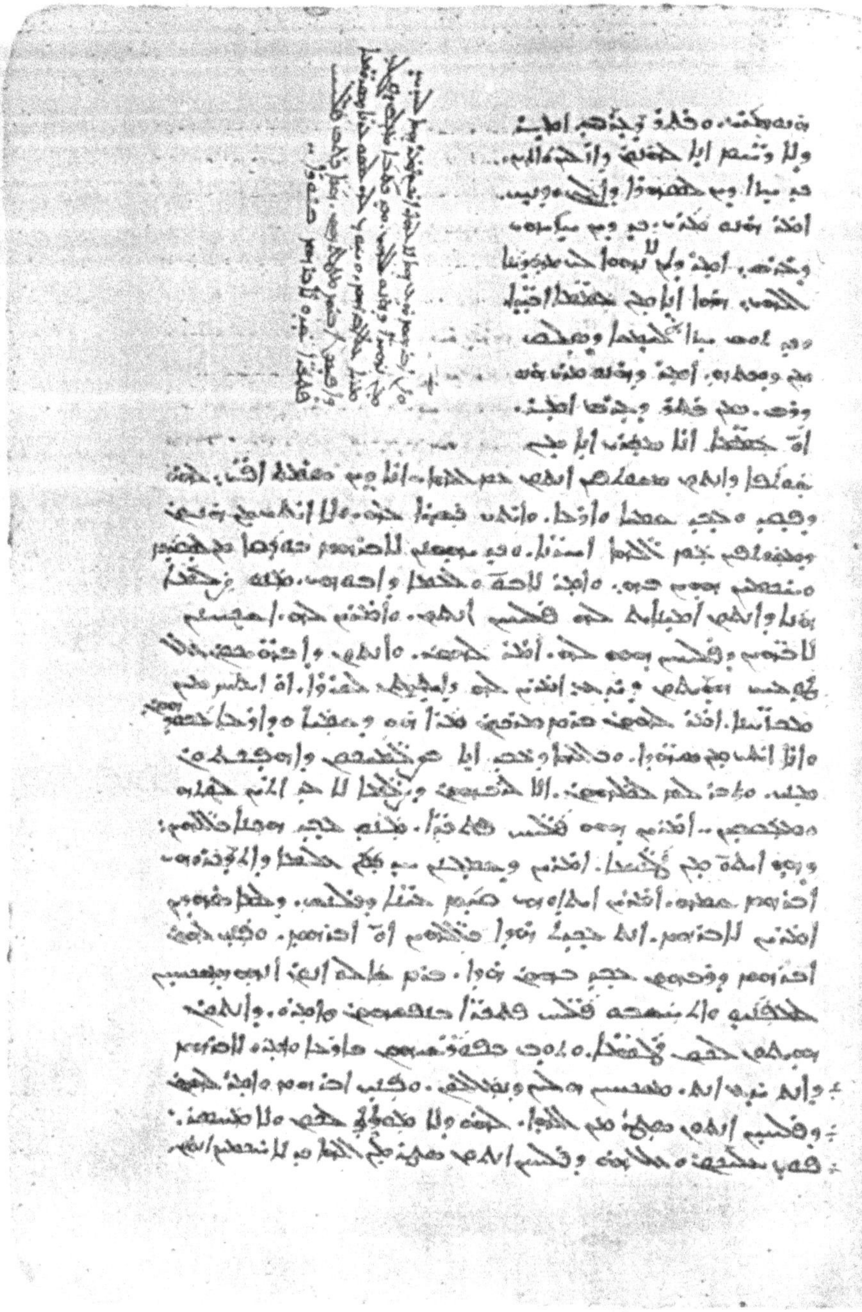

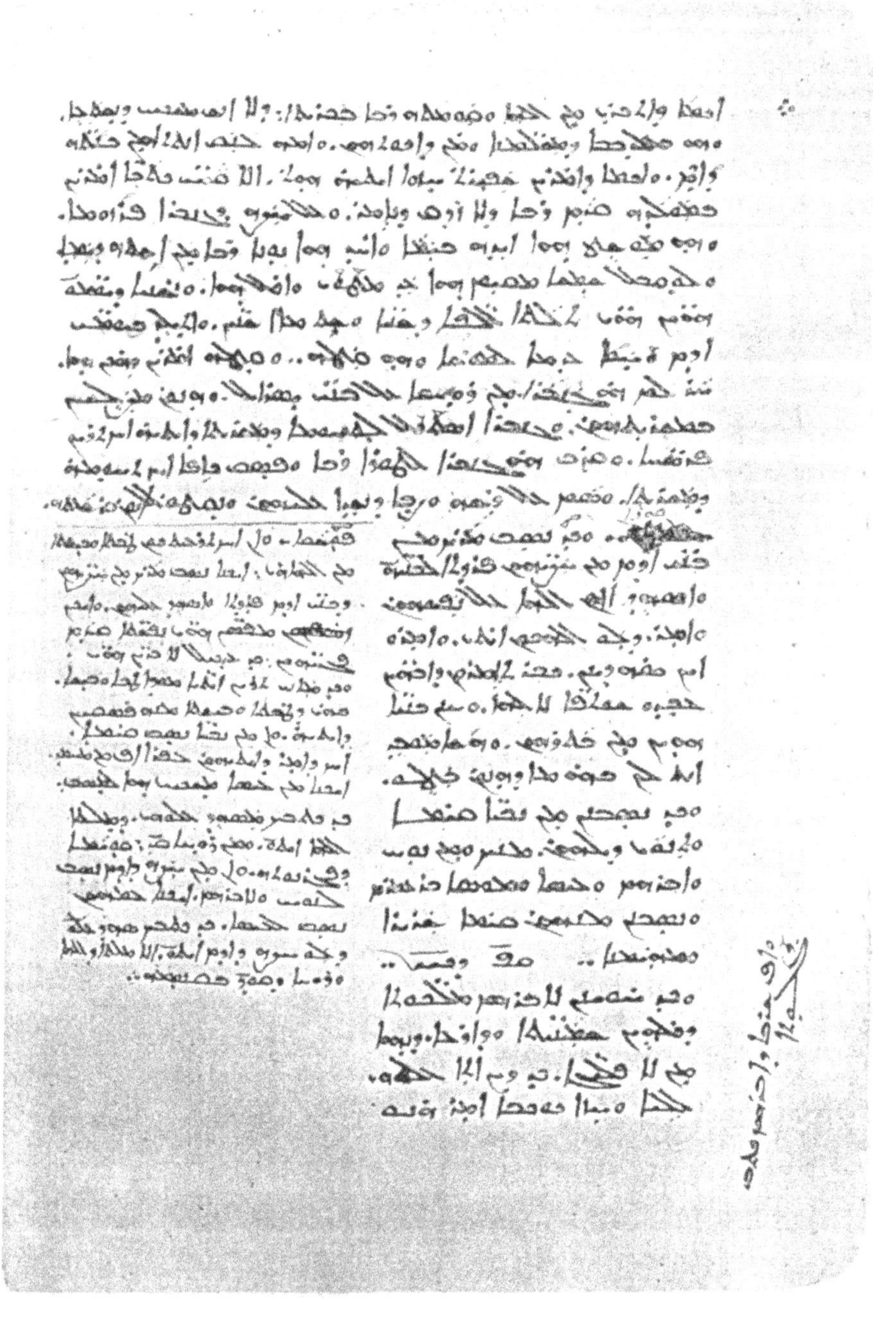

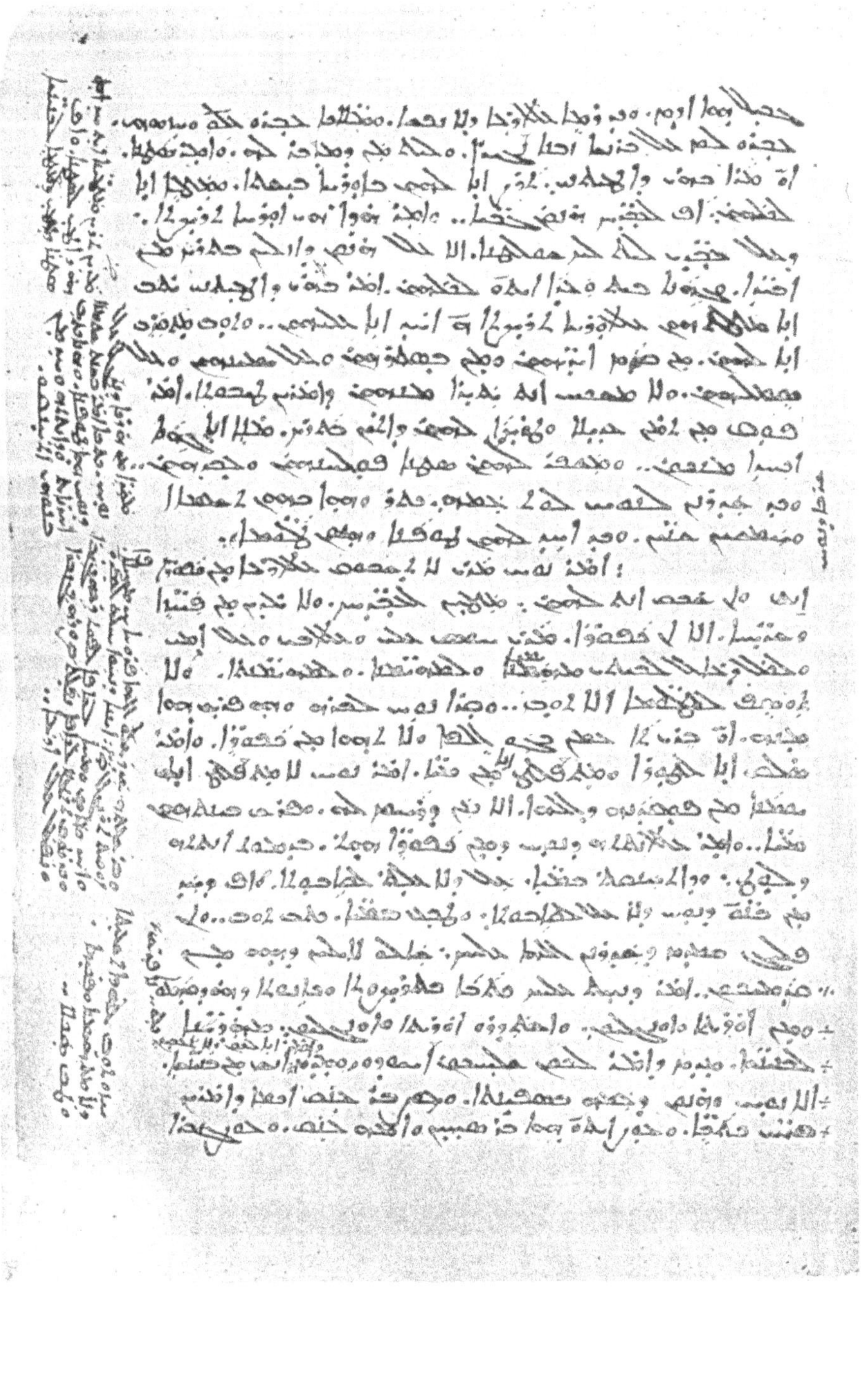

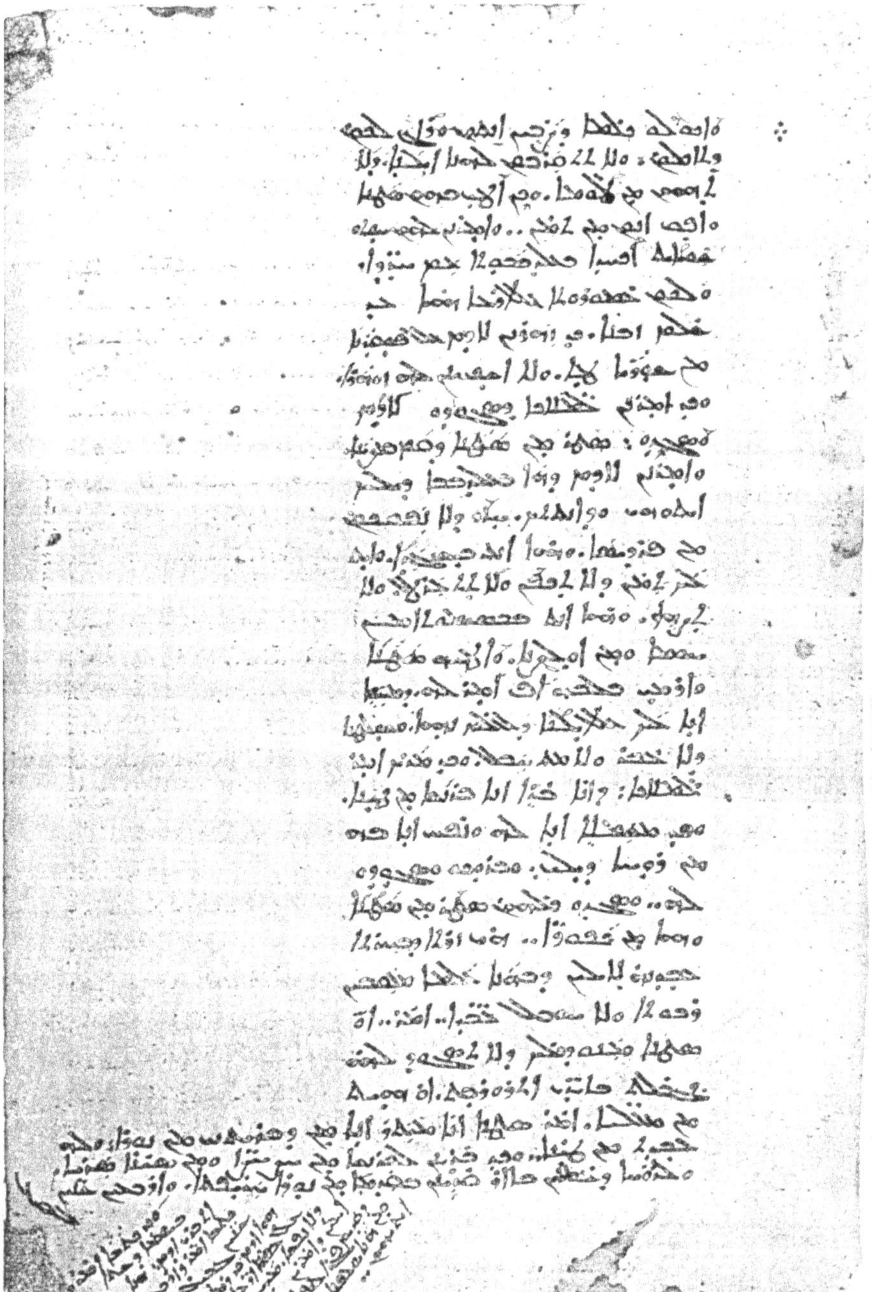

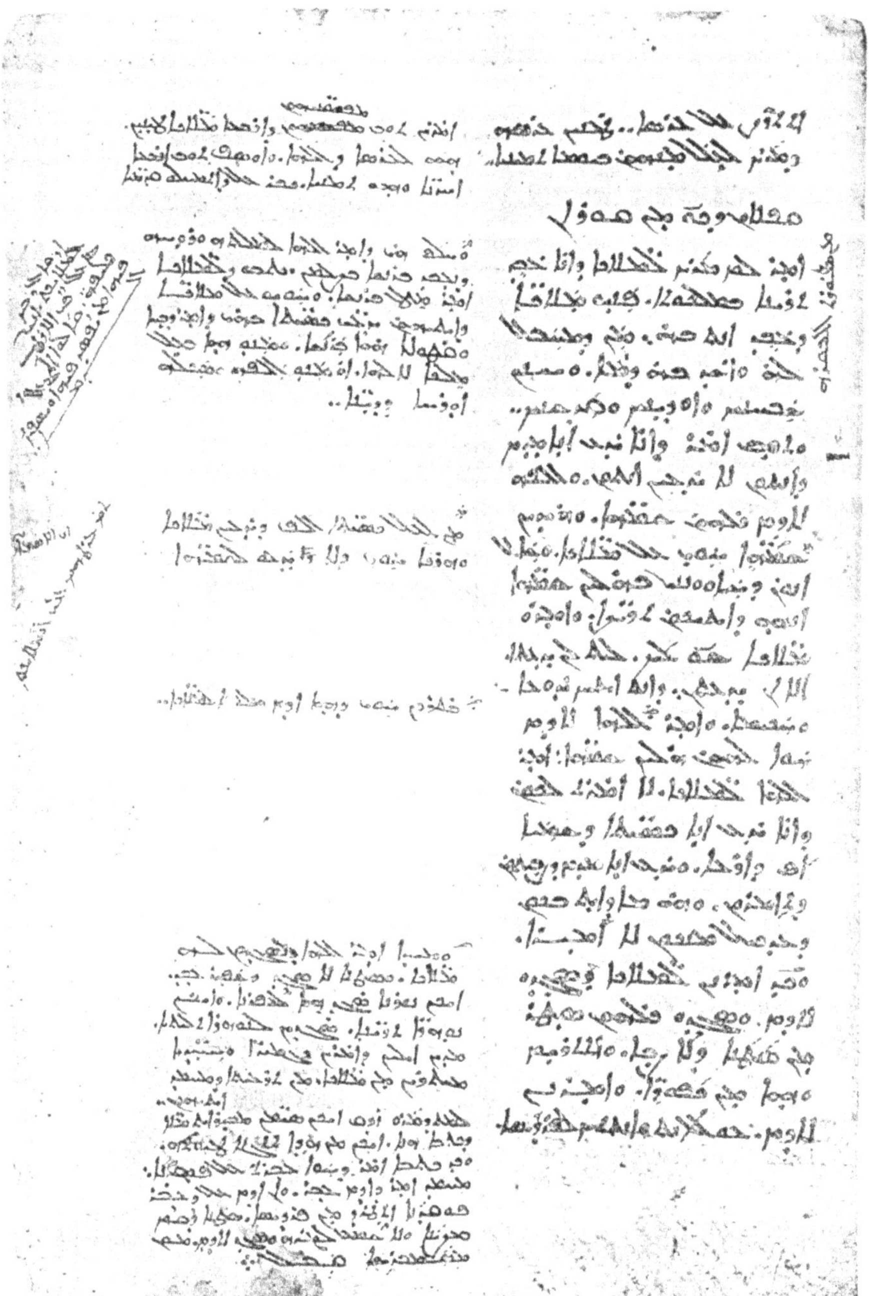

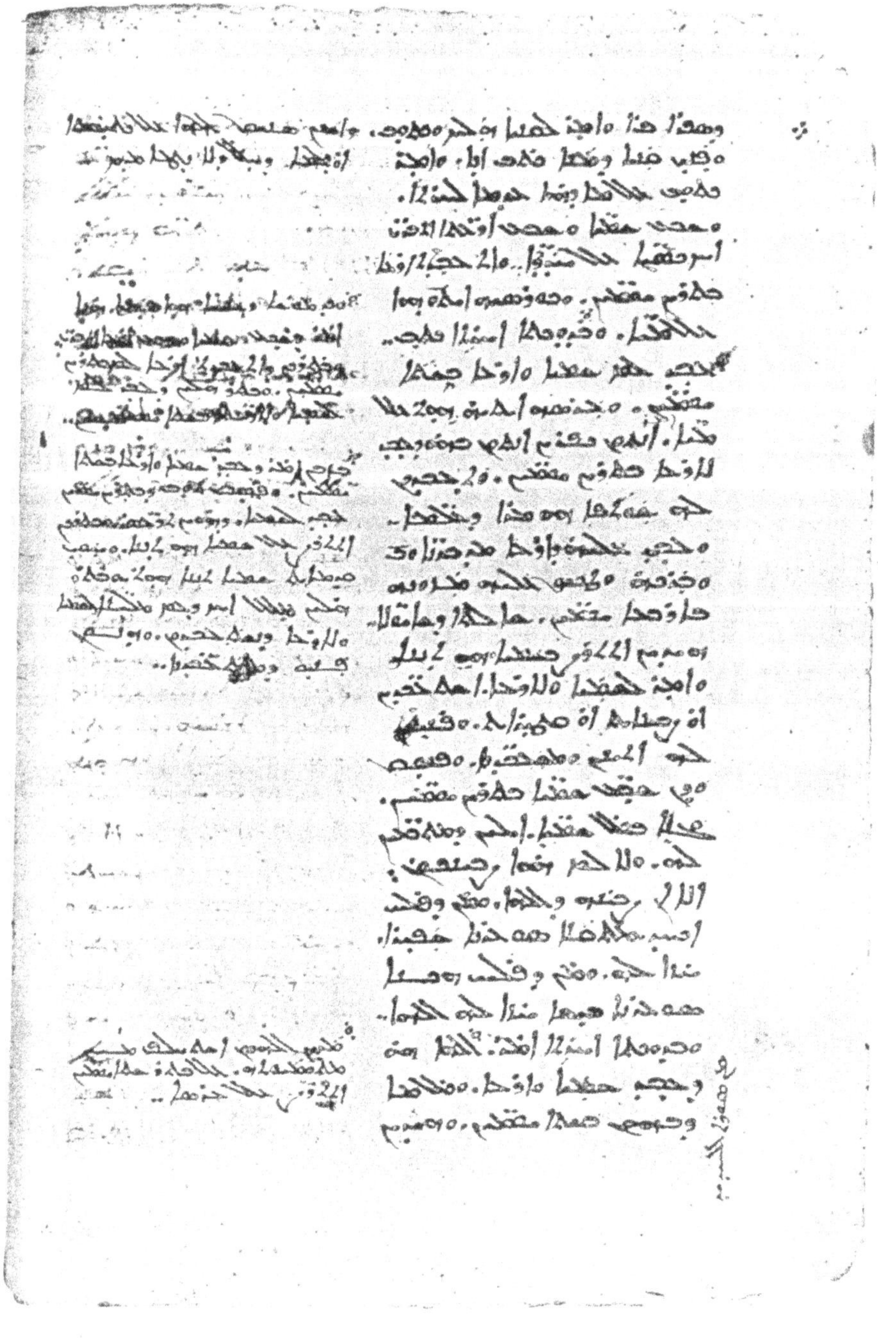

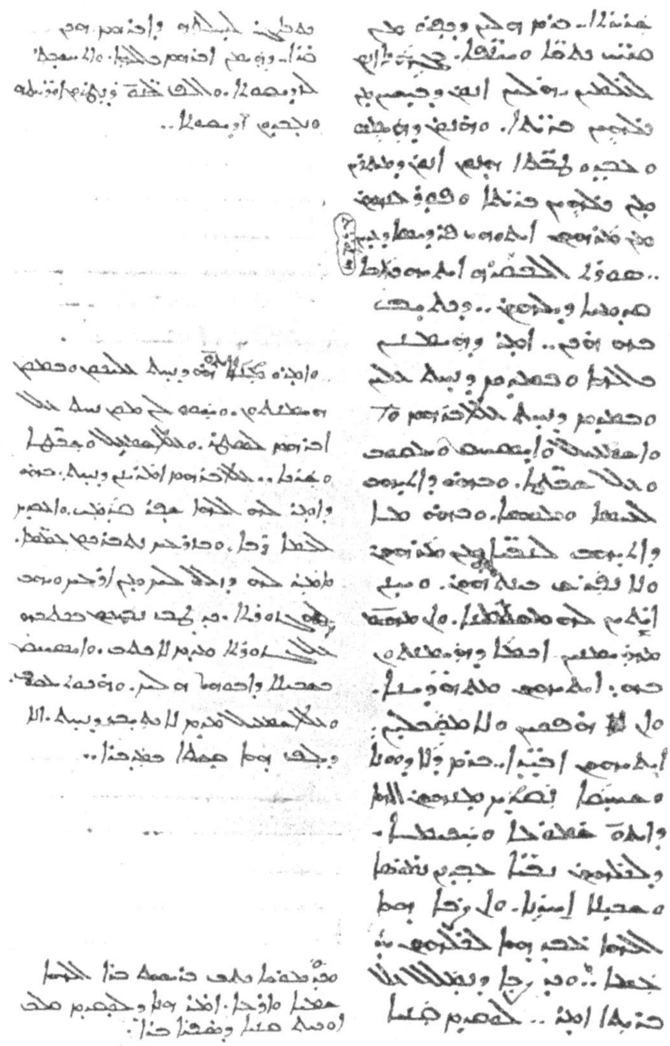

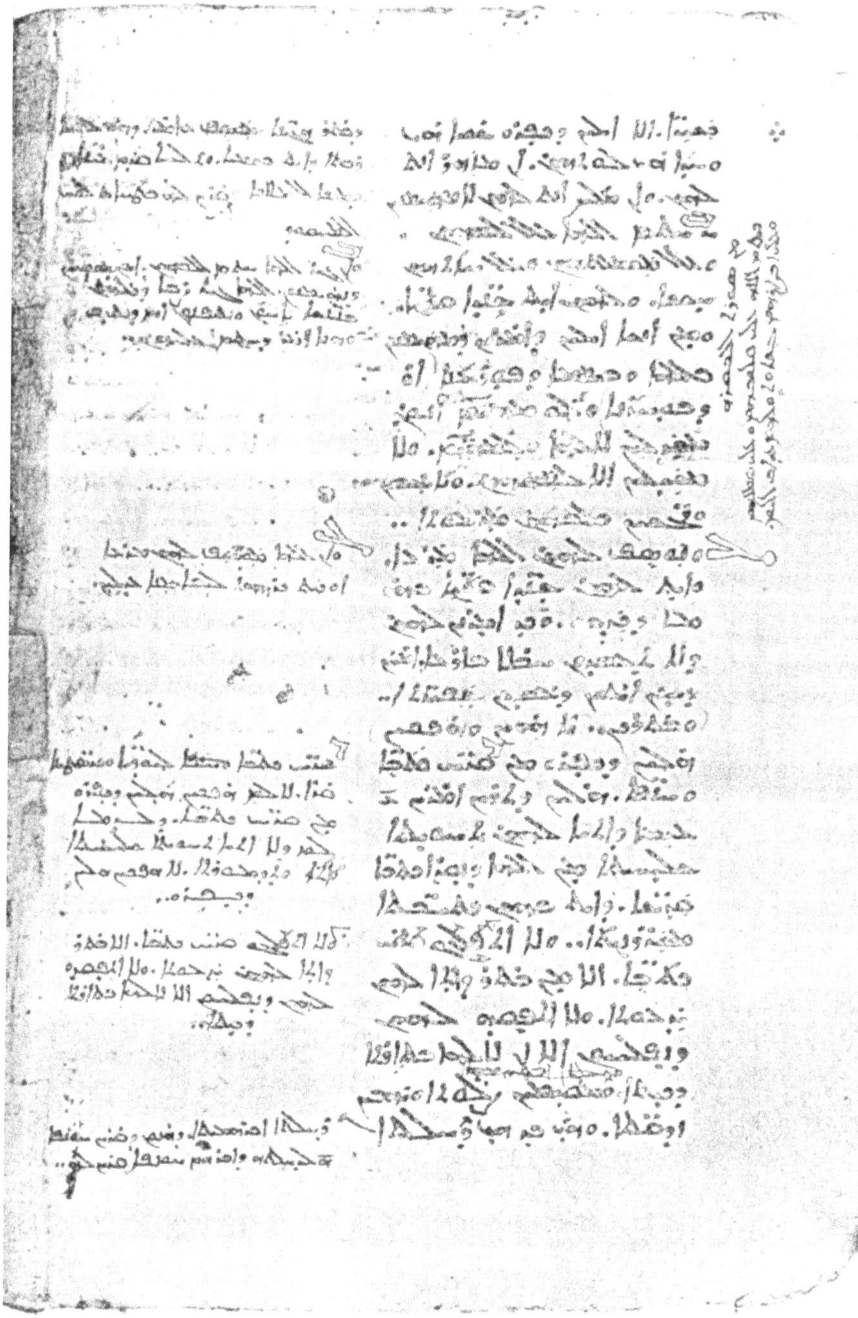

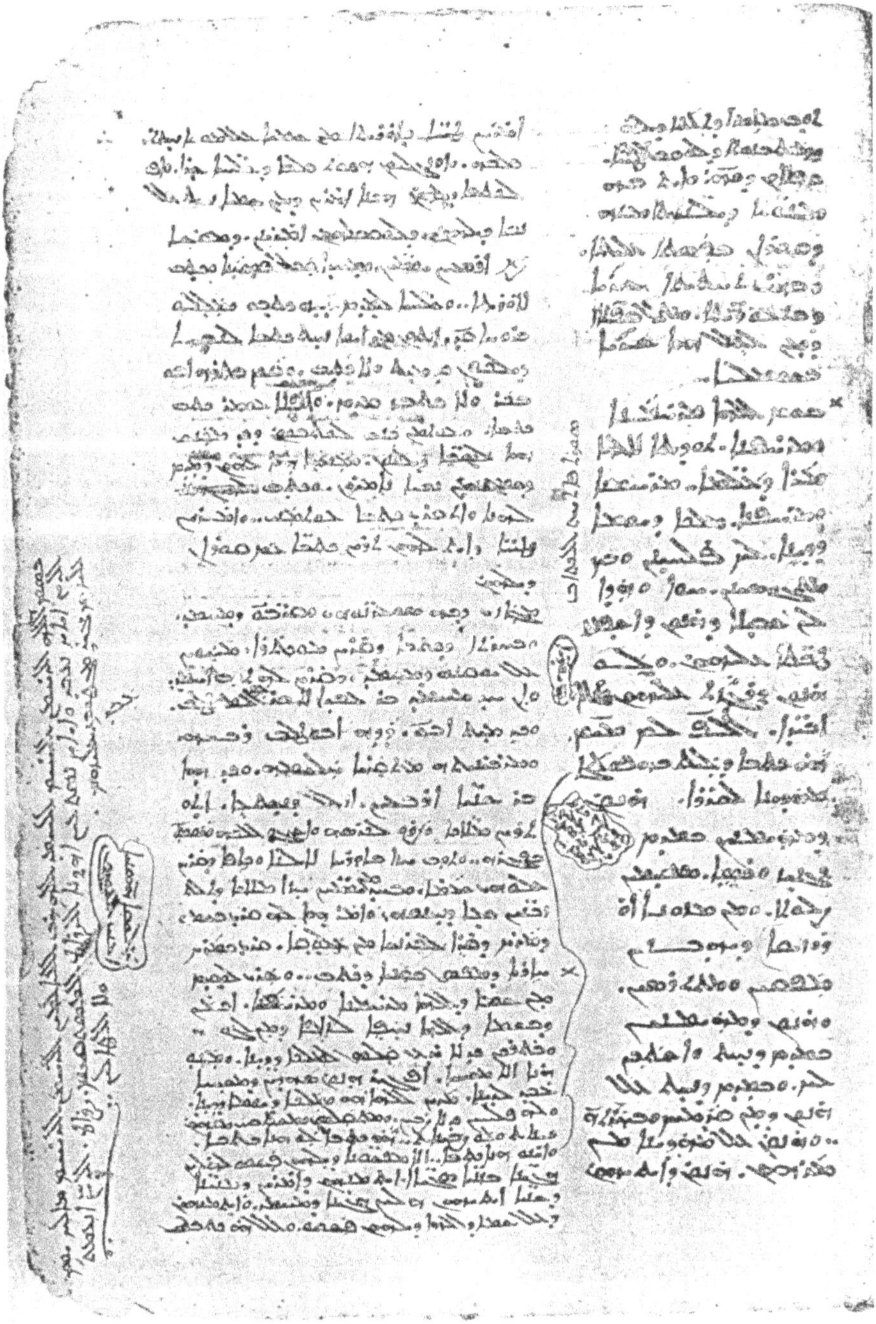

SUPPLEMENTARY NOTE

While the above pages were in the press, the authorities of Harvard University—to whom I here take the liberty to tender my sincerest thanks—were so kind as to place at my disposal, through the intermediary of my friend Dr. Rendel Harris, a manuscript described as "Harvard University Semitic Museum No. 4019" and containing all the controversial works of Barṣalībi mentioned by Baumstark in his *Geschichte der Syrischen Literatur* (p. 297). This manuscript formerly belonged to Dr. R. Harris, in whose collection it was numbered 83. On folio 47b we are informed that it was transcribed in Mardin, Saturday, March 14, 1898, by the priest Gabriel, from a manuscript dated 1913 of the Greeks (AD 1502) and written in the monastery of Mar Abel and Mar Abraham, near Midyād, in Ṭur ʿAbdīn. So far as our present study is concerned we venture to make the following remarks.[97]

A

The Harvard manuscript exhibits all the errors of the copyist of our manuscript to which we have drawn attention (with the exception of the grammatical slip in Ḳurʾān IV, 9 and *imart* in XVII, 94), and we do not deem it useful to repeat them here, but we will tabulate the fresh mistakes into which the copyist of the Harvard manuscript has fallen, and which the copyist of our manuscript was shrewd enough to avoid:

(*a*) In Ḳurʾān I, 7 read ܘܟܠ for ܘܒܠ (folio 48a and possible also our manuscript *primâ manu*). (*b*) In II, 3 the letter *hé*, which stood in the original manuscript as an abbreviation for ܗܝܡܢܘ has been wrongly read as the pronoun ܗܘܢ and erroneously added to the preceding word, which has thus become ܘܡܫܬܗܘܢ (folio 48b). (*c*) In XLI, 10 read ܘܗܝ for ܘܗܘ (folio 49b). (*d*) In XLI, 10 read ܘܦܫܘ for ܘܦܫܝܢ (folio 49b). (*e*) In XLII, 11 read ܘܡܠܠ for ܘܡܠܐ (folio 49b). (*f*) In XXI, 56 read ܠܗ for ܠܗܕܐ (folio 53a). (*g*) In XXI, 57 read ܒܕܡ for ܐܒܕܡ (folio 53a). (*h*) In XXI, 71 read ܬܠܒܘܬܐ for ܟܒܘܬܐ (folio 53a). (*i*) In XXI, 72 read ܒܕ ܒܕܡܗ for ܒܕܒܕܡܗ (folio 53b). (*j*) In III, 43 read ܒܒܬܩܘܢ for ܒܬܒܩܘܢ (folio 55a). (*k*) In X, 94 read ܠܟ for ܠܡ (folio 56b). (*l*) In LIII, 9 read ܡܘܕܒܐ for ܡܘܕܒܬܐ (folio 57a). (*m*) In XXVIII, 30 possibly read ܓܡܣܝܐ for ܬܡܣܝܐ (folio 57a) and ܬܡܣܝܐ of our manuscript, but this may possibly be due to the fact that the Ḳur'ān might have read التيمن for الايمن. (*n*) In LXII, 12 read ܕܒܫܘܒܚܬܗ for ܕܒܫܘܦܚܬܗ (folio 58b). (*o*) In LXXVI, 17 read ܠܗܘܢ for ܠܗܝ (folio 59b).

B

On the other hand, the Harvard manuscript contains readings that tend to improve both the text and the translation of our manuscript. In the translation given above we have taken account of all these improvements for the benefit of the English reader. Two such readings are mentioned under A; the others are:

(*a*) In Ḳur'ān XX, 114 before the word *Zuhhāra* the particle ܠܐ (folio 50b) is missing in our manuscript. (*b*) In XXXVIII, 77 for ܡܢܝܚܗ (folio 51a) our manuscript reads erroneously ܡܢܝ. (*c*) In the traditional verse about Adam, the Harvard manuscript (folio 51a) has ܚܕ for our ܘܚܕ. (*d*) In XXIII, 103 our manuscript omits after *Lā* the verb ܗܘܐ (folio 56b). (*e*) In III, 43 the verb ܘܗܘܐ (folio 57a) corrects our pronoun ܘܗܘ. (*f*) In XVII, 96 the copyist of our manuscript has by homoioteleuton omitted after ܕܐܡܪ the following sentence:

ܒܪܢܫܐ ܫܠܝܚܐ ܕܝܠܗ ܘܐܡܪ ܕܫܕܪ ܐܠܗܐ

"(. . . said), Has God sent a man as His apostle? And he said '[*sic*] . . .'" (folio 57a). The *wāw* before the verb *imar* seems to be erroneous.

C

Some other lexicographical and grammatical features worth mentioning are: (*a*) the word ܦܣܩܬܐ is used in Harvard (folio 56b) concerning III, 106, while our manuscript has (apparently be a later hand) ܥܘܠܝܢ. The first reading seems to be a wrong transliteration of the Arabic الفاسقون, which has been rendered into *'awālīn* (the reading of our manuscript) by an owner or a copyist, and possibly not by the first translator himself, unless the word were to be ܦܣܝܩܬܐ, "the cut off, or rejected ones." (*b*) In IV, 19 Harvard has ܕܢܦܫܟܘܢ (folio 57a) and our manuscript ܕܢܦܫܟܘܢ. (*c*) Both manuscripts have the erroneous readings ܣܓܕܬܗܘܢ for ܣܓܕܬܗ in XVII, 93 and ܬܚܕܪܬܐ (folio 58b) for ܬܚܕܪܐ in XC, 4.

D

The Garshūni words and phrases taken from the text of the Ḳur'ān and written mostly on the margins of our manuscript are absent in the Harvard copy. This bears out the opinion that we expressed concerning their origin: that they were due to some owners or late copyists.

E

The first half of the story of ʿAuṣ or ʿAuj b. Aʿnaḳ is in the Harvard manuscript also (folio 52a) written in the first column, and the second half in the second column. Evidently the blunder goes back to a very early manuscript, and it is even possible that it is due to Barṣalībi himself, who discovered it in time and promptly corrected it. What seems to render this view possible is the fact that both manuscripts break the sentence with the same word, and that the heading: "Ḳur'ān" is written in both of them in the body of the text immediately after the part of the story told in the first column, in order to show that it is not to be taken as Ḳur'ānic. The story forms a part of the didactic side of the work of Barṣalībi, like the first long note found in the second column of the first page.

F

Leaves 4b–6a of the Harvard manuscript contain an index of the contents of all three discourses of Barṣalībi against the Muslims. On folio 5b the third discourse is introduced in this index as follows: "Third discourse against the Muslims, containing various parts of the Ḳur'ān in the first column, with their refutation in the second column." Our manuscript is deficient here, and some leaves have disappeared from it that probably contained this index with the above statement.

Notes

1. *Leaves from three Ancient Ḳur'āns.*
2. Pp. 26–47.

3. It would be in place here to remark that the Harvard manuscript (see below) has an erroneous *wāw* after the verb (fol. 59b). This grammatical blunder does not deserve much attention as it cannot possibly be ascribed to Barṣalībi.

4. Tabari, *Tafsīr*, XIX, 37 (edit. Cairo). Zamakhshari, *Kashshāf*, II, 1222 (edit. Calcutta). Baiḍāwi, *Anwār*, II, 544 (edit. Bulak, AH 1296).

5. From *Baṣā-ir al-Ḳudamā* of Tawḥīdi who died in AD 1009, folio 191[a] of Arab. manuscript 827 of the John Rylands Library. This work is rare, and I know only of one other copy preserved in Cambridge, no. 134 (p. 21 in Prof. Browne's *Hand-List* of 1900), cf. Brock, II, 695. Our manuscript is more fully described below, pp. 301–302. On folio 218[a] Tawḥīdi informs us that many anomalies in the reading of the Ḳur'ān were in very early times attributed to the considerable number of the non-Arab population whose conversion to Islam goes back to the time of 'Ali b. a. Tālib. On folio 264[a] a variant of transposition of words is recorded in Ḳur'ān L, 18, on the authority of the Caliph Abu Bakr himself.

6. Exemplar or complete copy of the Ḳur'ān.

7. Yākūt, *Irshād*, VI, 301–302 (edit. Margoliouth).

8. R. Guest, in *Governors and Judges of Egypt*, by Kindi, p. 18.

9. Miskawaihi's *Experiences of Nations*, I, 285 (of the text).

10. The information that the *Mathālib* contain Ḳur'ānic variants I owe to Mr. F. Krenkow, whose acquaintance with the scattered remnants of early Arabian poetry and prose is possibly unique.

11. About Ibn Mas'ūd's Ḳur'ān we will recall the words of Diyārbakri (*Tārikh al-Khamīs*, edit. Cairo, 1302, I, 305): "If the Ḳur'ān of Ibn Mas'ūd had remained in the hands of the people, it would have caused a schism in the faith, on account of the disgraceful anomalies that it contained."

12. Some stress is laid on the importance of the controversial works of Abu Ḳurra in the *Century Supplement* of J.R.A.S., 1924, pp. 233 sqq.

13. Assemani, *Biblioth. Orient*, III, I, 212.

14. John of Phenek, pp. 141 and 175 of my edition (*Sources Syriaques*, vol. ii., Leipzig, 1908).

15. Folios 53[b] and 59[b] of the Syriac manuscript 61 of the John Rylands Library.

16. *Risàlah* or "Apology," edit. Muir, pp. 70 sqq. Casanova in *Mohammed et la fin du monde*, 2ème fascicule, *Notes Complémentaires*, p. 119 writes: "Il faut, je crois, dans l'histoire critique du Coran, faire une place de premier ordre au Chrétien Kindite."

17. The birthplace of Barṣalībi.

18. Cf. Nöldeke's *Gesch. des. Qorāns*, I, 255 (edit. Schwally).

19. Chron. Arab., p. 194 (edit. Beirut).

20. Some writers endeavor to give to the verb *jama'a* the sense of "to learn by

heart" (*Gesch. d. Qorāns*, II, 6). If this meaning can be applied to the "collection" of 'Abdal-Malik and Ḥajjāj, why not also to the "collection" of 'Uthmān?

21. *Tārikh al-Khulafā*, p. 227 (edit. Jarrett).

22. *Khiṭaṭ*, II, 454 (edit. Būlāk).

23. *Intiṣār*, IV, 73 (edit. Būlāk).

24. *Raf'al-Iṣr* in Kindi's *Kitāb al-Umarā*, p. 315 (edit. Guest).

25. IV, 463 (Tornberg).

26. *Wafayāt*, I, 183 (text of Baron de Slane).

27. This manuscript was recently acquired by me in the East and was part of a collection where it was numbered Mingana 122.

28. This date is possibly that of the original from which the treatise was transcribed.

29. Wrongly spelt "Khuthaim" in Ṭabari 3, 4, 2553. See about him, Ibn Rabban's *Book of Religion and Empire*, p. 72 (of my edition); Ibn Ḳutaibah's *Ma'ārif*, p. 36; Ibn Dur., p. 112; *Fihrist*, p. 225; Dhahabi's *Ṭabaḳāt*, p. 2 (edit. Wiistenfeld), etc.

30. *Wa yaḳūlu ila an ta'tiyana Ḳirā' at ul al-Ḥajjāji*. The manuscript has corrections and additions on the margins by at least two different owners, and these words dealing with Ḥajjāj are by one of them and are as usual followed by a *ṣaḥḥ*.

31. It is useful here to remark that Tawḥīdi makes mention in his *Baṣā'ir* (ibid., fol. 291[a]) of an unconclusive discussion that took place between learned *Ḳurrā'* before Ḥajjāj concerning the right reading and interpretation of Ḳur'ān VIII, 17, and ends by deploring the fact that a beautiful saying of the Prophet has not found room in the sacred text, as if Ḥajjāj was responsible for the insertion into the text of the Ḳur'ān of this or that verse. On folio 268[b] Tawḥīdi—to whom we actually owe a treatise on the art of writing (Brock, I, 244)—gives currency to an important and significant tradition to the effect that Ḥajjāj was the first man in Islam who wrote on papyrus: *awwal man Kataba fi l'Ḳarāṭīs*. The more I study Ḥajjāj the more I become convinced that he is one of the greatest men that Islam has ever produced. Was it not also in his time that Arabic coinage first came into use?

32. *Tafsīr*, XI, 96.

33. The author quotes also this verse as from the Ḳur'ān in chapter XXIV of the second discourse, but with the substitution of "*thy* Lord" for "*the* Lord."

34. Paradise of heaven; = Arab. *Jannah*.

35. God.

36. Cf. Bukhāri, *Ṣaḥīḥ*, IX, 134 sq. (edit. Cairo, AH 1313).

37. *Gesch. des Qorāns*, I, 234–62 (edit. Schwally).

38. Ṭabari, *Annales*, I, 89–90. Mas'ūdi, *Murūj*, I, 35 (edit. Bulāk), etc.

39. *Annales*, I, 29–30. *Tafsīr*, XXIX, 107. Ibn al-Athīr, *Kāmil*, I, 6–7 (Būlāk). Cf. Rāzi, *Mafātīḥ* (Cairo, 1278), VI, 330; Maḳdisi, *Baḍ'* (edit. Huart), I, 161.

40. *Annales*, I, 50.

41. Ṭabari, *Tafsīr*, II, 13. Zamakhshari, I, 114. Baiḍāwi (s.v.), etc.

42. *Tafsīr*, ibid., p. 15.

43. See also Hughes's *Dictionary of Islām*, p. 256 sq. In Bukhāri (IV, 187 edit. Cairo), and others, Syria is on the left-hand side of the Ka'bah.

44. If this were his intention it would indeed have been the depth of stupidity on his part. See a scathing saying of the Prophet concerning "the east" in Bukhāri, IV, 190 (edit. Cairo).

45. *Annales*, I, 192 and 501. *Tafsīr*, XII, 23. Ibn al-Athīr, *Kāmil*, I, 35 (Bulāḳ).

46. I.e., presumably the Ḳur'ān of the beginning of the verse.

47. I.e., dualists (?)

48. Or: he.

49. Written *'Īsa* and not *Īshō'*. Note his mention before Moses.

50. I.e., *Muslims* = resigned.

51. See foreword.

52. This verse is taken from the second column.

53. See foreword. Cf. XLI, 11.

54. There is no other place in the Ḳur'ān. See foreword.

55. So the translator understood the *Jinns*.

56. See foreword.

57. Or: the one who loves him.

58. LXVI, 10.

59. This is not found in the Ḳur'ān but is found in the Tradition possibly under the influence of LXVI, 10.

60. XI, 45.

61. In Syriac *'Īsa* (as above) and not *Īshō'*. Note that here also Jesus precedes Moses.

62. Doubtful meaning.

63. In Syriac here also *'Īsa* and not *Īshō'*.

64. Here also it is spelt *Īsa*, and it precedes Moses.

65. Spelt *'Īsa*.

66. Spelt *'Īsa*.

67. Or: reconciliation.

68. Here also *'Īsa*.

69. Here also *'Īsa*.

70. Here also *'Īsa*.

71. Here also *'Īsa*.

72. Here also *'Īsa*.

73. Or: whom.

74. Or: it.

75. Or: it.

76. Or: of.

77. Or: he turned from straying away from the path of God.

78. This verse is more exactly quoted below. Is it possible that there was another Ḳur'ānic verse worded in this way?

79. See foreword.

80. Syriac: *hagrān* (from *hagar*).

81. Translation of *Jinn* which in XV, 27 (see above) has been rendered by "Spirit that dwells in the air."

82. About this passage see foreword.

83. Length? (doubtful meaning.)

84. See foreword.

85. See foreword.

86. See foreword.

87. Or: apostle.

88. Between this verse and the next is a large heading "Prayer of the Muslims" which is: "O God, pray over Muḥammad and over the children of his paternal uncle, and bless Muḥammad and the children of his paternal uncle, as Thou hast prayed over, and blessed, and hadst mercy upon Abraham and the children of his paternal uncle; for He is high and glorious."

89. See foreword.

90. Lit. liver.

91. See foreword.

92. Here also spelt *'Īsa* and not *Īshō'*.

93. A Persian word in the Persian plural form meaning "couches."

94. The Kāfūr (Camphor) of our Ḳur'āns, the right meaning of which no one has ever understood. See Ṭabari, *Tafsīr*, XXIX, 128.

95. The *Zanjabīl* of our Ḳur'āns, generally translated by "ginger."

96. The *Salsabīl* of our Ḳur'āns.

97. We take the Syriac words that follow in the order in which they occur in the text. The references are to the Harvard manuscript.

3.5

The Orthography of the Samarqand Qur'ān Codex

Arthur Jeffery and Isaac Mendelsohn

The Library of Columbia University has recently acquired a copy of the Pissareff photographic reproduction of the famous Samarqand Codex of the Qur'ān,[1] which has made it possible for the writers to take up the long overdue task of a reexamination of the text of this unusually important codex.

This codex was introduced to the attention of the learned world in 1870 by a notice in Petzholdt's *Neuer Anzeiger für Bibliographie und Bibliothekswissenschaft*, where, in the number for that year, on p. 372 we read:

> 818 Aus St Petersburg
>
> hat die kaiserliche öffentliche Bibliothek von dem General-Gouverneur von Turkestan, Generaladjutanten v. Kaufmann in Samarkand, ein sehr werthvolles Geschenk, nämlich einen alten bisher in der Moschee Chodscha-Achrar aufbewahrten Koran in kufischer Schrift ohne Punkte und Vocalzeichen, erhalten, der über 1200 Jahre alt und von Osman selbst geschrieben sein soll.

The local legend regarding this codex is that it was brought to Samarqand by Khoja Akhrar himself, when he removed there from Tashkent, and when his mosque was built there this venerable codex was placed therein. Khoja Akhrar, whose real name, it seems, was ʿUbaidallah, lived in Tashkent in the latter half of the fifteenth century, and was, toward the end of his life, the local Pīr of the Nakshbandiyya Order of Dervishes. His possession of the codex was due to a disciple of his Order, who, after accomplishing the duties of the Pilgrimage to Mecca, decided to extend his journey to Constantinople and return home from there. While in Constantinople it so happened that by the use of a prayer taught him by his Pīr, he was instrumental in curing the caliph of that day of a dread disease. In gratitude for the cure the caliph offered him anything he might choose to take from the Treasury. He chose the ancient Qur'ān said to have belonged to the third caliph 'Uthmān, and indeed to have been the copy that he was reading when he was murdered, the stains of his blood being visible on the pages that were open at the moment the murderers attacked him. This precious volume he brought with him to Tashkent, where for many years it was exhibited as an object for the veneration of pious Muslims, but when the head of the Fraternity removed to Samarqand the codex accompanied him there. In the Khoja's mosque at Samarqand it lay in public and was stroked and kissed by the pious as a source of blessing.[2]

Von Kaufmann's letter that accompanied the gift to the Imperial Library in St. Petersburg has been preserved, and gives an account of the acquisition of the manuscript. It is addressed to the Minister of Public Instruction, and is accompanied by two depositions made by the 'Ulamā' at the Khoja Akhrar Mosque.

Chancellery of the Governor General of Turkestan,
Division—24th October 1869.
Journal: No. 182. City of Samarqand

His Excellency, the Minister of Public Instruction.

The Commander of the Zariavshansky District has handed over to me a Qur'ān, written on parchment in Kufic characters without diacritical points or vowels, which previously was in the possession of the Mosque of Khoja Akhrar in Samarqand. Being aware of the great value of this Qur'ān, and its sacredness in the eyes of the Muslims, Major General Abramov commissioned the Commander of the Samarqand District, Lietuenant Colonel Sierov, to investigate whether the acquisition by us of that manuscript would in any way violate the religious susceptibilities of the community. The 'Ulamā' of the Mosque and certain honourable citizens testified:

1) that this Qur'ān, though it was permanently deposited in the Mosque of Khoja Akhrar, did not really belong to it, but was

regarded as the possession of the Crown, being the property of the Emir of Bokhara.

2) that this Qur'ān is at present of no importance either to the Muslim community or to the Mosque. Formerly (indeed, very long ago) it used to attract many worshippers, but lately only the Emirs arriving at Samarqand have worshipped before it.
3) that nobody is able to read it, and that for many years it has been lying around without any use.

Thereupon Major General Abramov received the book, and in return for it donated from his own money 500 kokans (100 roubles), with which the clergy of Samarqand were completely satisfied.

In view of the fact that such a book may, from a bibliographical point of view, be of great value to the scholarly world, I hasten to send the Qur'ān thus acquired to your Excellency, together with the depositions of the two 'Ulemā' of the Mosque of Khoja Akhrar, Mullah 'Abdul Jalīl and Mullah Mughīn Muftī, as arranged by me, describing the origin of the Qur'ān and how it came to the Mosque of Akhrar, and I humbly ask you, Sir, to deliver the book with the enclosed depositions, in my name, as a gift to the Imperial Library.

Signed—Adjutant General von Kaufmann.
Countersigned—Director of Chancellery Major General Gomzin.
Correct: Secretary Diakov.

The accompanying depositions of the two mullahs give the story as outlined above, and repeat the claim that it was the Qur'ān of 'Uthmān. As a goodly number of other Qur'āns, however, have at various time turned up in different parts of the Islamic world, all purporting to show the traces of the blood of the third caliph 'Uthmān upon certain pages, and thus be the genuine 'Uthmānic Codex, the *Imām*, which he was reading at the time of his death, this may only be pious legend first invented for this particular codex at Samarqand itself. That it came there from Constantinople, is not, however, unlikely.

In 1891 in volume VI of the *Zapiksi Vostochnago Otdieleniia Imperatorskago Russkago Archeologicheskago Obshchestva* (St. Petersburg, 1892), pp. 63–133, A. Shebunin gave an account of the codex, and made a detailed examination of the peculiarities of its orthography. The publication of this article gave rise to a great deal of discussion as to the relationship of the text represented in this codex to that in the ordinary lithographed editions in use throughout the Muslim world. So great indeed was the interest excited that in 1905 S. Pissareff was encouraged to publish a facsimile edition, which he did by photographic process after having carefully inked in those placed on some of the folios where the writing had been almost obliterated by the greasy hands of the faithful stroking the pages to secure blessing. Only fifty copies of this facsimile seem to have been made, of which only twenty-five were offered for sale (Chauvin, *Bibliographie*, X, no. 94). The reproduction is printed on *papier d'ivoire* 50 cm × 67 cm, with all the decorations of the original reproduced in color. The title page reads:

> Coran Coufique de Samarcand écrit d'après la tradition de la propre main du troisième calife Osman (644–656), qui se trouve dans la Bibliothèque Impériale publique de St Pétersbourg. Edition faite avec l'autorisation de l'Institut archéologique de St Pétersbourg, par S. Pissareff. St Pétersbourg, 1905. (Fac-simile.)

Muslim savants have frequently asserted that Pissareff in his reinking of the dulled folios deliberately made alterations in the text, but an examination of the facsimile shows that while some mistakes due to ignorance have been made here and there in the process of reinking, there are no adequate grounds for this charge of deliberate alteration.

When Shebunin made his study of the orthography of the codex he used Flügel's Qur'ān as his standard for the text, and the first edition of Nöldeke's *Geschichte des Qorans* as his authority for the older Kūfic form of text. There was, of course, nothing else for him to do, for the *Muqniʿ* of ad-Dānī had not then been printed, even Mūsā Jārullah's text of the *ʿAqīla* of ash-Shāṭibī was only published at Kazan in 1908, and the oriental lithographs of the Qur'ān available to him differed so much among themselves in matters of orthography, that though they might have been preferable to Flügel, in that they did offer some consistent form of Oriental tradition, Shebunin had nothing to guide him in his choice among them. At present, however, we are in a better position, and so in 1926, when publishing the first fasciculus of the third part of the new edition of Nöldeke's *Geschichte des Qorans*,

Bergsträsser announced his intention of taking up a fresh examination of the Samarqand Codex in the light of our more advanced knowledge of the early Qur'ānic orthography.[3] His untimely death left this, as so many other promised studies, uncompleted, and it is a peculiar pleasure to be able in this present study to carry to completion a plan that he had long had in mind.

Unfortunately we are now dependent entirely on the Pissareff facsimile, as the original codex has disappeared. Indian Muslims had been much angered at the attention given to this codex and its supposed deviations from the standard text, and had made many attempts to have the codex given back to the Muslim community. In 1917 they succeeded in getting the consent of the Bolshevik leaders to the return of the codex to its former resting place, and somewhat later it was handed over to the Muslim leaders in Petrograd for transmission to Samarqand. In volume LI of the *Revue du Monde musulman* (1922), p. 10 we find the notice:

Restitution aux musulmanes du Caron d'Osman.

> Et pour mieux attirer les bonnes dispositions du monde musulman, le Gouvernement bolsheviste, par decret du 9 décembre 1917 (No 6 art. 103), ordonnait de restituer au Congrès regionale des Musulmanes de Pétrograd qui en avait fait la demande le Coran très sacré d'Osman, qui avait autrefois été deposé à la Bibliothèque nationale de Pétrograd après son transfert de Samarkande.

Since then nothing has been heard of it. Mūsā Jārullah in a private letter informs us that he has heard of it being seen at Tashkent, its original home, but it has been impossible to get confirmation of this rumour. ʿAbdallah az-Zandjānī, on the other hand, in his *Tārīkh al-Qur'ān* (Cairo, 1936), p. 46, asserts that it was taken from Petrograd to England and stored there, but one may suspect that this is merely a confusion with the transfer to the British Museum of the Codex Sinaiticus.[4]

From the Pissareff facsimile and the article of Shebunin in the *Zapiski*, however, since Shebunin's study, which was made from the actual text of the codex before it had been retouched, enables us to correct in places mistaken reinkings, we can make with fair success the needed reexamination.

Originally the codex was a complete Qur'ān, written on thick, strong parchment folios averaging 68 × 53 cm in size, with the written portion averaging 50 × 44 cm. Only 353 folios were left, however, when General von Kaufmann secured the codex, and of these only fifteen were quite whole without any paper mending, namely, folios 210, 214, 215, 218–20, 232–35, 237, 238, 240, 243, and 246. Many folios had been damaged by dampness, and others were worn, and had been mended with paper, a thick, soft cotton-paper, which looks very much like parchment. Sixty-nine folios, which were missing entirely, had been replaced by folios made of this paper. The portions of the text which survive in the codex are:

Ff.	Sūrah		From verse		to Verse[5]	
1–32	II	al-Baqarah	7/6	wa lahum	177/172	bi 'llāhi
33–34			179/175	ḥāyāt	187/183	'uḥilla
35			213/209	Allāhu'lladhīna	217/214	wa'l-masjidi'l-ḥarām.
36			231	ḍirāran	233	rizquhum
37–42			256/257	bi'ṭ-ṭāghūt	273/274	fa'inna'llāha
43–45			282	ya'ayyuha		end of Sūrah.
46–57	III	Āl ʿImrān	36/31	Maryama	92/86	ḥatta
58			97/91	sabīlan	102/97	Allāha
59–67			105/101	lahum	148/141	Allāhu thawāb
68–89			154/148	fī buyūtikum IV an-Nisā'	29/33	takūna.
90–92	IV	an-Nisā'	33/37	'aqadat	43/46	aw'ala
93–94			72/74	minkum	77/79	ittaqā
95–97			81/83	barazū	90/92	us-salama
98–112			92/94	mu'mimatin wa'in.	145/144	id-darki
113–89	V	Al-Mā'idah	85/88	al-muḥsinīn VII al-A'rāf	106/103	qāla'in
190–204	XI	Hūd	47/49	'a'ūdhu	121/122	lā
205	XII	Yūsuf	19	biḍā'atan	23	ma'ādha
206	XIV	Ibrāhīm	39/41	li'llāhi	44/46	'aqsamtum
207–13	XV	al-Ḥijr	7	bi'l-malā'ikati	86	ul-'alīmu
214–29	XVI	an-Naḥl	7	'illa	101/103	wa'idha
230			114/115	fa kulū	119/120	dhālika
231–36	XVII	al-'Isrā		Bismillāh	48/51	al-'amthāla
237–57			56/58	aḍ-ḍurri XVIII Kahf	77/76	fīha
258–60	XVIII	Kahf	82/81	wa mā	105	waznan
261–65	XIX	Maryam	3/2	Khafiyyan	44/45	ta'budi
266–86			52/53	min XX ṬaHa	135	mutarabbiṣ
287–90	XXVI	ash-Shu'rā'	63	fa'nfalaqa	117	'inna
291			130	wa 'idha	142	ṣāliḥ

292–95			155	yaumin	202	fa ya'tiyahum
296–99	XXVII	an-Naml		Bismillah	22	bi mā
300			28	fa 'alqih	34	'a'izzata
301–306			44	ḥasibathu	80/82	uṣ-ṣumma
307–21	XXXVI	Yā Sīn	12/11	'inna XXXVII aṣ-Ṣāfāt	75/73	al-mujībūn
322–32	XXXVII	aṣ-Ṣāfāt	91/89	'alā XXXVIII Ṣad	29/28	'ilaika
333	XXXIX	az-Zamar	6/8	khalaqakum	8/11	thumma 'idha
334	XL	al-Mu'min	4	Allāhi	7	al-Jaḥīmi
335			51/54	āmanū	57/59	'akbaru
336–38			67/69	min turābin	83	fariḥū
339–45	XLI	Fuṣṣilat	5/4	wa min	39	'nnahu
346–53	XLII	ash-Shūrā	21/20	shara'ū XLIII az-Zukhruf	11/10	maitan

The paper leaves, which were later additions and may be neglected for our purpose of comparison, are the following:

Ff.	Sūrah		From verse		to Verse	
1–2r	II	al-Baqarah	7/6	wa lahum	17/16	ẓulumātin lā
8			54/51	ur-raḥīmu	60/57	min rizqi
13–15			84/77	wa 'aqīmū	96/90	bi muzaḥziḥihi
33–34			179/175	ḥayātun	187/183	'uḥilla
35			213/209	Allāhu'lladhīna	217/214	wa'l-masjidi 'l-ḥarām
36			231	ḍirāran	233	rizquhunna
37–42			256/257	bi'ṭ-ṭāghūt	273/274	fa 'inna 'llāha
43–45			282	ya 'ayyuha		end of Sūrah.
59–63	III	Āl 'Imrān	105/101	lahum	128/123	laisa
76			186/183	taṣbirū	190/187	il-'albābi
88	IV	an-Nisā'	24/28	'illa	25/29	musāfiḥātin
100–102			97/99	fa tuhājirū	106	wa' staghfiri
120	V	al-Mā'idah	108/107	'adnā	110	aṭ-ṭīni
124			119	fīha VI al-'An'ām	3	jahrakum
129–30	VI	al-'An'ām	22	taz'umūna	31	wa hum
142			77	ra'ā	81	ma'ashraktum
150–65			107	bi wakīlin VII al-'A'rāf	3/2	'auliyā'a
168–70	VII	al-'A'rāf	18/17	la'amla'anna	31/29	'ādama
179			57/55	la'allakum	63/61	'awa'ajibtum
181–82			68/66	wa'ana	74/72	wa tanḥitūna

Folio 90 containing IV 33/37 'aqadat to 36/40 seems to have been added still more recently than the foregoing paper leaves. Folios 2, 6–7, 46–58, 89, 92, 112, 183, 315, and 316 consist of approximately half paper and half original parchment, according to Shebunin. Unfortunately it is not possible to distinguish in the facsimile where this paper mending begins or ends, so that it is always possible that some of the peculiarities of orthography that we note are due to the later hand that did the mending, and not to the original scribe of the codex, for where we cannot check from Shebunin's remarks or from the style of the writing, we are at a loss.

THE SCRIPT

As can be seen from the facsimiles, the script is large, straight, and well-proportioned Kūfic (i.e., the style of writing that became specialized in Kūfa for the writing of Qur'āns), and is fairly uniform. On some folios, particularly in the early part of the second sūrah and the beginning of the seventeenth (ff. 231 ff.), the writing is in a smaller more rapid hand, but Shebunin is doubtless right in thinking that they are even so by the hand of the original scribe, and not the work of another hand. The scribe has his own peculiarities. At times his *Kāf* is hardly to be distinguished from a *Ṭā'*. His *'Ain* at times has an open head both medially and finally, and sometimes is confusingly like (ىد) when it occurs initially or medially. In the case of *Hamza* he is quite uncertain about the *kursī*, sometimes providing one and at others not, as, for example, in (سيئة) and (شيئة), and often using an *Alif* as *kursī* where we should expect a *Wāw* or a *Yā'*, while final *Hamza* is very commonly neglected altogether. A final *Yā'* may turn to the left as we normally expect (على) or may turn in under to the right in the fashion that has become common in writing Urdu (علے).

On the whole, diacritical points are few, though every now and again for a few folios they become relatively numerous. These diacritical points where they occur are certainly contemporary with the original writing, at least in the great majority of cases. They are not in form dots but strokes (″ة for ة), but this is more in appearance than in reality, for with the broad cut reed pen necessary to produce letters the thickness employed in this codex, the pressure above a letter that with our pens could produce a dot naturally produced a thin line. Thus there will be one thin stroke above for a *Nūn* or *Fā'* or *Ghain*, two above for a *Ṭā'* or *Qāf*, and three above for a *Thā'* or *Shīn*, and so on, with corresponding strokes below for the *Bā'*, *Yā'*, and *Jīm*. Occasionally there are mistakes in the putting of these strokes, as when on folio 23v a medial *bā'* is marked with a stroke above instead of below, or on folio 26v where a *tā'* is marked with one stroke only instead of two, or on 22r where a *thā'* has but two strokes instead of three, or 32v where a *lām* is wrongly marked with a stroke beneath. These, however, are purely scribal mistakes, and have no significance. Indeed it is just possible that they are due to Pissareff's inking in, though so far as one can judge they seem to go back to the original scribe. By far the commonest letter to be marked is *Nūn*, seldom when it occurs initially, but very commonly when it occurs medially or finally or in the ending *-nā*. The next most commonly marked letter is *Tā'*. Some letters, such as *Dhāl*, *Ẓā'*, *Ḍād*, and *Ghain*, are very rarely pointed.

Other signs such as the *shadda*, *sukūn*, *waṣla*, and the like, and the *hamza* where there is no *kursī* indicating its presence, are entirely lacking, and there are no signs to indicate the vowels. The scribe has no scruples about breaking up words, filling out his line with as many letters of a word as he needs, and finishing the word on the next line that he begins.

VERSE DIVISION

The verse division of this codex is in general that of the Kūfan School, but the scribe was somewhat careless. Where he does mark the verse endings his ending is usually that of the Kūfans, but he will frequently run on for verse after verse without remembering to put in any sign of verse ending. The sign he uses is the commonly known series of oblique parallel strokes ////, sometimes more, sometimes fewer, and in one or two places only a single oblique stroke; but their number has no significance. At the conclusion of roughly ten verses he places a colored rosette, sometimes accompanied by the strokes indicating a verse ending (as at II, 81/75, 111/105; IV, 111, etc.), but more frequently not. Sometimes he forgets his rosette altogether (cf. II, 109/103), and occasionally he has a blank space left for a rosette but nothing has been filled in (e.g., III, 180/176), and at II, 171/170 where a rosette would normally appear he has just drawn a black circle around his strokes (////). At XXVII,

68/70; XXXVII, 60/58, 182 the strokes are at the end of the verse and the rosette appears in the margin against that line of writing. These colored rosettes seem to have been put in later than the original writing of the codex.

The following peculiarities of his verse marking may be noted:

II, 102/96. The normal Kūfan ending of the verse of *ya'lamūna* is not marked, but one is marked within the verse after *khalāqin* where € has a pausal sign ج, and the lithographs with the Sajāwandī system of pausal signs have قف .

109/103. A rosette comes after *lahum* where no verse ending, or even pause, comes in any of the known systems. After the next word *ul-ḥaqq*, however, there is a pausal mark صلے in €, and a ق in the Sajāwandī system.

III, 145/139. Besides the normal verse ending at *ash-shākirīna*, there is here another at *mu'ajjalan* where € has a pausal sign قلے , and the Sajāwandī system a ط .

IV, 12/13. There is a verse ending marked after the first *dain*, where Flügel ends verse 13, and where € has a pausal sign ج, and Sajāwandī a ط . There is also a verse ending marked after the second *dain*, where Flügel ends verse 14, and where € has قلے and Sajāwandī ط .

V, 81/83. In the middle of the verse there is an ending marked after *yubayyitūna*, where € has only a pausal صلے and Sajāwandī a ج . The normal sign for verse ending probably came after *wakīlan* as it should, but the page is defective here.

141/140. After having noted no verse endings at the end of 139 or 140 or at the normal ending of 141, there is one placed after *al-mu'minīna* in the middle of verse 141/140, where € has only a pausal ج and Sajāwandī a ط .

VI, 73/72. Besides the mark at the normal verse ending after *ul-khabīru*, one is marked after *fa yakūnu* where Flügel ends his verse 72, but where € has only a ج and Sajāwandī a ط .

VII, 89/87. There is no mark at the normal ending after *al-fātiḥīna*, but within the verse one is placed after *'īlman*, where € has only a pausal ج, and Sajāwandī a ط .

XI, 86/87, 88. There is no mark at the normal ending of the verse after *bi ḥafīẓin*, nor at the normal ending of verse 87/89, that is, after *ur-rashīdu*, but within 86 one is marked after *mu'minīna* where Flügel ends verse 87, but where ϵ has only a ج and Sajāwandī a ق.

XVI, 23/24, 25. Besides the normal verse ending after *al-mustakbirīna* one is marked after *yu'linūna* where Flügel ends verse 24, but where ϵ has only a قلے and Sajāwandī a ط.

91/93. Besides the normal verse ending after *raf'alūna* one is marked after *kafīlan*, where ϵ has only a pausal sign ج and Sajāwandī a ط.

XVII, 35/37. Besides the normal verse ending after *ta'wīlan*, one is marked after *il-mustakīmi* where ϵ has only a ج and Sajāwandī a ط.

82/84. Besides the normal verse ending after *khasāran*, one is marked also after *lil-mu'minīna* where ϵ expressly marks it لا to show no pause is to be made, and Sajāwandī does likewise.

XVIII, 2. There is no mark at the normal verse ending after *ḥasanan*, but there is one after *al-mu'minīna* where neither ϵ nor Sajāwandī mark any pause.

98. Besides the normal pause at the verse ending after *ḥaqqan*, one is marked after *dakkā'a* where ϵ has only صلے and Sajāwandī a ق.

XIX, 17. There is no mark at the normal verse ending after *sawiyyan*, but one is marked in the middle of the verse after *ḥijāban*, where no pausal sign is given in ϵ or Sajāwandī.

41/42. There is no mark at the normal ending of the verse nor after the next (v. 42/43) but in the middle of verse 41/42 one is marked after *Ibrāhīma*, where ϵ has only the sign ج and Sajāwandī a ط.

XX, 53/55. Besides marking the normal verse ending after *shatta* there is one marked also after *subulan*, where no pausal sign at all is given in either ϵ or Sajāwandī.

86/88. Besides marking the usual verse ending after *mau'idī*, two other verse endings are marked within the verse; one after *'asifan* where Flügel marks the end of his verse 88, and where ϵ has a ج and Sajāwandī a ق; and another after *ḥasanan* where ϵ has a ج and Sajāwandī a ط. But in compensation no mark occurs here at the normal ending of verse 87/90 after *as-Sāmirī*, where Flügel also marks no verse ending.

88/90. The verse ending is marked after *Mūsā*, whereas it ought normally to come after the next word, *fa nasiya*. This is doubtless merely a scribal error.

123/121, 122. Besides marking the normal verse ending after *yashqā*, one is also marked after *hudan* where Flügel ends his verse 121, but where neither ϵ nor the Sajāwandī sytem has any mark of pause.

XXXIX, 7/9, 10. Besides the mark for the normal verse ending after *iṣ-ṣudūri* there is one marked also after *ta'malūna*, where Flügel ends his verse 9, but where ϵ has only a صلے and Sajāwandī a ط.

XLII, 48/47. Besides marking the normal verse ending after *kafūrun*, one is also marked after *ḥafīẓan* where ϵ has only a pausal صلے and Sajāwandī a ط.

The most striking fact in this list is the number of coincidences of verse endings in the Codex with those adopted by Flügel in his text. There are further coincidences in that II, 40/38, 67/63, 78/73; III, 38/33, 131/126, 196; IV, 3, 27/32, 41/45, 118; V, 101; VI, 66; VII, 105/103; XI, 74/77, 82/84, 118/120; XIV, 43/44; XVII, 104/106; XVIII, 2, 23, 32/31, 84/83; XX, 33/34, 72/75, 78/81, 87/90, 92/94, 106, 116/115; XL, 53/56, 73/74; and XLII, 32/31 this codex has no verse endings marked where Flügel marks none but ϵ does.[6] Since we are entirely in the dark as to the source from which Flügel drew his verse divisions, these coincidences are significant. Flügel's verse endings agree with none of the known systems whose tradition has come down to us, nor with any that we have been able to trace in the Masoretic literature under the section *Ru'ūs al-Ayy*, and it has been generally assumed that he selected his verse endings on an arbitrary system of his own. The number of agreements between his system and that followed in this codex, however, suggest that he may have been following the system of some manuscript in his possession that may have followed some divergent Oriental tradition. It must be admitted, however, that the table Shebunin constructs of the divergences between this Samarqand Codex and the Flügel text in the matter of verse endings is equally long and imposing, so that it is obvious that the question of Flügel's system of verse division awaits further elucidation.

In placing the rosettes at roughly ten verses apart, the scribe was following the ancient practice of indicating the *'ushr* or tenths, which is possibly the earliest of the various systems of verse grouping. It is clear that he was following a system and not just counting verses, for in many places his rosette comes where it ought to come on the Kūfan system of marking the tens, whereas between two rosettes he himself has marked more or less than ten verse endings. For example, in sūra XVIII there is a rosette at verse 10 after *rashadan* and another at verse 20 after *abadan*, where they would normally come according to the Kūfan system, but in the codex only seven verses are marked between them. As these rosettes are witness to an early *'ushr* system it is worthwhile listing them, though with the remark that the witness is not as perfect as it might have been, for the scribe has often forgotten to put in a rosette in places where, even on his own counting, he has gone well beyond ten verses. The list following is corrected from that of Shebunin.

Folio 4v after *ṣādiqīna* (II, 31/29); 7v after *ẓālimūna* (51/48); 9v after *ya'tadūna* (61/58); 11r after *yaf'alūna* (71/66); 12v after *khālidūna* (81/75); 16v after *ya'lamūna* (101/95); 18v after *lahum* (109/103); 19r after *ṣādiqīna* (111/105); 21r after *al-khāsirūna* (121/115); 23r after *al-'ālamīna* (131/125); 28r after *ta'lamūna* (151/146); 29v after *ajma'īna* (161/156); 47r after *yashā'u* (III, 40/35); 53r after *ta'lamūna* (71/64); 56r after *ash-shāhidīna* (81/75); 58v after *kāfirīna* (100/95); 66r after *aẓ-ẓālimīna* (140/134); 69v after *al-mu'minīn* (160/154); 74r after *khābirun* (180/176); 79r after *tufliḥūna* (200); 86v after *mubīnan* (IV, 20/24); 103v after *ḥakīman* (111); 109r after *ḥamīdan* (131/130); 113v after *mu'minūna* (V, 88/90); 117r after *raḥīmun* (98); 123v after *al-ḥakīmu* (118); 126r after *yalbisūna* (VI, 9); 128r after *tushrikūna* (19); 133r after *mustakīmin* (39); 137v after *mubīnin* (59); 140r after *yakfurūna* (70/69); 144v after *bi kāfirīna* (89); 167r after *as-sājidīna* (VII, 11/10); 171v after *ya'lamūna* (32/30); 174r after *aẓ-ẓālimīna* (41/39); 177r after *yajḥadūna* (51/49); 184r after *musrifūna* (81/79); 187r after *jāthimīna* (91/89); 189r after *al-kāfirīna* (101/99); 190v after *muftarūna* (XI, 50/52); 193r after *mujībun* (61/64); 195r after *Ya'qūba* (71/74); 197r after *bi qarībin* (81/83); 199r after *wadūdun* (90/92); 201r after *ḥaṣīdun* (100/102); 203r after *murībin* (110/112); 205r after *az-zāhidīna* (XII, 20); 207r after *al-'awwalīna* (XV, 10); 208r after *bi-rāziqīna* (20); 209r after *'ajma'ūna* (30); 210r after *al-mukhlaṣīna* (40); 211v after *al-ghābirīna* (60); 212r after *al-'ālamīna* (70); 213r after *al-mursalīna* (80); 214r after *tusīmūna* (XVI, 10); 215r after *yukhlaqūna* (20); 217v after *al-muttaqīna* (30/32); 219v after *fa yakūnu* (40/42); 222r after *al-ḥakīmu* (60/62); 224r after *qadīrun* (70/72); 226v after *ḥīnin* (80/82); 228r after *tadhak-karūna* (90/92); 229v after *mushrikūna* (100/102); 232r after *'alīman* (XVII, 10/11); 233v after *maḥẓūran* (20/21); 234v after *baṣīran* (30/32); 235v after *'aẓīman* (40/42); 237v after *kabīran* (60/62); 239r after *tafḍīlan* (70/72); 240r after *naṣīran* (80/82); 241v after *yanbū'an* (90/92); 243r after *qatūran* (100/102); 244v after *takbīran* (111); 246r after *rashadan* (XVIII, 10/9); 248r after *'abadan* (20/19); 250v after *'amalan* (30/29); 252r after *ṭalaban* (41/39); 254r after *'aḍudan* (51/49); 256r after *saraban* (61/60); 257r after *'imran* (71/70); 259r after *saddan* (94/93); 260v after *waznan* (105); 263r after *maqḍiyyan* (XIX, 21); 264v after *ḥayyan* (31/32); 265v after *Ibrāhīma* (41/42); 267r after *shai'an* (60/61); 268r after *ṣiliyyan* (70/71); 269v after *maddan* (79/82); 270r after *'iddan* (89/91); 271r after *rikzan* (98); 272r after *yā Mūsā* (XX, 11); 273r after *al-'ūlā* (21/22); 273v after *'azrī* (31/32); 274v after *yā Mūsā* (40/42); 275v after *al-'ūlā* (51/53); 276v after *iftarā* (61/64); 278r after *'abqā* (71/74); 279v after *ihtadā* (82/84); 281r after *Mūsā* (91/93); 282v after *zurqan* (102); 283v after *dhikran* (113/112); 284v after *hudan* (123/121); 286r after *'abqā* (131); 287v after *ta'budūna* (XXVI, 70); 289r after *lil-muttaqīna* (90); 289v after *shāfi'īna* (100); 291v after *ar-raḥīmu* (140); 293r after *'ajma'īna* (170); 294r after *il-'ālamīna* (180); 295r after *mu'minīna* (190); 295v after *al-mujrimīna* (200); 297v after *al-mursalūna* (XXVII, 10); 299v after *al-ghā'ibīna* (20); 300r after *ir-raḥīmi* (30); 301v after *yuṣliḥūna* (48/49); 303r after *ul-mundharīna* (58/59); 305v after *ul-'awwalīna* (68/70); 306v after *ul-'alīmu* (78/80); 308r after *muhtadūna* (XXXVI, 21/20); 309v after *yarji'ūna* (31); 310v after *il-mashḥūni* (41); 312r after *yansilūna* (51); 313r after *mustaqīmun* (61); 314v after *mālikūna* (71); 317v after *ud-dīni* (XXXVII, 20); 318v after *ṭāghīna* (30/29); 319v after *al-mukhlaṣīna* (40/39); 320r after *yatasā'alūna* (50/48); 320v after *ul-'aẓīmu* (60/58); 321v after *yuhra'ūna* (70/68); 322v after *aṣ-ṣāliḥīna* (100/98); 323v after *il-muḥsinīna* (110); 324r after *Hārūna* (120); 324v after *'il Yāsīna* (130); 325r after *il-māshḥūni* (140); 326r after *shāhidūna* (150); 326v after *il-mukhlisīna* (160); 327r after *ya'lamūna* (170); 328r after *yaṣifūna* (180); 329v after *al-aḥzābi* (XXXVIII, 11/10); 330v after *ul-miḥrāba* (21/20); 336v after *ya'lamūna* (XL, 70/72); 338v after *tunkirūna* (81); 340r after *ṭā'i'īna* (XLI, 11/10); 342r after *turja'ūna* (21/20); 346v after *ul-kabīru* (XLII, 22/21); 348v after *shakūrin* (33/31); 350r after *il-'umūri* (43/41); 352v after *ul-'umūru* (53).

Shebunin notes rosettes also on folio 3r after II, 21/19; folio 288r after XXVI, 80; and folio 344v after XLI, 31, where none are visible on the pages of the Pissareff facsimile. On the other hand, he omits to catalog, those on folio 18v, folio 58v, and folio 254r, which are there quite plainly in the facsimile. It is possible that these omissions on his part are purely mistakes due to oversight, and it is also probable that the rosettes that are missing in the Pissareff facsimile may be due to further deterioration of the codex between the time when Shebunin examined it and Pissareff's work in reproducing it.

Within the rosettes are crudely formed Arabic letters used as numerals, which once doubtless noted the numbers of the *a'shār* in the original codex in its complete form, but which now, with so many folios of the original missing, present no sort of sequence. In the Columbia copy of the facsimile folios 138, 139, 141, 143, 194, 197, 207, 209, 210, 218, 231, 238, 239, 276, 291, and 295 have been bound in back to front, that is, the recto is the verso and vice versa, which only adds to the confusion.

A comparison with the Kūfan and Baṣran *'ushr* marks in the lithographed Qur'āns of Cairo and Stambul reveals that the system in this codex does not agree with the later systems of either of these cities, coinciding sometimes with a Baṣran *'ushr* mark, sometimes with a Kūfan, and sometimes, perhaps more often, with neither. The lithographs, it is true, do not always agree with one another on the matter, but none of the several examined showed any marked connection with the system here.

At the end of a sūrah there is a colored band of decoration stretching right across the page to separate the end of one sūrah from the beginning of another. Such are preserved on folios 79r, 244v, 271r, 316r, 328r, and 352v. If the last words of the sūrah do not fill out a complete line, the scribe fills in what remains of the line with this colored decoration, so that his *Bismillah* for the next sūrah will start at the beginning of a line. There is no rubric of any kind at the head of a new sūrah. Each new sūrah begins directly with the *Bismillah*, and there is no pause mark or space between it and the first words of the verse to follow. The so-called Mystic Letters are found, and again there is no break between the *Bismillah* and these letters or between them and the beginning of the verse. Needless to say, since there is no rubric at the head of a sūrah there is no name or number attached to the sūrah.

No pausal signs are used in the codex, and there are no marginal indications of *ajzā'* or other liturgical divisions.

ORTHOGRAPHY

Shebunin in his account of the orthography compared this text with that of Flügel, but as Flügel followed no known Oriental tradition of *Rasm* in preparing his text, a comparison on that basis is almost valueless. Compared with Flügel's text this Samarqand Codex presented a great number of peculiarities, but when we compare it with the rules for Qur'ānic orthography given in the *Muqni'* of ad-Dānī,[7] and the Egyptian government text (€), which attempt to follow consistently the Kūfan masoretic tradition of *Rasm al-Maṣāḥif* in Qur'ānic orthography, we find that this codex, while presenting numerous deviations, yet follows the general Kūfan system with fair consistency. Where it deviates it presents numerous points of interest, so that a detailed comparison is of a certain importance.

Only what remains of the original folios can be used in this comparison, and unfortunately our comparison will be to some extent vitiated by an element of uncertainty not present in Shebunin's case. He, as already mentioned, was able to make his comparison directly from the codex, where it was possible to distinguish the places where the folios had been mended, but this distinction is not possible on the facsimile, which is all we now have available. The folios that Shebunin notes as being entirely paper may be rejected, and indeed they are generally distinguishable by the difference in handwriting, but where the parchment leaves have been mended to a greater or lesser extent with paper patches, the patching does not show up in the facsimile, and though it is sometimes possible to distinguish the later hand that filled in the writing on these patches, there yet remains an element of uncertainty that is unfortunate but inescapable.

In a later number of the *Zapiski* (vol. XIV, 1901, pp. 119–54) Shebunin published an examination of another ancient codex of the Qur'ān, no. 534 of the collection in the Khedivial Library at Cairo, which in many respects was closely similar to the Samarqand Codex in matters of orthography. This codex had also been restored at various times, and not always by skillful hands, but it still has 248 original parchment leaves, besides 34 imitation parchment leaves, 61 leaves taken from another codex and inserted to fill in missing passages, and 219 paper leaves supplied to complete the volume.

We may label this codex (C) and from the evidence of the original portions of the 248 parchmant leaves as they were scrutinized by Shebunin, use its evidence to check with the peculiarities we have before us in the Samarqand Codex.

II, 22/20. اندادا is written without the medial *alif*, that is, انددا. So in 165/160 and XLI, 9/8.

24/22. الحجارة without the medial *alif*. So in 74/69; XI, 82/84; XV, 74.

25/23. جنت is written with the final *alif*, that is, جنات, contrary to *Muqni'* 23–25, which says that this word should have the final *alif* only in XLII, 22/21. In this codex, however, it is written with the final *alif* in III, 136/130, 195/194, 198/197; IV, 122/121; V, 119; XV, 45; XVI, 31/33; XVIII, 31/30; XIX, 61/62; XX, 76/78; XXVI, 134; XXXVI, 34; XXXVII, 43/42, but elsewhere without the alif, even in XLII, 22/21, though the defective state of the folio at this point makes the reading a little uncertain. C has it always with the *alif*. منها is written مها, but possibly this is on the paper portion, and in any case would be a scribal error without textual significance.

26/24. اراد without the medial *alif*.

28/26. فاحيٰكم is written with the *alif*, that is, فاحياكم compared to XLI, 39. In € the *alif* of احيا is omitted before pronominal suffixes in this sūrah only, the *alif* being written in احياها in V, 35; XLI, 39 and in احياكم in XXII, 66/65. The only one of these passages extant in this codex is XLI, 39, where, however, it is written احيها without the *alif*. In C the *alif* is generally written before suffixes.

30/28. جاعل without the *alif*. So normally in C.

35/33. شئتما without the *hamza*, that is, شتما.

38/36. هداى without the medial *alif*. € normally writes this without the *alif* before pronominal suffixes, but here and at XX, 123/122 it has the *alif*, obviously to distinguish هُدَاىَ from هُدَى, but the more primitive writing may well have been as here without the *alif* (*see Muqni'*, 68), though this codex has it in XX, 123/122, as does C.

41/38. كافر without the *alif*.

49/46. سوء has an *alif* for the *hamza*, that is, سوا quite irregularly.

53/50. الفرقان without the medial *alif*. So in C.

54/51. باتخاذكم without the medial *alif*. So يؤخذكم (bis) in V, 89/91, يؤاخذ in XVI, 61/63, يؤخذهم in XVIII, 58/57, and تؤخذنى in XVIII, 73/72.

61/58. طعام without the *alif*. So طعمه in V, 96/97, but with the *alif* in V, 95/96, XVIII, 19/18, as invariably in Є and C.

قثائها without the medial *alif*.

64/61. من is omitted before الخسرين, but this is probably merely a scribal error, if not due to a mistake on a paper patch in the folio.

65/61. خسئين has the *alif* but no *kursī* for the *hamza*.

68/63. فارض without the *alif*.

69/64. فاقع without the *alif*.

74/69. كالحجارة without the *alif*. See under 24/22.

78/73. امانى without the *alif*. So in 111/105 and IV, 123/122. C agrees.

83/77. احسانا without the *alif*. So C. Є has it here but is without it elsewhere.

99/93. ءايت with the *alif* of the feminine plural, and so in IV, 140/139; XVII, 101/103; XVIII, 17/16; XIX, 58/59; XXVII, 1, 12; XXXVI, 46; XL, 56/58, 69/71, but elsewhere without, as normally in Є. Shebunin noted the same inconsistency in C.

102/96. مروت with the *alif*, though the corresponding هروت is without, as in Є. *Muqni'* 23 says that there was variation among the codices as to this *alif*.

يعلمان without the *alif*, as in C, and as it should be according to *Muqni'* 18.

حتى is written حتا, and so in IV, 15/19, 18/22; VII, 38/36, 40/38; XVII, 34/36; XVIII, 60/59, 70/69, 86/84; XXVII, 18, 32; XXXVI, 39; XLI, 20/19, though elsewhere it is written normally, as is invariably the case in C.

بضارين without the medial *alif*.

خلق with the *alif*, but in III, 77/71 without the *alif*, as normally in Є.

108/102. سئل is written سائل. There were numerous variant readings recorded for this word, so that this may be an ancient variant in the text.

109/103. كفار without the *alif*. So in III, 91/85, but with the *alif* in II,

161/156 and IV, 18/22. C has it without the *alif*, though according to *Muqni'*, 13, 16 it ought to be written with the *alif* save in XIII, 42.

111/105. امانيهم without the medial *alif*. See 78/73.

119/113. بشيرا. The text has here some word ending in صرا, but the edge of the folio is lost. There is no known variant here, so possibly this is to be taken as a mistake.

124/118. جاعلك without the *alif*, as in 30/28. So in III, 55/48.

اماما without the *alif*. So in XV, 79 and XXXVI, 12/11. € writes it with the *alif* save in XVII, 71/73 where it agrees with this text. C writes without *alif*.

126/120. وارزق. What is written seems to be ارزوق, but doubtless it is merely an error in the rewriting.

128/122. مناسكنا without the first *alif*. € has it here, but writes it without in 200/196.

133/127. ءابائك without the second *alif*, that is, ءابٰئك. So in XXVII, 67/69 and XXXVII, 17, though elsewhere with the *alif*, as in € . C also varies in this matter.

136/130. الاسباط without the medial *alif*. So in 140/134 and III, 84/78. C agrees.

139/133. اتحاجوننا without the medial *alif*. C agrees.

145/140. بتابع without the *alif* (bis).

156/151. اصٰبتهم with the *alif*. So in IV, 72/74, 73/75; III, 172/166; XI, 81/83; III, 146/140; XLII, 30/29; XI, 89/91; V, 106/105; III, 165/159, 166/160. € differs in its treatment of the *alif* in this word. In اصاب and اصابت it always has it (as does this codex in XI, 89/91, the only place we can test); has it in اصابك, اصابه, اصابها (where we cannot test it in this text), but omits it in اصٰبكم (which in this text has it in III, 166/160; IV, 73/75; XLII, 30/29); has it in اصابهم (as does this text), but omits it in اصٰبتكم and اصٰبتهم (where this text has it in III, 165/159; IV, 72/74; V, 106/105; II, 156/151).

158/153. شعائر without the *alif*. So C, and so € save in this verse.

جناح without the *alif*, but with it in V, 93/94; IV, 23/27, 128/127. Both € and C write it with the *alif* throughout.

166/161. الاسباب without the medial *alif*. So C, and so € save in this verse.

171/166. لايعقلون is written طعقلون with no room for the لا. This looks very much like the original writing, but it must be merely a scribal error.

172/167. ءامنوا. The *nūn* has been omitted by scribal error.

176/171. شقاق without the medial *alif*, but is written with it in 137/131; IV, 35/39; XI, 89/91; XXXVIII, 2/1. Both C and € have it throughout.

177/172. البرّ من ءامن is written البر لمن ءامن, but it may be due to a reinking.

III, 39/33. فنادته without the medial *alif*.

40/35. امرٲتى without the medial hamza, that is, امرتى, though elsewhere it is written regularly. C always has the *alif* as *kursī* for the *hamza*.

عاقر without the *alif*. So in XIX, 5, 8/9.

50/44. بـٔاية written باىة with two *kursis* for the *yā'*. See 58/51. Shebunin notes that cases of this superfluous *kursī* occur in C in various forms of the word ءاية.

52/45. انصار without the medial *alif*, though it is written with it in 192/189, and in انصارى in this verse. C writes it with the *alif* when it is without pronominal suffixes, but without it when it has the suffixes.

58/51. الايٰت is written with two *kursis* for the *yā'*. So also in 70/63. See on verse 50/44, where the superfluous *kursī* occurs in the singular form.

61/54. تعالوا without the *alif*. So also in 64/57, though it is written with it in 167/160 and V, 104/103. C always has the *alif*.

65/58. تحاجون without the *alif*. So in 66/59 and تحجوكم in 73/66.

69/62. طائفة without the *alif*, that is, طئفة, though written with it in 72/65; IV, 113; and III, 154/148.

75/68. بقنطار without the medial *alif*. So in IV, 20/24.

بدينار without the medial *alif*. C would normally be without.

75/69. الامّيّن is written with two *yā's*, that is, الاميين as in many old codices.

78/72. The words وما هو من عند الله are omitted by the scribe, obviously by error, thinking he had already written them.

79/73. عبادا written without the *alif*, that is, عبدا. So in VII, 32/30; XVII, 17/18, 30/32, 96/98; XIX, 61/62, 82/85; XXVII, 15, 59/60; XXXVII, 111, 122, 132, 171; XXXIX, 7/9; XLII, 23/32, 25/24, 27/26 bis, 52, but elsewhere with the *alif*, as at XXXVI, 30/29; XXXVII, 40/39, and so on. ϵ has the *alif* written throughout save عبد in XLIII, 19/18; عبدى in LXXXIX, 29; عبدنا in XXXVIII, 45; and لعبدته in XIX, 65/66. C normally writes with the *alif*.

ربنين is written with the *alif*. C commonly has the *alif* in words of the form فعّال.

83/77. السموت with the first long *alif*. So 133/127, 180/176; IV, 131/130, 132/131; VI, 12, 75; XI, 107/109; XVIII, 14/13, 26/25, 51/49; XX, 4/3; XXVII, 65/66; XXXVI, 81; XLI, 12/11; XLII, 49/48, 53, though elsewhere he writes as ϵ with no long *alif*. C always omits the long *alif*. ϵ has second long in XLI, 12/11.

87/81. الملئكة with the medial *alif*. So in XV, 30; XVII, 92/94; XX, 116/115; XLI, 30, but elsewhere without as ϵ. C generally has it without the *alif*.

88/82. العذاب. The final ب has been omitted by error.

92/86. تنالوا without the medial *alif*.

133/127. سارعوا written without the medial *alif*.

134/128. العافين without the *alif*.

136/130. جزاوهم is written without any *waw*, that is, جزاهم. So in IV, 93/95, but see XX, 76/78.

138/132. بيان written with the *alif*, which would be the normal writing in C.

140/134. نداولها without the *alif*.

144/138. افاين is written افين, which is peculiar, but see *Muqni'* 50.

146/140. استكانوا without the medial *alif*.

147/141. اسرافنا without the medial *alif*. So in IV, 6/5. C would normally omit it.

اقدامنا without the medial *alif*. So in XLI, 29. So normally in C.

154/148. مضاجعهم without the medial *alif*. So in IV, 34/38. So normally in C.

155/149. الجمعان without the *alif*, agreeing with *Muqni'* 18. In 166/160, however, it is with the *alif* as in ϵ.

156/150. يحي is written يحيى with the *kursī* for a *yā'* before the final ى. So in XV, 23 and XXXVI, 11/12, 78, though elsewhere it follows ع with only a final ى. C is inconsistent in writing this word.

158/152. لالى is written لاالى, which may be a mistake of the scribe, though C has it written thus in XXXVII, 68/66.

159/153. رحمة is written رحمت contrary to *Muqni'* 82.

شاورهم without the *alif.*

160/154. على written without the *alif.*

علا is written علا. So in IV, 17/21, 85/87; V, 92/93, 99, 117; VI, 93; XVIII, 15/14; and in III, 179/173. This form is never found in C.

167/160. نافقوا is written without the *alif.*

قتالا without the alif. C and ع always have the *alif.*

لاتّبعنكم is written لااتّبعنكم with an extra *alif*; see *Muqni'* 18.

168/162. اطاعونا is written without the *alif*, that is, اطعونا.

172/166. استجابوا without the medial *alif.* So in XLII, 38/36, but with it in III, 195/193.

174/168. ذو فضل is written ذوا فضل. Probably a scribal error, though Shebunin notes that this superfluous *alif* occurred four times in C, in XL, 15; LIII, 6; LXV, 7; and LXXXV, 15 in the case of this word ذو.

175/169. تخافوهم is written without the *alif.* So in IV, 34/38.

178/172. يزدادوا is without the *alif.* So ازدادوا in IV, 137/136 and XVIII, 25/24.

183/179. بقربان is written without the *alif* on the analogy of بقنطار and so on above. It would normally be written without in C.

195/193. عمل is with the medial *alif*, where ع has it without. In this word ع has the *alif* only in VI, 135, عامل.

195/194. هاجروا is written without the *alif.* So in IV, 89/91 and XVI, 41/43.

198/197. للابرار is written without the *alif*, that is, للابر'ر, though it has the *alif* in 193/191 as ع and C have throughout.

200. صابروا without the *alif.*

رابطوا without the *alif.*

IV, 1. رجالا is written without the *alif*, that is, رجٰلا. So in VII, 48/46 and XVI, 43/45, but elsewhere with the *alif* as € and C.

الارحام without the *alif*.

3. طاب is written طيب, which was said to be the writing in 'Uthmān's Codex. *Muqni'* 71.

4/3. شىء is written شاى as it was written in the Codex of Ibn Mas'ūd (see *Muqni'* 45). So in VI, 38, 91, 93; XI, 57/60, 101/103; XV, 21; XVI, 35/37, 75/77, 89/91; XVIII, 70/69; XX, 50/52. € has it thus only in XVIII, 23 but C has this form in VI, 38, 93; XVIII, 23, 70/69; XX, 50/52. Elsewhere in this codex as in C it is written normally, as in €. [In VI, 93 it is شىٔ, everywhere else شىٔ.]

6/5. النكاح is written without the *alif*.

بدارا is written without the *alif*.

7/8. الوٰلدان (bis) is written without either *alif*, that is, الوٰلدٰن. See *Muqni'* 18.

15/19. حتى is written حتا. See II, 102/96.

16/20. والذان is written والّذٰن without the *alif*.

19/23. كرها is mistakenly written كوها, but this may be due to the reinking.

عاشروهن is written without the *alif*.

20/24. استبدال is without the *alif*.

23/27. خلتكم is written with the alif, that is, خالتكم.

25/29. متخذٰت is followed by an عند that does not belong there. It is quite obviously a scribal error and not a textual variant.

اخدان is written without the *alif*.

36/40. ذى is written ذا, which *Muqni'* 110 notes from some Kūfan codices.

الصاحب is written without the *alif*.

مختالا is written without the *alif*, that is, مختٰلا.

75/77. الظالم without the *alif*. So in 97/99; XVI, 28/30; XVIII, 35/33; XXXVII, 113.

92/94. فصيام without the *alif*. So in V, 95/96, 89/91. € and C always write with *alif*.

93/95. فجزاؤه as in III, 136/130 is written فجزاه without any *waw*.

94/96. مغانم is written without the medial *alif*.

107. يختانون is written يختنون without the medial *alif.*
 خوّانا is without the *alif.* So C would normally write it without the *alif.*
115. يشاقق is written without the medial *alif.* € has the *alif* in this word save in XVI, 27/29 where in this codex also it is written without the *alif.*
119/118. ءاذان is written ءاذن without the medial *alif.* So in XVII, 46/48 and XVIII, 11/10, but in XVIII, 57/55 it has the medial *alif* as € has all through.
125/124. ابرهيم is written ابرهم without the *yā'*. So in XIX, 41/42, 58/59. € has it thus in Sūrah II only, but elsewhere with the *yā'* (see *Muqni'* 36). In C it is apparently always written with the *yā'*.
128/127. اعراضا is written without the *alif.* So in VI, 35. C would normally omit *alif.*
137/136. اعراضا is written اامنوا with two *alifs*, but perhaps by mistake. ليغفر is wrongly written ليغفم with م for ر, but this is possibly due to the reinking.
140/139. يستهزأ is written with *waw*, that is, يستهزؤ. This و for the *kursī* of the *hamza* is an understandable writing, but *Muqni'* 60 expressly lists this verse as one of the places where there was an *alif* as *kursī* in all the early codices.
 جامع is written without the *alif.*
142/141. كُسَالَى is written كسلى without the *alif*, which is possibly the original writing since there are textual variants كَسْلَى and كُسْلَى (see Abū Ḥayyān *Baḥr* III, 337; Ibn Ḫālawaih 26) that assume an original form without *alif* from which these could be derived.

V, 89/91. يؤاخذكم (bis) without the *alif.* So in XVI, 61/63; XVIII, 58/57, 73/72.
 اطعام is written اطعم without the *alif.* € is inconsistent in writing this word, writing it with *alif* here and in LVIII, 4/5, but without *alif* in XC, 14. As C also would seem to have written it without the *alif* this may well have been the original writing.
90/92. الانصاب without the *alif*, as would be the normal writing in C also.
94/95. تناله is written without the medial *alif*, that is, تنله.
 رماحكم without the *alif*, as would be normal in C also.

95/96. عدل منكم. There is only an unintelligible writing here, which looks like ملسه, but is possibly due to the reinking process, where the original was too faint to be properly traced.

96/97. للسيارة is written without the *alif*, that is, للسيٰرة.

106/105. فاصٰبتكم is written with the medial *alif*, but as this *alif* comes at the end of a line, that may be the explanation. See II, 156/151.

فيقسمان without the *alif* here and in the next verse, contrary to € but in agreement with the regulation in *Muqni'* 18.

107/106. فـٰاخران يقومان are both without the *alif*, agreeing in this with *Muqni'* 18.

111. الحواريين is without the *alif* here and in verse 112, though it had it in III, 52/45 as €.

116. علٰم is written علام with the *alif*. So in C.

VI, 6. مدرارا is written without the *alif*. So in XI, 52/54. This would be normal in C.

7. قرطاس without the *alif* here and in verse 91. So C would normally write.

14. فاطر is without the *alif*.

17. كاشف is without the *alif*.

18. القاهر without the *alif* here and in verse 61.

36. إليه is wrongly written by the scribe as الله, though this again may be a case of wrong reinking of faded letters.

37. قادر is without the *alif*. So in verse 65 and in XVII, 99/101. € is inconsistent in writing this word. Generally € writes it as here with the *alif*, but without it in XXXVI, 81; XLVI, 33/32; LXXV, 40. See *Muqni'* 14.

38. بجناحيه is without the *alif*, as it is in C.

38. امثالكم is without the medial *alif*. € is inconsistent, writing it generally as here with the *alif*, but without it in XXIV, 35; XXV, 9/10, 39/41; XXIX, 43/42; XLVII, 3, 10/11, 35/40; LVI, 23/22, 61; LIX, 21; LXXVI, 28. Tis Codex has it without the *alif* in XVI, 74/76 and XVII, 48/51 also, in both of which passages € has the *alif*.

50. خزائن is written without the medial *alif*. So in XV, 21; XVII, 100/102; and XXXVIII, 9/8.

52. حسابك is written without the medial *alif*, but حسابهم has it as ع. C is without the *alif* in LXV, 8.

59. مفاتح is written without the medial *alif*. So C would normally omit the *alif*.

مبين is written مبن with only one *kursī*, but doubtless by error.

71/70. اعقابنا is written اعقبٰنا without the *alif*.

حيران without the *alif*. So probably in C.

74. اصناما is without the medial *alif*. So in XXVI, 71. C would normally omit it.

85. إلياس is written إليٰس without the *alif*. C writes it with the *alif* here but without it in XXXVII, 123, where this text has the *alif* as ع.

91. قراطيس without the medial *alif* as in the singular form in verse 7.

92. مبارك without the *alif*. So in XIX, 31/32. This would agree with *Muqni'* 19, 82. The writing in ع is inconsistent, having it with *alif* here and at verse 155/156; XIX, 32; XXI, 50/51; XXIII, 29/30, but without it in XXIV, 35, 61; XXVIII, 30; XXXVIII, 29/28; XLIV, 3/2; and L, 9.

92. يحافظون is without the *alif*.

93. باسطوا is without the *alif*, that is, بسٰطوا.

94. شركٰؤا is written شركاء here, as normally in IV, 12/15 and VI, 100. ع has the *waw* ending only here and at XLII, 21/20. See *Muqni'* 61.

96. فالق is written فلق without the *alif*, which is perhaps the original writing, for there are textual variants فَلَقَ and فَلَّق (Abū Ḥayyān *Baḥr* IV, 185; Kirmānī *Bayān* 79), which could only have arisen from a form without the *alif*.

الاصباح is without the *alif*. So C would normally have written.

حسبانا is without the *alif*. So in XVIII, 40/38.

99. نبات is written نبٰت without the *alif*, though it has the *alif* in XVIII, 45/43 and XX, 53/55. C is without it in LXXVIII, 15. ع has the *alif* throughout.

99. متراكبا is written without the medial *alif*.

قنوان is without the *alif*. C would normally omit it also.

اعناب is without the *alif*, which is perhaps the original writing, for ع has it without the *alif* in all passages save this and II, 266/268. So C would normally write it without the *alif*.

100. بنت is written with the *alif*, which again is possibly original, for € has it with the *alif* everywhere save here and at XVI, 57/59 and LII, 39 (see *Muqni'* 23). C always has it with the *alif*, and in this codex it is with it in XVI, 57/59.

تعلى is written تعالى with the *alif*, and so in XVII, 43/45 also, though without *alif* as € in XXVII, 63/64 and XX, 114/113. *Muqni'* 19 says it should be without the *alif*.

104. بصائر is written بصير without the *alif*. So in XVII, 102/104. C would agree.

VII, 10/9. مكنكم is written مكناكم with the *alif*.

17/16. شمائلهم is written without the *alif*, though in XVI, 48/50 it has it.

32/30. خالصة is without the *alif*. So in XVI, 66/68.

38/36. كلّما is written كلّ ما with the elements separated. There was some dispute as to how this should be written. In *Muqni'* 79 and *Manār al-Hudā* 11, the rule is given that this separated form should be written only in XIV, 34/37, but € has it separated in IV, 91/93 and XXIII, 44/46, though joined everywhere else. C has it joined in V, 64/69 but separated in LXVII, 8.

ادّاركوا is written without the *alif*, which may be original, for save in this passage € omits the *alif* (*Muqni'* 13), and there were textual variants here (Ibn Ḫālawaih 44; Kirmānī Bayān, 85) that could only have arisen from a form without the *alif*.

40/38. الخياط is written الخيط without the *alif*, which may be original for there were textual variants (Abū Ḥayyān *Baḥr* IV, 297, 298) that assume an original form without an *alif*.

43/41. هدٰنا (bis) is written with but one *kursī*, هدانا.

46/44. الاعراف is written without the *alif* here and in 48/46. So C would have omitted *alif*.

54/52. تبارك is without the *alif*, agreeing with *Muqni'* 19 and with C. € writes it without in LV, 78 and LXVII, 1. See on XLI, 10/9.

57/55. سحابا is written without the *alif*.

ثقالا is without the *alif*, as would be normal also in C.

66/64. سفاهة is without the *alif*. So in the next verse.
77/75. فعقروا has been mistakenly written twice by the scribe.
79/77. رسالة is written without the *alif*. C would normally omit the *alif* also.
85/83. الميزان is without the *alif*. So also in XI, 84/85, 85/86. C also without the *alif*.

XI, 53/56. بتارکی is written بترکی without the *alif*, and so لتارکوا in XXXVII, 36/35.
56/59. بناصيتها is without the *alif*.
63/66. اتنی is written with the *alif*, that is, اتانی. C would normally write as € here.
75/77. اوه is written with the *alif*, that is, اوّاه. C often kep the *alif* in such forms.
77/79. سیء is written سای apparently on the analogy of شای for شیء. C writes it as in €.
82/84. عليها is written with the *alif*, that is, عاليها and so in XV, 74.
84/85. المكيال is without the *alif* here and in the next verse.
87/89. لأنت is mistakenly written لاأنت. Doubtless a scribal error.
88/90. اخالفكم is without the *alif*.

XV, 23. نحی is written with the extra letter نحيی. See III, 156/150.
79. لبامام is written without the *alif*, that is, لبامم. See II, 124/118.
86. الخلق is written with the *alif*, that is, الخلاق, against the rule of *Muqni'* 18, but on the analogy of علام in V, 116.

XVI, 14. مواخر is written without the *alif*.
25/27. اوزارهم is without the *alif*, as is اوزر, here and in XX, 87/90.
كاملة is without the *alif*.
26/28. القواعد is written without the medial *alif*, though it has it in II, 127/121. € is with *alif* here and at II, 127/121, but without it at XXIV, 60/59. C is normally without the *alif* in such forms.
61/63. يستئخرون is written with alif as *kursī* for the *hamza*, that is, يستأخرون.
65/67. احيا is written احی. C agrees with €.

66/68. سائغا is written سٰئغا without the *alif.*

80/82. اقامتكم is without the *alif.*

اصوافها is without the *alif.*

80/82. اوبارها is written without the *alif.* So normally C.

اشعارها is without the *alif.* So normally C.

89/91. شیٔ is written شای. See IV, 4/3.

90/92. إیتائی is written without the *alif*, that is, إیتی. See *Muqni'* 50.

92/94. ادبی is written ادبا.

117/118. متع is written متاع with the *alif*, though it is without it in III, 185/182, 197/196; V, 97/96; XVI, 80/82; XXXVI, 44; XLII, 36/34. This is not a word where Shebunin notes any inconsistency in C, which would normally write it without the *alif.*

XVII, 5. الدیار is written without the *alif.* This is perhaps the original writing for ع writes it without the *alif* everywhere save in this verse, and this codex and C have it consistently without the *alif.*

15/16. وازرة is written وٰزرة without the *alif.* So in XXXIX, 7/9.

18/19. العاجلة is without the *alif.*

23/24. كلاهما is written كلهما without the *alif. Muqni'* 100, 101 notes that the early codices differed on the spelling here.

24/25. ربّانی is written ربّنی without the *alif.*

35/37. بالقسطاس is without the *alif.* So in XXVI, 182, doubtless on the analogy of such forms as قرطاس, VI, 7.

38/40. سیّئه is written سیّاه, probably by scribal error.

40/42. اصفٰكم is written اصفاكم with the *alif.*

64/66. شاركهم is without the *alif.* So normally would C write.

68/70. جانب is written جنب without the *alif.* So in XXXVII, 8 and بجنبه here in verse 83/85.

حاصبا is written حصبا without the *alif.*

69/71. قاصفا is written قصفا without the *alif.*

79/81. نافلة is written نفلة without the *alif.*

82/84. خسارا is written خسرا without the *alif.*

84/86. شاكلته is without the *alif.*

93/95. سبحان is written سبحٰن without the *alif.* This is possibly original for ع has the *alif* here alone. See *Muqni'* 18, 101. C omits the *alif.*

100/102. الاتفاق is without the *alif.*
107/108. للاذقان is written للاذقن without the *alif* here and in the next verse.
110. بصلاتك is written بصلتك without the *alif*, which is perhaps the original writing, for there were textual variants here (see Zamakhshari on the verse, and as-Suyūṭī's *Durr* IV, 208), and ᵋ shows much inconsistency in writing the word صلوة when it has attached pronouns. C seems usually to have had the *alif.*
تخافت is written تخفت without the *alif.*

XVIII, 16/15. يهيّئ is written يهيا. See *Muqni'* 54.
18/17. إيقاظا is written without the medial *alif.*
ذراعيه is without the medial *alif.*
بسط is written باسط with the *alif.* ᵋ has the *alif* in V, 28/31 but writes the word without it elsewhere. C would normally omit the *alif.*
فرارا is written فرّرا without the *alif.*
22/21. رابعهم and سادسهم and ثامنهم are all without the *alif.*
23. فاعل is written فعل without the *alif.* This would be normal in C.
29/28. سرادقها is written سردقها without the *alif.*
31/30. اساور is written اسور without the *alif.*
ثيابا is without the *alif.*
الارائك is written الارئك without the *alif*, here and in XXXVI, 56.
34/32. يحاوره is without the *alif*, here and in verse 37/35.
37/35. صاحبه is written صحبه without the *alif.*
46/44. ثوابا is without the *alif* here, though with it in other occurrences, as in ᵋ and in C.
47/45. بارزة is written برزة without the *alif.*
نغادر is without the *alif*; and so يغادر in verse 49/47.
49/47. حاضرا is written حضرا without the alif.
53/51. مواقعوها is without the medial *alif*, which is perhaps original, as ᵋ is without it in LVI, 75/74.
62/61. جاوزا is written جوزا without the first *alif.* ᵋ is inconsistent, having the *alif* here and in II, 249/250 and XLVI, 16/15, but without in VII, 138/134 and X, 90.

64/63. ءاثارهما is written without the *alif.* So in XL, 82, though elsewhere with the *alif* as in XXXVI, 12/11, where € writes without any *alif.*

69/68. صابرا is written صبرا without the *alif.*

96/95. سَاوَى is written سُوى without the *alif*, as would be normal with C.

XIX, 10/11. ليال is written ليل without the *alif.* So would C normally write.

11/12. المحراب is without the *alif* here and in XXXVIII, 21/20, but with it in III, 39/33.

13/14. حنانا is written حننا without the *alif.*

14. جبّارا is written جبّرا without the *alif* here and in verse 32/33, but with it in XI, 59/62.

17. حجابا is written حجبا without the *alif* here, but with it in VII, 46/44; XVII, 45/47; and XLII, 51/50.

29/30. فاشارت is written without the *alif.*

37/38. الاحزاب is without the *alif* here and in XXXVIII, 11/10, 13/12; XL, 5.

54/55. صادق is written صدق without the *alif.*

59/60. اضاعوا is written without the medial *alif.*

71/72. واردها is without the *alif.*

73/74. مقاما is written مقما without the *alif*, but has it in II, 125/119; XVII, 79/81; and XXXVII, 164.

75/77. مكانا is written مكنا without the *alif*, though elsewhere it has the *alif* as €. C is inconsistent in its treatment of this word.

83/86. تؤزّهم is written تاوزهم, but this seems a scribal error.

97. بلسانك is written without the *alif*, and so in XXVI, 195, but elsewhere with the *alif* as in €. C is inconsistent, sometimes having the *alif* and sometimes not.

XX, 12. طوًى is written طاوى with the *alif*, which is perhaps original, for there were textual variants طَاوِى and طَاوًى (Marandī, 141; Abū Ḥayyān, VI, 231; Ibn Jinnī, 49; Kirmānī, 150), which assume an original *alif* in the text.

39. بالساحل is written بالسحل, without the *alif.*

47/49. فأتياه is written فاتيه, though probably only by error.

63/66. هٰذٰن is written with the second *alif*, that is, هذان, which is perhaps original, for € has the *alif* in XXII, 19/20. See *Muqni'* 18.

63/66. لسٰحرٰن is written with the second *alif*. It is so written in C also, and is probably the original form. See *Muqni'* 18.

66/69. حبالهم is written حبٰلهم without the *alif*.

69/72. الساحر is written السٰحر without the *alif*, possibly the original form, for ع is without it in all places save here. See *Muqni'* 21.

71/74. خلٰف is written with the *alif*, that is, خلاف, though *Muqni'* 12 says it should be written without the *alif*, and it is thus without in XVII, 76/78.

76/78. جزاءُ is written with the *waw*, that is, جزاؤ. See III, 136/130. Shebunin notes that C sometimes wrote with the *waw* and sometimes without. See *Muqni'* 61, 106.

85/87. السامرى is written السٰمرى without the *alif* here and in verse 87/90. This is perhaps original, though ع writes it with *alif* in verses 85/87 and 87/90, but in verse 95/96 without, as does this codex.

94/95. يبنؤمّ is written يابنؤمّ. *Muqni'* 81. There were textual variants here (see Marandī and Kirmānī 154), which show that there was confusion even in the earliest codices. C writes as here.

97. عاكفا is written عٰكفا without the *alif*.

106. قاعا is written قٰعا without the *alif*.

108/107. الاصوات is written without the *alif* of the feminine plural ending, which is probably original for ع has the *alif* here contrary to the rule of *Muqni'* 23, though elsewhere, as at XXXI, 19/18, it follows the rule.

121/119. يخصفان is without the *alif*, in accordance with the rule in *Muqni'* 18.

129. لزاما is written لزٰما without the *alif*.

130. اطراف is written اطرٰف without the *alif*.

XXVI, 92. اين ما is written joined, that is, اينما, which is probably correct, for *Manār* 11 and *Muqni'* 77 are against ع here. C separates here and at XL, 73/74; LVII, 4; LVIII, 7/8, but joins in XXXIII, 61.

114. بطارد is written بطٰرد without the *alif*.

165. الذكران is without the *alif*. So in XLII, 50/49.

XXVII, 19. ضاحكا is written ضحكا without the *alif.*
32. قاطعة is without the *alif*, that is, قطعة.
44. قوارير is written قورير without the *alif.*
45/46. فريقان is without the *alif*, probably correctly; see *Muqni'* 18.
49/50. تقاسموا is without the *alif.*
57/58. امرآته is written امرته, but possibly by mistake.
60/61. حدائق is written حدئق without the medial *alif.*
61/62. قرارا is written قررا without the *alif.* C is inconsistent, writing it with the *alif* in XXXVIII, 60 and without it in XL, 39/42.
حاجزا is written حجزا without the *alif.* C normally omits the *alif.*
67/69. تربا is written ترابا with the *alif*, which is perhaps the original form. € is inconsistent, having the *alif* everywhere save in XIII, 5; XXVII, 67/69; and LXXVIII, 40/41. See *Muqni'* 20. C always has the *alif.*
اباؤنا is written ابؤنا without the *alif*, but in the next verse with it as €. It is without it also in XXXVII, 17. See II, 133/127.
73/75. لذو is written لذوا. Shebunin notes that C often had this superfluous *alif.*
75/77. غائبة is written غئبة without the *alif.*

XXXVI, 14/13. بثالث is without the *alif*, that is, بثلث, which is perhaps original.
22/21. لا is mistakenly written الا.
39. منازل is written منزل without the *alif.*
40. سابق is written سبق without the *alif.*
51. الاجداث is without the *alif.*
73. مشارب is without the *alif.*

XXXVII, 6. الكواكب is written الكوكب without the *alif.* So normally in C.
7. مارد is written مرد without the *alif*, as would normally be the case in C.
10. ثاقب is without the *alif.*
11. لازب is written لزب without the *alif.* So normally in C.
16. عظما is written عظاما with the *alif* here and in verse 53/51. C always has the *alif.* € is inconsistent, though it spells it generally without the *alif.*
25. تناصرون is without the *alif.*

30/29. طغين is written with the alif, which is perhaps correct. € has the *alif* in XXXVIII, 55 and LXXVIII, 22 against *Muqni'* 23 and طاغون with the *alif* in LI, 53 and LII, 32 in accordance with *Muqni'* 24.

32/31. غوين is written with the *alif*, possibly correctly, as € has the *alif* in all passages save this.

36/35. لشاعر is written لشعر without the *alif*.

38/37. لذائقوا is without the *alif*.

57/55. نعمة is written نعمت in accordance with the rule in Ibn Abi Dāwūd's *Kitāb al-Maṣāḥif*, p. 214, but against *Muqni'* 82, 83 and *Manār* 12. C also writes it with ت here as also in XXXI, 31/30 and LII, 29.

75/73. نادٰنا is written without *kursī* for the *alif*, that is, نادٰنا. So in C.

99/97. ذاهب is written ذهب without the *alif*.

102/101. المنام is written without the *alif*.

106. البلٰؤا is written البلاء, which is perhaps original. See Ibn Abi Dāwūd, p. 214 and *Muqni'* 62.

176. افبعذابنا is written without the *alif*.

177. صباح is written صبح without the *alif*. So C would normally omit the *alif*.

XXXVIII, 12/11. الاوتاد is written الاوتد without the *alif*.

18/17. الاشراق is without the *alif*.

22/21. خصمان is without the *alif*, probably correctly. See *Muqni'* 18.

بغى is written بغا.

XL, 4. البلذ is written with the *alif*, that is, البلاذ. It is not one of the words that Shebunin marks as taking the *alif* in C.

XLI, 10/9. وبٰرك is written with the *alif*, contrary to C and € and the rule in *Muqni'* 19. See VII, 54/52.

16/15. نحسات is written نحسٰت without the *alif*.

29. اضلانا is written اضلّنا without the *alif*, agreeing with *Muqni'* 18.

31. اولياؤكم is written اولیٰكم probably correctly. See *Muqni'* 40.

XLII, 22/21. واقع is written وٰقع without the *alif.* € is inconsistent, writing it with *alif* here and at VII, 171/170 and LXX, 1, but without the *alif* elsewhere.

روضات is without the *alif*, which is probably original.

33/31. رواكد is written روٰكد without the *alif.*

40/38. جزاؤا is written without the final alif, that is, جزاؤ, which is possibly the original form; but see *Muqni'* 61.

48/47. الانسٰن is written with *alif*, as it is in C.

XLIII, 8/7. مضى is written مضا.

****

The general principles of the orthography are thus those of the Kūfan School as set forth by ad-Dānī in the *Muqni'*, and followed for the most part by the € text. It is noticeable, however, that this Samarqand Codex agrees with the *Muqni'* not a few times where € departs from its instructions, notably in not expressing the *alif* of the dual ending. In other respects, as Shebunin noted for the C text, it has correspondences with what we know of the old Baṣran Codex, so that we may safely say that the text is ʿIrāqī in type, as against the Syrian or Ḥijāzī tradition. Where we are able to check its readings against those listed in the *Muqni'*, pp. 106 ff. as characteristic of the great Metropolitan Codices, we find that it is almost always in agreement with those of ʿIrāq as against those of the other centers, even in such readings as ذا for ذى in IV, 36/40 and انجٰنا for انجيتنا in VI, 63, where the Kūfan reading is opposed by all the other codices. The one exception is in XXXVI, 35, where it reads عملته with € and Baṣra and the majority of codices, against the عملت, which *Muqni'* 113 gives as the reading in the Kūfan Codex. An ʿIrāqī origin is also indicated by the writing شاى, which was characteristic of the codex of Ibn Masʿūd, so long influential at Kūfa. It agrees with the ʿIrāqī Codices in often omitting an *alif* when *hamza* follows (*Muqni'* 24), in reading اولىكم in XLI, 31 (*Muqni'* 40), in writing ملائه (*Muqni'* 40), in reading اناى in XX, 130 (*Muqni'* 51) and جزؤا in XX, 76/78 even against € (*Muqni'* 61, 106), and in reading شركاؤا in XLII, 21/20 (*Muqni'* 61), though it disagrees with ʿIrāq on this word in VI, 94.

On the other hand, it disagrees with the ʿIrāqī Codices in reading سبحٰن for سبحان in XVII, 93/95 (*Muqniʿ* 18), in reading قرءنا without the *alif* in XLIII, 3/2 (*Muqniʿ* 20), perhaps in reading جنت for جنات in XLII, 22/21 (*Muqniʿ* 25), though the page of the manuscript is defective here, in reading اولاء with € and the Madīnan Codex (*Muqniʿ* 51), and in reading جزاء instead of جزؤا in XVIII, 87/88 (*Muqniʿ* 61) to agree again with € and the Madīnan Codex. It disagrees with all the codices in reading البلوا in XXXVII, 106 (*Muqniʿ* 62), and has one curious agreement with ʿUthmān's Codex, the *Imām*, in reading طيب for طاب in IV, 3 (*Muqniʿ* 71), though it definitely disagrees with what is recorded of the readings of ʿUthmān's *Imām* in other passages, for example, in writing the second *alif* in هٰذان in XX, 63/66 (*Muqniʿ* 16).

Other peculiarities, in so far as they are not pure errors, whether of the original scribe, or made during the process of one or other of the renovations of the text, seem to be nothing more than the natural peculiarities of a scribe working at a time when the minutiae of orthography were not so firmly fixed as they later became. One can thus safely date the codex earlier than the time of ad-Dānī († AH 444), by whose time most of these minutiae had become fixed. The fact that its peculiarities are of the Baṣra-Kūfa circle suggests that it must date from a time when the tradition of those schools was beginning to take its characteristic form, and this would point to the third Islamic century. Shebunin wanted to date both this codex and C in the second or late first Islamic century, but this would seem too early. The fact that it has no vowel points does not necessarily point to a very early date, for Ibn Abī Dāwūd († AH 316) in his *Kitāb al-Maṣāḥif*, pp. 141 ff., records the prejudice there was in many circles against putting any marks, whether to distinguish consonants or vowels, in codices of the Qurʾān. In this codex, as already mentioned, the marks to distinguish consonants are by the original scribe, and not, as in some of the fragments of early codices known to us, inserted by later hands, and though the scribe of this codex is spasmodic in his marking of them, the fact that he marks any would point to a date later than that of the earliest codices. Thus we shall be safe in assigning the codex to some centre in ʿIrāq, probably Kūfa, early in the third Islamic century.

NOTES

1. See I. Mendelsohn, "The Columbia University Copy of the Samarqand Kufic Qur'ān," in *Moslem World* for October, 1940.

It was purchased from a local Russian bookseller, and is apparently one of the twenty-four copies of Pissareff's work that were put on the market, the other twenty-four having been presented to important libraries and institutions. It is an excellent copy, clean and complete. The reproduction, it may be mentioned, is the exact size of the original, is on heavy paper, and has an additional ornamental title page, with the inscription Kalām Sharīf, besides the title page in Russian and French.

2. Eugene Schuyler, *Turkistan* (1876), vol. I, pp. 256, 257; Landsell, *Russian Central Asia* (1885), vol. I, p. 582.

3. *Geschichte des Qorantexts*, p. 8, n. 1.

4. In *Moscow News* for June 12, 1941, V. Nagel has an article on rare manuscripts in the Leningrad Library, and mentions this codex as though it were still there (p. 20).

5. The verse numbering is given both according to the Kūfan tradition of verse numbering as represented in the Egyptian Standard Edition of AH 1344 = AD 1925 hereafter referred to as the ع text, and according to Flügel. Thus 213/209 means that the verse is 213 in the ع text and 209 in that of Flügel, which is the verse numbering quoted in most European works and almost all European translations of the Qur'ān. Where both texts agree only one number is written.

6. The number of cases may even be more numerous than this, for in many cases the end of a verse comes at the edge of a folio, and as the edges are badly broken it is often not possible to ascertain whether any mark for the end of the verse was there or not. In such cases we have assumed that it was, but this may be wrong.

7. *Orthographie und Punktierung des Koran: zwei Schriften von Abū ʿAmr ʿUṯmān ibn Saʿīd ad-Dānī*, herausgegeben von Otto Pretzl. Istanbul, 1932.

3.6

Some Additions to A. Jeffery and I. Mendelsohn, and Some Pages from the Samarqand Qur'ān Codex

Ibn Warraq

1. Introduction

Jeffery and Mendelsohn (J&M, henceforth) have rendered scholars an enormous service in their painstaking examination of the Samarqand Quran Codex (SQ, henceforth). As J&M explain,

> Many folios of the SQ Codex were damaged by dampness, and others were worn, and had been mended with paper, a thick, soft cotton-paper, which looks very much like parchment. Sixty-nine folios, which were missing entirely, had been replaced by folios made of this paper.

However, J&M chose to ignore the paper leaves for their purpose of comparison since they were later additions. We do not know how much later, but certainly not a great deal later. And for that reason I have picked some examples from the paper leaves; they retain their scientific interest and cannot be dismissed a priori. My other examples come from the parchment. I have chosen instances of differences between the latter codex and the Cairo Qur'an, even where the differences are often due, very probably, to

[i] scribal errors,
[ii] damage to the parchment,
[iii] poor or false restoration or repair to the codex,
[iv] tinkering with individual letters, or words for unknown reasons, or
[v] genuine variants.

First, it must be remembered that we are working with bad photos; we do not have the original parchment or codex in front of us. Second, most of the discrepancies of the SQ are due to false restoration, not to scribal errors. Real variants are much more frequent than scribal errors! It is often claimed that all discrepancies from the Cairo Qur'an that we find in manuscripts are mistakes, scribal errors. This is certainly not true, since, in the earliest manuscripts, we have several discrepancies on practically every page, and we cannot suppose that the scribes were so careless with so important a book as the Qur'an. Although scribal errors do, of course, exist, most discrepancies should be taken seriously as being variants. If one finds in a manuscript a discrepancy from the Cairo Qur'an occurring not just once but over and over again, then we must examine it carefully, and cannot lightly dismiss it as a "scribal error." Still, we do not know much about the role of Qur'an copyists in early times: Dr. Elisabeth Puin[1] has, in her research on manuscripts from Ṣanʿāʾ, discerned about twenty different "hands" (scribes); each scribe apparently having his own system of putting the diacritical marks (by "system" I mean: to which letters and how frequently they actually add the diacritical dots). One wonders how many scribes really understood what they were writing or copying, and whether and to which extent they tried to make sense of the text and even to make changes.

2. Kinds of Variants

What is a variant? It is not as easy as one thinks to define a variant in a concise way, to be of use to scholars working with Arabic manuscripts. Here is an attempt at a preliminary, working definition of a variant. First, a variant, or a word to be counted as a variant, must be a recognizable Arabic word that makes grammatical sense in the context but which is a different word from that used in the Cairo Qur'an of AH 1324 (= AD 1923?). Of course, the variant may well be a synonym; in other words, it will make no difference to the sense.

The variant could be a totally different word, giving a different sense. The basic shape or form of Arabic words without the dots or vowelling is called a *rasm*. In some old manuscripts, we have the same *rasm* as in the

Cairo Qur'an, but the *rasm* is pointed or dotted differently, most of the time giving the sentence a different meaning.

In some cases, one finds in manuscripts a different word than that in the Cairo Qur'an but which, though not a strict synonym, does not essentially change the overall meaning of the sentence.

Or we could have an orthographic variant, such as the word *šay'un*, meaning "thing, something," and with the negative, "nothing," which is written in modern printed Qur'ans with the letters *šīn* (ش), *yā* (ى), and a *hamza* (ء). But in many older manuscripts we find the orthographic variant where the same word is written *šīn* (ش), *alif* (ا), *yā* (ى), but certainly no *hamza* since it was invented at a later stage. We have such a variant in my example {4} (frame 299, line 2 of the SQ), in sura VI, verse 93 of the word *šay'un*. The pronunciation remains the same. Another, frequent kind of orthographic variant is the so-called defective writing.

A long vowel, most of the time an *alif*, is lacking in contrast to the Cairo Qur'an, where the word concerned is written *with* the *alif*. I give several occurences of this kind in my examples below. To distinguish it from a pure *reading*, a variant must be visible on the parchment or paper. Readings often depend on "reading" literature (*Qira'āt* literature), interpretations, and not on observations resulting from close examination of manuscripts.

We also find cases in some early manuscripts where whole words, or even whole verses, have been left out but cannot be assumed to be scribal errors. They could, for instance, indicate that the manuscript concerned represents the Qur'an at a stage when the contents were not fixed, or standardized.

Then we have cases where words have been added. In other instances, the sura order is different.

The whole of section 2 above represents an earlier version of this article (Markus Gross and Karl-Heinz Ohlig, ed., *Vom Koran zum Islam* [Berlin: Verlag Hans Schiler, 2008], pp. 582–605), where, in trying to give some general description of variants to be found in Qur'anic manuscripts, and even more ambitiously trying to arrive at a taxonomy of variants, I conflated what is to be seen in manuscripts, that is, the physical evidence for the discrepancies from the Cairo Qur'an, with the quite separate question of the semantic significance of the discrepancies. We would perhaps approach our enquiry in three steps.

The first step or task is to record what one sees in the manuscripts. Variants could be due to transposition, or there could be words, verses, or whole passages that are different from the Cairo Qur'an, or are not to be found in the Cairo Qur'an, or there are words and passages missing in the manuscripts. The next stage is to decide whether the latter cases represent genuine textual variants, or simply orthographical variants. The final step comes when we begin to decide on the significance of these variants, and whether there are semantic consequences having legal or theological implications.

3. The Samarqand Codex

I was able to obtain a microfilm of the Samarqand Codex from the Princeton University Firestone Library.[2] The microfilm is a positive film of 731 frames. The first three frames and the last one (frame 731) consist of :

- Frame 1: the words in Arabic, *kalām šarīf.*
- Frame 2: a text in Russian and French, which says: "Kufic Qur'an of Samarqand written, according to tradition, by the third Caliph Uthman [644–656] himself, and which is to be found in the Imperial Public Library of St Petersburg. Edition prepared with the authorisation of the Archaeological Institute of St. Petersburg, by S. Pissaref, St Petersburg [facsimile], 1905."
- Frame 3: a text in Russian reading: "Printed with the permission of the Archaeological Institute of St Petersburg, Director of Institute. Print run of 50 copies, those on sale will be 500 roubles each. Printed in St Petersburg."
- Frame 731: someone's handwritten notes in English recording twelve or so folio numbers and whether they are on the right side or left side.

In between we have various suras of the Qur'an (frame 4 [Qur'an II, verse 7] to frame 730 [Qur'an XX, verse 95], [thus 727 pages of Qur'anic verses]). The frames, thus, do not follow the numerical order of the suras, since in between frame 4 and frame 730 there are also verses from suras XXVI, XXVII, XXXVI, XXXVII, XXXXIX, XL, XLI, and XLII.

In the following pages, I give examples of differences from the Cairo Qur'an to be found in folios of the SQ. Numbers in square brackets refer to the frame numbers on the film of the SQ, obtained from Princeton's Firestone Library. I have also occasionally made comparisons of the SQ with other printed Qur'ans, which are listed in my introduction, pp. 45–46.

4. Variants in the Samarqand Codex

{1} Sura II, 283–84 [SQ 93, on paper] two Allahs missing.

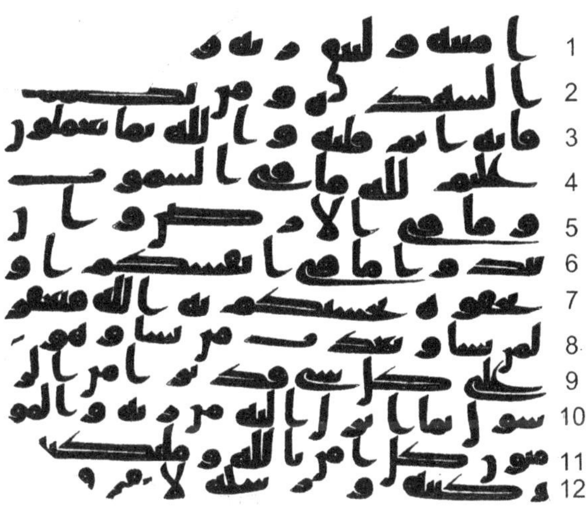

verse 283, line 1. After the word *wa-l-yattaqi*, there should be the word *–llāha*. Despite this lack, the sentence makes sense, and thus we can take it to be a genuine variant.

(verse 283, line 2. Note the defective writing of *šahādata*, that is, there is an *alif* missing. However, it is written defectively in the Cairo Qur'an as well, though, interestingly, it is written *plene*, with an *alif*, in the M. Ali and Marmaduke Pickthall Qur'ans. See pp. 45–46 of my introduction.)

verse 284, line 7. Note the defective writing of *yuḥāsibkum*, that is, there is an *alif* missing. We can take this to be an orthographic variant.

verse 284, line 8. After the words *man yašāʾu*, there should be *wa-llāhu*; instead we have *wa-huwa*. This is a genuine variant, though the meaning of the sentence is not changed in any way.

In the following chapters, the Cairo Qu'an is shown for comparison in the transcription by Zirker, followed by Arabic script, and finally Pickthall's translation. All forms mentioned above are shaded in gray.

Zirker: 283. wa-ʾin kuntum ʿalā safarin wa-lam taǧidū kātiban fa-rihānun-maqbūḍatun fa-ʾin ʾamina baʿḍukum baʿḍan fa-l-yuʾaddi llaḏī ʾtuminaʾamānatahū wa-l-yattaqi llāha rabbahū walā taktumū š-šahādata wa-manyaktumhā fa-ʾinnahū ʾāṯimun qalbuhū wa-llāhu bi-mā taʿmalūna ʿalīmun

وَإِن كُنتُمْ عَلَىٰ سَفَرٍ وَلَمْ تَجِدُوا كَاتِبًا فَرِهَانٌ مَّقْبُوضَةٌ فَإِنْ أَمِنَ بَعْضُكُم بَعْضًا فَلْيُؤَدِّ الَّذِي اؤْتُمِنَ

أَمَانَتَهُ وَلْيَتَّقِ اللَّهَ رَبَّهُ وَلَا تَكْتُمُوا الشَّهَادَةَ وَمَن يَكْتُمْهَا فَإِنَّهُ آثِمٌ قَلْبُهُ وَاللَّهُ بِمَا تَعْمَلُونَ عَلِيمٌ

Pickthall: If ye be on a journey and cannot find a scribe, then a pledge in and (shall suffice). And if one of you entrusteth to another let him who is trusted deliver up that which is entrusted to him (according to the pact between them) and let him observe his duty to Allah. Hide not testimony. He who hideth it, verily his heart is sinful. Allah is Aware of what ye do.

Zirker: 284. li-llāhi mā fī s-samāwāti wa-mā fī l-ʾarḍi wa-ʾin tubdū mā fīʾanfusikum ʾaw tuḫfūhu **yuḥāsibkum** bihi llāhu fa-yaġfiru li-man yašāʾu wayuʿaḏḏibu man yašāʾu **wa-llāhu** ʿalā kulli šayʾin qadīrun

لِّلَّهِ مَا فِي السَّمَاوَاتِ وَمَا فِي الْأَرْضِ وَإِن تُبْدُوا مَا فِي أَنفُسِكُمْ أَوْ تُخْفُوهُ يُحَاسِبْكُم بِهِ اللَّهُ فَيَغْفِرُ لِمَن

يَشَاءُ وَيُعَذِّبُ مَن يَشَاءُ وَاللَّهُ عَلَىٰ كُلِّ شَيْءٍ قَدِيرٌ

Pickthall: Unto Allah (belongeth) whatsoever is in the heavens and whatsoever is in the earth; and whether ye make known what is in your minds or hide it, Allah will bring you to account for it. He will forgive whom He will and He will punish whom He will. Allah is Able to do all things.

{2} Sura III, 37 [SQ 95]

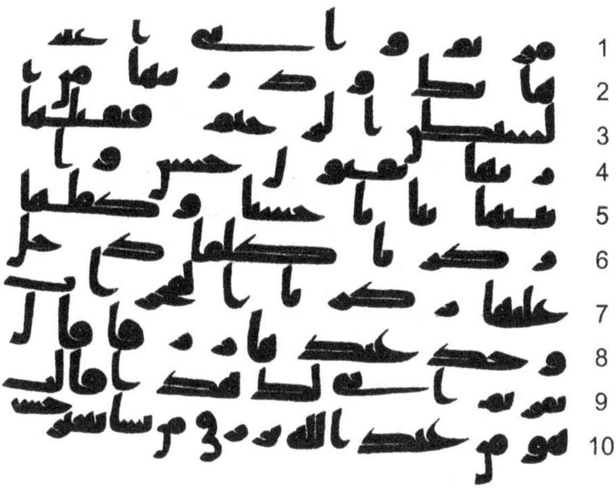

line 10. The words *ʾinna-llāha* are missing after *ʿindi-llāhi*. This is a real variant (lacunae variant), but the meaning remains the same.

Zirker: 3, 37. fa-taqabbalahā rabbuhā bi-qabūlin ḥasanin wa-ʾanbatahānabātan ḥasanan wakaffalahā zakariyyā kullamā daḫala ʿalayhā zakariyyā lmiḥrābawağada ʿindahā rizqan qāla yā-maryamu ʾannā laki hāḏā qālathuwa min ʿindi llāhi ʾinna llāha yarzuqu man yašāʾu bi-ġayri ḥisābin

فَتَقَبَّلَهَا رَبُّهَا بِقَبُولٍ حَسَنٍ وَأَنبَتَهَا نَبَاتًا حَسَنًا وَ كَفَّلَهَا زَ كَرِ يَّا كُلَّمَا دَخَلَ عَلَيْهَا زَ كَرِ يَّا الْمِحْرَابَ

وَ جَدَ عِندَهَا رِزْ قاقَالَ يَامَرْيَمُ أَنَّى لَكِ هَـذَاقَالَتْ هُوَ مِنْ عِندِاللهِ إِنَّ اللهَ يَرْزُ قُ مَن يَشَاءِ بِغَيْرِ حِسَابٍ

Pickthall: And her Lord accepted her with full acceptance and vouchsafed to her a goodly growth; and made Zachariah her guardian. Whenever Zachariah went into the sanctuary where she was, he found that she had food. He said:

O Mary! Whence cometh unto thee this (food)? She answered: It is from Allah. Allah giveth without stint to whom He will.

{3} Sura III, 78 [SQ 111]

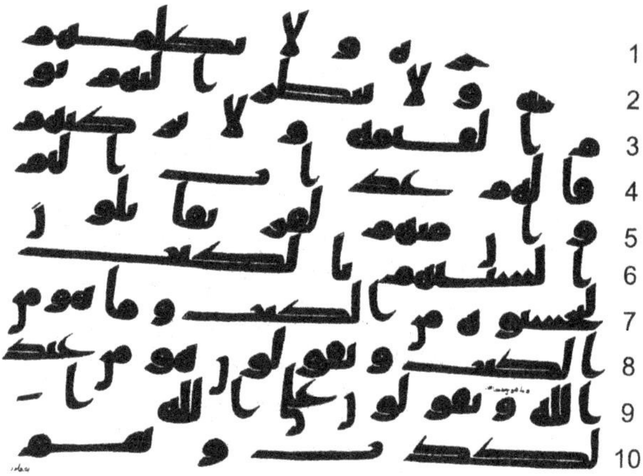

line 9. The words *mā huwa min ʿindi llāhi* are missing after *min ʿindi llāhi wa*. A real, lacunae variant, the phrase “when it is not from Allah” has been left out, without drastically changing the overall meaning.

Zirker: 3, 78. wa-ʾinna minhum la-farīqan yalwūna ʾalsinatahum bi-l-kitābili-taḥsabūhu mina l-kitābi wa-mā huwa mina l-kitābi wa-yaqūlūna huwamin ʿindi llāhi **wa-mā huwa min ʿindi llāhi** wa-yaqūlūna ʿalā llāhi l-kaḏibawa-hum yaʿlamūna

وَإِنَّ مِنْهُمْ لَفَرِيقًا يَلْوُونَ أَلْسِنَتَهُم بِالْكِتَابِ لِتَحْسَبُوهُ مِنَ الْكِتَابِ وَمَا هُوَ مِنَ الْكِتَابِ

وَيَقُولُونَ هُوَ مِنْ عِندِ اللَّهِ وَمَا هُوَ مِنْ عِندِ اللَّهِ وَيَقُولُونَ عَلَى اللَّهِ الْكَذِبَ وَهُمْ يَعْلَمُونَ

Pickthall: And Lo! there is a party of them who distort the Scripture with their tongues, that ye may think that what they say is from the Scripture, when it is not from the Scripture. And they say: It is from Allah, when it is not from Allah; and they speak a lie concerning Allah knowingly.

{4} Sura VI, 93 [SQ 299]

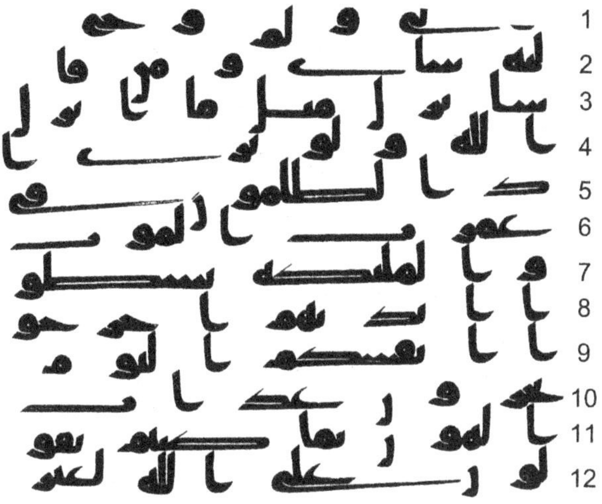

line 1. The letter *yāʾ* in the word *yuḥa* seems to be missing, but probably due to damage to the codex.

line 2. The word *šay'un* is written with a *šīn*, *alif*, and *yā*, whereas it is written with the letters *šīn*, *ya*, and a *hamza* in the Cairo Qur'an. An orthographic variant. However, Christoph Luxenberg has pointed out[3] that the terminal *nūn* in Syriac resembles the final retroflex *yā* in Arabic, and which has been read either as a final "ā" or as a final "y" or "ī." This Syriac reading gives in this case a reading "SH-Ā-N." Instead, of course, it is read, incorrectly according to Luxenberg, as *šay'un* with a fictive medial *hamza*.

lines 5, 6, 7. Defective writings of *ẓālimūna*, *ġamarāti*, and *malāʾikatu*, respectively. However, the Cairo Qur'an is also written defectively. Given J&M's discovery of the number of coincidences of verse endings in SQ with those adopted by Flügel in his text, it is interesting to note that these coincidences do not stretch to defective writing, since *all three* of the above words are written *plene* in the Flügel Qur'an.

line 7. The word *bāsiṭū* is written defectively, though the Cairo Qur'an is written *plene*, that is, with an appropriate *alif*. We could count this as an orthographic variant.

line 12. The last word on this line should read *ġayra* but instead we have a *rasm*, which could be read as *li-ġayri*. The letter *lam* was added later as an attempt at a "correction."

Zirker: 6, 93. wa-man ʾaẓlamu mimmani ftarā ʿalā llāhi kaḏiban ʾaw qālaʾūḥiya ʾilayya wa-lam yūḥa ʾilayhi šayʾun wa-man qāla sa-ʾunzilu miṯla māʾanzala llāhu wa-law tarā ʾiḏi ẓ-ẓālimūna fī ġamarāti l-mawti wa-l-malāʾikatubāsiṭū ʾaydīhim ʾaḫriǧū ʾanfusakumu lyawma tuǧzawna ʿaḏāba l-hūni bi-mākuntum taqūlūna ʿalā llāhi ġayra l-ḥaqqi wakuntum ʿan ʾāyātihī tastakbirūna

وَمَنْ أَظْلَمُ مِمَّنِ افْتَرَى عَلَى اللهِ كَذِبًا أَوْ قَالَ أُوحِيَ إِلَيَّ وَلَمْ يُوحَ إِلَيْهِ شَيْءٌ وَمَن قَالَ سَأُنزِلُ مِثْلَ مَا أَنزَلَ اللهُ

وَلَوْ تَرَى إِذِ الظَّالِمُونَ فِي غَمَرَاتِ الْمَوْتِ وَالْمَلآئِكَةُ بَاسِطُواْ أَيْدِيهِمْ أَخْرِجُواْ أَنفُسَكُمُ الْيَوْمَ

تُجْزَوْنَ عَذَابَ الْهُونِ بِمَا كُنتُمْ تَقُولُونَ عَلَى اللهِ غَيْرَ الْحَقِّ وَكُنتُمْ عَنْ آيَاتِهِ تَسْتَكْبِرُونَ

Pickthall: Who is guilty of more wrong than he who forgeth a lie against Allah, or saith: I am inspired, when he is not inspired in aught; and who saith: I will reveal the like of that which Allah hath revealed? If thou couldst see, when the wrongdoers reach the pangs of death and the angels stretch their hands out, saying: Deliver up your souls. This day ye are awarded doom of degradation for that ye spake concerning Allah other than the truth, and scorned, His portents.

{5} Sura VI, 135–36 [SQ 320]

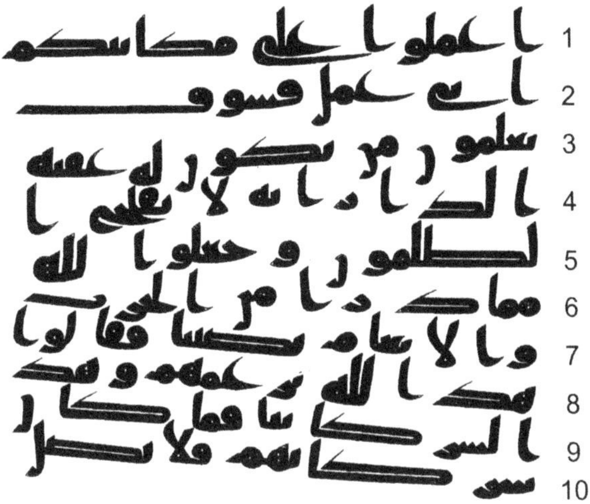

line 2. *ʿāmilun* is defectively written: an orthographic variant.

lines 3, 5. *āqibatu* and ẓālimūna, respectively: defectively written, but also defectively written in Cairo Qur'an, but, again, written with the *alifs* in the Flügel text.

line 10. The *li-* in *li-šurkāʾihim* seems to be missing.

Zirker: 6,135. qul yā-qawmi ʿmalū ʿalā makānatikum ʾinnī ʿāmilun fa-saw-fataʿlamūna man takūnu lahū ʿāqibatu d-dāri ʾinnahū lā yufliḥu ẓ-ẓālimūna

قُلْ يَا قَوْمِ اعْمَلُوا عَلَىٰ مَكَانَتِكُمْ إِنِّي عَامِلٌ فَسَوْفَ تَعْلَمُونَ مَن تَكُونُ لَهُ عَاقِبَةُ الدَّارِ إِنَّهُ لَا يُفْلِحُ الظَّالِمُونَ

Pickthall: Say (O Muhammad): O my people! Work according to your power. Lo! I too am working. Thus ye will come to know for which of us will be the happy sequel. Lo! the wrongdoers will not be successful.

Zirker: 6, 136. wa-ǧaʿalū li-llāhi mimmā ḏaraʾa mina l-ḥarṯi wa-l-ʾanʿāminaṣībanfa-qālū hāḏā li-llāhi bi-zaʿmihim wa-hāḏā li-šurakāʾinā fa-mā kāna li-šurakāʾihim fa-lā yaṣilu ʾilā llāhi wa-mā kāna li-llāhi fa-huwa yaṣilu ʾilāšurakāʾihim sāʾa mā yaḥkumūna

وَجَعَلُواْ لِلهِ مِمَّا ذَرَأَ مِنَ الْحَرْثِ وَالأَنْعَامِ نَصِيبًا فَقَالُواْ هَـذَا لِلهِ بِزَعْمِهِمْ وَهَـذَا لِشُرَكَآئِنَا فَمَا كَانَ

لِشُرَكَآئِهِمْ فَلاَ يَصِلُ إِلَى اللهِ وَمَا كَانَ لِلهِ فَهُوَ يَصِلُ إِلَى شُرَكَآئِهِمْ سَاءَ مَا يَحْكُمُونَ

Pickthall: 136. They assign unto Allah, of the crops and cattle which He created, a portion, and they say: "This is Allah's" in their make believe "and this is for (His) partners in regard to us." Thus that which (they assign) unto His partners in them reacheth not Allah and that which (they assign) unto Allah goeth to thee (so-called) partners. Evil is their ordinance.

{6} Sura VI, 139–41 [SQ323]

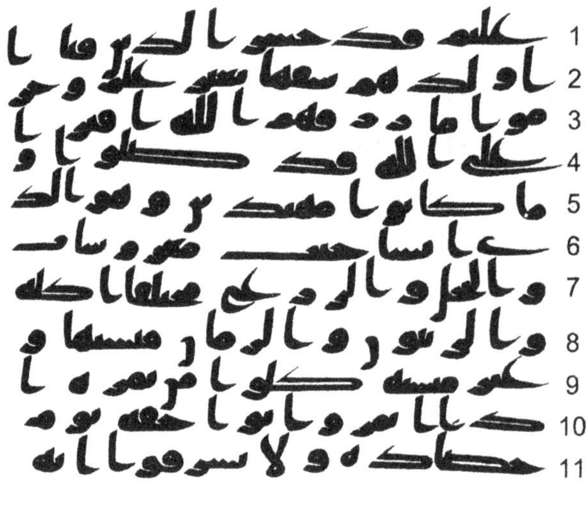

line 1. The letter *wāw* is missing from *qatalū*, very probably due to an incorrect restoration.

line 2. *awlādahum* is defectively written, as also in Cairo Qur'an, but, again, written with the *alif* in the Flügel text where it is in verse 141.

line 6. Interestingly, the Samarqand manuscript here has the plene writing, that is, with the *alif*, which is lacking in defective writing for the word *maʿrūšātin*. The Cairo Qur'an is defective, whereas the Flügel text, like SQ, is written plene (Flügel VI, 1420). An orthographic variant.

line 6. The words *wa ġayra maʿrūšātin* are missing. A lacunae variant.

lines 8, 9. The words *mutašābihan* and *mutašābihin* are defectively written, as in the Cairo Qur'an, but with *alifs* in Flügel (VI, 142).

6, 139

Zirker: wa-qālū mā fī buṭūni hādihi l-ʾanʿāmi ḫāliṣatun li-dukūrinā wamuḥarramunʿalā ʾazwāğinā wa-ʾin yakun maytatan fa-hum fīhi šurakāʾu sayağzīhimwaṣfahum ʾinnahū ḥakīmun ʿalīmun

وَقَالُواْ مَا فِي بُطُونِ هَـٰذِهِ الأَنْعَامِ خَالِصَةٌ لِّذُكُورِنَا وَمُحَرَّمٌ عَلَىٰ أَزْوَاجِنَا وَإِن يَكُن مَّيْتَةً فَهُمْ فِيهِ شُرَكَاءُ

سَيَجْزِيهِمْ وَصْفَهُمْ إِنَّهُ حِكِيمٌ عَلِيمٌ

Pickthall: And they say: That which is in the bellies of such cattle is reserved for our males and is forbidden to our wives; but if it be born dead, then they (all) may be partakers thereof. He will reward them for their attribution (ordinances unto Him). Lo, He is Wise, Aware.

6, 140

Zirker: qad ḫasira lladīna qatalū ʾawlādahum safahan bi-ġayri ʿilmin waḥarramū mā razaqahumu llāhu ftirāʾan ʿalā llāhi qad ḍallū wa-mā kānūmuhtadīna

قَدْ خَسِرَ الَّذِينَ قَتَلُواْ أَوْلاَدَهُمْ سَفَهًا بِغَيْرِ عِلْمٍ وَحَرَّمُواْ مَا رَزَقَهُمُ اللهُ افْتِرَاءً عَلَى اللهِ قَدْ ضَلُّواْ وَمَا كَانُواْ

مُهْتَدِينَ

Pickthall: They are losers who besottedly have slain their children without knowledge, and have forbidden that which Allah bestowed upon them, inventing a lie against Allah. They indeed have gone astray and are not guided.

6, 141

Zirker: wa-huwa llaḏī ʾanšaʾa ǧannātin **maʿrūšātin** wa-ġayra maʿrūšātin wan-naḫla wa-z-zarʿa muḫtalifan ʾukuluhū wa-z-zaytūna wa-r-rummāna **mutašābihan** wa-ġayra **mutašābihin** kulū min ṯamarihī ʾiḏā ʾaṯmara wa-ʾātūḥaqqahū yawma ḥaṣādihī wa-lā tusrifū ʾinnahū lā yuḥibbu l-musrifīna

وَهُوَ الَّذِي أَنشَأَ جَنَّاتٍ مَّعْرُوشَاتٍ وَغَيْرَ مَعْرُوشَاتٍ وَالنَّخْلَ وَالزَّرْعَ مُخْتَلِفًا أُكُلُهُ وَالزَّيْتُونَ

وَالرُّمَّانَ مُتَشَابِهًا وَغَيْرَ مُتَشَابِهٍ كُلُوا مِن ثَمَرِهِ إِذَا أَثْمَرَ وَآتُوا حَقَّهُ يَوْمَ حَصَادِهِ وَلَا تُسْرِفُوا إِنَّهُ لَا يُحِبُّ

Pickthall: He it is Who produceth gardens trellised and untrellised, and the date palm, and crops of divers flavour, and the olive and the pomegranate, like and unlike. Eat ye of the fruit thereof when it fruiteth, and pay the due thereof upon the harvest day, and be not prodigal. Lo! Allah loveth not the prodigals.

{7} Sura VII, 68–70 [SQ 370]

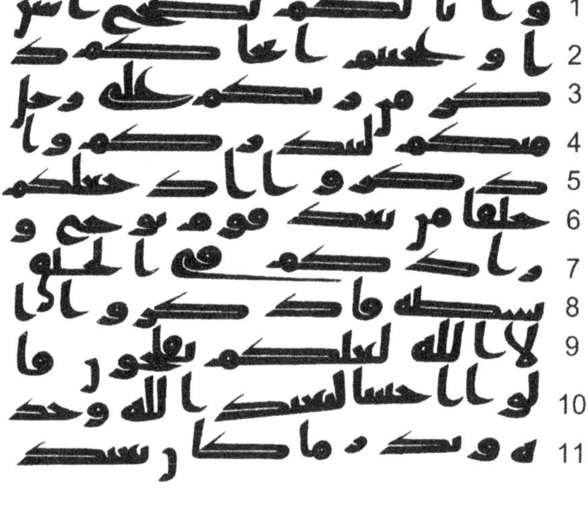

line 1. *nāsiḥun* is defectively written. Cairo Qur'an is with an *alif.*

line 2. Where the Cairo Qur'an has *ʾan ğāʾ-kum* [two words *ʾan* and *ğāʾ* plus the suffix *kum*], in the Samarqand manuscript the words are joined together so that the rasm looks like *ʾanğāʾkum*.

verse 69, line 8. We have *basṭatan* written with the letter *sīn* instead of the letter *ṣād*. An orthographic variant. Interestingly, in the Saudi Qur'an (Saudi II) a tiny *sīn* has been written over the letter *ṣād*, to indicate that it should be pronounced as a *sīn* and not a *ṣād*. Again, interestingly, in the Flügel text (verse 67) this word is written, like the SQ, with a *sīn*. All the other Qur'an listed in my introduction, pp. 45–46 spell the word with a *ṣād*, but often with a tiny *sīn* written over the *ṣād*.

7, 68

Zirker: ʾuballiġukum risālāti rabbī wa-ʾana lakum **nāṣiḥun** ʾamīnun

أُبَلِّغُكُمْ رِسَالاتِ رَبِّي وَأَنَا لَكُمْ نَاصِحٌ أَمِينٌ

Pickthall: I convey unto you the messages of my Lord and am for you a true adviser.

7, 69

Zirker: ʾa-wa-ʿağibtum **ʾan ğāʾakum** ḏikrun min rabbikum ʿalā rağulinminkum li-yunḏirakum wa-ḏkurū ʾiḏ ğaʿalakum ḫulafāʾa min baʿdi qawminūḥin wa-zādakum fī l-ḫalqi **basṭatan** fa-ḏkurū ʾālāʾa llāhi laʿallakumtufliḥūna

أَوَعَجِبْتُمْ أَنْ جَاءَكُمْ ذِكْرٌ مِنْ رَبِّكُمْ عَلَى رَجُلٍ مِنْكُمْ لِيُنْذِرَكُمْ وَاذْكُرُوا إِذْ جَعَلَكُمْ خُلَفَاءَ مِنْ

بَعْدِ قَوْمِ نُوحٍ وَزَادَكُمْ فِي الْخَلْقِ بَسْطَةً فَاذْكُرُوا آلاءَ اللَّهِ لَعَلَّكُمْ تُفْلِحُونَ

Pickthall: Marvel ye that there should come unto you a Reminder from your Lord by means of a man among you, that he may warn you? Remember how He made you viceroys after Noah's folk, and gave you growth of stature. Remember (all) the bounties of your Lord, that haply ye may be successful.

7, 70

Zirker: qālū ʾa-ǧiʾtanā li-naʿbuda llāha waḥdahū wa-naḏara mā kāna yaʿbuduʾābāʾunā fa-ʾtinā bi-mā taʿidunā ʾin kunta mina ṣ-ṣādiqīna

فَتَقَبَّلَهَا رَبُّهَا بِقَبُولٍ حَسَنٍ وَأَنبَتَهَا نَبَاتًا حَسَنًا وَكَفَّلَهَا زَكَرِيَّا كُلَّمَا دَخَلَ عَلَيْهَا زَكَرِيَّا الْمِحْرَابَ

وَجَدَ عِندَهَا رِزْقًا قَالَ يَامَرْيَمُ أَنَّى لَكِ هَـٰذَا قَالَتْ هُوَ مِنْ عِندِ اللهِ إِنَّ اللهَ يَرْزُقُ مَن يَشَاءُ بِغَيْرِ حِسَابٍ

Pickthall: They said: Hast come unto us that we should serve Allah alone, and forsake what our fathers worshipped? Then bring upon us that herewith thou threatenest us if thou are of the truth.

{8} Sura VII, 73 [SQ 373]

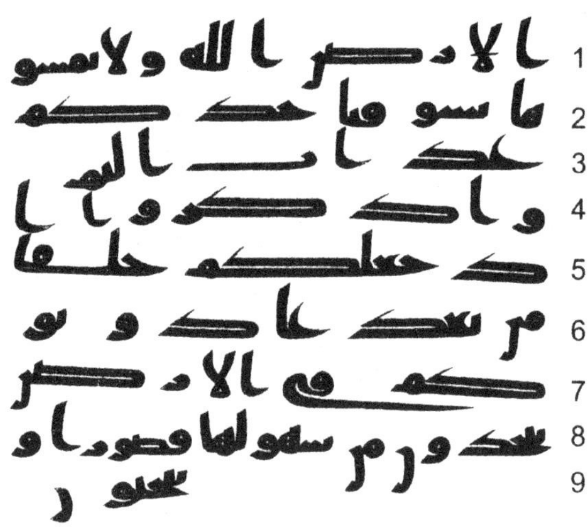

line 1. The Samarqand Codex has written *fī-l-ʾarḍi* (with the definite article in front of *ʾarḍi*), though the Cairo has only *fī ʾarḍi* (i.e., no definite article). Only the latter is grammatically correct. Perhaps the scribe was confusing it

with the next verse, which does indeed have the same word but this time with the definite article. However, in this folio, one can clearly see that someone has put a stroke through the *lam* and *alif*, in order to correct this mistake.

Zirker: 7, 73 wa-ʾilā ṯamūda ʾaḫāhum ṣāliḥan qāla yā-qawmi ʿbudū llāha mālakum min ʾilāhin ġayruhū qad ǧāʾatkum bayyinatun min rabbikum hāḏihīnāqatu llāhi lakum ʾāyatan fa-ḏarūhā taʾkul *fī ʾarḍi* llāhi wa-lā tamassūhā bisūʾin fa-yaʾḫuḏakum ʿaḏābun ʾalīmun

وَإِلَى ثَمُودَ أَخَاهُمْ صَالِحًا قَالَ يَا قَوْمِ اعْبُدُوا اللهَ مَا لَكُم مِّنْ إِلَهٍ غَيْرُهُ قَدْ جَاءَتْكُم بَيِّنَةٌ مِّن رَّبِّكُمْ

هَذِهِ نَاقَةُ اللهِ لَكُمْ آيَةً فَذَرُوهَا تَأْكُلْ فِي أَرْضِ اللهِ وَلَا تَمَسُّوهَا بِسُوءٍ فَيَأْخُذَكُمْ عَذَابٌ أَلِيمٌ

Pickthall: And to (the tribe of) Thamud (We sent) their brother Salih. He said: O my people! Serve Allah. Ye have no other God save Him. A wonder from your Lord hath come unto you. Lo! This is the camel of Allah, a token unto you; so let her feed in Allah's earth, and touch her not with hurt lest painful torment seize you.

{9} Sura VII, 76–77 [SQ 375]

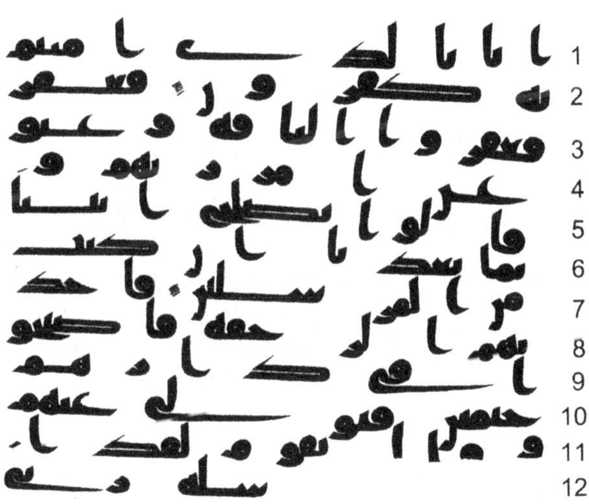

lines 2/3. The word *fa ʿaqarū* is written twice. A scribal error.

7, 76

Zirker: qāla llaḏīna stakbarū ʾinnā bi-llaḏī ʾāmantum bihī kāfirūna

فَعَقَرُوا النَّاقَةَ وَعَتَوْا عَنْ أَمْرِ رَبِّهِمْ وَقَالُوا يَا صَالِحُ ائْتِنَا بِمَا تَعِدُنَا إِن كُنتَ مِنَ الْمُرْسَلِينَ

Pickthall: Those who were scornful said: Lo! In that which ye believe we are disbelievers.

7, 77

Zirker: fa-ʿaqarū n-nāqata wa-ʿataw ʿan ʾamri rabbihim wa-qālū yā-ṣāliḥuʾtinā bi-mā taʿidunā ʾin kunta mina l-mursalīna

فَعَقَرُوا النَّاقَةَ وَعَتَوْا عَنْ أَمْرِ رَبِّهِمْ وَقَالُوا يَا صَالِحُ ائْتِنَا بِمَا تَعِدُنَا إِن كُنتَ مِنَ الْمُرْسَلِينَ

Pickthall: So they hamstrung the she camel, and they flouted the commandment of their Lord, and they said: O Salih! Bring upon us that thou threatenest if thou are indeed of those sent (from Allah).

{10} Sura XXVI, 91 [SQ 588]

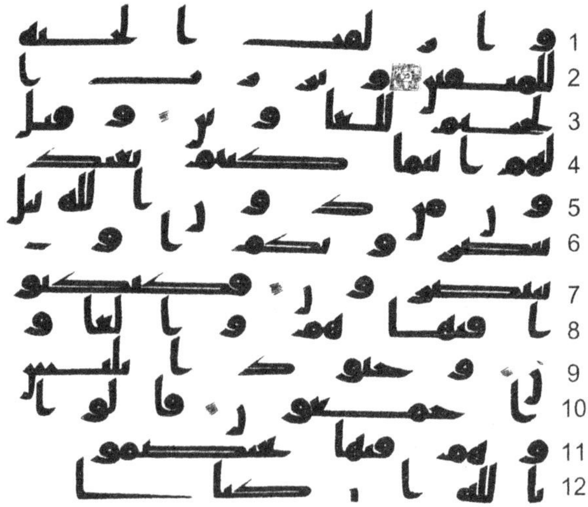

line 3. Take note of the plene writing of *li-l-ġāwīna*, as in the Cairo Qur'an. But both the Pickthall and M. Ali Qur'ans have the defective writing.

line 4. The Cairo Qur'an has two words *'ayna mā* after the words *wa-qīla lahum*. Here they seem to be joined together, giving us a real orthographic variant. But, once again, the Flügel text follows SQ in having the words joined together.

line 5. Instead of the word *hal* after *Allāh*, we have another *rasm*. This was very probably an attempt at restoration gone wrong.

line 12. After the word *kunnā* we should have *lafī* but do not seem to; again this is due to damage and false restoration: the *fā* and part of the *yā* are lost, and the restorer has falsely connected the *lam* to the rest of the retroflex *yā*.

26, 91–97

26, 91

Zirker: wa burrizati l-ǧahīmu li-l-ġāwīn^{a}

وَبُرِّزَتِ الْجَحِيمُ لِلْغَاوِينَ

Pickthall: And hell will appear plainly to the erring.

26, 92

Zirker: wa qīla lahum ʾayna mā kuntum taʿbudūn^{a}

وَقِيلَ لَهُمْ أَيْنَ مَا كُنتُمْ تَعْبُدُونَ

Pickthall: And it will be said unto them: Where is (all) that ye used to worship.

26, 93

Zirker: min dūni llāhi **hal** yanṣurūnakum ʾaw yantaṣirūn[a]

مِن دُونِ اللَّهِ هَلْ يَنصُرُونَكُمْ أَوْ يَنتَصِرُونَ

Pickthall: Instead of Allah? Can they help you or help themselves?

26, 94

Zirker: fa-kubkibū fīhā hum wa-l-ġāwūn[a]

فَكُبْكِبُوا فِيهَا هُمْ وَالْغَاوُونَ

Pickthall: Then they will be hurled therein, they and the seducers.

26, 95

Zirker: wa-ǧunūdu ʾiblīsa ʾaǧmaʿūn[a]

وَجُنُودُ إِبْلِيسَ أَجْمَعُونَ

Pickthall: And the hosts of Iblis, together.

26, 96

Zirker: qālū wa-hum fīhā yaḫtaṣimūn[a]

قَالُوا وَهُمْ فِيهَا يَخْتَصِمُونَ

Pickthall: And they will say, when they are quarrelling therein:

26, 97

Zirker: ta-llāhi ʾin kunnā la-fī ḍalālin mubīn^{in}

تَاللَّهِ إِن كُنَّا لَفِي ضَلَالٍ مُّبِينٍ

Pickthall: By Allah, of a truth we were in error manifest.

{11} Sura XXXVII,171–79 [SQ 665]

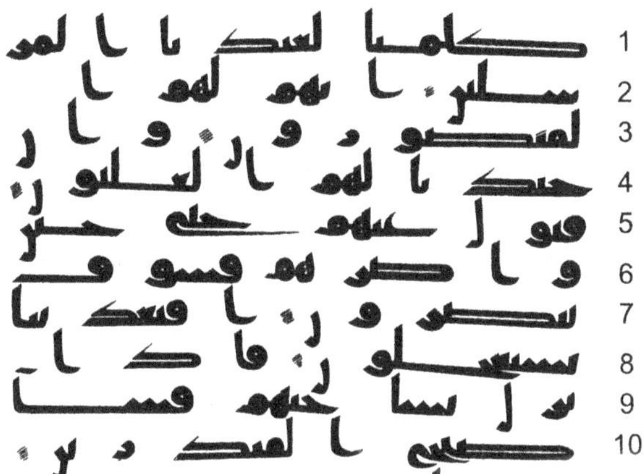

line 1. Defective writing of *li-ʿibādinā*: an orthographic variant.

line 6. The letter *bāʾ* is missing from the word *ʾabṣir* (hum). Compare the word *ʾabṣir*, correctly written on line 12. Probably caused by damage to the SQ.

line 7. The word is defectively written from the middle of the word *a-fa-bi-ʿaḏābinā*. An orthographic variant.

line 10. Defective writing of *ṣabāḥu*: an orthographic variant.

37, 171–77

37, 171

Zirker: wa-la-qad sabaqat kalimatunā li-ʿibādinā l-mursalīn[a]

وَلَقَدْ سَبَقَتْ كَلِمَتُنَا لِعِبَادِنَا الْمُرْسَلِينَ

Pickthall: And verily Our word went forth of old unto Our bondmen sent (to warn)

37, 172

Zirker: ʾinnahum la-humu l-manṣūrūn[a]

إِنَّهُمْ لَهُمُ الْمَنصُورُونَ

Pickthall: That they verily would be helped.

37, 173

Zirker: wa-ʾinna ǧundanā la-humu l-ġālibūn[a]

وَإِنَّ جُندَنَا لَهُمُ الْغَالِبُونَ

Pickthall: And that Our host, they verily would be the victors.

37, 174

Zirker: fa-tawalla ʿanhum ḥattā ḥīnin

فَتَوَلَّ عَنْهُمْ حَتَّى حِينٍ

Pickthall: So withdraw from them (O Muhammad) awhile,

37, 175

Zirker: wa-ʾabṣirhum fa-sawfa yubsirūna

وَأَبْصِرْهُمْ فَسَوْفَ يُبْصِرُونَ

Pickthall: And watch, for they will (soon) see.

37, 176

Zirker: ʾa-fa-bi-ʿaḏābinā yastaʿǧilūna

أَفَبِعَذَابِنَا يَسْتَعْجِلُونَ

Pickthall: Would they hasten on Our doom?

37, 177

Zirker: fa-ʾiḏā nazala bi-sāḥatihim fa-sāʾa ṣabāḥu l-munḏarīna

فَإِذَا نَزَلَ بِسَاحَتِهِمْ فَسَاءَ صَبَاحُ الْمُنذَرِينَ

Pickthall: But when it cometh home to them, then it will be a hapless morn for those who have been warned.

{12} Sura XXXVIII, 3–6 [SQ 667]

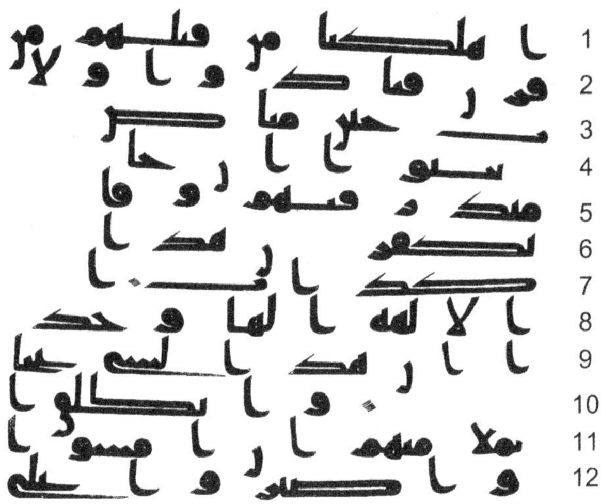

line 4. The word *ʿağibū* should begin with a *ʿayn* but the rasm is incorrect. We can see how the *ʿayn* at the beginning of a word is written in the Samarqand Qu'ran in the last word on line 12: *ʿalā*. The strange *ʿayn* is very probably due to incorrect restoration.

line 5. We have the word *fīhum* instead of *minhum*. A real variant but meaning remains the same.

line 8. The word *ʾilāhan* is written defectively; the Cairo Qu'ran is also defective; but note the way that word is written in the Pickthall Qu'ran. There is also an *alif* lacking after the letter *wāw* in the word *wāḥidan*. The Flügel Qu'ran does have the *alif.*

38, 3–6

38, 3

Zirker: kam ʾahlaknā min qablihim min qarnin fa-nādaw wa-lāta ḥīna manāṣ^{in}

كَمْ أَهْلَكْنَا مِن قَبْلِهِم مِّن قَرْنٍ فَنَادَوا وَّلَاتَ حِينَ مَنَاصٍ

Pickthall: How many a generation We destroyed before them, and they cried out when it was no longer the time for escape!

38, 4

Zirker: wa-ʿ**ağibū** ʾan ğāʾahum mundirun **minhum** wa-qāla l-kāfirūna hāḏā sāḥirun kaḏḏābᵘⁿ

وَعَجِبُوا أَن جَاءهُم مُّنذِرٌ مِّنْهُمْ وَقَالَ الْكَافِرُونَ هَذَا سَاحِرٌ كَذَّابٌ

Pickthall: And they marvel that a warner from among themselves hath come unto them, and the disbelievers say: This is a wizard, a charlatan.

38, 5

Zirker: ʾa-ğaʿala l-ʾālihata **ʾilāhan wāḥidan** ʾinna hāḏā la-šayʾun ʿuğābᵘⁿ

أَجَعَلَ الْآلِهَةَ إِلَهًا وَاحِدًا إِنَّ هَذَا لَشَيْءٌ عُجَابٌ

Pickthall: Maketh he the gods One God? Lo! that is an astounding thing.

38, 6

Zirker: wa-nṭalaqa l-malaʾu minhum ʾani mšū wa-ṣbirū ʿalā ʾālihatikumʾinna hāḏā la-šayʾun yurādᵘ

وَانطَلَقَ الْمَلَأُ مِنْهُمْ أَنِ امْشُوا وَاصْبِرُوا عَلَى آلِهَتِكُمْ إِنَّ هَذَا لَشَيْءٌ يُرَادُ

Pickthall: The chiefs among them go about, exhorting: Go and be staunch to your gods! Lo! this is a thing designed.

Notes

1. I owe Dr. Elisabeth Puin a special word of thanks. She has worked for many years on Qur'anic manuscripts, and the fruit of her groundbreaking research will be published soon in the Inarah Insitute Series. She looked through my article with characteristic thoroughness and analytical clarity, and thereby saved me from countless errors and embarrassment. She made many suggestions, all of which I have adopted. But she cannot be held responsible, of course, for any errors that remain.

2. The catalog record from Princeton's own online catalog is as follows:

Title: *Qur'an.*

Samarkandsk̄ii kufichesk̄ii ***Qur'an*** [microform], popredan̄iiu pisannyi sobstvennoruchno tret′im kh*alif*om Osmanom (644–656) inakhodiashch̄iisia v Imperatorskoi S-Peterburgskoi publichnoi bibl̄iotek; izdano pri S-Peterburgskom arkheologicheskom institut S. Iv. Pisarevym (faksimile) . . .

Coran coufique de Samarcand, écrit d'après la tradition de la propre main du troisième c*alif*e Osman (644–656) qui se trouve dans la Bibliothèque impériale publique de St. Petersbourg . . .

Published/Created: St. Petersbourg, 1905.

Physical Description: 1. facsim.: 706 p. 52 x 70 cm.

Location: RECAP: Use in Firestone Microforms only. Use recap button

Call Number: MICROFILM 674

Status: Not Charged.

The transliteration is incorrect. The reconstructed Russian title would be: Самаркандский Ҡуфический Ҡоран.

3. Christoph Luxenberg, "Relikte syro-aramäischer Buchstaben in frühen Qur'ankodizes im Hijâzi und Kûfi-Duktus" (Relics of Syro-Aramaic Letters in Early Qur'an Codices in Hijâzi and Kufic Style), in *Der frühe Islam* (Early Islam), 1st ed. (Berlin: Verlag Hans Schiler, 2007), pp. 377–414.

Part 4

Variants

4.1

The Qur'ān Readings of Zaid b. 'Alī

Arthur Jeffery

One of the as yet untouched problems of the textual criticism of the Qur'ān is that of the Shī'a *Qirā'āt*. It is well known that there was considerable Shīʿa opposition to the official 'Uthmānic text. On the one hand, this is expressed in the tradition that 'Alī had made a recension of the Qur'ān earlier than that of 'Uthmān, earlier indeed than the supposed first recension that was made by Abū Bakr. Thus in Ya'qūbī, *Historia*, II, 152 (ed. Houtsma) we read—"It is said that ʿAlī b. Abī Ṭālib was making an edition of the Qur'ān when the Prophet of God passed away, and he brought it along on a camel and said—'this is the Qur'ān that I have edited.'" Ya'qūbī then goes on to give a list of the sūras as arranged in this recension of 'Alī. If we can believe Ibn an-Nadīm (*Fihrist*, p. 28), this Codex of 'Alī, lacking but a few leaves, was still in the hands of the 'Alīd family when he wrote. On the other hand, this opposition appears in the charges of the Shīʿas that in the 'Uthmānic recension much material favorable to the *Ahl-al-Bait* was omitted and other passages were reworded so as to conceal their claims. Thus we have the *Sūrat an-Nūrain*, published by Kazem Beg in the *Journal asiatique* for 1843, and numerous textual suggestions, as that *umma* in many places ought to be read *a'imma*, that *āl-ʿImrān* in III, 30 ought to be read *āl-Muḥammad*, and so on.

That this Shīʿa objection to the 'Uthmānic recension of the text was very early is evident from the fact that Sunnī orthodoxy found it necessary to invent traditions in which 'Alī is made to express his unqualified approval of the text published by 'Uthmān.[1]

Now we are quite sure, as a result of modern investigations, that the text published by the Caliph ʿUthmān was only a choice out of many rival texts, and we have no conviction that the text chosen by him as the official text for Islām was in all respects the best possible text. The texts of Ibn Masʿūd and of Ubai b. Kaʿb, for example, had at least a claim to consideration. It may well be that there was a text associated with ʿAlī and the *Ahl al-Bait* which also had a claim to consideration. The problem is whether we can arrive at their text. The information that we have about ʿAlī's Codex is suspect,[2] and such Shīʿa inventions as the *Sūrat an-Nūrain*, the *Sūrat al-Wilāya*, and the text emendations mentioned above, not to speak of those quoted in such Shīʿa works as the *Kāfī* of al-Kulīnī, are more than suspect. Is there any other possibility of reaching back to an early Shīʿa text tradition?

If we turn to the notices of the variant readings given in the commentaries and *qirāʾāt* books we find a considerable number of such variants ascribed to ʿAlī and still more to ʿAbd ar-Raḥmān as-Sulamī (†85), who is said to represent ʿAlī's tradition as to Qur'ān reading (Ibn al-Jazarī, *Ṭabaqāt*, no. 1755). There are also not a few readings ascribed to various members of the *Ahl al-Bait*, for example, to al-Ḥasan, al-Ḥusain, Mḥd b. al-Ḥanafīya, Jaʿfar aṣ-Ṣādiq, Mḥd al Bāqir, and so on, and these not only in Shīʿa commentaries and sources. Most prominent among them, however, are the readings ascribed to Zaid b. ʿAlī (†122).

Zaid b. ʿAlī was the brother of Mḥd al Bāqir and the great grandson of ʿAlī, being the son of Zain al-ʿĀbidīn, who was the son of al-Ḥusain the second son of ʿAlī. He is thus in direct succession in the *Ahl-al-Bait*. He is an important figure for two reasons: first because he gave his name to the sect of the Zaidites, and second because he is the earliest of the *Ahl al-Bait* to figure in any prominent way as a theologian and writer.[3] A whole compendium of jurisprudence goes under his name, and his elucubrations on the Qur'ān are frequently quoted. A very brief examination of the *Corpus Juris di Zaid ibn Ali*, published by Griggini, suffices to show that a great mass of opinions, deductions, and decisions of later Zaidite authorities have been fathered on him, but with regard to the exegetical material we may be on sounder ground. He was apparently particularly interested in Qur'ānic matters, and was given the title *ḥalīf al-Qur'ān*, and though it is very possible that later materials was here also fathered on him, it has been several times suggested that in the Qur'ānic readings that go under his name, we may have preserved to us very ancient material from the Shī'a tradition.

This question it was impossible to study more closely until the readings of Zaid b. 'Alī were assembled. Such an assemblage is offered to scholars in the pages which follow. The most important sources that have been utilized are the Qur'ān commentaries and *qirā'āt* works, though the lexicons and philological works have also been consulted. The most useful commentaries have been the following—the *Kashshāf* of az-Zamakhsharī, the *Jāmi' al-Bayān* of aṭ-Ṭabarī, the *Mafātīḥ al-Ghaib* of ar-Rāzī, the *Ma'ālim at-Tanzīl* of al-Baghawī, the *Baḥr* of Abū Ḥayyān, the *Fatḥ al-Qadīr* of al-Alūsī, and the two volumes so far published of the commentary of al-Qurṭubī. Of *qirā'āt* books besides the Ibn Khālawaih and Ibn Jinnī edited by the late Professor Bergsträsser,[4] the most important source has been al-'Ukbari's *I'rāb al-Qirā'āt ash-Shādhdha*, a manuscript of which is now in the collection of Dr. Mingana at Selly Oak. The lexicons and the philological works rarely give a reading that is not to be found in the commentaries, though they are often helpful in ascertaining its exact meaning.

The readings have not been grouped but are arranged in the order of the sūras of the Qur'ān, the verse numbering being that of Flügel, which is the most convenient for purposes of reference. Where a reading is also given from other readers I have generally mentioned the most important of them who agree therein with Zaid b. 'Alī. In most cases the variant is easily intelligible from the form itself when compared with the *textus receptus* (*TR*), but where there might be a possibility of doubt, a note has been added to indicate what the difference of meaning is. I have also thought it worthwhile to indicate those passages where the sources expressly note that Zaid b. 'Alī agreed with the *TR*, or with one or other of the seven canonical readers against another well-known reading.

The Ambrosiana manuscript folio 289, to which my attention was called by Strothmann's notice (*Der Islam*, XIII, 11), contains a section on the special *qirā'āt* of Zaid b. 'Alī. Through the kindness and courtesy of the editor of the *Rivista* I was able to procure photostats of this section. On examination, however, it proved to contain nothing more than a word-for-word reproduction of the material in the *Baḥr* of Abū Ḥayyān referring to the readings of Zaid b. 'Alī. Moreover it is only a fragment commencing with Sūra LXXVII, 35.

It is always possible that more material may come to light. My own discovery of the complete manuscript of al-'Ukbari's *I'rāb al-Qirā'āt ash-Shādhdha*, which has been the richest of all sources for uncanonical readings of Zaid, was a pure accident. In working through the commentaries one frequently comes across references to the lost works of al-Ahwāzī, al-Mahdawī, and Ibn ʿAṭīya, which apparently contained numerous readings from Zaid b. 'Alī. Should these works ever come to light we could probably increase manifold this present list of variants. Also it is very possible that in the specifically Shīʿa sources there may be rich material. Those that I have been able to examine here have not made any notable contribution, but they have been few, for it is peculiarly difficult to procure Shīʿa texts. Shīʿa sheikhs with whom I have conversed in this city of Cairo have assured me that in Persia there are great stores of manuscripts material on Shīʿa exegesis and Qur'ānic science that are as yet practically unknown to Western scholarship. I do not doubt that if this material could be examined we might find some profitable sources for a more complete collection of variants.

It is matter of congratulation that so large a selection of variants as we have here has been preserved to us, but in passing judgment on Zaid's readings we must remember that these are only what has been preserved to us in Sunnī sources, whose custom, as we know from Abū Ḥayyān (*Baḥr*, VII, 268) was only to record such variant readings as were not too far removed from the accepted consonantal text.

Sūra I.

1: الحَمْدِ لِلّه – الحَمْدُ لِلّه as read by al-Ḥasan and Muʿādh. It is explained as لاتباعها اللام.

رَبَّ – رَبِّ taken either as على المدح or because الحمدُ لِلّه is equivalent to نحمدُ اللهَ.

2: الرحمنَ الرحيمَ – الرحمنِ الرحيمِ naturally after reading رَبَّ.

3: مَلَكَ يَوْمَ – مَالِكِ يَوْمِ (i.e., *māḍī*). So read by Abū Ḥaiwa and Abū'ṣ-Sammāl.

4: نُعْبُدُ – نَعْبُدُ agreeing with Ibn Waththāb and ʿUbaid b. ʿUmair.

5: صِرَاطًا مُسْتَقِيمًا – الصراطَ المستقيمَ so read by al-Ḥasan, aḍ-Ḍahhāk, and Naṣr b. 'Alī.

6: مَنْ – الَّذِينَ as was read by Ibn Masʿūd. That is, "whoever" instead of "those who."

7: غَيْرِ – وَلَا as read by 'Alī, Ubai, and Jaʿfar aṣ-Ṣādiq. It is a grammatical simplification.

Sūra II.

1: لَارَيْبٌ – لَارَيْبَ taking it as لَا with the meaning of ليس instead of لا النافية للجنس.

6: غُشَاوَةٌ – غِشَاوَةٌ as was read by al-Ḥasan. An alternative voweling.

14: طِغْيَانِهِمْ – طُغْيَانِهِمْ an alternative form (*lugha*). So read by Abū Nahīk.

15: اشْتَرَوِا – اشْتَرَوُا so read by Yaḥyā b. Yaʿmar and Ibn Abī Isḥāq, this being the original form for فى التقاء الساكنين.

16: ظُلْمَاتٍ – ظُلُمَاتٍ as read by al-Ḥasan.

17: صُمًّا بُكْمًا عُمْيًا – صُمٌّ بُكْمٌ عُمْىٌ taking them as a second *mafʿūl*. It was so read by Ubai and Ibn Masʿūd.

19: يُخَطِّفُ – يَخْطَفُ, that is, II form explained as تكثير مبالغة لا تعدية. وَٱلَّذِينَ مَنْ قَبْلَكُمْ – وَٱلَّذِينَ مِنْ قَبْلِكُمْ the مَنْ being taken as تاكيد to the الذين.

22: اُعْتِدَتْ – أُعِدَّتْ a reading given also from Ibn Masʿūd, Ibn as-

Samaifaʿ, and Abūʾl-ʿĀliya, deriving it from عتد, which is synonymous with اعدّ .

23: بَشِّرِ - بُشِّرَ, that is, passive taken as following on أُعْتِدَتْ. So read by Abūʾl-Jawzāʾ.

مُطَهَّرَةٌ - مُطَهَّرَاتٌ perhaps suiting a little better the ازواج, and so read by Ibn Masʿūd; or مُطَّهِّرَةٌ as read by Ibn Qais.

24: يُضِلُّ بِهِ كثيرًا وَيَهْدِى به كثيرًا وما يُضِلُّ به إلّا الفَاسِقِين - يُضَلُّ بِهِ كثيرٌ ويُهْدَى به كثيرٌ وما يُضَلُّ الّا الفَاسِقُونَ, that is, a passive construction instead of making Allah the subject direct. So read by Ubai, Ibn Masʿūd, and Ibn Abī ʿAbla.

28: خَلِيفَةً - خَلِيقَةً, that is, "creatures" instand of "a viceregent."

30: عَلَّمْتَنَا - أَعْلَمْتَنَا a synonym, so read by Ubai and Ibn Masʿūd.

34: مُسْتَقَرٌّ - مُسْتَقِرٌّ as read by Abū Nahīk, using the active participle instead of the passive participle and probably meaning "an abiding" rather than "an abode."

39: تَلْبِسُوا - تُلْبِسُوا, that is, "do not cover" instead of "do not confuse," so read by Abū Shaikh.

46: نَجَّيْنَاكُمْ - أَنْجَيْتُكُمْ, which was the reading of an-Nakhaʿī and Abū Shaikh, putting the verb I singular instead of I plural.

يَسُومُونَكُمْ - يُسَوِّمُونَكُمْ with Abū Razīn., that is, II form instead of I form.

58: يُخْرِجْ لَنَا مِمَّا تُنْبِتُ ٱلْأَرْضُ - يَخْرُجْ لَنَا مِمَّا تَنْبُتُ ٱلْأَرْضُ. Same meaning.

65: تَشَابَهَ - تَشَابَهُ so read by Ubai and Abū Nahīk.

66: كادوا he read here with Imāla like Ibn Abī Isḥāq.

69: قَسَتْ - قَسَا dual, as read by Ubai and Ibn Masʿūd.

قَسْوَةً - قَسَاوَةً so read by Ibn Masʿūd.

79: تُرَدُّونَ - يُرَدُّونَ a change of person, as read by al-Ḥasan.

83: مُصَدِّقًا - مُصَدِّقٌ taking it as *ḥāl*. So read by Ibn Masʿūd and Ubai.

97: لَمَثْوَبَةٌ - لَمَثُوبَةٌ an alternative form, so read by Qatāda.

103: تُبَيِّنَ - تَبَيَّنَ making it passive, as read by Abū Nahīk and others.

105: لَنْ يُدْخَلَ ٱلْجَنَّةُ - لَنْ يَدْخُلَ ٱلْجَنَّةَ passive so read by Abū Shaikh and others.

111: بَدِيعَ - بَدِيعُ governed by an أَغْنَى understood. So read by Ibn as-Samaifaʿ.

118: ذِرِّيَّتِي - ذُرِّيَّتِي so read by Yaḥyā b. Yaʿmar.

120: ٱضْطَرُّهُ - أَضْطَرُّهُ (imperfect). So Ibn ʿAbbās and others.

123: يَتْلُوا and يُعَلِّمُهُمْ and يُزَكِّيهِمْ - نَتْلُوا and نُعَلِّمُهُمْ and نُزَكِّيهِمْ making the address personal. So Abū Nahīk read.

143: مُوَلَّاهَا - مُوَلِّيهَا as read by Abū'l-ʿĀliya and others.

145: أَلَا ٱلَّذِينَ - إِلَّا ٱلَّذِينَ, that is, "are there not those" for "except those."

156: والمَلَائِكَةُ وَٱلنَّاسُ أَجْمَعُونَ - وَٱلْمَلَائِكَةِ وَٱلنَّاسِ أَجْمَعِينَ taking it as *maʿṭūf* to لعنةُ not to اللهِ. So read by al-Ḥasan and Abū Nahīk.

159: الفَلْكِ - الفُلْكِ a variant voweling, given from Abū Nahīk and others.

161: تَبَرَّ - تَبَرَّأَ so read by 'Alī, Jaʿfar b. Mḥd, and Shaiba.

165: نَتْبَعُ - نَتَّبِعُ, that is, I form instead of VIII but with same meaning. So read by Abū Shaikh.

166: يَنْعَقُ - يَنْعِقُ an alternative form, so read by Abū Nahīk and Abū Shaikh.

170: أَصبرهُمْ - أَصْبَرَهُمْ so read by Abū Nahīk and others.

180: وَإِنْ تَصُومُوا - وَأَنْ تَصُومُوا so Abū ʿImrān, reading "if ye fast" instead of "that ye should fast."

183: الرَّفَثُ - الرفُوثُ plural as read by Ibn Masʿūd.

192: نُسُكٍ - نُسْكٍ an alternative form, so read by al-Ḥasan, an-Nakhaʿī, and others.

سَبَعَةٍ - سَبْعَةً a grammatical interpretation (see Alūsī, II, 72), so read by Ibn Abī ʿAbla.

193: لَاجِدَالَ - لَاجِدَالٌ taking it as لا with the meaning of ليس, as read by ʿIkrima, al-Ḥasan, and Abū Jaʿfar.

205: زَلَلْتُمْ - زَلِلْتُمْ an alternative form, so read by Muʿādh and Abūʾs-Sammāl.

209: لِمَا - لَمَّا as read by Abū Nahīk, that is, "when" instead of "to what," an easier construction.

233: يُتِمَّ الرَّضَاعَةَ - يُتِمَّ الرَّضْعَةَ an alternative form, so read by Mujāhid and Muʿādh.

كِسْوَتُهُنَّ - كُسْوَتُهُنَّ an alternative form read by as-Sulamī and Ṭalḥa.

234: يُتَوَفَّوْنَ - يَتَوَفَّوْنَ a synonym, so read by ʿAlī, as-Sulamī, and others.

235: خِطْبَةِ - خِطَبَاتِ plural, which is perhaps simpler here. It was so read by Abūʾl-ʿĀliya and others.

238: فَنِصْفُ - فَنُصْفُ an alternative form, read by ʿAlī, as-Sulamī, and others.

242: لِلْمُطَلَّقَاتِ - لِلْمُطَلَّقَةِ, that is, singular as read by Ubai and Ibn Masʿūd.

248: سَعَةً - سِعَةً an alternative form, so read by Abūʾl-Jawzāʾ, Abū Shaikh, and Abū ʿImrān.

بَسْطَةً - بُسْطَةً an alternative form read by Abū ʿImrān and Muʿādh.

250: بِنَهَرٍ - بِنَهْرٍ the more usual form, read thus by Ḥumaid b. Qais, Mujāhid, and others.

257: الرَّشَدُ - الرُّشْدُ an alternative form, so read by as-Sulamī, al-Ḥasan, and Abū Nahīk.

261: كَيْفَ أَنْشِزُهَا ثُمَّ أَكْسُوهَا - كَيْفَ نُنْشِزُهَا ثُمَّ نَكْسُوهَا, that is, "I" instead of "we," as was also read by Ubai and some others.

266: يَقْدُرُونَ - يَقْدِرُونَ an alternative form.

273: نُكَفِّرُ - يُكَفِّرُ so read by Al-Aʿmash and Abū'ṣ-Sammāl, "we shall expiate" for "it will expiate."

282: وَأَشْهِدُوا - وَأَشْهِدُوا so read by Muʿādh and Abū ʿImrān.

285: يُفَرِّقُ - نُفَرِّقُ with الله as subject, so read by Qatāda, al-Jaḥdarī, and Ya'qūb.

Sūra III

2: القَيَّامِ - القَيُّومِ as read by Jaʿfar aṣ-Ṣādiq and others.

27: تَقِيَّةً - تُقَاةً, that is, *maṣdar* of II form, so read by al-Ḥasan and Ya'qūb.

28: مُحْضِرًا - مُحْضَرًا active participle as read by Abū Nahīk.

30: ذُرِّيَّةٌ - ذُرِّيَّةً taking it as beginning a new clause. So read by Ibn Qais and Abū ʿImrān.

32: فَتَقَبَّلْهَا رَبَّهَا - فَتَقَبَّلَهَا رَبُّهَا, that is, imperative. So read by Mujāhid and others.

أَنْبِتْهَا and أَنْبَتَهَا - كَفِّلْهَا and كَفَّلَهَا, that is, imperative and involving زكرياءَ. So read by Mujāhid and others.

34: بِكِلْمَةٍ - بِكَلِمَةٍ so read by Abū'ṣ-Sammāl.

36: تُكَلِّمَ - تُكَلِّمَ, that is, a *takhfīf* form read by Abū'l-Jawzā' and others.

40: وِجِيهًا - وَجِيهًا an alternative form, so read by Muʿādh and Abū Nahīk.

45: حَسَّ - أَحَسَّ a dialectal form. So read by Abū Nahīk.

50: فَأُوَفِّيهِمْ - فَنُوَفِّيهِمْ "I shall reward them" instead of "we shall reward them," so read by Ubai and Ibn Masʿūd.

79: نُقْبَلَ - يُقْبَلَ "we shall" instead of "he will." So read by Abū Nahīk and ʿĪsā b. ʿUmar.

82: نُخَفِّفُ عَنْهُمُ ٱلْعَذَابَ - يُخَفَّفُ عَنْهُمُ ٱلْعَذَابُ, that is, "we shall lighten the punishment for them" instead of "the punishment shall be lightened for them." So read by Abū Nahīk and others.

84: لَنْ نُقْبِلَ تَوْبَتَهُمْ - لَنْ تُقْبَلَ تَوْبَتُهُمْ, that is, "we shall never accept their repentance" instead of "their repentance will never be accepted." Same readers as in verse 82.

85: تَقْبَلَ.....مِلْءَ - يُقْبَلَ.....مِلْءُ same active construction by same readers as in previous verse.

86: يُنَالُوا ٱلْبِرَّ حَتَّى يُنْفِقُوا - لَنْ تَنَالُوا ٱلْبِرَّ حَتَّى تُنْفِقُوا مِمَّا تُحِبُّونَ وَمَا تُنْفِقُوا مِمَّا يُحِبُّونَ وَمَا يُنْفِقُوا.

90: وَضَعَ - وُضِعَ active for passive. So read by Muʿādh and Abū ʿImrān.

107: يُنْصَرُوا - يُنْصَرُونَ taking it as *ma ʿṭūf* to يولوكم. So Ubai and Ibn Masʿūd.

141: قَوْلَهُمْ - قَوْلُهُمْ making it the subject not the predicate of كان. So Mujāhid and Qatāda.

164: فَارِحِينَ - فَرِحِينَ and alternative form, so read by Ibn as-Samaifaʿ and Abū Nahīk.

Sūra IV

2: حَوْبًا - حُوبًا an alternative form, read by al-Ḥasan and Qatāda.

3: صدقتهن - صَدُقَاتِهِنَّ (singular) so read by Ibn Waththāb and Mālik b. Dīnār.

4: قِوَامًا - قِيَامًا as read by Ubai.
12: النُّصْفُ - النِّصْفُ See II, 238. He read so throughout the Qur'ān.
23: تَعْضِلُوهُنَّ - تَعْضُلُوهُنَّ alternative form, so read by Abū Nahīk.
لِتُذْهِبُوا - لِتَذْهَبُوا alternative form, so read by Ibn Qais al-Ḥanafī.
41: بِٱلْبُخُلِ - بِٱلْبُخْلِ alternative form, so read by ʿĪsā ath-Thaqifī and al-Ḥasan.
47: تَضَلُّوا - تَضِلُّوا alternative form, so read by Ubai and Ibn Waththāb.
74: لَيُبْطِئَنَّ - لَيُبَطِّئَنَّ, that is, IV form as read by Mujāhid and others.
80: مَشِيدَةٍ - مُشَيَّدَةٍ as read by 'Alī and al-Jaḥdarī.
83: طَاعَةً - طَاعَةٌ as accusative so read by al-Ḥasan and Naṣr b. ʿĀṣim.
86: يَكْفِي - يَكُفَّ from الكفاية. So Ubai and Ibn Masʿūd.
90: رَكَّسَهُمْ - أَرْكَسَهُمْ, that is, II form instead of IV. So read by Ubai and Ibn Masʿūd.
94: فَتَحْرِيرُ رَقَبَةً مُؤْمِنَةً - فَتَحْرِيرُ رَقَبَةٍ مُؤْمِنَةٍ. So read by Abū ʿImrān.
فَصِيَامَ - فَصِيَامُ accusative, that is, meaning فَلْيَصُمْ صِيَامَ, so read by Abū Ḥaṣīn.
96: مُؤْمَنًا - مُؤْمِنًا passive participle so read by 'Alī, ʿIkrima, and Abūʾl-ʿĀliya.
97: الضَّرَرِ - الضَّرَرُ an alternative form, so read by Muʿādh.
102: تُنْفَصَرُوا - تَنْفُصُرُوا passive as read by Abū Nahīk.
يُفْتِنَكُمْ - يَفْتِنَكُمْ, that is, IV form with same meaning, as read by Abūʾl-Jawzā'.
115: يُوَلِّهِ - نُوَلِّهِ "he" instead of "we," as read by al-Aʿmash.
117: تَدْعُونَ - يَدْعُونَ "ye will" instead of "they will," as read by Abū Rajāʾ, and others.

147: ظَلَمَ – ظُلِمَ, that is, active for passive so read by al-Ḥasan, Qatāda and others.

156: شَبَّهَ – شُبِّهَ, that is, active for passive as read by Ibn Mas'ūd and Abū Nahīk.

175: أَنْ لَا تَضِلُّوا – أَنْ تَضِلُّوا making it negative, as read by Ibn Mas'ūd and Ubai.

Sūra V

1: أَحْلَلْتُ لَكُمْ بَهِيمَةَ – أُحِلَّتْ لَكُمْ بَهِيمَةُ so read by Ubai and Ibn Mas'ūd.

"I have allowed you" instead of "ye are allowed."

3: أَحْلَلْتُمْ – حَلَلْتُمْ, that is, "I have made you free" for "ye are free." So read by Ubai and Ibn Mas'ūd.

يُجْرِمَنَّكُمْ – يَجْرِمَنَّكُمْ IV form for I. So read by Ibn Mas'ūd, al-A'mash, Ibn Waththāb, and others.

4: النَّصْبِ – النُّصُبِ an alternative form, read also by al-Ḥasan and others.

26: يُخَافُونَ – يَخَافُونَ, that is, IV form, so read by Mujāhid, Ibn Jubair, and others.

30: لَأَقْتُلَنْكَ – لَأَقْتُلَنَّكَ, that is, with *takhfīf.*

33: فَطَّوَّعَتْ – فَطَوَّعَتْ, that is, for فَتَطَوَّعَتْ, or some said he read فَطَاوَعَتْهُ like al-Ḥasan.

35: مِنْ اِجْلِ – مِنْ أَجْلِ alternative form, so read by 'Amr b. Fā'id and Abū Ja'far.

38: تَقْدُرُوا – تَقْدِرُوا alternative form regularly read by him.

45: لِلْكُذُبِ - لِلْكَذِبِ as Muʿādh., that is, "to liars" instead of "to a lie."
46: لِلسُّحُتِ - لِلسُّحْتِ an alternative form, read by an-Nakhaʿī and Khārija.
54: يَفْتَتِنُوكَ - يَفْتِنُوكَ so read by Abū ʿImrān.
65: وَعُبَّدَ الطَّاغُوتِ - وَعَبَدَ ٱلطَّاغُوتَ an alternative plural form, so read by al-Aʿmash and others, meaning "worshippers of aṭ-Ṭāghūṭ."
82: يَنْتَهُونَ - يَتَنَاهَوْنَ, that is, VIII form "they did not abstain from," instead of VI "they forbade not," so read by Ubai and Ibn Masʿūd.
97: أَحَلَّ لَكُمْ صَيْدَ ٱلْبَحْرِ وَطَعَامَهُ - أُحِلَّ لَكُمْ صَيْدُ ٱلْبَحْرِ وَطَعَامُهُ, that is, "He made lawful" for "there is made lawful," active for passive.

Sūra VI

1: الحَمْدِ لِلّه - الحَمْدُ لِلّه. See I, 1.
9: لَبَّسْنَا - لَلَبَسْنَا so read by Abū'l-Jawzā' and Abū'l-Mutawakkil.
27: وَقَفُوا - وُقِفُوا "they stand" for "they are set," so read by Abū Nahīk and Ibn as-Samaifaʿ.
فَلَا نُكَذِّبُ - وَلَا نُكَذِّبَ so read by Muʿādh and Ibn Masʿūd, though from Ibn Masʿūd we also have the reading نُكَذِّبَ.
33: يَكْذِبُونَكَ - يُكَذِّبُونَكَ, that is, "contradict" instead of "accuse of lying."
38: طَائِرٌ - طَائِرٍ so read by Ibn Abī ʿAbla, Abū Razīn, and others, taking it as *maʿṭūf*.
39: يُضِلَّهُ - يُضْلِلْهُ an alternative form. So read by Muʿādh.
45: والحمدِ - والحمدُ as in I, 1.
46: نَصْرِفُ - نُصَرِّفُ an alternative form, so read by al-Jaḥdarī, ʿIkrima, and others.

49: نُمِسُّهُمُ ٱلْعَذَابَ - يَمَسُّهُمُ ٱلْعَذَابُ, that is, "we shall cause punishment to fall," instead of "punishment will fall." So read by al-Jaḥdarī.

59: حَبَّةٍ and رَطْبٍ and يَابِسٍ - حَبَّةٌ and رَطْبٌ and يابسٌ taking them as not *ma'ṭūf*, so read by Ibn Abī Isḥāq.

61: لَا يُفْرِطُونَ - لَا يُفَرِّطُونَ, that is, "they are not to be escaped" instead of "they fail not," so read by Abū'l-Jawzā'.

63: خِفْيَةً - خُفْيَةً as read by Ibn Mas'ūd and Abū'l-Mutawakkil.

73: الصُّوَرِ - الصُّورِ taking it as the plural of صورة, as read by al-Ḥasan, 'Amr b. 'Ubaid, and others.

99: خُضَرًا - خَضِرًا, that is, "herbs" instead of "green vegetables." So read by Mu'ādh.

يُخْرَجُ مِنْهُ حَبٌّ - نُخْرِجُ مِنْهُ حَبًّا "from which the grain is brought forth" for "from which we bring forth grain." So read by Abū Nahīk.

105: دُرِسَتْ - دَرَسْتَ or دُرِّسَتْ "it has been deeply studied" for "thou hast studied deeply."

Sūra VII

9: مَعَآئِشَ - مَعَايِشَ as al-A'raj and some lines from Ibn 'Āmir and Nāfi'.

19: سَوْءَتِهِمَا - سَوْآتِهِمَا, that is, singular as al-Ḥasan and Mujāhid.

مَلِكَيْنِ - مَلَكَيْنِ "two kings" not "two angels." So Ibn Jubair and as-Zuhrī.

25: رِيَاشًا - رِيشًا plural as read by al-Ḥasan, Qatāda, and Mujāhid.

26: يَفْتِنَنَّكُمْ - يَفْتِنْكُمْ, that is, without the توكيد as read by Abū Nahīk and Abū Ḥaṣīn.

41: الحمدُ as in I, 1.

50: رَحْمَةً - رَحْمَةٍ taking it as in apposition to عِلْمٍ. So read by Abū Nahīk.

51: فَنَعْمَلَ - فَنَعْمَلُ taking it as *ma'ṭūf* to نُرَدُّ. So read by al-Ḥasan and Abū'l-'Āliya.

71: تَأْكُلْ - تَأْكُلُ as Abū Ja'far, Abū's-Sammāl, and others.

103: اَقُولَ - اَقُولُ as Abū Nahīk and others.

155: هُدْنَا - هِدْنَا as Mujāhid.

164: مَعْذِرَةً he agrees here with *TR* against the more common reading مَعْذِرَةٌ.

165: بَئِيسٍ - بَئْسٍ (Ḥay. IV, 412) as Ya'qūb and 'Īsā b. 'Umar.

Sūra VIII

1: يَسْـَٔلُونَكَ عَنِ ٱلْأَنْفَالِ - يَسْـَٔلُونَكَ ٱلْأَنْفَالَ as Ibn Mas'ūd and others.

14: وَأَنَّ - وَإِنَّ as al-Ḥasan and Sulaimān at-Taimī.

32: ٱلْحَقَّ - ٱلْحَقُّ as al-A'mash, that is, taking it as a *mubtada'*.

42: عَبْدِنَا - عُبُدِنَا, that is, a plural of عَبْد.

43: بِٱلْعُدْوَةِ (bis) - بِٱلْعَدْوَةِ an alternative form read by al-Ḥasan and Qatāda.

ٱلْقُصْوَى - الْقُصْيَا, which was the dialectal form of Tamīm.

أَسْفَلَ - اسْفَلُ the simpler grammatical construction.

60: سَوَاءٍ - سِوَاءٍ an alternative form, so read by Abū Nahīk.

Sūra IX

3: رَسُولَهُ - رَسُولُهُ taking it as *ma'ṭūf* to اللهُ, as read by al-Ḥasan, ʿĪsā b. ʿUmar, and Ibn Abī Isḥāq.

8: يُظْهَرُوا - يَظْهَرُوا, that is, passive.

12: إِيمَانَ - أَيْمَانَ following the reading of al-Ḥasan and Ibn ʿĀmir.

13: بَدُوكُمْ - بَدَؤُوكُمْ, that is, without *hamza*.

14: نَشْفِ - يَشْفِ "we" instead of "he," making Allah the personal subject.

15: وَيَذْهَبُ - وَيُذْهِبْ I form, read thus by Muʿādh and Ibn Dharr.

يَتُوبَ - يَتُوبُ as al-Aʿraj and many others.

17: شَاهِدُونَ - شَاهِدِينَ making it begin a new clause, as read by Abū Shaikh and Abū ʿImrān.

خَالِدِينَ - خَالِدُونَ accusative after a verb understood, as read by Muʿādh and Abū Nahīk.

25: رَحْبَتْ - رَحُبَتْ, which is said to be dialect of Tamīm.

26: سِكِّينَتَهُ - سَكِينَتَهُ an alternative form, as read by Ibn Qais and Ibn Dharr.

37: زَيَّنَ لَهُمْ سُوءَ - زُيِّنَ لَهُمْ سُوءُ taking it as active and not passive. It was thus read by Ibn Masʿūd.

42: لَوُ - لَوِ as al-Ḥasan and al-Aʿmash.

54: يُقْبَلَ - تُقْبَلَ as Ibn Hurmuz, Ṭalḥa, and al-Aʿmash.

نفقتُهُم - نَفَقَاتُهُمْ singular as Ibn Hurmuz and al-Aʿmash.

61: أُذُنٌ خَيْرٌ - أُذُنُ خَيْرٍ as al-Ḥasan and Mujāhid.

67: نَعْفُ – he supported the reading of *TR* against the more common يُعْفَ.

نُعَذِّبْ طَائِفَةً - again he supports *TR* against the common reading تُعْذَبْ طَائِفَةٌ.

91: الْمُعْذِرُونَ - الْمُعَذِّرُونَ, that is, تخفيف as Ya'qūb and many others.

119: الَّذِينَ خَالَفُوا - الَّذِينَ خُلِّفُوا as Ja'far aṣ-Ṣādiq and others.

رَحْبَتْ - رَحُبَتْ as in verse 25.

120: الصَّادِقَيْنِ - الصَّادِقِينَ dual, as read by Mu'ādh and Ibn as-Samaifa'.

121: يُغِيظُ - يَغِيظُ, that is, IV form.

125: اَيَّكُمْ - اَيُّكُمْ taking it as على تقدير فعل, as read by 'Ubaid b. 'Umair.

Sūra X

23: يَنْشُرُكُمْ - يُسَيِّرُكُمْ as was read in the Damascus Codex.

حِيطَ - أُحِيطَ, that is, I form as read by Ubai and Ibn Mas'ūd.

24: مَتَاعَ - supporting *TR* against the more common reading مَتَاعُ.

25: وَتَزَيَّنَتْ - وَازَّيَّنَتْ as in the codices of Ubai and Ibn Mas'ūd.

31: تَتْلُوا - تَبْلُوا, that is, "shall recount" instead of "shall prove," so read by Ḥamza and al-Kiṣā'ī, al-A'mash, and Ya'qūb.

الْحَقَّ - الْحَقِّ taking it as على المدح with al-Ḥasan.

36: يَهْتَدِي - يَهِدِّي the regular VIII form, so read by Ibn as-Samaifa'.

38: تَصْدِيقَ and تَفْصِيلَ - تَصْدِيقُ and تَفْصِيلُ, the easier grammatical form after لكن, and so read by 'Īsā b. 'Umar and Abū Rajā'.

52: اَثَمَّ - اَثُمَّ, that is, "there" instead of "then," as read by Ibn Mas'ūd.

Sūra XI

1: فَصَلَتْ - فُصِّلَتْ, giving it the meaning of فرقت ('Ukb. II, 21) as read by al-Jaḥdarī, 'Ikrima, and others.

3: يُمْتِعْكُمْ – يُمَتِّعْكُمْ III form as read by Ibn Muḥaiṣin, Mujāhid, and others.

5: تَثْنَوْنِي صُدُورُهُمْ – يَثْنُونَ صُدُورَهُمْ, that is, "their breasts deter me" instead of "they fold up their breasts," so read by Mujāhid, Ja'far aṣ-Ṣādiq, al-Jaḥdarī, Naṣr b. 'Āṣim, and others.

17: نَزَّلَ – أَنْزَلَ with the same meaning.

18: يُوفِي – نُوَفِّ, that is, from أَوْفَى.

19: بَطَلَ – بَاطِلٌ taking it as a verb the subject of which would be the following words.

43: مَجْرَيهَا وَمَرْسَيهَا – مَجْرِيهَا وَمُرْسِيهَا taking them as *ẓurūf*, as did Ibn Mas'ūd, 'Īsā b. 'Umar, and al-A'mash.

48: تَسْئَلَنِّي – تَسْئَلْنِ the more emphatic form, read by Warsh, Abū Ja'far, and Shaiba.

74: يعْقُوبُ he supported the *TR* here against the more common يعقوبُ.

80: أَطْهَرَ – أَطْهَرُ as al-Ḥasan, 'Īsā b. 'Umar, and many others. It was a reading over which there were famous grammatical discussions, c.f. *Mughnī* II, 101 and the commentaries.

89: نَفْعَلَ and نَشَؤُا – تَفْعَلَ and تَشَؤُا, that is, "thou" referring to Shu'aib himself rather than "we" referring to the people.

115: تُنْصَرُوا – تُنْصَرُونَ taking it as accusative *ma'ṭūf* to فَتَمَسَّكُمْ, thus instead of "ye shall not be helped" it will be "lest ye be not helped." It was so read by Ibn Mas'ūd.

Sūra XII

5: تَقُصَّ - تَقْصُصْ, which is said to have been the form in the dialect of Tamīm and so read by Abū'l-Jawzā' and Abū ʿImrān.

11: تَأْمَنَّا - he is said to have read this بالادغام بغير اشمام as did Abū Jaʿfar, ʿAmr b. ʿUbaid, and az-Zuhrī.

12: يُرْتَعْ وَيُلْعَبْ - يَرْتَعْ وَيَلْعَبْ, that is, passive "there will be revel and playing" instead of "he will revel and play."

13: لَيَحْزُنِّى - لَيَحْزُنُنِى the contracted form, as read by al-Aʿraj and Ibn Muḥaiṣin.

18: كَذِبًا - كَذِبٍ taking it as *ḥāl*, as read by Ibn Abī ʿAbla and ʿĪsā b. ʿUmar.

23: هِئْتُ - هَيْتَ as also read by Ibn Abī Isḥāq. It only differed from the reading attributed to 'Alī, Ibn ʿAbbās, and Hishām in being read with *tashīl* of the *hamza*.

25: عَذَابًا أَلِيمًا - عَذَابٌ أَلِيمٌ making it cognate accusative, that is, يُعَذَّبُ عَذَابًا أَلِيمًا ʿĪsā b. ʿUmar also so read.

33: السَّجْنُ - السِّجْنُ, which was Ya'qūb's reading, that is, "imprisonment," rather than "prison."

45: أَمَةٍ - أُمَّةٍ as read by al-Ḥasan and Qatāda. Cf. *LA*., XVII, 363 and the *Amālī* of al-Qālī, II, 301.

49: تَعَّصِرُونَ - يَعْصِرُونَ VIII form. The reading of تاء for ياء was Kūfan.

72: صَوْغَ - صُوَاعَ one of many attempts to interpret this word of foreign origin. This reading is also attributed to Ibn Masʿūd and Yaḥyā b. Waththāb.

Sūra XIII

4: يُسْقَى – he here supported *TR* against the more usual reading تُسْقَى.

10: عَالِمُ – عَالِمَ taking it as accusative على المدح as read by ʿĪsā b. ʿUmar and others.

12: مِنْ أَمْرِ – بِأَمْرِ a reading also attributed to ʿAlī, Ibn ʿAbbās, Jaʿfar aṣ-Ṣādiq, and ʿIkrima.

18: بِقَدَرِهَا – بِقَدْرِهَا an alternative form, read by al-Ḥasan and others.

19: أَفَمَنْ – أَوَمَنْ same meaning.

26: يَقْدِرُ – يَقْدُرُ as in all other occurrences of this verb.

30: يَايْئَسِ – يَتَبَيَّنْ a reading given from ʿAlī, Ibn ʿAbbās, al-Jaḥdarī, Ibn Masʿūd, and many others. As ييايئس meaning "despair" is very difficult here, the other reading is an attempt to avoid the difficulty by reinterpreting the skeleton consonantal text.

Sūra XIV

6: وَيُذَبِّحُونَ – يَذْبَحُونَ omitting the و and reading I form with the same meaning.

11: فَاطِرِ – فَاطِرَ taking it as على المدح.

21: يَقْدِرُونَ – يَقْدُرُونَ an alternative form.

24: بَرَزُوا – بُرِّزُوا as Abū Nahīk and others. "They were brought out," instead of "they issued forth."

40: أَفْئِدَةً مِنَ ٱلنَّاسِ تَهْوِى إِلَيْهِمْ – إِفَادَةً مِنَ ٱلنَّاسِ تَهْوَى إِلَيْهِمْ, that is, "a group of the people kindly affectioned towards them" instead of "hearts of the people incline towards them." In this case افادة is a derivative from وفد not from فيد (Abū Ḥayyān, V, 433).

41: الحمدِ - الحمدُ as in I, 1.

42: رَبُّنَا - رَبَّنَا taking it as a *khabar*, as read by Mḥd b. 'Alī and al-Ḥūsain b. 'Alī.

لِوَلَدَىَّ - لِوَالِدَىَّ making the reference to Ismā'īl and Isḥāq. It was so read by Ibn Mas'ūd, Ubai, az-Zuhrī, and others, especially of the Ahl al-Bait.

47: كَادَ - كَانَ as 'Alī, Ibn Mas'ūd, Ubai, and many others. It eases the statement from "did" to "almost did."

49: بُرِّزُوا - بَرَزُوا as in verse 24.

Sūra XV

2: رُبَتَمَا - رُبَمَا an alternative form, read by Ṭalḥa and Abū's-Sammāl.

6: نَزَّلَ - نُزِّلَ active which necessitates الذكرَ. Others say he read نَزَلَ with ذكرُ.

8: نَزَلَ الملائكةُ - نُنَزِّلُ المَلَائِكَةَ, that is, "the angels descended" instead of "we send down the angels."

47: سُرُرٍ - سُرَرٍ an alternative form, read by Abū's-Sammāl and others.

56: يَقْنُطُ - يَقْنَطُ an alternative form, so read by Ibn Ya'mar, Ibn Sīrīn, and others.

66: إِنَّ - أَنَّ making it begin a new sentence. So read by al-A'mash.

86: الخَالِقُ - الخَلَّاقُ the reading of al-A'mash and al-Jaḥdarī.

Sūra XVI

2: تُنَزَّلُ الملائكةُ - يُنَزِّلُ المَلَائِكَةَ, that is, passive so read by al-Aʿmash and Abū Bakr.

5: دِفٌ - دِفْءٌ without *hamza* as read by az-Zuhrī, and by Ḥamza and Hishām in Pause.

10: تَسِيمُونَ - تُسِيمُونَ I form, but taken as having the same meaning as IV. So read by Ibn Jubair.

28: السُّقْفُ - السَّقْفُ, which was Mujāhid's reading. It is an alternative form.

32: خَيْرٌ - خَيْرًا as Abū Nahīk, making it begin a sentence and not governed by قالوا.

لَنِعْمَةُ دَارِ - لَنِعْمَ دَارُ taking it as a noun in construction. So Ibn Qais.

68: نَسْقِيكُمْ - نُسْقِيكُمْ supporting the reading of Nāfiʿ, Ibn ʿĀmir, and al-Ḥasan.

77: يَقْدُرُ - يَقْدِرُ as usual (similarly in verse 78).

Sūra XVII

4: عُلِيًّا - عُلُوًّا or some said عِلِيًّا as Ubai and Ibn Masʿūd.

5: عَبِيدًا - عِبَادًا the reading of al-Ḥasan, an alternative plural form.

7: لِيَسُوُّوا - some say he read لِنَسُوًّا supporting the reading of Yaʿqūb and al-Kiṣā'ī.

17: أَمَّرْنَا - أَمَرْنَا as was read by a great number of readers outside the Seven.

24: أُفًّا - أُفٍّ an alternative form, so read by Ḥumaid b. Qais, ʿĪsā b. ʿUmar, and al-Jaḥdarī.

32: يَقْدُرُ - يَقْدِرُ as elsewhere.

35: تُسْرِفْ - يُسْرِفْ supporting the reading of Ḥamza, al-Kiṣā'ī, al-Aʿmash, and others.

38: تَقْفُو - تَقْفُ preserving the و though still constructing it as *majzūm*, a dialectal form.

40: سَيِّآتُهُ - سَيِّئُهُ, that is, plural as read by Ubai and Ibn as-Samaifaʿ.

45: عُلِيًّا - عُلُوًّا see verse 4.

59: يُدْعَوْنَ - يَدْعُونَ, that is, passive. So read by Abū Nahīk and Abūʾl-Mutawakkil.

61: مُبْصِرَةٌ - مُبْصِرَةً taking it as a *khabar* to a suppressed *mubtada'*. as read by Ibn Masʿūd and ʿAlī b. al-Ḥūsain.

62: After للناس he added وَلِيَعْمَهُوا فِيهَا as did ʿAlī b. al-Ḥūsain and Mḥd. b. 'Alī.

84: شِفَاءً وَرَحْمَةً - شِفَاءٌ وَرَحْمَةٌ taken as *ḥāl*, so read by Abū Nahīk and ʿĪsā b. ʿUmar.

104: عَلِمْتُ - عَلِمْتَ supporting the reading of at-Kiṣā'ī and al-Aʿmash. The reading is also attributed to 'Alī.

107: فَرَّقْنَاهُ - فَرَقْنَاهُ as read by Ubai, Ibn Masʿūd, 'Alī, and many others.

Sūra XVIII

1: الحمدِ - الحمدُ as in I, 1.

5: بَاخِعُ نَفْسِكَ - بَاخِعٌ نَفْسَكَ taking it as a construct. So read by Qatāda and Saʿīd b. Jubair.

18: بِوَرِقِكُمْ - he here supported *TR* against the rival readings.

19: يَظَّهَرُوا - يُظْهَرُوا passive. So read by Ibn Masʿūd.

25: يُشْرِكُ - تُشْرِكْ supporting the reading of Ibn ʿĀmir, a reading which had also Baṣran support.

34: مِنْهَا - مِنْهُمَا supporting the reading of the Meccan, Madīnan, and Syrian codices.

36: لَٰكِنَّا هُوَ he had some peculiar way of pronouncing this.

42: الحَقِّ - الحَقُّ taking it as *ta'kīd*, as read by Abū Ḥaiwa, Ibn Abī ʿAbla, and others.

43: الرِّيَاحُ - الرِّيحُ singular as read by al-Ḥasan, Ibn Muḥaiṣin, Ṭalḥa, and others.

47: وَوُضِعَ ٱلْكِتَابُ - وَوَضَعَ الكِتَابَ constructing it as active. So read by Ibn Qais.

51: مَصْرِفًا - مَصْرَفًا taking it as a *maṣdar*, so read by Ibn Yaʿmar and ʿĪsā b. ʿUmar.

70: لِتُغْرِقَ اَهْلَهَا - لِتَغْرَقَ اَهْلُهَا supporting the Kūfan reading of Ḥamza, Khalaf, and Al-Aʿmash. It is also attributed to Ubai, Ṭalḥa, and others.

73: زَكِيَّةً - he here supports *TR* against the common reading زَاكِيَةً .

83: فَأَتْبَعَ - he supports *TR* against the more common فَاتَّبَعَ .

84: حَمِئَةٍ - حَامِئَةٍ as was read by Ibn Masʿūd, al-Ḥasan, and others.

102: اَفَحَسِبَ - اَفَحَسْبُ taking it as *muḍāf* to الذين. It is attributed to ʿAlī, ʿIkrima, Mujāhid, and others.

Sūra XIX

5: خَفَّتِ ٱلْمَوَالِي – خِفْتُ ٱلْمَوَالِيَ a reading attributed to 'Uthmān, Mḥd b. 'Alī, ʿAlī b. al-Ḥūsain, and others.

11: تُكَلِّمُ – تُكَلِّمَ as read by Ibn Abī ʿAbla, taking the ان in الا as *khafīf* and not governing the verb.

25: تَسْقُطْ – تُسَاقِطْ the reading attributed to Ubai and Abū Ḥaiwa.

34: وَلَدَتْ – وُلِدْتُ, that is, making Maryam the subject. So read by Abū Nahīk and others.

35: قَوْلَ – he agreed here with *TR* against the numerous other readings.

Sūra XX

33: أُشْرِكْهُ – أَشْرِكْهُ supporting the reading of Ibn ʿĀmir and al-Ḥasan.

72: كَيْدَ سِحْرٍ – كَيْدُ سَاحِرٍ a reading given also from Ibn Masʿūd and Mujāhid, taking كيدَ as the direct object of صنعوا.

83: تَطْغُوا – تَطْغَوْا as read by Abū Nahīk and others, that is, from طَغَا not طَغَى.

86: إِثْرِى – أَثَرِى as read by Ruwais and some lines of tradition from Abū ʿAmr.

90: بِمَلْكِنَا he supported *TR* here against the usual Kūfan reading.

96: تِبْصِرُوا – يَبْصُرُوا making the person "ye" instead of "they"; the *kasra* as the vowel of the imperfect, however, is irregular.

134: نَذِلَّ and نَخْزَى – نُذَلَّ and نُخْزَى so read by ʿIkrima and Ibn as-Samaifaʿ, taking it as passive.

Sūra XXI

2: مُحْدَثٍ - مُحْدَثًا taken as *ḥāl*. So read also by Abūʾl-Jawzāʾ.

31: رَتْقًا - رَتَقًا an alternative form, which was also read by al-Ḥasan, Abū Ḥaiwa, and ʿĪsā b. ʿUmar.

48: مِثْقَالَ - مِثْقَالُ supporting the Madinan reading of Nāfiʿ and Abū Jaʿfar.

58: تَوَلَّوا - تَوَلَّوْا meaning تَتَوَلَّوْا as read by ʿĪsā b. ʿUmar, Abū Rajāʾ, and others.

80: لِتُحْصِنَكُمْ – he supported *TR* here against the more common لِنُحْصِنَكُمْ.

95: حَرَامٌ - حَرُمَ taking it as a verb, a reading attributed to Ibn ʿAbbās, Aḍ-Ḍaḥḥāk, Qatāda, ʿIkrima, and others.

98: حَصَبُ - حَطَبُ a reading taken back to ʿAlī, Ibn as-Zubair, Ubai, ʿĀʾisha, and many others. The two words mean practically the same, and حصب in this form occurs only here.

Sūra XXII

2: تَرَى ٱلنَّاسَ - تُرَى النَّاسُ passive. So read by ʿIkrima, Abū Rajāʾ, and others.

3: يَتَّبِعُ - يُتْبِعُ the *takhfīf* form, read by Abū Nahīk and Abūʾl-Mutawakkil.

9: نُذِيقُهُ - أُذِيقُهُ making it "I" instead of "we." Some, however, say that he read فَأُذِيقُهُ.

28: رِجَالًا - رُجَّالًا the reading of al-Ḥasan, ʿĪsā b. ʿUmar, and others. It is an alternative plural form.

32: فَتَخْطَفُهُ - فتخطّفه so read by Muʿādh, Abū Nahīk, and others.

38: يَنَالَ اللهَ - يُنَالُ اللّٰهُ followed by يُنَالُهُ for يَنَالُهُ, that is, passive. So read by Ibn Qais and Abūʾl-Jawzāʾ.

71: النَّارُ - النَارَ accusative by *ikhtiṣāṣ* (see Zam.) read thus by Ṭalḥa, Ibn Abī ʿAbla, and Abūʾl-ʿĀliya.

Sūra XXIII

14: عِظَامًا and العِظَامَ - عَظْمًا and العَظْمَ (singular) supporting the reading of Ibn ʿĀmir.

15: لَمَيِّتُونَ - لَمَائِتُونَ the reading of Ibn Muḥaiṣin, Ibn Abī ʿAbla, and others.

21: نُسْقِيكُمْ - نَسْقِيكُمْ supporting the reading of Nāfiʿ, Ibn ʿĀmir, and Yaʿqūb, a reading which some authorities gave also from Ibn Masʿūd and al-Ḥasan.

29: الحمدُ - الحمدِ as in I, 1.

52: رَبْوَةٍ - رَبَاوَةٍ an alternative form, said to have been read by as-Sulamī and al-Ashhab.

69: سَامِرًا - سُمَّارًا an alternative form of plural so read by Ibn ʿAbbās, Abū Rajāʾ, and others.

تَهْجُرُونَ - تُهَجِّرُونَ II form, the reading of Ibn Masʿūd, Ibn ʿAbbās, ʿIkrima, and many others.

113: أَنَّهُمْ - إِنَّهُمْ supporting the reading of Ḥamza and al-Kisāʾī.

Sūra XXIV

3: حَرُمَ – حُرِّمَ, that is, active of I form with much the same meaning. So read by Ibn Qais.

14: تَلِقُونَهُ – تَلَقَّوْنَهُ, which is given as the reading of ʿĀʾisha and Ibn ʿAbbās, taking it as the imperfect of a verb ولق (Abū Ḥayyān, VI, 438).

25: يُوفِيهِمُ – يُوَفِّيهِمُ IV form, so read by Abūʾl-Mutawakkil and Abūʾl-Jawzāʾ.

35: نَوَّرَ السَّمٰوَاتِ والارضَ – نُورُ السَّمٰوات والأَرْضِ as read by ʿAlī, as-Sulamī, and others.

دُرِّىءٌ – دُرِّيٌّ an attempt to reproduce the original form. Quite a number of readers so read it with the *hamza*.

تُوقَدُ – يُوقَدُ supporting the Kūfan reading.

52: طَاعَةً مَعْرُوفَةً – طَاعَةٌ مَعْرُوفَةٌ so read by al-Yazīdī, al-Jaḥdarī, and ʿĪsā b. ʿUmar, taking it as the object of the verb تقسموا.

57: عَوَرَاتٍ – عَوْرَاتٍ a dialectical form, so read by Abū Nahīk and Ibn Dharr.

Sūra XXV

9: نَأْكُلُ – يَأْكُلُ making the reference to the people themselves, not to the Prophet. It was the usual Kūfan reading.

19: نُتَّخَذَ – نَتَّخِذَ, that is, passive. Al-Ḥasan's reading and also so read by many others.

60: الرحمنِ – الرحمٰنُ taking it as a *ṣifa* going back to الحى.

63: يَذْكُرَ – يَذَّكَّرَ, which was the usual Kūfan reading.

Sūra XXVI

2: بَاخِعُ نَفْسِكَ - بَاخِعٌ نَفْسَكَ as in sūra XVIII, 5.

12: يَضِيقَ and يَنْطَلِقَ - يَضِيقُ and يَنْطَلِقُ taking them as *ma'ṭūf* to يكذبون in verse 11. It was the reading of Ya'qūb, Ṭalḥa, al-A'raj, 'Īsā b. 'Umar, and many others.

56: حَاذِرُونَ he supports *TR* here against the other common reading حَذِرُونَ.

149: فَارِهِينَ he supports *TR* against the more common reading فَرِهِينَ.

Sūra XXVII

15: الحمدِ - الحمدُ as in I, 1.

84: أَنَّ - he supports *TR* against the other common reading إِنَّ.

Sūra XXVIII

10: جُنُبٍ - جُنْبٍ as Qatāda and al-Ḥasan, though some said he and they read جَنْبٍ.

34: يُصَدِّقُنِي - يُصَدِّقُونِي plural as read by Ubai and Ibn Qais.

35: عَضُدَكَ - عُضُدَكَ an alternative form read by Qatāda, Shaiba, and al-Ḥasan.

48: سِحْرَانِ - he supported *TR* here against the more common سَاحِرَانِ the *TR* being the usual Kūfan reading.

49: أَتَّبِعْهُ - أَتَّبِعُهُ as read by Mu'ādh, Abū'l-Mutawakkil, and others.

82: يَقْدِرُ - يَقْدُرُ as usual.

Sūra XXIX

11: خَطَايَاهُمْ - خِطَايَاهُمْ a dialectal form, so read by Abān b. Taghlib.

16: تَخْلُقُونَ - تَخَلَّقُونَ as 'Alī, as-Sulamī, and Ibn az-Zubair, meaning تَتَخَلَّقُونَ though some said he read تُخَلِّقُونَ, a reading which is also given from as-Sulamī.

58: لَنُبَوِّئَنَّهُمْ - لَنُثْوِيَنَّهُمْ supporting the reading of the Kūfans Ḥamza, al-Kiṣā'ī, Khalaf, and al-Aʿmash, a reading covered also by the names of 'Alī, Ibn Masʿūd, and Ṭalḥa. Instead of "will surely inform them" they read "we will surely lodge them."

62: يَقْدِرُ - يَقْدُرُ as elsewhere.

63: الحمدُ - الحمدِ as in I, 1.

Sūra XXX

35: يَقْنَطُونَ - يَقْنُطُونَ an alternative form, so read by Ibn Sīrīn, Abān, and others.

36: يَقْدِرُ - يَقْدُرُ as elsewhere.

49: يُحْيِي - نُحْيِي making Allah speak in the first person; so read by Abū Nahīk, Muʿādh, and others.

Sūra XXXI

8: خَالِدِينَ - خَالِدُونَ taking it not as still governed by إِنَّ but as the *khabar* of a هُمْ understood. It was so read by Muʿādh, Abū Nahīk, and others.

17: تُصَعِّرْ he supported *TR* as against the other common reading تُصَاعِرْ .
19: نِعْمَةً - نِعَمَهُ supporting the reading of Ibn Kathīr, Ibn 'Āmir, and others, though some say he read نِعْمَةً.
24: الحمدِ - الحمدُ as in I, 1.
26: كَلِمَةُ - كَلِمَاتُ singular. As read by Abū Nahīk and Ibn Qais.

Sūra XXXII

5: عَالِمِ - عَالِمُ followed by العزيزِ الرحيمِ, taking it as *badal* to the pronoun in اليه. It was thus read by al-Jaḥdarī, Abū'l-Mutawakkil, and Ibn Qais.
11: تَرْجِعُونَ - تُرْجَعُونَ supporting the reading of Ya'qūb and Ibn Muḥaiṣin.
12: نَكَسُوا رُؤُسَهُمْ - نَاكِسُوا رُؤُسِهِمْ, that is, verb and its object, so read by Abū Nahīk and Ibn Qais.

Sūra XXXIII

20: يَسَّاءَلُونَ - يَسْئَلُونَ, that is, VI form, as read by Ruwais, Qatāda, and al-Jaḥdarī.
27: تَطَوْهَا - تَطَؤُهَا as read by Abū Ja'far.
28: أُمْتِعْكُنَّ - أُمَتِّعْكُنَّ IV form as read by Abū'l Jawzā', Abū's-Sawwār, and others.
30: تَأْتِ - يَأْتِ taking the subject as feminine. So read by Ya'qūb and al-Jaḥdarī.
نُضَاعِفْ لَهَا العَذَابَ - يُضَاعَفْ لَهَا ٱلعَذَابُ as was read by Ibn Muḥaiṣin.

34: يُتْلَى - تُتْلَى taking the subject as feminine. So read by Abū'l-Jawzā' and others.

37: زَوَّجْنَاكَهَا - زَوَّجْتُكَهَا a reading given from Ahl al-Bait.

40: لَكِنْ - لَكِنَّ the reading of Ibn Abī ʿAbla and others, with رسولُ instead of رسولَ taking it as the *khabar*.

خَاتَمَ - he supported *TR*, as did ʿAlī and al-Ḥasan, against the more common خَاتِم but naturally read خَاتَمُ to agree with رسولُ.

49: إِذْ - إِنْ as Ubai, Abū'l-Mutawakkil, and Abū Nahīk.

Sūra XXXIV

3: أَصْغَرُ and أَكْبَرُ - أَصْغَرَ and أَكْبَرِ, that is, *jarr* and *muḍāf* to something understood (Abū Ḥayyān, VII, 258), so read by Abū's-Sawwār, Abū'l-Jawzā', and others.

7: يُنَبِّئُكُمْ - يُنَبِّيكُمْ, that is, with *takhfīf*, or some say he read يُنْبِئُكُمْ IV form.

18: رَبَّنَا بَاعِدْ - رَبُّنَا بَاعَدَ, as read by Yaʿqūb and many others, reading as a verb of which رَبُّنَا is the subject.

19: صَدَّقَ - he supports *TR* as the Kūfan reading, along with Ibn ʿAbbās, Qatāda, and Ṭalḥa, against the more common صَدَقَ.

إِبْلِيسُ ظَنَّهُ - إِبْلِيسَ ظَنُّهُ changing around the subject and object as read by az-Zuhrī, Ibn as-Samaifaʿ, and others.

38: يَقْدِرُ - يُقَدِّرُ as elsewhere.

47: عَلَّامُ - عَلَّامَ taking it as still governed by إِنَّ. So read by ʿĪsā b. ʿUmar Ibn Abī Isḥāq, and others.

Sūra XXXV

3: غَيْرُ - غَيْرِ supporting the reading of Ḥamza and other Kūfans.
11: يَصْعَدُ - يُصَعِّدُ II form but with much the same meaning.
25: مُخْتَلِفًا - مُخْتَلِفَةٌ to make it congruent with شَجَرَات. It was so in the Codices of Ubai and Ibn Masʿūd.
30: لِبَاسُهُمْ - لِبَاسَهُمْ taking it as *ma'ṭūf* to the previous accusative, so read by Muʿādh and Ibn Qais.
31: الحمدُ - الحمدِ as in I, 1.

Sūra XXXVI

8: فَأَغْشَيْنَاهُم - فَأَعْشَيْنَاهُمْ with ع, that is, "we blinded them" instead of "we will cover them." It is attributed to a large number of readers from Ibn ʿAbbās downward.
41: ذُرِّيَّتَهُمْ - ذُرِّيَّاتِهِمْ plural supporting the reading of Nāfi', Ibn ʿĀmir, and Ya'qūb.
78: خَلْقَهُ - خَالِقَهُ, that is, "his creator" instead of "his creation." So read by Muʿādh, Abū Nahīk, and others.
81: الخَلَّاقُ - الخَالِقُ supporting al-Ḥasan's reading.
83: تُرْجَعُونَ - تَرْجِعُونَ taking it as active, the reading of Ya'qūb and Ibn Muḥaiṣin.

Sūra XXXVII

6: بِزِينَةٍ ٱلْكَوَاكِبِ - بزينةٍ كَوَاكِبُ taking كواكب as a khabar to a هم understood. It was so read by Abū Nahīk and others.

56: بِمَائِتِينَ - بِمَيِّتِينَ so read by Muʿādh and Abū Nahīk and others.

104: نَادَيْنَاهُ - نَادَيْنَاهُ أَنْ with omission of أَنْ, as was read also by Ubai, Muʿādh, and others.

126: اللهَ رَبَّكُمْ وَرَبَّ – he supported *TR* as the Kūfan reading against the more common اللهُ رَبُّكُمْ وَرَبُّ.

182: والحمدِ - والحمدُ as in I, 1.

Sūra XXXVIII

22: تَسْعٌ وَتَسْعُونَ – تِسْعٌ وَتِسْعُونَ as read by Ibn Masʿūd, al-Ḥasan, and Ayyūb as-Sakhtiyānī.

32: مِسَاحًا بِالسَّاقِ - مَسْحًا بِالسُّوقِ using an alternative *maṣdar* from مسح as read by Ubai, Muʿādh, and others, and then the singular "leg" instead of "legs," as did Abū'ṣ-Sammāl and Abū'l-Jawzā'.

64: تَخَاصُمَ - تَخَاصُمُ as Ibn Abī ʿAbla and others, taking it as still governed by إِنَّ.

Sūra XXXIX

1: تَنْزِيلَ - تَنْزِيلُ as Ibn Abī ʿAbla and ʿĪsā b. ʿUmar and others, understanding a verb like اِقْرَأْ before it.

5: كَذُوبٌ كَفُورٌ - كَاذِبٌ كَفَّارٌ, which would mean much the same. So read by Ubai, Abū'ṣ-Sawwār, and others.

30: الحمدِ - الحمدُ as in I, 1.

53: يَقْدُرُ - يَقْدِرُ as elsewhere.

54: تَقْنُطُوا - تَقْنَطُوا an alternative form, so read by Ibn Sīrīn, Abān, and others.

68: الصُّوَرِ - الصُّورِ as read by Qatāda and al-Ḥasan.

فَصُعِقَ - فَصَعِقَ passive as read by Ibn as-Samaifa', Ibn Ya'mar, al-Jaḥdarī, and Abū Ḥaiwa.

قِيَامًا - قِيَامٌ taking it as *ḥāl*, as read by Mu'ādh, 'Īsā b. 'Umar, and others.

74: الحمدِ - الحمدُ as in I, 1.

Sūra XL

4: يَغُرَّكَ - يَغْرُرْكَ with *idghām* as read by 'Ubaid b. 'Umair and others.

8: جَنَّةَ - جَنَّاتِ singular as in the Codex of Ibn Mas'ūd and read by al-A'mash.

27: يُظْهَرَ فِى ٱلْأَرْضِ ٱلْفَسَادُ - يُظْهِرَ فى ٱلْأَرْضِ ٱلْفَسَادَ passive as Mu'ādh, Abū Nahīk, and Ibn Dharr.

39: فَأَطَّلِعَ - he supports *TR*, which is peculiar to Ḥafṣ among the Seven, against the more common فَأَطَّلِعُ.

62: سَيُدْخَلُونَ - سَيَدْخُلُونَ supporting the Meccan reading which was also read by Abū Ja'far, Abū Bakr, and Ruwais.

64: خَالِقَ - خَالِقُ taking it as *ikhtiṣās*, so read by 'Īsā b. 'Umar and others.

66: صِوَرَكُمْ - صُوَرَكُمْ an alternative form read by al-Ḥasan, Qatāda, and many others.

67: الحمدِ - الحمدُ as in I,1.

73: والسَّلَاسِلَ يَسْحَبُونَ - والسَّلَاسِلُ يُسْحَبُونَ taking it as active, and the noun in accusative. So read by Ibn Mas'ūd, Ibn Waththāb, 'Īsā b. 'Umar, and so on.

Sūra XLI

3: بَشِيرٌ وَنَذِيرٌ - بَشِيرًا وَنَذِيرًا taking them as *ṣifa* to كِتَابٌ in verse 2. So read by Muʿādh, Abū Nahīk, and others.

9: سَوَاءٍ - سَوَاءً taking it as a *na't* to اربعة. So read by al-Ḥasan, ʿĪsā b. ʿUmar, and others.

18: نَحْشُرُ أَعْدَاءَ - يُحْشَرُ أَعْدَاءُ supporting the reading of Nāfiʿ and Yaʿqūb.

Sūra XLII

5: فَرِيقٌ (bis) - فَرِيقًا taking each as accusative, after a verb افترقوا suppressed. So read by ʿĪsā b. ʿUmar and others.

9: فَاطِرِ - فَاطِرُ connecting it with the الى الله of the previous verse. It was thus read by Abū Nahīk, Muʿādh, and others.

10: يَقْدِرُ - يَقْدُرُ as elsewhere.

13: وُرِّثُوا - اورِثوا as read by Abūʾl-Mutawakkil and Abūʾl-Jawzāʾ.

22: مَوَدَّةً - المَوَدَّةَ.

نَزِدْ - يَزِدْ making it more impersonal, as read by al-Ḥasan, al-Jaḥdarī, and others.

33: يَعْلَمَ - يَعْلَمُ supporting the Madīnan reading.

Sūra XLIII

4: أَنْ - إِذْ where some of the Seven read إِنْ.

17: يُنَشَّؤُا - he supports *TR* as the Kūfan reading against the more common يَنْشَؤُا.

18: أُنُثًا - إِنَاثًا an alternative form, so read by Abū'ṣ-Sammāl, Abū ʿImrān, and others.

سَيَكْتُبُ شَهَادَتَهُمْ - سَتُكْتَبُ شَهَادَتُهُمْ, that is, "he will write down their witness" instead of "their witness shall be written down." So read by Mujāhid and many others.

35: يَعْشُوا - يَعْشُ as read by Abū'ṣ-Sawwār and Ibn Qais.

49: يَنْكِثُونَ - يَنْكُثُونَ an alternative form, read by Abū Ḥaiwa, Muʿādh, and others.

61: لَعَلَمٌ - لَعِلْمٌ attributed to Ibn ʿAbbās, Abū Huraira, and a great many of the older readers.

Sūra XLIV

3: نَفْرُقُ كُلَّ أَمْرٍ حَكِيمٌ - يُفْرَقُ كُلُّ أَمْرٍ حَكِيمٍ, though some said that he read يَفْرِقُ كُلَّ أَمْرٍ حَكِيمٌ. In both cases he, like several other readers, takes حكيمٌ as the subject, of the verb, not as a *ṣifa* to امر.

4: أَمْرٌ - أَمْرًا, which is the reading one would naturally expect.

5: رَحْمَةٌ - رَحْمَةً as al-Ḥasan and others, taking it as *khabar* of some word like تِلْكَ understood.

21: أَنَّ - إِنَّ as Ibn as-Samaifaʿ, ʿĪsā b. ʿUmar, and others.

47: فَاعْتُلُوهُ - فَاعْتِلُوهُ supporting the reading of Nāfiʿ, Ibn Kathīr, Ibn ʿĀmir, and Yaʿqūb.

51: مُقَامٍ - مَقَامٍ (an alternative form) supporting the reading of Nāfiʿ, Ibn ʿĀmir, Abū Jaʿfar, and al-Aʿmash.

Sūra XLV

4: الرِّيحِ - الرِّيَاحِ supporting the usual Kūfan reading.

13: لِنَجْزِىَ قَوْمًا - لِيَجْزِىَ قَوْمًا supporting the reading of Ibn ʿĀmir, Ḥamza, and al-Kiṣā'ī.

18: وَلِىَّ - وَلِىَّ taking it as still governed by the إِنَّ. So read by ʿĪsā b. ʿUmar and Ibn Qais.

20: سَوَاءٌ he supported *TR* as the Kūfan reading against the more common سَوَاءٌ.

23: نَحْيَا - نُحْيَا (others write it as نُحْىَ) as read by Abū'ʾs-Sawwā and others. يُهْلِكْنَا - يُهْلِكُنَا a difficult *majzūm*, but so read by Abū Shaikh and Abū ʿImrān.

24: حُجَّتَهُمْ - حُجَّتُهُمْ taking it as the subject of كان not the object. So read by al-Ḥasan, Abū Ḥaiwa, Ibn Abī Isḥāq, and others.

Sūra XLVI

3: أَثَارَةٍ - أَثَرَةٍ an alternative form. So read by ʿIkrima, as-Sulamī, al-Ḥasan, and others, though some gave him as reading أَثْرَةٍ as Ubai, aḍ-Ḍaḥḥāk, Abū Rajā', and as-Sulamī.

8: يُفْعَلُ - يَفْعَلُ taking it as active as read by Ibn Abī ʿAbla and others.

15: نَتَقَبَّلُ – he supported *TR* as against the more common reading يُتَقَبَّلُ.

24: تُدَمِّرُ - يَدْمُرُ as read by Muʿādh and Ibn Qais.

يُرَى – he supported *TR* as the Kūfan reading against the more common تَرَى.

32: بِقَادِرٍ - يَقْدِرُ taking it as a verb, as read by al-Jaḥdarī, Ya'qūb, ʿĪsā b. ʿUmar, and others.

35: بَلَاغٌ - بَلَاغًا as accusative after a verb understood. So read by al-Ḥasan and many others.

Sūra XLVII

2: نُزِّلَ - نَزَّلَ active the reading of Ibn Masʿūd, Abū Nahīk, and others.

22: أُنْزِلَتْ سُورَةٌ مُحْكَمَةٌ وَذُكِرَ فِيهَا ٱلْقِتَالُ - نَزَلَتْ سُورَةٌ مُحْكَمَةٌ وَذَكَرَ فِيهَا ٱلْقِتَالَ though some say that he read the first part نزلَتْ سُورَةٌ مُحْكَمَةٌ.

27: سَوَّلَ - سُوِّلَ passive as read by Ibn as-Samaifaʿ, al-Jaḥdarī, and Abū Nahīk.

Sūra XLVIII

10: يَنْكُثُ - يَنْكِثُ an alternative form, so read by Abū'ṣ-Sammāl, Abū Ḥaiwa, and others.

فَسَيُؤْتِيهِ - فَسَنُؤْتِيهِ supporting the reading of Nāfi', Ibn Kathīr, and Ibn ʿĀmir.

16: يُسْلِمُونَ - يُسْلِمُوا taking it as *manṣūb* after an أَن understood. So read by Ubai, Ibn Masʿūd, and others.

21: تَقْدِرُوا - تَقْدُرُوا as elsewhere.

29: شَطْئَهُ - شَطَاءَهُ as Naṣr b. ʿĀṣim and Ibn Waththāb, though others say that he read شَطَهُ as al-Jaḥdarī and Ibn Abī Isḥāq.

Sūra XLIX

2: فَتَحْبَطَ - أَنْ تَحْبَطَ as read by Ibn Masʿūd.
9: آقْتَتَلَا - آقْتَتَلُوا (dual) as read by Ubai, Ibn Masʿūd, and ʿUbaid b. ʿUmair.
10: بَيْنَ اِخْوَتِكُمْ وَاِخْوَانِكُمْ - بَيْنَ اَخَوَيْكُمْ as read by al-Ḥasan, Yaʿqūb, and others.
17: اِذْ هَدٰيكُمْ - اَنْ هَدٰيكُمْ as read by Ibn Masʿūd and Abū Nahīk.

Sūra L

8: تَبْصِرَةٌ - تَبْصِرَةً taking it and ذكرى as nominative as read by Abūʾs-Sawwār and others.
43: تَتَشَقَّقُ - تَشَقَّقُ writing it in full, though some say that he read تَنْشَقِقُ like Ubai and Ibn Qais.

Sūra LI

9: يَأْفِكُ عَنْهُ مَنْ اَفَكَ - يُؤْفَكُ عَنْهُ مَنْ اُفِكَ though some said he read يَافَكَ as Qatāda, Muʿādh, and others, and some said his reading was only in the يافك without any change in the اُفِكَ.
44: الصَّعْقَةُ - الصَاعِقَةُ supporting the reading of al-Kiṣāʾī and Ibn Muḥaiṣin.

Sūra LII

7: وَاقِعٌ - لَوَاقِعٌ as read by Ubai, Abū Nahīk, and others.

13: يُدْعَوْنَ - يُدَعُّونَ IV form, as read by 'Alī as-Sulamī and Ibn as-Samaifaʿ.

45: يُصْعَقُونَ he supports *TR* here against the common reading يَصْعَقُونَ.

Sūra LIII

9: قَادَ - قَابَ a synonym.

22: ضَيْزَى - ضِيزَى as read by Ubai, Muʿādh, and others.

26: شَفَاعَتُهُ - شَفَاعَتُهُمْ singular pronoun on the ground that مَلَك is singular. So read by Ubai, Ibn Qais, and others.

32: لِيَجْزِيَ and لِنَجْزِيَ - يَجْزِيَ and نَجْزِيَ making Allah speak in the first person. It was read thus by Abū Nahīk, Muʿādh, Ibn Qais, and others.

38: وَفَى - وَفَّى so read by Ibn as-Samaifaʿ, Saʿīd b. Jubair, Abū Nahīk, and others.

Sūra LIV

3: مُسْتَقِرٍّ - مُسْتَقَرٌّ taking it as a *ṣifa* to أَمْرٍ. So read by Abū Jaʿfar.

4: مُزَّجَرٌ - مُزْدَجَرٌ with *idghām*, though others say that he read مُزْجَرٌ.

6: نُكِرَ - نُكُرٍ taking it as a verb in the passive. So read by Mujāhid, Qatāda, al-Jaḥdarī, and others.

10: إِنِّي - أَنِّي as read by al-Aʿmash, ʿĪsā b. ʿUmar, Ibn Abī Isḥāq, and others.

12: فَجَرْنَا - فَجَّرْنَا the reading of Ubai, Ibn Masʿūd, al-Jaḥdarī, and others.

14: بِأَعْيُنَّا - بِأَعْيُنِنَا with *idghām*, as read by Abūʾs-Sammāl and al-Aʿmash.

38: بُكْرَةَ عَذَابٍ - بُكْرَةً عَذَابٌ, that is, with *iḍāfa*, as read by Abūʾs-Sammāl and Abūʾl-Jawzā'.

Sūra LV

8: تَخْسِرُوا - تُخْسِرُوا or, some said, تَخْسَرُوا.

24: الْمُنْشِآتُ - الْمُنْشَآتُ supporting the reading of Ḥamza, as did Ṭalḥa and al-Aʿmash.

31: سَيَفْرُغُ - سَنَفْرُغُ supporting the reading of the Kūfans, as did Abū Ḥaiwa.

33: اسْتَطَعْتُمَا - اسْتَطَعْتُمْ (dual).

35: نُرْسِلُ عَلَيْكُمَا شُوَاظًا مِنْ نَارٍ وَنُحَاسًا - يُرْسَلُ عَلَيْكُمَا شُوَاظٌ مِنْ نَارٍ وَنُحَاسٌ

active with Allah as the speaker. This was the reading of Ibn Masʿūd, ʿĪsā b. ʿUmar, and others, save that they read يُرْسِلُ, which some gave also from Zaid b. 'Alī.

Sūra LVI

3: خَافِضَةً رَافِعَةً - خَافِضَةٌ رَافِعَةٌ taking it as *ḥāl* as did al-Yazīdī, al-Ḥasan, and many others.

4: رَجَّتِ - رُجَّتِ active, which necessitates الارضَ. So Muʿādh and Abū Nahīk.

5: بَسَّتِ - بُسَّتِ active, which necessitates الجبالَ. So Muʿādh and Abū Nahīk.

15: سُرُرٍ - سُرَرٍ as elsewhere.

20: فَاكِهَةٌ - فَاكِهَةٍ as the *mubtada'* of a لهم understood. So as-Sulamī.

21: لَحْمٌ - لَحْمٍ constructed the same as فاكهةٌ above.

78: المُطَّهِّرُونَ - المُطَهَّرُونَ for المُتَطَهِّرُونَ as read by al-Ḥasan and 'Abdallāh b. 'Aun, taking it as an active participle.

Sūra LVII

9: أَنْزَلَ - يُنَزِّلُ as Ubai, Ibn Qais, and others.

10: قَبْلَ - مِنْ قَبْلِ as read by Ibn Masʿūd and Abūʾl-Mutawakkil.

13: أَنْظِرُونَا - أُنْظُرُونَا supporting the Kūfan reading of Ḥamza, al-Aʿmash, and Ibn Waththāb.

Sūra LVIII

8: يُنْبِيهِمْ - يُنَبِّئُهُمْ or some said يُنْبِئُهُمْ IV form.

Sūra LIX

5: قَوْمًا - قَائِمَةً as Ibn Masʿūd, al-Aʿmash, and Ṭalḥa, though others give it as قُوَّمًا also attributed to Ibn Masʿūd and Ṭalḥa.

17: خَالِدَانِ - خَالِدَيْنِ taking it as a new beginning and not as still governed by إِنَّ. It was so read by Ibn Masʿūd, al-Aʿmash, and Ibn Abī ʿAbla.

Sūra LX

3: نَفْصِلُ - يَفْصِلُ with mere change of person, as read by Abū Ḥaiwa, Ibn Abī ʿAbla, and others.

4: بُرَآءُ - بُرَاءُوا as read by Abūʾs-Sammāl, Abūʾs-Sawwār, and others.

Sūra LXI

4: يُقَاتَلُونَ - يُقَاتِلُونَ passive.

5: زَاغُوا he read with *imāla* here as Ḥamza and Abū Nahīk.

11: تُؤْمِنُونَ and تُجَاهِدُونَ - تُؤْمِنُوا and تُجَاهِدُوا, as Ubai, Abū Nahīk, and others, taking them as governed by a *lām al-'amr* understood. (Alūsī, XXVII, 79.)

Sūra LXII

1: الْقَدُّوس – الْقُدُّوسِ an alternative form, so read by Abūʾd-Dīnār al-Aʿrābī.

5: حَمَلُوا - حُمِّلُوا active of I form to make it correspond with the following يَحْمِلُ. So read by Yaḥyāb. Yaʿmar, Abū Nahīk, and others.

9: الْجُمْعَةِ - الْجُمُعَةِ, which was the form in the dialect of Tamīm, and was read by Al-Aʿmash, Abū Ḥaiwa, and quite a number of early readers.

Sūra LXIII

3: فَطَبَعَ اللهُ - فَطُبِعَ as read by al-Aʿmash, though some said he read طَبَعَ without the اللهُ, as read by Abū Nahīk and Abū Rajāʾ.

Sūra LXIV

3: صِوَرَكُمْ - صَوَّرَكُمْ the reading of Al-Aʿmash and Abū Razīn, a dialectal form.

9: نَجْمَعُكُمْ - يَجْمَعُكُمْ making Allāh speak in the first person. So read by Ya'qūb, ash-Sha'bī, and others.

نُكَفِّرْ - يُكَفِّرْ supporting the reading of Nāfi', Ibn ʿĀmir and Abū Jaʿfar.

Sūra LXV

1: فِي قُبُلِ عِدَّتِهِنَّ - لِعِدَّتِهِنَّ a much discussed reading of Ubai, which was read also by Mujāhid, Jaʿfar b. Mḥd, ʿAlī b. al-Ḥūsain, and so on and was attributed to Ibn ʿAbbās, 'Uthmān, and even to the Prophet himself.

3: بَالِغُ أَمْرِهِ he supported this reading, which is peculiar to Ḥafṣ among the Seven, but was also read by Ya'qūb, Ibn Abī ʿAbla, and Ṭalḥa, as superior to the common reading.

Sūra LXVI

8: تَوْبًا نَصُوحًا - تَوْبَةً نَصُوحًا, apparently intending the same meaning.

Sūra LXVII

8: تَمِيزُ - تَمَيَّزُ taking it as I form with apparently the same meaning. It was so read by Ibn Abī ʿAbla and al-Jaḥdarī.

Sūra LXVIII

39: بَالِغَةً - بَالِغَةٌ taking it as *ḥāl*. It was so read by al-Ḥasan.

Sūra LXIX

5: فَهَلَكُوا - فَأُهْلِكُوا active, that is, "they perished" for "they were destroyed."

11: طَغَى - طَغَا as Ibn Qais and Ibn Dharr.

Sūra LXX

38: يَدْخُلَ - يُدْخَلَ active the more normal construction, and so read by al-Ḥasan, Yaḥyāb. Ya'mar, Ṭalḥa, and many others.

Sūra LXXI

21: كِبَارًا - كُبَّارًا an alternative form used by Ibn Muḥaiṣin and others.

25: غُرِّقُوا - أُغْرِقُوا II form.

29: لِوَلَدَيَّ - لِوَالِدَيَّ, that is, "to my two sons" instead of "to my two parents," so read by Ibn Mas'ūd, az-Zuhrī, an-Nakha'ī, and others including Al-Ḥūsain b. 'Alī.

Sūra LXXII

1: أُحِيَ - أُوحِيَ from وُحِيَ, which is said to have the same meaning. So read by Ubai, Ibn Abī 'Abla. al-Jaḥdarī, and others.

28: لِيُعْلَمَ - لِيَعْلَمَ passive as read by az-Zuhrī, an-Nakhaʿī, Mujāhid, and others.

Sūra LXXIII

3: نُصْفَهُ - نِصْفَهُ an alternative form, attributed to 'Alī and al-Aṣma'ī.
9: رَبَّ - رَبُّ taken على المدح so read by Ubai, Abū'ṣ-Sammāl, and others.
14: تُرْجَفُ - تَرْجُفُ passive. So read by Muʿādh, Abū'ṣ-Sammāl, and others.
17: يَوْمُ نَجْعَلُ - يَوْمًا يَجْعَلُ so read by Ibn Qais.
20: وَنُصْفَهُ - وَنِصْفَهُ as in verse 3.

Sūra LXXIV

29: لَوَّاحَةً - لَوَّاحَةٌ taking it as *ḥāl*, as read by al-Ḥasan, ʿĪsā b. ʿUmar, and others.
36: إِذْ أَدْبَرَ he supported *TR* here against the more common إِذَا دَبَرَ.

Sūra LXXV

7: بَرَقَ - بَرِقَ supporting the reading of Nāfi' and Abū Jaʿfar.
8: خُسِفَ - خَسَفَ passive as read by Abū Ḥaiwa, Ibn Abī ʿAbla, and others.
22: نَضِرَةٌ - نَاضِرَةٌ as read by Ubai, Abū Nahīk, and others.
39: فَخَلَقَ مِنْهُ ٱلزَّوْجَانِ - فَجَعَلَ مِنْهُ ٱلزَّوْجَيْنِ as read by Abū'l-'Āliya, Abū Nahīk, and Abū'l-Mutawakkil.

40: بِقَادِرٍ - يَقْدُرُ as a verb. So read by Abū Rajā' and al-Jaḥdarī. See XLVI, 32.

Sūra LXXVI

16: قَدَّرُوهَا - قُدِّرُوهَا passive as read by ash-Sha'bī, Ibn Ya'mar, al-Jaḥdarī, and others.

21: عَالِيَهُمْ - عَالِيهُمْ taking it as a *mubtada'* of which ثِيَابُ is the *khabar*. It was so read by Ibn Mas'ūd, Ṭalḥa, and al-A'mash.

Sūra LXXVII

6: عُذْرًا he supports *TR* against the reading عُذُرًا of al-Ḥasan, which was supported by many ancient authorities.

نُذْرًا - نُذُرًا supporting the non-Kūfan reading along with many ancient authorities.

35: يَوْمُ - يَوْمَ said to be a dialectal way of treating يوم before a لا (Abū Ḥayyān, VIII, 407). It was so read by al-A'mash and quite a number of ancient authorities.

36: يُؤْذَنُ - يَأْذَنُ (active) so read by Mu'ādh, Abū Nahīk, Abū's-Sawwār, and others.

Sūra LXXVIII

23: لَابِثِينَ - لَبِثِينَ supporting the reading of Ḥamza, as did Ibn Mas'ūd, Ṭalḥa, and others.

Sūra LXXIX

36: بَرَزَتِ ٱلْجَحِيمُ لِمَنْ تَرَى - وَبُرِّزَتِ ٱلْجَحِيمُ لِمَنْ يَرَى, that is, instead of "hell shall be brought out for him who sees," he read "hell has appeared to him whom thou seest" (that is, Mḥd). So read by ʿIkrima, Abū Nahīk, Mālik b. Dīnār, and attributed to ʿĀʾisha.

Sūra LXXX

1: عَبَّسَ - عَبَسَ perhaps a little stronger word. So read by Abū Nahīk and al-Jaḥdarī.

2: ءَان - أَنْ as al-Ḥasan, ʿĪsā b. ʿUmar, and others.

34: المُرْءُ - المَرْءُ an alternative form, so read by Muʿādh, Abū Nahīk, and Abū Ḥaṣīn.

Sūra LXXXI

8: سَأَلَتْ - سُئِلَتْ active the reading of 'Alī, Ibn Masʿūd, and attributed to a number of ancient authorities.

Sūra LXXXII

19: يَوْمُ - يَوْمَ supporting the reading of Ibn Kathīr, Abū ʿAmr and Ya'qūb.

Sūra LXXXIII

6: يَوْمٌ - يَوْمَ taking it as *khabar* to a ذَٰلِكَ understood. So read by Ubai, Ibn Qais, and others.

24: يُعْرَفُ - تَعْرِفُ, that is, "there will be recognized" instead of "thou wilt recognize," and masculine, because the feminine ending of نضرة is considered figurative (مجازى).

26: خَاتَمُهُ - خِتَامُهُ supporting the reading of al-Kiṣā'ī, a reading attributed to 'Alī, 'Alqama, and others.

Sūra LXXXIV

9: يُقْلَبُ - يَنْقَلِبُ, that is, passive of I form instead of VII form, so read by Abū Nahīk and Mu'ādh.

Sūra LXXXV

8: نَقِمُوا - نَقَمُوا as read by Abū Ḥaiwa, Ibn Abī 'Abla, and al-Jaḥdarī.

22: مَحْفُوظٌ - مَحْفُوظٍ supporting the Madīnan reading of Nāfi', as did Ibn Muḥaiṣin and al-A'raj.

Sūra LXXXVI

6: مَدْفُوقٍ - دَافِقٍ passive participle instead of active participle.

Sūra LXXXVIII

23: إِلَّا – أَلَا the reading of Qatāda, al-Jaḥdarī, Saʿīd b. Jubair, and others.

Sūra LXXXIX

19: تَحَاضُّونَ – تُحَاضّون III form but same meaning, as read by Ibn Masʿūd, ʿAlqama, and others.
27: يٰأَيَّتُهَا – يٰأَيُّهَا masculine.

Sūra XC

6: لُبَدًا – لُبْدًا, which was the reading of Abū Jaʿfar, Mujāhid, and Ibn Muḥaiṣin.

Sūra XCI

13: نَاقَةَ – نَاقَةٌ the more natural construction, so read by Abūʾs-Sammāl, Abūʾl-Jawzā', and others.

Sūra XCII

14: تَلَظَّى – تَتَلَظَّى the complete form, as read by Ibn Masʿūd, ʿĪsā b. ʿUmar, Ṭalḥa, and others.

Sūra XCIV

7: فَٱنْصَبْ - فَٱنْصِبْ as read by Jaʿfar b. Mḥd.

8: فَٱرْغَبْ - فَرَغِّبْ as Ibn as-Samaifaʿ, Ibn Abī ʿAbla, Al-Jaḥdarī, and others.

Sūra XCV

2: سِينِينَ - سَيْنَاء a more usual form, but out of rhyme here. It was attributed to ʿUmar.

Sūra XCVI

16: نَاصِيَةٍ - نَاصِيَةً so also كَاذِبَةً and خَاطِئَةً taking them على الشتم. So read by Abū Ḥaiwa, Ibn Abī ʿAbla, ʿĪsā b. ʿUmar, and others.

Sūra XCIX

7: يَرَهُ - يُرَهُ passive, a reading given from a great many ancient authorities and particularly from Ahl al-Bait.

Sūra C

5: فَوَسَطْنَ - فَوَسَّطْنَ perhaps a little stronger expression, so read by Qatāda and others.

Sūra CI

3: يَوْمَ – يَوْمُ taking it as a *khabar*. So read by Abūʾs-Sammāl and others.

Sūra CIII

2: خُسْرٍ – خُسُرٍ an alternative form, so read by Ibn Hurmuz, ʿĪsā b. ʿUmar, and others.

Sūra CIV

4: الحُطَمَةِ – الحَاطِمَةِ making it a participle. So read by Ibn Masʿūd, Abū Ḥaiwa, and others.

5: الحُطَمَةُ as in verse 4.

Sūra CVII

3: يَحُضُّ – يُحَاضُّ, that is, III form as in LXXXIX, 19.

Sūra CXI

4: حَمَّالَةَ الحَطَبِ – he supports *TR* against the more common reading حَمَّالَةُ الحَطَبِ.

Sūra CXII

1: أَحَدٌ - أَحَدُ as read by al-Ḥasan, Naṣr b. ʿĀṣim, Abūʾs-Sammāl, and others.

From this collection of material the one outstanding conclusion is that Zaid b. ʿAlī had a decidedly eclectic taste in readings. There are occasions when he champions the text of Ḥafṣ, which is our *textus receptus*, against all other readings,[5] and there are other occasions when he champions the Kūfan reading where it differs from Ḥafṣ, against the received reading of the other metropolitan codices,[6] so that we have here some slight justification for those who class him as belonging to the Kūfan school (though by others he is included in the Madīnan school). On the other hand, he not infrequently chooses the reading favored by some other school as against the Kūfan, and in his choice shows a most catholic taste. This might have been expected, of course, as his *qirāʾa* must have been formed before the fixing of even the first stages of the systems of the Seven.

As to the connection of his *qirāʾa* with the *Shīʿa* text, three points are to be noticed. First, it is true that he sometimes agrees with characteristic readings of the *Ahl al-Bait*,[7] but on the other hand, he is not quoted as supporting some of the most characteristic of such readings. It is true that we have only fragmentary information as to his readings, and moreover only from Sunnī sources, which could not be expected to have great enthusiasm for reporting readings peculiar to the Shīʿas,[8] so it may well be that he supported very many other Shīʿa readings even where no mention of his name occurs in our sources. Second, it is noteworthy how often he agrees with readings of Ibn Masʿūd,[9] whose text as we learn from other sources was in high favor with the Shīʿas, though apparently quite unconnected with the text of ʿAlī. Third, there must be taken into account the numerous variants where he agrees with al-Ḥasan al-Baṣrī,[10] which must be weighed as an offset to peculiarly Shīʿa leanings.

It will be noted how few readings there are where Zaid b. ʿAlī stands by himself. Some of the readers who agree with him in particular readings are later than him in time, and may possibly have learned their readings from his tradition, though this is not likely in very many cases. The much more likely theory is that he and they are both drawing from a common tradition. The impression one gains from a consideration of Zaid's readings as a whole is that he was not attempting to form a special tradition of his own, as may be said of the Seven or of such readers as ʿĪsā b. ʿUmar or al-Jaḥdarī, but made independent choice of what he considered best among the various types of oral tradition current in his time.

That the text tradition was still fluid in his time is perfectly clear, but it will be noticed that his textual variants show far fewer cases where the variant depends on a different consonantal text from that current today, than is the case in the variants collected from the codices of Ubai and Ibn Masʿūd.[11] Indeed it will have been noticed that there are not a few instances where his readings have the appearance of being corrections of a written text that lay before him. This postulates a definite stage in the process of crystallization of the tradition, but as there were various types of written text current at an early period in Islam, it is not necessary to assume that he must have had before him some early form of the present 'Uthmānic text.

If the theory that his readings represent early Shīʿa tradition were true, it might have been expected that his readings would have been related to the Codex of 'Alī, if to any, but the cases known to us where his readings agree with those attributed in our sources to 'Alī are too few to admit of any such connection being established. Further investigation may throw more light on this problem, but it must be confessed that the evidence of the collection given here gives at most meager support to any attempt at ascertaining the early Shīʿa textual tradition. At the present stage in our investigation of the textual history of the Qur'ān the value of this collection lies in the much more general sphere of evidence for the wide range of variants that was still possible at the time of Zaid. Critical investigation of this matter will only be possible when we have so collected the readings of a number of the more important early readers.

NOTES

1. *Itqān*, 140, 141.

2. Nöldeke-Schwally, II, 9.

3. Strothmann, "Das Problem der literarischen Personlichkeit Zaid b. 'Alī," *Der Islam* XIII (1923).

4. *Ibn Ḫālawaih's Sammlung nichtkanonischer Koranlesarten*, Stambul, 1934 (Bibliotheca Islamica VII): *Nichtkanonische Koranlesarten im Muḥtasab des Ibn Ginni*, 1933 (Sitzungsberichte der Bayerischen Akademie der Wissenschatten, 1933, no. 2).

5. Cf. VII, 164; IX, 67; X, 24; XI, 74; XIII, 4; XVIII, 18, 83; XIX, 35; XX, 90; XXI, 80; XXVI, 56,149; XXVII, 84; XXVIII, 48; XXXI, 17; XXXIV, 19; XXXVII, 126; XL, 39; XLIII, 17; XLV, 4, 20; XLVI, 24; LII, 45; LXV, 3; LXXIV, 36; LXXVII, 6; CXI, 4.

6. Cf. XVII, 35, 104; XVIII, 70; XXIII, 113; XXIV, 35; XXV, 9, 63; XXIX, 58; XXXV, 3; LV, 31; LVII, 13; LXXVIII, 23.

7. Eg. I, 7; II, 16, 161; III, 2; XIII, 12; XIV, 42; XIX, 5; XXXIII, 37; LXXI, 29; XCIX, 7.

8. I have gone carefully through the great Shīʿa commentary of aṭ-Ṭabarsī, but found it to contain nothing new under this head.

9. I, 6; II, 17, 22, 23, 24, 30, 69, 183, 242; III, 50, 107; IV, 86, 90, 154, 175; V, 1, 3, 82; VI, 27, 63; VIII, 1; IX, 37; X, 23, 24, 52; XI, 43, 115; XII, 72; XIII, 30; XIV, 42, 47; XVII, 4, 61, 107; XVIII, 10, 84; XX, 72; XXIII, 21, 69; XXXV, 25; XXXVIII, 22; XL, 8, 73; XLVII, 2; XLVIII, 16; XLIX, 2, 9, 17; LIV, 12; LV, 35; LVII, 10; LIX, 5, 17; LXXVI, 21; LXXVIII, 23; LXXXI, 8; LXXXIX, 19; XCII, 4; CIV, 4.

10. I, 1, 5; II, 156, 192, 193, 257; IV, 2, 41, 83, 147; V, 4; VI, 73; VII, 19, 25, 51; VIII, 43; IX, 3, 12, 42, 61; X, 31; XI, 80; XII, 45; XIII, 18; XVI, 68; XVII, 5; XVIII, 43, 84; XX, 33; XXI, 31; XXII, 28; XXIII, 21; XXV, 19; XXXIII, 40; XXXVI, 81; XXXIX, 68; XL, 66; XLI, 9; XLII, 22; XLIV, 5; XLV, 24; XLVI, 3, 35; XLIX, 9; LVI, 78; LXVIII, 39; LXX, 38; LXXIV, 29; LXXX, 2; CXII, 1.

11. A preliminary collection of them will be found in Bregsträsser's *Geschichte des Qorantexts*, pp. 60–94. A much larger collection has been made by the present writer and will be published in his forthcoming work, *Materials for the Textual History of the Qur'ān*.

4.2

Further Qur'ān Readings of Zaid b. 'Alī

Arthur Jeffery

In volume 16 of the *Rivista* the courtesy of the editor enabled us to print a collection of variant readings to the Qur'ān text which were attributed to Zaid b. 'Alī. Since the publication of that collection access to new sources, particularly to photographs of the Escorial manuscript of al-Marandīs *Qurrat 'Ain al-Qurrā'*, the Stambul manuscript of al-Farrā's *Ma'ānī al-Qur'ān*, and the Azhar manuscript of al-Kirmānī's *Kitāb Shawādhdh al-Qirā'āt wa'khtilāf al-Maṣāḥif*, the photographs of all of which we owe to the kindness of Dr. Otto Pretzel of Munich, has brought to light a considerable number of new readings which ought to be brought to the notice of interested scholars, as well as certain additions and corrections to the material given there. Again we are indebted to the editor for the hospitality of the pages of the *Rivista* in publishing this new material.

The material is arranged according to the sūra order of the Qur'ān, and the verse numbering is that of the standard Egyptian text (which follows the Kūfan system of verse numbering), followed, where there is a difference, by the numbering of the Flügel edition of the text of the Qur'ān.

Sūra I

2/1: رَبِّ - others said he read رَبُّ and consequently الرحمنُ and الرحيمُ.

4/3: مَـٰلِكِ - مَلَكَ as read by Abū Ḥanīfa, taking it as a verb, with يَوْمَ as its object.

Sūra II

14/13: لَاقُوٓا - لَقُوا as Abū Ḥanīfa and Ibn as-Samaifa'. So in v. 71.

16/15: ٱشْتَرَوِا - ٱشْتَرَوُا and so in II 86/80, 175/170; III 177/171, etc.

20/19: يَخْطَفُ - some say he read يُخْطِفُ.

أُظْلِمَ - أَظْلَمَ as Ibn Qais and aḍ-Ḍaḥḥāk.

24/22: أَعِدَّتْ - others say he read أُعْدِتُ (but this is probably a mistake for أُعِدْتُ from عاد).

25/23: مُطَهَّرَةٌ - but others say he read مُطْهِرَةٌ as Ibn Qais and Abū Ḥaṣīn.

32/30: أَنَّكَ - إِنَّكَ.

35/33: حَيْثَ - حَيْثُ and so wherever it occurs in the Qur'ān.

42/39: تَلْبِسُوا - others say he read تُلَبِّسُوا.

48/45: تُقْبَلُ - يُقْبَلُ as read by Ubai and Ibn ʿAbbās, and supporting the reading of the Meccans and Baṣrans.

49/46: أَنْجَاكُمْ - نَجَّيْنٰكُمْ as Ibn Khuthaim and Abū Ḥaṣīn.

51/48: وَعَدْنَا - وٰعَدْنَا supporting the Baṣrans. So in VII 142/138 and XX 80/82.

61/58: تُنْبِتُ - but others said he read تَنْبِتُ.

70/65: الْبَاقَرَ - ٱلْبَقَرَ, which some gave from Kirdāb and Ibn Miqsam, beside the alternative الْبَاقِرِ. Others say Zaid b. 'Alī read الْبَوَاقِرِ.

تَشَٰبَهَ - some say he read تَشَابَهُ as Ubai, others تَتَشَابَهُ.

80/74: تَمْسَسْنَا - تَمَسَّنَا, though some said he read تَمِسَّنَا.

83/77: إِحْسَانًا - حُسْنًا as Ibn Khuthain, al-Jaḥdarī, and others.

94/88: فَتَمَنَّوِا - فَتَمَنَّوُا. So also in LXII 6.

102/96: يَضِرُّهُمْ - يَضُرُّهُمْ.

مُلُكِ - مُلْكِ and so wherever this word occurs.

106/100: نُنْسِخْ - نَنْسَخْ as Ibn ʿĀmir and Ibn Abī ʿAbla.

نَنْسَاهَا - نُنْسِهَا as Muʿādh, Ibn Qais, Ubai, and ʿAlī.

109/103: تَبَيَّنَ - others said he read بُيِّنَ .

110/104: فَمَا - وَمَا as Abū Jaʿfar.

119/113: وَلَا تَسْئَلْ - وَلَا تُسْئَلُ as Ibn ʿAbbās, Nāfiʿ, and many others.

124/118: ذِرِّيَّتِي - ذُرِّيَّتِي and so in all occurrences of this word in all its various forms.

125/119: مَثْوَبَةً - مَثَابَةً as in v. 103/97.

126/120: فَأُمْتِعُهُ - فَأُمَتِّعُهُ as Qatāda, Ibn Muḥaiṣin, and others.

128/122: مُسْلِمِينَ - مُسْلِمَيْنِ as al-Ḥasan and Ibn ʿAbbās.

أَرْنَا - أَرِنَا as Ibn Kathīr. Likewise in IV 153/152 and XLI 29; and أَرْنِي in II 260/262 and VII 143/139.

129/123: يُزَكِّيهِمْ - some said he read يُزَكِّهِمْ taking it as جواب الأمر.

135/129: مِلَّةَ - مِلَّةِ as al-Aʿraj.

139/133: أَتُحَاجُّونَّا - أَتُحَاجُّونَنَا as Ibn Muḥaiṣin and al-Aʿmash.

143/138: يَتْبَعُ - يَتَّبِعُ as Ibn Qais and Abūʾl-Mutawakkil.

144/139: حَيْثَ - حَيْثُ as Ibn Khuthaim. See v. 35/33.

147/142: ٱلْحَقَّ - ٱلْحَقُّ as ʿAlī, Muʿādh, and Abū Ḥaṣīn.

149/144: يَعْمَلُونَ - تَعْمَلُونَ as Ubai, Ibn Khuthaim, and the Baṣrans.

158/153: يَطُوفَ - يَطَّوَّفَ as Ubai and ʿĪsā b. ʿUmar.

164/159: ٱلْفُلُكِ - ٱلْفُلْكِ . So in all other occurrences of this word.

165/160: يَحِبُّونَهُمْ - يُحِبُّونَهُمْ as Abū Rajāʾ.

يُرَى - يَرَى as Ibn Khutaim, Abū Razīn, and others.

166/161: رَأَوِا - رَأَوُا . Likewise in X 54/55, XXVIII 64, XXIV 33/32, and XLII 44/43.

171/166: صُمًّا بُكْمًا عُمْيًا - صُمٌّ بُكْمٌ عُمْيٌ as in v. 17/16, like Ubai and Ibn Masʿūd.

185/181: أَنْزَلَ فِيهِ ٱلْقُرْآنَ – أُنْزِلَ فِيهِ ٱلْقُرْآنُ as Ibn as-Samaifa'.

197/193: فَلَا رَفُوثٌ – فَلَا رَفَثَ. So read also by Ibn Masʿūd and al-Aʿmash.

198/194: الْمَشْعِرِ – ٱلْمَشْعَرِ as al-Jaḥdarī and Abū'ʾs-Sammāl.

205/201: يهلك ٱلْحَرْثُ وَٱلنَّسْلُ – يُهْلِكَ ٱلْحَرْثَ وَٱلنَّسْلَ.

210/206: ظُلَلٍ – ظُلَلٍ. See also the reading of Ibn Masʿūd and Ubai ظِلَالٍ.

226: يُقْسِمُونَ – يُؤْلُونَ as Ubai and Ibn ʿAbbās.

233: تُضَارُّ – تُضَارَّ as given by some from Ibn Kathīr and Abū ʿAmr.

يُتَمَّ ٱلرِّضَاعَةُ – others say he read يُتِمَّ ٱلرِّضَاعَةَ.

237/238: تَنْسَوِا – تَنْسَوُا.

يَعْفُوِا – يَعْفُوَا (?).

238/239: وَٱلصَّلَوٰةَ – وَٱلصَّلَوٰةِ as ʿĀʾisha, al-Jaḥdarī, and others.

249/250: غَرْفَةً – غُرْفَةً as the reading of Nāfiʿ, Ibn Kathīr, and Abū ʿAmr.

254/255: خُلَّةٌ and شَفَعَةٌ – خُلَّةٌ and شَفَاعَةٌ (though he read بَيْعٌ as *TR*).

255/256: ٱلْقَيَّامُ – ٱلْقَيُّومُ as ʿUmar, ʿAlqama, and Ibn Masʿūd, but others said القَيِّمْ.

259/261: فَمَوَّتَهُ – فَأَمَاتَهُ as Muʿādh and Abū Mijlaz.

نُنْشِزُهَا – others say he read نَنْشُرُهَا.

277: آتَوِا – آتَوُا. Likewise is IX 5, 11 and XXII 41/42.

280: ذَا عُسْرَةٍ – ذُو عُسْرَةٍ as in the codices of Ubai and ʿUthmān.

تَصَدَّقُوا – he supported *TR* here against the more common reading تَصَّدَّقُوا.

282: فَتُذَاكِرَ – فَتُذَكِّرَ as Zaid b. Aslam and Ibn Khuthaim, though others said he read فَتُذَكِّرُ as Ḥamza, al-Aʿmash, and Ṭalḥa.

283: فَرُهُنٌ – فَرِهَٰنٌ as Ubai, az-Zuhrī, and others.

Sūra III

28/27: يَتَّخِذُ - يَتَّخِذ . So read also by Aḥmad b. Ḥanbal.
45/40: بِكِلْمَةٍ - بِكَلِمَةٍ as Abū's-Sammāl.
64/57: كِلْمَةٍ - كَلِمَةٍ as Abū's-Sammāl.
71/64: تَلْبَسُونَ - تَلْبِسُونَ or some said تَلَبِّسُوا as ʿUbaid b. ʿUmair.
85/79: يُقْبَلَ – others say that he read نَقْبَلَ as abū Razīn and Abū ʿImrān.
90/84: تُقْبَلَ تَوْبَتُهُمْ – others said his reading was تَقْبَلَ تَوْبَتَهُمْ as Abū ʿImrān.
91/85: فَلَنْ يُقْبَلَ – others said فَلَنْ يَقْبَلَ as Abū ʿImrān.
119/115: لَاقَوْكُمْ - لَقُوكُمْ . See II 113.
161/155: أَنْ يُغَلَّ - أَنْ يَغُلَّ supporting Nāfiʿ and some Kūfans.
لِلنَّبِيِّ - لِنَبِيٍّ.
195/194: قُتِلُوا وَقَاتَلُوا - قَاتَلُوا وَقُتِلُوا as Ḥamza and al-Kiṣā'ī.

Sūra IV

3: فَوَاحِدَةٌ - فَوَاحِدَةً as Abū Ja'far and others.
4/3: صَدُقَٰتِهِنَّ – others said he read صُدُقَاتِهِنَّ as Ibn Abī ʿAbla.
10/11: سَيُصِلُونَ - سَيَصْلَوْنَ as Ibn ʿĀmir and Abū Bakr from ʿĀṣim.
15/19: فاشهدوا - فَاسْتَشْهِدُوا as ʿUbaid b. ʿUmair.
42/45: عَصَوِا - عَصَوُا.
66/69: إِلَّا قَلِيلًا - إِلَّا قَلِيلٌ as Ibn Masʿūd, Anas, and the Syrian codices.
79/81: فَمَنْ نَفْسُكَ فَبِذَنْبِكَ وَأَنَا قَدَّرْتُهَا عَلَيْكَ وَأَرْسَلْنَاكَ - فَمِنْ نَفْسِكَ وَأَرْسَلْنَاكَ as Ubai, but some said his only addition was the أَنَا قدرتها عَلَيْكَ.
84/86: يَكُفَّ – others said he read يَكُفُّ and others يُكِفَّ.

95/97: الضَّرَرِ – some said he read الضَّرِّ as ʿUbaid b. ʿUmair.

114: يُؤْتِيهِ – نُؤْتِيهِ as Ḥamza and the Baṣrans.

117: أَوْثَانًا – إِنَٰثًا which was said to be in the Codex of ʿĀʾisha.

137/136: لِيَهْدِيهِمْ – لِيَهْدِيَهُمْ.

142/141: يُرَوْنَ – يُرَآءُونَ.

154/153: تَعَدُّوا – تَعْدُوا as some of the Madīnan readers.

155/154: فَبِنَقْضِهِمْ – فَبِمَا نَقْضِهِم others said he read نَقْضُهُمْ and consequently كُفْرُهُمْ and قَتْلُهُمْ and قَوْلُهُمْ.

157: إِلَّا ٱتِّبَاعُ – إِلَّا ٱتِّبَاعَ. Said to be so read among the Banī Tamīn.

Sūra V

1: حُرْمٌ – حُرُمٌ as al-Ḥasan and Ibn Waththāb.

2: ٱلْهَدِيَّ – ٱلْهَدْىَ. So read by ʿUbaid b. ʿUmair.

2/3: شِنْآنُ – شَنَئَانُ or some said شَنْآنُ as az-Zuhrī and al-Ḥasan. So in v. 11.

6/8: أَرْجُلَكُمْ – he supported *TR* here against the alternative readings.

6/9: فَأَمُّوا – فَتَيَمَّمُوا as Ubai and others, but some said he read فَتَأَمَّمُوا.

13/16: فَبِنَقْضِهِمْ – فَبِمَا نَقْضِهِمْ as Ubai and Abū Mijlaz. See also IV 155/154.

28/31: لَأَقْتُلُكَ – لَأَقْتُلَنَّكَ as Ibn Khuthaim and Ibn Qais.

32/35: فَسَادًا – فَسَادٍ as al-Ḥasan and Muʿādh.

42/46: لِلسُّحْتِ – but others said he read لِلسَّحْتِ.

45/49: وَٱلْأُذْنُ بِٱلْأُذْنِ – وَٱلْأُذُنَ بِٱلْأُذُنِ as Nāfiʿ and Abū Jaʿfar. So in IX 61, XXXI 6, and LXIX 12.

51/56: فَهُوَ مِنْهُمْ – فَإِنَّهُ مِنْهُمْ as Ubai b. Kaʿb.

60/65: وَعَبَدَ ٱلطَّٰغُوتَ – others said he read وَعُبِدَ ٱلطَّاغُوتُ.

64/69: طُغْيَانًا - طِغْيَانًا as Ibn Khuthaim and an-Nakhaʿī, and similarly in all other occurrences of this word.

96/97: حُرِّمَ عَلَيْكُمْ صَيْدُ - حَرَّمَ عَلَيْكُمْ صَيْدَ as Muʿādh and Abū Mijlaz.

Sūra VI

6: مِدْرَارًا - دِرَارًا.

9: لَلَبَسْنَا - لَبَّسْنَا as Ibn Muḥaiṣin, or some said لَبَسْنَا.

23: تَكُن - يَكُن as Mujāhid, thereby supporting the Kūfan reading.

59: حَبَّةٍ - but others said he read حَبَّةٌ and only رطبٌ and يابسٌ in *raf'*.

61: يُفَرِّطُونَ - others say he read يُفْرِطُونَ as al-Aʿraj and ʿUbaid b. ʿUmair.

63: أَنْجَانَا - he agreed with *TR* as the Kūfan reading against the more common reading أَنْجَيْتَنَا.

64: يُنَجِّيكُمْ - he agreed with *TR* as the Kūfan against the usual يُنْجِيكُمْ.

65: نُصَرِّفُ - نَصْرِفُ. So read also by al-Jaḥdarī.

70: نُرَدُّ - نَرْتَدُّ as Ibn Masʿūd.

91: تَجْعَلُونَهُ and تُبْدُونَهَا and تُخْفُونَ - he read with ياء in these as the Meccans, Baṣrans, and Ubai.

98: فَمُسْتَقَرٌّ - فَمُسْتَقِرٌّ as the Meccans and Baṣrans.

99: His reading here necessarily involves مُتَرَاكِبٌ.

110: طُغْيَنِهِمْ - طِغْيَانِهِمْ as Ibn Khuthaim and Abūʾl-Mutawakkil.

115: مُبَدِّلَ - مُبْدِلَ the reading of Ubai.

125: حَرَجًا - حَرِجًا as al-Ḥasan and the Madīnan readers.

135: مَكَانَتِكُمْ - مَكَانَاتِكُمْ and so in XI 95, 122; XXXVI 67; and XXXIX 40.

142: حَصَادِهِ - he agreed with *TR* against the alternative حِصَادِهِ.

Sūra VII

20/19: سَوْءَاتِهِمَا – others said سَوَأَتُهُمَا, as Ibn Qais.
27/26: يَفْتِنَنَّكُمْ – others say his reading was يُفْتِنَنَّكُمْ and others يُفْتِنْكُمْ.
34/32: آجَالُهُمْ – أَجَلُهُمْ the reading of Ubai.
40/38: تُفَتَّحُ – تُفْتَحُ as Ubai and the Baṣrans.
يُدْخَلُونَ – يَدْخُلُونَ.
59/57: إِنِّي – أَنِّي as Nāfiʿ, Ibn Kathīr, and Abū ʿĀmr.
139/135: بَٰطِلٌ – بَطَلَ taking it as the *māḍī* of the verb.
146/143: ٱلرُّشْدِ – ٱلرَّشَدِ as Muʿādh and Ibn Qais.
172/171: تَقُولُوا – يَقُولُوا as Ibn Muḥaiṣin and the Baṣrans. So also in v. 173/172.
202/201: يَمُدُّونَهُمْ – يُمِدُّونَهُمْ as the Madīnans.

Sūra VIII

9: مُرْدِفِينَ – مُرْدَفِينَ as the Madīnans and Ibn Abī ʿAbla.
46/48: تَذْهَبَ – يُذْهَبْ.
60/62: تُرْهِبُونَ – يَرْهَبُونَ.
61/63: فَٱجْنَحْ – فَٱجْنُحْ.
66/67: ضَعْفًا – he supported *TR* against the more common ضُعْفًا.
70/71: ٱلْأَسْرَىٰ – ٱلْأُسَارَىٰ as Abū ʿĀmr.

Sūra IX

13: بَدَءُوكُمْ – others said بَدَوْكُمْ as read by Abū ʿImrān and Abū Ḥaṣīn.
40: وَكَلِمَةُ – وَكَلِمَةَ as al-Ḥasan and the Baṣrans.

47: زَادَكُمْ - زَادُوكُمْ as Ubai and Ibn Abī ʿAbla.
75/76: لَنُصْدِقُنَّ - لَنَصَّدَّقَنَّ.

Sūra X

61/62: لَا أَصْغَرَ and لَا أَصْغَرِ - لَا أَكْبَرَ and لَا أَكْبَرِ.
81: ءَآلسِّحْرُ - آلسِّحْرُ as Muʿādh, Ṭalḥa, and Ibn Khuthaim.
90: جَوَّزْنَا - جَٰوَزْنَا as al-Ḥasan, Muʿādh, and al-Jaḥdarī.
103: نُنْجِ - he supported *TR* here as the Kūfan reading.

Sūra XI

15/18: يُوَفِّ - نُوَفِّ as al-Aʿmash and Ṭalḥa.
111/113: تَعْمَلُونَ - يَعْمَلُونَ. So read also by Abūʾl-Mutawakkil.

Sūra XII

31: حَاشَا لِلَّهِ - حَٰشَ لِلَّهِ as many of the Baṣrans.
65: نُزَادُ - نَزْدَادُ.

Sūra XIII

19: أَنْزَلَ إِلَيْكَ مِنْ رَبِّكَ آلْحَقَّ - أُنْزِلَ إِلَيْكَ مِنْ رَبِّكَ آلْحَقُّ. So read by Kirdāb.
33: زَيَّنَ لِلَّذِينَ كَفَرُوا مَكْرَهُمْ - زُيِّنَ لِلَّذِينَ كَفَرُوا مَكْرُهُمْ as Ibn Abī ʿAbla.
36: أَنْزَلَ إِلَيْكَ - أُنْزِلَ إِلَيْكَ as Kirdāb.

Sūra XIV

32/37: سَخَّرَ (quater) – سُخِّرَ as Ibn Abī ʿAbla and Muʿādh.
50/51: قَطِرَانٍ – قِطْرٍ آنٍ as Ibn ʿAbbās, Saʿīd b. Jubair, and others.

Sūra XV

56: يَقْنَطُ – others say يَقْنِطُ as the Baṣrans.

Sūra XVI

2: يُنَزِّلُ ٱلْمَلَـٰٓئِكَةَ – some say he read يَنْزِلُ ٱلْمَلَائِكَةُ others تَنَزَّلُ ٱلْمَلَائِكَةُ as the Baṣrans.
10: شَجَرٌ – شِجَرٌ, which was the reading of Ubai.

Sūra XVII

3: ذُرِّيَّةَ – ذِرِّيَّةَ as Zaid b. Thābit and Abū Ja'far.
13: مُبْصِرَةً – مَبْصَرَةً as Ubai and Ibn Khuthaim. So in v. 59/61 and in XXVII 13.
36/38: تَقْفُ – but others say he read تَقُفْ as Muʿādh and Abū Mijlaz.
68/70: يَخْسِفَ and يُرْسِلَ – نَخْسِفُ and نُرْسِلَ as Ubai, supporting the Meccan and Baṣran reading.
69/71: يُعِيدَكُمْ and فَيُرْسِلَ and فَيُغْرِقَكُمْ – نُعِيدَكُمْ and فَنُرْسِلَ and فَنُغْرِقَكُمْ as Ubai, supporting the Meccan and Baṣran reading.
71/73: نَدْعُو – يُدْعَى as Ibn Khuthaim and Ibn Qais.
102/104: مَثْبُورًا – لَمَثْبُورًا, which was the reading of Ubai.

Sūra XVIII

19/18: بِوَرِقِكُمْ others say he read بِوَرْقِكُمْ as was read by several of the Baṣrans and Kūfans.
27/26: مُبْدِلَ ـ مُبَدِّلَ, which was the reading of Ubai.
45/43: تَذْرِيهِ ـ تَذْرُوهُ as Ibn Abī 'Abla, a reading sometimes given from Ibn Mas'ūd.
47/45: تُسَيَّرُ ٱلْجِبَالُ ـ نُسَيِّرُ ٱلْجِبَالَ as Ibn Kathīr, Ibn 'Āmir, and Abū 'Amr.
96/95: ٱلصُّدُفَيْنِ ـ ٱلصَّدَفَيْنِ as Ubai, supporting the Meccan and Baṣran reading.

Sūra XIX

1: كهيعص – he read with *imāla* of the هاء as Ubai.
51/52: مُخْلَصًا – he supported *TR* as the Kūfan reading against the more common مُخْلِصًا.
63/64: نُوَرِّثُ ـ نُورِثُ as al-Ḥasan, Qatāda, and Ibn Abī 'Abla.
72/73: نُنْجِى ـ نُنَجِّى as al-Kisā'ī and al-A'mash.

Sūra XX

1: طه ـ طِهِ, which was the reading of Abū Mijlaz and Abū Razīn.
52/54: عِنْدَ ٱللّٰهِ ـ عِنْدَ رَبِّى.
63/66: إِنَّ هٰذَيْنِ ـ إِنْ هٰذَانِ as Abū 'Amr and Ibn Khuthaim.
84/86: أُولَى ـ أُولَاءِ as 'Īsā b. 'Umar.
أَثَرِى – but some said he read أَثْرِى as Mu'ādh.
96: بَصِرْتُ ـ بَصُرْتُ as al-Ḥasan and Abū'l-Mutawakkil.
98: وَسَّعَ ـ وَسِعَ.

Sūra XXII

3: وَيَتَّبِعُ كُلَّ – his reading here should be وَيَتْبَعُ كُلَّ as read by Muʿādh.
31/32: فَتُخَطَّفُهُ – فَتَخْطَفُهُ as read by the Madīnans.
36/37: ٱلْمُعْتَرِى – ٱلْمُعْتَرَّ as al-Ḥasan.
39/40: قُتِّلُوا – يُقَـٰتَلُونَ, though some said قَاتَلُوا like Ibn Masʿūd.
45/44: أَهْلَكْتُهَا – أَهْلَكْنَـٰهَا as the Baṣrans.

Sūra XXIII

2: صَلَوَاتِهِمْ – صَلَاتِهِمْ as Ubai and Abū Razīn.
14: عِظَـٰمًا – others said عُظْمًا.
20: سَيْنَا – سَيْنَاءَ the reading of al-Aʿmash.
22: ٱلْفَلِكِ – ٱلْفُلْكِ (though elsewhere he read ٱلْفُلُكِ).
60/62: إِنَّهُمْ – أَنَّهُمْ the reading of Al-Aʿmash.
87/89: ٱللَّهُ – لِلَّهِ as the Baṣrans. So also in v. 89/91.

Sūra XXIV

1: فَرَّضْنَاهَا – فَرَضْنَـٰهَا as the Meccans and Baṣrans.
31: عَوَرَاتِ – عَوْرَاتِ as Ibn ʿAbbās and al-Aʿmash, but others said عِوَرَاتِ as Abū ʿImrān.

Sūra XXV

8/9: يَأْكُلُ – others said he read here يَأْكُلُ.
40/42: مُطِرَتْ – أُمْطِرَتْ as Ubai and Muʿādh.
69: يُضَاعِفُ لَهُ ٱلْعَذَابُ – يُضَـٰعَفْ لَهُ ٱلْعَذَابُ as Ṭalḥa.

Sūra XXVI

3/2: بَاخِعٌ نَفْسَكَ - but some said he read بَخْعٌ نَفْسَكَ.

Sūra XXVII

36: أَتُمُدُّونِّي - أَتُمِدُّونَنِ as Ḥamza and Ya'qūb.
51/52: إِنَّا - أَنَّا as the non-Kūfan readers.
52/53: خَاوِيَةٌ - خَاوِيَةً as 'Īsā b. 'Umar and others.
66/68: بَلْ أَدْرَكَ - بَلِ ادَّارَكَ as Abū 'Amr and Ibn Kathīr.

Sūra XXVIII

35: عَضَدَكَ – others say he read عُضُدَكَ.

Sūra XXIX

17/16: تَخْلَفُونَ - تَخْلُقُونَ (with ف instead of ق) .
46/45: أَنْزَلَ - أُنْزِلَ as was read by Abū'l-Barhasīm.
50/49: ءَايَتٌ – he agreed with *TR* against the more common آيَةٌ.

Sūra XXX

2/1: غَلَبَتِ - غُلِبَتِ as read by 'Alī, Ibn 'Abbās, and al-Ḥasan.
11/10: يَرْجِعُونَ - تُرْجَعُونَ as the Baṣrans.

Sūra XXXI

6/5: لِيُضِلَّ - لِيَضِلَّ as the Meccans and Baṣrans.
18/17: تُصَعِّرْ – others said he read تُصَاعِرْ as Nāfiʿ, Abū ʿAmr, and Ḥamza.
27/26: وَٱلْبَحْرُ - وَٱلْبَحْرَ as the Baṣran readers.

Sūra XXXII

7/6: خَلَقَهُ - خَلْقَهُ as Ubai and the Ḥijāzī readers.

Sūra XXXIII

31: يَقْنُتْ - تَقْنُتْ as al-Jaḥdarī and Yaʿqūb.

Sūra XXXIV

3: أَصْغَرُ and أَكْبَرُ – others say he read here أَصْغَرٍ and أَكْبَرٍ (with *tanwīn*).
10: وَٱلطَّيْرَ - وَٱلطَّيْرُ as some of the Baṣran readers.
11/10: سَٰبِغَٰتٍ - صَابِغَاتٍ as Abū'l-Mutawakkil.
12/11: ٱلرِّيحَ - ٱلرِّيحُ as Ubai and Ibn Abī ʿAbla.
15/14: لِسَبَإٍ - لِسَبَأَ as Abū ʿAmr and al-Yazīdī.
23/22: أَذِنَ - أُذِنَ as the Kūfans and Baṣrans.
فُزِّعَ - فُرِعَ (or فُرِّغَ ?) as al-Ḥasan and Muʿādh.
38/37: مُعَٰجِزِينَ - مُعْجِزِينَ as Ubai and Ibn Kuthaim.

Sūra XXXV

9/10: ٱلرِّيَٰحَ - ٱلرِّيحَ as the Kūfans.
10/11: ٱلْكَلِمُ ٱلطَّيِّبُ - ٱلْكَلَامَ ٱلطَّيِّبَ .

28/25: أَلْوَانَهَا – أَلْوَانُهُ as Ibn as-Samaifa' and Ibn ʿUmair.
33/30: يُدْخَلُونَهَا – يَدْخُلُونَهَا as the Baṣrans.
43/41: وَلَا يُحِيقُ ٱلْمَكْرَ ٱلسَّيِّئَ – وَلَا يَحِيقُ ٱلْمَكْرُ ٱلسَّيِّئُ.

Sūra XXXVI

9/8: سَدًّا (bis) – سُدًّا as Ubai, 'Alī, and the non-Kūfan readers.
33: ٱلْمَيِّتَةُ – ٱلْمَيْتَةُ as the Kūfans.
55: شُغْلٍ – شُغُلٍ as Ubai and the readers of the Ḥijāz.
62: جُبُلًّا – جِبِلًّا as many of the Baṣran readers.
67: مَكَانَاتِهِمْ – مَكَانَتِهِمْ as Abū Bakr, al-Ḥasan, and others.
68: تَعْقِلُونَ – يَعْقِلُونَ as the Madīnans and many Syrians.
83: تُرْجَعُونَ – others said يُرْجَعُونَ. So Ibn ʿUmair and the friends of Ibn Masʿūd.

Sūra XXXVII

6: بِزِينَةٍ ٱلْكَوَاكِبِ – others said بِزِينَةٍ ٱلْكَوَاكِبَ as many of the Kūfan readers.
102: يَا أَبَاهُ فَٱفْعَلْ مَا أُمِرْتَ – يَا أَبَتِ ٱفْعَلْ مَا تُؤْمَرُ.

Sūra XXXVIII

50: جَنَّاتُ – جَنَّاتِ as Abū Ḥaiwa and al-Jaḥdarī.
53: يُوعَدُونَ – تُوعَدُونَ as Ubai and Ibn Khuthaim.

Sūra XXXIX

29/30: سَالِمًا - سَلَمًا as the Meccans and Baṣrans.
30/31: مَيِّتٌ and مَائِتٌ - مَيِّتُونَ and مَائِتُونَ as al-Ḥasan and others.

Sūra XLI

16/15: لِيُذِيقَهُمْ - لِنُذِيقَهُمْ.

Sūra XLII

20/19: يُؤْتِهِ - نُؤْتِهِ as some of the Baṣrans.
23/22: يَبْشُرُ - يُبَشِّرُ as the Meccans and Baṣrans.
حُسْنَى - حُسْنًا as Ibn Masʿūd and al-Jaḥdarī.
41/39: بَعْدَ مَا ظُلِمَ - بَعْدَ ظُلْمِهِ. So read also by ʿUbaid b. ʿUmair.

Sūra XLIII

19/18: سَتُكْتَبُ شَهَادَتُهُمْ - others said he read سَنَكْتُبُ شَهَادَتَهُمْ as Ibn Abī ʿAbla and Abū'l-Barhasīm.
33/32: سَقْفًا - سُقُفًا as the Meccans and Baṣrans.
37/36: لَيَصُدُّونَهُمْ - لَيَصِدُّونَهُمْ.

Sūra XLIV

4/3: يُفْرَقُ كُلُّ - but some said he read نَفْرُقُ كُلَّ.
53: وَآسْتَبْرَقَ - وَإِسْتَبْرَقٍ as Ibn Muḥaiṣin and Ibn Khuthaim.

Sūra XLV

6/5: يُؤْمِنُونَ – He supported *TR* against the Kūfan تُؤْمِنُونَ.
19/18: وَٱللَّهُ – وَٱللَّهَ.
24/23: إِلَّا ٱلدَّهْرُ – إِلَّا دَهْرٌ which was the reading of Ubai and Ibn Masʿūd.
نَحْيَا – نُحْيَا as ʿUbaid b. ʿUmair.

Sūra XLVI

9/8: يُوحَى – يُوحِي as the reading of ʿUbaid b. ʿUmair.
25/24: يُرَى إِلَّا مَسَٰكِنُهُمْ – ترى إِلَّا مَسَاكِنَهُمْ which was the reading of 'Alī.
تُدَمِّرُ كُلَّ – but others said he read يَدْمُرُ كُلُّ as Ibn ʿUmair.

Sūra XLVII

25/27: أَمْلَى – أُمْلِي as Abū ʿAmr, Muʿādh, and Ṭalḥa.
37/39: يُخْرِجْ – نُخْرِجُ as Hārūn from Abū ʿAmr, though others said that he read يَخْرُجْ as Ubai.

Sūra XLVIII

9: لِتُؤْمِنُوا – لِيُؤْمِنُوا as the Meccans and Baṣrans. So also in the following verbs he read with بياء.

Sūra L

9: وَنَزَّلْنَا – وَأَنْزَلْنَا as Ubai and Ibn Qais.
44/43: تَشَقَّقُ – others said he read تَنْشَقُّ.

Sūra LI

46: وَقَوْمَ – وَقَوْمِ as Ubai and the Kūfans.

Sūra LII

13: دُعَاءً – دَعًّا.
21: وَأَتْبَعْنَاهُمْ ذُرِّيَّاتِهِمْ – وَٱتَّبَعَتْهُمْ ذُرِّيَّتُهُمْ as ʿAlī and Abū ʿAmr.
28: أَنَّهُ – إِنَّهُ as the Madīnans, al-Ḥasan, and ʿAlī.
30: نَتَرَبَّصُ بِهِ رَيْبَ – some said he read يَتَرَبَّصُ بِهِ رَيْبُ as Abū ʿImrān, not يُتَرَبَّصُ as Muʿādh.

Sūra LIII

42/43: وَإِنَّ – وَأَنَّ as Ibn Qais and Ibn Abī ʿAbla. Likewise إِنَّ for أَنَّ in v. 47/49 and إِنَّهُ for أَنَّهُ in vv. 43/44, 44/45, 45/46, 48/49, 49/50, and 50/51.
50/51: عَادَ لُّولَى – عَادًا ٱلْأُولَى with *idghām* as the Madīnans and Baṣrans.

Sūra LIV

12: ٱلْمَاءَانِ – ٱلْمَاءُ as Ubai, ʿAlī, and al-Jaḥdarī.
49: بِقَدْرٍ – بِقَدَرٍ.

Sūra LV

9/8: تُخْسِرُوا – but others said he read تَخْسُرُوا.

Sūra LVI

2: كَاذِبَةً – كَاذِبَةٌ as al-Yazīdī, taking it as *hōl*.
32/31: فَاكِهَةٌ كَثِيرَةٌ – فَٰكِهَةٍ كَثِيرَةٍ and so necessarily مَقْطُوعَةٌ and مَمْنُوعَةٌ in v. 33/32 and فُرُشٌ مَرْفُوعَةٌ in v. 34/33.

Sūra LVII

8: أُخِذَ مِيثَاقُكُمْ – أَخَذَ مِيثَاقَكُمْ as many of the Baṣrans.

Sūra LVIII

6/7: فَيُنْبِئُهُمْ – فَيُنَبِّئُهُمْ.
7/8: وَلَا أَقَلَّ – وَلَا أَدْنَىٰ as Ubai, Muʿādh, and Ibn Qais.
ثَلَٰثَةٍ and خَمْسَةٍ – ثَلَاثَةٌ and خَمْسَةٌ as Ubai and Ibn Abī ʿAbla.

Sūra LX

3: يَفْصِلُ – others said he read نُفْصِلُ as Ibn ʿUmar ath-Thaqafī and Ibn Fāʾid.
11: فَعَاقَبْتُمْ – but others say he read فَعَقَّبْتُمْ.

Sūra LXI

6: بَعْدِيَ – بَعْدِي as the readers of Ḥijāz and Baṣra.
14: أَنْصَارًا لِلَّهِ – أَنْصَارَ ٱللَّهِ as the Ḥijāzī and Baṣran readers.

Sūra LXIII

10: وَأَكُونَ - وَأَكُنْ as the Baṣran readers.

Sūra LXVI

4: زَاغَتْ - صَغَتْ as Ibn Masʿūd and ʿAlī.

Sūra LXVII

1: ٱلْمُلْكُ - ٱلْمُلْكُ as Muʿādh and Abū Mijlaz.
2: لِيَبْلُوَكُمْ - لِيَبْلُوكُمْ as as-Sāmirī from al-Yazīdī.
11: بِذُنُوبِهِمْ - بِذَنْبِهِمْ as Muʿādh and Ibn Qais.

Sūra LXVIII

2: بِنِعْمَةِ - others said he read بِنَعَمَةِ.
14: أَنْ - أَأَنْ ء, which was the alternative reading.

Sūra LXIX

5: فَهَلَكُوا - فَأُهْلِكُوا as Ubai. So also in v. 6.

Sūra LXXI

15/14: سَمَاوَاتٍ طِبَاقًا - سَمَاوَاتِ طِبَاقٍ with *iḍāfa*. (Note that Ibn Masʿūd and Ibn Abī ʿAbla read the طِبَاقٍ but without *iḍāfa*.)
22/21: كُبَّارًا - others said he read كِبَّارًا.

Sūra LXXII

3: جَدًّا رَبُّنَا - جَدُّ رَبِّنَا as 'Ikrima and Ibn Jubair.
23/24: فَأَنَّ - فَإِنَّ as Ṭalḥa and ʿĪsā b. ʿUmar.

Sūra LXXIII

9: ٱلْمَشَارِقِ وَٱلْمَغَارِبِ - ٱلْمَشْرِقِ وَٱلْمَغْرِبِ as Ubai and Ibn Qais.

Sūra LXXV

22: نَاضِرَةٌ - some said he read نَضْرَةٌ the reading given from Ubai.
37: تَكُ - يَكُ as al-Ḥasan.

Sūra LXXVI

21: واستَبْرَقٌ - وَإِسْتَبْرَقٍ as Abū ʿAmr and others.
ثِيَابُ سُنْدُسٌ - ثِيَابُ سُنْدُسٍ as Abū Ḥaiwa and Ibn Abī ʿAbla.
24: إِثْمًا - ءاثِمًا.
وَلَا كَفُورًا - أَوْ كَفُورًا.
مِنْهَا - مِنْهُمْ as Ubai and Abūʾl-Mutawakkil.
28: شَدَّدْنَا - شَدَدْنَا.
30: يَشَاؤُنَ - تَشَاءُونَ as Ubai and Abūʾl-Mutawakkil.

Sūra LXXVII

23: فَقَدَّرْنَا - فَقَدَرْنَا as Ubai and Ibn Khuthaim.

Sūra LXXIX

11: نَاخِرَةً - نَخِرَةً as the Kūfan readers.

Sūra LXXXI

6: سُجِرَتْ - سُجِّرَتْ as the Meccans and Baṣrans.

Sūra LXXXIV

19: لَيَرْكَبُنَّ - لَتَرْكَبُنَّ as Ibn Khuthaim.

Sūra LXXXVIII

11: لَا تُسْمَعُ فِيهَا لَاغِيَةٌ - لَا تَسْمَعُ فِيهَا لَاغِيَةً as Ubai and the Meccan and Baṣran readers.

Sūra LXXXIX

8/7: نَخْلُقْ مِثْلَهَا - يُخْلَقْ مِثْلُهَا as Ibn Abī ʿAbla.

Sūra XCI

15: فَلَا - وَلَا as Ubai and some of the codices.

Sūra XCVII

5: مَطْلِعِ - مَطْلَعِ as some gave from Abū ʿAmr and Abūʾs-Sammāl.

Sūra CVII

3: يَحُضُّ – others say he read تُحَاضُّ as Yaḥyā b. Yaʿmar.

In this collection again it will be noticed that the great majority of variants are variants in interpretation of the 'Uthmānic text. In a number of cases, however, we find variants which depend on a different consonantal text, in some of which he stands alone. It seems very probable that new accessions of material may show a considerable increase in such variants, and make clear that Zaid exercised considerable freedom in his treatment of the text. In a number of uncanonical variants it will be noticed that he agrees with readings attributed to 'Alī, but with none of the extreme Shī'a readings. What is more remarkable is the number of readings where he agrees with the text of Ubai b. Kaʿb. This fact needs further elucidation.

The *Ṭabaqāt* books consider Zaid b. 'Alī as being a Madīnan reader, which would account for the general agreement of his text with that of 'Uthmān, who, if we are right, canonized the Madīnan tradition. This makes it all the more interesting to note the great number of cases where his reading agrees with that of the various Baṣran readers, particularly in cases where the Baṣrans and Meccans agreed against the other schools.

The happy chance which brought to light the manuscripts of al-Marandī and al-Kirmānī may yet hold, and bring to us still earlier sources, that may enable us to understand even more clearly the state of the Qur'ān text in the early part of the second century of Islam.

4.3

The Qur'ān Readings of Ibn Miqsam

Arthur Jeffery

The main stages in the process of the fixation of the *Textus Receptus* of the Qur'ān are fairly clear. After an early period during which there were many types of text in circulation the Caliph 'Uthmān canonized officially the Madīnan type of text, and ordered the destruction of all other codices than those that were written according to the text of his now officially canonized *Imām*. As this, however, was a bare consonantal text, with no punctuation, no points to distinguish similar consonants, and no vowel or other orthographic signs, there was still considerable liberty of interpretation. A beginning at the settling of some of these difficulties was made in the Caliphate of ʿAbd al-Malik, at the instigation of his famous official al-Ḥajjāj b. Yūsuf, under whom we again hear of the destruction of nonconforming codices. In the succeeding years the tradition as to pointing the *ḥurūf*, and as to the *qirāʾā*, or vowelling of them, naturally tended to crystallize under the succession of great teachers, whose systems would be transmitted by their pupils, until in AH 322, these traditions came to be fixed in the well-known Seven Systems by a decision of the Wazīrs Ibn Muqlah and Ibn ʿĪsā, acting under the guidance of the great savant Ibn Mujāhid. A century later, when ad-Dānī (†444) was writing, the two canonical *riwāyas* from each of these Seven had been decided on, though by what process we do not at present know. The gradual dominance in the succeeding centuries of the Kūfan tradition of Ḥafṣ from the School of ʿĀṣim, has given us the *mashhūr*, the *Textus Receptus* that is to be found in the vast majority of lithographs of the Qur'ān in circulation at the present day. No official canonization of this text tradition of Ḥafṣ has ever been made, but his was the type of text that won recognition and spread throughout the Muslim world, being adopted everywhere save in North Africa, where the Madīnan text tradition of Warsh, of the School of Nāfiʿ, still survives, though it is gradually disappearing even there. Thus it is now becoming rare to find any Muslim savant acquainted with the text traditions of any of the Seven save Ḥafṣ.

In the days of Ibn Mujāhid (†324) the problems of *ḥurūf* and *qirāʾā* were still being debated in the schools, and we have a fairly long list of famous teachers of Qur'ānic science who transmitted an *ikhtiyār*, that is, their independent judgment on how the skeleton consonantal text should be pointed and vowelled for correct recitation. By this time, however, the criteria for judgment on readings were already beginning to assert themselves, namely, (1) *muṣḥaf*; (2) *ʿarabiyya*; (3) *imjāʿ*. That is, any suggested reading was scrutinized to see whether it could be derived from the accepted consonantal text, whether it was defensible linguistically as being in accordance with the normal rules of Arabic language, and whether it gave a meaning that fitted the generally accepted interpretation of the text. The readings of Ibn Shanabūdh and of Ibn Miqsam that came under judgment at his instigation were thus in a sense test cases as to the continued legitimacy of *ikhtiyār*, and the range within which, if legitimate, it could be allowed freedom. Khalaf b. Hishām (†229), who was one of the two *rāwīs* later chosen to represent the Kūfan tradition of Ḥamza, and who was thought by some to have merited a place in the Seven rather than al-Kiṣā'ī, had an *ikhtiyār*, and this was approved. But how far could such an approval of *ikhtiyār* be allowed to go? Both Ibn Shanabūdh and Ibn Miqsam claimed the same freedom as was allowed Khalaf, but they were haled before the authorities and forced to disavow their readings.[1] It is thus of some importance to study what their readings actually were. Of Ibn Shanabūdh we know little more than the list[2] of reproved readings that was reported at his trial, but in the case of Ibn Miqsam a goodly number of his readings have been preserved in the commentaries and the various *qirāʾāt* books.

Though we today know Ibn Miqsam only as a specialist in the Qur'ānic sciences, his reputation among his own people was as a philologer, and Yaqūt in the *Irshād al-Arīb* and as-Suyūṭī in the *Bughyat al-Wuʿāt*, write of him as such. He was trained in the Kūfan grammatical school and was a prominent pupil of the famous Thaʿlab (†291), whose *Amālī* he heard and transmitted.[3] Ibn Khallikān's story of him represents him as being consulted, along with Ibn Duraid and Ibn al-Anbārī, by the Qāḍī Abū ʿAmr Muḥammad b. Yūsuf on certain philological questions,[4] and both Yaqūt and al-Khaṭīb quote him as authority on literary and philological matters.[5] Among his works[6] whose titles have come down to us are an Introduction to the Art of Poetry (*al-Madkhal ilā ʿIlm ash-Shiʿr*), an Arabic Grammar and some special grammatical studies, such as a treatise on words masculine and feminine, and one on words ending in *alif maqṣūra* or *alif mamdūda*, as well as a more general philological treatise *at-Taisīr fīʾl-Lugha*. It is possible that his work titled *Akhbār Nafsihi* is, as Flügel thinks, autobiographical, though in the *Fihrist* it has quite another title, and he seems to have made one venture into the arena of theological controversy in a Refutation of the Rationalists (*ar-Radd ʿalāʾl-Muʿtazila*).

Al-Khaṭīb, II, 206, gives us a list of the famous teachers under whom he studied the Kūfan grammatical tradition:

Abūʾs-Sarī Mūsā b. al-Ḥasan al-Jalājalī, †287: (al-Khaṭīb, XIII, 49, 50).
Abū Muslim al-Kajjī, †292: (Ibn al-ʿImād, II, 210).
Muḥammad b. ʿUthmān b. Abī Shaiba, †287: (Ibn Ḥajar, *Lisān*, V, 280).
Mūsā b. Isḥāq al-Anṣārī, †297: (Ibn al-ʿImād, II, 226, 227).
Abūʾl-ʿAbbās Thaʿlab, †291: (Yāqūt, *Irshād*, II, 133–54).
al-Ḥasan b. ʿAlawaihi al-Qaṭṭān, †298: (al-Khaṭīb, VII, 375).
Muḥammad b. Yaḥyā al-Marwazī, †298: (al-Khaṭīb, III, 422, 423).
Muḥammad b. al-Laith al-Jawharī, †297: (al-Khaṭīb, III, 196).

Idrīs b. ʿAbd al-Karīm al-Ḥaddād, †292: (al-Khaṭīb, VII, 14, 15) to whom as-Suyūṭī, *Bughya*, 36 adds Yaḥyā b. Muḥammad b. Saʿīd, †318 (see al-Khaṭīb, XIV, 231–34), and Yāqūt, *Irshād*, I, 141, adds Aḥmad b. Sulaimān al-Maʿbadī, †292, who through ʿAlī b. Thābit was a pupil of Abū ʿUbaid. Among his pupils in this philological learning we find Ibn Rizqawaih and Ibn Shādhān (Yāqūt, *Irshād*, VI, 498), to whom al-Khaṭīb, II, 206, adds ʿAlī b. Aḥmad ar-Razzāz, and the Ṣūfī al-Ḥūsain b. ash-Shujāʿ.

Our interest, however, is in his contributions to Qur'ānic science, and it is fortunate that not only do Yāqūt and al-Khaṭīb deal largely with this matter in their accounts of him, but we have an even fuller account of this aspect of his work in the *Ghāya* of Ibn al-Jazarī,[7] who supplements the account in al-Khaṭīb by material from a number of excellent sources, including the *Jāmiʿ al-Bayān* of ad-Dānī, and the *Kāmil* of al-Hudhalī.

His full name according to these sources was Muḥammad b. al-Ḥasan b. Yaʿqūb b. al-Ḥasan b. al-Ḥūsain b. Muḥammad b. Sulaimān b. Dāwūd b. ʿUbaidallāh b. Miqsam,[8] Abū Bakr, al-Muqriʿ al-Aṭṭār, and his dates are AH 265–354,[9] and they record that while he was accounted as trustworthy (*thiqa*) as a transmitter of Ḥadīth,[10] and famed for his wide knowledge of philology,[11] he was even more famous in Qur'ānic lore. Certainly in the lists of his works by far the largest number are concerned with various branches of Qur'ānic science. The most famous of them was doubtless his *al-Anwār fī Tafsīr al-Qur'ān* (or *fī ʿIlm al-Qur'ān*), which is specially mentioned as being excellent in the fields both of *Tafsīr* and *Maʿānī*. He had a book on the codices, *Kitāb al-Maṣāḥif*, which may very well have been of the same nature as the *Maṣāḥif* books of Ibn Abī Dāwūd and Ibn Ashta. Three of his works would seem to have dealt with matters of the Qur'ānic Massorah, namely, a work on Pause (*Kitāb al-Waqf wa'l-Ibtidā'*), one on verse numbering ('Adad at-Tamām), and a manual for scribes writing Qur'āns (*al-Laṭā'if fī Jamʿ Hijā' al-Maṣāḥif*).[12] The *Kitāb Mufradātihi* given in the lists,[13] was probably a work on the unique expressions in the Qur'ān, and the book *al-Muwaḍḍaḥ* may have been of similar nature. More important, however, were his works on the readers and their readings. One such is apparently a general work titled *Iḥtijāj al-Qurrā' fī 'l-Qirā'āt*,[14] another was on the great metropolitan systems, *al-Intiṣār li Qurrā' al-Amṣār*, and besides these there were attributed to him three works on the Seven, a large treatise, *Kitāb as-Sabʿa fī 'Ilalihā 'l-Kabīr*, a medium-sized *Kitāb as-Sabʿa al-Awsaṭ*, and a small work, *Kitāb al-Aṣghar*, known also as *Shifā' aṣ-Ṣudūr*.[15]

Ibn al-Jazarī has preserved for us the list of his teachers in *qirā'āt*—Idrīs b. ʿAbd al-Karīm, †292 (*Ghāya*, no. 717):

Dāwūd b. Sulaimān (*Ghāya*, no. 1253).

Ḥātim b. Isḥāq of Mosul, †after 300 (*Ghāya*, no. 920).

Abū'l-ʿAbbās al-Muʿaddil, †301 (*Ghāya*, no. 3542).

Abū'l-ʿAbbās b. al-Faḍl ar-Rāzī, † c. 290 (*Ghāya*, no. 2562).

Aḥmad b. Faraḥ, †303 (*Ghāya*, no. 437).

ʿAbdallāh b. Muḥammad b. Bakkār (*Ghāya*, no. 1748).

Muḍār b. Muḥammad (*Ghāya*, no. 3613).

ʿAlī b. al-Husain al-Fārisī, (*Ghāya*, no. 2210), four of whom were also the teachers of Ibn Shanabūdh.

His accuracy and reliability were admitted by ad-Dānī, and adh-Dhahabī specially commends his knowledge as one of the best Kūfan authorities on *qirā'āt*, whether the canonical variants or the strange and uncanonical ones. He had an *ikhtiyār* that was recorded in the *Kāmil* of al-Hudhalī, and was transmitted from him by Abū'l-Faraj ash-Shanabūdhī, and became the object of a refutation by Ibn Durustawaih.[16] What was held against him was that he went on reading *ḥurūf* that were contrary to the general consensus. Yāqūt gives as an example of this his reading in sūra XII, 80: *nujabā*, where the usual reading is *najiyyan*, so that he interpreted the verse, "So when they despaired of him, they withdrew as noble men," where the general consensus (*ijmāʿ*) interprets it as "they withdrew whispering." Apparently he had a goodly number of such readings, which were possible interpretations of the skeleton consonantal text, and were linguistically defensible, but which his opponents declared were his own invention, and not only were contrary to *ijmāʿ* but had no *isnād*, that is, were not readings handed down from any of the famous early readers.

The stir caused by his reading and teaching his *ikhtiyār* in this matter finally led to his being brought before the civil authorities. In the presence of an assembly of the readers and the jurists the charge was made against him that he taught that any reading that the consonantal text would bear and that was good Arabic was a reading that could legitimately be used in the prayer service or elsewhere. This was objected to on four grounds, (1) that it was heretical innovation (*bidʿa*), (2) that it associated with the Book of Allāh falsities that did not belong thereto, (3) that such mischievous opinions gave a handle to the defamers of Islam, (4) that it was making a choice of readings by way of investigation and personal judgment instead of holding fast to the received tradition. The civil authorities accepted the charges as proved and called on him to repent and to retract. He, however, claimed the right to his *ikhtiyār*, arguing that Khalaf b. Hishām[17] had a well-known *ikhtiyār* that was permitted and not reproved, and that Abū ʿUbaid[18] and Ibn Saʿdān[19] were also known to have an *ikhtiyār*, to which apparently no exception was taken. If in their cases this was something that was permitted and not reproved, why should it be considered in his case as something objectionable? If his liberty in this matter was to be curtailed, why should nothing be done to prevent the transmission of their *ikhtiyār*? The answer is very interesting to us. We know now from our collections of variants handed down from these readers that they exercised true *ikhtiyār*, but the labors of Ibn Mujāhid had been to limit *ikhtiyār* and canonize the systems of the Seven, so that the reply to Ibn Miqsam was that Khalaf's *ikhtiyār* was that he had abandoned some of the readings of Ḥamza, and in their place chose to use readings of Nāfiʿ of the Madīnan School, and that neither Abū ʿUbaid nor Ibn Saʿdān had chosen readings outside the readings of the Imāms, that is, of the Seven, and that had he limited his *ikhtiyār* to the same range this would have been permitted him also and not reproved. In other words, we have in his case a clear proof of the official nature of this stage in the development of the process of canonization of the text of the Qur'ān. This stage is that of the limitation of *ikhtiyār*. Ibn Shanabūdh was condemned because he persisted in using readings from the old pre-ʿUthmānic Codices,[20] such as those of Ibn Masʿūd and Ubai, while Ibn Miqsam was condemned for his insistence that while he accepted the ʿUthmānic consonantal text he still claimed the right of private judgment as to its interpretation.

Under threat of the civil authorities he agreed to recant, a document to that effect was drawn up, and this was signed by not a few of the Qurrāʾ who were present at the assembly. Like all forced recantations, however, it had little effect, for the later writers all record that it was said that he continued using his peculiar readings till the day of his death, and even had a following who accepted his readings. Al-Khaṭīb, who quotes at length from *Kitāb al-Bayān* of Abū Ṭāhir b. Abī Hishām, the close friend of Ibn Mujāhid, an account of the trial, says that Ibn Mujāhid labored hard to persuade him to accept the limitation of *ikhtiyār* in accordance with the written judgment against him, but quite unsuccessfully.[21] The new stage in canonization, however, could not long be resisted,[22] and we have an interesting light on the prejudice felt against those who resisted the imposition of this new stage, in the story that circulated and is contained in all the biographies of Ibn Miqsam,[23] of how a certain Abū Aḥmad al-Faraḍī dreamed one night that he was in the mosque praying with the people, when he saw Ibn Miqsam also praying but with his back turned to the *qibla*, which was symbolic of his habit of going contrary to the Imāms in his readings.

Should we someday recover the *Kāmil* of al-Hudhalī it is possible that we might be able to get a complete picture of the *ikhtiyār* of Ibn Miqsam. The *qirā'āt* works that we have were for the most part written after the limitation in the range of *ikhtiyār* had come to be accepted, and consequently where they mention the readings of Ibn Miqsam they are for the most part merely such readings as also had the support of other authorities. As the majority of them, however, are outside the systems of the Seven, they have considerable importance as a witness to the teaching of the Kūfan School before the fixing of the Seven. Our collection of them is here arranged according to the order of the sūras for reasons of practical convenience.

Sūra I

4/3.*māliki*—He supported the *TR* against the alternative *maliki*.

Sūra II

14/13. *laqū*—*lāqawū* as Zaid b. ʿAlī and Ibn as-Samaifaʿ.
19/18. *ḥadhara*—*ḥidhāra* as Ubai and Abū'-s-Sammāl.
20/19. *yakhṭafu*—*yukhaṭṭifu* as al-Ḥasan and al-Jaḥdarī.
25/23. *tajrī*—*yajrī* (and so throughout the Qur'ān).
30/28. *yasfiku*—*yusaffiku* as Ibn Ghazwān ʿan Ṭalḥa.
innī—*inniya* as Nāfiʿ, Ibn Kathīr, and Abū ʿAmr (and so every similar final *-nī* in the Qur'ān).
38/36. *khaufun*—*khaufa* as al-Ḥasan, Mujāhid, and many others, here and where it occurs elsewhere.
40/38. *'dhkurū*—*'dhdhakkarū* as Ibn Masʿūd.
55/52. *jahratan*—*jaharatan* as al-Ḥasan, Ḥumaid, and Abū Razīn.
aṣ-ṣāʿiqatu—*aṣ-ṣaʿqatu* as ʿAlī, ʿUmar, and ʿUrwa b. az-Zubair.

61/58. *yaqtulūna—yuqattilūna* as ʿAlī, al-Ḥasan, and Abū Mijlaz.

63/60. *wa'dhkurū—wa'dhdhakkarū* as Abū ʿImrān al-Jawnī.

69/64. *tasurru—yasurru.*

70/65. *al-baqara—al-bāqira* as Zaid b. ʿAlī.
tashābaha—yashshābahu as al-Ḥasan, Mujāhid, and Ibn Abī ʿAbla.

74/69. *qaswatan—qasāwatan* as Abū Ḥaiwa and Zaid b. ʿAlī.

83/77. *ḥusnan—ḥasanan* as Ḥamza, al-Kiṣā'ī, and Yaʿqūb.

85/79. *taqtulūna—tuqattilūna* as al-Ḥasan, Abū Mijlaz, and az-Zuhrī.

87/81. *taqtulūna—tuqattilūna* as al-Ḥasan and Abū Mijlaz.

88/82. *ghulfun—ghulufun* as Ibn Muḥaiṣin and Ibn ʿAbbās, though some said that he read with *TR* here.

91/85. *taqtulūna—tuqattilūna* as al-Ḥasan and Abū Mijlaz.

120/114. *tarḍā—yarḍā.*

122/116. *'dhkurū—'dhdhakkarū* as Abū ʿImrān.

140/134. *ta'malūna—ya'malūna* as Qatāda, Mujāhid, and al-Ḥasan.

173/168. *famani*—He supported the *TR* against the more common *famanu.*

182/178. *mūṣin—muwwaṣin*, that is, the Kūfan and Baṣran reading.

184/180. *faʿiddatun—faʿiddatan* as ʿUbaid b. ʿUmair.
fidyatun—fidyatan.

185/181. *faʿiddatun—faʿiddatan.*
al-yusra and *al-ʿusra*, *al-yusura*, and *al-ʿusura* as Abū Jaʿfar and al-Ḥasan.
walitukmilū—walitukammilū as Abū Bakr, Yaʿqūb, and al-Ḥasan.

187/183. *wa'btaghū—wa'ttabiʿū*, as Ibn ʿAbbās and al-Ḥasan.

189/185. *al-buyūta*—He supported *TR* here and throughout the Qur'ān, against the alternative reading *al-biyūta.*

196/192. *fa-fidyatun—fa-fidyatan.*

198/194. *fa'dkurū—fa'dhdhakkarū* as Abū ʿImrān. So in vv. 200/196, 203/199, 231, and 239/240.

205/201. *yuhlika—yahlaka* as al-Ḥasan and Abū Ḥanīfa.

210/206. *ẓulalin—ẓilālin* as Ubai and Ibn Masʿūd.
wal malā'ikatu—wal-malā'ikati as Ibn as-Samaifaʿ, al-Ḥasan, and Qatāda.
quḍiya 'l-amru—qaḍāi 'l-amri as Ubai and Ibn Masʿūd.

211/207. *sal—is'al*, and so wherever this occurs in the Qur'ān.

212/208. *zuyyina—zayyana* as Mujāhid, al-Ḥasan, and Ḥumaid b. Qais.
216/212. *kurhun—karhun* as as-Sulamī.
219/216. *kabīrun—kathīrun* as Ḥamza, al-Kiṣā'ī, and al-A'mash.
akbaru—aktharu as Mu'ādh and Zaid b. Aslam.
229. *yakhāfā—yukhāfā* as Ḥamza and Ya'qūb.
233. *tuḍārra—tuḍārru* as Mu'ādh, Ibn Khuthaim, and Zaid b. 'Alī.
236/237. *qadaruhu* (bis)—He supported *TR* against the more common *qadruhu.*
237/238. *fa-niṣfu—fa-naṣafu* as al-Ḥasan.
tansawu—tanāsawi as Ibn Abī 'Abla. So in all similar cases of final *wāw*—before a *waṣl*, he read *wī*—as against the *wū* of the *TR*, or the *wā* supported by al-A'mash.
256/257. *ar-rushdu—ar-rashādu* as as-Sulamī.
265/267. *ukulahā—uklahā* as Nāfi', Ibn Kathīr, and Abū 'Amr.
269/272. *yu'ta—yūti* as Abū Razīn and az-Zuhrī.
276/277. *yamḥaku* and *yurbī—yumaḥḥiku* and *yurabbī.*
280. *fa-naẓiratun—fa-naẓratun* as Mujāhid and al-Ḥasan.
maysaratin—maysuratin as Nāfi' and Ḥamza.
282. *tijāratan ḥāḍiratan*—He agreed with *TR* against the more common reading *tijāratun ḥāḍiratun.*
283. *kātiban—kitāban* as Ubai, Ibn 'Abbās, and al-Ḥasan.
285. *wa-kutubihi—wa-kitābihi* as Ḥamza and al-Kiṣā'ī.

Sūra III

10/8. *tughniya—yughniya* as as-Sulamī, Mu'ādh, and Abū'l-Mutawakkil.
11/9. *ka-da'bi—ka-da'abi.*
12/10. *satughlabūna—sayughlabūna* supporting the Kūfan reading.
13/11. *fi'atun—fi'atin* as al-Ḥasan, az-Zuhrī, and Mujāhid.
14/12. *zuyyina li'n-nāsi ḥubbu—zayyana li'n-nāsi ḥubba*, as Mujāhid and al-Jaḥdarī.
18/16. *shahida 'llāhu—shuhadā'u 'llāhi* as Ubai, al-Jaḥdarī, and Ibn as-Samaifa'.

21/20. *yaqtulūna—yuqattilūna* as al-Ḥasan and Abū Mijlaz: and in the second occurrence *yuqātilūna* as some of the Kūfan readers.

28/27. *tuqātan—taqiyyatan* as Ibn ʿAbbās, Mujāhid, ad-Ḍaḥḥāk, and others.

37/32. *kaffalahā*—He agreed with *TR* against the alternative reading *kafalahā*.

48/43. *yuʿallimuhu*—He agreed with *TR* against the more common reading *nuʿallimuhu*.

49/43. *annī—inni* as the Madīnan readers.

81/75. *ātaytukum—ātaynākum* as Abū Jaʿfar and al-Ḥasan.

90/84. *tuqbala—yuqbala*.

101/96. *tutlā—yutlā* as Ibn Masʿūd.

103/98. *wa'dhkurū—wa'dhdhakkarū* as Abū ʿImrān.

104/100. *waltakun—walyakun* as Ibn Masʿūd and an-Nakhaʿī.

112/108. *yaqtulūna—yuqattilūna* as al-Ḥasan and Abū Mijlaz.

115/111. *yafʿalū—tafʿalū* supporting the non-Kūfan reading.

116/112. *tughniya—yughniya* as as-Sulamī.

140/134. *qarḥun* (bis)—*qurḥun* as Ḥamza, al-Kiṣā'ī, and Ṭalḥa.

145/139. *nu'tihi* (bis)—*yu'tīhi* as al-Mufaḍḍal and az-Zaʿfarānī. *sanajzī—sayajzī* as al-Aʿmash and Ibn Khuthaim.

147/141. *qaulahum—qauluhum* as al-Ḥasan, Qatāda, Ḥumaid, and others.

154/148. *kullahu—kulluhu* as the Baṣrans and Ṭalḥa.

156/150. *qutilū—quttilū* as al-Ḥasan, and so in v. 169/163, and *quttiltum* for *qutiltum* in v. 158/152.

178/172. *yaḥsabanna—taḥsabanna* as Ibn ʿAbbās, Mujāhid, and Ḥamza. So in v. 180/175.

181/177. *sanaktubu—sayaktubu* as al-Ḥasan, al-Aʿraj, and al-Aʿmash. *naqūlu—yaqūlu* as al-Aʿmash.

188/185. *taḥsabannahum—yaḥsabannahum* as Ibn Kathīr and Abū ʿAmr.

Sūra IV

5/4. *allatī—allātī* as al-Ḥasan, Abū Razīn, and Ibn Khuthaim.

10/11. *sayaṣlauna—sayuṣallauna*.

11/12. *yūṣīkum—yuwaṣṣīkum* as al-Ḥasan and Abū Razīn.
12/15. *yūrathu—yuwarrithu* as al-Ḥasan and ʿIkrima.
23/19. *yaḥillu—taḥillu* as al-Jaḥdarī and Abū Ḥaiwa.
27/32. *tamīlū—yamīlū* as al-Ḥasan, Qatāda, and Ibn Khuthaim.
30/34. *nuṣlīhi—nuṣallīhi.*
32/36. *was'a'lū—wasalū* as Ibn Kathīr and al-Kiṣā'ī.
42/45. *tusawwā—tassawwā* as Nāfiʿ, Ibn ʿĀmir, and al-Ḥasan.
46/48. *'l-kalima—'l-kalāma* as Muʿādh, ʿAlī, and Abū Nahīk.
92/94. *khaṭa'an* (bis)—*khaṭā'an* as al-Ḥasan, Shaiba, and Abū ʿImrān, though some sources give him as reading *khiṭā'an*.
fa-diyatun musallamatun—fadyatun muslamatun.
101/102. *taqṣurū—tuqaṣṣirū* as az-Zuhrī, al-Ḥasan, and Abū'l-Mutawakkil.
153/152. *aṣ-ṣāʿiqatu—aṣ-ṣāʿqatu* as Ibn Muḥaiṣin.
154/153. *ta'dū—ta'addū* as Warsh and other Madīnan readers.

Sūra V

27/30. *la-aqtulannaka—la-uqattilannaka* as al-Ḥasan and Abū Mijlaz.
28/31. *li-taqtulanī—li-tuqattilanī* as al-Ḥasan and Abū Mijlaz.
45/49. *walʿayna—walʿaynu* as Anas and al-Kiṣā'ī.
60/65. *waʿabada 'ṭ-ṭāghūta—waʿubbada 'ṭ-ṭāghūti* as ʿIkrima and al-Aʿmash.
67/71. *risālatahu—risālātihi* as Nāfiʿ, Ibn ʿĀmir, and al-Ḥasan.
70/74. *yaqtulūna—yuqattilūna* as al-Ḥasan and Abū Mijlaz.
71/75. *takūna—yakūna* as al-Ḥasan, but some said he read *yakūnu*.
95/96. *taqtulū* and *qatalahu* and *qatala—tuqattilū* and *qattalahu* and *qattala* as al-Ḥasan and Abū Mijlaz.
110. *siḥrun—sāḥirun* as the general Kūfan reading.

Sūra VI

7. *siḥrun—sāḥirun* as Aḍ-Ḍaḥḥāk.
22. *naḥshuruhum* and *naqūlu—yaḥshuruhum* and *yaqūlu* as Yaʿqūb.
23. *takun—yakun* as Ḥamza, al-Kiṣā'ī, and Yaʿqūb.

44. *fatahnā—fattahnā* as Abū Jaʿfar and Shaiba.
46. *bihi—bihu* as al-Aʿmash and al-Musayyibī.
47. *baghtatan au jahratan—baghatatan au jaharatan* as al-Ḥasan and Abū Jaʿfar.
55. *li-tastabīna sabīlu—li-yastabīna sabīlu* as Ḥamza and al-Kiṣāʾī.
58. *la-quḍiya—la-qaḍā*, and so in every other occurrence.
61. *tawaffathu—tawaffāhu* as Ṭalḥa, al-Aʿmash, and Abū Razīn.
71/70. *ʾstahwathu—ʾstahwāhu* as Ḥamza and al-Aʿmash.
74. *āzara—āzaru* as al-Ḥasan, Yaʿqūb, and Ḥumaid.
91. *qadrihi—qadarihi* as al-Ḥasan and Abū Mijlaz.
92. *ṣalātihim—ṣalawātihim* as al-Ḥasan.
99. *mutashābihin—mushtabihin.*
thamarihi—thumurihi as Ibn ʿAlī Lailā and Ibn Saʿdān.
100. *wa-kharaqū—wa-kharraqū* as Nāfiʿ and Abū Jaʿfar of Madīna.
101. *takun—yakun* as Ibn Waththāb and an-Nakhaʿī.
108. *ʿadwan—ʿuduwwan* as al-Ḥasan, Yaʿqūb, and Qatāda.
110. *nuqallibu—yuqallibu* as Abūʾl-Mutawakkil.
nadharuhum—yadharuhum as Abūʾl-Mutawakkil and Ibn Qais.
124. *risālatahu—risālātihi*, the non-Meccan reading.
125. *ḍayyiqan—ḍayqan* as Ibn Kathīr, Ḥumaid, and Muʿādh.
ḥarajan—ḥarijan as Nāfiʿ, al-Ḥasan, and Abū Jaʿfar.
130. *yaʾtikum—taʾtikum* as al-Hasan and al-Aʿraj.
135/136. *takūnu—yakūnu* as Hamza, al-Kiṣāʾī, and al-Aʿmash.
137/138. *zayyana—zuyyina* with following *qatlu*, as Ibn ʿĀmir and al-Ḥasan.
139/140. *khāliṣatun—khāliṣuhu* as Ibn ʿAbbās, Ibn Masʿūd, and ʿIkrima.
maytatan—mayyitatun (?), as Shaiba and Muʿādh. So in v. 145/146.
141/142. *ukuluhu—ukluhu* as Nāfiʿ and Ibn Kathīr.
151/152. *taqtulū* (bis)—*tuqattilū* as al-Ḥasan and Abū Mijlaz. So in v. 156/157.
153/154. *wa-anna hādhā—wa-an hādhā* as Ibn ʿĀmir and Yaʿqūb.
160/161. *ʿashru amthālihā—ʿashrun amthāluhā* as Yaʿqūb, al-Jaḥdarī, and Abū Razīn.

Sūra VII

3/2. *tadhakkarūna—tatadhakkarūna* as as-Sulamī and Ibn ʿAbbās.

26/25. *rīshan—riyāshan* as Ibn ʿAbbās, al-Ḥasan, and Qatāda.

40/38. *tufattaḥu—yuftaḥu* along with a majority of the Kūfan readers. *al-jamalu—al-jummalu* as Ibn ʿAbbās and ʿIkrima.

44/42. *naʿam—naʿim* as al-Kiṣāʾī and al-Aʿmash.

54/52. *yughshī—yughashshī* as the generality of the Kūfans. *ash-shamsa wa ʾl-qamara wa ʾn-nujūma musakhkharātin—ash-shamsu wa ʾl-qamaru wa ʾn-nujūmu musakhkharātun* as Ibn ʿĀmir and Ibn Abī ʿAbla.

58/56. *nuṣarrifu—yuṣarrifu* as Ibn Waththāb and an-Nakhaʿī.

69/67. *wa ʾdhkurū—wa ʾdhdhakkarū* as Abū ʿImrān. So also in vv. 74/72, 86/84, 171/170.

73/71. *thamūda—thamūdin* as al-Aʿmash and al-Ḥasan.

88/86. *qāla—wa-qāla*. So in v. 109/106.

105/103. *ʿalā an—ʿalayya an* as al-Ḥasan, Qatāda, and the Madīnans.

127/124. *ālihataka—ilāhataka* as al-Ḥasan, Qatāda, and Ibn Muḥaiṣin.

128/125. *yūrithuhā—yuwarrithuhā* as al-Ḥasan, Ibn Masʿūd, and Ibn Waththāb.

137/133. *yaʿrishūna—yuʿarrishūna* as Muʿādh and Ibn Abī ʿAbla.

138/134. *yaʿkufūna—yuʿakkifūna* as Muʿādh and Ibn Abī ʿAbla.

145/142. *saʾurīkum—saʾuwarrithukum* as Abūʾl-Mutawakkil.

150/149. *yaqtulūnanī—yuqattilūnanī* as al-Ḥasan and Abū Mijlaz.

164. *maʿdhiratan*—He supported *TR* against the more common *maʿdhiratun*.

172/171. *dhurriyatahum—dhurriyātihim* as the Madīnans and Baṣrans. *taqūlū—yaqūlū* as Ibn Muḥaiṣin, Abū ʿAmr, and Ubai. So in v. 173/172.

202/201. *yuqṣirūna—yuqaṣṣirūna* as az-Zuhrī and al-Jaḥdarī.

Sūra VIII

15. *laqītum—lāqītum*. So also in v. 45/47 and in XLVII, 4.

17. *taqtulūhum—tuqattilūhum* as al-Ḥasan and Abū Mijlaz.

26. *wa ʾdhkurū—wa ʾdhdhakkarū* as Abū ʿImrān.
30. *yaqtulūka—yuqattilūka* as al-Ḥasan and Abū Mijlaz.
35. *ṣalātuhum—ṣalawātuhum* as al-Ḥasan and Ibn Abī ʿAbla.
39/40. *wa-yakūna—wa-yakūnu* as al-Aʿmash.
42/44. *ḥayya—ḥayiya* as Nāfiʿ, Yaʿqūb, and Abū Jaʿfar.
45/47. *wa ʾdhkurū—wa ʾdhdhakkarū* as Abū ʿImrān.
52/54. *ka-daʾbi—ka-daʾabi.*
60/62. *turhibūna—yurahhibūna* as as-Sulamī and Abūʾl-Mutawakkil.

Sūra IX

4. *yanquṣūkum—yanquḍūkum* with *ḍād* as ʿIkrima, Muʿādh, and Ibn as-Samaifaʿ.
8. *taʾbā—yaʾbā.*
11. *nufaṣṣilu—yufaṣṣilu.*
25. *tughni—yughni.*
35. *fa-tukwā—fa-yukwā* as Abū Ḥaiwa, Abūʾs-Sammāl, and Ibn Qais.
37. *yuḍallu—yuḍillu* as Yaʿqūb, al-Ḥasan, and Sallām.
40. *kalimatu—kalimata* as Yaʿqūb, al-Ḥasan, and Zaid b. ʿAlī. Others say that in this verse he read both *kalimata* and *kalimatu* as *kalimāt.*
54. *tuqbala—yuqbala* as Ḥamza, al-Kiṣāʾī, and Zaid b. ʿAlī.
58. *yalmizuka—yalmuzuka* as Yaʿqūb and al-Ḥasan.
70/71. *thamūda—thamūdin* as al-Aʿmash.
atathum—atāhum.
98/99. *as-sauʾi—as-suʾi* as the Meccans and Baṣrans.
111/112. *yuqātilūna—yuqatttilūna* as al-Ḥasan and Abū Mijlaz.
fa-yaqtulūna wa-yuqtulūna—fa-yuqattilūna wa-yuqattalūna as al-Ḥasan and Abū Mijlaz.
117/118. *kāda yazīghu*—He supported *TR* against the more common *kāda tazīghu.*

Sūra X

10/11. *ani ʾl-ḥamdu—anna ʾl-ḥamda* as Ibn Muḥaiṣin, Mujāhid, and Yaʿqūb.

18/19. *yushrikūna—tushrikūna* as the Kūfans in general.
24/25. *taghna—yaghna* as al-Ḥasan and Qatāda.
33/34. *kalimatu—kalimāta* as the Madīnan and Syrian readers. So in v. 96.
58/59. *fal-yafraḥū—fal-tafraḥū* as Ruwais, al-Ḥasan, and Qatāda.
71/72. *fa-ajmiʿū—faʾjmaʿū* as Ruwais and al-Jaḥdarī.
76/77. *la-siḥrun—la-sāḥḥirun* as Mujāhid and Saʿid b. Jubair.
79/80. *sāḥirin—saḥḥārin* as the majority of the Kūfans.
101. *tughnī—yughnī*, which is given by some from al-Aʿmash.

Sūra XI

5. *yathnūna—yathnūnī* as Ibn Quṭais.
7/10. *siḥrun—sāḥirun* as the majority of the Kūfans.
15/18. *nuwaffi—yuwaffi* as Zaid b. ʿAlī and Abūʾl-Mutawakkil.
27/29. *bādiya—bādiʾa* as Abū ʿAmr, ʿĪsā ath-Thaqifī, and al-Ḥasan.
31/33. *tazdarī—yazdarī.*
37/39. *tukhāṭibnī—tukhāṭibannī.*
40/42. *kullin*—He supported *TR* against the more common *kulli.*
46/48. *ʿamalun ghayru—ʿamila ghayra* as Ibn ʿAbbās and ʿIkrima.
51/53. *ajriya—ajrī* as al-Ḥasan and the Kūfans.
61/64. *thamūda—thamūdin* as al-Aʿmash, al-Ḥasan, and Ibn Waththāb, and similarly *li-thamūdin* for *li-thamūda* in v. 68/71.
80/82. *ruknin—rukunin* as Ibn as-Samaifaʿ and Abū Ḥaṣīn.
95/98. *buʿdan—buʿudan* as Abū Ḥaiwa and some of the Baṣrans.
104/106. *nuʾakhkhiruhu—yuʾakhkhiruhu* as al-Ḥasan and other Baṣran readers.
111/113. *wa-inna—wa-in* as al-Ḥasan, supporting the Ḥijāzī reading.
119/120. *kalimatu—kalimātu* as Khārija ʿan Abī ʿAmr.

Sūra XII

10. *lā taqtulū—lā tuqattilū* as al-Ḥasan and Abū Mijlaz.
ghayābati—ghayābāti as the Madīnan readers.
12. *yartaʿ—yartaʿi* as the Madīnan readers.

45. *unabbi'ukum—ātī'kum* as Ubai and al-Ḥasan.
80. *najiyyan—nujabā'*.
90. *yattaqi—yattaqī* as some of the Meccan readers.
102/103. *nūḥīhi—yūḥīhi*.

Sūra XIII

3. *yughshī—yughashshi* as the majority of the Kūfans.
4. *'l-ukuli—'l-ukli* as the Ḥijāzī reading. So in v. 35, *ukluhā* for *ukuluhā*.
7/8. *hādin—hādī* as the Meccan reading.
8/9. *taghīḍu—yaghiḍu* as al-Ḥalawānī ʿan Abī ʿAmr.
11/12. *wālin—wālī* as some of the Meccan and Baṣran readers.
16/17. *tastawī—yastawī* as the Kūfans.
33. *hādin—hādī* as some of the Meccans and Baṣrans.
34. *wāqin—wāqī* as some of the Meccans and Baṣrans.
43. *baynī—bayniya* as Ibn al-Munādhirr.
wa man ʿindahu ʿilmu 'l-kitābi—wa-min ʿindihi ʿulima 'l-kitābu as al-Ḥasan and Mujāhid.

Sūra XIV

9. *thamūda—thamūdin* as al-Aʿmash.
19/22. *khalaqa s-samāwāti wa 'l-arḍa—khāliqu 's-samāwāti wa 'l-arḍi* as the Kūfans generally.
30/35. *li-yuḍillū—li-yaḍillū* as the Meccans and Baṣrans.

Sūra XV

15. *sukkirat—sukirat* as al-Ḥasan, Mujāhid, and the Meccan readers.
41. *ʿalayya—ʿaliyyun* as Yaʿqūb and al-Ḥasan.
72. *sakratihim—sakarātihim* as Ibn Abī ʿAbla.

Sūra XVI

12. *wa 'sh-shamsa wa 'l-qamara—wa 'sh-shamsu wa 'l-qamaru* as Ibn ʿĀmir, Abū Ḥaiwa, and others.
28/30. *tatawaffāhum—yatawaffāhum* as the Kūfans generally.
40/42. *fa-yakūnu—fa-yakūna* as Ibn ʿĀmir and al-Kiṣā'ī.
59/61. *sū'i mā—sū'in mā.*
97/99. *falanuḥyiyannahu—falayuḥyiyannahu* as Ibn Munādhirr ʿan Nāfiʿ, and similarly for *lanajziyannahum* he read *layajziyannahum.*
115/116. *'l-maytata—'l-mayyitata* as Abū Jaʿfar, Shaiba, and Muʿādh.
124/125. *juʿila 's-sabtu—jaʿala 's-sabta* as al-Ḥasan, Muʿādh, and Abū Ḥaiwa.
127/128. *ḍayqin—ḍayyiqin.*

Sūra XVII

2. *tattakhidhū—yattakhidhū* as Abū ʿAmr, Ibn ʿAbbās and Mujāhid.
12/13. *mubṣiratan—mabṣaratan*, likewise in v. 59/61 and in XXVII, 13. *kulla—kullu* as Abū Mijlaz and Abū's-Sammāl.
13/14. *wa-kulla—wa-kullu* as Abū Mijlaz, Abū's-Sammāl, and Muʿādh.
16/17. *amarnā—ammarnā* as al-Ḥasan, ʿAlī, and Zaid b. ʿAlī.
18/19. *yaṣlāhā—yuṣallīhā* as Abū Ḥaiwa and Abū'l-Barhashīm.
23/24. *yablughanna—yablughānni* as the Kūfans generally. *uffin—uffa* as the Meccan and Syrian readers.
31/33. *taqtulū—tuqattilū* as al-Aʿmash and Ibn Waththāb. So in v. 33/35. *khiṭ'an—khiṭā'an* as al-Ḥasan, Shaiba, and others.
59/61. *mubṣiratan—mabṣaratan* as Ubai, Zaid b. ʿAlī, and Qatāda.
93/95. *qul—qāla* as the Meccan and Syrian readers.
97/99. *naḥshuruhum—yaḥshuruhum.*
106/107. *faraqnāhu—farraqnāhu* as Ubai, Ibn Masʿūd, al-Ḥasan, and others.
110. *bi-ṣalātika—bi-ṣalawātika* as al-Ḥasan and Khalaf.

Sūra XVIII

5/4. *kalimatan—kalimatun* as al-Ḥasan, Ibn Muḥaiṣin, and Ibn Abī ʿAbla.

33/31. *ukulahā—uklahā* as Nāfiʿ, Ibn Kathīr, and Abū ʿAmr.

33/32. *fajjarnā—fajarnā* as Yaʿqūb, al-Aʿmash, and Sallām.

47/45. *nusayyiru ʾl-jibāla—tusayyaru ʾl-jibālu* as Ibn Kathīr, Ibn ʿĀmir, and Abū ʿAmr.

51/49. *ashhadtuhum—ashhadnāhum* as Abū Jaʿfar, Shaiba, and Abū Mijlaz.

52/50. *yaqūlu—naqūlu* as Ḥamza, al-Aʿmash, and Ṭalḥa.

71/70. *li-tughriqa ahlahā—li-tugharriqa ahlahā* as al-Ḥasan and Abū Rajāʾ.

73/72. *ʿusran—ʿusuran* as Abū Jaʿfar, al-Ḥasan, and Shaiba.

102. *afa-ḥasiba—afa-ḥasbu* as ʿAlī, ʿIkrima, and Mujāhid.

109. *madadan—midādan* as Ibn Masʿūd, al-Ḥasan, and Ibn ʿAbbās.

Sūra XIX

5. *khiftu ʾl-mawāliya—khaffati ʾl-mawālī* as ʿAlī and Saʿīd b. Jubair.

6. *yarithunī wa-yarithu—yarithnī wa-yarith* as Abū ʿAmr and al-Kiṣāʾī.

58/59. *idhā tutlā ʿalayhim āyātu—idhā yutlā jamīʿu āyāti.* The *yutlā* for *tutlā* was read also by al-Ḥasan and Ibn Muḥaiṣin.

59/60. *aṣ-ṣalāta—aṣ-ṣalawāti* as Ibn Masʿūd, al-Ḥasan, and aḍ-Ḍaḥḥāk.

63/64. *nūrithu—nuwarrithu* as al-Ḥasan, Qatāda, and Ibn Abī ʿAbla.

90/92. *tanshaqqu—yanshaqqu*, and so for *takhirru* he read *yakhirru.*

Sūra XX

77/79. *an asri—ani ʾsrī* as the readers of al-Ḥijāz.

97. *tukhlafahu—tukhallifahu* as al-Ḥasan and the Meccan and Baṣran readers.

114/113. *yuqḍā ilayka waḥyuhu—naqḍiya ilayka waḥyahu* as Ibn Masʿūd and al-Ḥasan.

130. *tarḍā—turḍā* as some of the Kūfans.
131. *zahrata—zaharata* as Ya'qūb and al-Ḥasan.

Sūra XXI

37/38. *khuliqa 'l-insānu—khalaqa 'l-insāna* as Ḥumaid, Mujāhid, and Abū Razīn.
40/41. *ta'tīhim—ya'tīhim* as al-A'mash and aḍ-Ḍaḥḥāk.
fa-tabhatuhum—fa-yabhatuhum as al-A'mash and aḍ-Ḍaḥḥāk.
58/59. *judhādhan—jidhādhan* as Abū Ḥaiwa and some of the Kūfans.
65/66. *nukisū—nukkisū* as Abū Ḥaiwa and Ibn Abī 'Abla.
67. *uffin—uffa* as Ibn 'Āmir, Ibn Kathīr, and Ya'qūb.
80. *li-tuḥṣinakum—li-yuḥaṣṣinakum* as Ḥumaid and Abū 'Imrān.
87. *naqdira—nuqaddira* as az-Zuhrī, Ḥumaid, and Yaḥyā b. Ya'mar.
103. *tatalaqqāhum—yatalaqqāhum* as aḍ-Ḍaḥḥāk.

Sūra XXII

9. *li-yuḍilla—li-yaḍilla* as the Meccans and Baṣran.
11. *khasira—khāsira*, which involves reading *'l-ākhirati*, as Mujāhid and some of the Baṣrans.
17. *yafṣilu—yufaṣṣilu*, and so in XXXII, 25 and LX, 3.
31/32. *fa-takhṭafuhu—fa-takhiṭṭifihi* as al-Ḥasan and al-A'mash.
36/37. *wa'l-budna—wa'l-buduna* as al-Ḥasan, Shaiba, and Ibn Abī Isḥāq.
fa'dhkurū—fa'dhdhakkarū as Abū 'Imrān.
65/64. *'l-fulka—'l-fuluka* as 'Īsā b. 'Umar, and, according to some, al-Ḥasan.

Sūra XXIII

2. *ṣalātihim—ṣalawātihim* as Ubai, al-Ḥasan, and Zaid b. 'Alī.
8. *li-amānātihim—li-amānatihim*, which was the Meccan reading.
14. *'iẓāman—'aẓman* as the Damascus readers.
63/65. *ghamratin—ghamarātin* as Ubai and Ibn Mas'ūd.

100/102. *kalimatun—kalimātun.*
106/108. *shiqwatunā—shaqāwatunā* as al-Ḥasan and the Kūfans.

Sūra XXIV

2. *ra'fatun—ra'afatun* as the Meccan reading.
7. *anna laʿnata—an laʿnatu* as Qatāda, Abū Rajā', and al-Ḥasan.
11. *kibrahu—kubrahu* as al-Ḥasan and many of the Baṣran readers.
21. *zakā—zakkā* as al-Ḥasan, Mujāhid, and Qatāda.
24. *tashhadu—yashhadu* as the majority of the Kūfans.
31. *ʿaurāti—ʿawarāti* as al-Aʿmash and Ibn Abī ʿAbla.
35. *tamsashu—yamsashu* as Ibn ʿAbbās, al-Ḥasan, and Ḥumaid.
45/44. *khalaqa kulla—khāliqu kulli* as the Kūfans.
57/56. *taḥsabanna—yaḥsabanna* as Ibn ʿAbbās, Mujāhid, and the Damascus readers.

Sūra XXV

8/9. *ya'kulu—na'kulu* as Zaid b. ʿAlī and the Kūfans.
25/27. *nuzzila 'l-malā'ikatu—nunzilu 'l-malā'ikata* as Ubai and the Meccan Codex.
67. *yaqturū—yuqtirū* as the Madīnan and Syrian readers.
68. *yaqtulūna—yuqattilūna* as al-Ḥasan and Abū Mijlaz.
74. *qurrata—qurrāti* as Ibn Masʿūd and Ibn Khuthaim.

Sūra XXVI

13/12. *yaḍīqu—yaḍīqa* as Zaid b. ʿAlī, Qatāda, and Ṭalḥa. So he read with them *yanṭaliqa* instead of *yanṭaliqu* as a consequence.
14/13. *yaqtulūnī—yuqattilūnī* as al-Ḥasan and Abū Mijlaz.
82. *khaṭī'atī—khaṭāyāya* as Ubai, al-Ḥasan and Abū Mijlaz, though some sources say he read here *khaṭī'ātī.*
184. *wa 'l-jibillata—wa 'l-jubullata* as al-Ḥasan, and Ibn as-Samaifaʿ.
198. *'l-aʿjamīna—'l-aʿjamiyyīna* as al-Ḥasan, al-Jaḥdarī, and Abū'l-Mutawakkil.

Sūra XXVII

11. *ḥusnan—ḥusunan.*
13. *siḥrun—sāḥirun*, see sūra V, 110.
31. *ta'lū—ta'allū.*
45/46. *thamūda—thamūdin* as al-Ḥasan, al-A'mash, and Ibn Waththāb.
49/50. *la-nubayyitannahu—la-yubayyitannahu* as Mujāhid and Ḥumaid.
63/64. *bushran*—He supported the *TR* as against the numerous other readings.
70/72. *ḍaiqin—ḍayyiqin* as in XVI, 127/128.
74/76. *mā tukinnu—mā takunnu* as Ibn Muḥaiṣin, Ḥumaid, and Abū'l-Mutawakkil, though some sources say he read *yakunnu* here and in XXVIII, 69.

Sūra XXVIII

15/14. *fa'staghāthahu—fa'sta'ānahu* as al-Ḥasan and aḍ-Ḍaḥḥāk.
19/18. *taqtulanī* and *qatalta—tuqattilanī* and *qattalta* as al-Ḥasan and Abū Mijlaz.
20/19. *li-yaqtulūka—li-yuqattilūka* as al-Ḥasan and Abū Mijlaz.
29. *jadhwatin—judhwatin* as the Kūfans.
33. *yaqtulūnī—yuqattilūnī* as al-Ḥasan and Abū Mijlaz.
34. *yuṣaddiqunī*—He supported *TR* against the more common *yuṣaddiqnī.*
66. *fa'amiyat—fa-'ummiyat* as Sa'īd b. Jubair.
69. *tukinnu—takunnu*, but see XXVII, 74/76.

Sūra XXIX

17/16. *takhluqūna—tukhalliqūna* as Abū Ḥanīfa and Zaid b. 'Alī.
25/24. *mawaddata baynikum—mawaddatun baynakum* as al-Ḥasan, al-A'mash, and Ibn Abī 'Abla.
50/49. *āyātun—āyatun* as al-Ḥasan, Ya'qūb, and some Kūfan readers.
55. *yaqūlu*—He supported *TR* against the alternative reading *naqūlu.*

Sūra XXX

46/45. *li-tajziya—li-yajziya.*

Sūra XXXI

3/2. *raḥmatan—raḥmatun* as Ḥamza, al-Aʿmash, and Ṭalḥa.
6/5. *li-yuḍilla—li-yaḍilla* as Ibn Kathīr, Abū ʿAmr, and Zaid b. ʿAlī.
16/15. *fa-takun—fa-tukanna.*
18/17. *tuṣaʿʿir—tuṣāʿir* as Nāfiʿ, Abū ʿAmr, and some Kūfan readers.

Sūra XXXII

7/6. *khalaqahu*—He supported *TR* against the non-Kūfan reading *khalqahu.*
17. *qurrati—qurrāti* as Ibn Masʿūd, Abū Huraira, and Abū Jaʿfar. See XXV, 74.
27. *taʾkulu—yaʾkulu* as some gave from Ḥamza and Abū Ḥaiwa.

Sūra XXXIII

9. *ʾdhkurū—ʾdhdhakkarū* as Abū ʿImrān.
13. *ʿawratun—ʿawiratun* as Ibn ʿAbbās, ʿIkrima, Mujāhid, and al-Ḥasan. So in this verse he read *bi-ʿawiratin* for *bi-ʿawratin.*
20. *yasʾalūna—yassāʾalūna* as Qatāda, al-Ḥasan, and Ibn Abī ʿAbla.
26. *taqtulūna—tuqattilūna* as al-Ḥasan, Abū Mijlaz, and Ibn Qais.
31. *taʿmal—yaʿmal* as some of the Kūfan readers.
41. *ʾdhkurū—dhdhakkarū* as Abū ʿImrān.
59. *yudnīna—yudayyina.*

Sūra XXXIV

3. *ʿālimi—ʿallāmi* as some of the Kūfan readers.
5. *alīmun*—He supported *TR* against the more common reading *alīmin.*

14/13. *minsa'atahu—minsa'tahu* as Ibn Dhakwān and some Damascus readers.

16/15. *ukulin—uklin* as Nāfiʿ, Ibn Kathīr, and Ibn Muḥaiṣin.

17/16. *nujāzī*—He supported *TR* against the more common reading *yujāzī*.

20/19. *ṣaddaqa*—He supported *TR* against the non-Kūfan reading *ṣadaqa*.

37/36. *jazā'u 'ḍ-ḍiʿfi—jazā'ani 'ḍ-ḍiʿfu* as Ibn Abī ʿAbla, Muʿādh, and Ruwais.

40/39. *yaḥshuruhum* and *yaqūlu*—He supported *TR* against the alternative readings *naḥshuruhum* and *naqūlu*, which were more commonly read.

43/42. *siḥrun—sāḥirun* as in V, 110 and XXVII, 13.

Sūra XXXV

3. *'dhkurū—'dhdhakkarū* as Abū ʿImrān.
ghayru—ghayri as read by many of the Kūfans.

4. *turjaʿu 'l-umūru—yurjaʿu 'l-umūru*. So likewise in LVII, 5.

8/9. *tadhhab—tudhhiba* as Abū Jaʿfar and Shaiba. It involves the reading of *nafsaka* for *nafsuka*.

36/33. *yuqḍā—yaqḍī* as Kirdāb.
najzī—yajzī as Shibil and Kirdāb.
yukhaffafu—tukhaffifu.

40/38. *bayyinatin—bayyinātin* as Nāfiʿ, Ibn ʿĀmir, and al-Ḥasan.

Sūra XXXVI

9/8. *fa-a'ghshaynāhum—fa-aʿshaynāhum*, with *ʿain* instead of *ghain*, as Ibn ʿAbbās, al-Ḥasan, and Abū Ḥanīfa.

12/11. *kulla—kullu* as Ibn Abī ʿAbla and Abū's-Sammāl. See XVII, 12/13, 13/14.

33. *al-maytatu—al-mayyitatu* as Nāfiʿ, Abū Jaʿfar, and Shaiba.

39. *wal-qamara—wal-qamaru* as Nāfiʿ, Ibn Kathīr, Abū ʿAmr, and al-Ḥasan.

41. *dhurriyyatahum—dhurriyyātihim* as Nāfiʿ, Ibn ʿĀmir, and Yaʿqūb.
62. *jibillan—jubullan* as al-Ḥasan, Zaid b. ʿAlī, and Ibn Abī ʿAbla.
82. *fa-yakūnu—fa-yakūna* as Ibn ʿĀmir, al-Kiṣāʾī, and Ibn Muḥaiṣin.

Sūra XXXVII

12. *ʿajibta—ʿajibtu* as Ibn Masʿūd and many of the Kūfans.
15. *siḥrun—sāḥirun* as in V, 110 and elsewhere.
94/92. *yaziffūna—yuzaffūna* as al-Aʿmash.

Sūra XXXVIII

5/4. *ʿujābun—ʿujjābun* as ʿAlī, as-Sulamī, and ʿĪsā b. ʿUmar.
17/16. *waʾdhkur—waʾdhdhakar*, and so in v. 41/40.
41/40. *bi-nuṣbin—bi-naṣabin* as al-Ḥasan, Yaʿqūb, and al-Jaḥdarī.
45. *ʿibādanā*—He agreed with *TR* against the Meccan reading *ʿabdanā*.

Sūra XXXIX

8/11. *li-yuḍilla—li-yaḍilla* as al-Ḥasan, Abū ʿAmr, and Ibn Kathīr.
23/24. *taqshaʿirru* and *talīnu—yaqshaʿirru* and *yalīnu*.
35/36. *aswaʾa—aswāʾa* as was given by some from Ibn Kathīr. So in XLI, 27.
59/60. *fa-kadhdhabta—fa-kadhdhabti*, and as a consequence he read also the following words *waʾstakbarti* and *kunti* as feminine. So Abū Ḥaiwa, Yaḥyā b. Yaʿmar, and al-Jaḥdarī.
61/62. *bi-mafāzatihim—bi-mafāzātihim* as al-Ḥasan and az-Zaʿfarānī.

Sūra XL

6. *kalimatu—kalimātu* as Muʿādh, Shaiba, and Ibn Abī ʿAbla.

26/27. *yuẓhira*—He supported *TR* against the Meccan reading *yaẓhara.*
28/29. *a-taqtulūna*—*a-tuqattilūna* as al-Ḥasan and Abū Mijlaz.
32/34. *'t-tanādi*—*'t-tanāddi* as Ibn ʿAbbās and aḍ-Ḍaḥḥāk.
35/37. *kulli qalbi*—*kulli qalbin* as az-Zuhrī and Abu Baḥriyya.
37/39. *fa'aṭṭaliʿa*—He supported *TR* against the generally followed *fa'aṭṭaliʿu.*
46/49. *adkhilū*— *udkhulū* as al-Ḥasan and the non-Kūfans.
62/64. *tu'fakūna*—*yu'fakūna* as Ṭalḥa b. Sammān.

Sūra XLI

13/12. *ṣāʿiqatan* and *ṣāʿiqati*—*ṣaʿqatan* and *ṣaʿqati* as an-Nakhaʿī and as-Sulamī.
thamūda—*thamūdin* as al-Aʿmash.
17/16. *ṣāʿiqatu*—*ṣāʿqatu* as in v. 13/12.
'l-hūni—*'l-hawāni.*
44. *ʿaman*—*ʿamin* as Ibn ʿAbbās and Ibn az-Zubair.
47. *thamarātin*—*thamaratin* as al-Ḥasan, Ṭalḥa, al-Aʿmash, and some of the Seven.

Sūra XLII

5/3. *takādu*—*yakādu* as Nāfiʿ, al-Kiṣā'ī, and al-Aʿmash.
20/19. *nu'tihi*—*yu'tihi* as az-Zaʿfarānī and Zaid b. ʿAlī.
23/22. *nazid*—*yazid* as Zaid b. ʿAlī and az-Zaʿfarānī.

Sūra XLIII

10/9. *mahdan*—He supported *TR* against the more common *mihādan.*
18/17. *yunashsha'u*—He supported *TR* against the non-Kūfan *yansha'u.*
24/23. *ji'tukum*—*ji'nākum* as Ubai, Abū Jaʿfar, Shaiba, and az-Zaʿfarānī.
36/35. *nuqayyiḍ*—*yuqayyiḍ* as al-Aʿmash and Yaʿqūb.
38/37. *baynī*—*bayniya* as Ibn Munādhirr and Ḥumaid.
57. *yaṣiddūna*—*yaṣuddūna* as Nāfiʿ, Ibn ʿĀmir, al-Kiṣā'ī, and also ʿAlī.

58. *jadalan—jidālan.*
61. *la-ʿilmun—la-ʿalamun* as Qatāda, aḍ-Ḍaḥḥāk, and Ibn ʿAbbās.
71. *tashtahīhi—yashtahīhi.*
84. *ilāhun*(bis)-*Allāhu* as Ibn ʿAbbās, Ibn Masʿūd, and Ibn as-Samaifaʿ.
85. *turjaʿūna*—He supported *TR* against the Meccan reading *yurjaʿūna.*

Sūra XLIV

7/6. *rabbi*—He supported *TR* along with al-Ḥasan against the non-Kūfan reading *rabbu.*
8/7. *rabbukum—rabbikum* as al-Ḥasan, Abū Ḥaiwa, and az-Zaʿfarānī, which involves *wa-rabbi.*
23/22. *fa'asri*—He supported *TR* against the Meccan and Madīnan *fa'sri.*

Sūra XLV

4/3. *āyātun—āyātin* as many of the readers of ʿIrāq.
12/11. *li-tajziya—li-yajziya.*
22/21. *li-tujzā kullu—li-yujziyā kulla* as al-Aʿmash and Ibn Qais.
31/30. *tutlā—yutlā.*

Sūra XLVI

7/6. *siḥrun—sāḥirun* as in V, 110 and elsewhere.
15/14. *dhurriyyatī—dhurriyyatiya* as al-Khuzāʿī.
16/15. *nataqabbalu*—He supported *TR* against the non-Kūfan *yutaqabbalu.*
21/20. *wa'dhkur—wa'dhdhakkar* as in XXXVIII, 17/16 and so on.

Sūra XLVII

2. *nuzzila—nazzala* as Ibn Masʿūd and Zaid b. ʿAlī.
31/33. *la-nabluwannakum* and *naʿlama* and *nabluwa—la-yabluwannakum* and *yaʿlama* and *yabluwa* as ʿAlī, Yaʿqūb, and az-Zaʿfarānī.

Sūra XLVIII

25. *tazayyalū—tazāyalū* as Ibn Masʿūd, Qatāda, and Ibn Abī ʿAbla.

Sūra XLIX

1. *tuqaddimū—taqaddamū* as Ibn ʿAbbās, aḍ-Ḍaḥḥāk, and Yaʿqūb.
12. *maytan—mayyitan* as Ibn Masʿūd, Nāfiʿ, and Ruwais.

Sūra L

32/31. *tūʿadūna*—He supported *TR* against the Meccan reading *yūʿadūna*.

Sūra LI

3. *yusran—yusuran* as Shaiba, al-Ḥasan, and Ṭalḥa.
23. *mithlamā—mithlumā* as the Kūfans and al-Ḥasan.
43. *thamūda—thamūdin* as in XLI, 13/12 and so on.
44. *'ṣ-ṣāʿiqatu—ṣ-ṣaʿqatu* as Mujāhid, Ḥumaid, and al-Kiṣā'ī. See II, 55/52.
46. *qauma—qaumu* as Abū'-s-Sammāl, Qatāda, and some Baṣrans.
47. *wa 's-samā'a—wa 's-samā'u* as Abū's-Sammāl and Mujāhid.

Sūra LIII

11. *kadhaba—kadhdhaba* as Abū Jaʿfar, al-Ḥasan, and al-Jaḥdarī.
26. *shafāʿatuhum—shafāʿātuhum* as Ubai and Ibn Abī ʿAbla.

Sūra LIV

7. *yakhrujūna—yukhrajūna*.
12. *qudira—quddira* as Abū Ḥaiwa and Abū ʿImrān.
37. *fa-ṭamasnā—fa-ṭammasnā*.

Sūra LV

12/11. *wa ʾr-rayḥānu—wa ʾr-rayḥāni* as the majority of the Kūfans.
24. *al-munshaʾātu—al-munassātu.*
56. *qablahum—min qablihim* as Abū ʿImrān. So also in v. 74.
70. *khayrātun—khayarātun* or some said *khayyirātun.*

Sūra LVI

2. *kādhibatun—kādhibatan* as al-Ḥasan, az-Zaʿfarānī, and Ibn Abī ʿAbla.
3. *khāfiḍatun rāfiʿatun—khāfiḍatan rāfiʿatan* as al-Ḥasan, al-Yazīdī, and Abū Ḥaiwa.
22. *ḥūrun ʿīnun—ḥūra ʿīnin.*
89/88. *fa-rauḥun—fa-rūḥun* as Ibn ʿAbbās, al-Ḥasan, and some of the Baṣrans.

Sūra LVII

16/15. *takhshaʿa—yakhshaʿa.*
18/17. *al-muṣṣaddiqīna wal-muṣṣaddiqāti*—He supported *TR* against the Meccan reading, which had one *shadda* only.
27. *raʾfatan—raʾafatan* as Ḥumaid and Ibn Muḥaiṣin.

Sūra LVIII

7/8. *akthara—akbara* as al-Ḥasan, az-Zuhrī, and ʿIkrima.

Sūra LIX

2. *yukhribūna—yukharribūna* as al-Ḥasan, Abū ʿAmr, and al-Yazīdī.
7. *dūlatan—daulatun* as ʿAlī and Ibn Qutais.
10. *ghillan—ghimran* as Ṭalḥa and al-Aʿmash.

Sūra LXI

6. *siḥrun—sāḥirun* as Ibn Masʿūd and many of the Kūfan readers.

Sūra LXII

10. *wa'dhkurū—wa'dhdhakkarū* as Abū ʿImrān.

Sūra LXIII

4. *tuʿjibuka—yuʿjibuka.*
9. *tulhikum—yulhikum.*
10. *wa akun—wa akūna* as Abū ʿAmr al-Ḥasan and al-Yazīdī.

Sūra LXV

4. *yusran—yusuran* as al-Ḥasan, Shaiba, and Abū Jaʿfar.
5. *yuʿẓim—yuʿaẓẓim.*

Sūra LXIX

14. *wa ḥumilati—wa ḥummilati* as al-Aʿmash and Ibn Abī ʿAbla.
18. *takhfā—yakhfā* as the majority of the Kūfans.
41. *tu'minūna—yu'minūna* as Yaʿqūb, al-Ḥasan, and Ibn Muḥaiṣin.
42. *tadhakkarūna—yadhakkarūna.*

Sūra LXX

4. *taʿruju—yaʿruju* as Ibn Masʿūd, al-Aʿmash, and al-Kiṣā'ī.
17. *nazzāʿatan*—He supported *TR* against the Kūfan reading *nazzāʿatun.*
23. *ṣalātihim—ṣalawātihim* as Ibn Masʿūd. So also in v. 34.
33. *bi-shahādātihim*—He supported *TR* against the more common *bi-shahādatihim.*

Sūra LXXI

5. *qaumī—qaumiya* as ʻIsā al-Ḥamdānī, Ḥumaid, and Yaʿqūb.
23/22. *waddan—wuddan* as Qatāda and Shaiba.

Sūra LXXII

2. *ʾr-rushdi—ʾr rashadi* as al-Ḥasan and Abū Mijlaz.
5. *taqūla—taqawwala* as Ubai, Yaʿqūb, and Abū Razīn.
17. *yaslukhu*—He supported *TR* against the more common reading *naslukhu.*

Sūra LXXIII

6. *waṭʾan—wiṭāʾan* as Mujāhid, Abū Ḥaiwa, and az-Zaʿfarānī.
20. *niṣfahu wa thuluthahu—niṣfihi wa thuluthihi* as the non-Kūfans.

Sūra LXXV

7. *bariqa—baraqa* as al-Ḥasan, Nāfiʿ, and Abū Jaʿfar.

Sūra LXXVI

4. *salāsila—salāsilan* as Nāfiʿ, al-Kiṣāʾī, and some Baṣran readers.

Sūra LXXVII

8. *ṭumisat—ṭummisat* as Ibn Khuthaim and al-Jaḥdarī.
9. *furiḥat—furriḥat* as Ibn Khuthaim and al-Jaḥdarī.
10. *nusifat—nussifat.*
32. *bi-shararin—bi-sharārin* or according to some sources *bi-shirārin. ka ʾl-qaṣri—ka ʾl-qaṣari* as Ibn ʿAbbās, al-Ḥasan, and Ibn Abī ʿAbla.

Sūra LXXVIII

4. *sa-yaʿlamūna—sa-taʿlamūna* as Ibn ʿĀmir, al-Ḥasan, and Abūʾl-ʿĀliya. So also in v. 5.
25. *ghassāqan*—He supported *TR* against the non-Kūfan *ghasāqan.*
29. *kulla—kullu* as Abūʾs-Sammāl, Ibn Khuthaim, and Ibn Abī ʿAbla.
37. *rabbi* and *ʾr-raḥmāni*—He supported *TR* against the alternative *rabbu* and *ʾr-raḥmānu.*

Sūra LXXIX

11. *nakhiratan—nākhiratan* as many of the Kūfans.
45. *mundhiru—mundhirun* as Ṭalḥa, Shaiba, al-Aʿraj, and al-Ḥasan.

Sūra LXXX

4. *fa-tanfaʿahu*—He supported *TR* against the usual reading *fa-tanfaʿuhu.*

Sūra LXXXI

5. *ḥushirat—ḥushshirat* as al-Ḥasan, Ibn Qais, and Abū ʿImrān.
8. *suʾilat—suyyilat* as Abū Jaʿfar.
10. *nushirat—nushshirat* as the Kūfan and Meccan readers.
11. *kushiṭat—kushshiṭat.*
21. *thamma—thumma* as Abū Jaʿfar, Abū Ḥaiwa, and Abūʾl-Barhasīm.

Sūra LXXXIII

13. *tutlā—yutlā* as Abū Ḥaiwa and Ibn Khuthaim.

Sūra LXXXIV

19. *la-tarkabunna—la-yarkabunna* as Abūʾs-Sammāl and Abūʾl-Mutawakkil.

Sūra LXXXVI

7. *yakhruju—yukhraju* as Ibn Abī ʿAbla, Ibn Sīrīn, and Ibn as-Samaifaʿ.
ʾṣ ṣulbi—ʾṣ-ṣulubi as Ibn Khuthaim and Ibn Abī ʿAbla.
9. *tublā—yublā.*

Sūra LXXXVII

16. *tuʾthirūna—yuʾthirūna* as Ibn Masʿūd, al-Ḥasan, and al-Jaḥdarī.

Sūra LXXXVIII

4. *taṣlā—tuṣlā* as Muʿādh, Abūʾs-Sammāl, and Abū Rajāʾ.

Sūra LXXXIX

9/8. *thamūda—thamūdin* as al-Aʿmash and Ibn Waththāb.
18/19. *taḥāḍḍūna*—He supported *TR* against the more common *tuḥāḍḍūna.*
25. *yuʾadhdhibu—yuʾadhdhabu* as al-Ḥasan, Yaʿqūb, and al-Kiṣāʾī.
26. *yūthiqu—yūthaqu.*

Sūra XCII

7. *lil-yusrā—lil-yusurā* as Abū Jaʿfar.
10. *lil-ʿusrā—lil-ʿusurā* as Abū Jaʿfar.
15. *yaṣlāhā—yuṣalliyahā.*
19. *tujzā—yujzā.*

Sūra XCIV

5. *yusran—yusuran* as Abū Ja'far, al-Ḥasan, and Shaiba.

Sūra XCVII

4. *tanazzalu—yunzalu.*

Sūra XCVIII

1. *ta'tiyahum—ya'tiyahum.*

Sūra XCIX

7. *yarahu—yurahu* as Ibn ʿAbbās, Zaid b. ʿAlī, and Abū Ḥaiwa.

Sūra C

9. *buʿthira—baʿthara* as Kirdāb and Abū Mijlaz.
10. *ḥuṣṣila—ḥaṣṣala* as Kirdāb, though other sources say he read *ḥaṣala* as Naṣr b. ʿĀṣim, Ibn Yaʿmar, and Saʿīd b. Jubair.

Sūra CII

6. *la-tarawunna—la-turawunna* as Ibn ʿĀmir, al-Kiṣā'ī, and Qatāda. *la-tarawunnahā—la-tara'unnahā* as al-Ḥasan, Abū Mijlaz, and Abū Ḥaiwa.

Sūra CIV

2. *jamaʿa*—He supported *TR* against the alternative reading *jammaʿa.*

Sūra CVII

5. *ṣalātihim—ṣalawātihim* as al-Ḥasan, Abū Mijlaz, and Abū Ḥaṣīn.

Sūra CXI

1. *lahabin*—He supported *TR* against the Meccan *lahbin*.
3. *sa-yaṣlā*—*sa-yuṣlā* as Ibn Masʿūd and Abū Ḥaiwa.
4. *ʾmraʾatuhu*—*murayʾatuhu* as Ibn Masʿūd, Ibn Abī ʿAbla, and Abū Ḥaiwa.

Sūra CXIV

2. *maliki*—*māliki* as Abū Ḥanīfa, Abū ʿImrān, and Abū Ḥaṣan.[24]

In this collection of some five hundred and fifty readings there are some that are persistent, that is, readings that he read throughout the Qur'ān, for example, *waʾdhdhakkarū* for *waʾdhkurū* where he preferred the use of Form V to that of Form I, where the meaning is much the same, though Form V is perhaps a little stronger; *thamūdin* for *thamūda* taking the name as grammatically a triptote not a diptote: *yuqattilūna* instead of *yaqtulūna*, and so in the other persons of this verb, taking the intensive Form II in preference to the simple verb, though the meaning is much the same: *aṣ-ṣaʿqatu* instead of *aṣ-ṣāʿiqatu*: *sāḥirun* "magician" instead of *siḥrun* "magic": *ṣalawātuhum* the plural instead of the singular *ṣalātuhum*: *mayyitatun* instead of *maytatun*, so that he probably read thus at II, 173/168 and V, 3/4, though it is not recorded from him at those passages: *ukl* for *ukul* so that again he probably read thus at XIII, 35 and XIV, 25/30, though it is not there recorded from him: *daʾab* for *daʾb*, so that this is probably to be read from him in VIII, 54/56 and XL, 31/32 also: *uffa* instead of *uffin*, so that he probably read thus also in XLVI, 17/16: *raʾafat* for *raʾfat* in the singular: *ḍayyiq* for *ḍayq*: *yusur* for *yusr* and *ʿusur* for *ʿusr*, so that he probably read thus also in XVIII, 88/87; LXV, 7; XCIV, 6, even though it is not recorded from him. Also since he read *yurjaʿu ʾl-umūru* in XXXV, 4 and LVII, 5 it is very probable that he would have read the same in the other passages where this phrase occurs, namely, II, 210/206; III, 109/105; VIII, 44/46; and XXII, 76/75, though no source so far examined mentions him reading thus in any of these passages. He shows a tendency to prefer intensive forms, for example, *yukhaṭṭif* instead of *yukhṭaf*:

yusaffik instead of *yasfik*: *yuwarrith* instead of *yūrith*: *nuṣallīhi* instead of *nuṣlīhi*: *ta'addū* instead of *ta'dū*: *fattaḥnā* instead of *fataḥnā*: and in XI, 7/10 *saḥḥār* for *sāḥir*. Also he tends to prefer an extra vowel instead of a *sukūn* in nominal forms such as *jaharat* for *jahrat*, *ḥasanan* for *ḥusnan*, *ghuluf* for *ghulf*, *baghatat* for *baghtat*, though there are instances of his choice falling in the other direction.

Since he was a follower of the Kūfan School it is not strange to find him in a goodly number of cases following the Kūfan reading where the *TR* departs therefrom, or supporting the *TR* as the Kūfan reading where the weight of authority was on the side of other metropolitan systems. Where he deviates from the common Kūfan reading in favor of some other metropolitan reading, he is most often in agreement with Madīnan readings of Nāfi' or Abū Ja'far. What is most striking, however, is the extent of his agreement with the readings of al-Ḥasan al-Baṣrī, particularly where al-Ḥasan's readings were not those later canonized as the Metropolitan readings from Baṣra accepted among the Seven. In one fifth of the readings collected here we find him in agreement with al-Ḥasan. Bergsträsser had recognized the importance of al-Ḥasan in the development of *qirā'āt*, and made a preliminary collection of his readings, *Die Koranlesung des Hasan von Basra*, in *Islamica* II (1926): 11–57, and it would be of no little interest to correct and supplement that collection from the newly available sources to which Bergsträsser did not have access in 1926.

The readings of Ibn Miqsam here given are for the most part quite intelligible in comparison with the *Textus Receptus* (*TR*), without commentary, but some points of interest are worth noting. Many of the readings are simply different possibilities of reading the text without in any way changing the meaning. Thus in II, 19/18 the meaning is "fear of death" whether we use the *maṣdar ḥadhar* or the noun *ḥidhār*: or in II, 210/206 *ẓulal* and *ẓilāl* are alternative plurals of *ẓullat* "an awning or covering": or in II, 256/257 *rushd* and *rashād* are alternative *maṣdars* of the prime verb. Other cases involve grammatical minutiae but again do not alter the meaning, for example, in II, 38/36 the meaning is "there is no fear" whether we read *fa lā khaufun* with *TR*, taking the *khaufun* as *marfū'* being the *ism* of the *lā*, or *khaufa* as *manṣūb* because following *lā li nafyi'l-jins*. So in VI, 135/136 the meaning is in both readings "whose will be the recompense," but *TR* reads *takūn* because it takes *ʿāqibat* as the subject, while Ibn Miqsam reads *yakūn*, taking *man* as the subject: or in XII, 10 where the meaning is "bottom of the well," whether we read singular with *TR* or plural with Ibn Miqsam: or XXI, 40/41 where the meaning is "will come upon you and confound you," whether the subject is taken as feminine with *TR*, or as masculine with Ibn Miqsam. Occasionally a fairly wide divergence in reading involves no difference in meaning, for example, in XXVIII, 15/14 both *faʾstaghāthahu* and *faʾstaʿānahu* mean "so he asked his help," and in LIX, 10 both *ghillan* and *ghimran* mean "rancour."

Sometimes there is a slight difference in meaning. This may be in the nature of a change necessitated by pause, for example, in VI, 74 *TR* reads, "when Abraham said to his father Āzar - 'dost thou take images as gods?'" and so *Āzara* is *majrūr* in apposition to *abīhi*, but Ibn Miqsam read, "when Abraham said to his father - 'Oh Āzar, dost thou take images as gods?'" where *Āzaru* is *marfūʿ* because vocative. The commonest cases of this kind are changes of person, for example, in XVIII, 51/49 *TR* reads "I made them not witnesses," but Ibn Miqsam, "We made them not witnesses": or XXXVII, 12 where *TR* reads "while thou marvellest," but Ibn Miqsam "while I marvel." Most frequently it is a change from "we" to "He," both referring to Allāh, as for example, XLIII, 36/35 where *TR* reads "We will chain a Satan to him," but Ibn Miqsam "He will chain a Satan to him." In our list there are twenty-six cases of this particular change, and Ibn Miqsam's reading may represent the original, for with the development of the theory that in Scripture it is always God who speaks, the reading "He" suggests at times that it is Muḥammad who is speaking, whereas the simple change to "We" saves the situation. There are, however, five cases in our list where Ibn Miqsam preferred the "We" reading where others read "He," so that this point cannot be pressed. Sometimes we find cases of a verb used in the indicative instead of the imperative, as "he said" instead of "say" in XVII, 93/95, or a nominal form used instead of a verbal, for example, XVIII, 102 where *TR* reads "do the infidels think that," but Ibn Miqsam "is the thought of the infidels that." There is a goodly number of cases of substitution between active and passive, which changes the wording but makes but little change in the meaning, for example, in XXI, 37/38 "man is created" if we read with *TR*, but "He created man" if we read with Ibn Miqsam: or "the present world is adorned" in II, 212/208 if we read with *TR*, but with Ibn Miqsam "He adorned the present world." A few readings are said to be dialectal, for example, *maysurat* instead of *maysarat* in II, 280: *qurḥ* for *qarh* in III, 140/134: *rīsh* and *riyāsh* in VII, 26/25: *judhādhan* and *jidhādhan* in XXI, 58/59.

As might be expected in the *ikhtiyār* of a famous philologer, many of the readings are on linguistic grounds preferable to those we have in the *TR*. Some cases of this sort are quite innocuous as, for example, the already mentioned reading *khaufa* for *khaufun* after *falā*, or such small points as *inniya* for *innī*; *anna ʾl-ḥamda* instead of *ani ʾl-ḥamdu* in X, 10/11, *bādiʾ* with the *hamza* instead of *bādī* in XI, 27/29, the use of pausal forms *hādi*, *wālī*, *wāqī* instead of *hādin*, *wālin*, *wāqin* in sūra XIII. Perhaps among these should be included the longer forms *ʾ-llātī* for *ʾ-llatī* in IV, 5/4, or *ḥayiya* for *ḥayya* in VIII, 42/44, or *salāsilan* in LXXVI, 4.

Others involve slight grammatical points where one can see that the philologer would regard the variant as superior to the *TR*. It would be a mistake to regard these variants as attempts to improve on the *TR*, for there was as yet no finally fixed *TR*, and we are still in the period of the *ikhtiyār*, where, since there was no established tradition as to what the original reading was, the great teachers were at liberty, within limits, to interpret the skeleton text. For example, we find *tuḍārru* instead of *tuḍārru* in II, 233, taking it as following the case of *tukallafu*: or *fiʾatin* instead of *fiʾatun* in III, 13/11, taking it as following on *fiʾatayni*, or *kulluhu* in III, 154/148, taking it as the *khabar* of *inna* where *TR* makes *lillāhi* the *khabar* and reads *kullahu* as *tawkīd* to *ʾl-amra* or a similar case in VI, 139/140 where the reading *khāliṣuhu* takes this as in apposition to *mā*, whereas the *TR* reading *khāliṣatun* makes it part of the *khabar*. The reading *bihu* instead of *bihi* in VI, 46 is on the ground that the vowel of the elision ought to be the *ḍamma* falling from the succeeding imperative and not the normal grammatical *kasra*. In IX, 70/71 *atāhum* instead of *atathum* is because the subject *rusul*, though a broken plural, yet refers to animate beings, and so ought to have a masculine form of the verb. The form with the *nūn emphaticus* in XI, 37/39 suggests a slight linguistic nuance, and the reading *yablughānni* in XVII, 23/24 is due to a feeling that the dual ought to be preserved after *biʾl-wālidayni.* Two interesting cases of a refusal of the *iḍāfa* as a point of grammatical nicety are in XVI, 59/61 and XXIX, 25/24.

In other cases the grammatical improvements involve a more radical change in interpretation of the skeleton text. In II, 210/206 the *wa quḍiya ʾl-amru* of *TR* is very awkward, and the reading *wa qaḍāʾi ʾl-amri*, following *wa ʾl-malā ʾikati* in the *jarr* case, makes a smooth and easy sentence, the decreeing being now, like the angels, part of that with which Allāh comes. Again in VII, 105/103 the *ʿalā* of the *TR* is clumsy and apparently superfluous, whereas the *ʿallayya* of Ibn Miqsam, "it is my duty," makes a much smoother reading. The change of a noun into a verb in XI, 46/48 where *TR* reads "it is a deed not right," and Ibn Miqsam "he has done what is not right," was probably the older reading, and the converse process in XIV, 19/22 (c.f. XXIV, 45/44), where he reads a participle as against the verb in *TR*, that is, "Creator of heaven and earth" instead of "He created heaven and earth," has much in its favor. In XXV, 74 and XXXII, 17 he read *qurrāt* in the plural instead of *qurrat*, and a comparison with XXVIII, 9/8 suggests that the plural is the better reading. So his reading of *thumma* for *thamma* in LXXXI, 21 avoids an awkwardness which is purely linguistic, for the meaning "there" gives a perfectly intelligible interpretation of the verse.

There are other readings, however, which are not merely points of grammatical nicety, but show a difference in understanding of how the text should be interpreted as to meaning. There are a good many of such readings, and it is of some interest to note that they do not at all support the charge made against him that he proposed all sorts of strange readings, merely on the ground that they were linguistically defensible readings of the consonantal text and without much regard to meaning. On the other hand, it is true that only such readings of his as would not greatly change the meaning of the text would be likely to have survived to us in the commentaries and later works. In XII, 45 *TR* reads *unabbi-ʾukum*, "I shall reveal to you (the interpretation)," but the reading of Ibn Miqsam was *ātīkum*, "I shall bring you." In XV, 41, if we read with *TR ʿalayya*, the meaning is "this is a way that is straight for me" (i.e., this, for me, is the straight path), but Ibn Miqsam's *ʿaliyyun* gives a meaning "this is a path exalted, straight." In II, 187/183 the *wa ʾbtaghū* of *TR* means "and desire (what Allāh has ordained for you)," but the *waʾ-ttabiʿū* of Ibn Miqsam is "and follow," which avoids the rather crudely expressed sex implication of the accepted reading. The *kathīr* and *akthar* in II, 219/216 instead of *kabīr* and *akbar*, that is, "much" instead of "great," involve no great change of meaning, but is perhaps a better reading, whereas in LVIII, 7/8 the change from *akthar* to *akbar* gives a less good reading. To read *kitāban* instead of *kātiban* in II, 283 is to understand it "and there is no written document," instead of "and there is no notary." In III, 18/16 *shuhadā'u 'llāhi* "witnesses of Allāh," instead of "Allāh hath borne witness," is a much more difficult reading, but as it comes from one of the old codices it may be the older reading. The substitution of the participle of Form VIII *mushtabih* for that of Form VI *mutashābih* in VI, 99 may have been a conscious effort to avoid *mutashābih* when this began to take on a specialized technical meaning in Qur'ānic science. A more interesting case is VII, 40/38, the famous verse about the camel going through the needle's eye, where *TR* reads "camel," but the *jummal*, in which Ibn Miqsam follows Ibn ʿAbbās, means a ship's rope. In VII, 145/142 the reading of *TR* is "I shall show you," but Ibn Miqsam "I shall cause you to inherit," that is, the abode of the evildoers. In XIII, 43 *TR* reads "and whoever has knowledge of the Book," which is difficult, because in referring to knowledge one would expect *lahu* not *ʿindahu*, and Ibn Miqsam's "and from Him comes understanding of the Book" is preferable. In XVIII, 109, the *madadan* of *TR* means "aid" or "auxiliary," but Ibn Miqsam's *midādan* is "ink," which is a reasonable understanding of the sense. In XIX, 5 Zachariah says, according to the *TR*, "I fear for the kindred after me," but Ibn Miqsam's reading means "kindred will decrease after me." The reading of *'llāh* for *ilāh* in both places in XLIII, 84, that is, the definite for the indefinite, looks like an attempt at improvement, and the change from the unusual word for "sign" *ʿilmun* in verse 61 of the same sūra, to the more usual *'alamun*, is certainly such, and so the *TR* in these cases may represent the older reading. In CXI, 4, however, *muray'atuhu* for *'mra'atuhu* may well have been original, for the diminutive of contempt suits well the whole spirit of this sūra, and was the reading in Ibn Masʿūd's Codex.

The reputation of Ibn Miqsam was that he kept to the text of the 'Uthmānic Codex, and confined his *ikhtiyār* to possible interpretations of this skeleton text, and this is borne out by the readings we have before us. Only in LV, 56 and 74 where he adds a *min* before the *qablahum*, in LIX, 10 where he reads *ghimran* instead of *ghillan*, in VII, 88/86 and 109/106 where he added a *wāw* before the *qāla*, and in XXV, 25/27 where for *nazala* he read *nanzil*, did he add anything to the consonantal text, though in this last case he had the support both of the Codex of Ubai and the Meccan Codex, while in XII, 45 his reading *ātīkum* instead of *unabbiʾukum* perhaps drops something, though he here again had the support of Ubai's Codex.

Ignace Goldziher's Olaus-Petri Lectures *Die Richtungen der islamischen Koranauslegung* opened up many problems in the investigation of the interpretation of the Qur'ān, and this study of Ibn Miqsam is but a continuation of that work in that it is an attempt to gain some picture of the state of *ikhtiyār* at the moment when official action was being taken to make it subject to the consequences of the canonization of the Seven Systems under Ibn Mujāhid.

Notes

1. See the note by Bräunlich in *ThLZ* 8 (November 1929): 531, and Massignon, *Passion d'al-Hallaj*, pp. 240–43.

2. Ibn an-Nadīm, *Fihrist*, pp. 31, 32; Ibn al-ʿImād, *Shadharāt adh-Dhahab*, II, 314; Ibn Khallikān in de Slane's translation, III, 16–18.

3. Ibn al-ʿImād, III, 16. Yāqūt, *Irshād*, V, 378 tells how the grammarian ʿAlī b. Muḥammad b. ʿUmair al-Kinānī transmitted from him the *Amālī* of Thaʿlab, so that the probabilities are that the *Majālis Thaʿlab* (or *Majālisāt Thaʿlab*), which is listed among his works, is his *riwāya* of these same *Amālī*: cf. *Fihrist*, p. 74.

4. De Slane's text, p. 703.

5. *Irshād* V, 300 quotes him for an opinion on the book of ʿAlī b. al-Mubārak al-Liḥyānī, a pupil of al-Kiṣāʾī and one of the teachers of Abū ʿUbaid al-Qāsim b. Sallām. Al-Khaṭīb, *Taʾrīkh Baghdād*, VII, 14 quotes him as authority for a certain literary matter regarding one of his other teachers, al-Ḥaddād.

6. Lists are given in the *Fihrist*, p. 33, Yāqūt's *Irshād*, VI, 501, and in as-Suyūṭī's *Bughya*, p. 36. See also Flügel, *Die grammatischen Schulen der Araber*, pp. 179, 180.

7. *Ghāyat an-Nihāya fī Ṭabaqāt al-Qurrāʾ*, II, 123–25, where he is no. 2945.

8. De Slane in his translation of Ibn Khallikān gives the name as Ibn Muqsim, but see *Tāj al-ʿArūs*, IX, 27, and Bevan's glossary to the *Naqāʾid*, p. 226.

9. As-Suyūṭī, *Bughya*, gives 354 but says that some said 353, and quotes ad-Dānī as putting it at 355. Ibn al-Athīr, *Chron.*, VIII, 418, 419, lists him under 354, as does Ibn al-ʿImād, III, 16, but in the *Fihirst*, p. 33 we have the statement that he died in 362.

10. The sole tradition recorded from him is one going back to az-Zuhrī about the Prophet entering Mecca, on the conquest of the city, wearing a *mighfar*, or metal helmet, on his head.

11. Both as-Suyūṭī and Ibn al-Jazarī quote adh-Dhahabī on the wide range of his philological learning.

12. So Yāqūt, *Irshād*, VI, 501, and as-Suyūṭī, *Bughya*, p. 36. Flügel, *Die grammatischen Schulen*, p. 180, goes quite astray over this title.

13. In the *Fihrist* this title is given as *Kitāb Infirādātihi*, and so may refer to some other subject, but the likelihood is that the title in the *Fihrist* is a mistake.

14. So as-Suyūṭī. In the *Fihrist* it is given as *Iḥtijāj al-Qirā'āt*, and Yāyūt on p. 499 calls it *al-Iḥtijāj li 'l-Qurrā'*, and on p. 501 *al-Iḥtijāj fi'l Qirā'āt.*

15. As three such books with these titles are also attributed to an-Naqqāsh (†352), it may be, as Flügel notes, that they are wrongly ascribed to Ibn Miqsam, whom one would not judge to have been particularly interested in the systems of the Seven.

16. *Radd ʿalā Ibn Miqsam fī Ikhtiyārihi*, according to the *Fihrist*, p. 63. Since Ibn Durustawaih died in 330 he must have written this *Radd* at the time of the famous process of condemnation of Ibn Miqsam.

17. He was one of the Ten, i.e., of the three beyond the Seven, whose systems almost reached the grade of canonicity. He began as a follower of the Kūfan reader Ḥamza, but came to differ from him in many places. On him see the *Fihrist*, p. 35, Ibn Qutaiba, *Maʿārif*, p. 180, and for his *ikhtiyār*, see *Ghāya*, I, 154, 274.

18. This is the famous savant Abū ʿUbaid al-Qāsim b. Sallām (†224). The *Fihrist*, p. 35, mentions his book on *Qirā'āt*, and for his *ikhtiyār* see *Ghāya*, I, 93; II, 18.

19. A Kūfan reader, †231, who had a book on *Qirā'āt* (*Fihrist*, pp. 35, 70). At first he followed the tradition of Ḥamza, but later worked out a tradition of his own, on which see as-Suyūṭī, *Bughya*, p. 45, and Ibn al-Jazarī, *Ghāya*, no. 3019.

20. This appears clearly in al-Khaṭīb's account of him (*Ta'rīkh Baghdād*, I, 280).

21. The accounts all say that Ibn Mujāhid insisted that Ibn Miqsam had been asked to produce proofs of the genuineness of the readings he followed, but had been unable to produce any proof (*ḥujjā*) either strong or weak, but this can only refer to the fact that his readings were lacking in *isnād*, that is, did not go back to any early

authority. Finally the decision was reached to leave him to Allāh, since in sūra XV, 9 Allāh promises that He Himself will care for the Qur'ān, since it was He who revealed it.

22. The date of the judgment against Ibn Miqsam is given by Ibn Miskawaihi as AH 322 (ed. Amedroz, I, 285), so that the official decision obtained by Ibn Mujāhid in favor of his Seven must have been a little earlier than that date.

23. See Yāqūt, *Irshād*, VI, 500, and Ibn Ḥajar, *Lisān al-Mīzān*, V, 131.

24. In the references to the verses quoted above the first numbers follow the standard Kūfan verse numbering as given in the Egyptian Standard Text of 1342, and the second numbers are the verse numbers of G. Flügel's edition.

4.4

Note for the Study of a "Shīʿī Qur'ān"

B. Todd Lawson

In 1936, Arthur Jeffery published his collection of the *qirā'āt* of Zayd b. ʿAlī (d. 122/740), son of the quietist Fourth Imām Zayn al-ʿĀbidīn (d. ca. 94/712) and eponym of the Zaydī sect of Shīʿī Islam. His interest in singling out these particular readings had been stimulated by three facts: (1) a codex of 'Alī was said to be in the hands of the Alid family when Ibn al-Nadīm wrote the *Fihrist*; (2) the existence of traditions in which 'Alī is made to express his unqualified approval of the text published by 'Uthmān; (3) the 'Uthmānic text was only one of many rival texts. His final opinion on the material that he had collected was that it really bore little resemblance to what could be thought of as a distinctly Shīʿī text: "a text associated with 'Alī and the *ahl al-bayt* which also had a claim to consideration." Nonetheless, he remained convinced that "one of the as yet untouched problems of the textual criticism of the Qur'ān is that of the Shī'a [*sic*] *Qirā'āt*."[1]

At the time Jeffery wrote this article, the extant literature on the subject was confined to three articles on the so-called Shīʿī suras[2] published in the *Dabistān*,[3] which had been proven forgeries, the study of Goldziher,[4] and a few remarks in the current edition of *Geschichte des Qorans*.[5] Jeffery discounted the material in *al-Kāfī*[6] as "more than suspect."[7] Unfortunately, he did not give explicit reasons for this assessment and one assumes that it merely represents the once fashionable and widespread practice of discounting, ipso facto, any dissident information coming from a recognizably Shīʿī source as so much sectarian propaganda.[8]

The judgment on such sources has, in recent years, become somewhat optimistic. The question of a distinctly Shīʿī attitude to the Qur'ān was treated at length in a series of articles which appeared in 1961–1962.[9] In 1968, an important study of Shīʿism appeared in which the specific problem of the Imāmi attitude toward the 'Uthmānic Codex was raised.[10] In 1969, Eliash revised Goldziher's conclusions.[11] The latter had thought that the Shīʿa claim that the 'Uthmānic Qur'ān is not the true Qur'ān as revealed to Muḥammad; that many verses which supported the claims of the Shīʿa had been omitted and the order of the suras altered. 'Alī possessed the complete Qur'ān, three times longer than the present text. This longer version disappeared with the Twelfth Imām. Until his return, all believers are required to follow the 'Uthmānic text.[12] From his study of the Shīʿī sources Goldziher had not taken into account, Eliash argued for the following adjustment of the above:

> The Qur'ān in the form accepted by the Sunnīs as the Holy Qur'ān revealed to the Prophet, is the same book accepted by the Imāmī-Shīʿa as the Holy Qur'ān. The Imāmī Shīʿa maintain that only the order of some of the suras as well as some of the odd verses, and not their content (except as far as differences which arose from various readings, *qirā'āt*, are concerned) was corrupted in the 'Uthmānic Codex. 'Alī and the eleven Imāms are the only ones after Muḥammad who know the right order. 'Alī's copy of the Qur'ān contained the suras and verses in their revealed order. It did not contain any additional revealed text and included 'Alī's explanatory notes. 'Alī's notes are revered by the Shīʿa to the same extent as the revealed text.[13]

Finally, Eliash stated: "It is beyond any doubt that at least as early as Kulīnī (*sic*; d. 329/940), the 'Uthmānic Codex had been accepted by the Imāmī *jurists*."[14]

In 1972, Kohlberg summarized much of the previous scholarship on the question and, in the process, drew our attention to some of the more interesting aspects of the problem.[15] Chief among these was the persistent suspicion in the writings of Shīʿī writers about the integrity of the so-called 'Uthmānic Qur'ān. He concluded his study as follows:

> [The attitude that the Qur'ān we have is corrupt[16]] seems to be the exception rather than the rule among modern Shiʿites, most of whom take a dia-

> metrically opposed view which totally rejects any doubts concerning the integrity of the Qur'ān. Their attitude is . . . that only some uncritical traditionists (*ḥashwiyya*) and the ascetists (*nussāk*) were led astray by the leaders of extreme sects in the beginning of Islam. . . . The internal discussion and dissension within the Imāmite community on the attitude to the 'Uthmānic Codex is a product of the intricate political and religious history of Shiʿism.[17]

By way of a footnote, the author hazarded the following speculation:

> It may not be entirely wrong to suppose that this insistence on the integrity of the Qur'ān and the regulation of all traditions to the contrary reflect the wish to find more common ground with Sunnite Islam. The fact is that some modern Sunnite scholars still accuse the Imamites of believing in the "omission theory."[18]

Kohlberg's final word was: "Various shades of opinion, however, persist to our own day, and we can agree with Prof. G. E. von Grunebaum that 'the Shiʿites themselves have never been able to agree on the alleged distortion of the sacred text by their adversaries.'"[19]

This conclusion may be found reproduced in the recent general work on Shīʿism by Momen.[20] In 1985, Mahmoud Ayoub raised the question of the authenticity of the present Qur'ān text according to the Shīʿa. Here it was again emphasized that the belief in the corruption of the present text is "extremist," and that the Buwayhid Shīʿī scholars had established that this belief was erroneous.[21] Just as recently, scholarship has more sharply defined a process of accommodation of belief to changing times by these tenth- and eleventh-century Shīʿī authors and that part of this accommodation involved denouncing previously held views on the corruption of the Qur'ān.[22] In what follows, I would like to ask about the contemporary Shīʿī attitude to the venerable topic of the corruption of the Qur'ān text. To do this, I would like to begin in the fourth/tenth century with the work of Kulaynī.

AL-KĀFĪ

Abū Ja'far Muḥammad b. Ya'qūb al-Kulaynī al-Rāzi al-Salsalī (d. 328/939 or 329/940) was the author of what is regarded as one of the four canonical *ḥadīth* books of the Shī'a, *al-Kāfī fī 'ilm al-dīn*.[23] This huge compendium of more than sixteen thousand reports (*akhbār*) traced to the Prophet or one of the members of the Holy Family revered by the Twelver Shī'a, was compiled over a period of twenty years. With special reference to the material in this work which upholds, either explicitly or implicitly, the deliberate alteration of the Qur'ān text by forces hostile to the claims of the Shī'a, opinion varies widely. Some authors have said that despite *Kāfī*'s enormous prestige, much of his material falls into the category of *khabar al-aḥād*, and therefore such statements are not absolutely compelling.[24]

Other views are that every *ḥadīth* in *Kāfī* is sound and trustworthy by virtue of its having been compiled during the period of the Lesser Occultation (873–939) and must have therefore had the approval of the Hidden Imām. Indeed some have referred to Kulaynī as the first deputy (*nā'ib*) of the Hidden Imām.[25] At the very minimum, therefore, the material cited below can be read with the secure knowledge that it was received by some, if not many, as trustworthy and veracious, to borrow a Sunnī term—*ṣaḥīḥ*.[26]

While all of the above-mentioned studies have referred to this work in the course of their analyses of the problem of the Shī'ī attitude toward the 'Uthmānic Codex, none has called sufficient attention to a specific type of *khabar* whose explicit and emphatic expression is thought to be worthy of notice. Several such reports may be found in a chapter of *Kāfī* titled in the edition at hand as "Various statements culled from the revelation (*tanzīl*) concerning guardianship (*walāya*)."[27] Such a chapter heading may in fact be the reason this material seems not to have been noticed previously inasmuch as there is no explicit reference to the "hot" words *taghyīr*, *taḥrīf*, *muḥarraf*, to name a few, usually associated with this subject. That the central concern of this chapter is stated to be *walāya* indicates just how important this idea is for the study of otherwise unlikely aspects of Shī'ism. In any case, containing no less than ninety-two separate reports, this is one of the more extensive chapters in the *Kitab al-ḥujja*, and all of its *akhbār* concur, in some way or another, that the present 'Uthmānic text is decidedly not the text revealed to the Prophet. For example, the next to last report in it has as its subject several verses, all of which are discussed in a conversation between the Eighth Imām and his disciple Muḥammad b. al-Fuḍayl. The exchange follows the formula of the Imām being asked about a verse, to which he replies by pointing out its original form (i.e., the standard text plus some reference to 'Alī or the *ahl al-bayt*). His questioner then seeks confirmation by asking: "Is this really Revelation (*hādhā tanzīl*)?" to which the response is always a brief and authoritative "*naʿm*."[28] Numerous other verses are discussed in this chapter which employ similarly explicit language. The type of report to which I would like to call attention is represented by the following three examples, presented here in Qur'ānic order.[29]

Example A ad 2:23[30]

[From ʿAlī b. Ibrāhīm[31] from Aḥmad b. Muḥammad al-Barqī from his father] from Muḥammad b. Sinān from ʿAmmār b. Marwān from Munakhkhal from Jābir:

> Abū Ja'far [i.e., the Fifth Imām, Muḥammad al-Bāqir, b. 57/676, d. 117/735] said:
>
> > Gabriel, upon him peace, came down with this verse to Muḥammad thus:[32] *And if you are in doubt about what we have revealed unto our servant (concerning 'Alī) then produce a sura the like thereof.*

Example B ad 2:59

From Aḥmad b. Mihrān from ʿAbd al-'Aẓīm b. ʿAbd Allāh from Muḥammad b. al-Fuḍayl from Abū Hamza from Abū Ja'far:

> Gabriel, upon him peace, came down with this verse to Muḥammad, may God bless him and his family, thus: *But those who did wrong against (the family of Muḥammad) changed the word which had been given them for*

> *another saying, and We sent down upon those who wronged (against the rightful claim of the family of Muḥammad) wrath out of heaven for their evil-doing.*[33]

Example C ad 2:90

From ʿAlī b. Ibrāhīm from Aḥmad b. Muḥammad al-Barqī from his father, from Muḥammad b. Sinān from ʿAmmār b. Marwān from Munakhkhal from Jābir from Abū Ja'far, upon him peace, he said:

> Gabriel, upon him peace, came down with this verse to Muḥammad, may God bless him and his family, thus:[34] *Evil is that for which they sell their souls: that they should disbelieve in that which God hath revealed (concerning 'Alī)*[35] *grudgingly . . .*

While these and various other examples of the Shīʿī "*qirā'āt*"[36] have been published in which the alleged omissions (indicated here by parentheses) have been noticed,[37] as far I am able to determine, the particular type of *khabar*, complete with *isnād* and *matn*, has not.[38] Surely by having the angel of revelation involved in the report we are meant to be in the presence of a unit of truth of the highest possible order, comparable to a *ḥadīth qudsī*,[39] or, as the title of this chapter plainly states, the Quranic revelation itself. The comments of Kulaynī's modern editor notwithstanding, these traditions cannot be taken as suggesting that the Shīʿī material merely "inheres" as the esoteric meaning of the verses in question. Nor, as the following will demonstrate, have these traditions been abandoned as irresponsibly promiscuous insults to the integrity of the Holy Text.

Examples A and C are related on the authority of the famous Shīʿī exegete ʿAlī b. Ibrāhīm al-Qummī (d. 307/919–920)[40] who was in fact one of Kulaynī's teachers. Qummī has apparently related this report from the Imām on the ultimate authority of Jābir b. al-Juʿfī (d. 128/745). There is of course no agreement in the sources on the reliability of Jābir.[41] It may be of some interest to note that in the published editions of Qummī's *Tafsīr*, the commentary on 2:23 is much less detailed than that which *Kāfī* repeats on his authority. There is no mention of Gabriel or 'Alī; Qummī is concerned with this verse only to gloss *rayb* as *shakk* and to identify the *shuhadā'*.[42] As for 2:59, Qummī does repeat the verse as given in the above example, but does not mention a "*nazala Jibrīl hākadhā khabar*."[43] It has not been possible to find his commentary on 2:90 in the expected place in available editions of the *Tafsīr*.

This interesting type of tradition does not figure in either of the two "authoritative" works of Shīʿī Qur'ān commentary, those of Ṭūsī (d. 460/1067) and Ṭabarsī (d. 548/1153).[44] We know, in any case, that the attitude of these authorities on the subject of the acceptability of the 'Uthmānic Codex was quite clear: it was to be accepted.[45] However, in what has been described as the third major stage in Shīʿī history,[46] we see that these traditions had remained viable, as a brief look at the following three separate works of exegesis from the Safavī period will confirm.

AL-ṢĀFĪ

This work was completed in 1664[47] by the famous student and son-in-law of the great Safavī philosopher Mullā Ṣadrā, Mullā Muḥammad b. Murtaḍā Muḥsin-i Fayḍ, known as Fayḍ al-Kāshī (d. 1091/1680). In the context of the Uṣūlī/Akhbārī debate as it was being articulated during his lifetime, Muḥsin Fayḍ was accounted among the Akhbāriyyūn.[48] He was also one of the teachers of the famous Muḥammad Bāqir Majlisī (d. 1110/1699), author of the *Biḥār al-anwār*, and the author of what is now regarded as one of the three canonical *ḥadīth* collections of later Ithnā-ʿasharī Shīʿism, *al-Wāfī*.[49] The full title of his commentary is *al-Ṣāfī fī tafsīr kalām Allāh al-wāfī*. In addition to fathering the pertinent sayings of the Prohpet and Imāms around a given verse, *Sāfī* also borrows from the very popular Sunnī commentary by Bayḍawī (d. 685/1286), *Anwār al-tanzīl*.

There seems to be no consensus on how to characterize Muḥsin Fayḍ's position in the *taḥrīf* debate. In this regard, some refer to him (together with Muḥammad Bāqir Majlisī) as an extremist,[50] while others call him a moderate.[51] And *Ṣāfī* is apparently sufficiently ambiguous on the question to enable another author to cite it in support of his own argument that the Shīʿa do not hold that the present Qur'ān is somehow defective.[52] *Ṣāfī* is introduced with twelve "prologues" (*muqaddamāt*), which contain the basic presuppositions informing the work.[53] The most extensive of these prologues is titled: "Concerning those traditions about the collection of the Qur'ān, its corruption, its augmentation and its diminution, and the explanation of this."[54]

Ayoub points out that Muḥsin Fayḍ claimed that the first transmitters of the exegetic tradition were limited in what they related by *taqiyya* ("pious dissimulation"), with the result that much of the true tradition might have been lost. "This, of course, left great scope for new ideas in *tafsīr* in the name of recovering the tradition."[55] One of the relevant passages in *Ṣāfī* is:

> The Qur'ān which is in our hands is not the entire Qur'ān sent down by God to Muḥammad. Rather, there is in it that which contradicts that which God had sent down. There is, moreover, in it that which was altered and changed. There were many things deleted from it, such as the name of 'Alī in many places and the phrase *Āl Muḥammad* (the family of Muḥammad), as well as the names of the "hypocrites," where they occur. . . . The Qur'ān, furthermore, was not arranged in accordance with the pleasure of God and his apostle.[56]

Later, however, Muḥsin Fayḍ appears to soften this position somewhat. This is explained by Ayoub as follows: Muḥsin Fayḍ was bound by tradition, as represented by such venerated Shī'ī scholars as Ṭūsī and Ṭabarsī who had insisted on the authenticity of the text. Ayoub explains, paraphrasing *Ṣāfī*:

> The Qur'ān as it now stands is the word of God which, if interpreted correctly, contains all that the community now needs in the way of legal sanctions and prohibitions, as well as the necessary proofs of the Imams' high office as its guardians and sole authorities on its exegesis. The Qur'ān which is in our hands must, [Muḥsin Fayḍ] argues, be followed during the occultation (*ghayba*) of the Twelfth Imām. It must be assumed that the true Qur'ān is with him.[57]

In light of these rather strong and undisguised statements, it is somewhat surprising that in his commentary for 2:23, Muḥsin Fayḍ does quote *Kāfī*, but not the *khabar* which is of interest here. Rather, it is a different tradition completely from the Seventh Imām, Mūsā al-Kāẓim (d. 183/799). The purpose is merely to identify those to whom the verse was addressed. No mention is made of an alternate reading, whether through *taḥrīf*, *tabdīl*, or any other process, let alone the one quoted above in which Gabriel is said to have brought the verse down as explicitly mentioning 'Alī.[58] In his commentary at 2:59, however, we find Muḥsin Fayḍ quoting the "*nazala Jibrīl*" *khabar* from al-Bāqir but *not* from *Kāfī*. He quotes directly from another great early master of Shīʿī commentary, Abū al-Nasr Muḥammad b. Masʿūd b. ʿAyyāsh al-Sulamī al-Samarqandī, known most widely as ʿAyyāshī (d. ca. late ninth/early tenth century CE).[59] Although the verse is given a typically Shīʿī interpretation, in his commentary for 2:90 we find neither mention of *taḥrīf* nor of the *khabar* quoted asbove from *Kāfī*.[60]

Nūr al-Thaqalayn

This work[61] was written by ʿAbd 'Alī al-Ḥuwayzī (d. 1112/1700), *Kitāb tafsīr nūr al-thaqalayn* (*Nūr*). Not much is known about his life, but as indicated by his *nisba*, he was from the small town of Ḥuwayza (the old headquarters of the Mushaʿshaʿ movement), near Aḥwāz in southwest Iran. His work contains none of the introductory material found in *Ṣāfī*; rather, it begins after a few words of doxology in veneration of the Prophet and the Imāms, with a discussion of the *Fātiḥa* by way of pertinent *ḥadīths*. The only known edition was edited by Hāshim al-Rasūlī al-Maḥallātī (the editor of ʿAyyāshī's *tafsīr*) and printed in Qum during the years 1963–1965. This edition is based on three manuscripts of varying completeness.[62] A preface by the highly regarded Shīʿī scholar Muḥammad Ḥusayn al-Ṭabāṭabāʾī refers to this commentary as "one of the best . . . if not the best" work of its kind.[63] The author of *Dharīʿa* complains about the *tafsīr*'s lack of organization,[64] and discusses briefly the history of its composition, stating that it was completed in 1656.[65] This indicates that the work was probably extant while Muḥsin Fayḍ was writing *Ṣāfī*, but it appears to have been unknown to him.

In the edition at hand, Quranic materials is set off from the text in bold type. Qur'ān 2:23 is mentioned solely in the above-mentioned *khabar*, introducing it only with *ʿan Jābir qāla*: . . .[66] The editor has made no attempt to distinguish the "Shīʿī" content of the report through the use of parentheses, or any other device. Indeed, the *fī ʿAlī* appears to be a natural part of the verse. This procedure is followed for the remaining two verses, both of which are introduced as coming from *Kāfī*.[67] The difference between the way our edition of *Kāfī* nad our edition of *Nūr* use this material is of course striking. Neither Ḥuwayzī, the author, nor Maḥallātī, the editor, has made any effort to explain away what might appear a troublesome *khabar*.

AL-BURHĀN

The title of this work is *Kitāb al-burhān fī tafsīr al-Qur'ān* (*Burhān*).[68] The author, al-Baḥrānī (d. 1107/1695 or 1109/1697, his date of birth is unknown), was born in a village in one of the districts of Baḥrayn. He is said to have been a compiler of *ḥadīth*s, comparable in his efforts only to Majlisī himself. He is also said to have written seventy-five works, mostly dealing with religious sciences.[69] The *Tafsīr* was written sometime during the reign of the Safavid Shāh Sulaymān or al-Ṣāfī (r. 1077/1666–1106/1694). The commentary contains introductory material similar to *Ṣāfī*, and, in addition to other *akhbār* which are not found in *Ṣāfī*, carries many of the same traditions which are adduced at corresponding verses in the more famous *tafsīr*.

For each verse or group of verses, the author lists a series of pertinent *akhbār* from the Prophet or the Imāms.[70] It begins with a number of reports against *tafsīr biʾl-raʾy*, and other reports which assert that only the Prophet and the Imāms were able to interpret the Qur'ān. "God taught the Prophet the literal text (*tanzīl*) and He taught ʿAlī its interpretation (*taʾwīl*)."[71] The author of this work laments that not withstanding such a statement, he finds the people of his time persistent in interpreting the Qur'ān without referring to the Imāms, and cites the works of Zamakhsharī (d. 539/1144) and Bayḍawī (d. 685/1286) as examples.[72]

In any case, Baḥrānī (or his editor) makes no attempt at setting off the Shīʿī material from verse 2:23, which is cited, complete with *isnād*, as it is found in *Kāfī*.[73] Baḥrānī treats 2:59 as part of a Quranic exegetical unit which includes all of the verses 2:58–62. In explanation of this unit, eleven *akhbār* of varying lengths are quoted, the second of which is our example B above.[74] Here, as was the case with *Nūr*, the Shīʿī material is reproduced as being an integral part of the text. In addition, the fifth *khabar* carries a similar reading, but through a different *isnād*: *ʿan Zayd al-Shihām ʿan Safwān, ʿan Abī Jaʿfar*.[75] To explain the final verse, 2:90,[76] Baḥrānī has brought forth three *akhbār*, the first one is the same one quoted by Muḥsin Fayḍ, the second is the one mentioned in *Kāfī*, and the third presents an interesting variant in the way opposition to the ʿUthmānic Codex may be expressed:

> ʿAyyāshī said Abū Jaʿfar, upon him peace, said this verse came down upon the Messenger of God, may God bless him and give him peace, thus: "EVIL IS THAT FOR WHICH THEY SOLD THEIR SOULS THAT THEY DISBELIEVE IN THAT WHICH GOD HATH REVEALED CONCERNING ʿALĪ GRUDGINGLY" and God said CONCERNING ʿALĪ, upon him peace. "GOD SENDS DOWN OF HIS BOUNTY UPON WHOM HE WILL OF HIS SERVANTS" that is ʿAlī (*yaʿnī ʿAlī*) God said "THEY HAVE INCURRED ANGER UPON ANGER" that is the Banī Umayya "FOR DISBELIEVERS A SHAMEFUL DOOM."[77]

CONCLUSION

Why Muḥsin Fayḍ would have been so selective in his use of such material is open to speculation. That it was selectivity, and not mere ignorance of the material in *Kāfī*, is confirmed by reference to the two other late Safavī works of *Tafsīr*, both of which employ these *akhbār*. If an edition of *Kāfī* containing such material was known to other authors who were, for all practical purposes, contemporaries of Muḥsin Fayḍ, it would most certainly have been known to Muḥsin Fayḍ. Whatever his reasons, it is clear that these commentators felt that such traditions had sufficient merit that they took the trouble to reproduce them in their works. It may also be conjectured that such material has continued to be looked upon as in some way edifying, inasmuch as all three commentaries have been published in recent editions,[78] in which there seems to be no attempt to "explain away" the explicit language of these *akhbār*. It is also worth mentioning that such "explosive" material continued to be reproduced during the three centuries which intervened between the original composition of these commentaries and their recent publication over the last thirty years. Not only was an edition of *Ṣāfī* published in lithograph in Tabrīz in 1869, but these traditions are found quoted in a manuscript *tafsīr* which was probably written shortly before 1844, by ʿAlī Muḥammad Shīrāzī, known as the Bāb.[79] The likelihood that such *akhbār* were known and regarded with a measure of respect by a large segment of the Shīʿī population at this time is strengthened by the fact that the Bāb did not come from a typical scholastic background, but was a member of the merchant class.[80]

The question that arises, therefore, is one partly answered by Kohlberg and others, namely: What is the Imāmi Shīʿī attitude to the *taḥrīf al-Qur'ān* problem? The answer thus far has been that the majority of Shīʿites hold that the Qur'ān we now have is the integral Qur'ān as communicated to the prophet Muḥammad. But it seems that Kohlberg based this conclusion mainly on the statement of one Hibat al-Din al-Shahrastānī, and the arguments of Ayatu'llah al-Khūʿī.[81] It is interesting to note that Khūʿī, who is one of the, if not *the*, leading *marjaʿ* of the Imāmi Shīʿī and is currently under house arrest in Iran,[82] quotes Muḥsin Fayḍ to support his position, but the work he cites is *al-Wāfī*, not the *tafsīr*.[83]

The question remains as to how representative such statements really are. The continued reproduction of these ʿ*nazala Jibrīl . . . hākadhā akhbār* would appear to support one of the conclusions of a recent study of the history of the Uṣūlī/Akhbārī dispute in Shīʿism which says that the writing of men like Mufīd, Murtaḍā, and Ṭūsī, whom Uṣūlīs regard as the fathers of their school, and all of whom argued strenuously in their works for the acceptance of the 'Uthmānic Codex, represents an accommodation to changing historical religio-political conditions.[84] It is suggested that this analysis will continue to be borne out with the continued study of Shīʿism, particularly in the little-known period between the thirteenth and sixteenth centuries.

Of course, it has already been recognized that the position on the *taḥrīf* question was conditioned by historical circumstances.[85] It is important to acknowledge, however, that the continued publication of these *akhbār* suggests that certain issues of the Uṣūlī/Akhbārī argument are still being debated. One of the things called for, therefore, is an in-depth, diachronic study of all the various commentaries on this section of *al-Kāfī*. In the meantime, it seems that it may not be entirely accurate to state that the Shīʿa have never been able to agree amongst themselves on the status of the Qur'ān. Rather, a more accurate characterization suggests itself: that the Shīʿa view the Qur'ān as being simultaneously flawed and inerrant—inerrant for the purposes of *fiqh* but deficient as an explicit guide to the recognition of the locus and bearer of *walāya*.

NOTES

1. Arthur Jeffery, "The Qur'ān Readings of Zaid b. 'Alī," *Rivista degli Studi Orientali* 16 (1936): 249–89. [This is reprinted as section 4.1 of the present volume.]

2. Garcin De Tassy, "Chapitre inconnu du Coran," *Journal asiatique* 13 (1842): 431–39; Mirzā Kazembeg, "Observations sur Chapitre inconnu du Coran," *Journal asiatique* 14 (1843): 371–429; W. St. Clair Tisdall, "Shīʿah Additions to the Koran," *Muslim World* 3 (1913): 227–41.

3. Muhsin Fānī (ascribed), *Dabistān-i Madhāhib*, 3 vols. English edition translated by David Shea and Anthony Troyer, Paris 1843 [see the more recent abridged edition published by Washington & London (Walter M. Dunne: Washington & London 1901), pp. 329–31].

4. Ignaz Goldziher, *Die Richtungen der Islamischen Koranauslegung* (Leiden: Brill, 1952 [first published 1920]), pp. 263–309.

5. See now Theoḍor Nöldeke et al., *Geschichte des Qorāns* (Hildesheim: Georg Olms, 1961), pp. 93–112.

6. Kulaynī, *al-Uṣūl min al-kāfi*, one of the four books accepted as having canonical status by the Shīʿa. It occupies the same place of authority for the Shīʿa as the *Ṣaḥīḥayn* of Bukhārī and Muslim do for Sunnī Muslims.

7. Jeffery, p. 250.

8. On Shīʿī *tafsīr* specifically: "Nöldeke charakterisiert sie nicht mit Unrecht als elendes Gewebe von Lügen und Dummheit." Goldziher, p. 309 citing *GdesQ*, p. xxix.

9. Daud Rahbar, "The Relation of Shīʿa Theology to the Qur'ān," *Muslim World*, 51 (1961): 92–98, 211–16; 52 (1962): 17–21, 124–28.

10. Abdoljavad Falaturi, "Die Zwölfer-Schia aus der Sicht eines Schiiten: Probleme ihrer Untersuchung," in *Festschrift Werner Caskel* (Leiden, 1968), pp. 62–95 (see esp. pp. 91–95).

11. Joseph Eliash, "The Shiʿite Qur'ān: A Reconsideration of Goldziher's Interpretation," *Arabica* 16 (1969): 15–24.

12. As summarized in ibid., pp. 15–16.

13. Ibid., p. 24.

14. Ibid. Italics added.

15. Kohlberg, "Some Notes on the Imāmī Attitude to the Qur'ān," *Islamic Philosophy and the Classical Tradition: Essays presented to R. Walzer*, ed. S. M. Stern, A. Hourani, and Y. Brown (Oxford: Cassirer, 1972), pp. 209–24.

16. The most recent representative of this view mentioned by Kohlberg is Ḥusayn b. Muḥammad Taqī al-Nūrī al-Ṭabarsī (d. 1320/1902), *Faṣl al-khiṭāb fī ithbāt taḥrīf kitāb rabb al-ārbāb*, n.p., 1298.

Al-Nūrī al-Ṭabarsī, who is better known for his *Mustadrak al-wasā'il*, held that Ibn Babāwayh (d. 381/991), Murtaḍā (d. 436/1044), and Ṭūsī (d. 460/1067), who figure among Eliash's jurists, are in the minority in their opposition to *taḥrīf*. He rejected al-Mufīd's equation of Qur'ān with *tafsīr* on grounds of inconsistency and argued, with Murtaḍā al-Ansārī (d.1281/1864, the sole *marjaʿ al-taqlīd* of the Shīʿī world from 1266/1850) "that the corruption of the Qur'ān does not imply that one should not follow its apparent (*zāhir*) meaning . . . especially in the sections dealing with practical religious duties . . . since there is no general knowledge that the apparent meaning was affected by the corruption." Further:

> In three introductory sections he attempts to prove that since the Gospels were corrupted, it is not impossible that the same fate should have befallen the Qur'ān. He also maintains that 'Alī had a copy of the Qur'ān which included additional material that was neither a "divine tradition" (*ḥadīth qudsī*) nor a commentary (*tafsīr*) . . . and hence must be regarded as having formed part of the original revelation. . . . [He] defines *taḥrīf* as "abandoning and omitting parts of the revelation" and says that most Imamites accepted the theory of *taḥrīf* thus defined. Ibn Babawayh (al-Ṣadūq) was "the first who introduced (*aḥdatha*) this opinion (i.e., the denial of *taḥrīf*) into the Shīʿa," and the implied accusation is that he was guilty of heretical innovation. (Kohlberg, p. 218)

17. Kohlberg refers to one Hibat al-Din al-Shahrastānī and the better known as-Khū'ī (on whom see below) as representative of "most modern Shīʿites," pp. 218–19.

18. See Kohlberg, p. 223 for the books by the Sunnī authors referred to. In this connection, it is worth noting that the modern edition of Ṭabarsī's *tafsīr* (see below), which argues against the falsification theory, was published by the *Dār al-taqrīb al-madhāhib al-islāmīya* (Centre for the reconciliation of the various sects of Islam)

and contains an introduction by Maḥmūd Shaltūt, erstwhile ecumenist Shaykh of Al-Azhar.

19. Kohlberg, p. 219 citing G. E. von Grunebaume, *Islam: Essays in the Nature and Growth of a Cultural Tradition* (London, 1955), p. 80.

20. Moojan Momen, *An Introduction to Shiʿi Islam: The History and Doctrines of Twelver Shiʿism* (Oxford: George Ronald, 1985), pp. 172–73:

> There is . . . considerable evidence that the early Shiʿa did not accept the standard text of the Qur'ān. Even as late as the time of Shakyh al-Mufīd [d. 413/1022], there was considerable discussion among the Shiʿa as to what had been omitted from the Qur'ān by the enemies of 'Ali, although by that time there was a consensus that nothing had been added. In other words, it was felt that although the standard text of the Qur'ān represented God's word with no human additions, part of the text extolling 'Ali and pointing to his Imamate had been excised by his enemies.
>
> Although most Shiʿis eventually took the view that nothing had been omitted or added to the Qur'ān, traces of the earlier view are enshrined among some of the *ḥadīth* and are even reproduced in some of the later books.

21. Mahmoud Ayouob, "The Speaking Qur'ān and the Silent Qur'ān," *Approaches to the History of the Interpretation of the Qur'ān*, ed. Andrew Rippin (Oxford: Clarendon Press, 1988), pp. 182 and 185.

22. Andrew Joseph Newman, *The Development and Political Significance of the Rationalist (usūlī) and the Traditionalist (akhbārī) Schools in Imāmī Shīʿī History from the Third/Ninth to the Tenth/Sixteenth Century A.D.*. 2 pts. in 2 vols. (Ann Arbor: UMI, 1988 [PhD UCLA 1986]). Pt. 1: pp. 39, 217–18, 409–12.

Kohlberg also draws attention to "al-Mufīd's careful formulations" which are in fact full of conditionals quite out of character with the rest of the book and supports the view that Ṭūsī was forced to express such views in order to conceal his true beliefs by saying that Ṭūsī "lived to witness the downfall of the Buwayhids and the resurgence of anti-Shiʿite sentiments . . . [and] was personally affected by these events: his house was burnt down and he had to flee Baghdad and spend the remaining twelve years of his life in exile in Najaf." Kohlberg, pp. 216 and 223 n. 92.

23. In what follows, reference is restricted to the first two volumes of this work: *al-Usūl min al-kāfī*. 2 vols. (Tehran: Dār al-Katub al-Islāmīya, 1374/1954). The other three works are *Man lā yaḥduruhu al-faqīh* by Ibn Babāwayh (d. 381/991); *Tahdhīb al-aḥkām* and *al-Istibṣār* by Ṭūsī (d. 460/1070).

24. So Murtaḍā (d. 436/1046) who "went further than many *mujtahidūn* by claiming that a tradition which is translated on the authority of a single person . . . cannot be cited as legal proof" (Kohlberg, p. 222 n. 70), and Majlisī (d. 1110/1700), ibid., p. 218. On the polemic revolving around the use of *akhbār al-aḥād*, see Newman, 1:42–49. See also "*Khabar al-wāḥid*," in the second edition of *The Encyclopedia of Islam* (*EI*²) and now Norman Calder, "Doubt and Prerogative: The emergence of an Imāmī Shīʿī theory of jurisprudence," *Studia Islamica* 70 (1989): 57–78. For other aspects of *ḥadīth* criticism in connection with this subject, see Kohlberg, p. 219.

25. Newman, pp. 47–49. Here Majlisi is quoted as saying that all *akhbār* in *Kāfī* and *Faqīh* are *ṣaḥīḥ*. Al-Qazwīnī is cited (from Khwānsārī) as saying that all *akhbār* in *Kāfī* are correct because they had been accepted by the Hidden Imām inasmuch as Kulayni had compiled the collection during the lesser occultation and that "*rawī*" in *Kāfī* refers to the Imām himself, while *ʿalim* refers to one of his deputies.

26. Or, as Kohlberg, p. 219: "The traditions, even if mostly forged, which implied that deliberate omissions had occurred grew out of the deep frustration and reflect widely held views among the Imamites."

27. *Bāb fīhi nukat wa nutaf min al-tanzīl fī ʾl-walāya: Kāfī*, 1:412–32. See ibid., p. 433 for the following chapter with the parallel title: *Bāb fīhi nukat wa nutaf min al-riwāya fī ʾl-walāya.*

28. *Kāfī*, 1:432–35, #91. See the varying definitions of *tanzīl* in the literature.

29. *Kāfī*, 1:417 cites examples A and C (nos. 26 and 25) in reversed order.

30. "Egyptian" verse numbers are used here; the editor of *Kāfī* refers to this verse as 2:21, the following as 2:56, and the last as 2:84.

31. Al-Qummī (d. 307/919–920), the author of one of the earliest Shīʿī works of *tafsīr*, a teacher, and frequent source of Kulaynī.

32. *Kāfī*, 1:417: *Nazala Jibrīl ʿalayhi al-salām ʿalā Muḥammad* [*sic*] *hākadhā.*

33. *Kāfī*, 1:423, #58. Cf. ibid., #57.

34. *Kāfī*, 1:417: *Nazala Jibril ʿalayhi al-salām bi-hādhihi ʾl-āya ʿalā Muḥammad ṣalā Allāh ʿalayhi wa-ālihi hākadhā.*

35. The parentheses are in the printed text to which the editor has commented as follows: *yaʿnī bi-hādhā ʾl-maʿnā nuzilat*, arguing that this was merely the esoteric meaning of this verse, but for the other two examples he adds only the sura and verse numbers. It is not clear whether we are supposed to understand the other statements as also representing only the esoteric understanding of the verses. This recalls the debate about whether the *muṣḥaf* of ʿAlī contained verses which were actually different from the ʿUthmānic Codex, or was valued by the Shīʿī community only for the First Imām's exegesis which it contained in the margins.

36. Classification of such verses as *qirāʾāt* (rather than, say, *muḥarrafāt*) may have served to defuse the whole controversy within a milieu in which variant readings were "tolerated."

37. Kohlberg, pp. 211–12 summarizes the introduction to the *Tafsīr al-Qummī* in which these and other alterations of the text are mentioned, but without the introductory *isnād* or mention of Gabriel.

38. Kohlberg, "An Unusual Shīʿī isnād," *Israel Oriental Studies* 5 (1975): 144–45 mentions a similar report in which Gabriel figures. But this report has nothing to do with the explicit text of the Qur'ān.

39. As already mentioned, al-Nūri al-Ṭabarsī (d. 1320/1902) is quite explicit about such a comparison claiming that 'Alī had a Qur'ān which contained material that was neither *aḥadīth qudsī* nor *tafsīr*, but rather revelation.

40. Not "the second half of the fourth/tenth century" as in Kohlberg, p. 211.

41. On Jābir especially see Kohlberg, "Unusual," p. 144, n. 13.

42. *Tafsīr al-Qummī* (Tabrīz 1315/1897), pp. 18–19.

43. E.g.: *wa qāla allāh: fabaddala ʿl-ladhīna ẓalamū ʿalā Muḥammad ḥaqqahum qawlan . . . Qummī*, p. 25. The *Tafsīr* of the Eleventh Imām, al-Ḥasan al-ʿAskarī (b. 232/846, d. 260/873), printed on the margin of this edition of Qummī, makes no mention of these reports in the appropriate places, or, as far as has been determined, elsewhere in the commentary.

44. Abū Ja'far Muḥammad b. Ḥasan, al-Tūsī, *al-Tibyān fī tafsīr al-Qur'ān*, introduction by Aghā Buzurg al-Tihrānī (Najaf, Maṭbaʿat al-ʿIlmiya, 1376–1383/1957–1963); Abū 'Alī, al-Ṭabarsī, *Majmaʿ al-bayān fī tafsīr al-Qur'ān* (Cairo: Dār al-taqrīb al-madhāhib al-Islāmīya, 1377/1957); for 2:23 see 1:118–22; 2:59, 1:235–36; 2:90, 315–18. In discussing these verses Ṭabarsī, for example, would rather quote material from such authorities as Abū ʿUbayda, Mujāhid, and Qatada than from Qummī or the Imāms.

45. Eliash, p. 21; we would not agree that Kulaynī be included in the statement here: "it becomes clear that Kulīnī [*sic*] and other Imāmī jurists . . . do not claim deliberate corruption of the contents of the 'Uthmānic Codex"; see also Kohlberg, p. 217.

46. Ayoub, p. 185.

47. Goldziher, p. 278.

48. We are advised, however, to avoid the common equivalence Akhbārī/literalist. See Henry Corbin, *En Islam iranien: Aspects spirituels et philosophiques*, 4 vols. (Paris: Gallimard, 1971–1972), 4:250.

49. The other two are *Wasāʾil al-shīʿa* by al-Ḥurr al-ʿĀmilī (d. 1104/1692) and *Biḥār al-anwār* by Muḥammad Bāqir Majlisī (d. 1110/1699).

50. Ayoub, p. 182.

51. Newman, 1:42.

52. Maulvi Muḥammad Ali, *The Holy Qur'ān* (Lahore 1935), pp. xci–xcii.

53. *Ṣāfī*, 1:15–78.

54. *Ṣāfī*, 1:40–55.

55. Ayoub, p. 186.

56. Translated in ibid., p. 190; cf. *Ṣāfī*, 1:49.

57. Ayoub, p. 190; cf. *Ṣāfī*, 1:55.

58. *Ṣāfī*, 1:102.

59. Died late third/ninth early tenth century; he was a contemporary of al-Qummī who converted from Sunnism to Shīʿism. His commentary, much of which is collected from such sources as *Ṣāfī*, the two Safavī commentaries referred to below, and *Biḥār al-anwār*, is published as: *Tafsīr ʿAyyāshī*, 2 vols. in 1, ed. Hāshim al-Rasūlī al-Maḥallātī (Qum 1380/1960).

60. *Ṣāfī*, 1:162–63.

61. ʿAbd 'Alī al-Ḥuwayzī, *Kitāb tafsīr nūr al-thaqalayn*, 5 vols., ed. Hāshim al-Rasūlī al-Maḥallātī (Qum: Maṭbaʿat al-Ḥikma, 1383–1385/1963–1965) (*Nūr*).

62. *Nūr*, 1:iv and 5:ii.

63. *Nūr*, 1:iii. ʿAllāma Sayyid Muḥammad Husayn al-Ṭabāṭabāʾī also wrote a brief introduction to *Tafsīr ʿAyyāshī* and is the author of *al-Mīzān fī tafsīr al-Qur'ān*, the first several volumes of which have appeared in English: *al-Mīzān: An Exegesis of the Qur'ān*, trans. Sayyid Saeed Akhtar Rizvi (Tehran: World Organization for Islamic Services, 1404/1984).

64. Muḥammad Muḥsin, Āghā Buzurg Ṭihrānī, *Al-Dharīʿa ilā taṣānif al-shīʿa*, 25 vols. (Tehran and Najaf: n.p., 1355/1936–1398/1978) (*Dharīʿa*), 24:345, #1967.

65. Ibid.

66. *Nūr*, 1:36, #55.

67. For 2:59 see *Nūr*, 1:70, #214; for 2:90, *Nūr*, 1:86, #286. It should be mentioned that while other *akhbār* are adduced for 2:59 and 2:90, 2:23 is carried in the single report, although other statements are brought forth to identify some of the features in it which are also common to other verses.

68. Al-Sayyid Hāshim al-Baḥrānī, *Kitāb al-burhān fī tafsīr al-Qur'ān*, 4 vols. (Tehran: Chāpkhānah Āftāb 1375/1955) (*Burhān*).

69. For a list of forty-three of these works see *Burhān*, 4:555–59. All that is known of his life is found in 4:555 where the editor has summarized the information on his biography from the *Luʾluʾat al-Baḥrayn* by Yūsuf al-Baḥrānī, apparently the only work which deals with this subject. It mentiones nothing of his early life or edu-

cation. Information about his writings is taken from *Dharīʿa*, 1:111. On this work specifically see ibid., 3:93, #294, where it is compared with a number of other works, some in manuscript, and others, like the *Tafsīr nūr al-thaqalayn.*

70. *Burhān*, 1:2–40.

71. Ibid., 1:3.

72. Ibid.

73. Ibid., 1:70, #3.

74. Ibid., 1:104, #2.

75. Ibid., 1:104, #5; this report does not employ the adverb *hākadhā.*

76. Strangely misnumbered as "33."

77. *Burhān*, 1:139, #3.

78. Another similar work is Abū al-Ḥasan al-Isfahānī, *Tafsīr mir'āt al-anwār wa mishkat al-asrār* (Tehran 1374/1954). On the gnostic dimension of such commentaries (including those of Baḥrānī and Isfahānī) see Corbin, in *Encylopedia of Islam*, 2nd. ed., 1:135–218 and 3:214–32.

79. Cambridge, Browne Collection, F 10, 33b; 72a; 87a. On this and other of the Bāb's commentaries see B. Todd Lawson, "The Qur'ān Commentary of Sayyid ʿAlī Muḥammad Shīrāzī, the Bāb," unpublished Ph.D. thesis. McGill University, 1987.

80. On the Bāb and the rise of the Bābī movement see now Abbas Amanat, *Resurrection and Renewal: The Making of the Babi Movement in Iran, 1844–1850* (Ithaca & London: Cornell University Press, 1989).

81. Kohlberg, pp. 218–19 and references.

82. Moojan Momen, *An Introduction to Shīʿī Islam*, p. 262; here Momen also says that Khūʿī opposed Khomeinī's early political activity.

83. *Al-Bayān fī tafsīr al-Qur'ān* (Beirut: Dār al-Zahrā, 1401/1980), p. 223. Khūʿī (2nd ed. Najaf 1966), pp. 215–54. Ayoub, p. 10 also singles out al-Khūʿī's position on the *taḥrīf* question but does not claim that this statement represents a Shīʿī consensus.

84. "Together these developments in doctrine and practice represented a significant alteraction, and, in some cases, an outright reversal of the dominant, Imāmī *akhbāriyya* generally anti-rationalist, individual-priented, non-authoritarian and anti-accommodationist tendencies as represented in both *al-Kāfī* and [*Man lā yaḥḍuruhu*] *al-Faqīh* [by al-Ṣadūq, Ibn Babāwayh]." Newman, 1:196.

85. Kohlberg, p. 219.

4.5

Variant Readings and Additions of the Imāmī-Šīʿa to the Quran[1]

Meir M. Bar-Asher

1. Preliminary Observations

In his groundbreaking book *Die Richtungen der islamischen Koranauslegung*, I. Goldziher delineated in detail the importance of variant readings (*qirāʾāt*) to the canonical codex of the Quran found in Muslim exegetical works on the Quran in general[2] and in Imāmī-Šīʿī exegesis in particular.[3] In this book as well as in later studies (such as those of J. Eliash,[4] E. Kohlberg,[5] and M. Ayoub[6]) examples are adduced of Quranic verses for which the Šīʿa presented alternative and unique variant readings. However, as far as I know, to date no comprehensive attempt has been made to collect all these Šīʿī variants in a single corpus. It is the aim of this article partially to fill this gap. This should prove useful both for scholars interested in the Quranic text and for those dealing with Quran exegesis in general and sectarian exegesis in particular. The list published here complements the thorough and important study of A. Jeffery, *Materials for the History of the Text of the Qurʾān*. Jeffery's study contains variant readings to the canonical text of the Quran collected from various sources, mostly of Sunnī origin; Šīʿī readings were for the most part ignored.

The article is divided into two parts. The first (sections 2–6) is devoted to a discussion of several underlying principles guiding the Imāmī-Šīʿī variant readings to the canonical text of the Quran: the nature of the variants, their status vis-à-vis the canonical text, and so on. The second part includes a list of the Šīʿī variant readings. This list is presented in the form of a synoptic table: the canonical verse is given on one side of the page while the Imāmī-Šīʿī variant reading is presented on the other. Each Šīʿī variant is followed by a citation of the sources where it is found, references to modern literature where the text is discussed, and brief notes explaining the doctrine behind the Imāmī-Šīʿī version.

It should be stressed here that this list includes only variants which have a specific Šīʿī character. Other variant readings found in Šīʿī Quranic commentaries are not included.[7]

The sources from which the variant readings and additions were collected are first and foremost those early Imāmī-Šīʿī Quran commentaries which have come down to us. These include in the first place the works of ʿAlī b. Ibrāhīm al-Qummī, Furāt b. Furāt b. Ibrāhīm al-Kūfī, Abū al-Naḍr Muḥammad b. Masʿūd al-ʿAyyāšī (all three flourished at the turn of the 3rd/9th century); Muḥammad b. Ibrāhīm b. Ǧaʿfar al-Nuʿmānī (d. ca. 360/971);[8] Abū Ǧaʿfar al-Tūsī (d. 460/1067), one of the greatest Imāmī scholars at the close of the Buwayhid period; and Abū ʿAlī al-Faḍl b. al-Ḥasan al-Ṭabrisī (d. 548/1153). In addition, other early nonexegetical Imāmī writings, which nevertheless include much exegetical material, were also used. Of these, special note should be made of *Baṣāʾir al-daraǧāt* by Muḥammad b. al-Ḥasan al-Ṣaffār al-Qummī (d. 290/903) and *al-Kāfī* by Abū Ǧaʿfar Muḥammad b. Yaʿqūb al-Kūlīnī (d. 329/941). Finally, later Imāmī works were also consulted, including exegetical writings such as *Tafsīr al-Burhān* by Hāšim al-Baḥrānī (d. 1107/1693 or 1109/1697) and *Tafsīr al-Ṣāfī* by Muḥammad b. Murtaḍā ("Muḥsin al-Fayḍ") al-Kāšānī (d. 1091/1680), and compilations of which the most important is *Biḥār al-anwār* by Muḥammad Bāqir al-Maǧlisī (d. 1110/1700).

The main Sunnī sources consulted for purpose of comparison are the most important exegetical commentaries on the Quran. These were supplemented by reference to Jeffery's book mentioned above. It should be emphasized that this comparison showed that typical Šīʿī variant readings to the text were only very rarely quoted by non-Šīʿīs.[9]

2. The Different Forms of Variant Readings or Additions

Until the mid-fourth/tenth century, most Imāmī-Šīʿī scholars held the view of the incompleteness of the Quran. One of the chief forms in which the Imāmī-Šīʿa voiced its disapproval of the canonical text of the Quran was to point out an alternative version to several dozen verses in it. The text held sacred by most Muslims, that is, that designated *Muṣḥaf ʿUṯmān* ("the 'Uthmanic Codex"—named after the caliph ʿUṯmān b. ʿAffān [d. 35/656], to whom Muslim tradition assigns its editing), is viewed by the Šīʿa as tendentious and decidedly anti-Šīʿī. This caliph and his associates, as claimed by the Šīʿa, were bent on eliminating from the canonical text as revealed to the Prophet Muḥammad all traces of Šīʿī legitimacy, that is, all references to the family of the Prophet (*ahl al-bayt*) and his heirs, the Šīʿī Imams; to the Šīʿī supremacy over the Islamic nation; and to certain Šīʿī doctrines. Revealing the "original" text is, in the eyes of the Šīʿa, a step in the direction of correcting the falsifications thus created.

Before introducing the different types of variants, it should be pointed out that starting with the end of the fourth/tenth century, some decades after the establishment of the Buwayhid dynasty (334/945–447/1055), doctrinal changes began to take place in the position of the Imāmī-Šīʿa. The period of sovereignty of the Buwayhid dynasty constitutes a golden era for the Imāmī-Šīʿa, whose prior history was marked by continual suppression and persecution. The legitimation accorded the Imāmī-Šīʿa under the Buwayhid brought about an important cultural turning point including far-reaching internal innovations in Imāmī doctrine, which included a gradual rejection of the view that the 'Uthmanic codex was incomplete.[10]

The variants and additions to the Quranic text which the Šīʿa upholds can be divided typologically into several categories:

A. Minor Alteration of a Word: Exchange or Addition of a Letter and/or Alteration of Vocalization

Instead of the version in the 'Uthmanic Codex in verse 45/29(28): *Hāḏā kitābunā yanṭiqu ʿalaykum bi-l-ḥaqq* . . . ("This is our book that speaks against you the truth . . ."), the Imāmī reading suggests *Hāḏā bi-kitābinā yanṭiqu ʿalaykum bi-l-ḥaqq* . . . ("This [i.e., Muḥammad or the Imams] who speaks against you the truth by the book . . .").[11] A similar example is the variant reading suggested for verse 78/40(41). Instead of the reading . . . *Wa-yaqūlu al-kāfir yā laytanī kuntu turāban* (". . . And the unbeliever shall say: 'O would that I were dust'") found in the canonical codex, some Imāmī traditions suggest the variant *turābiyyan*.[12] While according to the canonical text the wish of the desperate unbeliever on the day of judgment is to be turned into dust (*turāban*), the variant reading suggests that he in fact hopes to become a Shiʿite (*turābiyyan*). This is a term used by the Shiʿites to refer to themselves, since one of ʿAlī's appellations was *Abū Turāb*.[13] It should be stressed, however, that in most exegetical traditions the term *turābiyyan* is presented as an interpretation of *turāban* and not necessarily as an alternative reading.[14]

B. Exchanging One Word for Another

The best example of this sort of alteration is the insertion of the word *aʾimma* ("Imams") in place of the word *umma* ("nation"/"people") found in the canonical text. This was done so as to introduce the doctrine of the *imāma* into the text of the Quran. For example, instead of *Kuntum ḫayra ummatin uḫriǧat li-l-nās* . . . ("You are the best nation ever brought forth to men . . .") in verse 3/110(106), the Imāmī tradition reads: *Kuntum ḫayra aʾimmatin* ("You are the best Imams").[15]

C. Rearrangement of Word Order

Many Imāmī commentators note that verse 11/17: *a-fa-man kāna ʿalā bayyinatin min rabbihi wa-yatlūhu šāhidun minhu wa-min qablihi kitāb Mūsā imāman wa-raḥmatan* . . . ("And what of him who stands upon a clear sign from his Lord and a witness from Him recites it, and before him is the Book of Moses for an ensample and a mercy . . .") is an example of a falsification. In the "original" version of the Quran it appeared, according to them, in the following order: *wa-yatlūhu šāhidun minhu imāman wa-raḥmatan*. The significant difference between the two verses is that in the Sunnī version the expression *imāman wa-raḥmatan* is disengaged from, and appears after, the expression *šāhidun minhu*, which, according to the Šīʿī tradition, relates to ʿAlī.[16]

D. Addition of Words

The Imāmī tradition holds that certain expressions were intentionally omitted from the Quran by the Sunnīs. Of these, two word clusters are particularly common:

a) *fī ʿAlī* ("about Ali").[17]
b) *āl Muḥammad* ("Muḥammad's family") or sometimes *āl Muḥammad ḥaqqahum* ("The rights of Muḥammad's family"), usually as the object of verbs derived from the root *ẓlm* ("to do injustice," "to usurp") often mentioned in the Quran. These additions are intended to show that the acts of injustice mentioned in some verses of the Quran are not neutral, but refer specifically to the usurpation of the rights of the Prophet's family and their offspring, that is, the Šīʿa itself.[18]

The same can be said for other typical Imāmī doctrines deduced from the text by way of word additions, or, as the commentator would have it, through "restoring" the "original" text by adding the words "omitted" by the editors. Thus, in several verses of the Quran, the words *fī walāyat ʿAlī* are added by Šīʿī commentators in order to read into the text the duty of *walāya* ("loyalty [to the house of ʿAlī]").[19] Similar to this is the addition of the words *ilā ağalin musamman* ("for a given period of time") to the *mutʿa* verse (4/24[28]), an addition intended to show the temporal nature of the marriage of pleasure (*nikāḥ al-mutʿa*), an issue on which Shiʿites and Sunnīs have disagreed throughout history.[20]

It should further be stressed that the variant readings and additions put forward by the Shiʿites are limited in scope. They never constitute an entire verse but consist only of the alteration or addition of a limited number of words. There is, however, one exception to this rule, when an entire verse found in the ʿUthmanic Codex is replaced in some sources by another. The verse in question is (26/214) *Wa-anḏir ʿašīrataka al-aqrabīna* ("And warn thy clan, thy nearest kin"); a tradition found in *TQ* in the name of Ǧaʿfar al-Ṣādiq states that the original verse descended from heaven was *Wa-rahṭaka minhum al-muḫliṣīn* ("and your most faithful men among them"). While in this tradition it is not clear whether these words should be taken as replacing the canonical verse or are merely an addition to it, in another Šīʿī tradition in *TQ*, brought in the name of Abū al-Ǧārūd,[21] the canonical verse is omitted altogether and only the words *Wa-rahṭaka minhum al-muḫliṣīn* are cited with no additional commentary. In *TF*, on the other hand, a third version is presented, which binds together the two above-mentioned verses. It appears that this last text represents a harmonizing tendency whereby both texts are accepted.[22]

3. How to Distinguish between Variant Readings and Exegetical Additions

The differentiation between variant readings and exegetical additions of the commentators or their sources is based primarily on terminology. In many places where the commentator suggests a Šīʿī version to a Quranic verse, he does so by using typical formulas. The Šīʿī version is followed by statements such as: *Nazala Ǧibrāʾīl/Ǧibrīl bi-hāḏihi al-āya hākaḏā* ("thus the verse was revealed by [the archangel] Gabriel");[23] *Hākaḏā nazalat* ("thus [the verse] was revealed");[24] or by stating explicitly that the version suggested was the reading of one of the Imams.[25] Sometimes even stronger expressions are used to stress that particular passages of the Quran as preserved by the Sunna are incorrect. These include statements formulated in the negative, such as: . . . *ʿalā ḫilāf mā anzala Allāh* ("[The verse in its canonical form] contradicts the form in which it was revealed")[26] or *fīmā ḥurrifa min Kitāb Allāh* "([This verse] is one of those falsified/altered in God's book"),[27] and so on.

In the absence of such firm indicators it is difficult to decide whether the alteration mentioned is a mere commentary or whether the exegete is in fact suggesting an alternative reading to the canonical text, despite the absence of typical expressions such as those mentioned above. A good example of such an uncertain case is found in the commentary to verses 81/8–9: *wa-iḏā al-mawʾūdatu suʾilat bi-ayyi ḏanbin qutilat* ("when the buried infant shall be asked for what sin she was slain"). Instead of explaining these verses as relating to the *mawʾūda* ("a buried infant"), (i.e., to the pre-Islamic custom of *waʾd*), it was understood as relating to *mawadda* ("love"), namely, the duty to love the family of the Prophet and the Imams.[28] However, since it is plainly stated in at least one tradition that the verse should be interpreted as relating to *mawadda* without the use of any formula common to the introduction of a Šīʿī variant reading, this seems to indicate an interpretation rather than a *qirāʾa*.[29]

In cases where it was difficult to decide whether the text refers to a variant reading or to an interpretation this has been noted in the list.

4. The Status of the Variant Readings within the Imāmī Quran Exegesis

The early Šīʿī criticism of the tendentious anti-Šīʿī nature of the ʿUthmanic Codex is categorical; formulas such as those cited at the beginning of section 3 brought proof to Imāmī commentators of the revealed truth. These expressions are intended to enhance the stature of the suggested Imāmī version and thus to underline its importance in the eyes of Šīʿī believers, while at the same time serving to reject and delegitimize the other readings, that is, those of the Sunnīs. On the basis of such a rejection of the Sunnī text one should naturally have expected the Šīʿa to insert these alternative versions and additions into the text of the Quran or at least to implement them in religious rulings and/or include them in the liturgy. However, in reality, as far as I know, almost no action was taken on the part of the Imāmī-Šīʿa to canonize their variant readings.[30] One exception to this rule is a late attempt reflected in a manuscript of the Quran discovered at the beginning of the twentieth century in the city of Bankipur in India, in which, besides the Šīʿī alternative versions to some of the Quranic verses, two apocryphal sūras were also included: *Sūrat al-walāya* ("the *Sūra* of loyalty [to the House of ʿAlī]") and *Sūrat al-nūrayn* ("the *Sūra* of the two lights [i.e., Muḥammad and ʿAlī]").[31]

This behavior on the part of the Šīʿa reveals a paradox. On the one hand, the Shiʿites are certain that the true version of the Quranic text is that known to them, but on the other hand, not only do they not reject the canonical codex, but they actually endorse it.[32]

This contradiction is typical of the Šīʿa in that, on the one hand, an uncompromising position of superiority was adopted on the theoretical-doctrinal level while, on the other hand, the constant fear of persecution from the hostile Sunnī environment brought about, on the practical level, a pragmatic attitude that included the adoption of the ʿUthmanic Codex. This tension and paradox in the Šīʿī tradition is reflected in many exegetical traditions in which Imāmī variants are mentioned. In some of them one finds the following situation: a disciple of a certain Imam is reading out of the (canonical) Quran in the presence of the Imam, but when he suddenly reaches a controversial verse he is stopped by the Imam who tells him that it was revealed in a different version. The Imam then proceeds to read the "true," that is, Šīʿī, version. However, as against these traditions that underrate the importance of the ʿUthmanic Codex, in others an opposing tendency is revealed: someone is reading out of the Quran in the presence of one of the Imams and inserts in his reading the Šīʿī version of the verse; at this point he is stopped by the Imam who instructs him to read according to the version followed by all the people (i.e., the canonical version) till the time when the "righteous savior" (the *qāʾim*) shall come with the correct version of the Quran, identical to the one that ʿAlī had possessed. Typical of this kind of tradition is the following:

> Someone read words (*ḥurūfan*) from the Quran not as is the custom (*laysa ʿalā mā yaqraʾuhā al-nās*) in the presence of Abū ʿAbd Allāh (Ǧaʿfar al-Ṣādiq) while I was listening (*wa-anā asmaʿu*).[33] Said Abū ʿAbd Allāh: Stop, cease this reading (*mah, mah, kuffa ʿan hāḏihi al-qirāʾa*), read as is customary until the coming of the *qāʾim* and when he comes, he shall read the book of God as it should be (*ʿalā ḥaddihi*) and shall produce the book which ʿAlī wrote. . . .[34]

This tradition shows that the common opinion held by the Šīʿa was that the ʿUthmanic Codex is less than perfect but so long as the world is ruled by the enemies of the Šīʿa—the Sunnīs—one has to uphold, against one's will, their canonical book. In the eschatological era, when the *qāʾim* will appear and correct the wrongs done to the Šīʿa, the question of the correct text of the Quran will also be settled.

5. The Imāmī Variant Readings and the Question of the Numerous *Qirāʾāt* (*Nazala al-Qurʾān ʿalā Sabʿat Aḥruf*)

The supremacy accorded by the Shiʿites to their variant readings raises another difficulty: what was their position on the Sunnī assertion according to which "The Quran was revealed according to seven words each of which is sufficient (*nazala al-qurʾān ʿalā sabʿat aḥruf; kullin šāfin kāfin*)." As is well known, at a very early stage this tradition was associated with the variant readings in the Quran, all of which are considered equally canonical.[35] At first sight it would seem that the Shiʿites rejected this interpretation since they believed in an Imāmī-Šīʿī version of the Quran that God had revealed to his Prophet Muḥammad, and accepting it would have meant accepting as valid other versions, thus undermining the superiority and exclusivity reserved for their own readings. However, it seems that on this question, too, the Shiʿites were not of one mind. Moreover, it appears that two contradictory approaches can be detected in the Šīʿa with regard to this issue, revealing a direct link between the attitude of the Šīʿī scholars to the integrity of the Quran and their attitude to variant readings. In the pre-Buwayhid period (3–4th/9–10th centuries), when the Šīʿa propagated the theory of falsification (*taḥrīf*) of the Quran, a categorical attitude was also adopted regarding alternative versions of Quranic verses; they were rejected. In one tradition brought by al-Kūlīnī in the name of his teacher ʿAlī b. Ibrāhīm al-Qummī, the Imam (Ǧaʿfar al-Ṣādiq) is asked: "People say that the Quran was revealed according to seven variant readings (*aḥruf*);[36] [Is that so?]." Al-Ṣādiq answers: "[No, these] enemies of God have lied[37] for [it is revealed] by one God according to one version (*ḥarf*)." A similar tradition is cited there in the name of al-Bāqir but with additional explanation that "the origin of the difference [between the versions] goes back to the transmitters (*wa-lākinna al-iḫtilāfa yaǧīʾu min qibal al-ruwāti*).[38]

On the other hand, in later periods, the Šīʿa rejected the view that the Quran was falsified and adopted another, less militant, view with regard to the issue of the numerous versions. A prime representative of this new attitude is Abū Ǧaʿfar al-Tūsī (mentioned above).

In his introduction to his commentary on the Quran, al-Tūsī approaches the question of the *qirāʾāt*. He cites the above-mentioned tradition about the seven *aḥruf* and, like his predecessors, points to its various interpretations. When faced with the issue of the numerous versions, he says:

> You should know that the accepted view among our brethren (*al-ʿurf min maḏhab aṣḥābinā*) is that the Quran was revealed to the Prophet in one version (*bi-ḥarf(!)*[39] *wāḥid ʿalā nabiyyin wāḥid*). However, it was agreed among them that one may accept a version handed down among the readers (*ġayra annahum aǧmaʿūʿalā ǧawāz al-qirāʾ bi-mā yatadāwalūhu al-qurrāʾ*) and that a man is free to choose which version he prefers. They also refrained from recommending one particular version (*wa-karihū taǧwīd qirāʾa bi-ʿaynihā*) and permitted only an approved version, [i.e.] one that had been approved among the readers (*bal aǧāzū al-qirāʾa bi-l-muǧāz allaḏī yaǧūzu bayna al-qurrāʾ*).[40]

This tolerant attitude prevalent among the Shiʿites, beginning with the Buwayhid period, seems quite understandable. Since the doctrine that propagated the imperfect character of the Quran was receding, Šīʿī scholars could now also adopt a positive attitude toward the issue of the numerous versions of the Quran and justify the Šīʿī version within this framework.[41] On the other hand, one should not rule out the possibility that the more tolerant position adopted here by the Šīʿa was tactical rather than reflecting their true beliefs. In other words, the wish to avoid a direct confrontation with the Sunna, a wish based (as in other issues) on *taqiyya* (precautionary dissimulation),[42] brought about an outward external decline in Šīʿī militant attitudes while internally the Shiʿites stuck to their view that only their version of the Quran was correct.

6. On the Similarity between the Imāmī-Šīʿī Variant Readings and the Jewish Midrash "Al Tikrei" (אַל תִּקְרֵי "Read Not")

The exegetical system employed by the Shiʿites with regard to variant readings is strongly reminiscent of the Talmudic method of exegesis knows as "*al tikrei*" ("read not").[43] This method entails a new interpretation of a biblical verse by altering the reading of a word (in a very similar fashion to that described above with relation to the Šīʿī alterations in the Quranic text). Of the many examples found in Talmudic literature I shall restrict myself to one well-known example:

> It was taught in the *Tannā debē Eliyyahū*:[44] Whoever repeats *hălāḵōt* (i.e., religious rulings) may rest assured that he is destined for the future world, as it is written: "his ways (*hălāḵōt*) are those of eternity (or 'of the world'—*ʿōlām*)" (Habakuk 3/6). Read not *hălīḵōt* but *hălāḵōt*.[45]

The exegete wishes to deduce from Scripture the idea that anyone who devotes his time to the study of religious laws and rulings (*hălāḵōt*) has a place in the world to come. This he does by suggesting that one read *hălāḵōt* instead of *hălīḵōt* in Scripture and then, by using this new reading, he reinterprets the verse so that the words "those of eternity (or of the world)" should point to the eternal world, that is, the world to come.

The small alteration in the word (in this case the omission of a letter and a change in vocalization) enabled the biblical exegete to insert into Scripture a new idea. It is, however, of great importance to note the difference between this system and that of the Šīʿa despite the technical similarity we have noted. Each of these systems has a totally different attitude to the status of interpretation with relation to the canon. The Talmudic interpreter has no intention of altering the meaning of Scripture and he does not believe even in theory that he has discovered the true original meaning of the verse. His readings have been, all along, an (allegorical) interpretation. On the other hand, the Šīʿī interpretation that does similar things with the Quranic verse sees in the version produced not just another exegetical possibility; in the eyes of the Shiʿites this is the original version.

List of Imāmī-Šīʿī Variant Readings and Additions to the Quran

Note: The following conventions are used in this list:

a) Words in boldface indicate an addition to the 'Uthmanic Codex
b) An asterisk before running number of a verse indicates a doubtful reading, that is, cases where it is difficult to decide whether these are an exegetical note or a "reconstruction" of the "original" text.

Verse	'Uthmanic Codex	Imāmī-Šīʿī Reading
1. 2/23(21)	وَإِنْ كُنْتُمْ فِي رَيْبٍ مِمَّا نَزَّلْنَا عَلَى عَبْدِنَا فَأْتُوا بِسُورَةٍ مِنْ مِثْلِهِ...	وَإِنْ كُنْتُمْ فِي رَيْبٍ مِمَّا نَزَّلْنَا عَلَى عَبْدِنَا **فِي عَلِيٍّ** فَأْتُوا بِسُورَةٍ مِنْ مِثْلِهِ... *K*, 1, 417, 26 (whence *B*, 1, 70, 3).
2. 2/59(56)	فَبَدَّلَ ٱلَّذِينَ ظَلَمُوا قَوْلاً غَيْرَ ٱلَّذِي قِيلَ لَهُمْ فَأَنْزَلْنَا عَلَى ٱلَّذِينَ ظَلَمُوا رِجْزاً مِنَ ٱلسَّمَاءِ...	فَبَدَّلَ ٱلَّذِينَ ظَلَمُوا **آلَ** **مُحَمَّدٍ حَقَّهُمْ** قَوْلاً غَيْرَ ٱلَّذِي قِيلَ لَهُمْ فَأَنْزَلْنَا عَلَى ٱلَّذِينَ ظَلَمُوا **آلَ مُحَمَّدٍ** **حَقَّهُمْ** رِجْزاً مِنَ السَّمَاءِ... *TʿA*, 1, 45, 49; *TQ*, 1, 48, 13 (reports the second addition only); *K*, 1, 423, 8; *B*, 1, 104, 2 and 5; *Ṣ*, 1, 96, 16–17; *BA*, 24, 222, 8 (cites *TʿA*); *ShA*, 235/3.
3. 2/90(84)	بِئْسَمَا ٱشْتَرَوْا بِهِ أَنْفُسَهُمْ أَنْ يَكْفُرُوا بِمَا أَنْزَلَ ٱللهُ...	بِئْسَمَا ٱشْتَرَوْا بِهِ أَنْفُسَهُمْ أَنْ يَكْفُرُوا بِمَا أَنْزَلَ ٱللهُ **فِي عَلِيٍّ**...

		TʿA, 1, 51, 71 (whence *B*, 1, 129, 3; *BA*, 36, 98, 38); *TF*, 60, 23; *K*, 1, 417, 25.
4. 2/91(85)	وإِذَا قِيلَ لَهُمْ آمِنُوا بِمَا أَنْزَلَ ٱللهُ...	وَإِذَا قِيلَ لَهُمْ آمِنُوا بِمَا أَنْزَلَ ٱللهُ **فِي عَلِيٍّ**... *TʿA*, 1, 51, 74 (whence *B*, 130, 2).
5. 2/143(137)	وَكَذٰلِكَ جَعَلْنَاكُمْ أُمَّةً وَسَطاً...	وَكَذٰلِكَ جَعَلْنَاكُمْ أَئِمَّةً وَسَطاً... *TQ*, 1, 63, 14–19 (whence *Rich*, 283).[46]
6. 3/28(27)	لاَ يَتَّخِذُ ٱلْمُؤْمِنُونَ ٱلْكَافِرِينَ أَوْلِيَاءَ مِنْ دُونِ ٱلْمُؤْمِنِينَ... إِلاَّ أَنْ تَتَّقُوا مِنْهُمْ تُقَاةً...	لاَ يَتَّخِذُ ٱلْمُؤْمِنُونَ ٱلْكَافِرِينَ أَوْلِيَاءَ مِنْ دُونِ ٱلْمُؤْمِنِينَ... إِلاَّ أَنْ تَتَّقُوا مِنْهُمْ تَقِيَّةً... *TʿA*, 1, 166, 24;[47] *T*, 2, 433 (= *MB*, 3, 54); *Ṣ*, 1, 253, 10.[48]
7. 3/33(30)	إِنَّ ٱللهَ ٱصْطَفَى آدَمَ وَنُوحاً وَآلَ إِبْرَاهِيمَ وَآلَ عِمْرَانَ عَلَى ٱلْعَالَمِينَ	إِن ٱللهَ ٱصْطَفَى آدَمَ وَنُوحاً وَآلَ إِبْرَاهِيمَ وَآلَ عِمْرَانَ **وَآلَ مُحَمَّدٍ** عَلَى ٱلْعَالَمِينَ *TʿA*, 1, 169, 34–35 and *TQ*, 1, 100, 12–14 (whence *B*, 1, 277–79; *Ṣ*, 1, 256, 13–14); Some sources read وآلَ مُحَمَّد instead of وَآلَ عِمْرَانَ (*TF*, 78; *T*, 2, 441, 5–6; *MB*, 3, 62, 10–11). Cf. also *JM*, 32;[49] *KQ*, 212 (with note 40).

8. 3/102(97)	يَا أَيُّهَا ٱلَّذِينَ آمَنُوا ٱتَّقُوا ٱللَّهَ حَقَّ تُقَاتِهِ وَلَا تَمُوتُنَّ إِلَّا وَأَنْتُمْ مُسْلِمُونَ	يَا أَيُّهَا ٱلَّذِينَ آمَنُوا ٱتَّقُوا ٱللَّهَ حَقَّ تُقَاتِهِ وَلَا تَمُوتُنَّ إِلَّا وَأَنْتُمْ مُسْلِمُونَ **لِرَسُولِ ٱللَّهِ ثُمَّ ٱلْإِمَامِ مِنْ بَعْدِهِ** *TʿA*, 1, 194, 119 (whence *B*, 1, 304–305, 4; *Ṣ*, 1, 285, 3–7).[50]
9. 3/110(106)	كُنْتُمْ خَيْرَ أُمَّةٍ أُخْرِجَتْ لِلنَّاسِ...	كُنْتُمْ خَيْرَ أَئِمَّةٍ أُخْرِجَتْ لِلنَّاسِ... *TʿA*, 1, 195, 128–29[51] and *TQ*, 1, 110, 1 (whence *B*, 1, 308–309; *Ṣ*, 1, 289, 19–290, 5); *TN*, 26, 18; cf. *Rich*, 282 and *KQ*, 212 (both cite *TQ*).
10. 3/123(119)	وَلَقَدْ نَصَرَكُمُ ٱللَّهُ بِبَدْرٍ وَأَنْتُمْ أَذِلَّةٌ...	وَلَقَدْ نَصَرَكُمُ ٱللَّهُ بِبَدْرٍ وَأَنْتُمْ ضُعَفَاءُ / قَلِيلٌ... *TʿA*, 1, 196, 133–34 (whence *B*, 1, 310, 2–3, *Ṣ*, 1, 295, 10) reads قَلِيلٌ instead of أَذِلَّةٌ whilst *TʿA*, ibid., 135 (= *B*, ibid. and *Ṣ*, ibid.) reads ضُعَفَاءُ.[52] The last version is also the one preferred by *TQ*, 1, 122, 14 (cf. *Rich*, 284); *T*, 2, 578; *MB*, 4, 188 and see also *JM*, 125.[53]
11. 4/24(28)	...فَمَا ٱسْتَمْتَعْتُمْ بِهِ مِنْهُنَّ...	... فَمَا ٱسْتَمْتَعْتُمْ بِهِ مِنْهُنَّ **إِلَى أَجَلٍ مُسَمًّى...** *TʿA*, 1, 234, 87–88 and *TQ*, 1, 136, 1 (whence *B*, 1, 360–61;

		Ṣ, 1, 346);[54] *T*, 3, 166;[55] *ĞB*, 5, 12–13; *Rich*, 13; *ShA*, 236/12.
12. 4/47(50)	يَا أَيُّهَا ٱلَّذِينَ أُوتُوا ٱلْكِتَابَ آمِنُوا بِمَا نَزَّلْنَا مُصَدِّقاً لِمَا مَعَكُمْ...	يَا أَيُّهَا ٱلَّذِينَ أُوتُوا ٱلْكِتَابَ آمِنُوا بِمَا أَنْزَلْتُ **فِي عَلِيٍّ** مُصَدِّقاً لِمَا مَعَكُمْ... *TʿA*, 1, 245, 148 (whence *B*, 1, 374, 4);[56] *TF*, 1, 105; *K*, 1, 417, 27.
13. 4/64(67)	...وَلَوْ أَنَّهُمْ إِذْ ظَلَمُوا أَنْفُسَهُمْ جَاءُوكَ...	...وَلَوْ أَنَّهُمْ إِذْ ظَلَمُوا أَنْفُسَهُمْ جَاءُوكَ **يَا عَلِيُّ**... *TQ*, 1, 142, 13 (whence *B*, 1, 389, 1).[57]
14. 4/66(69)	...وَلَوْ أَنَّهُمْ فَعَلُوا مَا يُوعَظُونَ بِهِ...	...وَلَوْ أَنَّهُمْ فَعَلُوا مَا يُوعَظُونَ بِهِ **فِي عَلِيٍّ** *K*, 1, 424, 60 (whence *B*, 1, 391, 2 and 3; *Ṣ*, 1, 369, 6–7 (cf. *TʿA*, 1, 256, 188).
15. 4/166(164)	لَٰكِنِ ٱللهُ يَشْهَدُ بِمَا أَنْزَلَ إِلَيْكَ...	لَٰكِنِ ٱللهُ يَشْهَدُ بِمَا أَنْزَلَ إِلَيْكَ **فِي عَلِيٍّ**... *TʿA*, 1, 285, 307; *TQ*, 1, 159, 3–5 (whcnce *B*, 1, 428, 1 and *Ṣ*, 1, 414, 6 [cites *TQ* only]; *BA*, 36, 99, 39). Cf. *Rich*, 285; *KQ*, 212.
16. 4/168(166)	إِنَّ ٱلَّذِينَ كَفَرُوا وَظَلَمُوا...	إِنَّ ٱلَّذِينَ كَفَرُوا وَظَلَمُوا **آلَ مُحَمَّدٍ حَقَّهُمْ**...

		TʿA, 1, 285, 307; *TQ*, 1, 159, 6 (whence *B*, 1, 428, 2–3; *Ṣ*, 1, 414, 11–12; *BA*, 36, 99, 39); *K*, 1, 424, 59; *ShA*, 236/11; *KQ*, 212.
17. 4/170(168)	يَا أَيُّهَا ٱلنَّاسُ قَدْ جَاءَكُمُ ٱلرَّسُولُ بِٱلْحَقِّ مِنْ رَبِّكُمْ فَآمِنُوا خَيْراً لَكُمْ وَإِنْ تَكْفُرُوا فَإِنَّ للهِ مَا فِي السَّمٰوَاتِ وَٱلأَرْضِ...	يَا أَيُّهَا ٱلنَّاسُ قَدْ جَاءَكُمْ ٱلرَّسُولُ بِٱلْحَقِّ مِنْ رَبِّكُمْ **فِي وَلَايَةِ عَلِيٍّ** فَآمِنُوا خَيْراً لَكُمْ وَإِنْ تَكْفُرُوا **بِوَلَايَتِهِ** فَإِنَّ لِلّٰهِ مَا فِي ٱلسَّمٰوَاتِ وٱلأَرْضِ...
		TʿA, 1, 285, 307 (whence *B*, 1, 428, 2; *Ṣ*, 1, 414, 15–16; *BA*, 36, 99, 39); *K*, 1, 424, 59.
18. 5/1	يَا أَيُّهَا ٱلَّذِينَ آمَنُوا أَوْفُوا بِٱلْعُقُودِ...	يَا أَيُّهَا ٱلَّذِينَ آمَنُوا أَوْفُوا بِٱلْعُقُودِ **ٱلَّتِي عَقَدْتُ عَلَيْكُمْ لِأَمِيرِ ٱلْمُؤْمِنِينَ عَلَيْهِ ٱلسَّلَامُ...**
		TQ, 1, 160, 10–11 (whence *B*, 1, 431, 9; *Ṣ*, 1, 417, 11–12).
19. 5/6(8)	يَا أَيُّهَا ٱلَّذِينَ آمَنُوا إِذَا قُمْتُمْ إِلَى ٱلصَّلَاةِ فَٱغْسِلُوا وُجُوهَكُمْ وَأَيْدِيَكُمْ إِلَى المَرَافِقِ وَٱمْسَحُوا بِرُؤُوسِكُمْ وَأَرْجُلَكُمْ...	يَا أَيُّهَا ٱلَّذِينَ آمَنُوا إِذَا قُمْتُمْ إِلَى ٱلصَّلَاةِ فَٱغْسِلُوا وُجُوهَكُمْ وَأَيْدِيَكُمْ إِلَى ٱلْمَرَافِقِ وَٱمْسَحُوا بِرُؤُوسِكُمْ وَأَرْجُلِكُمْ...
		TʿA, 1, 298, 50, and 299, 50[58] (whence *B*, 1, 450–54 and *Ṣ*, 424–26 who cite other Šīʿī and non-Šīʿī sources); *K*, 3, 29–31; *T*, 3, 447–53;[59] *MB*, 6, 34, 37–38; *MQ*, 1, 302–303;[60]

		ĞB, 6, 126–31; *KḤT*, 1, 597–98. Cf. also *Rich*, 7–8.
20. 5/67(71)	يَا أَيُّهَا ٱلرَّسُولُ بَلِّغْ مَا أُنْزِلَ إِلَيْكَ مِنْ رَبِّكَ...	يَا أَيُّهَا ٱلرَّسُولُ بَلِّغْ مَا أُنْزِلَ إِلَيْكَ مِنْ رَبِّكَ **فِي عَلِيٍّ...**
		TQ, 2, 201, 9 (Cf. *Ṣ*, 1, 460, 2–3; ibid., 462, 7; ibid., 463, 3–4, *Rich*, 285); *B* (citing *Kašf al-Ġumma*) provides an alternative variant reading: أَنَّ عَلِيًّا مَوْلَى ٱلْمُؤْمِنِينَ (cf. *JM*, 40).
21. 6/93	... وَلَوْ تَرَى إِذْ ٱلظَّالِمُونَ فِي غَمَرَاتِ ٱلْمَوْتِ...	...وَلَوْ تَرَى إِذْ ٱلظَّالِمُونَ **آلَ مُحَمَّدٍ حَقَّهُمْ** فِي غَمَرَاتِ ٱلْمَوْتِ...
		TQ, 1, 211, 8 (whence *B*, 1, 542, 6).
22. 6/159(160)	إِنَّ ٱلَّذِينَ فَرَّقُوا دِينَهُمْ وَكَانُوا شِيَعاً...	إِنَّ ٱلَّذِينَ فَارَقُوا دِينَهُمْ وَكَانُوا شِيَعاً...
		TʿA, 1, 385, 131 (whence *B*, 1, 565, 3; *Ṣ*, 1, 560, 3–4; *BA*, 9, 389). Cf. *TQ*, 1, 222, 10 (cited in *B*, ibid. and in *Ṣ*, ibid.);[61] *T*, 4, 328; *MB*, 8, 244, 2; cf. *MQ*, 1, 366; *ĞB*, 8, 104; *KḤT*, 2, 64. See also *JM*, 42.
23. 7/172(171)	وَإِذْ أَخَذَ رَبُّكَ مِنْ بَنِي آدَمَ مِنْ ظُهُورِهِمْ ذُرِّيَّتَهُمْ وَأَشْهَدَهُمْ عَلَى أَنْفُسِهِمْ أَلَسْتُ بِرَبِّكُمْ...	وَإِذْ أَخَذَ رَبُّكَ مِنْ بَنِي آدَمَ مِنْ ظُهُورِهِمْ ذُرِّيَّتَهُمْ وَأَشْهَدَهُمْ عَلَى أَنْفُسِهِمْ أَلَسْتُ بِرَبِّكُمْ **وَأَنَّ مُحَمَّداً رَسُولَ ٱللهِ [نَبِيُّكُمْ] وَأَنَّ عَلِيًّا أَمِيرُ ٱلْمُؤْمِنِينَ...**

		TʿA, 2, 41, 113–14[62] (whence *B*, 2, 50; *BA*, 9, 256).
24. 9/40	فَأَنْزَلَ ٱللهُ سَكِينَتَهُ عَلَيْهِ وَأَيَّدَهُ بِجُنُودٍ...	فأنْزَلَ ٱللهُ سَكِينَتَهُ عَلَى رَسُولِهِ... *TʿA*, 2, 89, 58 (whence *B*, 2, 128, 10; *Ṣ*, 1, 702, 12–15; *BA*, 19, 80, 23).[63]
25. 9/105(106)	وَقُلْ ٱعْمَلُوا فَسَيَرَى ٱللهُ عَمَلَكُمْ وَرَسُولُهُ وَٱلْمُؤْمِنُونَ...	وَقُلْ ٱعْمَلُوا فَسَيَرَى ٱللهُ عَمَلَكُمْ وَرَسُولُهُ وَٱلْمَأْمُونُونَ... *K*, 1, 424, 62 (whence *B*, 2, 157, 7 and *Ṣ*, 1, 727, 4–5).[63a]
26. 9/117(118)	لَقَدْ تَابَ ٱللهُ عَلَى ٱلنَّبِيِّ وَٱلْمُهَاجِرِينَ وَٱلأَنْصَارِ ٱلَّذِينَ ٱتَّبَعُوهُ فِي سَاعَةِ ٱلْعُسْرَةِ...	لَقَدْ تَابَ ٱللهُ بِٱلنَّبِيِّ عَلَى ٱلْمُهَاجِرِينَ وَٱلأَنْصَارِ ٱلَّذِينَ ٱتَّبَعُوهُ فِي سَاعَةِ ٱلْعُسْرَةِ *TQ*, 1, 297, 16 (whence *B*, 2, 168, 1 [with 2, 132]; *Ṣ*, 1, 736, 3–7 cites besides *TQ*, *MB*, and *Kitāb al-Iḥtiǧāǧ*); *MB*, 10, 156, 30.[64]
27. 9/118(119)	وَعَلَى ٱلثَّلَاثَةِ ٱلَّذِينَ خُلِّفُوا حَتَّى إذا ضَاقَتْ عَلَيْهِمْ ٱلأَرْضُ...	وَعَلَى الثَّلَاثَةِ ٱلَّذِينَ خَالَفُوا حَتَّى إِذا ضَاقَتْ عَلَيْهِمْ ٱلأَرْضُ... *TʿA*, 2, 115, 152; *TQ*, 1, 297, 18–19 (both sources as well as other sources [such as *K* and *MB*] are cited in *B*, 2, 168–69; *Ṣ*, 1, 737, 13–16; *BA*, 21, 237,

		22); *T*, 5, 316, 16; *MB*, 11, 153, 17. See also Jeffery, who provides this variant as the one preferred by ʿAlī (*JM*, 187), who according to others read ٱلْمُخَلَّفِينَ. This was also the reading of the Kūfan reader al-Aʿmaš [ibid., 319] and of Ǧaʿfar al-Ṣādiq [ibid., 333]. Cf. *KḤT*, 2, 218 who gives, besides the variants mentioned[65] above, the reading وَخَلَّفُوا.
28. 16/24(26)	وَإِذَا قِيلَ لَهُمْ مَاذَا أَنْزَلَ رَبُّكُمْ قَالُوا أَسَاطِيرُ ٱلْأَوَّلِينَ	وَإِذَا قِيلَ لَهُمْ مَاذَا أَنْزَلَ رَبُّكُمْ **فِي عَلِيٍّ** قَالُوا أَسَاطِيرُ ٱلْأَوَّلِينَ *TF*, 234; *TʿA*, 2, 257, 17–18 (whence *B*, 2, 363; *Ṣ*, 1, 920; *BA*, 36, 104, 47–48); *TQ*, 1, 383, 16–17.
29. 16/90(92)	إِنَّ ٱللَّهَ يَأْمُرُ بِٱلْعَدْلِ وَٱلْإِحْسَانِ وَإِيتَاءِ ذِي ٱلْقُرْبَى...	إِنَّ ٱللَّهَ يَأْمُرُ بِالْعَدْلِ وَالْإِحْسَانِ وَإِيتَاءِ ذِي ٱلْقُرْبَى **حَقَّهُ**... *TʿA*, 2, 267, 60 (whence *B*, 2, 381, 5; *Ṣ*, 1, 937, 8–10; *BA*, 7, 129).[66]
30. 16/92(94)	...تَتَّخِذُونَ أَيْمَانَكُمْ دَخَلًا بَيْنَكُمْ أَنْ تَكُونَ أُمَّةٌ هِيَ أَرْبَى مِنْ أُمَّةٍ...	...تَتَّخِذُونَ أَيْمَانَكُمْ دَخَلًا بَيْنَكُمْ أَنْ تَكُونَ أَئِمَّةٌ هِيَ أَزْكَى مِنْ أَئِمَّتِكُمْ... *TʿA*, 2, 268, 64 and *TQ*, 1, 389, 17 (both cited in *B*, 2, 382–83; *Ṣ*, 1, 939, 3–6).

31. 17/60(62)	...وَمَا جَعَلْنَا الرُّؤْيَا ٱلَّتِي أَرَيْنَاكَ إِلَّا فِتْنَةً لِلنَّاسِ وَٱلشَّجَرَةَ ٱلْمَلْعُونَةَ فِي ٱلْقُرْآنِ...	...وَمَا جَعَلْنَا ٱلرُّؤْيَا ٱلَّتِي أَرَيْنَاكَ إِلَّا فِتْنَةً **لَهُمْ لِيَعْمَهُوا فِيهَا** وَٱلشَّجَرَةَ ٱلْمَلْعُونَةَ فِي ٱلْقُرْآنِ... *TQ*, 2, 21, 19–21 (whence *B*, 2, 425, 12 [who, however, retains the word لِلنَّاسِ]; *Ṣ*, 1, 916, 7–9 [with the omission of the word لِلنَّاسِ], i.e., he reads إِلَّا فِتْنَةً لَهُمْ لِيَعْمَهُوا]);[67] Jeffery (*JM*, 55) gives the reading إِلَّا فِتْنَةً لَهُمْ as the reading of Ibn Masʿūd.
32. 17/82(84)	وَنُنَزِّلُ مِنَ ٱلْقُرْآنِ مَا هُوَ شِفَاءٌ وَرَحْمَةٌ لِلْمُؤْمِنِينَ وَلَا يَزِيدُ الظَّالِمِينَ إِلَّا خَسَاراً	وَنُنَزِّلُ مِنَ ٱلْقُرْآنِ مَا هُوَ شِفَاءٌ وَرَحْمَةٌ لِلْمُؤْمِنِينَ وَلَا يَزِيدُ ٱلظَّالِمِينَ **آلَ مُحَمَّدٍ حَقَّهُمْ** إِلَّا خَسَاراً *TʿA*, 2, 315, 155 (whence *B*, 2, 443, 2 [and see also 3–4 ibid.]; *Ṣ*, 1, 987, 3–5.
33. 17/89(91)	وَلَقَدْ صَرَّفْنَا لِلنَّاسِ فِي هٰذَا ٱلْقُرْآنِ مِنْ كُلِّ مَثَلٍ فَأَبَى أَكْثَرُ ٱلنَّاسِ إِلَّا كُفُوراً	وَلَقَدْ صَرَّفْنَا لِلنَّاسِ فِي هٰذَا ٱلْقُرْآنِ مِنْ كُلِّ مَثَلٍ فَأَبَى أَكْثَرُ ٱلنَّاسِ **وَلَايَةَ عَلِيٍّ** إِلَّا كُفُوراً *TʿA*, 2, 317, 166[68] (whence *B*, 445, 4; *Ṣ*, 1, 989, 10–11; *BA*, 36, 105, 50).[69] Cf. *K*, 1, 425, who reads here بِوَلَايَةِ عَلِيٍّ.
34. 18/29(28)	...إِنَّا أَعْتَدْنَا لِلظَّالِمِينَ نَاراً...	...إِنَّا أَعْتَدْنَا لِلظَّالِمِينَ **آلَ مُحَمَّدٍ حَقَّهُمْ** نَاراً...

		TʿA, 2, 326, 28 and *TQ*, 2, 35, 6 (cited also ibid., 282, 11). These two commentaries, as well as other sources, cited in *B*, 2, 465–66; *Ṣ*, 2, 13, 3–4 reports this addition from *TQ* and *K* (see *K*, 1, 425, 64).
*35. 20/115(114)	وَلَقَدْ عَهِدْنَا إِلَى آدَمَ مِنْ قَبْلُ فَنَسِيَ...	وَلَقَدْ عَهِدْنَا إِلَى آدَمَ مِنْ قَبْلُ **كَلِمَاتٍ فِي مُحَمَّدٍ وَعَلِيٍّ وَفَاطِمَةَ وَٱلْحَسَنِ وَٱلْحُسَيْنِ وَٱلأَئِمَّةِ عَلَيْهِمُ السَّلَامُ مِنْ ذُرِّيَّتِي** فَنَسِيَ... *K*, 1, 416, 23 (whence *B*, 3, 45, 3 and *Ṣ*, 2, 80, 5–7).
36. 22/52(51)	وَمَا أَرْسَلْنَا مِنْ قَبْلِكَ مِنْ رَسُولٍ وَلَا نَبِيٍّ...	وَمَا أَرْسَلْنَا مِنْ قَبْلِكَ مِنْ رَسُولٍ وَلَا نَبِيٍّ **وَلَا مُحَدَّثٍ** *TQ*, 2, 86, 2 (whence *B*, 3, 98, 1); *BD*, 320, 3 and 321, 8 (whence *BA*, 26, 31 and ibid., 80, 41 [cites al-Kiššī]; *K*, 1, 177 (cited in *Ṣ*, 2, 129, 8–9). See also Jeffery, who indicates that this addition was found in the codices of Ubayy b. Kaʿb (*JM*, 148) and ʿAbd Allāh Ibn ʿAbbās [ibid., 202]).[70]
37. 25/8(9)	...وَقَالَ الظَّالِمُونَ إِنْ تَتَّبِعُونَ إِلَّا رَجُلًا مَسْحُوراً	...وَقَالَ ٱلظَّالِمُونَ **لِآلِ مُحَمَّدٍ حَقَّهُمْ** إِنْ تَتَّبِعُونَ إِلَّا رَجُلًا مَسْحُوراً *TF*, 291; *TQ*, 2, 111, 18 (whence *B*, 3, 156, 1 [see also ibid., tradition no. 3]; *Ṣ*, 2, 187, 3–5).

*38. 25/28(30)	يَا وَيْلَتَي لَيْتَنِي لَمْ أَتَّخِذْ فُلَانًا خَلِيلًا	يَا وَيْلَتَي لَيْتَنِي لَمْ أَتَّخِذِ ٱلثَّانِيَ خَلِيلًا *B*, 3, 163, 4 (citing Muḥammad b. al-ʿAbbās).[71]
39. 25/74	وَٱلَّذِينَ يَقُولُونَ رَبَّنَا هَبْ لَنَا مِنْ أَزْوَاجِنَا وَذُرِّيَّاتِنَا قُرَّةَ أَعْيُنٍ وَٱجْعَلْنَا لِلْمُتَّقِينَ إِمَامًا	وَٱلَّذِينَ يَقُولُونَ رَبَّنَا هَبْ لَنَا مِنْ أَزْوَاجِنَا وَذُرِّيَّاتِنَا قُرَّةَ أَعْيُنٍ وَٱجْعَلْ لَنَا مِنَ ٱلْمُتَّقِينَ إِمَامًا *TQ*, 2, 117, 15–17 (whence *B*, 177 [citing other sources as well]; *Ṣ*, 2, 207, 2–6); *TF*, 295, 2; *T*, 7, 512, 5; *MB*, 19, 128, 16. Cf. *Rich*, 284; *KQ*, 212.[72]
40. 26/214	وَأَنْذِرْ عَشِيرَتَكَ ٱلْأَقْرَبِينَ	وَأَنْذِرْ عَشِيرَتَكَ ٱلْأَقْرَبِينَ وَرَهْطَكَ مِنْهُمُ ٱلْمُخْلَصِينَ *TQ*, 2, 124, 7 and ibid., 126, 1; *TF*, 302, 22–23;[73] *MB*, 19, 188, 22; *B*, 3, 189–92 and *Ṣ*, 2, 227, 1–17[74] provide several sources for this addition, among whom *TQ*. See also *ǦB*, 19, 121, 5 and 25. Cf. Jeffery, who provides two other additions to this verse: a) وَهُمْ أَهْلُ بَيْتِكَ وَمَنِ ٱتَّبَعَكَ مِنَ ٱلْمُؤْمِنِينَ فَإِنْ عَصَوْكَ وَرَهْطَكَ مِنْهُمُ ٱلْمُخْلَصِينَ فَقُلْ (*JM*, 68 with the corrigenda, p. 358).

		b) وَهُمْ أَهْلُ بَيْتِكَ مِنَ الْمُؤْمِنِينَ فَإِنْ عَصَوْكَ وَرَهْطَكَ مِنْهُمُ الْمُخْلِصِينَ فَقُلْ (Ibid., 189). Both variants are attributed to ʿAlī and to ʿAbd Allāh b. Masʿūd.
41. 26/227(228)	...وَسَيَعْلَمُ ٱلَّذِينَ ظَلَمُوا أَيَّ مُنْقَلَبٍ يَنْقَلِبُونَ	...وَسَيَعْلَمُ ٱلَّذِينَ ظَلَمُوا **آلَ مُحَمَّدٍ حَقَّهُمْ** أَيَّ مُنْقَلَبٍ يَنْقَلِبُونَ *TQ*, 2, 125, 12–13 (whence *B*, 3, 194, 4; *Ṣ*, 2, 230, 17–18). See also *Rich*, 285.
42. 33/71	... وَمَنْ يُطِعِ ٱللَّهَ وَرَسُولَهُ فَقَدْ فَازَ فَوْزاً عَظِيماً	...وَمَنْ يُطِعِ ٱللهَ وَرَسُولَهُ **فِي وَلَايَةِ عَلِيٍّ [وَوَلَايَةِ] ٱلْأَئِمَّةِ مِنْ بَعْدِهِ** فَقَدْ فَازَ فَوْزاً عَظِيماً *TQ*, 2, 198, 1–3 and *K*, 1, 414, 8 (whence *B*, 3, 340, 1–2 and *Ṣ*, 2, 369, 5–7).
43. 37/143–44	فَلَوْلَا أَنَّهُ كَانَ مِنَ ٱلْمُسَبِّحِينَ لَلَبِثَ فِي بَطْنِهِ إِلَى يَوْمِ يُبْعَثُونَ	فَلَوْلَا أَنَّهُ كَانَ مِنَ **ٱلْمُقَرَّبِينَ** لَلَبِثَ فِي بَطْنِهِ إِلَى يَوْمِ يُبْعَثُونَ *TF*, 265, 3–6.[75]
*44. 41/33	وَمَنْ أَحْسَنُ قَوْلاً مِمَّنْ دَعَا إِلَى ٱللهِ وَعَمِلَ صَالِحاً وَقَالَ إِنَّنِي مِنَ ٱلْمُسْلِمِينَ	وَمَنْ أَحْسَنُ قَوْلاً مِمَّنْ دَعَا إِلَى ٱللهِ وَعَمِلَ صَالِحاً **وَهُوَ صَبِيٌّ** وَقَالَ إِنَّنِي مِنَ ٱلْمُسْلِمِينَ

		T'A, 1, 279, 286[76] (whence *B*, 4, 111, 1).
45. 42/13(11–12)	...كَبُرَ عَلَى ٱلْمُشْرِكِينَ مَا تَدْعُوهُمْ إِلَيْهِ...	...كَبُرَ عَلَى ٱلْمُشْرِكِينَ بِوَلَايَةِ عَلِيٍّ مَا تَدْعُوهُمْ إِلَيْهِ يَا مُحَمَّدُ مِنْ وَلَايَةِ عَلِيٍّ *K*, 1, 418, 32 (whence *Ṣ*, 2, 509, 10–12) and cf. *TF*, 387, who provides a similar variant without indicating explicitly that this is an addition.
46. 43/38(37)	حَتَّىٰٓ إِذَا جَآءَنَا قَالَ يَا لَيْتَ بَيْنِي وَبَيْنَكَ بُعْدَ ٱلْمَشْرِقَيْنِ فَبِئْسَ ٱلْقَرِينُ	حَتَّىٰٓ إِذَا جَآءَنَا [يَعْنِي فُلَانًا وَفُلَانًا](77) يَقُولُ أَحَدُهُمَا لِصَاحِبِهِ حِينَ يَرَاهُ يَا لَيْتَ بَيْنِي وَبَيْنَكَ بُعْدَ ٱلْمَشْرِقَيْنِ فَبِئْسَ ٱلْقَرِينُ *TQ*, 2, 286, 13–15[78] (whence *Ṣ*, 2, 530 7–9); according to another tradition in *Ṣ*, (ibid., 1.5) the sole difference in the Šīʿī reading is the usage of the dual form, i.e., جَآءَانَا ("the two of them came") instead of جَآءَنَا ("he came").[79]
47. 43/39(38)	وَلَن يَنفَعَكُمُ ٱلْيَوْمَ إِذ ظَّلَمْتُمْ أَنَّكُمْ فِي ٱلْعَذَابِ مُشْتَرِكُونَ	وَلَنْ يَنْفَعَكُمْ ٱلْيَوْمَ إِذْ ظَلَمْتُمْ آلَ مُحَمَّدٍ حَقَّهُمْ أَنَّكُمْ فِي ٱلْعَذَابِ مُشْتَرِكُونَ *TQ*, 2, 286, 15–16 (whence *Ṣ*, 2, 530, 10) and see also *B*, 4,

		143, 3 citing Muḥammad ibn al-ʿAbbās.[71]
48. 45/29(28)	...هٰذَا كِتَابُنَا يَنْطِقُ عَلَيْكُمْ بِٱلْحَقِّ...	...هٰذَا بِكِتَابِنَا يَنْطِقُ عَلَيْكُمْ بِالْحَقِّ... *TQ*, 2, 295, 14–17 (whence *B*, 4, 169, 1; *Ṣ*, 2, 3–8. Both of them cite other sources in support of this reading. See also *Rich*, 281).[80]
49. 47/2	وَٱلذين آمَنُوا وَعَمِلُوا الصَّالِحَاتِ وَآمَنُوا بِمَا نُزِّلَ عَلَى مُحَمَّدٍ...	وَٱلَّذِينَ آمَنُوا وَعَمِلُوا ٱلصَّالِحَاتِ وَآمَنُوا بِمَا نُزِّلَ عَلَى مُحَمَّدٍ فِي عَلِيٍّ *TQ*, 2, 301, 12–13 (whence *B*, 4, 181; *Ṣ*, 2, 562, 6).
50. 47/9(10)	ذٰلِكَ بِأَنَّهُمْ كَرِهُوا مَا أَنْزَلَ ٱللهُ فَأَحْبَطَ أَعْمَالَهُمْ	ذٰلِكَ بِأَنَّهُمْ كَرِهُوا مَا أَنْزَلَ ٱللهُ فِي عَلِيٍّ فأَحْبَطَ أَعْمَالَهُمْ *TQ*, 2, 302, 10–11 (whence *B*, 4, 182, 1 [and see also tradition no. 2 citing Muḥammad ibn al-ʿAbbās];[71] *Ṣ*, 2, 563, 15–18 [cites, in addition to *TQ*, *MB* who reads here فِي حَقِّ عَلِيٍّ ; see *MB*, 26, 32, 19]).
51. 47/26(28)	ذٰلِكَ بِأَنَّهُمْ قَالُوا لِلَّذِينَ كَرِهُوا مَا نَزَّلَ ٱللهُ	ذٰلِكَ بِأَنَّهُمْ قَالُوا لِلَّذِينَ كَرِهُوا مَا نَزَّلَ ٱللهُ فِي عَلِيٍّ *TQ*, 2, 302, 10–11 and *K*, 421, 43 (whence *B*, 4, 187, 2 and *Ṣ*, 2, 570, 2–5); cf. *MB*, 26, 44, 7.

52. 50/24(23)	أَلْقِيَا فِي جَهَنَّمَ كُلَّ كَفَّارٍ عَنِيدٍ	**يَا مُحَمَّدُ يَا عَلِيُّ** أَلْقِيَا فِي جَهَنَّمَ كُلَّ كَفَّارٍ عَنِيدٍ *TF*, 439, 20–440, 2.[81]
53. 62/10–11	...وَٱبْتَغُوا مِنْ فَضْلِ ٱللهِ... وَتَرَكُوكَ قَائِماً قُلْ مَا عِنْدَ ٱللهِ خَيْرٌ مِنَ ٱللَّهْوِ...	... وَٱبْتَغُوا فَضْلَ ٱللهِ **عَلَى ٱلْأَوْصِيَاءِ**... وَتَرَكُوكَ **مَعَ عَلِيٍّ** قَائِماً قُلْ **يَا مُحَمَّدُ** مَا عِنْدَ ٱللهِ **مِنْ وَلَايَةِ عَلِيٍّ وَٱلْأَوْصِيَاءِ** خَيْرٌ مِنَ ٱللَّهْوِ... **لِلَّذِينَ ٱتَّقَوْا** *Iḥt*, 124–25 (whence *B*, 4, 335, 9 and *BA*, 86, 278).
54. 70/1–2	سَأَلَ سَائِلٌ بِعَذَابٍ وَاقِعٍ لِلْكَافِرِينَ...	سَأَلَ سَائِلٌ بِعَذَابٍ وَاقِعٍ لِلْكَافِرِينَ **بِوَلَايَةِ عَلِيٍّ...** *K*, 1, 422, 47 (whence B, 4, 381, 1, 4, and 5; *Ṣ*, 2, 742, 10–11).
55. 72/23(24)	إِلَّا بَلَاغاً مِنَ ٱللهِ وَرِسَالَاتِهِ وَمَنْ يَعْصِ ٱللهَ وَرَسُولَهُ	إِلَّا بَلَاغاً مِنَ ٱللهِ وَرِسَالَاتِهِ **فِي عَلِيٍّ** وَمَنْ يَعْصِ ٱللهَ وَرَسُولَهُ **فِي وَلَايَةِ عَلِيٍّ...** *K*, 434, 91[82] (whence *Ṣ*, 2, 753, 5–7).
56. 78/40(41)	...وَيَقُولُ ٱلْكَافِرُ يَا لَيْتَنِي كُنْتُ تُرَاباً	...وَيَقُولُ ٱلْكَافِرُ يَا لَيْتَنِي كُنْتُ **تُرَابِيًّا** *TN*, 27, 17–18.[83]

List of Abbreviations

B Hāšim b. Sulaymān . . . al-Baḥrānī al-Tawbalī, *Kitāb al-Burhān fī tafsīr al-Qurʾān*, Tehran, n.d., 5 volumes.

BA Muḥammad Bāqir al-Mağlisī, *Biḥār al-anwār*, Beirut 1403/1983, 100 volumes.

BC *Le Coran* (*al-Qurʾān*), translated from Arabic by Régis Blachère, Paris 1980.

BD Abū Ğaʿfar Muḥammad b. al-Ḥasan al-Ṣaffār al-Qummī, *Baṣāʾir al-darağāt*, Tibrīz 1380h.

BS M. M. Bar-Asher, *Studies in Early Imāmī-Šhīʿī Qurʾān Exegesis (3rd–4th / 9th–10th Centuries*), PhD Dissertation, Jerusalem 1991 (in Hebrew).

ĞB Abū Ğaʿfar Muḥammad b. Ğārīr al-Ṭabarī, *Ğāmiʿ al-bayān ʿan taʾwīl āy al-Qurʾān*, Cairo 1388/1968, 12 volumes.

Iḫt Abū ʿAbd Allāh Muḥammad al-Ḥāriṯī al-Baġdādī (al-šayḫ al-Mufīd), *Kitāb al-Iḫtiṣāṣ*, Najaf 1390 / 1971.

JM A. Jeffery, *Materials for the History of the Text of the Qurʾān*, Leiden 1937.

K Abū Ğaʿfar Muḥammad b. Yaʿqūb al-Kūlīnī, *al-Kāfī*, ed. ʿAlī Akbar al-Ğaffārī, Tehran 1377–1381h, 8 volumes.

KB E. Kohlberg, *Belief and the Law in Imāmī-Shīʿism, Variorum* (Collected Studies Series), Aldershot 1991.

KḤT Abū al-Qāsim Ğār Allāh Maḥmūd b. ʿUmar al-Zamaḫšarī, *al-Kaššāf ʿan ḥaqāʾiq ġawāmiḍ al-tanzīl*, 1403/1983, 4 volumes.

KQ E. Kohlberg, "Some Notes on the Imamite Attitude to the Qurʾān," in *Islamic Philosophy and the Classical Tradition, Essays Presented to R. Walzer*, ed. S. M. Stern, A. Hourani, and V. Brown, Oxford 1972, pp. 209–24.

MB Abū ʿAlī al-Faḍl al-Ṭabrisī, *Mağmaʿ al-bayān fī tafsīr al-Qurʾān*, Beirut 1374–1377/1954–1957, 6 volumes.

MQ Abū Zakariyyāʾ Yaḥyā b. Muḥammad al-Farrāʾ, *Maʿānī al-Qurʾān*, Cairo 1980, 3 volumes.

N Abū al-ʿAbbās Aḥmad b. ʿAlī al-Nağāšī, *Riğāl al-Nağāšī*, Qumm 1407h.

Rich I. Goldziher, *Die Richtungen der islamischen Koranauslegung*, Leiden 1920.

Ṣ Muḥammad b. al-Murtaḍā (= "Muḥsin al-Fayḍ") al-Kāšānī, *Kitāb al-Ṣafī fī tafsīr al-Qur'ān*, Tehran, n.d., 2 volumes.

ShA W. St. Clair Tisdall, "The Shī'ah Additions to the Koran," *Moslem World* 3 (1913): 227–41.

T Abū Ǧa'far Muḥammad b. al-Ḥasan al-Tūsī, *al-Tibyān fī tafsīr al-Qur'ān*, Najaf 1376–1385/1957–1965, 10 volumes.

T'A Abū al-Naḍr Muḥammad b. Mas'ūd b. 'Ayyāšī al-Sulamī al-Samarqandī, *Tafsīr al-'Ayyāšī*, ed. Hāšim al-Rasūlī al-Maḥallātī, Qumm 1380h, 2 volumes.

T'A (1) *Tafsīr al-'Ayyāšī*, manuscript no. 4153 of the India Office Library, London.

TF Furāt b. Ibrāhīm al-Kūfī, *Tafsīr Furāt*, Najaf 1410/1990.

TN *Tafsīr al-Nu'mānī*, a treatise on the Quran attributed to Muḥammad b. Ibrāhīm b. Ǧa'far al-Kātib al-Nu'mānī incorporated in: *Biḥār al-anwār*, vol. 93, pp. 1–97.

TQ 'Alī b. Ibrāhīm al-Qummī, *Tafsīr al-Qummī*, ed. al-Ṭayyib al-Mūsawī al-Ǧazā'irī, Najaf 1386–1387h, 2 volumes.

Notes

*The first part of this article is a revised and extended version of sections of my doctoral thesis (see the list of abbreviations under *BS*). The list of Šī'ī readings incorporated in the second part is published here for the first time. I would like to express my gratitude to Professor E. Kohlberg, who read an earlier draft of this article and made valuable comments. In addition, I would like to thank him for drawing my attention to the variant readings nos. 1, 25, 35, 45, 53, and 54 in the appended list. I am also grateful to Dr. T. Ilan for her assistance in translating this paper from the Hebrew.

1. The English translation of the Quranic verses cited in this article is that of A. Arberry, *The Koran Interpreted*, Oxford University Press, 1983 (2nd edition). Verses are cited in the numbering of both the common Egyptian and G. Flügel's editions. Where the two differ, the Egyptian edition is cited first and Flügel's second. In citations from other sources the first numeral appearing after the abbreviation of the source name indicates the number of the volume (or part—in works divided into

parts), the second indicates the page number, and the third, the tradition number (in works divided into numbered traditions) or the line number (in other works).

2. *Rich*, pp. 1–54.

3. Ibid., pp. 279–85.

4. "The 'Shiʿite Qurʾān,' a Reconsideration of Goldziher's Interpretation," *Arabica* 16 (1969): 15–24.

5. See his article in the list of abbreviations under *KQ*.

6. "The Speaking Qurʾān and the Silent Qurʾān: A Study of the Principles and Development of Imāmī Tafsīr," in *Approaches to the History of the Interpretation of the Qurʾān*, ed. A. Rippin, Oxford University Press, 1988, pp. 177–98.

7. For example, an alteration such as the reading *yaḍuǧǧūn* ("to scream," "to cause a row") instead of *yaṣiḍḍūn* in verse 43/57: *Wa-lammā ḍuriba bnu Maryam maṯalan iḏā qawmuka minhu yaṣiḍḍūn*) "And when the son of Mary is cited as an example, behold thy people turn away from it . . .") (*TQ*, 2, 286, 5; *TF*, 403, 12) or *wa-ġayri al-ḍḍāllīn* instead of *wa-lā al-ḍḍāllīn* (". . . not those who are astray") on verse 1/7 (see, e.g., *TʿA*, 1, 24, 28), which are variations that have no bearing on the Šīʿī doctrine.

8. For a detailed survey of the last four commentators and their works see *BS*, pp. 35–68.

9. See, for example, nos. 7, 11, 22, and 27 in the appended list.

10. I have dealt with some of the changes that occurred in the Šīʿa during the Buwayhid period in *BS*, chapter 3, pp. 69–82.

11. *TQ*, 2, 295, 14. The nature of this alteration has been dealt with in detail by Goldziher (*Rich*, p. 281), who cites this tradition in its entirety.

12. See, for example, *TN*, 27, 17–18, which expressly states that the version in this verse has been altered/falsified (*fa-ḥarrafūhā*) to *turāban*. See by way of comparison the tradition adduced by Kohlberg in his article cited in the following note (p. 351).

13. On this designation and its different interpretations, see E. Kohlberg, "*Abū Turāb*," *KB*, ch. 6, pp. 347–52. (= *Bulletin of the School of Oriental and African Studies* 41, no. 2 [1978]).

14. See, for example, *TQ*, 2, 402, 14–15; *Ṣ*, 2, 783, 5–11; *B*, 4, 423, 1–3 and also Kohlberg, ibid., p. 251.

15. See the sources in the appended list, no. 9.

16. See: *TN*, 9–12, which combines this interpretation within the suggested alteration, and similarly *TʿA*, 1, 142, 12; cf. *TQ*, 1, 324, 14, which cites this verse as an example for *taʾḥīr fī al-taʾlīf* ("a late editing"), but does not define it outright as a forgery.

17. See nos. 1, 3, 4, 12, 14, 15, 20, 28, 49, 50, 51, and 55 in the appended list, and also Goldziher, *Rich*, p. 285.

18. See nos. 2, 16, 21, 32, 34, 41, and 47 in the appended list, and Goldziher, ibid.

19. See nos. 17, 33, 42, 45, 53, and 54 in the appended list.

20. This issue has recently been thoroughly dealt with by A. Gribetz, *Strange Bedfellows: Mutʿat al-nisāʾ and Mutʿat al-Ḥajj—A Study Based on Sunnī and Šīʿī Sources of Tafsīr, Ḥadīth and Fiqh* (*PhD Dissertation*), Jerusalem 1991. The textual variants of this verse are discussed in detail on pp. 65–67 and 171–73 of this dissertation. See also Blachère (*BC*, p. 109), who, in his French translation of the Quran, renders this verse according to both Sunnī and Šīʿī versions. See also his note on this verse, ibid., p. 108.

21. On the *Zaydī-Ǧārūdī* material found in *TQ* see *BS*, pp. 50–56.

22. See the sources for this in the appended list, no. 40.

23. See *TʿA*, 2, 326, 28. For similar versions, see ibid., 1, 45, 49 and also *TQ*, 2, 111, 18.

24. See, for example, *TQ*, 1, 142, 14; 1, 297, 16; 2, 21, 19.

25. See, for example, *TʿA*, 1, 194, 119; 1, 195, 128; *TQ*, 1, 389, 17.

26. See *TQ*, 1, 10, 3–16, which cites as an example for such verses 3/110 and 25/74. See also the note of the editor (al-Ṭayyib al-Mūsawī al-Ǧazāʾirī) to *TQ*, 1, 5.

27. See, for example, *TQ*, 2, 295, 14.

28. See *TQ*, 2, 407, 10; *TF*, 541–42. It should, however, be noted that among other interpretations, al-Qummī (*TQ*, ibid.) also brings one that remains loyal to the plain meaning of the text.

29. This is clearly discernible from one tradition in *TF*, 542 (the last tradition there), which reads *yaʿnī mawaddatanā*. The use of *yaʿnī* (= i.e.) may stress the fact that this is an interpretation rather than a variant reading.

30. Two verses should be excluded from this rule: in the first (no. 11), the temporal nature of the *mutʿa* marriage is stressed by the addition of the words *ilā aǧalin musamman* (see section 2.D above); in the second (no. 19) the vocalization indicates a difference between the Sunna and the Šīʿa concerning laws of purification prior to prayer.

31. This sugject was already noted by scholars in the nineteenth century. See a summary of this subject in *BS*, pp. 32–33.

32. See by way of comparison Goldziher, *Rich*, p. 281.

33. The speaker is Sālim b. Abī Salma (died 137/754); a Kūfan, *mawlā* of *Banū ʿIǧl*; a transmitter of traditions from the Imams Zayn al-ʿĀbidīn, al-Bāqir, and al-Ṣādiq (*N*, p. 188).

34. *BD*, 193, 3. With minor alterations the tradition is also found in *K*, 2, 633, 23.

35. The word *aḥruf* in this tradition has been interpreted as synonymous with *qirāʾāt*; see by way of comparison Goldziher, *Rich*, p. 37ff.

36. *K*, 2, 630, 13. The context indicates that here too the word *aḥruf* is synonymous with *qirāʾāt*.

37. This can also be translated in the imperative: "Deny (*kaḏḏibū*) the (words of these) enemies of God."

38. *K*, ibid., tradition no. 12. See also Muḥammad Ibn Babawayhi, *Risāla fī al-iʿtiqādāt*, p. 100, l. 6–7; and Abū al-Qāsim al-Mūsawī al-Ḫūʾī, *al-Bayān fī tafsīr al-qurʾān*, p. 177. Al-Ḫūʾī (a modern Šīʿī authority) maintains also the view that there is only one authoritative version of the Quran.

39. The word *ḥarf* has been translated here, according to context, as synonymous with *qirāʾa* (see note 35).

40. *T*, 1, 7. Al-Ṭabrisī (*MB*, 1, 23–26) uses similar wording and may in fact be dependent on al-Tūsī. It should be noted that al-Tūsī is cautious in his attitude toward the tradition of the seven *aḥruf* / *qirāʾāt*; although he stresses that these are the opinions of the opponents of the Šīʿa (*wa-rawā al-muḫālifūna lanā*) he nevertheless does not reject it altogether.

41. See the beginning of section 2, note 10.

42. For more about the *taqiyya* consideration with relation to variant readings, see *Kitāb al-iḥtiǧāǧ* by Aḥmad b. Abī Ṭālib al-Ṭabrisī, cited in *BA*, 93, 120, 18–121, 1.

43. Literally: "Do not read," that is, a certain word in Scripture should not be read the way it appears in the text but slightly altered, thus rendering a new meaning to the verse (see below).

44. That is, an external tannaitic tradition (*Baraithā*) attributed to the Prophet Elijah.

45. *The Babylonian Talmud: Megillah*, 29b., translated into English by I. Epstein, London 1938, vol. 10, p. 174 (with slight modifications). The Hebrew of this *baraitha* runs as follows:

"תנא דבי אליהו: כל השונה הלכות בכל יום מובטח לו שהוא בן העולם הבא, שנאמר 'הליכות עולם לו'; אל תקרי 'הליכות' אלא 'הלכות'"

For other examples of this kind of midrash s.v. "al-tikrei" (אל תקרי) in *Talmudic Encyclopedia*, Jerusalem 1949, vol. 2, pp. 1–2; and v. "al tikrei," in *Encyclopedia Judaica*, vol. 2, p. 776.

46. It should be noted that the tradition that reads أَئِمَّةٌ instead of أُمَّةٌ is unusual. Most of the traditions in fact interpret the word أُمَّةٌ as pertaining to the Imams, but do not state that it involves a variant reading (see, for example, *TʿA*, 1, 62–63; *TF*,

62, 7–14; *T*, 2, 7–8; *MB*, 2, 10–11; *B*, 1, 159–60; *Ṣ*, 1, 147–48). The tradition in *TQ*, on the other hand, contains the explicit formula *innammā nazalat* ("so was [the verse] revealed"). The tradition in *TN* (27, 15–17) even states that the verse as it appears in the canon is counterfeit.

47. The variant in this verse shows the importance of one's behaving in accordance with *taqiyya*. The traditions in *TQ*, 1, 100 and *TN*, 29, 9–16 (cited also in *B*, 1, 275) maintain that the verse deals with *taqiyya*, but do not state in so many words that this is a variant reading. On this see E. Kohlberg, "Some Imāmī-Šīʿī Views on *Taqiyya*," *KB*, ch. 3, pp. 395–402 (= *Journal of the American Oriental Society* 95, no. 3 [1975]), and for the matter at hand see particularly p. 396 with note 6.

48. Al-Ṭūsī, and following him al-Ṭabrisī, both state that the reading تَقِيَّةً is the version held by some important readers, including al-Ḥasan al-Baṣrī, al-Farrāʾ (see also *MQ*, 1, 205), and Muǧāhid. Further on, these two commentators maintain the importance of behavior in accordance with *taqiyya* (*T*, 435; *MB*, ibid.). A similar attitude is also found in the writings of al-Kāšānī (*Ṣ*, ibid.); see also: *ĞB*, 3, 230 and *KḤT*, 1, 422.

49. Jeffery (ibid.) states that this variant reading was included in the Codex of ʿAbd Allāh b. Masʿūd, and that it was "also given from the Imams of *Ahl al-Bayt*"; see also *B*, 1, 279, 17.

50. Two traditions state categorically that the canonical version is identical with the reading of the Imam Zayd, while ʿAlī's version (which is, according to these traditions, similar to the version "revealed by the [archangel] Gabriel to Muḥammad") includes the additions brought here.

51. These two traditions clearly state that this is a Šīʿī reading, but see by way of comparison tradition no. 130, which has the canonical version. The interpretation of the verse there is also devoid of any Šīʿī characteristics.

52. The variation in this verse is the result of the doctrine of *ʿiṣma* (immunity of prophets [and in Imāmī-Šīʿī doctrine of the Imams also] from error and sin). The Imāmī commentators found it inconceivable that God should describe the Prophet and his army in the Battle of Badr which is the subject of this verse) as أَذِلَّةٌ ("humiliated"), a definition which suggests denigration of the Prophet. The variants قَلِيلٌ ("few") or ضُعَفَاءُ ("weak") reflect in the eyes of the commentators the real situation in which the Prophet and his warriors found themselves, and at the same time do not create doctrinal difficulties from the *ʿiṣma* point of view. For further details see *BS*, pp. 96 and 146.

53. Jefferey (ibid.) states that this version was included in the Codex of Ubayy b. Kaʿb.

54. On the significance of this addition and its position in the Sunnī-Šīʿī controversy, see above, section 2.D and note 20.

55. Al-Ṭūsī states that the addition to this verse held by the Šīʿa is included in the codices of some important readers (*qurrāʾ*) such as Ibn ʿAbbās, Ibn Masʿūd, and Ubayy b. Kaʿb. The same is implied by Jeffery (*JM*, 36, 126, 197, 246, 255, 288).

56. The two textual variations provided by the last source are: 1. بِمَا نَزَّلْنَا عَلَى عَبْدِنَا (tradition no. 3) and 2. .. فِي عَلِيٍّ نُوراً مُبِيناً (ibid., 373, 1).

57. Against this tradition, which views the additional words as part of the "original" text (as indicated by the words *hā-kaḏā nazalat* in *TQ*, ibid.), other traditions regard these words as an exegetical addition. See *B*, 1, 390, 7; 390, 14.

58. Some of the sources quoted here only hint at this variant reading while others deal with it explicitly and extensively. As suggested in the introduction, this verse is the focus of a judicial controversy between the Sunna and the Šīʿa. The issue at hand was the syntactical position of the word وَأَرْجُلَكُمْ ("and your feet") in this verse. The reading held by the Sunna maintains that the word is in the accusative case: وَأَرْجُلَكُمْ, that is, it is regarded as a third direct object of the verb فَاغْسِلُوا ("and wash") joining the two previous ones وُجُوهَكُمْ وَأَيْدِيَكُمْ ("your face and hands"). The Sunnī commandment, which maintains that one should wash his feet as well before prayer, is derived from this. The Šīʿa, on the other hand, maintains that the reading وَأَرْجُلِكُمْ is in the dative case, joining the word بِرُؤُوسِكُمْ ("your heads") as a second indirect object to the verb فَامْسَحُوا ("and wipe"). Thus the Imāmī doctors deduced that it is sufficient for the believer to wipe his head and feet and he is not obliged to wash them. However, some Imāmī scholars maintained that one should follow the Sunnī ruling out of considerations of *taqiyya*. For this issue see the words of al-Tūsī (*al-Istibṣār fi-mā ʾḫtulifa min al-aḫbār*, vol. 1, ch. 37, pp. 64–66, and particularly his conclusion on p. 66, lines 5–8, quoted here): "And this tradition (mentioned above, dealing with the obligation to wash one's feet) corresponds with (the system of) the Sunnīs and is maintained through *taqiyya*, since it is well known and without doubt that according to our Imams, may they rest in peace, one should (only) wipe (!) his feet (*fa-hāḏā ḫabar muwāfiq li-l-ʿāmma wa-qad warada mawrida al-taqiyya li-anna al-maʿlūm allaḏī lā yataḫāğu fīhi al-šakku min maḏāhibi aʾimmatinā ʿalayhim al-salām al-qawlu bi-l-masḥ ʿalā al-riğlayn.*"

59. It should be noted that the editor of *al-Tibyān* (Aḥmad Ḥabīb Quṣayr al-ʿĀmilī) not only cites the Šīʿī exegetical traditions that support the Šīʿī doctrine but also vocalized the controversial word in the accusative (i.e., وَأَرْجُلَكُمْ) according to these same traditions (see *T*, 3, 447, 14).

60. Al-Farrāʾ presents two traditions according to which the ruling demanding the washing of feet is not embedded in the Quranic text (precisely according to the Šīʿī doctrine), but is only a custom (*sunna*) of the Prophet.

61. It should be stressed that in *TQ* (ibid.) the verb فَرَّقُوا ("caused dissention") is explained with the help of the verb فَارَقُوا ("left, abandoned") without being regarded as a variant reading. Nevertheless, the uniqueness of the Šīʿī alteration فَارَقُوا > فَرَّقُوا becomes clear through al-Qummī's comment further down: فَارَقُوا أَمِيرَ ٱلْمُؤْمِنِينَ وَصَارُوا شِيعاً ("They abandoned the Commander of the faithful and became sects"). However, compare al-Tūsī's comment (*T*, 4, 328), who states that both readings, despite the difference between them, are close in meaning.

62. The word نَبِيُّكُمْ is found in square brackets in the source itself; such brackets are used there for additions found (only) in some manuscripts on which this edition is based (and compare *TʿA*[1], 131a, l. 19, where this word is absent altogether).

63. All these three works cite as a source for this reading both *TʿA* and *K*; it should be stressed that the anti-Sunnī intention is clearly reflected in the Šīʿī reading. This verse (according to both Šīʿī and Sunnī commentators) recalls Abū Bakr's sojourn with Muḥammad in the cave when they were fleeing the people of Mecca. The Šīʿī tradition seeks, however, to remove all ambiguity from the word عَلَيْهِ ("on him") found in the canonical text that may be interpreted as referring to Abū Bakr as well; such an interpretation would elevate him to a position where he too received divine revelation (*sakīna*). It therefore reads the words عَلَى رَسُولِهِ ("upon his Messenger") stressing that Muḥammad alone received divine revelation. See also *T*, 5, 223 and *MB*, 10, 55, which discuss, in connection with this verse, the episode of Muḥammad's hiding in the cave, without referring to the above-mentioned variant reading. Contrast the version mentioned by Jeffery (*JM*, 214), which, according to him, was included in the Codex of Ḥafṣa (the daughter of ʿUmar): وَأَنْزَلَ سَكِينَتَهُ عَلَيْهِمَا وَأَيَّدَهُمَا بِجُنُودٍ ("Then [God] sent down on both of them his Shechina, and confirmed the two of them with legions . . ."); for a detailed discussion of other aspects of this verse, see *BS*, 79–80; 96–97.

63[a]. See the note on this tradition (in *K*, ibid., n. 6) explaining the variant reading *maʾmūnūn* as referring to the Imams, "who are protected from and immune to sin (*wa-hum al-maʾmūnūn ʿan al-ḫaṭaʾ al-maʿṣūmūn*). It should be emphasized that both *TW* (1, 304, 10–11) and *TʿA* (2, 108–109) interpret this verse as referring to the Imams (or to ʿAlī alone), without, however, adopting the variant itself.

64. In this verse (like the previous one [9/40]) the Šīʿī version reflects the wish to harmonize the Quranic text with the doctrine of *ʿiṣma*. The Imāmī traditionists could not accept the idea that the Prophet be treated on an equal footing with the *muhāǧirūn* ("the Emigrants") and the *anṣār* ("the Helpers"), against whom the wrath of God receded, or as the verse has it: "God had turned towards the Prophet and the Emigrants and the Helpers." The idea that God was angry with his Prophet Muḥammad is unthinkable. The difficulty

was overcome by a simple emendation in the version of the verse, namely, . . . *bi-l-nabiyyi ʿalā al-muhāǧirīn wa-l-anṣār* ("[God] through the Prophet turned towards the Emigrants and the Helpers"). This small emendation not only averts the possibility that Muḥammad is the object of the wrath of God but also elevates him to the position of *šafīʿ* ("intercessor"), whose intervention persuades God to accept the repentance of others.

65. In order to clarify the idea behind the Šīʿī version, one should review the way in which this verse is interpreted in the general Muslim Quranic exegesis. All viewed the verse cluster 116/115–119/118 in the 9th Sūra as referring to the behavior of some of Muḥammad's believers during the expedition to Tabūk (in the year 8/630). But the Sunnī and Šīʿī commentators are divided on the reading and interpretation of certain words in this verse cluster. With regard to the verse under discussion, the Sunnī commentators read: وَالثَّلاثَةِ الَّذِينَ خُلِّفُوا ("And the three who were left behind") and identify the three anonymous persons mentioned here as three of the *anṣār* (on the various traditions relating to this issue and to the identification of these *anṣār* as Hilāl b. Umayya, Kaʿb b. Mālik, and Mirāra b. al-Rabīʿ, see *ǦB*, 11, 52–56). The Imāmī tradition, on the other hand, which reads here خَالَفُوا, identifies these men as persons who disobeyed the prophet: *ʿUṯmān wa-ṣāḥibāhu* ("ʿUthmān and his two companions")—a code word indicating most likely the two Caliphs Abū Bakr and ʿUmar (on the use of code words of this kind in Imāmī Quranic exegesis, see I. Goldziher, "Spottnamen der ersten Chalifen bei den Schiʿiten" in Ignaz Goldziher, *Gesammelte Schriften*, Hildesheim 1970, vol. 4, pp. 295–308; and recently *BS*, pp. 104–106). It should further be emphasized that the Imāmī commentators defend the superiority of their version by pointing out the drawbacks of the Sunnī version. Had the Sunnī version (according to which the three men were left behind [*ḥullifū*] against their will) been the correct one, it would have been inappropriate for God to be angry with them (*law kānū ḥullifū mā kāna ʿalayhim min sabīl*) (*TʿA* [ibid.], and see also al-Qummī [*TQ*, 1, 296, 1] who reads *wa-lam yakun ʿalayhim min ʿayb*). Moreover, the context in general, which suggests that God forgave them their behavior, would not have been altogether clear. Over and against this, according to the Šīʿī reading here (i.e., خَالَفُوا), God's forgiveness to the sinners receives added significance. Finally, it should be noted that traditions identifying the three men in a similar manner to the Sunnī tradition are also found in Šīʿī sources (see, e.g., *TʿA*, 2, 115, 159; *TQ*, 1, 296, 15–16 whence *B*, 2, 169, 6; *Ṣ*, 1, 728, 4–5 and tradition 3 ibid. [the citation is from *Nahǧ al-Bayān*]).

66. The tradition found in al-ʿAyyāšī adds that the reading that includes the word حَقَّهُ is ʿAlī's; Zayd, on the other hand, opts for the verse as found in the canonical codex. It should be noted that the addition of the word حَقّ ("rights") to different Quranic verses

is common in the Šīʿī readings, which protest against the usurpation of Šīʿī rights (see nos. 2, 16, 22, 32, 34, 37, 41, and 47 in the list). Further still, Šīʿī tradition that does not have these additions interprets the above-mentioned verse (based on the expression *ḏī al-qurbā* ["kinsmen"] found in it), as referring to the family of the Prophet and/or to the Šīʿa in general (see, e.g., *TQ*, 1, 388, 17–18; *TF*, 236; *T*, 6, 419, 4–5).

67. In *TʿA*, 2, 297, 93 a tradition similar to the one found in *TQ* is presented, but nowhere is it mentioned that the words added to the canonical version are a variant reading. It should be stressed that in both Sunnī and Šīʿī exegesis this verse has been interpreted as referring to the Umayyad dynasty. On the importance of this verse among the group of Quranic verses referring to the Umayyads, see the detailed comment of Goldziher in *Rich*, pp. 266–67 and also in his *Muslim Studies*, vol. 2, pp. 111–12.

68. The tradition including this addition is absent from *TʿA* (1).

69. It should be noted that the last three sources bring the version found in *TʿA* with a slight alteration: بِوَلَايَةِ instead of وَلَايَةِ. Furthermore, the two last sources (*B* and *Ṣ*) cite *K* as the source for this addition. However, see by way of comparison tradition 3 in *B* (ibid.), which leaves unaltered the canonical version but adds that the verse was revealed in connection with the *walāya*.

70. The term مُحَدَّث ("one to whom God has spoken and whom he has taught"), which the Šīʿa reads in the canonical verse, seeks to incorporate in the Quran the idea that the Imams, too, are party to some form of revelation. On this issue see E. Kohlberg, "The Term *Muḥaddath* in Twelver Shīʿīsm," *KB*, ch. 5, pp. 39–47 (= *Studia Orientalia Memoriae D. H. Baneth Dedicata*, Jerusalem 1979); and recently: Y. Friedmann, *Prophecy Continuous: Aspects of Aḥmadī Religious Thought and Its Medieval Background*, Berkeley, Los Angeles, London, 1989, pp. 82–86; and see also *BS*, 139–40 with note 158 (pp. 282–83).

71. Known as Ibn al-Ǧuḥām, an Imāmī scholar of the 3–4th/9–10th centuries, who wrote a number of works, including a commentary on the Quran of which fragments only have survived (see *N*, 379). As for the derogatory appellation al-ṯānī, it is usually used in Imāmī literature with reference to ʿUmar ibn al-Ḫaṭṭāb. It should be noted that the word *fulān* is also often used with reference to ʿUmar, but since it is found here in the Quranic text itself, it was substituted by another "code word" alluding to him. (On attributes and appellations aimed at him, see the references to Goldziher and *BS* at note 65.) It should be noted further that this verse, like its predecessor *yā laytanī ttaḫaḏtu maʿa al-rasūl sabīlan* ("Would that I had taken a way along with the Messenger") has been interpreted as words of regret uttered by the enemies of the Šīʿa on the day of judgment. A tradition found in *TQ*, 2, 113, 5–6 stresses that according to the interpretation of the Imam Abū Ǧaʿfar (al-Bāqir), the

sinner who regrets the wrongs he has committed against the Šīʿa utters on the day of judgment: *Yā laytanī ttaḫadtu maʿa al-rasūl ʿAliyyan waliyyan* ("Would that I had taken, with the Messenger, ʿAlī as an ally").

72. This verse with its two versions has been interpreted as referring to the family of the Prophet (e.g., *TF*, 292–95; *TQ*, 2, 117, 13–21). However, the verse that combines a variant reading is preferred by the commentators. According to the Šīʿī version the translation would be: "Give us an Imam from among the believers" (*wa-ǧʿal lanā min al-muttaqīna imāman*), while according to the other reading, the translation is: "and make us a model (an Imam) to the God fearing."

73. On the differences between the three last sources with regard to this verse, see above, end of section 2.D.

74. Attention should be paid to the tradition cited in *B*, 190, 2, where the text is: *wa-anḏir ʿašīrataka al-aqrabīna ay rahṭaka al-muḫliṣīna*, the additional words being understood as an exegetical addition, as is clear from the explanatory word *ay*.

75. This version is found in the commentary to verse 21/87; *TF* is the only source where this variant was found. The meaning of the variant مُسَبِّحِينَ > مُقِرِّينَ is clarified when one studies the way in which the tradition in Furāt interprets the relevant verses: Jonah's punishment (being swallowed by a fish), which is the topic of these two verses, was not only the result of his attempted escape from God's mission, but came about more particularly because, alone among all the heavenly and earthly creatures, he refused to express his loyalty (*walāya*) to ʿAlī, when required to do so. "Had he persisted in his stubborn refusal, and had he not joined those who confess (*al-muqirrīn*) their loyalty to ʿAlī, he would have been left within the stomach of the fish till the day of the resurrection." It is clear from this that since the verse was interpreted as referring to the duty of loyalty to ʿAlī, the verb found in the canonical version *al-musabbiḥīn* ("the praisers") was no longer suitable. This verb is used only to refer to God and not to anyone of flesh and blood; the alternative Šīʿī verb *al-muqirrīn* can easily be employed for humans as well.

76. This tradition is found in the commentary on verse 4/137(136).

77. The three words within square brackets are exegetical additions, as can be inferred from the explanatory word *yaʿnī*.

78. The addition that al-Qummī presents under the guise of words of revelation (*nazalat hātāni al-āyatāni hā-kaḏā*) refers to Abū Bakr and ʿUmar. This is hinted at both in the words of the commentator: *yaʿnī fulānan wa-fulānan* and in the employment of the dual form in the word *aḥaduhumā* in the verse itself.

79. Al-Kāšānī (like *TQ*) interprets this verse as referring to "the extortionist" (*al-ġāšim*) and "Satan" (*al-šayṭān*), who are none other than Abū Bakr and ʿUmar.

See by way of comparison also the traditions cited in *B*, 4, 142–43, which also denigrate these two men, without suggesting textual alterations in the canonical text of the Quran.

80. On the meaning of the alteration suggested by the Šīʿa to this verse, see above, section 2.A, note 11.

81. Several traditions in *TF* (436–40) and in other sources (*TQ*, 2, 324–26; *B*, 223–27 and *Ṣ* 2, 260, 13–19) interpret this verse as referring to Muḥammad and ʿAlī. But only this tradition in *TF* suggests that this interpretation be incorporated into the text of the Quran.

82. The tradition in *K* defines explicitly the first addition as a (prophetic) revelation (*tanzīl*).

83. As mentioned above (section 2.A), the term تُرَابِيًّا has been interpreted as referring to ʿAlī without suggesting a variant reading in the Quranic text (see note 14 above). Nevertheless, some traditions have incorporated this expression into the Quranic text (such as the tradition from *TN* cited here, and see also note 12 above).

P.S.

Since the initial publication of the present article in 1993, a key work in the field of Imāmī-Šīʿī *qirāʾāt* has come out: *Revelation and Falsification: The Kitāb al-qirāʾāt of Aḥmad b. Muḥammad al-Sayyārī* (*Critical Edition with an Introduction and Notes*) by E. Kohlberg and M. A. Amir-Moezzi (Leiden, 2009). This work contains numerous other cases of Imāmī-Šīʿī variant readings.

Appendix A

Abbreviations

AcO	*Acta Orientalia*. Copenhagen.
AO	*Ars Orientalis*. Washington, DC, Ann Arbor, 1954–.
BSOAS	*Bulletin of the School of Oriental and African Studies*. London, 1917–.
CODCH	*The Concise Oxford Dictionary of the Christian Church*. Edited by E. A. Livingstone. Oxford, 1980.
CSCO	*Corpus scriptorum christianorum orientalium*. Edited by J. B. Chabot, I. Guidi, et al. In six sections: Scriptores Aethiopici; Scriptores Arabici; Scriptores Armeniaci; Scriptores Coptici; Scriptores Iberici; Scriptores Syri (various publishers). Paris, Leuven, 1903–.
EI	*Encyclopaedia of Islam*. Edited by M. T. Houtsma et al. 4 vols. Leiden and London, 1913–1934.
EI^2	*Encyclopaedia of Islam*, 2d ed. Edited by H. A. R. Gibb et al. Leiden and London, 1960–.
EQ	*Encyclopaedia of the Qur'ān*, 6 volumes. Leiden, Netherlands: Brill, 2001–.

ER	*Encyclopedia of Religion*. Edited by M. Eliade. New York: Macmillan, 1993.
GAL	C. Brockelmann. *Geschichte des Arabischen Literatur*, 2d ed. 2 vols. Leiden, 1943–49; Supplementbände. 3 vols. Leiden, 1937–42.
GAS	Fuat Sezgin. *Geschichte des arabischen Schriftums*. Leiden, 1967–.
GdQ/GdK	Theodor Nöldeke. *Geschichte des Qorans*. Göttingen, 1860. 2d ed. Edited by Friedrich Schwally, G. Bergstrasser, and O. Pretzl. 3 vols. Leipzig, 1909–1938.
IC	*Islamic Culture*. Hyderabad, 1927–.
IJMES	*International Journal of Middle East Studies*. Middle East Studies Association of North America, New York. Vol. 1, 1970–.
JA	*Journal asiatique*. Paris, 1822–.
JAATA	*Journal of the American Association of Teachers of Arabic*.
JAL/ZAL	*Journal for Arabic Linguistics*. Wiesbaden.
JAOS	*Journal of the American Oriental Society*. New Haven, Ann Arbor, 1842–.
JESHO	*Journal of the Economic and Social History of the Orient*. Paris, 1957–.
JNES	*Journal of Near Eastern Studies*. Oriental Institute, University of Chicago. Vol. 1, 1942–. Supersedes *American Journal of Semitic Languages and Literatures*.

JPHS	*Journal of the Pakistan Historical Society*
JRAS	*Journal of the Royal Asiatic Society.* London, 1834–.
JSAI	*Jerusalem Studies in Arabic and Islam.* Jerusalem, 1979–.
JSS	*Journal of Semitic Studies.* Oxford, 1956–.
MW	*Muslim World.* Hartford Seminary Foundation, Hartford, CT. Vol. 1, 1911–. Published as *Moslem World,* 1911– 1947.
Or.Ltz.	*Orientalistische Literaturzeitung,* Berlin. Vols. 1–8, 1898–1905.
REI	*Revue des Etudes Islamiques.* Paris.
REJ	*Revue des Etudes Juives.*
RHPR	*Revue d'Histoire et de Philosophie Religieuses.* Strasbourg.
RHR	*Revue de l'histoire des religions. Annales du Muséé Guimet.* Paris. Vol. 1, 1880–.
RSO	*Rivista degli studi orientali.* Rome. Vol. 1, 1907–.
RSPT	*Revue des Sciences Philosophiques et Théologiques.* Paris.
RSR	*Revue des sciences religieuses.* Strasbourg, 1921–.
SBWA	*Sitzungsberichte der Philosophisch-Historischen Klasse der Kaiserlichen Akademie der Wissenschaften.* Vienna, 1848–.

SEI	*Shorter Encyclopaedia of Islam.* Edited by H. A. R. Gibb and J. H. Kramers. Leiden, 1953.
SI	*Studia Islamica.* Paris, 1953–.
TGUOS	*Transactions of the Glasgow University Oriental Society.* Glasgow.
THES	*Times Higher Education Supplement.* London.
TLS	*Times Literary Supplement.* London.
Wellhausen *Reste*	J. Wellhausen. *Reste arabischen Heidentums*, 2d ed. Berlin, 1897.
WI	*Die Welt des Islams.* Berlin, 1913–.
WZKM	*Wiener Zeitschrift für die Kunde des Morgenlandes.* Vienna.
ZA	*Zeitschrift für Assyriologie und verwandte Gebiete.* Vols. 1–19, Berlin 1886–1905/06.
ZAL/JAL	*Zeitschrift für Arabische Linguistik.* Wiesbaden.
ZATW	*Zeitschrift für alttestamentliche Wissenschaft.*
ZDMG	*Zeitschrift der deutschen Morgenlandischen Gesellschaft.* Leipzig, Wiesbaden, 1847–.

Appendix B

Glossary

Abū l -Qāsim. Father of Qasim, that is, Muhammad, the Prophet; a **kunya** for Muhammad, the Prophet.

adab. *Belles-lettres*; refinement, culture.

'adālah. Probity; synonym of **ta'dīl**.

adīb. Writer of **adab**; man of letters.

'ahd. Covenant, treaty, engagement.

Ahl al-Bayt. The people of the house, Muhammad's household (the family of the Prophet).

ahl al-Ḥadīth. Those collecting and learned in the **Ḥadīth**.

Ahl al-Kitāb. "People of the Book," especially Christians and Jews.

ahl al-ra'y. People of reasoned opinion; those using their own opinion to establish a legal point.

ahl as-ṣuffa. The people of the bench, of the temple at Mecca; they were poor strangers without friends or place of abode who claimed the promises of the Apostle of God and implored his protection.

akhbār. Reports, anecdotes, history.

'alām. Signs, marks, badges.

amān. Safe conduct.

amārāt al-nubūwwa. Marks of prophethood.

ʿāmm. Collective or common words.

anṣār. The helpers; early converts of Medina, and then later all citizens of Medina converted to Islam; in contrast to the Muhajirun, or exiles, those Muslims who accompanied the Prophet from Mecca to Medina.

ʿaqīqah. The custom, observed on the birth of a child, of leaving the hair on the infant's head until the seventh day, when it is shaved and animals are sacrificed.

ʿarabiyyah. The standard of correct Arabic usage of the sixth and seventh centuries CE, as envisaged by the eighth-century grammarians.

ʿaṣabiyyah. Tribal solidarity.

asbāb al-nuzūl. The occasions and circumstances of the Koranic revelations.

aṣḥā b al-nabī. Companions of the Prophet. (A single companion is a **sahabi**.)

assonance. A repeated vowel sound, a part rhyme, which has great expressive effect when used internally (within lines), for example, "An old, mad, blind, despised and dying king," Shelley, "Sonnet: England in 1819." It consists in a similarity in the accented vowels and those which follow, but not in the consonants, for example, creep/feet skin/swim. Examples in the Koran at VI, 164; XVII,15; and so on, for example, *wa-lā taziru wāzir -atun wizra ukhrā.*

Awā'il. The ancients; the first people to do something.

āyah (pl. **āyāt**). Sign, miracle; verse of the Koran.

ayyām al-ʿArab. "Days" of the Arabs; pre-Islamic tribal battles.

bāb. Subchapter, especially in **Ḥadīth** literature.

basmalah. The formula "In the name of God, the Merciful, the Compassionate" (*bi-ʿsmi ʿillahi ʿl-Rahmani ʿ l-Rahim*).

bint. Girl; daughter of.

ḍaʿīf (pl. **ḍuʿafā'**). Weak, as classification of a **Ḥadīth**; traditionist of dubious reliability.

dalā'il. Proofs, signs, marks.

dār. Abode.

Dār al-Ḥarb. The Land of Warfare, a country belonging to infidels not subdued by Islam.

Dār al-Islām. The Land of Islam, the Islamic world.

dhimmah. Security, pact.

dhimmī. Non-Muslim living as a second-class citizen in an Islamic state; Christian or Jew.

diglossia. A situation where two varieties of the same language live side by side. The two variations are high and low: High Arabic and Low Arabic.

dīn. Religion.

dīwān. Register; collection of poetry by a single author or from a single tribe.

du'ā'. Prayer; generally used for supplication as distinguished from ṣalāt, or liturgical form of prayer.

faḍā'il. Merits.

fakhr. Boasting, self-glorification, or tribal vaunting.

faqīh (pl. **fuqahā'**)**.** One learned in **fiqh**.

fātiḥah. The first **sura** of the Koran.

fiqh. Islamic jurisprudence.

al-fiṭaḥl. The time before the Flood.

fitnah. Dissension, civil war; particularly the civil war ensuing on the murder of the Caliph 'Uthmān.

fuṣḥā. The pure Arabic language.

futūḥ. Conquests; the early Islamic conquests.

ghārāt. Raids.

gharīb. Rare, uncommon word or expression; a rare tradition, or such traditions as are isolated, do not date from one of the companions of the Prophet, and are only from a later generation.

ghazwah (pl. **ghazawāt**)**.** Early Muslim military expeditions or raiding parties in which the Prophet took part; synonym of **maghāzī**.

ḥabl. Covenant, treaty, engagement.

Ḥadīth. The corpus of traditions of the sayings and doings of the Prophet.

ḥadīth (with a small initial)**.** Such a tradition.

ḥajj. The annual pilgrimage to Mecca in the month of Dhu 'l-Hijjah.

ḥalāl. Licit, permitted; opposite of **ḥarām**.

ḥanīf. A Koranic term applying to those of true religion; seeker of religious truth.

ḥaram. Sacred enclave; especially those of Mecca and Medina.

ḥarām. Forbidden, illicit; opposite of **ḥalāl**.

ḥarakāt. Vowels.

ḥasan. Category of **ḥadīth** between sound (ṣaḥīḥ) and weak (ḍaʿīf).

hijrah (hijra). Muhammad's migration from Mecca to Medina in 622 CE.

ḥukm. Judgment.

ibn. Son of.

i ʿjāz. Inimitability of the Koran.

ijāzah. License given by a scholar to his pupil, authorizing the latter to transmit and teach a text.

ijmāʿ. Consensus; the consensus of the Islamic community.

illah (pl. **ilal).** Cause; defect; especially a gap in the chain of authentic transmission of a **ḥadīth**.

imām. Leader, especially a religious leader; leader in communal prayer.

Injīl. The Gospel.

Iʿrāb. Usually translated as "inflection," indicating case and mood, but the Arab grammarians define it as the difference that occurs, in fact or virtually, at the end of a word, because of the various antecedents that govern it.

isnād. Chain of authorities; in particular in **Ḥadīth** and historical writings.

isrāʿ. Journey by night; the famous night journey of Muhammd to Jerusalem.

Jāhiliyyah. Period before Muhammad's mission; era of ignorance; pre-Islamic period.

jihād. Holy war.

jizyah. Poll tax; capitation tax.

kāfir. Unbeliever.

kāhin. Pre-Islamic soothsayer.

kalāla. (a) one who dies leaving neither parent nor child, or, all the heirs with the exception of parents and children; (b) a bride, daughter-in-law, or sister-in-law.

kalām. Scholastic theology.

karshūnī. Syriac alphabet adapted to suit the Arabic language.

khabar (pl. **akhbār**)**.** Discrete anecdotes, reports.

khafī. Sentences whose meanings are hidden.

khajī. Sentences in which other persons or things are hidden beneath the plain meaning of a word or expression contained therein.

khāṣṣ. Words used in a special sense.

khāṣṣīya (pl. **khaṣā'iṣ**)**.** Privilege, prerogative, feature, trait.

khaṭīb. Orator; person pronouncing the Friday **khuṭbah**.

khulq. Disposition, temper, nature.

khuṭbah. Oration; address in the mosque at Friday prayers.

kiblah. *See* **qiblah**.

kissa. *See* **qiṣṣah**.

kitāb (pl. **kutub**)**.** Writing, Scripture, book; in **Ḥadīth**, a division approximating a chapter.

kufic. Style of Arabic script, used in early Koran codices.

kunya (konia, kunyah). A patronymic or name of honor of the form Abu N or Umm N (father or mother of N).

kussas. *See* **quṣṣāṣ**.

mab 'ath. Sending; the Call, when Muhammad was summoned to act as God's Prophet.

maghāzī. Early Muslim military expeditions or raiding parties in which the Prophet took part.

majlis (pl. **majālis**)**.** Meeting, session, scholarly discussion.

manāqib. Virtues, good qualities.

mansūkh. Abrogated.

mashhūr. Well known, widely known; a statement handed down by at least three different reliable authorities.

mathālib. Defects.

matn. Main text; narrative content.

mawlā (pl. **mawālī**). Client, non-Arab Muslim.

Midrash (Hebrew for "exposition or investigation"). A Hebrew term for the method of biblical investigation or exegesis by which oral tradition interprets and elaborates on the scriptural text. This investigation became necessary because the written law in the Pentateuch (the first five books of the Old Testament) needed to be reinterpreted in the light of later situations and disagreements. The Midrashim are usually divided into two broad groups:

1. **Halakha Midrash**, which is the scholastic deduction of the oral law (Halakha) from the written law; the totality of laws that have evolved since biblical times regulating religious observances and conduct of the Jewish people; they tend to be rather dry and legalistic.

2. **Haggada Midrash**, which consists of homiletic works whose purpose is edification rather than legislation; while less authoritative than halakhic ones, they are often highly imaginative stories, with a great deal of charm.

mi ʿrāj. Ascent; the Prophet's vision of heaven.

Muʿallaqah (pl. **Muʿallaqāt**). A collection of supposedly pre-Islamic poems.

mu'awwal. Words that have several significations, all of which are possible.

mubtada'. Beginnings.

mufakharah. Contests of vaunting; a war of words constituting a literary genre.

mufaṣṣal. Set forth or described minutely or in great detail.

mufassar. Explained. A sentence that needs some word in it to explain it and make it clear.

muḥaddith Ḥadīth. Scholar, collecting and studying the **Ḥadīth**.

muhājirūn. Those who went with the Prophet from Mecca to Medina at the time of the *hijrah*.

muḥkam. Perspicuous; a sentence the meaning of which there is no doubt.

mujmal. Sentences that may have a variety of interpretations.

muruwwah. Manliness, chivalry, prowess; the qualities of the ideal pre-Islamic Arab.

musannaf. Classified, systemized compilation. **Ḥadīth** compilations arranged according to subject matter.

muṣḥaf. Koran codex.

mushkil. Sentences that are ambiguous.

mushtarak. Complex words that have several significations.

musnad. Work of **ḥadīth** in which individual **ḥadīth** can be attributed to the Prophet himself.

mut'ah. Temporary marriage.

mutakallim. Scholastic theologian.

mutashābih. Intricate sentences or expressions, the exact meaning of which it is impossible for man to ascertain.

mutawātir. A report handed down successively by numerous companions, which was generally known from early times and to which objections have never been raised.

Mu'tazilah. Theological school that created speculative dogmatics of Islam.

nabī. Prophet.

nahḍah. Renaissance.

nasab (pl. **ansāb**). Genealogy.

nāsikh. Passage in the Koran or Sunnah that abrogates another passage.

nuqaṭ. The diacritical points, the function of which is to differentiate letters of the basic ***rasm***; there are seven letters that are the unmarked members of pairs where the other member has over-dotting.

Peshitta (Pšiṭṭā). The official text of the Bible in Syriac.

Poetical koinē. The written but not spoken language common to pre-Islamic poetry. (Not a happy term, as Rabin says (chap. 3.4) since the Greek *koinē* was a spoken language; thus Classical Arabic resembles more closely the status of Homeric Greek.)

Qaddarites. A group of teachers during ther Abbasid period who championed free will against the theory of predestination.

Qāḍī. Judge of a sharī'ah court.

qara'a 'alā. Literally, read aloud to; study under.

qāri' (pl. **qurrā'**). Reader, reciter of the Koran.

qiblah. Direction of prayer.

qirā'ah. Recitation of the Koran; variant reading of the Koran.

qiṣṣah (pl. **qiṣaṣ**). Story, fable, narrative tale; the narrative tales of the Koran.

qiyās. Analogy; the process of arriving at a legal decision by analogy.

quṣṣāṣ. Storytellers, relaters of **qiṣaṣ**.

Rāshidūn. The first four caliphs (the orthodox or rightly guided caliphs), that is, Abū Bakr, 'Umar, 'Uthmān, and 'Alī.

rasm. The basic (unpointed) form, shape, or drawing of the individual word.

rasūl. Messenger; apostle.

rāwī (pl. **ruwāh**). Reciter, transmitter.

ra'y. Opinion.

rijāl (sing. **rajul**). Men; trustworthy authorities in **Ḥadīth** literature.

risālah (pl. **rasā'il**). Epistle.

riwāyah. Transmission (of a nonreligious text); recension; variant reading in poetry.

Ṣadaqa. Alms, charitable gift; almsgiving, charity; legally prescribed alms tax.

Ṣaḥābah. The group of the Companions of the Prophet.

ṣaḥīfah (pl. **ṣuḥuf**). Page leaf; in the plural: manuscripts, documents containing **Ḥadīth** material.

ṣaḥīḥ. Sound (category of **Ḥadīth**); name of the **Ḥadīth** collections of al-Bukhārī and Muslim.

saj'. Balanced and rhyming prose.

sarāyā. Early Muslim military expeditions at which the Prophet was not present.

shādhdh. Peculiar; especially unacceptable variants of the Koranic text.

shamā'il. Good qualities; character, nature.

sharī'ah. The corpus of Islamic law.

shawāhid. Piece of evidence or quotation serving as textual evidence.

Shī'ah. Sect that holds that the leadership of the Islamic community belongs only to the descendants of 'Alī and Fāṭima.

Shu'ūbiyyah. Anti-Arab political and literary movement, especially strong in Iranian circles.

sīra/sīrah (pl. **siyar**). Biography, especially of the Prophet.

Sitz im leben (German: situation or place in life). A term used initially in biblical criticism to signify the circumstances (often in the life of a community) in which a particular story, saying, and so on, was created or preserved and transmitted.

stanza/strophe. Some poems are divided into groups of lines that stricly speaking are called "stanzas"; though in popular language they are often called "verses." The stanza will have a predominating meter and pattern of rhyme. For example, the Omar Khayyam stanza has four iambic pentameters, rhyming AABA; it receives its name from its use by E. Fitzgerald in his translation of the *Rubaiyat.*

sunnah. Way, path; customary practice; usage sanctioned by tradition; the sayings and doings of the Prophet that have been established as legally binding.

sura/sūrah. A chapter of the Koran.

ṭabaqāt. Historical works organized biographically.

tābi'ūn (sing. **tābi'**). Followers, the generation after the Prophet's companions (**ṣaḥā bah**).

ta 'dīl. Confirming the credibility of a **muḥaddith**.

tafsīr. Koranic exegesis.

tafsīr bi'l-ma'thūr. Interpretation or exegesis of the Koran following tradition.

tafsīr bi'l-ra'y. Interpretation or exegesis of the Koran by personal opinion.

tajwīd. The art of reciting the Koran, giving each consonant its full value, as much as it requires to be well pronounced without difficulty or exaggeration.

tanzīl. The divine revelation incorporated in the Koran; occasionally, the inspiration of soothsayers.

ta'rīkh. History.

tawḥīd. The doctrine of the unity of God.

ta'wīl. Interpretation; sometimes used as a synonym for **tafsīr**; later acquired specialized sense of exposition of the subject matter of the Koran, in contrast to the more external philological exegesis of the Koran, which was now distinguished as **tafsīr**.

ummah. Folk; the Islamic community.

Ur- (German origin; prefix). Primitive, original.

uṣūl. The fundamentals of jurisprudence.

waḍū'. Ablution.

warrāq. Paper seller, stationer, bookseller, copyist.

zakāh. Alms tax of prescribed amount.

zuhd. Asceticism.

Appendix C
Conversion Chart

The left-hand column gives Flügel's numbers; the corresponding numbers in the Egyptian text are obtained by adding or subtracting as shown. At the points of transition this applies only to part of a verse in one of the editions.

I	1–6	+1	III *cont.*	180–90	+3	VII *cont.*	28–103	+2
II	1–19	+1		191–93	+2		103–31	+3
	19–38	+2		194	+1		131–39	+4
	38–61	+3		196–98	+1		140–43	+3
	61–63	+4	IV.	3–5	+1		144–46	+2
	63–73	+5		7–13	–1		147–57	+1
	73–137	+6		14	–2		166–86	+1
	138–72	+5	–	15	–3		191–205	+1
	173–212	+4		16–29	–4	VIII	37–43	–1
	213–16	+3		30–32	–5		44–64	–2
	217–18	+2		32–45	–4		64–76	–1
	219–20	+1		45–47	–3	IX	62–130	–1
	236–58	–1		47–48	–2	X	11–80	–1
	259–69	–2		49–70	–3	XI	6	–1
	270–73	–3		70–100	–2		7–9	–2
	273–74	–2		100–106	–1		10–22	–3
	274–77	–1		118–56	+1		22–54	–2
III	1–4	+1		156–70	+2		55–77	–3
	4–18	+2		171–72	+1		77–84	–2
	19–27	+1		174–75	+1		84–87	–1
	27–29	+2	V	3–4	–1		88–95	–2
	29–30	+3		5–8	–2		96–99	–3
	30–31	+4		9–18	–3		99–120	–2
	31–43	+5		18–19	–2		120–22	–1
	43–44	+6		20–35	–3	XII	97–103	–1
	44–68	+7		35–52	–4	XIII	6–18	–1
	69–91	+6		53–70	–5		28–30	+1
	92–98	+5		70–82	–4	XIV	10–11	–1
	99–122	+4		82–88	–3		12–13	–2
	122–26	+5		88–93	–2		14–24	–3
	126–41	+6		93–98	–1		25–26	–4
	141–45	+7		101–109	+1		27–37	–5
	146–73	+6	VI	66–72	+1		37	–4
	174–75	+5		136–63	–1		37–41	–3
	176–79	+4	VII	1–28	+1		41–42	–2

XIV *cont.*	42–45	–1	XXII *cont.*	26–43	–1	XL *cont.*	33–39	–2
	46–47	–2		43–77	+1		40–56	–3
	47–51	–1	XXIII	28–34	–1		56–73	–2
XVI	22–24	–1		35–117	–2		73–74	–1
	25–110	–2		117	–1	XLI	1–26	+1
	110–28	–1	XXIV	14–18	+1	XLII	1–11	+2
XVII	10–26	–1		44–60	+1		12–31	+1
	27–48	–2	XXV	4–20	–1		31–42	+2
	49–53	–3		21–60	–2		43–50	+1
	53–106	–2		60–66	–1	XLIII	1–51	+1
	106–108	–1	XXVI	1–48	+1	XLIV	1–36	+1
XVIII	2–21	+1		228	–1	XLV	1–36	+1
	23–31	+1	XXVII	45–66	–1	XLVI	1–34	+1
	31–55	+2		67–95	– 2	XLVII	5–16	–1
	56–83	+1	XXVIII	1–22	+1		17–40	–2
	83–84	+2	XXIX	1–5I	+1	L	13–44	+1
	85–97	+1	XXX	1–54	+1	LIII	27–58	–1
XIX	1–3	+1	XXXI	1–32	+1	LV	1–16	+1
	8–14	–1	XXXII	1–9	+1	LVI	22–46	+1
	27–76	–1	XXXIII	41–49	+1		66–91	+1
	77–78	–2	XXXIV	10–53	+1	LVII	13–19	+1
	79–91	–3	XXXV	8–20	–1	LVIII	3–21	–1
	91–93	–2		20–21	+1	LXXI	5–22	+1
	93–94	–1		21–25	+2		26–29	–1
XX	1–9	+1		25–34	+3	LXXII	23–26	–1
	16–34	–1		35–41	+2	LXXXIV	32	–1
	40–41	–1		42–44	+1		33	–2
	42–63	–2	XXXVI	1–30	+1		34–41	–3
	64–75	–3	XXXVII	29–47	+1		41–42	–2
	75–79	–2		47–100	+2		42–51	–1
	80–81	–3		101	+1		54–55	+1
	81–88	–2	XXXVIII	1–43	+1	LXXVIII	41	–1
	89–90	–3		76–85	–1	LXXX	15–18	+1
	90–94	–2	XXXIX	4	–1	LXXXIX	1–14	+1
	94–96	–1		5–9	–2		17–25	–1
	106–15	+1		10–14	–3	XCVIII	2–7	+1
	115–21	+2		14–19	–2	CI	1–5	+1
	122–23	+1		19–63	–1		5–6	+2
XXI	29–67	–1	XL	1–2	+1		6–8	+3
XXII	19–21	–1		19–32	–1	CVI	3	+1

Appendix D

List of Contributors

Daniel Baggioni, until his tragic death in a car accident in 1998, was a professor in the Department of French Language at the UFR LACS of the University of Provence, France. Baggioni was interested in all aspects of sociolinguistics and the history of linguistic theories, and was the author of *Langues et nations en Europe* [Languages and Nations in Europe] (Paris: Payot, 1997).

Meir M. Bar-Asher is a professor of Arabic and Islamic Studies at the Department of Arabic Language and Literature, the Hebrew University of Jerusalem. He specializes in Qur'ān Exegesis and in Shī'i studies. His recent publications are *Scripture and Exegesis in Early Imami Shī'ism* (Jerusalem and Leiden, 1999) and *The Nusayri-Alawi Religion: An Enquiry into Its Theology and Liturgy* (written with A. Kofsky) (Leiden, 2002). Professor Bar-Asher is currently the chair of the Institute of Asian and African Studies at the Hebrew University.

Arthur Jeffery (1892–1959), professor of Semitic Languages at Columbia University and at Union Theological Seminary, was one of the great scholars of Islamic Studies. Apart from numerous articles in learned journals, Jeffery wrote two works that are considered definitive in their respective domain, in 1937 *Materials for the History of the Text of the Qur'ān: The Old Codices* and in 1938 *The Foreign Vocabulary of the Qur'ān*. The latter was a tour de force that reviewed about 275 words in the Koran that were regarded as foreign. This survey led Jeffery to examine texts in Ethiopic, Aramaic, Hebrew, Syriac, Greek, Latin, and Middle Persian, among other languages. His research led him to look for and at manuscripts in the Middle East, including Cairo. Other works included *The Qur'ān as Scripture* (1952).

Pierre Larcher (1948–). Born in Paris, Larcher received his PhD in 1996. He is professor of Arabic Linguistics at the University of Aix-en Provence, France, and teacher and researcher at IREMAM (CNRS). He travelled, taught, and carried out field research for eleven years in Syria, Libya, and Morocco. Larcher is the author of numerous articles in learned journals like *Arabica* and one book, *Le Système verbal de l'arabe classique* [*The Verbal System in Classical Arabic*] (Aix-en-Provence: University of Provence Publications, 2003). His translations of pre-Islamic Arabic poetry into French (*Les Mu'allaqât. Les Sept poèmes préislamiques* [Saint-Clément de Rivière: Fata Morgana, 2000]; *Le Guetteur de mirages. Cinq poèmes préislamiques* [Paris-Arles: Sindbad-Actes Sud, 2004]) have won him much praise.

B. Todd Lawson is associate professor of Islamic Thought in the Department of Near and Middle Eastern Civilizations, University of Toronto, Ontario, Canada.

Isaac Mendelsohn was associate prolessor of Semitic Languages at Columbia University. He edited *Religions of the Ancient Near East: Sumero-Akkadian Religious Texts and Ugaritic Epics* (New York: Liberal Arts Press, 1955). His other publications include *Slavery in the Ancient Near East: A Comparative Study of Slavery in Babylonia, Assyria, Syria, and Palestine, from the Middle of the Third Millennium to the End of the First Millennium* (New York, 1949).

Alphonse Mingana (1881–1937). Mingana was a great scholar of Arabic, especially Syriac. He was a member of the Chaldaean Church in Iraq, where he was also professor of Semitic Languages and Literature in the Syro-Chaldaean Seminary at Mosul. He collected invaluable Arabic and Syriac manuscripts that became the foundation for the famous Mingana Collection, now housed in

Birmingham, UK. The last twenty years of his life were spent in England where he taught Semitic Languages. His essays were collected in *Woodbrooke Studies: Christian Documents in Syriac, Arabic, Garshuni* (1927).

Theodor Nöldeke (1836–1930). The growing interest in Islamic studies in Europe led the Parisian Academie es Inscriptions et Belles-Lettres in 1857 to propose as the subject for a prize monography "a critical history of the text of the Coran." The subject attracted the young German scholar Nöldeke, who had already published the year before a Latin disquisition on the origin and composition of the Koran. Nöldeke won the prize, and an enlarged German version of the prizewinning work was published in Göttingen in 1860 as *Geschichte des Qorāns*. It became the foundation of *all* later Koranic studies. It is still referred to and is considered an indispensable tool for further research on the Koran. Some of his essays were gathered and published as *Sketches from Eastern History*.

Michael Schub was lecturer in Arabic language and literature at Yale University for three years. He now teaches at Trinity College in Hartford, Connecticut.

Friedrich Schulthess (1878–1922) studied theology and Oriental languages at Basel, Göttingen, Strassburg, and Zürich, and became a professor of Semitic philology successively at Göttingen, Königsberg, Strassburg, and Basel. His writings include *Christlich-palästinische Fragmente aus der Omajjaden-Moschee zu Damaskus* (1905), *Kalila und Dimna, syrisch und deutsch* (1911), *Die Machtmittel des Islams* (1922), and he edited and translated Diwan *des arabischen Dichters Hatim Tej nebst Fragmenten* (1897).

www.ingramcontent.com/pod-product-compliance
Lightning Source LLC
Chambersburg PA
CBHW031926090426
42811CB00040B/2393/J
* 9 7 8 1 5 9 1 0 2 4 2 9 3 *